Mar ⊥
La

THE TRAGEDY
OF CHILE

Contributions in Political Science
SERIES EDITOR: *Bernard K. Johnpoll*

AMERICAN DEMOCRATIC THEORY: Pluralism and Its Critics
William Alton Kelso

INTERNATIONAL TERRORISM IN THE CONTEMPORARY WORLD
Marius H. Livingston, with Lee Bruce Kress and Marie G. Wanek, editors

DOVES AND DIPLOMATS: Foreign Offices and Peace Movements in Europe and America in the Twentieth Century
Solomon Wank, editor

BELIEVING SKEPTICS: American Political Intellectuals, 1945-1964
Robert Booth Fowler

LOCKE, ROUSSEAU, AND THE IDEA OF CONSENT: An Inquiry into the Liberal Democratic Theory of Political Obligation
Jules Steinberg

JUDICIAL CRAFTSMANSHIP OR FIAT?: Direct Overturn by the United States Supreme Court
Howard Ball

THE NEW LEFT IN FRANCE: The Unified Socialist Party
Charles Hauss

Robert J. Alexander

THE TRAGEDY
OF CHILE

Contributions in Political Science, Number 8

GREENWOOD PRESS
Westport, Connecticut • London, England

Library of Congress Cataloging in Publication Data

Alexander, Robert Jackson, 1918-
    The tragedy of Chile.

    (Contributions in political science ; no. 8
ISSN 0147-1066)
    Bibliography: p.
    Includes index.
    1. Chile--Politics and government--1970-
2. Chile--Politics and government--1920-1970.   I. Title.
II. Series.
F3100.A34   320.9'83'064   77-91101
ISBN 0-313-20034-3

Library of Congress Catalog Card Number: 77-91101
ISBN: 0-313-20034-3
ISSN: 0147-1066

First published in 1978

Greenwood Press, Inc.
51 Riverside Avenue, Westport, Connecticut 06880

Printed in the United States of America

10 9 8 7 6 5 4 3 2 1

TO HELEN MARTIN

Contents

PREFACE   ix
INTRODUCTION   xi

PART ONE: TRADITIONAL CHILE AND ITS TRANSFORMATION   1
  1 The Evolution of Traditional Chile   3
  2 The First Assault on Traditional Chile: 1920-1932   10
  3 The 1932-1938 Alessandri Period   17
  4 The Second Assault on Traditional Chile: The Radical Period   26
  5 The Ibañez-Jorge Alessandri Interregnum   39

PART TWO: THE REVOLUTION IN LIBERTY   53
  6 Characteristics of the ''Revolution in Liberty''   55
  7 PDC Politics in the Frei Administration   58
  8 The Politics of the Opposition   66
  9 Military and Constitutional Issues During the Frei Regime   78
 10 Rural Reform   85
 11 Economic Policies of the Christian Democratic Government   98
 12 Labor and Communal Issues   108
 13 The 1970 Election   118

PART THREE: THE CHILEAN ROAD TO SOCIALISM   129
 14 The Nature of ''The Chilean Road to Socialism''   131
 15 Nationalization   145
 16 The Agrarian Revolution   160
 17 Economic Policies and Problems of the Unidad
      Popular Government   173
 18 Organized Labor During the Allende Regime   194
 19 Foreign Relations of the Allende Regime   209
 20 The ''Boycott,'' the CIA, and Other Yankee Activities   217
 21 Freedom of the Press, and Other Constitutional Issues   237

22   The Politics of the Unidad Popular and Its Allies   251
23   The Politics of the Opposition   278
24   Allende and the Military   288
25   Onset of the Fatal Crisis: October 1972-June 29, 1973   301
26   Culmination of the Crisis: The Last Weeks of the
          Allende Regime   314

PART FOUR: THE CULMINATION OF THE TRAGEDY OF CHILE   329
27   The Coup   331
28   The Politics of the Military Junta   339
29   The Politics of the Opposition Under the Junta   357
30   The Foreign Policy of the Junta Regime   371
31   The Cultural Blight of the Junta Regime   385
32   Economic Policies of the Junta Regime: The Shock Treatment   395
33   Economic Policies of the Junta Regime: Long-Run Effects   411
34   Labor Under the Junta Regime   426
35   The Nature of Chile's Tragedy   444

APPENDIX 1: The 91 Firms   449
APPENDIX 2: The Military's Stated Reasons for Overthrowing Allende 453

NOTES   455
ANNOTATED BIBLIOGRAPHY   483
INDEX   495

Preface

I first visited Chile in 1946–1947, spending almost six months there collecting material for my Ph.D. dissertation, "Labor Relations in Chile." I have subsequently made more than a dozen additional visits and have written several other books dealing in whole or in part with Chile. Until 1973, Chile was my "favorite" Latin American country.

The present book is therefore written with a great deal of personal commitment, and even some passion, although I have tried to keep the latter in check in the writing. I have a point of view about what has happened in Chile in recent years. I see it as a profound tragedy of significance for all of Latin America, and even for the world as a whole. Chile had a kind of society and a quality of life that are rare in the world. It is the disappearance of these that is Chile's tragedy. When Chilean democracy was destroyed, the whole world was the loser.

The tragedy of Chile did not begin on September 11, 1973, when the Military Junta government came to power, but at least three years earlier, when Salvador Allende was elected president. Its roots are still further back in time, in the judgment and policy errors of the leaders of the Christian Democratic party and government, which made it impossible for them to win continuation in office in the 1970 election. In the pages that follow, I attempt to trace how this tragedy came to pass.

Much of what I say here is based on my observations of the country over the years; my judgments and conclusions certainly are. However, I have tried to offer verification for facts and figures from as varied a group of sources as possible.

Of course, I have incurred many debts of gratitude during the writing and publication of this book. First, I owe much to the hundreds of friends and acquaintances, on all levels of society, whom I have in Chile. Over the years they have answered my almost interminable questions, and frequently have offered me hospitality and kindness as well as information. To name any of these people would be to exclude others, so it is best to extend them a general word of thanks rather than individual expressions of gratitude.

I also owe much to those who have helped to get this book into print. In this connection, I should particularly mention Betty Pessagno, who edited the manuscript for Greenwood Press, the publishers.

I must thank the *Christian Science Monitor* for permission to print, in a revised version, an article that originally appeared in their pages, and that constitutes the chapter on the cultural impact of the Junta regime in the present book.

Finally, as always, my family—my wife Joan and my children Tony and Meg—have tolerated me as I wrote the book. By now, they are used to my typing away when they would prefer me to be doing something else, but I thank them nonetheless.

Robert J. Alexander
New Brunswick, N.J.
September 1977

Introduction

On September 11, 1973, the armed forces seized power in Chile. Although military coups are not unusual in Latin America, they are unusual in Chile. This particular coup represented the culmination of a process that had been underway for several years. The result of this process, and its denouement in September 1973, may well be the destruction of a way of life and a polity that have made Chile almost unique in Latin America, giving her a distinctive place among the world's nations.

The 1973 coup was not entirely unexpected, either by Chileans or by outsiders who knew the country well. Nonetheless, it was a profound shock for both the nation's citizens and its friends. Not only did it reverse a forty-year tradition of military subordination to civilian authority, but the ferocity with which the armed forces acted once they had seized power was entirely unexpected and difficult for the civilian population to understand and explain.

Until shortly before September 11, 1973, Chile's society and conduct of public affairs had been characterized by diversity of opinion, freedom of discussion, tolerance, and a pride of the general population in the ability of a constitutional and democratic political system to adapt to change, even to abrupt change. Over a long period of time, too, Chile had made considerable, if sporadic, economic progress. It had become one of the more highly industrialized nations of Latin America. The standard of living of large elements of its population had continued to rise, in spite of nagging inflation, periodic balance-of-payments crises, and the continuing poverty of a substantial part of its people. During the latter half of the 1960s, the tempo of change quickened. For a while it appeared that a series of long-overdue reforms would be accomplished within the constitutional democratic system, while bringing the benefits of reform and economic development to elements that had previously been on the fringes of Chilean society and polity. These hopes proved illusory.

As the tragedy that culminated in the coup of September 1973 and its aftermath unfolded, the unique characteristics of Chile tended to be eroded. Growing intolerance and extremism at both ends of the political spectrum undermined the broad consensus in favor of political democracy and a more or less gradual process of transforming the society that had characterized most elements in Chilean politics. The confraternity among political leaders of almost all currents of opinion, which assured that none would try totally to eliminate any other, increasingly gave way to demands that one or another part of the polity be eliminated once and for all. To a growing extent, hatred took the place of rivalry and antagonism.

All of these trends, plus an insurmountable economic crisis, led to a virtually complete breakdown of Chilean politics and government during the middle months of 1973. This situation culminated in the coup of September 11, after which the trends that had been growing in previous years found full expression. Repression, persecution, torture, and even murder became commonplace. Victors sought revenge upon the vanquished. Civil liberties disappeared; the structure that had protected the rights of the individual was destroyed, at least for the time being. The government proclaimed its intention of "extirpating" political tendencies that represented at least a third of the nation's citizenry.

All of this is the "tragedy of Chile." The present volume is an attempt to describe and explain how the growing crisis developed, what finally provoked the coup of September 11, 1973, and what the results of that coup have been.

Because the events of the early 1970s represent such a radical departure from Chilean tradition and historical experience, a picture of the historical evolution of the country is given in the first chapters of this book, as background for recent events. These chapters sketch the characteristics of what we call "traditional Chile" and then trace the process by which this traditional society evolved and profoundly changed. Particular emphasis is given to the post-World War I period when traditional aristocratic Chile was transformed into a country with much greater economic diversity and social mobility, and with a political system in which virtually all elements of the population participated, at least to some degree.

Following this historical background is a discussion of the attempts made in the latter half of the 1960s to step up the pace of economic, social, and political change. These attempts were still within the spirit of tolerance, pluralistic politics, and free competition of ideas that was the most valuable tradition Chile had inherited from its past. This discussion constitutes the second part of this volume. The last two parts of the book trace the course of events that overtook Chile in the 1970s. One of these deals at some length with the so-called Popular Unity (Unidad Popular) regime of President Salvador Allende, and the other with the military regime that seized power with the overthrow and death of Allende in September 1973.

This approach will emphasize that the tragedy of Chile did not begin on September 11, 1973. It will also underscore the profound nature of the change that occurred in the country in the 1970s and the loss this change represents not only to the great majority of the Chileans, but to all people who believe in a free society.

PART ONE:
TRADITIONAL CHILE AND ITS TRANSFORMATION

1

The Evolution of Traditional Chile

Chile was a small, poor, and rather unimportant backwater of the Spanish colonial empire in America from the early sixteenth to the early nineteenth century. It extended from the southern edge of the Pacific Desert about a thousand miles south to the vicinity of the present city of Valdivia, occupying the valley and narrow coastal strip between the high cordillera of the Andes and the Pacific Ocean. Its Spanish-descended inhabitants, as well as those Indians who had been brought under their control, were engaged mainly in agriculture. Precious metals existed in only the most modest quantities, so that the area did not greatly inspire the avarice or even the interest of the Spaniards.

A substantial proportion of the Spanish immigrants who came to Chile during the colonial period were hardy Basque farmers and merchants. They became the nucleus of the agrarian-commercial ruling class that was to take over full control of the country with the exit of the Spaniards in the first decades of the nineteenth century. Even today a large part of the Chilean aristocracy is of Basque origin, although not everyone with a Basque name is an aristocrat.

Large parts of present-day Chile remained in the hands of the Indians, particularly the Mapuche or Araucanians. Their resistance to conquest by the Europeans became legendary, and they remained dominant in the islands and in the Patagonia region that today make up one-third of the country's territory. They also continued to control the region around present-day Temuco, which even now is commonly referred to as "the frontier" and continues to be the home of most surviving Indians.

An aristocratic pattern emerged in colonial Chile. Although Spaniards from the "mother country" continued to hold the principal posts in the governmental and church hierarchies, the economy of the colony was in the hands of Chileans of more or less pure Spanish descent. They held the land, on which people of more markedly Indian background worked under generally servile conditions. They were the merchants, and even the artisans, as well as the lower clergy and government bureaucracy. The effect of the independence movement was to transfer political and ecclesiastical power to those who already held economic and social power.

THE EARLY DECADES OF INDEPENDENCE

As was true in virtually all of the Spanish-American countries, political life was exceedingly turbulent in Chile during the first years of independence from 1810 to 1833. Even during the struggle against Spain, two rival parties began to develop, and their internecine quarrels on some occasions imperilled the struggle for independence.

The two factions that emerged were the Liberals and Conservatives, although in the beginning they did not have those names. They clashed on a number of important issues. With regard to the church, the Liberals sought to reduce its privileges and influence, while the Conservatives supported their maintenance. They also differed on economic policy, with the Liberals tending to be free traders and the Conservatives more inclined to favor protectionism. Finally, they were in disagreement concerning the form of government the new republic should have, with the Liberals advocating some form of federalism and the Conservatives supporting a more centralized state.

The first leader to emerge in Chile after independence was the Liberal caudillo Bernardo O'Higgins, who assumed the title supreme director. He was finally forced to resign in 1823 and went into exile in Peru, where he died many years later. During the 1820s, power tended to swing back and forth between the two groups, as the result of frequent insurrections and coups, and an occasional election. This instability was reflected in the frequent adoption of a new constitution.

RISE AND FALL OF THE PORTALES REPUBLIC

One of the more remarkable figures in Chilean history, Diego Portales, brought this period of turbulence and near anarchy to an end in the 1830s and helped establish a pattern of government and society that was to persist (albeit greatly transformed) for almost a century. Like Alexander Hamilton, Portales believed in a strong central government in which the president would have great power. Like Hamilton, too, Portales succeeded in rallying the great majority of the economically powerful interests behind the idea of establishing such a form of government. Another parallel between the two men is that neither ever became president; they achieved no position higher than the cabinet, but each exercised extraordinary power and influence in that post. Finally, both men met tragic deaths at the hands of political opponents.

The kind of regime which evolved in the Constitution of 1833 (which was to a large degree inspired, if not written, by Diego Portales), was that of a highly centralized republic. Within this national government the president was given extensive powers not only to administer but also to legislate. His power was curbed by two unique provisions: every eighteen months, he had to go to Congress for permission to maintain a standing army and navy; and each year he had to get congressional permission to allow the armed forces to stay within 50 kilometers of the capital city when the legislature was in session. Congress also had control over the budget. These three provisions were to generate considerable difficulties for the two outstanding presidents of the following century, José Manuel Balmaceda and Arturo Alessandri.

The groundwork for a form of government and society unique in Latin America was laid during the Portales era. For almost nine decades following the promulgation of the 1833 Constitution, political power remained in the hands of the rural-commercial aristocracy, and the electorate was severely restricted by literacy and property franchises. Nonetheless, there was only one case in which the presidency was not transferred as the result of a more or less orderly election. During this long period, the Chilean aristocracy was much like that of Great Britain in that it showed a surprising flexibility, a capacity for adjusting to fundamental reforms, and a willingness to concede just enough so as not to have to concede everything.

From 1831 to 1861, the presidency was in the hands of three strong and relatively conservative presidents: Generals Joaquín Prieto (1831-1841) and Manuel Bulnes (1841-1851) and lawyer Manuel Montt (1851-1861). They made ample use of the extensive powers of the presidency and "managed" elections to their taste. This era in Chilean history is known as the Conservative Republic. During this period, Chile remained essentially an agricultural country. It largely met its own needs for foodstuffs and had modest surpluses for export. The middle decades of the century witnessed substantial development of copper mining, and for a few years Chile was the world's largest exporter of copper, albeit a modest one.

The Conservative Republic came to an end in 1861 with the inauguration of President José Joaquín Pérez (1861-1871). This change came about largely as a result of a split in the Conservative forces during the administration of President Manuel Montt. Feeling himself challenged by the church, Montt sought to limit its powers. This policy brought about a division in the Conservative party and the establishment of the so-called Montt-Varista party, or Partido Nacional, which in future years became rather closely associated with the Liberals.

The period 1861 to 1891 is generally known as the Liberal Republic. One trend of this era was toward weakening the power of the presidency, with Congress insisting on its right to approve ministers named by the president and to remove them when it was unhappy with them. President Pérez and his three successors, Federico Errázuriz Zañartu, Aníbal Pinto, and Domingo Santa María, tended increasingly to concede to congressional demands. The weakening of the presidency may also have been reflected in the fact that President Pérez was the last to serve two five-year terms. Thereafter, no president served more than one term.

A second trend during the Liberal Republic was the curtailment of the power of the church. Its control over education, over keeping vital statistics, and over cemeteries was abolished. The clerical-anticlerical controversy reached its greatest height during the Santa María administration (1881–1886).

A third political trend that was to have considerable future significance was the establishment of two new parties, representing new elements in politics. The first of these was the Radical party, which was founded in 1857 during Montt's second term but which did not hold its first national convention until 1888. It was a militantly anticlerical breakaway from the Liberals. It soon came to be the principal spokesman for the white collar workers, small merchants, and other middle-class elements, as well as the party par excellence of the German Protestant farmers in the Valdivia-Puerto Montt region in the south.

The second new party was the Partido Democrático which was set up in the late 1880s by dissident left-wing Radicals. It soon proclaimed itself a socialist party, establishing contacts with the Socialist International. The Partido Democrático became the spokesman for a substantial group of artisans and other manual workers, including the nitrate miners in the north and the coal miners in the region near Concepción. It remained relatively small because most manual workers were still illiterate and therefore did not have the vote. However, it was a portent of things to come.

The Liberal Repubic was notable for at least two other developments, one of which was the geographical expansion of the country. After a series of conflicts with the Mapuche in the Temuco area, peace was finally made in the 1880s. As a result, the Mapuche were largely confined to a limited part of the region, and Chilean landlords moved in to establish grazing and grain-growing farms in much of the area.

At the same time, Chile was pushing its sovereignty further south. Particularly in the face of Argentina's drive to occupy all of the southern part of the continent to the east of the Andes, the Chileans felt the need to assure their control of the whole west coast, as well as of a large part of Patagonia and the island of Tierra del Fuego in the southernmost tip of the continent. For many decades, the conflicting claims of Chile and Argentina in those areas were to disturb the relations between the two republics.

Chile also extended its limits to the north during the Liberal Republic.

Chilean entrepreneurs, often in partnership with British interests, were increasingly penetrating the nitrate regions of Bolivia and Peru in the Pacific Desert area, particularly from the 1860s on. Finally, in 1879 economic rivalries in those regions provoked a war between Chile on the one hand and Bolivia and Peru on the other. Chile won the war, with the result that it annexed the Bolivian province of Antofagasta and the Peruvian province of Tarapacá, while also extending its effective control to the Peruvian provinces of Tacna and Arica, although their final disposition was left open for later settlement. An agreement on the Tacna-Arica question was not reached until 1929.

The acquisition of Antofagasta and Tarapacá helped transform the Chilean economy. Natural nitrates existed in these areas in abundance, and the demand for them grew steadily and rapidly in the decades after Chile acquired these areas. Nitrates came to account for the overwhelming majority of Chilean exports and to provide most of the government's income. The nitrate bonanza made it possible for the government, still largely controlled by agrarian interests, to reduce nearly all other kinds of taxation, particularly that on agriculture. At the same time, the growth of the nitrate mining industry greatly expanded the market for agricultural goods from the more southerly parts of the republic.

THE REVOLUTION OF 1891 AND
THE PARLIAMENTARY REPUBLIC

Conflicts over the relative powers of the president and Congress, as well as over policy towards the nitrate industry, finally resulted in a civil war in 1891. At the beginning of that year, Congress refused to authorize the maintenance of the standing armed forces and to allow the army to be billeted within 50 kilometers of Santiago. It also refused to enact a government budget. President José Manuel Balmaceda defied Congress by keeping the military under arms, keeping the army garrison in Santiago, and continuing to spend money even without authorization of the legislature. These actions provided the excuse, if not the reason, for Congress to lead a revolt against President Balmaceda. The navy supported Congress and took the legislative leaders to the northern provinces, where they recruited a new army. The regular army remained loyal to Balmaceda.

The civil war was a bloody one and lasted for almost nine months. The Balmaceda faction lost, and the rebel army entered Santiago shortly before the end of the president's term, on September 18, 1891. President Balmaceda remained in the presidential palace until his term had officially expired, and then committed suicide.

The triumphant rebel forces then inaugurated the so-called Parliamentary Republic. Without officially changing the Constitution, Congress resolved that hence forward it would have the right to censure ministers and ministries, and that in the event of censure these would have to abandon their posts. This practice was followed for the next thirty-three years.

The Parliamentary Republic has often been compared to the Third and Fourth Republics of France because ministries changed with exceeding frequency; one that lasted four or five months was considered aged. Congressmen became experts at blackmailing the president, demanding patronage and other privileges on the threat to vote to censure the cabinet if these concessions were not made. As in the French Third and Fourth Republics, too, parties and factions within parties multiplied profusely. Not only did the Liberals divide into several factions, but from time to time the Radicals and Conservatives, and even the Democráticos, did also. The parliamentarians played a veritable game of musical chairs in the search for ministerial jobs, even if these were held for only a few weeks or even days. There were few members of Congress of any importance who did not serve as minister at least once during this period.

Inevitably, the lines among the parties became somewhat blurred during much of the Parliamentary Republic. The need to get together enough factions to command a majority in Congress brought about the most unlikely alliances among parties which presumably were bitter ideological and philosophical opponents. In time, widespread discontent with the parties and with the parliamentary system developed.

The Parliamentary Republic marked no change in political control of the country by the landed aristocracy. In spite of the slow but steady rise of the Radical and Democrático parties in the urban areas, most of Chile remained rural, and most members of Congress represented—or sometimes headed— local political machines which drew their finances and political support from the local aristocracy. They dedicated themselves to defending the interests of these rural oligarchs. Continued aristocratic control was greatly facilitated by extensive rigging of elections.

UNDERMINING OF OLIGARCHICAL CONTROL

Principally as a result of the nitrate boom, the economy of Chile expanded rapidly during the Parliamentary Republic. Successive governments spent revenues derived from the nitrate taxes on public works and on expanding the government bureaucracy. Chile's ability to import grew with the expansion of its exports, quickening the activities of the commercial sector. The cities grew and were modernized—streets were paved, and gas and electricity, potable water supplies, and modern sewerage systems were installed. Hence, an increasing proportion of the population was brought into the money economy, particularly in the urban areas, and the market expanded. During the first two decades of the twentieth century, artisan shops and small factories began to provide some of the manufactured goods to meet the needs of this growing market.

Economic expansion and growth began to produce significant changes in the class structure of Chilean society. The period of the Parliamentary Republic saw marked expansion of both the wage-earning working class and various "middle sectors," such as white collar workers, artisans, small manufacturers, and government employees. As the middle- and working-class elements grew, they became more discontented with the social, economic, and political conditions prevalent in the republic. At about the turn of the century an organized labor movement began to appear, with formation of "brotherhoods" and "resistance societies" among nitrate miners, port workers, artisans, factory workers, and even white collar employees. There were more strikes, particularly in the ports and mining areas; some of them were accompanied by great violence, especially on the part of the authorities. The "social question" became an important issue of public debate, and various suggestions were made for legislation to deal with it.

This discontent also found political expression. The Radical party grew substantially during the first two decades of the twentieth century and became the party par excellence of those middle-class elements who sought reform. The Partido Democrático also grew, although less notably, attracting many followers among wage workers in the mining areas and in the major cities. In 1912, a more radical group split off from the Partido Democrático to form the Partido Socialista Obrero, which was ultimately to become the Communist party. Its strength was greatest in the nitrate mining areas, where it found its outstanding leader in a labor jour. 'ist, Luis Emilio Recabarren; and in Santiago, where its principal figure w, s & worker, Manuel Hidalgo.

Even the older parties were influenced by these developments. One wing of the Liberal party showed at least some sympathy with the aspirations of the workers and tended with increasing consistency to ally itself with the Radical party. Even some Conservatives were influenced by Catholic social ideas, and favored action on behalf of the workers. These Conservatives, however, were alienated from the more progressive Liberals as well as from the Radicals, Democráticos, and Socialists because of those groups' anti-church attitudes.

World War I stimulated all of these trends. After a short depression in the latter part of 1914, the war years were a period of intense economic activity, growth of manufacturing industry, and substantial inflation. Strikes were very frequent. Discontent with continued oligarchical domination of the country's political system and with the parliamentary system grew sharply. This rising tide of discontent emerged strongly during the parliamentary elections of 1916 and 1918, and reached its culmination in the historical presidential election of 1920.

2

The First Assault on Traditional Chile: 1920-1932

The election of 1920 marked the beginning of a period of upheaval in Chilean political life which has some striking parallels to the late 1960s and early 1970s. The years 1920–1932 witnessed the launching of fundamental social and political reforms, and a breakdown of constitutional government. It was the only period in the twentieth century prior to 1973 in which the military took and held control of the government for a considerable period of time.

THE ELECTION OF 1920

The election of 1920 resulted in a fundamental shift in political power, i.e., control over the executive branch of the Chilean government passed from the hands of the landed and commercial oligarchy to those of middle sectors, in alliance with some dissident elements of the old aristocracy. Never again, with the possible exception of the short presidency of President Emiliano Figueroa (1925–1927), was the presidency to be in the control of the traditional ruling classes, although they would continue to have a veto power in Congress for at least another forty-five years.

There were two candidates in the 1920 election, one of whom favored basic changes and the other who wanted to maintain the status quo. The candidate of the reform elements was Arturo Alessandri Palma, and the nominee of the opponents of change was Luis Barros Borgoño.

Arturo Alessandri was the grandson of an Italian immigrant who had made a small fortune in the maritime industry and other activities. On his mother's side he was descended from one of the most distinguished families of the late colonial and early republican periods. He had been a member of the Chamber of Deputies for nearly twenty years and had first been a minister in 1897 when he was not yet thirty years of age. In the Chamber he had been one of the worst abusers of the weaknesses of the parliamentary system.

Before 1916, few would have considered Alessandri a viable presidential candidate. In that year, he was elected to the Senate from the province of Tarapacá, where he ran against Arturo del Rio, boss of one of the most repressive and retrograde political machines in the republic. Del Rio had dominated the province virtually since it had been taken from Peru in the War of the Pacific. During this campaign, waged at considerable risk to his own life, Alessandri had awakened the imagination of the humbler citizenry. He emerged from the campaign not only with the sobriquet the Lion of Tarapacá, but also as the recognized spokesman for the discontented elements in national politics.

During his campaign for the presidency in 1920, Alessandri enunciated a list of demands for reform. He urged enactment of a labor code to protect the rights and improve the conditions of the working classes, as well as a more equitable tax system, including the introduction of an income tax. He promised to work for separation of church and state, and for rapid expansion of the public education system.

Alessandri massed behind his candidacy the bulk of the middle class. He also had the support of substantial elements of the organized labor movement, although most workers did not have the right to vote. The Alianza Liberal, which backed his candidacy, consisted of his faction of the Liberals, as well as the Radicals, the Partido Nacional, and the majority faction of the Partido Democrático.

Alessandri's opponent, Luis Barros Borgoño, on the other hand, had the staunch support of the economic Right. Barros Borgoño was a seasoned Liberal politician who had been a leader in the revolution against Balmaceda in 1891. The Unión Nacional, which backed his candidacy, consisted of a large Liberal party element as well as the Conservative party and a dissident faction of the Partido Democrático.

The election was extremely close, and under the electoral college system that existed at the time, there was some doubt as to who had won. During the several months in which the final decision was being made, there were rumblings of a general strike, a massive descent of workers on Santiago to defend Alessandri's cause, and even a possible military coup if his victory was not recognized. At last, it was decided that Alessandri had been the victor by one electoral vote. The traditional ruling group of Chile thus demonstrated its capacity to concede enough so as to avert a holocaust that might deprive it of everything.

ALESSANDRI'S FIRST PERIOD, 1920–1924

Alessandri was not able to complete his whole five-year term. The passions that had been aroused during the 1920 campaign did not abate thereafter.

His right-wing opponents, who controlled the Senate from 1920 until March 1924, took every opportunity presented by the parliamentary system to force him to change cabinets frequently, while at the same time obstinately refusing to enact any of the reform legislation he demanded. This situation rapidly converted Alessandri, the old manipulator of the parliamentary system, into its sworn enemy. He placed abolition of parliamentarianism at the top of his list of proposed reforms.

Meanwhile, the country faced a disastrous economic situation. After the boom of the World War I years, the nitrate industry virtually collapsed just about the time of Alessandri's inauguration. The Germans had developed a practical method of making synthetic nitrates, after they were cut off by the Allied blockade from Chilean supplies of natural nitrates. Demand for and prices of natural nitrates plunged during the first half of the 1920s. The collapse of the nitrate market was catastrophic for Chile. Unemployed miners streamed out of the northern provinces and had to be accommodated by the government in the center of the republic. Government revenues, which had been drawn almost completely from taxes on nitrates and sales taxes, declined massively. The whole of the Chilean economy was in crisis, which vastly complicated Alessandri's political problems.

The growing strains between the president and Congress reached crisis proportions in 1924. At the beginning of the year, when Congress threatened to use the old device of not renewing authorization for billeting the armed forces near Santiago, Alessandri threatened to resign and he vividly painted the dire consequences for the oligarchs. His opponents backed off temporarily, agreeing to certain modifications of the parliamentary system and passing a law introducing an income tax for the first time.

Soon afterwards, congressional elections were held. Alessandri had great hope that the election would give him a majority in the Senate, which would then proceed to enact the reforms he had so long been advocating. He won the election, but Congress proved no more anxious to pass the legislation he demanded when it had a supposedly pro-Alessandri majority than when his opponents controlled the upper house.

The final crisis came early in September over the issue of paying members of Congress a salary for the first time. Alessandri had had this proposal on his list of reforms, so as to permit people of humble financial means to occupy seats in the legislature. However, the bill was introduced and debated at a particularly inappropriate moment. The budget remained unpassed, and the salaries of both civil servants and the military had not been paid for some weeks. At this point, a group of young officers protested by attending a session of the Senate in which the congressional pay bill was being debated. At the session, the young men ostentatiously rattled their swords. This event, which came to be known as the "Rattling of the Sabres," precipitated a constitutional crisis. When Alessandri sought to discipline the young military men, he met resistance from their superiors. He therefore negotiated with the leaders of the military group.

President Alessandri and his civilian supporters supposedly reached a compromise with the military. It was agreed that he would present Congress with a list of more than a dozen bills, including measures not only for salary increases for the military and for speeding up promotion procedures, but also for several key items Alessandri had been advocating since becoming president—a bill legalizing unions, and two bills providing the basis for a social security system, among others. Once these bills became law, Alessandri was assured, the military men would "return to the barracks."

After a weekend of feverish negotiations between Alessandri and the party and parliamentary leaders of Alianza Liberal, it was agreed to rush the proposal through Congress. This was done on September 8, 1924, in one continuous session of Congress, during which all the proposals sent by Alessandri were rushed through the three stages of parliamentary debate and action. Once this was done, however, the military announced that instead of ceasing political activities, they would continue their Military Junta in order to "safeguard" the advances made. Alessandri, regarding this move as a betrayal of the agreement he had made with the young military men, resigned the presidency, taking refuge in the United States Embassy and leaving the country two days later.

ALESSANDRI'S RESTORATION

The events of early September 1924 marked the beginning of a period of more than seven years of military interference in politics. This was the first such period in Chile during the twentieth century, and the only one before the military coup of September 11, 1973.

For the three and a half months following Alessandri's resignation, the country was ruled by a Government Junta consisting of two generals and an admiral. The Military Junta of young officers, which had been responsible for the crisis of September, remained in existence during most of this period. Finally, on January 23, 1925, a further coup, led by the Military Junta's two principal figures, Colonels Marmaduque Grove and Carlos Ibáñez, overthrew the Government Junta.

The young military invited Arturo Alessandri, who was then in Italy, to return to the presidency, which he did, arriving back home in March 1925. During the next six months he ruled by decree, since Congress, which had been dissolved soon after Alessandri's resignation, was not called back into session. Alessandri was able to enact most of the reform program he had been pushing since 1920. A new constitution, substituting presidentialism for parliamentarianism and separating church and state, was drawn up and then adopted by popular referendum; a Central Bank was established; and the government began to put into effect the laws legalizing unions and to establish a social security system.

Alessandri continued to have difficulties with the young military men, particularly with Colonel Carlos Ibáñez, who served as his minister of war in 1925. Finally, when Ibáñez refused to step aside as a candidate for president in the elections called for later in the year, Alessandri once again, at the end of September 1925, withdrew from the presidency.

THE IBÁÑEZ REGIME

Although Alessandri's second resignation served its purpose of blocking the immediate candidacy of Colonel Ibáñez for the presidency, it did so for only a year and a half. In elections held six weeks after Alessandri's departure, Emiliano Figueroa was chosen president, with the support of all existing political parties. His only competitor was Alessandri's minister of health, José Santos Salas, a kind of stand-in for Ibáñez.

Figueroa made the mistake of keeping Colonel Ibáñez as minister of war. From that vantage point, the colonel exercised increasing influence on the government and its policies, and finally in May 1927, Figueroa resigned, paving the way for the election of Colonel Ibáñez to the presidency. His only competitor was Elías Laferte, a leader of the Communist party, whom Ibáñez had placed in forced residence on Easter Island, far out in the Pacific, and who did not learn he had been a candidate until after the election was over.

President Ibáñez ruled as a military dictator. Virtually all legal opposition to his regime was supressed, freedom of the press was nonexistent, and political parties were allowed to function only to the degree that they would not offer serious opposition to the regime. The Communist party was outlawed.

During its first two and half years, the Ibáñez regime rode the wave of prosperity of the late 1920s. It carried out large programs of public works, borrowing money copiously from abroad to finance many of them. It also sought to come to grips with the problems of the nitrate industry by organizing a monopoly firm, Compañía Salitrera de Chile (COSACh), in which the government and private mining companies were partners.

In some ways, the Ibáñez government continued the work of Alessandri. It was during the Ibáñez period that legal recognition was extended to a large part of the labor movement and that the system of government-supervised collective bargaining provided for in the legislation of September 1924 became the rule. It was during this period, too that the social security system was firmly established. In 1931, the country's labor legislation was brought together in a Labor Code. Ibáñez also resolved the long-standing border dispute with Peru over the Tacna-Arica question in 1929, bringing to an end negotiations that had been reopened by Alessandri in 1921.

Ultimately, the Ibáñez dictatorship fell victim to the Great Depression. So long as relative prosperity prevailed in the late 1920s, political resentment and opposition resulting from his dictatorial methods were not sufficient to bring him down. When the economy collapsed, however, his days in power were numbered.

Growing unrest found expression in attempted military coups, strikes, and public demonstrations. Finally, on July 28, 1931, Ibáñez resigned and shortly afterwards went into exile.

THE 1931–1932 INTERREGNUM

A civil-military provisional regime took over after the overthrow of Ibáñez. In the election campaign that began soon after Ibáñez's ouster, Juan Esteban Montero, a member of the Radical party who had been Ibáñez's last minister of interior and had contributed substantially to his leaving office, won in a poll in which his most important competitor was Arturo Alessandri.

Like Ibáñez, Montero was faced with the disastrous economic situation precipitated by the Depression, about which he was able to do very little. In addition, he met growing opposition because of his refusal to dissolve the Congress; the Congress was a holdover from the dictatorship and had been largely handpicked by Ibáñez. Among Montero's most vocal critics were members of a group of small radical parties, most of them proclaiming some kind of socialist orientation, which had made their appearance after the fall of Ibáñez. Finally, there was plotting in the armed forces, in which there were competing political currents—from sympathizers with the fallen dictator to vaguely "socialist" elements.

The economic crisis, together with accumulated social, political, and military discontent, led to Montero's overthrow on June 4, 1932. The rebels on this occasion were a heterogeneous alliance of socialistic and Ibáñista elements in the armed forces, leaders of the new socialist parties, and civilian followers of Ibáñez. They proclaimed a "Socialist Republic."

This new regime lasted only a bit more than three months; it can be divided into two periods. During the first twelve days, its principal figures were Colonel Marmaduque Grove and Eugenio Matte, leader of the largest of the new socialist parties. They rallied extensive support among organized labor, particularly among the unions legally recognized under the legislation of September 1924, and made many promises concerning basic reforms, few if any of which they had time to carry out. This phase of the Socialist Republic marked the organized workers' first massive incursion into Chilean politics. The Grove-Matte regime made its appeals directly to the workers, and the majority of the workers demonstrated strong support for the short-lived Junta de Gobierno. The socialist-minded middle-class political leaders and the leaders of the legal trade unions who rallied behind the Grove-Matte version of the Socialist Republic were to be the two basic elements which were to form the Socialist party in the following year.

The second part of the Socialist Republic was the hundred days dominated by Carlos Dávila, the principal civilian follower of General Ibáñez. His regime issued a long series of decrees to deal with the economic crisis, the most important of which authorized the government temporarily to "intervene" or take over and keep functioning any enterprise that had been forced by the economic situation to close its doors. (This decree was revived forty years later and was applied under widely different circumstances by the government of President Salvador Allende.)

On September 13, 1932, the Socialist Republic was brought to an end by a military insurrection led by General Bartolomé Blanche. Elections were held two months later. This campaign reflected basic changes in the nature of Chilean politics, which were not to find full expression until three decades later. Although older patterns would partially reassert themselves in the years between, the election of 1932 foreshadowed issues and forces in 1964 and thereafter.

The two principal candidates in the 1932 presidential election were Arturo Alessandri and Marmaduque Grove. Alessandri retained an aura of the reformer and was supported principally by the middle-class Partido Radical. The traditional oligarchical political groups looked upon him, at best, as the lesser evil. His opponent, Marmaduque Grove, also mustered considerable middle-class, particularly lower middle-class, backing, but his campaign was directed largely at the working class, to which he had become a species of idol. Unfortunately for Grove, a large proportion of his working-class followers were still deprived of the franchise by literacy requirements.

There was no substantial right-wing candidate in this election, a situation that was to be repeated more than thirty years later.

In this contest, Alessandri was the easy winner. With his assumption of the presidency once again on December 24, 1932, Chile's first period of military domination of government and politics in this century came to an end. There began a period of more or less democratic constitutional government which was to last until September 11, 1973.

3
The 1932-1938 Alessandri Period

Arturo Alessandri faced substantially different circumstances when he came back to power in December 1932 from those he had confronted a dozen years earlier. He had to deal with armed forces that had become more or less accustomed to making and unmaking governments. He had to deal with a situation in which the political center of gravity had shifted substantially to the Left, with new forces bringing pressures on and seeking a major voice in the policies of government.

In one respect, the situation Alessandri encountered in 1932 was similar. In 1932, Chile was faced with a major economic crisis, much as it had been in 1920. The world Depression presented at least as many problems as had the post-World War I collapse of the nitrate mining industry. Nevertheless, in 1932 Alessandri had much better instruments for dealing with these problems as a result of the Constitution of 1925 and the existence of the Central Bank, for which he had been principally responsible, than he had had twelve years earlier.

Alessandri's chief tasks in his administration of the 1930s were to restore civilian-controlled constitutional and democratic government, and to resolve the economic crisis in which the country was immersed. His political, economic, and social policies during the 1932-1938 period were largely subordinated to the achievement of these two goals.

REASSERTION OF CIVILIAN CONTROL

Certainly, one of Alessandri's major achievements during the 1930s was the reestablishment of civilian control over the government and political life of the country. This accomplishment lasted four decades, during which Chile attained an almost unique position among the Latin American republics.

Alessandri demonstrated much political skill in his effort to curb the political appetites of the armed forces. He started off by moving very energetically the very day he took office. When the major generals followed what was then the usual custom of presenting their pro forma resignations upon the inauguration of a new president, Alessandri accepted all but one of these resignations. The only one he rejected was that of General Marcial Urrutia, whom he strongly trusted personally and was sure was as anxious as he to keep the armed forces at their professional tasks instead of in political activity.

For about a year, only one general was on active service in the Chilean army. Thereafter, Alessandri exercised great care in his selection of colonels and brigadiers for promotion, so as to avoid putting in positions of command those who might use their posts to subvert the government. Alessandri also had confidence in the commanders of the navy and the Carabineros (the militarized national police). These were Admiral Olegario Reyes del Rio and General Humberto Arriagada.

Another method Alessandri used to keep civilian control over the military was to seek to short-circuit plotting before it had time to mature. On one occasion, when he heard reliable information of a movement commencing in the air force, he called the officers involved to the president's office and presented them with the evidence he had. In addition to giving them a severe dressing down, he informed them that if there was any indication of a mutiny on the part of the air force, the full power of the army would be used against them. By that time, he had sufficient control over the army to make this threat effective.

A third tactic Alessandri used was to encourage (with the cooperation of the navy and the Carabineros), a paramilitary group, the Milicia Republicana, to act as a check on the army, the principal source of concern during the first years of the administration. Although the Milicia had come into existence before Alessandri's inauguration, he got the navy and Carabineros to issue it arms, including machine guns, and to cooperate with its units in various parts of the country. Alessandri was fully aware of the danger that the Milicia Republicana itself would get involved in politics, and when it gave some evidence that it might indeed do so, the organization was dissolved.

Finally, on several occasions Alessandri got "special powers," from Congress, as provided for in the Constitution. These powers authorized him to move swiftly, and without all of the exigencies required by the constitutional guarantees, to crush any threatened political move in the armed forces.

Alessandri's policies towards the armed forces were successful. Although there was considerable plotting by discontented elements of the military, particularly with civilians associated with Carlos Ibáñez, and even involving Ibáñez himself, such conspiracies produced few results. Only one serious rebellion against the government occurred during the Alessandri administration in February 1936, and it was quickly suppressed. By the end of his term, the president had firm control over the armed forces.

ECONOMIC POLICIES

Alessandri's second major task was to come to grips with the economic crisis. For this purpose he relied very heavily on Gustavo Ross, who was his minister of finance during most of this administration. Ross, considered something of a financial wizard, succeeded in getting the economy back on fairly solid ground by the end of the Alessandri administration. Undoubtedly, the partial recovery of other parts of the world economy from the Great Depression in the latter half of the 1930s had something to do with this accomplishment.

The Alessandri-Ross economic policies were a combination of orthodoxy and innovation. On the one hand, Ross sought successfully to balance the national budget, to resume payment on the foreign debt, and to otherwise restore Chile's "good reputation" in foreign financial circles, especially in Great Britain. On the other hand, the Alessandri regime of the 1930s undertook the first deliberate effort to industrialize the country, through substantial increases in tariff protection for Chilean manufacturing and very modest government help for financing new enterprises. These policies were to be intensified and expanded in the following decades.

In addition to following a protectionist policy, the administration gave other evidence of economic nationalism. Thus, it forced the U.S.-owned electric company which served much of central Chile, including Santiago, to turn over part ownership to the Chilean government. Similarly, in reorganizing the nitrate industry, the Alessandri regime established a government-owned firm as the sole exporter of that industry's products.

The Alessandri-Ross economic policies resulted in a considerable degree of prosperity by the end of the administration. Manufacturing was growing, and unemployment was reduced to relatively minor proportions. On the negative side, the rate of inflation began to accelerate again and would be a major preoccupation of the next seven administrations. Also, the great majority of the population remained very poor, a substantial proportion of it remaining largely out of the market economy.

Some modest advances were made in social reform during this period. The most important measure was a preventive medicine program established to deal particularly with tuberculosis and venereal diseases, two of the major scourges of the country. A modest public housing program was launched, and a minimum salary system was instituted for white collar workers. Notable progress was made in the field of education, with emphasis placed on the construction of new school buildings.

THE EMERGENCE OF NEW POLITICAL FORCES

During the Alessandri administration of the 1930s, new political forces—the Socialist and Communist parties, and a reorganized trade union movement—assumed major importance.

The Socialist party (Partido Socialista) emerged following the fall of the Ibáñez regime. At this time, several small socialist parties came together to support the Socialist Republic during the short period in which it was controlled by Colonel Grove and Eugenio Matte, head of one of the new socialist parties. They also joined forces in support of Grove's candidacy in the election of 1932.

In April 1933, the founding convention of the new Partido Socialista de Chile took place in Santiago. It brought together Acción Revolucionaria Socialista, Orden Socialista, Partido Socialista Marxista, and Partido Socialista Unificado. Although the formation of the Partido Socialista was the work of these smaller parties, its mass base was found in the legalized unions established in conformity with the labor legislation of September 8, 1924. Both the Communists and anarchists, who had dominated the labor movement before 1924, refused to allow unions under their control to seek recognition. As a result, the new unions formed under the law were established in defiance of the older political groups. With the end of the Ibáñez dictatorship, the leaders and members of the legal unions found their own political expression in the new socialist parties, and finally in the Partido Socialista de Chile. Thus, from its inception the Partido Socialista was in opposition to the Communists.

A little more than two years later, the Partido Socialista was joined by most members of Izquierda Comunista, the Trotskyite Communist party that had been stronger in the labor movement and general politics than the Stalinist Partido Comunista de Chile. With this merger, the anti-Communist bias of the socialists was strengthened, particularly in the labor movement.

From the beginning, the Socialist party was one of the country's major political organizations. In this respect, it took a position alongside the Conservative, Liberal, and Radical parties. It was indisputably the majority force in the organized labor movement, especially after the entry of the labor elements of Izquierda Comunista. It had an exceedingly active and combative youth organization, which during the late 1930s challenged the attempt of the Nazi party to "seize control of the streets." The militancy and enthusiasm of the party won the admiration of visiting socialists from other countries.

The Socialist party had certain weaknesses which, although they did not hamper its growth during the 1930s, were to be exceedingly serious in the following two decades. The principal one was the extreme personalism and "prima donna" attitudes of many of its leaders. Each of the small parties that joined to form the Socialist party had had one or two outstanding figures in its leadership. Once the parties merged into a single organization, these men tended constantly to jockey for leadership and prestige. The party did not have sufficient time to resolve this situation before it was called upon to join the government succeeding that of President Alessandri. Indeed, its tradition of factionalism was never completely overcome.

Another element contributing to the Socialist party's factionalism was the heterogeneous nature of its membership and leadership. The party was made up of social democrats, who were more or less indistinguishable in their ideas from those who made up the bulk of the Social Democratic parties of Europe; Marxist-Leninists, who although having tactical and strategic differences with the Communist party, nonetheless shared with it the ultimate objective of establishing a one-party "proletarian" dictatorship; and opportunists who were attracted to the party more by the possibility of making a career within its ranks than by its ideas and program.

Another element on the Left that became important in national politics during the Alessandri administration was the Communist party (Partido Comunista de Chile). The Communist party had suffered considerably at the hands of the Ibáñez dictatorship and had come out of that period split into two rival organizations, one Stalinist and one Trotskyite. The party gained considerable ground in the latter part of the Alessandri regime primarily because of a change in the political line of the Communist International.

During the early 1930s the Communists, in conformity with the extremely sectarian "Third Period" of the Communist International, were isolated in national politics. Advocating a position of immediate revolution and denouncing all other elements on the left as "social fascists," they were strongly opposed to the Socialist Republic of 1932 and for some time after that would not ally themselves with other parties or groups. At the same time, they controlled a small faction of the labor movement, the Federación Obrera de Chile, which consisted of legally unrecognized unions.

With the advent of the Popular Front tactic of the Communist International, the party was no longer politically isolated. The Comintern apparently picked Chile as one of the major countries in Latin America in which a serious effort would be made to establish a Popular Front. Under the direction of the Comintern representative, the Peruvian Eudosio Ravines, the Chilean Communist party began to court other elements on the Left, particularly the Radical party. Through a variety of techniques—including lionizing certain Radical politicians in the Communist daily newspaper, helping to finance and man campaigns of some of the Radical leaders, supporting fellow travelers against rival Radical politicians within the party's ranks, and backing the Radicals against the Socialists on crucial issues—the Communists succeeded in ingratiating themselves with an appreciable element within the Radical party.

The result was that the Communist party began to grow in the late 1930s, gaining representation not only in the Senate and Chamber of Deputies, but also in municipal councils. After the unification of the labor movement in December 1936, their influence in the trade unions began to expand considerably.

In the last two years of the Alessandri regime, the organized labor movement became a significant political factor in Chile. After the adoption of the Popular Front line, the Communists were willing to merge their faction of the labor movement with others, and they began an intensive campaign for trade union unity. This campaign was aided by the increasing hostility of all elements of the labor movement towards the Alessandri administration. This antagonism reached a high point when the government broke a strike of railroad workers in February 1936.

The upshot of these developments was the congress of December 1936 which established the Confederación de Trabajadores de Chile (CTCh). This meeting was attended by delegates from the Confederación Nacional de Sindicatos Legales, controlled by the Socialists, as well as the Communists' Federación Obrera de Chile, the anarchosyndicalist Confederación General de Trabajadores, and independent unions. Although the anarchosyndicalists finally decided not to participate in the CTCh, the new confederation nonetheless represented the overwhelming majority of the organized labor movement, which grew substantially during the late 1930s.

The CTCh frankly believed in political participation for the trade unions. As a result, virtually from its inception, the CTCh joined the Popular Front, and had representatives at its congresses and in its executive bodies.

THE PARTIDO NACISTA

One other new force in Chilean politics in the 1930s, the Partido Nacista, proved to have a shorter life than the Socialist and Communist parties and the CTCh. This party was modeled on the European fascist parties, particularly that of Germany. It was headed by a somewhat erratic German-Chilean firebrand, Jorge González von Mareés. It had special appeal to the German-descended people of the southern part of central Chile, but also won recruits among other sectors of the population. It had most of the accoutrements of a fascist party, including uniformed storm troopers, and various symbols.

For some time, the Nacistas were a considerable source of worry not only to the parties of the Left, but also to the Alessandri administration. The president was particularly concerned with their close association with ex-dictator Carlos Ibáñez. As the election campaign of 1938 approached, the Nacistas formed the principal shock force behind the presidential candidacy of General Ibáñez.

However, the Nacistas virtually committed suicide. On September 5, 1938, they attempted a violent seizure of power, when their storm troopers temporarily seized the University of Chile, almost across the street from the presidential palace, La Moneda, and the Social Security building, katty-corner from La Moneda. They apparently believed they would have the support of some of the Santiago garrison, but the armed forces remained loyal to the regime. As a result, the Nacistas were easily ousted from the University of Chile, although not without casualties on both sides. It proved more difficult to remove them from the Social Security building. This was not accomplished until late in the afternoon, when the Carabineros made a frontal attack on the edifice, during which all but two of the besieged Nacistas were killed. Certainly, some of these were murdered after they had surrendered. The killings clouded Alessandri's reputation for the rest of his life, even though he had not ordered them.

As a result of the events of September 5, General Ibáñez withdrew as a presidential candidate, a factor which gave the election to the other anti-government nominee, Pedro Aguirre Cerda. At the same time, the Nacista party was discredited. Although it lingered on under another name for three or four years, it declined rapidly after September 5, 1938.

THE POPULAR FRONT

The Popular Front had finally been organized in the middle of 1936. Its chief advocates were the Communists, and there was strong opposition to it within both the Radical and Socialist parties. A strong faction of the Radicals wanted to continue to cooperate with President Alessandri, who had been their candidate in 1932 and with whom they had had close relations for more than a decade before that. For his part, Alessandri was very anxious to keep the Radicals in his government, but he met strong resistance from within the Conservative and Liberal parties, led by Gustavo Ross among others.

The Radical party had serious doubts about developing a close association with the parties to their Left, that is, the Socialists and Communists. Those Radicals opposed to the formation of the Popular Front were led by Pedro Aguirre Cerda and those who favored it were headed by Juan Antonio Ríos.

The Radicals finally decided to join the Popular Front, partly because of

President Alessandri's growing reliance on the Conservatives and Liberals for a majority in Congress, and his difficulties in getting those two parties to agree to give the Radicals equal representation in the government. Another factor was the real prospect the Popular Front gave for the election of a Radical as president in the 1938 election.

Within the Socialist ranks there was also strong opposition to formation of a Popular Front. Most Socialists innately distrusted the Communist party, both on the basis of ideological opposition to forming an alliance with the "bourgeois" Radicals and undoubtedly also on the basis of well-founded suspicions that in any Radical-Socialist-Communist alliance the Radicals and Communists would join forces against the Socialists. Growing hostility against President Alessandri within organized labor and generally on the Left, however, ultimately pushed the Socialists towards the Popular Front. So, too, did the possibility that the Popular Front candidate in the 1938 election might be the Socialist Marmaduque Grove.

The railroad strike of February 1936, Alessandri's harsh suppression of it, and the unanimous reaction on the Left against the government's attitude finally cast the die in favor of the Popular Front. Final negotiations for its formation were begun within days of the end of the strike, and after a few weeks the details of the new alliance had been worked out. It consisted of the Radical, Democrático, Socialist, and Communist parties and the CTCh.

The Popular Front made modest gains in the congressional elections of 1937, and as the presidential election year of 1938 approached, it was increasingly clear that the Front had a good chance of winning. The Front's nomination, therefore, became a hotly contested plum.

The Popular Front presidential nominee was chosen at a convention in April 1938. The Radicals' candidate was Pedro Aguirre Cerda, who had won his party's endorsement in primaries held earlier. The Socialists were unanimous in support of Grove. The Radicals and Socialists had almost equal representation at the convention, and the casting vote obviously lay with the Communists, who made it clear they did not like Grove as the nominee. Hence, the Socialists finally agreed to support Pedro Aguirre Cerda.

THE 1938 ELECTION

Throughout most of the 1938 presidential campaign, there were three nominees: Aguirre Cerda for the Popular Front; Carlos Ibáñez backed by his own party, Alianza Popular Libertadora, the Nacistas, and a small dissident Socialist group; and Gustavo Ross, the government nominee. Under these circumstances, the major probabilities lay with Ross.

General Ibáñez, who had returned to Chile from exile in the middle of Alessandri's term, set about organizing the forces that might bring him back to office, while at the same time engaging in some conspiratorial activity. In 1937, the Communists proposed that Ibáñez be invited to join the Popular Front, but both Radicals and Socialists rejected this notion. As a result, Ibáñez launched his candidacy with the backing of the three small groups already mentioned. He had little chance of winning, but the campaign would serve to reestablish him as an important element in national politics. As we have noted, he finally withdrew after the frustrated uprising of September 5, 1938.

Gustavo Ross was an unfortunate candidate from the government's point of view. He had a cold and imperious personality, and completely lacked charisma. He was nominated in spite of objections by President Alessandri, whose original idea had been to keep the Radicals in the government alliance and to offer the presidential nomination to someone from their ranks. Alessandri's Conservative and Liberal allies flatly rejected this idea and insisted on the candidacy of Ross, in whose conservative (if not reactionary) bona fides they had full confidence.

In spite of Alessandri's warnings that times had changed, the forces backing Ross counted on the traditional machinations of Chilean politics to elect their candidate. They depended on the landlords' ability to get their peasants to the polls to vote for the nominee the landlords favored; as well as on ability of vote-buying to influence large segments of both the urban and rural voters. They apparently did not foresee, as President Alessandri did, that voters might accept the bribes offered them by Ross's supporters and go into the voting booth and cast their ballot for Aguirre Cerda.

Aguirre Cerda won only by a margin of 227,720 votes to 218,609. Many of Ross's supporters charged fraud in the counting and urged Alessandri not to recognize Aguirre Cerda's victory. The president refused this suggestion and used his influence with the military to assure a peaceful transfer of power. This took place on December 24, 1938.

4

The Second Assault on Traditional Chile: The Radical Period

Between 1938 and 1952, four Radicals served as Chile's chief executive: Pedro Aguirre Cerda, Juan Antonio Ríos, Alfredo Duhalde, and Gabriel González Videla. The Radical party, Chile's largest political organization during this period, dominated the country's politics.

This fourteen-year period is crucial to an understanding of the tragedy Chile experienced in the 1970s. For one thing, those who formed the Unidad Popular of the 1970s saw this period as a direct antecedent to their own period in power. Lessons were drawn from the experiences of the earlier period concerning what to do and what not to do during the Allende regime. Strikingly different lessons were drawn by different elements in and around the Unidad Popular.

Second, it was during this period that leaders of the Socialist and Communist parties received their first experiences as ministers and other top government officials. Salvador Allende, for instance, served for some time as minister of health in Aguirre Cerda's administration.

Third, these fourteen years in power exhausted the Radical party. At the end of the period, it was somewhat unfairly discredited, and although the party made a brief recovery in the late 1950s, its fourteen years in control largely destroyed the party as the principal spokesman for the Chilean middle class and as the fulcrum of national politics.

Finally, during those years Chile underwent most of the process of import substitution industrialization. By the end of the period, manufacturing firms had been established to produce domestically nearly all the consumers' goods that formerly had been imported. At that point, a new strategy was required for the continuation of the country's economic development. More than a decade was to pass before such a new strategy was decided upon and adopted.

THE AGUIRRE CERDA ADMINISTRATION

The Popular Front government of Pedro Aguirre Cerda took office on December 24, 1938, and during its less than three years in office made notable economic and social changes. Some of these changes were in conformity with the platform on which the government had been elected, and others were more the result of circumstances which the Popular Front regime encountered.

Less than a month after Aguirre Cerda was inaugurated, the country suffered one of the worst earthquakes on record, centered in the cities of Chillan and Concepción, some 300 miles south of Santiago. The disaster required emergency action. After the first relief efforts had been carried out, the government established two new organizations, the Corporación de Reconstrucción y Auxilio (Reconstruction and Relief Corporation), and the Corporación de Fomento de la Producción (Production Development Corporation—CORFO). The first agency lasted only briefly, since its task was a limited one, but the Corporación de Fomento became a very important fixture of the Chilean government. It was to play a major role in the administration of President Salvador Allende, albeit a role that was not foreseen by its founders.

CORFO became the government's principal vehicle for fostering the country's economic development. In its early years, it drew up three extensive programs for developing key sectors of the economy: light and power, industry, and agriculture. Although the exigencies of World War II, which broke out before the end of the first year of the Aguirre Cerda regime, prevented the immediate full implementation of these programs, a basis was laid during this period for the policies and programs that would be followed during the rest of the Radical era.

In the field of energy and power resources, CORFO established programs in two sectors: electricity and petroleum. In the first, it organized a subsidiary, Empresa Nacional de Electricidad, S.A. (ENDESA), which had the dual objectives of providing electricity to those parts of the country which were badly served or had no electricity at all, and once this had been achieved, to develop a national electric grid, absorbing into it the existing privately owned electric companies. These objectives were largely achieved over the next thirty years.

In the petroleum field, too, CORFO established a subsidiary for the exploration and exploitation of oil reserves in the extreme southern part of the country. At the same time, it organized another subsidiary for refining the petroleum from the Chilean oil fields and abroad, while also giving aid to a second privately owned company for the same purpose. The first oil was discovered and began to be exploited in the years immediately following World War II.

In the manufacturing sector, CORFO encouraged the merging of small companies into larger ones, helping to finance the larger enterprises so that they could produce on an economical scale. This device was employed for home appliances, copper products, and pharmaceuticals, among others. In some cases, CORFO became a stockholder in these firms and in others it merely helped to finance them.

In addition, CORFO laid plans for more ambitious enterprises, the most important of which was the country's first modern steel plant, established at Huachipato, not far from Concepción. This plant was planned during World War II, with the cooperation of the Koppers Coke Company of the United States; it began production in 1947. Planned originally to turn out over 300,000 tons of steel a year, it was expanded several times in the succeeding decades.

CORFO had a more modest agricultural program, confining its efforts mainly to helping finance the importation of machinery, equipment, and other inputs in the agricultural sector. More extensive programs were hampered by the land distribution pattern that persisted in the country and about which little was done until the latter half of the 1960s.

The most important social change of the Aguirre Cerda regime was the very rapid expansion of the trade union movement. During the years of the Popular Front government and immediately thereafter, most of the organizable urban workers were brought into the labor movement. The government actively encouraged unionization and helped to break the power that employers in some sectors, notably the coal industry, had over the legal unions in those areas. Within six years after Aguirre Cerda's inauguration, trade union membership had at least doubled.

Unionization in that period was confined to the urban areas. During the first months of 1939, largely under the guidance of the Socialist and Communist parties, strong efforts were made to organize rural workers' unions, but in May 1939 President Aguirre Cerda issued a decree forbidding legal recognition of any more unions among these workers. One must suppose that this move was taken because of the fear that violent reaction among rural landlords might imperil the regime.

The politics of the Popular Front regime was marked by violent shocks between the Socialist and Communist parties. As a result of the pro-German neutrality of the Soviet Union during most of the first two years of World War II, the Chilean Communist party took the position that the conflict was an "imperialist war" in which the workers and people of Chile had no interest; it particularly attacked "Yankee imperialism." The Socialists, on the other hand, were pro-Allied. Minister of Production Oscar Schnake, who had been secretary general of the Socialist party from its establishment until he accepted the cabinet post, wanted to get whatever aid he could from the United States for economic development programs that were being developed under the aegis of his ministry and CORFO.

As a result of these differing positions, the Socialists and Communists carried on bitter polemics. Schnake and the Socialists demanded the expulsion of the Communists from the Popular Front, and when the Radicals would not agree, the Socialists themselves formally withdrew from the Front. In the congressional elections of 1941, they had their own candidates apart from those of the Front. The relations between the Socialists and Communists reached a low point in this period.

Meanwhile, the Socialist party experienced the first of several significant splits that were to take place during the 1940s. This dissidence first became evident in the party's Fifth Congress in December 1939, when a group led by César Godoy Urrutia and Natalio Berman demanded that the Socialist party withdraw from the Popular Front government. Although they were strongly defeated, the dissidents continued to be exceedingly critical of the party leadership. In April 1940 they withdrew to form a new party, the Partido Socialista de Trabajadores (PST).

The PST lasted only four years. Although at the time it was formed, the Communists had denounced Godoy Urrutia and his followers as Trotskyites and had carried out a strong press campaign against them, the new party quickly took a pro-Communist direction. In June 1944, the remaining members of the PST were accepted into the Communist party, and Godoy Urrutia immediately emerged as one of the principal leaders of the Partido Comunista.

These bitter political struggles created grave problems for Aguirre Cerda. They may well have contributed to his premature death on November 25, 1941. By that time, the Popular Front had for practical purposes ceased to exist.

THE ELECTION OF 1942

As a result of President Aguirre Cerda's death, new presidential elections were necessary in conformity with the Constitution. The Radical party candidate was Juan Antonio Ríox, who had been Aguirre Cerda's chief contender within the party's ranks four years earlier. After some discussion, the Socialists rather grudgingly threw their support to Ríos, as did the Communists and the smaller parties that had been in the Popular Front.

The Radical leader's opponent in the campaign was General Carlos Ibáñez who had the endorsement not only of his own followers, but also of the Conservative party and the majority of the Liberal party. At the beginning of the short campaign, the ex-dictator's chances of winning seemed very good.

Former President Arturo Alessandri liked neither Ibáñez nor Ríos. He had never forgiven Ríos for having been Ibáñez's closest associate within the Radical party during the dictatorship and for having plotted against

Alessandri's own regime on at least one occasion. In the end, however, Alessandri threw his support to Ríos in order to prevent the greater evil of the ex-dictator returning to power. As a result, he organized a split within the Liberal party ranks, taking a substantial element from that party into the forces supporting Juan Antonio Ríos. Ríos did win the 1942 election, but his margin of victory was a narrow one.

THE JUAN ANTONIO RÍOS PERIOD

Ríos, the second president of the Radical period, was also destined to die in office. He filled out only about four years of his six-year term.

The most controversial issue of Ríos' term centered on what stand Chile should take in World War II. Although Ríos' sympathies were with the Allies, he had grave reservations about taking Chile officially into the war. On the one hand, he deeply resented U.S. pressure on him and his government to take this step, pressure he thought infringed upon Chile's national sovereignty. In the second place, Ríos had serious worry that Chile's formal entry into the war might leave the country's 3,000-mile coastline open to raids from German submarines or surface ships known to be operating in the Pacific Ocean. With strong popular support for the Allies and for Chilean entry into the conflict, however, the government finally declared war on Germany and Japan.

The Socialist party suffered yet another division during the Ríos presidency. This schism arose over the same issues as those which split the party in 1940: whether the party should participate in the government, as well as what relations it should have with the Communist party. Marmaduque Grove led a movement in the Ninth Congress of the party in January 1943 which favored membership in the cabinet of President Ríos and close relations with the Communist party, looking towards eventual merger with the Partido Comunista. After this congress, difference between the Grove position and that favored by Salvador Allende, the party secretary general, and Bernardo Ibáñez, secretary general of the Confederación de Trabajadores de Chile, who opposed entry into the government and close association with the Communists, intensified. It culminated in the Fourth Extraordinary Congress of the party, held in August 1943, at which the Grove position was completely defeated. Grove thereupon withdrew from the Socialist party and formed the Partido Socialista Auténtico (PSA).

The Communists again encouraged the division with the Socialist ranks, this time siding with Grove against the Allende-Ibáñez faction. In May 1947, the majority of the PSA leadership voted to join the Communist party, although Grove himself soon afterwards returned to the Socialist party.

Social problems occupied a good deal of President Ríos' time, particularly after the close of World War II. During the war, both Socialists and Communists within the labor movement had tried to prevent strikes that would seriously cripple the supplying of war material to the Allies; they had no such restraint once the conflict was over. Inflation was increasingly serious during and immediately after the war, and there was very great pressure within the trade union movement for wage readjustments.

A series of strikes took place in the months immediately following the war. Some of these, particularly walkouts in the mining industry, were illegal, that is, they were called before all procedures called for in the Labor Code had been exhausted. President Ríos became increasingly concerned with this situation. The climax of these developments came under Vice-President Alfredo Duhalde, who had taken over the government with the onset of what proved to be President Ríos' fatal illness. Duhalde ordered that legal recognition be withdrawn from two mine workers' unions that had engaged in illegal strikes. After two general strikes and a meeting at which police fired on those present, Duhalde offered concessions. These events also produced a split in the Confederación de Trabajadores de Chile, with a majority CTCh under Communist domination and a minority CTCh under Socialist control.

THE ELECTION OF 1946

With the death of President Ríos in July 1946, another presidential election was held on September 4, 1946. This election, and the events of the next few months, were an important precedent for the Unidad Popular experience of the early 1970s and likely had considerable impact on the thinking of those who were to lead the Unidad Popular.

The Radicals, the Communists, and the small Christian Democratic party called Falange Nacional joined in supporting the candidacy of Gabriel González Videla. He was a Radical leader who had been courted by the Communists for several years and was considered the principal figure in the left wing of the Radical party. He had been a contender for the party's nomination in the 1942 election but had been passed over in favor of Ríos.

González Videla had three opponents in the 1946 election: Eduardo Cruz Coke for the Conservatives, Fernando Alessandri (son of Arturo Alessandri) for the Liberals, and Bernardo Ibáñez for the Socialists. González Videla received a plurality, but not an absolute majority, in the popular election. Thus, in accordance with the Constitution, the issue of choosing between him and Eduardo Cruz Coke, the runner up, was thrown into a joint session of Congress.

After the September 4 election, negotiations were conducted between the leading candidate and those forces whose support would give him victory in

Congress. (In some ways, these negotiations were similar to those which would take place twenty-four years later, when Salvador Allende also won a plurality but not a majority in the popular vote.) Arturo Alessandri took a leading part in persuading the Liberals to back González Videla. The full details of these negotiations are still not known, but the net result was that when he took office, González Videla appointed Liberals as well as Radicals and Communists to his first cabinet. He assumed office on November 3, 1946.

THE FIRST PHASE OF THE GONZÁLEZ VIDELA REGIME

The coalition cabinet included representatives of perhaps Chile's most conservative party (Partido Liberal), of the principal middle-class party, the Radicals, and of the Communist party. This cabinet continued in office from early November 1946 until early April 1947. This experience was to leave a deep impression on the Chilean left.

This was the first time that the Chilean Communist party participated in a cabinet. They sought to use their membership in the González Videla government to expand and consolidate their power and influence in the labor movement, and in the country's general politics.

As a result of the split in the CTCh, a bitter struggle was waged for control of the labor movement. The Communists sought to use the government to expand the CTCh faction under their control and to weaken that under the control of their Socialist rivals. The Communists' general technique was to ignore the laws with regard to legal union recognition and collective bargaining when these laws did not favor them. When unions under their control conducted illegal strikes, the minister of labor and even the president hastened to deal with the union leaders, even though they were in defiance of the law. On the other hand, when Socialist-controlled unions did the same thing, the law was strictly applied to them. In various sectors where Socialists controlled the unions, the Communists organized rival groups and demanded that the minister of labor and the president deal with them, in spite of the fact that the law provided for only one legal labor group in each firm or part of the economy.

The Communists also sought to terrorize their opponents, particularly in the labor movement, physically attacking and even murdering anarchosyndicalist, Socialist, and other trade union leaders who resisted Communist influence. The Communists mounted organized attacks on those circulating hostile literature or putting up Socialist or other posters.

Meanwhile, in the inner circles of the government, the Communists were exerting increasing pressure on President González Videla to follow a foreign policy in conformity with the Communist party's official line. These were the early days of the Cold War, and to the Communists the United States had taken the place of Hitler's Germany as "the enemy" and the object of their attack. González Videla resisted this pressure and became increasingly dubious about his Communist allies.

GONZÁLEZ VIDELA'S BREAK WITH THE COMMUNISTS

The tension between the Communists on the one hand, and President González Videla and the other parties in the cabinet on the other, finally erupted in April 1947. The immediate occasion for the break was the municipal elections, which caused considerable worry among both Radicals and Liberals. The Liberals lost considerable ground to the other major right-wing party, the Conservatives, which most Liberals tended to attribute to the fact that they were in a government together with the Communist party. The Radicals also lost much ground, the Communists gained substantially, while the Socialists, who were perhaps the most strongly antigovernment party contesting the elections, recouped many of their earlier losses. Thus, both Radicals and Liberals had reason to doubt the political wisdom of continued association with the Communist party. After a week's hesitation following the municipal elections, the Liberal party withdrew its members from the president's cabinet. The Radical ministers then turned in their resignations. When the Communist ministers refused to resign, the president dismissed them.

This was the beginning of a major conflict between President González Videla and his erstwhile allies, the Communists. Signs of the coming struggle were evident on the night the Communists were forced out of the government. They organized marches around the center of Santiago, with the marchers chanting *No se puede gobernar, sin apoyo popular* ("It is impossible to govern without popular support"), which obviously was intended to mean "without Communist support."

Within a few weeks, Communist-controlled unions throughout the country began a series of strikes, especially in key sectors such as the coal mines. González Videla, rightly or wrongly, concluded that these were revolutionary strikes designed ultimately to bring down the government. He felt that the Communists saw themselves in a position roughly equivalent to that of their comrades in Eastern Europe during this same period, who through a combination of different kinds of pressures brought down popularly elected governments in which they were in a minority and substituted for them completely Communist-controlled regimes.

If this was indeed the thinking of the Communists of Chile at that time, they overlooked one essential difference between their situation and that of their Eastern European confreres: although they had been in González Videla's cabinet, they had never had control over the Ministry of Interior and Ministry of Defense, such as the Communists in East European countries had been able to obtain through the influence of the occupying Russian forces. Thus, when the Chilean Communists forced an open showdown with President González Videla, they lost out.

The political strikes called by the Communists were defeated by the government, in part with the help of the Socialists, who from being the most bitter opponents of the González Videla regime became its closest allies. Once the strikes were defeated, González Videla submitted to Congress the so-called Law for the Defense of Democracy. This Draconian measure outlawed the Communist party and removed those who were registered as Communists from voter lists. This law also made Communists ineligible for election to offices in the unions and allowed the president to sequester Communists in isolated parts of the republic.

The controversy over the Law for the Defense of Democracy produced the last of the three major splits that plagued the Socialist party during the 1940s. Although the majority of the party members in Congress and in the National Executive of the party favored the proposed law, a strong minority, led by former Socialist Youth leader Raúl Ampuero and by Senator Salvador Allende, opposed it vigorously. The Ampuero-Allende group also opposed any further participation by the Socialists in González Videla's cabinet, which they had entered a few months after his break with the Communists.

This new schism resulted in the formation of the Partido Socialista Popular (PSP) by the Ampuero-Allende group. Ampuero, who became secretary general of the PSP, sought to impose a much stronger discipline on the new group than had been characteristic of the Socialists, and to commit it to Marxism-Leninism, a position the Socialists had never taken before.

Another result of the quarrel between González Videla and the Communists was a new law concerning unionization of rural workers. During their honeymoon with the administration, the Communists had been active in organizing new unions among agricultural workers, and a few of these had been legalized. These rural workers' unions were formed into a national federation. González Videla sought to put a halt to this activity by enacting new legislation. Although the new law ostensibly authorized legalization of rural unions, its conditions for legal recognition were so rigorous that it was practically impossible for any union of agricultural workers to gain legal standing. The law effectively curtailed rural unionization for several years.

OTHER ASPECTS OF THE GONZÁLEZ VIDELA REGIME

The González Videla administration was a period of intensive economic development. The plans of the Corporación de Fomento, which had been held up because of World War II, were put into execution. The steel plant at Huachipato went into operation, a new plant for smelting minerals was opened at Paipote, three major hydroelectric projects were opened at Sauzal, Abanico, and Pilmaiquén, and major progress was made in expanding oil exploration and exploitation in the far south. At the same time, CORFO pushed the expansion of older branches of industry, such as pharmaceuticals, metal fabricating, textiles, and paper production; several of the newer industries, notably household furnishings and equipment, were also expanded considerably with CORFO's help.

By the end of the González Videla administration, Chile had nearly completed a major phase of its economic development. This was the process of industrialization through establishment of manufacturing firms to produce goods the country previously had imported. Although some import substitution could still be undertaken, it was not sufficient to constitute a major impetus to further industrialization and general economic development.

With the virtual end of import substitution, new strategies and programs were needed. It was necessary to expand the internal market by bringing into it the substantial rural population that remained outside the market and by raising the real purchasing power of lower income groups in the urban economy. It was also necessary to develop programs for export of some industrial goods, through a process of rationalizing Chilean industry and making at least major sectors of it competitive in international markets.

In order to facilitate such basic changes in economic development strategy and programs, important basic reforms were required by the end of the González Videla period. These included agrarian reform, tax reform, modifications of labor and social security legislation, and steps to make both labor and management more efficient. It took more than a decade after the end of the Radical period before the country's political leaders came to realize the urgency of such changes. In the meantime the country suffered a period of comparative economic stagnation.

In additon to the Law for the Defense of Democracy, another major political change took place during the González Videla administration. This was the enactment of a constitutional amendment extending women the right to vote in congressional and presidential elections. A law passed during the 1930s administration of Arturo Alessandri had given them this right in municipal elections. The women first cast their votes for national candidates in the 1952 presidential election. Their vote represented a major and very important expansion of the franchise, which had continued to be limited to a relatively small part of the country's adult population.

THE ELECTION OF 1952

The fourteen-year period of Radical party rule came to an end in the presidential election of 1952. The years immediately preceding this election had been marked by increasing popular disillusionment with the Radical party, and to a considerable degree with all of the existing political parties. The sources of this disillusionment were the apparently chameleon-like nature of the Radicals and most other parties, demonstrated in the González Videla period by the fact that in his six years in office, González Videla had almost every party in his government at one time or another; by a persistent inflation with which the party politicians seemed unable to cope; and perhaps, insofar as the Radicals were concerned, a general feeling on the part of the electorate that it was "time for a change."

The chief beneficiary of the voters' mood was Carlos Ibáñez. The one-time dictator had been elected a senator in 1949, and in the following years his prestige had grown as that of the party leaders had declined. Increasingly, his period in office tended to be remembered not for its dictatorship, but for the economic prosperity of its early years. He now appeared as a somewhat grandfatherly figure, and his aversion for the traditional parties and politicians was well known.

A heterogeneous group of parties gathered around the Ibáñez candidacy. He was first proclaimed a candidate by the Partido Agrario Laborista, hitherto a small party with no well-defined ideology. He was then endorsed by a splinter of the Radicals, the Partido Radical Doctrinario, and a splinter group of the Democráticos. Finally, he was supported by the Partido Socialista Popular.

The PSP backing was on the face of it very strange. Ibáñez and the Socialists had long been enemies, and they shared little in political ideas and programs. The PSP support for Ibáñez can only be explained in opportunistic terms; indeed, that was the explanation Raúl Ampuero and other PSP leaders offered. They argued that Ibáñez was going to win whether or not they supported him. Second, they said, he had no particular program, and if the PSP was with him, they could supply him with one to their liking. Finally, whatever dictatorial tendencies he might once again demonstrate could be better fought from within his camp than from the opposition.

Many members of the PSP, led by Senator Salvador Allende, opposed its endorsement of Carlos Ibáñez. Allende headed a faction of the PSP which defected and rejoined the Partido Socialista de Chile (PSCh), the other faction resulting from the 1948 split in the party. Soon after he rejoined the PSCh, Allende was approached by the Communists (who were still illegal), who offered to support him if he became the PSCh presidential candidate. Considerably overestimating the backing the Communists could provide, the Partido Socialista de Chile leaders accepted the Communist offer and named Allende as their nominee.

This was one of the more bizarre switches in Chilean politics in recent decades. Almost overnight the Partido Socialista de Chile was converted from the most anti-Communist party in all of Chilean politics into the closest Communist ally. As the next two decades were to prove, the change in Socialist attitude was to be a long-run one, in spite of its unexpectedness and extra-ordinary swiftness.

The two other candidates in the election were the nominee of the again united Conservative and Liberal parties, Arturo Matte Larraín, a son-in-law of the late Arturo Alessandri who had died in 1950; and the nominee of the Radical party, Pedro Enrique Alfonso.

Carlos Ibáñez won the 1952 election decisively. Taking office in December 1952, he ended the Radical party's long period of control of the presidency. Ibáñez's ascension to power marked the end of a well-defined period in the political, economic, and social evolution of Chile.

LESSONS FROM THE RADICAL PERIOD

The parties of the Left learned many lessons from the fourteen-year ex-perience of the Radical period. From the Popular Front experiment, all of the Leftist parties—Socialists, Communists, and even many Radicals—concluded that any future coalition of the far Left had to carry out far-reaching changes in the economy, society, and polity of Chile, and not be satisfied with modest reforms. Many tended to look back at the Aguirre Cerda period as a lost opportunity for making much more sweeping changes than had actually been accomplished. It became increasingly an article of faith among Socialists and Communists that the Popular Front had not moved fast or far enough, and even that it had been a "betrayal" of those who had voted for it.

The Socialists drew several additional conclusions from the experience of the Radical period. One was that they never again wanted to be in a situation in which the Communists and Radicals would be able to take advantage of them, as they were convinced had happened during the Popular Front period. Thus, in subsequent decades they were to insist that any presidential candi-date from the far Left had to be drawn from one of the "proletarian" parties, which in practice meant from the Socialist party since no Communist stood a chance of election.

Another lesson the Socialists learned was the great danger of a head-on confrontation with the Communist party. The bitter and even violent struggle between Socialists and Communists in between 1946 and 1952, had demon-strated the ability of the Communists, with their much more disciplined or-ganization, extensive financial resources, and vituperative propaganda machine, to destroy the careers of Socialist leaders who collided with them. Two examples were Oscar Schnake and Bernardo Ibáñez. As a result of this experience, the Socialist leadership—and to a less degree their rank and file—developed a profound inferiority complex vis-à-vis the Communist party. Although the old enmities did not die easily and flared up periodically for many years, the Socialists believed they could never again risk another all-out confrontation with them such as they had during the 1940s. With regard to the trade union movement, the Socialists now felt that in the name of "labor unity" they had to acquiesce in the maintenance of a single central organization for the trade unions. The Communists were therefore able to control this central labor body, even though until the late 1960s numerically they were vastly inferior to the Socialists.

For their part, the Communists came to the conclusion that they had pushed President González Videla too hard during the early part of his administration. They had forced him to break drastically with them, although he had no intention of doing so even after he removed them from his cabinet. After 1952, the Communists developed a more subtle approach in their dealings with their allies. Hence, in the period of the Unidad Popular government of the early 1970s, they were cautious not to push President Allende into a position where he would have to choose between them and his own followers.

Many Socialists, especially Salvador Allende, likely drew another lesson from the Radical experience, particularly the González Videla period. Practically all of the far Left ultimately felt that González Videla had "betrayed" the Communists, the political group that had been most responsible for putting him in power. There is good reason to believe that Allende and others in the Socialist leadership came to the conclusion that if they attained the presidency, they would never attempt to crush elements instrumental in bringing them to power. This determination may have been behind Allende's extreme reluctance as president to break with any element among his followers.

When the Radicals looked back at the González Videla experience, they undoubtedly considered González Videla's turnabout the principal cause of the decline of their party. They, too, felt that their party could never again afford a decisive break with the Communists and far Left in general, which González Videla had had. While this element in the party was not dominant during much of the succeeding decade and a half, it was in control from the late 1960s until the end of the Allende regime.

5

The Ibañez-Jorge Alessandri Interregnum

A dozen years elapsed between the end of Radical party control and the beginning of the period of accelerated social and economic change of the late 1960s and early 1970s. This interregnum, which covered the presidencies of General Carlos Ibáñez (1952–1958) and Jorge Alessandri (1958–1964), was a period of almost imperceptible economic growth, mounting social ferment, and important political changes.

PROMISE AND PERFORMANCE OF THE SECOND IBÁÑEZ REGIME

General Carlos Ibáñez returned to power on so large a wave of personal popularity that, had he so chosen, he could well have initiated the kind of societal changes that in fact began more than a decade later. His popularity cut across class lines, and for the first time, on a substantial scale, rural workers voted contrary to their landowners' wishes, in support of General Ibáñez. Ibáñez had wide enough backing that he could have begun massive changes in the countryside and could have extended Chilean control over copper mining, the country's major export industry.

But Ibáñez did not come to power in 1952 as a reformer, in spite of his opponents' fears and his supporters' hopes. It would appear that his ambition in his second presidency was to vindicate himself in history, to overcome the association of his name with the only dictatorship Chile had had in the twentieth century. He succeeded in this ambition, and he seemingly wished for nothing more. He made no moves for reforms in the rural sector, and his reorganization of the mining industry was a modest one by any standards.

His style of government was exceedingly personalistic. He did not work with any consistency with any of the established political parties, and he changed ministers and ministries with disconcerting frequency.

In the early part of his administration, President Ibáñez governed with a coalition of the elements that had backed his candidacy—Partido Agrario Laborista, Partido Socialista Popular, and Partido Feminino. After a year the Socialistas Populares withdrew from the government and eventually went over to the opposition. For the rest of his term, the only party which was clearly Ibáñista was the Partido Agrario Laborista, which lost most of its electoral force in the last years of the administration. Ibáñez's cabinets were composed mainly of Agrarios Laboristas and independents.

A major concern of the Ibáñez regime was inflation, which had risen to over 90 percent a year. A mission organized by the Klein-Sachs firm of New York City was brought to Chile and recommended a more or less orthodox anti-inflation program, which was put into practice. The result was that the inflation of the latter part of the administration was considerably less than in 1952–1953, although it remained a very serious problem.

A number of important measures were passed during the first years of the Ibáñez government. Perhaps the most significant was a law which reorganized the copper industry. This law, carried out in 1955, simplified the tax structure of the industry, which had grown somewhat chaotically in the preceding decades. It also gave incentives to the copper mining companies to expand their activities. More than fifteen years later, the administration of President Salvador Allende was to insist that under this law the copper companies had been able to make "excess profits" which were superior to the value of the compensation owed to the companies when they were expropriated in 1971. As a result, the Allende regime refused to pay any compensation whatsoever.

The copper reorganization statute authorized the government to establish a new system of labor relations in the industry. Accordingly, a decree-law was issued which gave legal recognition to the Copper Workers' Confederation, the only national industrial union to receive such recognition. The law also provided that union leaders be given the right to conduct union business while still receiving their wages or salaries from the mining companies.

Other important measures during the first years of the Ibáñez regime included a law establishing a family allowance system, one calling for dismissal pay for workers scaled according to their seniority, another establishing the Banco del Estado, and a statute reorganizing the government's low-cost housing program and establishing the Corporación de la Vivienda to administer it.

In the last years of his administration, President Ibáñez's relations with Congress were somewhat strained. He did not have the support of a majority of Congress, and several pieces of legislation were passed which did not have his support, notably a measure repealing the Law for the Defense of Democracy.

At least one notable event in Chilean foreign relations took place early in the Ibáñez administration: the visit of President Juan Perón of Argentina. Perón had openly favored Ibáñez's election in 1952, and had expressed his pleasure at his victory. At that time, there was rather widespread sympathy for Perón in Chile, particularly among the workers, both because of the social program he had enacted and the strong anti-Yankee stand he had taken for a number of years. Therefore, when the Chilean president invited Perón to visit Chile a few months after the beginning of the Ibáñez administration, there was considerable popular enthusiasm and expectation. Perón suceeded in completely destroying this sympathy among the rank-and-file Chileans by presuming to lecture them on how they should conduct their political affairs, and himself offering to subsidize one of the conflicting factions in the pro-Ibáñez Partido Feminino. To some degree, history was to repeat itself twenty years later in the Allende administration with the visit of Fidel Castro.

REORGANIZATION OF ORGANIZED LABOR

Fears that General Ibáñez might attempt to establish the kind of domination over the labor movement that Perón had instituted in Argentina were a major factor in unifying Chilean organized labor in the early months of the Ibáñez regime. Another factor was the rapprochement during the 1952 election between the Communists and the Partido Socialista de Chile, the Socialist faction with the largest influence in organized labor. This unification of labor was to have great portent for the future.

Moves to form a new central labor body had been under way for some time before Ibáñez returned to power. They had been initiated by the Socialist-controlled Confederación de Trabajadores de Chile, with help from the strongly anti-Communist Organización Regional Inter Americana de Trabajadores (ORIT), with which CTCh was affiliated. It was originally proposed that the new group should consist of those unions belonging to the Socialist-controlled faction of CTCh, in addition to a number of independent unions and the remnants of the anarchosyndicalist Confederación General de Trabajadores (CGT). Unions under the control of the Communist party were to be excluded from the new central labor body.

Naturally, the communists objected strongly to these preliminary agreements. They insisted upon the need for "real labor unity" which would include them. Although the Communists' campaign was at first ignored, those who were planning for the new central labor body finally agreed to Communist participation in view of the alliance of the Communist party and PSCh in the 1952 election and Ibáñez's victory in that contest, which aroused widespread fears throughout the labor movement. By that time, the Socialists of the PSCh were thoroughly exhausted by their fight with the Communists and sought peace at almost any cost. As a result, they made relatively little effort to challenge a considerable overrepresentation of Communist strength in the founding congress of the Central Única de Trabajadores de Chile (CUTCh), which met in December 1952.

Perhaps the crucial battle in this founding congress was over the issue of international affiliation. The original intention of those who had planned for the new organization was that it would join ORIT and its parent body, the International Confederation of Free Trade Unions (ICFTU). The Communists naturally opposed this move and urged affiliation to the Communist-controlled World Federation of Trade Unions (WFTU), while a few of the Catholic delegates sought to have CUTCh join the International Federation of Christian Trade Unions. The issue was resolved by a decision that CUTCh should remain independent of any international grouping.

CUTCh did not have legal recognition, since the Chilean Labor Code did not provide for any legal central labor body. However, it did have considerable, and growing, influence. It increasingly tended to speak for the Chilean labor movement as a whole, and its periodic congresses served as testing grounds for the relative influence of various political groups within the labor movement.

CUTCh and a number of equally "unlegal" national industrial federations helped to strengthen the influence of the Communist party in the organized labor movement. Since these organizations did not have legal recognition, the unions affiliated with them could not pay dues or make other contributions to them. As a result, they had to get subsidies from outside the labor movement to maintain offices and paid staffs. This particular fact played into the hands of the Communist party.

From the late 1930s on, the Communist party had had substantial financial resources. Funds it had received both from abroad and from within the country had been invested in a number of business enterprises, and the income from these businesses had provided the party with a sizable treasury. With its relative affluence, the Communist party was able to maintain a considerable cadre of full-time leaders who worked in the labor movement. It was they who maintained the organizations of the industrial federations, and to some degree they constituted the staff of CUTCh. No other political group had a comparable cadre of full-time people in the labor movement—at least until the mid-1960s, when the Socialist party became more affluent and was able to maintain a somewhat comparable group of trade union activists.

These full-time labor officials were in a position to intervene in all kinds of labor disputes. Elected officials of the legally recognized unions—with the exception of the Confederation of Copper Workers after 1955—were supposed to conduct their trade union activities in their leisure time, after eight hours on their regular jobs. Therefore, it was quite important that when a situation developed in a plant whose union was affiliated with an industrial federation or with CUTCh, an official from a federation or the CUTCh could come and negotiate on behalf of the workers involved. For the Communists it was of unique importance that the officials who were in a position to do this were usually members of their party. This was a major factor in the Communists' dominance of the higher echelons of the labor movement during the 1950s and 1960s.

Another important element was the reticence of the non-Communists, and particularly the Socialists after 1952, to challenge inflated Communist representation at congresses of the industrial federations and CUTCh. Through more or less fictitious representation from more or less nonexistent unions, the Communists were able to have a representation at such meetings out of all proportion to their real influence in the rank and file and the genuine base unions of the labor movement during most of this period. Only in the latter part of the 1960s did the Communists really extend their control over genuine lower echelon organizations in organized labor.

THE FAR LEFT ALLIANCE

One of the most significant political trends during the Ibáñez administration was the consolidation of the Socialist-Communist alliance that first formed around Salvador Allende's presidential candidacy in 1952. This alliance was originally given the name Frente del Pueblo (Front of the People) and in 1955 was rechristened Frente Nacional del Pueblo, with Allende serving as its president. At that time, an effort was made to form a much broader front, bringing in the Partido Socialista Popular and some other elements that had originally supported Ibáñez in 1952, as well as the Radical party. However, the Radicals and former Ibáñista forces refused to have anything to do with one another.

The Partido Socialista Popular was generally opposed to the revival of anything resembling the Popular Front of the 1930s. Instead, they argued in favor of a coalition of all "proletarian" parties, excluding from this combination such "bourgeois" groups as the Radical party and the Falange Nacional, which Communists and others would have liked to see included.

The thesis of the Partido Socialista Popular won out on March 1, 1956, with the formation of the Frente de Acción Popular (FRAP). It consisted of the Partido Socialista de Chile, Partido Socialista Popular, Partido Communista, and the two factions into which the Democráticos were divided, that is, the Partido Democrático del Pueblo and the Partido Democrático de Chile. For more than a decade, FRAP was to play a major role in national politics.

The unification of the forces of the far Left, further strengthened with the reunification of the Socialists, was facilitated by the alienation of the PSP from the Ibáñez government. This process of alienation was completed in the so-called Sixteenth Congress of the PSP in 1955, which openly declared the PSP to be in the opposition.

The PSP had been able to capitalize on its association with Ibáñez, so long as that lasted. For example, in the parliamentary elections of 1953, the party won four Senate and nineteen Chamber of Deputies seats. In those same elections, the Partido Socialista de Chile won four deputies. However, the PSCh continued to have substantial influence in the organized labor movement in various parts of the country, while the labor strength of the PSP lay principally with the copper miners.

After extensive negotiations, it was decided to reunite the two Socialist parties. This reunification was accomplished at a congress called the Seventeenth Ordinary Congress; after the merger, in July 1957, the two parties became the Partido Socialista de Chile.

Raúl Ampuero became secretary general of the newly reunited Socialist Party and for almost a decade put his stamp upon the organization. Hence, like the PSP, the party sought to impose stricter discipline on its members than had been customary in Socialist ranks. Moreover, under Ampuero's leadership the reunited PSCh was committed, as the PSP had been, to Marxism-Leninism, although there was by no means a uniform interpretation among the party's members and leaders concerning the exact meaning of "Marxism-Leninism."

FOUNDATION OF THE CHRISTIAN DEMOCRATIC PARTY

During the Ibáñez administration, the Christian Democratic party (Partido Demócrata Cristiano—PDC) was established as the result of the fusion of three different groups with a Social Christian orientation. The oldest and most important element was the Falange Nacional which had its origins in the youth movement of the Conservative party in the 1930s. Many of the leaders of the Conservative Youth of those years had studied abroad, particularly in Belgium, and had been influenced by a number of leading advanced Catholic thinkers of the period, especially Jacques Maritain. They were therefore unhappy with the Conservative party's defense of the economic and social status quo. This discontent reached fever pitch during the presidential campaign of 1938, when the Conservative Youth refused to support the party's candidate, Gustavo Ross. When their seniors sought to discipline them, the youth element broke away from the Conservative party to form their own party, under the name Falange Nacional. During the 1940s and most of the 1950s, the Falange grew slowly, gaining some influence on the fringe of the labor movement and electing a number of its leaders to the Senate and Chamber of Deputies. It had representation for short periods in the cabinets of Presidents Juan Antonio Ríos and Gabriel González Videla and of Vice-President Alfredo Duhalde. In the 1957 congressional elections, it demonstrated considerable growth by electing one senator and fourteen deputies.

The second element forming the PDC was the Partido Conservador Social Cristiano. It had originated in a further split in the Conservative party in

1949, led by the party's 1946 presidential candidate, Eduardo Cruz Coke. During the 1950s, the party suffered several splits, with most of its leaders, including Cruz Coke, returning to the ranks of the more orthodox Conservative party. In 1957, the Partido Conservador Social Cristiano elected only one deputy in the congressional elections.

The third element of the PDC was the Partido Nacional Cristiano, a party established in 1952 by people of Social Christian orientation for the purpose of supporting the candidacy of Carlos Ibáñez. It, too, suffered splits, and a large group, headed by deputy José Musalem, broke with Ibáñez and went into the opposition.

In 1955, these parties joined to establish the Federación Social Cristiana, and in June 1957, this federation was converted into the new party, the Partido Demócrata Cristino. It had its baptism of fire in the 1958 presidential election.

OTHER POLITICAL DEVELOPMENTS DURING THE IBÁÑEZ REGIME

Early in 1958, the Law for the Defense of Democracy, which had been passed a decade earlier to outlaw the Communist party, was repealed through an alliance of all elements in Congress except the Liberals and Conservatives. It permitted the Communists once again to function openly and to run candidates under their own banners, but it had no effect on Communist participation in FRAP.

Another major political change during the Ibáñez regime, also effected early in 1958, was a basic alteration in the electoral law which greatly extended the franchise, practically eliminating the literacy requirement for voting. It also provided for a single ballot on which the names of all candidates appeared, in place of a system in which each party had a separate ballot, with the voter having to choose one to place in an envelope and deposit in the voting box. This electoral law made nearly all Chileans over the age of twenty-one eligible to vote, which meant that by the early 1960s about 3.5 million of the 7.5 million Chileans were potential voters. Although the number of actual registered voters continued to be well below the number who were eligible, the 1958 reforms brought into the political arena in their own right elements that had previously been outside of it.

These changes were especially important in the rural areas where illiteracy was concentrated. Previously, the literacy requirement had played into the hands of those landlords who wished to have their tenants and laborers vote for candidates whom the landlords favored. In such cases, the electoral officials tended to regard the peasants involved as "literate" regardless of whether they actually were. Thus, the illiterate peasants had the right to vote only if the landlords were fairly certain they would vote for candidates chosen by the landlords. This was one of the main factors that had kept the

Conservative and Liberal parties among the country's largest parties for so long. It is not a coincidence that these two parties declined abruptly, and then disappeared, in less than a decade after the establishment of a nearly universal adult franchise.

THE ELECTION OF 1958

Some of the changes noted above were reflected in the presidential election of 1958. The traditional Right united its forces behind the candidacy of Jorge Alessandri, one of the sons of the late President Arturo Alessandri. Jorge Alessandri was a businessman and engineer, who had also been active in politics from time to time over the previous thirty years. He had served as president of the major paper company, the Cia. de Papeles y Cartones, for a long time and was widely known as a good employer. He had a simple, even austere, manner, despite his considerable wealth. The respect and prestige he commanded gave him electoral support which to some degree at least cut across class lines.

His principal opponent in the election was Salvador Allende, who was supported by the Frente de Acción Popular, consisting of the reunited Socialists, the Communists, and the Democráticos. He had been active in politics for nearly thirty years and had been a deputy, senator, or minister during that time. Although he was an elegant dresser and had a reputation for liking good wine, fine food, and pretty women, Allende nonetheless had become very popular among the Socialist rank and file, most of whom were workers, and had the support of virtually all elements of the far Left.

One minor candidate contested the vote of the far Left with Allende and may have been responsible for Allende's defeat in the 1958 election. This was a radical priest, Antonio Zamorano, who pictured himself as being to the Left of the FRAP nominee. Had the votes cast for him gone to Allende, the FRAP candidate would have received the plurality.

The more serious candidates who trailed Alessandri and Allende were those of the new Christian Democratic party and the Radical party. In its first national contest, the PDC received over 20 percent of the vote for its candidate Eduardo Frei, whereas the Radical party, which until 1952 had been the country's largest party, received only slightly more than 15 percent for its nominee Luis Bossay, who came in fourth among five contestants.

The election results gave a narrow plurality to Alessandri, who received 369,309 votes, or 31.5 percent of the total. Allende got 356,493 votes, or 28.35 percent; Frei, 255,769, or 20.70 percent; Bossay, 192,077 or 15.55 percent; and Zamorano, 41,304 votes, or 3.34 percent of the total.[1] A few weeks after the popular vote, Alessandri's election was confirmed by a vote of Congress. He took office on November 4, 1958.

THE POLICIES OF THE JORGE ALESSANDRI REGIME

The Jorge Alessandri administration is usually regarded as a conservative regime. When compared with what came later, it was extremely moderate. Alessandri was elected president by the Chilean Right and governed principally with their assistance. Alessandri himself always resented the picture of his administration as one that had merely defended the status quo. Most of all, he resented foreign criticism of it along these lines, especially criticism originating in the United States. Alessandri liked to point out that the housing and agrarian programs of his administration were the type of reforms Chile needed, rather than the much more drastic ones that came after he left office.

As was true of all of Chile's recent presidents, Alessandri was plagued by the problem of continuing inflation. As a symbolic indication of his government's struggle against the rising price level, Alessandri substituted a new currency unit, the escudo, for the old Chilean peso, with the escudo being worth 1,000 pesos. At the outset, the value of the escudo was fixed at $1 (U.S.). During the first half of his administration, Alessandri succeeded in reducing the rhythm of inflation, but subsequently it again began to increase.

The most important social program of the Jorge Alessandri administration was a massive attack on the housing problem, particularly in the urban areas. Most of the squatter colonies then existing in and around the Santiago area were replaced by government housing projects, some in the form of four- or five-story apartment buildings, others in colonies of individual houses. Although subsequently squatter colonies were again to proliferate, the Alessandri administration was the first one to launch a massive attack on this problem.

Much less significant was the Agrarian Reform Law of 1962 which was the Alessandri government's response to the Alliance for Progress's insistence on the need for land redistribution programs throughout Latin America. Although ostensibly a measure to begin the transformation of the rural land tenure system, the conditions under which the land could be expropriated under the law were so extensively qualified, and the procedures were so complicated, that in fact very few properties were affected by the 1962 Agrarian Reform Law during the balance of the Alessandri administration.

The Alessandri government sought to promote the industrialization of the country, and to this end, it established the Commercial Agricultural Enterprise (Empresa de Comercio Agrícola—ECA). The purpose of the ECA was to help establish industries for processing agricultural products and for stimulating commercial fishing. Partly through the aid of the Corporación de Fomento, a cellulose products industry was established during this period.

In the area of foreign policy, in 1960 Chile entered the Latin American

Free Trade Area (LAFTA), the first tentative effort to establish a common market in Latin America. In addition, Chile participated in establishing the Alliance for Progress.

POLITICAL DEVELOPMENTS DURING THE JORGE ALESSANDRI ADMINISTRATION

Congressional support for the Alessandri administration came from the Liberal, Conservative, and Radical parties. During the first part of the regime, President Alessandri, who prided himself on not being affiliated with any political party (in contrast to his father and his brothers Fernando and Eduardo, who were lifelong Liberals), had cabinets consisting principally of independents. During the second half of his administration, however, the three parties supporting his government were usually represented in the cabinet.

The most significant political development of the period was the rapid rise in the strength of the Christian Democratic party. In the municipal elections of April 1963, the Christian Democrats supplanted the Radicals as the party with most votes, receiving 455,522 votes, or 22.8 percent of the total, compared with 431,470 votes, or 21.5 percent, for the Radicals. No other party had more than 13 percent of the vote in that contest.[2] In this election, the Christian Democrats demonstrated strength in areas where they had never been strong before. Most notably, they received a plurality in the largely German areas of the southern part of central Chile, where the Protestantism of the German-Chileans had until then made this region a bulwark of the still anticlerical Radical party. With the 1963 election, it became evident that the Christian Democrats had a real chance of winning the 1964 presidential contest.

The strength of the Christian Democratic party came in part from the decline in the fortunes of the Radical party, which had begun with their ignominious defeat in the 1952 presidential election. The middle-class elements that had traditionally supported the Radicals shifted their loyalty and votes to the Christian Democrats, who like the Radicals were on the Center-Left of the political spectrum, and unlike them did not then appear to be so hopelessly factionalized between a left and a right wing.

Another factor in the rise of the Christian Democrats was the vacuum created in the Left by the continuing alliance of Socialists and Communists. Before 1952, those workers, intellectuals, and middle-class people who favored fundamental changes in Chilean society, but were opposed to the Communist party, found their natural home in the ranks of the Socialist party. After 1952, however, when the Socialists shifted from being a strongly anti-Communist party to the most reliable allies of the Communists, these groups began to feel alienated from the Socialists. Many of them turned to the Christian Democratic party, as is demonstrated by the growing influence of the Christian Democrats in the organized labor movement.

THE ELECTION OF 1964

It was clear during the election campaign of 1964 that Chile was about to undergo very fundamental reforms. The basic issues of the campaign were: under whose auspices were these changes going to take place, and what would these changes be. There were three candidates. The Christian Democrats once again offered the name of Eduardo Frei; the Frente de Acción Popular nominated Salvador Allende for the third time; and the Radicals, Conservatives, and Liberals named Julio Durán, a Radical party leader.

As the campaign developed, there were various shifts of political forces. One was a split in the ranks of the Partido Democrático Nacional (PADENA), an affiliate of the Frente de Acción Popular, with the dissident group, the Nueva Izquierda Democrática, throwing its support behind Frei's candidacy. A more important development was the crisis within the Radical-Conservative-Liberal coalition, the so-called Frente Democrático (Democratic Front). As the result of a by-election for deputy in Curicó, which the Frente Democrático had hoped to win but had lost ignominiously, Julio Durán withdrew from the race, and the Radical party officially withdrew from the Frente. Subsequently, the Conservative and Liberal parties somewhat grudgingly endorsed Frei as the "lesser evil."

The Christian Democrats were anxious to keep Durán in the race, fearing that without a Radical candidate in the field many members of that party might vote for Allende. After extensive conversations, Durán agreed to return to the contest, this time as the candidate only of his own Radical party.

The principal campaign slogan of the Christian Democrats was "Revolution in Liberty." They promised a long list of reforms, including the "Chileanization" of the mining industry, the enactment of a meaningful agrarian reform law, the passage of legislation to facilitate the formation of legal trade unions among rural workers, and the establishment of legal organizations, representing neighborhood groups, particularly in the urban slum areas, which would have a role in municipal government and would undertake civic improvement programs of their own.

Even before the presidential election campaign began the Christian Democrats had conducted an intensive organizing effort among lower income people. It concentrated on the peasants, as well as on the residents of the squatter colonies and housing projects in the cities. Among the latter the party organized a network of neighborhood committees and other organizations that not only were active in a partisan political sense, but also undertook a variety of self-help projects in their neighborhoods.

The FRAP coalition proposed even more sweeping reforms than did the

Christian Democrats, including the nationalization of the mining industry. During the campaign, however, it sought to downplay the association of its candidate Salvador Allende and other FRAP leaders with the Cuban regime of Fidel Castro.

Both the Christian Democrats and FRAP spent unprecedented amounts of money on the campaign. Both sides undoubtedly received aid from abroad, the Christian Democrats from sympathetic groups in West Germany and other European countries as well as from the United States, and FRAP from Cuba and other Communist-controlled countries.

When the votes were counted, Frei had won a clear majority, with 1,409,072 votes, or 56 percent of the total; Allende had received 977,902 votes, or 39 percent and Durán had come in a very poor third, with 125,293, or about 5 percent of the total.[3]

THE CHILEAN ECONOMY, 1952–1964

The twelve-year period encompassing the administrations of Presidents Carlos Ibáñez and Jorge Alessandri was, on balance, one of economic stagnation. Julio Cesar Jobet has noted the contrast between this period and the decade and a half preceding it:

Only beginning in 1939, with the triumph of the Popular Front and the creation of the Corporación de Fomento de la Producción (CORFO) was the policy of economic independence adopted, involving an ample expansion of industry: electrification, steel production, petroleum, cellulose; and the technical improvement of various productive activities. Private initiative on the part of the national bourgeoisie promoted the metallurgical industry and textiles, principally. In 1952 the labor force employed in manufacturing reached 204,000 persons. In the decade of 1940–50 there were important advances in the industrial field. In the period 1940–45 industry generated 15.4% of the gross product; and in 1956, 19.6%. But the process of growth stopped beginning in 1953.[4]

As noted earlier, the fundamental reason for this economic slowdown was that it could no longer be maintained on the basis of import substitution and that a new strategy of development had to be devised. Such a new strategy, based on amplifying the existing market both domestically and abroad, required important reforms: land redistribution, accompanied by a shift in government investment priorities in the direction of agriculture; rationalization of management and development of a more skilled work force; changes in the tax structure; and emphasis on the development of industries that could sell a substantial proportion of their output abroad.

Very little progress in these directions was made during the 1952–1964 period. Agrarian reform did not even become a major political issue in Chile until the Alliance for Progress made it one. Only a slight beginning was made in the organization of rural workers into unions, which might have been another way of forcing modernization of the agricultural sector. However, some beginnings were made in three areas of reform: improving the quality of management, raising the skills of the work force, and reorganizing the social security system. The Instituto Chileno de Administración Racional de Empresas (Chilean Institute of the Rational Administration of Firms—ICARE) was established in the early 1950s with the support of Chilean entrepreneurs and help from the U.S. foreign aid program. ICARE began an extensive program to train middle and lower management people in modern techniques, and it undertook some pilot projects for reorganizing firms along more efficient lines.

In the field of vocational education, the most notable progress was in expanding the Universidad Técnica del Estado, which had been established during the González Videla administration. It carried out not only university-level training of engineers and other professionals, but also a wide range of programs for training skilled workers, semi-professional technicians, and foremen.

Finally, legislation passed at the end of the González Videla period and put into operation by the Ibáñez administration made some effort to rationalize the social security system. Its health services were consolidated into the Servicio Nacional de Salud, and a number of funds and services providing retirement and other benefits for workers were consolidated into the Servicio Nacional de Seguro Social, covering most manual workers. These were efforts to make the social security system less expensive and more efficient in delivering services to its clients, and they had only limited success.

These modest beginnings of reform were not sufficient to establish a new basis for continuing economic development. Much more fundamental changes were going to be necessary before this would be possible.

CHILE'S DEVELOPMENT LEVEL BY THE MID-1960s

By the 1960s, Chile could be accurately described (as Fernando Monckenberg puts it) as "an underdeveloped country on the way to development." In terms of gross national product, in 1969 it was sixth among nineteen Latin American countries (Cuba excluded) with a per capita product of $585, which compared with $851 for Argentina at the top and $92 for Haiti at the bottom. In terms of a broader concept of economic development used by the Institute of Social Development of the United Nations, based on fifty different items such as income, consumption of electricity, kilometers of paved highway, production of steel, and number of radios, Chile had a point total of 60 compared to that of 111 for the United States, at the top of the list. Illiteracy was officially estimated at only 10 percent, which may have been an understatement.[5]

Chile thus had made considerable economic and social progress, but had a considerable distance to go. The still difficult social conditions were illustrated by Fernando Monckenberg's study of the province of Curicó, in the heart of the agricultural region of the Central Valley, in 1968. He found that 16 percent of the housing in that province could be classified as good, 34 percent acceptable, 14 percent bad and 36 percent very bad. He found that 44 percent of the population had adequate water supply and 56 percent did not; 32 percent had adequate sewage disposal, 37 percent had bad facilities, and 31 percent very bad ones. He also found that 21 percent of the heads of families were illiterate and 40 percent had less than three years of primary education. Finally, he discovered that 71 percent of the children had parasites.[6] In terms of adequateness of diet, Monckenberg commented that "we cannot say that in Chile there was hunger, but there was malnutrition."[7]

GROWING PRESSURE FOR CHANGE

By the end of the Ibáñez-Jorge Alessandri period, there was widespread consensus on the need for sweeping economic and social changes in Chile. The political institutions had altered in such a way as to facilitate basic reforms.

Considerable peasant support for Ibáñez in 1952 and growing demands for effective legalization of peasant unions were two indications of growing pressure for reform from a sector that had theretofore been the most conservative in Chilean society. Other evidences of the growing support for change were the high vote received by Allende in the 1958 presidential election and the rapid rise of the Christian Democratic party in the late 1950s and early 1960s.

The changes in the electoral law provided an important vehicle for making fundamental reform the order of the day. In 1920, when Arturo Alessandri was elected president for the first time, and even in 1939, at the time of the triumph of the Popular Front, the right to vote was limited to a relatively small part of the adult population. In contrast, by 1964, this right had been extended to the great majority of adult Chileans. It was now possible for workers, peasants, and middle-class elements supporting programs of basic reforms to elect governments committed to changes much more vast than those suggested (and certainly more profound than those actually carried out) by Alessandri and Aguirre Cerda.

Thus, the Ibáñez-Jorge Alessandri period was one in which sentiment for adopting drastic measures to deal with these problems grew. In the years that followed, Chile's democratic and constitutional system was to be sorely tested by the process of enacting fundamental social and economic changes. The failure of this system to resist the pressures generated by rapid change is what we have called The Tragedy of Chile.

PART TWO:
THE REVOLUTION IN LIBERTY

6

Characteristics of the "Revolution in Liberty"

Between November 1964 and November 1970, the Christian Democratic government of President Eduardo Frei carried out what it called the Revolution in Liberty—a program of extensive social change, nationalism, and economic development conducted in the context of the traditional institutions of Chile's democracy. The philosophical basis of the program was one of extending democracy into parts of the society in which it did not yet apply. This concept was usually described as communitarianism, and although it remained ill-defined, with almost as many interpretations as there were interpreters, all versions of the idea shared the same premise: that the basic purpose of communitarianism was to involve all elements of the community in resolving the community's problems.

To this end, the Christian Democratic regime sponsored the formation of new organizations of rank-and-file citizens, organizations that had previously been lacking. These included unions of agricultural workers, which could participate in determining the living and working conditions of their members; and local groups in both urban and rural areas—neighborhood *juntas,* mothers' clubs, youth groups—which would serve as the lowest level of self-government in the municipalities and undertake programs for improving conditions in local areas.

The communitarian thrust of the Christian Democratic regime also involved efforts to give workers a greater say in running the enterprise for which they worked. The major move in this direction was the beginning of an agrarian reform which would transfer the larger part of the country's arable land to the peasants, either individually or in cooperatives.

Much discussed, although not acted upon by the Frei government, were measures to extend the communitarian concept to manufacturing and commercial enterprises. No agreement was reached concerning just how this objective was to be realized, but Radomiro Tomic, the PDC candidate in the 1970 election, promised that it would have high priority in the second Christian Democratic administration, which he hoped to head.

At the same time that it was creating fundamental changes to expand democracy in the society, the Frei government took steps to get the process of economic development going again. In the mining area, it combined this effort with a program to bring the copper and nitrate industries under the control of firms in which the Chilean government had a majority stock interest. By the end of the Frei government, an extensive program to increase copper output by at least 75 percent was underway. The government had also started projects for expanding the pulp and paper, metallurgical, and chemical industries, all of which were planned as moves to develop new "nontraditional" exports. Finally, the rural reform programs were accompanied by heavy government investments in agriculture and the infrastructure of the rural areas.

Thus, both the social and economic programs of the Christian Democratic regime were designed to expand the markets for Chilean products. Rural unionization and agrarian reform served to expand the internal market for products of the nation's industries. At the same time, the Frei government's projects in mining and manufacturing had among their purposes the expansion of foreign markets. Government investments in agriculture were designed to expand both domestic and foreign markets for Chilean goods.

All of these programs were initiated to get Chile beyond the post-import substitution crisis in which it had been since the end of the Radical period. Unfortunately for the Christian Democrats, the benefits of these measures were not scheduled to have a favorable impact on the economy until after the end of the Frei administration. Since the Christian Democrats lost the presidential election of 1970, they did not have the opportunity to enjoy the favorable political effects of much of what they carried out under President Frei. They lost the election mainly because Frei had miscalculated the importance of continued Socialist-Communist control of the labor movement, his administration's inability to deal adequately with the inflation, and the nature of the PDC election campaign in 1970.

Throughout the PDC's period in power, the democratic regime remained fully intact. The three branches of government operated normally, and in spite of the fact that his party did not control the Senate, President Frei was able, through adroit political maneuvering, to get most of the administration's basic legislative program through Congress, although sometimes belatedly. Freedom of speech, press, and other means of expression remained intact.

During this period, at least two political factors were developing which augured ill for the future. One factor was the growing polarization of public opinion: all elements to the Left of the PDC were joining in a new coalition, the Unidad Popular; many of those on the Right were reacting violently to the Christian Democratic government reforms, leading many to argue that the PDC was "worse than the Communists"; and on both the far Left and the far Right, extremist groups dedicated to the use of force to seize power, the Movimiento de Izquierda Revolucionaria (MIR) and the Patria y Libertad, respectively, were emerging.

The second political factor was the growing politicization of the armed forces. Late in 1969, an abortive military mutiny was led by General Roberto Viaux, and about a year later, an attempt was made to kidnap the commander-in-chief of the army, General René Schneider, which resulted in the general's death.

7

PDC Politics in the Frei Administration

Internal tensions within the Christian Democratic party go far to explain the policies—and sometimes the lack of apparent policy—of the Frei administration, and also contribute to an understanding of the defeat of the party in the 1970 election campaign.

THE VICTORIES OF 1964 AND 1965

Much of the thinking and actions of the leaders of the Christian Democratic party during its years in power was influenced by the party's striking electoral victories at the outset of its tenure in power. It won two sweeping triumphs within six months, which may have given the PDC leaders an over-optimistic picture of their party's possibilities for the future. Moreover, the election of Eduardo Frei had been a smashing victory. He had gotten substantially more than an absolute majority in the popular vote in September 1964, and thus Congress did not have to make the final choice as it had had to in several recent elections. This triumph was succeeded in March 1965 by an even more outstanding one. In the congressional elections of that month, the Christian Democratic party achieved an absolute majority in the Chamber of Deputies—the first party to do so in a hundred years. It elected 82 of the 150 members of the lower house. It did almost as well in the elections for the Senate, putting twelve new party members in office. Indeed, the party leaders had underestimated the PDC's chances in the senatorial race and therefore did not have enough candidates to win all the posts to which the popular vote entitled them. However, because only part of the Senate was elected in 1965, and most of the holdovers belonged to the Right and Left opposition, the PDC did not gain a majority in the upper house.

The two victories in succession undoubtedly gave the party and government leaders more confidence in their popularity than was justified. The inability or unwillingness of the Right to offer a viable opponent to Frei in the presidential election, and the almost complete collapse of the Conservative and Liberal parties in the congressional contest six months later, convinced the Christian Democrats that they no longer needed to worry about a serious opposition to their Right. This proved to be a serious error.

The Christian Democrats' assessment of the effect of these two victories on the Left opposition was perhaps even more seriously wrong. Because the party had done quite well in working-class districts that had previously been virtual fiefdoms of the Socialists and Communists, the Christian Democrats tended to feel that they could go over the heads of Socialist and Communist trade union leaders who still dominated the labor movement. This was a major mistake.

THE QUESTION OF COALITION

The magnitude of the Christian Democrats' victories of 1964 and 1965 was undoubtedly influential in their decision to reject the idea of a coalition cabinet until it was too late for the formation of such a government. Finally, the only party with which they might coalesce was the tiny Partido Democrático Nacional.

The logic of Chilean politics at the time the party acceded to power pointed to a PDC-Radical coalition. It would have had an overwhelming majority in the Chamber of Deputies and would have been only one short of a majority in the Senate, thus greatly facilitating the task of getting legislation through Congress. It would have broadened the support of the regime in public opinion in general. The logic of such a coalition was that the PDC and Radicals represented the Center-Left in Chilean politics. Although the Radicals had traditionally been faction-ridden, thus causing them to form alliances with both Right and Left, ideologically they represented a position not too far different from that of the Christian Democrats. What is more, both the Partido Demócrata Cristiano and the Radicals drew their support largely from the middle elements of the population, and in addition, each had some backing in the working class and in the upper social and economic circles.

Of course, it is a truism that politics is not always governed by rationality. There is no guarantee that had the Radicals been offered a chance to participate in the government they would have accepted such an invitation. However, the important fact is that they were never offered this chance.

Several factors on the Radical side might have stood in the way of a coalition with the Christian Democrats. Certainly one of these was the lingering anticlericalism in the Radical ranks and the tendency of some Radicals to look upon the Christian Democrats as a "confessional," or church-controlled, party. Another factor might well have been their reluctance to be a minority partner in a government dominated by the PDC, the party that was their chief rival for the constituencies they both cultivated. Finally, the Radicals had traditionally worked closely with the Communist party and favored an alliance with it rather than with the Christian Democrats.

On the other hand, the Radicals had always been hungry for jobs and had tended to seek government posts to satisfy this hunger. Similarly, their long-standing role as the chief spokesman for government employees might have convinced the Radicals of the wisdom of participating in the administration, so as to protect that part of their political base.

All of these pros and cons are purely academic, for no overture was ever made to the Radicals. Some members of the top leadership of the Christian Democratic party kept insisting on the advisability of making a rapprochement with the Radicals, but whenever they raised the issue, they were voted down.

Aside from the "insolence of office" arising from the PDC's electoral victories, the Christian Democrats refused to bring the Radicals into the government because of opposition on ideological grounds by left-wing elements within the PDC; until well along in the Frei administration, they were a powerful element in party councils. Another possible reason for their refusal was their unwillingness to share the prerogatives of office—which the party had obtained for the first time, in its own right—with any outside group. The results of this refusal were disastrous for the PDC. The Radical party gravitated increasingly towards the left-wing opponents of the Frei administration and became part of the Unidad Popular coalition behind the candidacy of Salvador Allende in the 1970 elections—although not without first suffering a serious internal split.

It was not until the last two years of the Frei administration, when the Christian Democrats' popular support had declined, that they finally decided to broaden the base of the government. By that time, it was too late to attract the Radicals. As mentioned earlier, the only party available as a coalition partner was the remnant of the old Partido Democrático Nacional (PADENA), which had a member of the cabinet during the last two years of the Frei administration. PADENA was by then a tiny party and as such represented no serious increase of support for the Christian Democratic administration.

INTERNAL FACTIONALISM

The Christian Democratic party's accession to power tended to exacerbate latent factional tendencies within the organization. The very magnitude of its victories in 1964 and 1965, particularly its congressional triumph, deepened these factional disputes more than they might otherwise have been. The eighty-two deputies elected by the party in March 1965 included many younger people whose thinking was considerably to the Left of the major leaders of the party and the government. This factionalism was relatively new for the Christian Democrats. Over the years, the Falange Nacional had suffered little from defections or the development of serious internal factional strife. Significantly, it was not the new elements which joined the Falange to form the PDC in 1957 that provided most of the dissident elements after 1964.

In part, the problem that arose after Frei took office was a generational one. By that time, the major party leaders, who had been rebels in their youth, were in their fifties and were no longer young or rebellious. Junior in age to the founders of the Falange were a couple generations of leaders who had a natural feeling of urgency about attaining top positions in the party and the government, and who had been influenced by different ideological beliefs from those which had brought the original founders of the Falange to set up their party.

The education of some of the new oppositionists within the PDC was of considerable importance in molding their attitudes, as had been that of the original founders of Christian Democracy in Chile. Like their political forebears, many of the younger leaders had gone to Europe to study, particularly at Catholic universities. They had come under the influence of more radical Catholic social thinkers than those who had influenced Frei and other major party figures. They returned home critical of the "conservatism" of their superiors within the party. In addition, these younger people were influenced by events of the 1960s, especially the Cuban revolution. Some had worked for the Castro government and as a result their ideas about the kind of revolution their country needed were very different from those of the older party chiefs.

Hence, in the early years of the Frei administration three distinct factions emerged within the Christian Democratic party and government: the so-called *Oficialistas* or *Freistas,* who were unequivocally associated with the administration and with President Frei in particular; the *Rebeldes,* who were in increasing disaccord with official policies and procedures; and the *Terceristas,* who stood somewhere in between these two groups.

THE *OFICIALISTAS*

During most of the Frei administration, the leadership of the party rested principally with the group that was closely associated with the president and loyally supported the PDC government. This *Oficialista* group had the backing of the great majority of the Christian Democratic members of Congress, of the party's most important trade union and peasant leaders, and of most of the local and regional organizations of the party.

The core of the *Oficialista* faction of the party consisted of those who had led the party since its inception, such as Bernardo Leighton, Jaime Castillo, Edmundo Pérez Zujovic, Tomás Reyes, and Ignacio Palma. There were also younger individuals, such as Renán Fuentealba and Patricio Aylwin. José Musalem, who had been the leader of the one-time pro-Carlos Ibáñez group that helped form the PDC in 1957, was also an important *Oficialista*.

There was by no means complete unanimity among the leaders and rank-and-file members of the *Oficialistas*. Some, for instance, thought that the party should try to bring the Radicals into the government. Some were considerably more unbending in their opposition to the *Rebeldes* and *Terceristas* than were other *Officialistas*. All agreed, however, that they should keep disagreements with the government completely to intraparty discussions and that the party was committed basically to supporting the government it had elected to office.

THE *REBELDES*

The *Rebeldes* were increasingly critical of the Frei government during its early years. They disagreed with the majority of the party on a number of ideological and strategic matters; these disagreements finally brought them into open confrontation with President Frei and his associates in the PDC.

Quite a few of the *Rebeldes* held positions within the government entities dealing with agrarian reform, particularly the Corporación de Reforma Agraria and INDAP. In those posts, they let it be known that they favored the establishment of collective farming on the land that was taken from the large landholders under the agrarian reform program. This point of view was rejected by most of the party, particularly by a majority of the peasant leaders of the PDC. These leaders did not reject communal ownership of some land where the crop involved made it impractical to subdivide the land into family-size plots, but were favorably disposed to granting family holdings where that was economically feasible.

The *Rebeldes* also favored the rapid establishment of the communitarianism advocated in a general way by the PDC. The party had no generally accepted definition of communitarianism, especially when applied to the manufacturing and commercial parts of the economy. In any case, the elements that followed President Frei did not feel that communitarianism was an issue of high priority for what they hoped would be only the first installment of an extended Christian Democratic party tenure.

The *Rebeldes* also disagreed with President Frei and his first minister of labor, William Thayer concerning the administration's labor policy. In this the *Rebeldes* had the support of the majority of the party leadership until shortly before they left the PDC ranks. Frei and Thayer favored basic revision of the Labor Code to permit legalization of labor federations and confederations, and to allow workers to establish as many federations in an industry and as many confederations on an overall basis as they wished to organize. The president and minister of labor favored an attempt to form a rival to the Socialist-Communist controlled Central Única de Trabajadores. The *Rebeldes* wanted to maintain the existing labor legislation and to work closely with the Communists and Socialists in the unions and CUTch.

Finally, the *Rebeldes* disagreed over political strategy. They supported an alliance with the Socialists and Communists in the 1970 election, and an orientation of the PDC in that direction in the maneuvers leading up to that election. The great majority of the party was opposed to any such alliance.

For the first two-thirds of the Frei administration, the *Rebeldes* largely dominated the PDC youth organization. They also tended to control the labor and peasant secretariats of the party, although the people who served in those bodies were not for the most part trade union or peasant leaders. Although the *Rebeldes* consisted principally of younger party leaders, a few members of the older generations joined forces with them—for example, Senator Rafael Gumucio, one of the founders of the Falange Nacional in the late 1930s, and Senator Alberto Jerez.

The *Rebeldes* finally broke with the party in May 1969. A number of their leaders were suspended from the PDC, and others withdrew voluntarily. A few *Terceristas* (among them Jacques Chonchol) left the party with them, and the secessionists formed a new party, the Movimiento de Acción Popular Unida (Movement of United Popular Action—MAPU).

THE *TERCERISTAS*

The element within the PDC which came to be known as the *Terceristas* generally sympathized with the *Rebeldes,* but were more cautious about creating a situation in which they might be forced to leave the party. They frequently sought to be a bridge between the *Rebeldes* and the *Oficialistas* who were fully supporting President Frei. They, like the *Rebeldes,* generally represented a younger element in the party. They did not have as much support as the *Rebeldes* within the PDC.

The *Terceristas* remained within the PDC during its period in power. It was not until almost a year after the defeat of the PDC candidate in the 1970 presidential election that they finally withdrew from the party and formed a new group, the Izquierda Cristiana.

THE DISSIDENTS AND PRESIDENT FREI

The dissident elements within the Christian Democratic ranks tended to grow during the first years of the Frei administration, partly as a result of the party's being in power. Inevitably, some became impatient with the difficulties the government was encountering in Congress and elsewhere in getting its program enacted.

By the latter part of 1967, the dissident PDC elements gained sufficient influence to present a serious embarrassment, if not a menace, to the administration. They finally provoked a direct intervention by President Frei, after which the power of the *Rebeldes* and *Terceristas* within the party apparatus was drastically reduced. From then on, neither group constituted a serious challenge to the *Oficialistas'* control of the party.

The occasion for the showdown between the president and the dissidents was the convention of the Partido Demócrata Cristiano in January 1968. For some months before that, the Executive Committee of the party had been in the hands of a majority that was unfriendly to Frei. One of the principal functions of the party congress was to resolve whether the critics of the PDC-led government should continue in the party leadership. President Frei decided the issue by making a dramatic appeal directly to the congress, urging it to reiterate the party's loyalty to the government it had elected and asking it to elect a leadership that could and would cooperate with the administration.

Frei's appeal was successful. By a vote of 278 to 202, on January 7, 1968, the PDC congress elected a new executive committee controlled by elements closely associated with Frei and headed by Jaime Castillo, ideologue of the *Oficialistas*.[1] Castillo was chosen on a temporary basis, largely because of his prestige and his clear alignment with Frei in the internal struggle in the party. He resigned six months later, in August 1968, at the meeting of the National Board of the PDC and was succeeded by Renán Fuentealba, who was to remain president of the party during most of the next five years.

This defeat of the administration's critics proved to be decisive. They never again were to occupy the top leadership positions within the party; their rank-and-file support declined precipitously; and when the *Rebeldes* and *Terceristas* finally quit the PDC ranks, they were in each case able to take only a small fraction of the party leadership and membership with them. In spite of their defections, the PDC remained the largest party in Chile by a wide margin.

DECLINE OF THE PDC ELECTORAL SUPPORT

The Christian Democratic party's declining electoral position during the latter part of the Frei administration no doubt fostered the development of party factionalism. Such a decline was not unique to political parties in Chile, but it nonetheless provoked discussion, and even controversy, within the party concerning its causes and possible remedies. Understandably, the

Oficialistas, Rebeldes, and *Terceristas* drew different conclusions from the election results.

President Frei had won the votes of about 55 percent of the electorate in 1964. However, since he was supported by parties other than his own, a better picture of the strength of the Christian Democrats as a party can be gained from the congressional elections of March 1965. These gave the Christian Democrats 42.3 percent of the total popular vote. The 1964–1965 elections marked the peak of the PDC's popularity.

Some attrition occurred in the municipal elections of March 1967. Although local issues in municipal contests may somewhat influence the final results, such elections are generally regarded as a kind of plebiscite on the government in power. In this instance, the PDC lost some ground, winning only 35.6 percent of the total vote.

Further decline took place in the congressional elections of March 1969. These gave the PDC only 31.1 percent of the total vote.[2] The number of deputies fell from 81 to 55—still by far the largest contingent in the lower house, but nonetheless representing a substantial decline. The PDC no longer commanded a majority in the Chamber of Deputies.

In terms of the internal controversies within the PDC, the 1969 congressional elections had particular significance. Among the Christian Democratic deputies who lost their seats, there were quite a few *Rebeldes* and *Terceristas.* As a result, when the *Rebeldes* broke with the party, they took with them only one member of the Chamber of Deputies and two senators; when the *Terceristas* broke away two years later, they took only six deputies.

8

The Politics of the Opposition

Throughout the Christian Democratic administration, President Frei and his party were faced with substantial opposition from both the Left and Right. Although the opposition was not able to completely block the programs of the Frei government, or even to alter them substantially, it was largely responsible for the fact that most of the president's crucial legislation was not finally enacted until the second half of his term.

Most of the opposition was represented in Congress. In addition, there emerged extremist extra-parliamentary groups of both the far Left and far Right which showed an increasing tendency to use deliberate violence and terrorism as their principal weapons.

During the Christian Democratic administration, both the Left and Right opposition to the Frei government underwent substantial changes in terms of their relative strength and of alignments among them, and their relationships with the Frei administration.

THE EMERGENCE OF THE PARTIDO NACIONAL

We have already referred to the disaster which overtook the traditional parties of the Right in the 1964 and 1965 elections. The Liberals and Conservatives had no candidate of their own in the presidential race, and they were decimated in the congressional elections six months later. In 1965, the Liberal party, which for much of its more than century-long history had been the country's largest party, won only six seats in the Chamber and none in the Senate, (although it still had five holdover senators) compared to twenty-eight seats in the Chamber and nine Senate seats in the 1961 election. The Conservatives did even worse than the Liberals. Whereas four years earlier they had elected four senators and seventeen deputies, in 1965 they won only three seats in the Chamber of Deputies and elected no senators, with only two holdovers in the upper house.

This decimation of the traditional Right persuaded both parties to forget old rivalries and differences and to merge their forces. A further argument for union was the fact that the old issues dividing the Liberals from the Conservatives had largely disappeared; during most of the preceding three decades, the two traditional parties had usually cooperated with one another.

The negotiations for the Liberal and Conservative party merger into a new organization also included a third group, the small Acción Nacional party, and some right-wing independents. A new party of the Right, the Partido Nacional, was launched on May 11, 1966, and officially registered as a party a month later.[1]

In a sense, the creation of the Partido Nacional was an act of desperation. At most, its protagonists hoped that they could thereby stop the process of total disintegration of the Right which seemed to be under way. The unification of Liberals and Conservatives did much more than that, however: it reversed the decline of the traditional Right and once again made it a serious force in national politics. Its revived power was amply demonstrated in the congressional elections of March 1969. At that time, the Partido Nacional emerged as the second largest party in the country, outdistanced only by the Christian Democrats. The Partido Nacional received approximately 20 percent of the vote, compared with somewhat more than 29 percent for the PDC, and succeeded in electing five senators and thirty-four deputies.[2]

During the Frei administration, the Partido Nacional developed a somewhat different constituency from the one it had before merging. It came to represent not only the economic powers-that-be, as had the Liberals and Conservatives, but also substantial elements in the middle and even lower middle class which were fearful of the economic and social changes initiated by the Christian Democratic regime. Its base was predominantly urban, in contrast to the traditional rural strongholds of the Liberals and Conservatives. Their power in the countryside had been eroded by the peasantry's increasing assertiveness in altering the institutions of rural society to their own benefit.

OTHER RIGHT-WING OPPOSITION

Two other opposition groups (which were largely outside but partly overlapped the party and parliamentary opposition on the Right) were the so-called economic Right, and the terrorist groups.

The economic Right consisted of the large landholders, larger industrialists, most of the important commercial interests, and some professionals. Some of the actions of the Christian Democratic regime damaged this group. Quite understandably, elements among them were opposed to the agrarian reform, and others were suspicious of the Chileanization program. Nearly all of them were suspicious of the PDC's reformist zeal, fearful of what might come next.

The economic Right's opposition for the most part was channeled through existing institutions. The landlord group, through the Sociedad Nacional de Agricultura and the new Confederation of Rural Employers set up under the Law of Peasant Unionization, made full use of the press and radio stations and other organs of expression at its disposal to protest alleged "abuses" of the agrarian reform program and otherwise to attack the government's actions in rural areas. They also lobbied with members of Congress and with administrative agencies. As had been traditional in Chile, the powerful economic and social interests conceded what they were forced to concede but fought to preserve what they could, without fundamentally challenging the existing political system.

The attitudes of the economic Right hardened during the Frei period. During those years, the opinion of the landlords or businessmen, and some politicians closely associated with them, was that the Christian Democrats were worse than the Marxists. Such an outlook further polarized national political life and partly accounted for the gravitation of this class to support Jorge Alessandri (who then was nearly eighty) in the election of 1970 in the hope of "getting revenge" for the damage to their interests which they thought had been done under Frei. It also helps explain why, later, many elements of the economic Right so adamantly resisted peaceful compromise in the crisis that developed under Allende.

An even more disturbing aspect of the Frei years was the emergence of a new right-wing extremist tendency. In the latter part of the Christian Democratic administration, a small but vocal and fanatical group called Patria y Libertad (Fatherland and Liberty) was formed. This largely secret group believed in violent confrontation with not only similar groups on the Left, but with virtually *all* elements of the Left and Center-Left. The most notorious of their adventures during these years was the murder of army commander-in-chief General René Schneider during the period between the presidential popular vote of September 4, 1970, and the final choice of Salvador Allende as president by Congress six weeks later. As subsequent investigation showed, both civilian and military elements were involved in the attack on General Schneider.

Like their left-wing counterparts, the right-wing extremists were mostly young men of the middle and upper classes who had contempt for the democratic process. They were convinced that armed action was the best vehicle for carrying out their objectives.

THE SOCIALIST PARTY

The party of three-time presidential candidate Salvador Allende, the Partido Socialista, was consistently in opposition throughout the Frei administration. As had been true throughout most of its history, it was plagued by factionalism; it suffered a split of some consequence during this period. In its efforts to outpace its Communist competitors, it also tended to drift increasingly to the Left.

Immediately after his defeat by Eduardo Frei in the 1964 election, Salvador Allende suggested to the Socialists that a new mass party be formed in order to confront the Christian Democrats on a more equal basis. He rejected the position of some of his colleagues who insisted that the traditional parties and the Christian Democrats were just "two faces of reaction." Instead, Allende argued that the PDC was in fact a mass party with a program and policies that for the time were progressive. Hence, the only effective means of confronting them in the 1965 congressional elections and thereafter would be to oppose them with another more progressive party with the kind of multiclass base which characterized the Christian Democrats in 1964-1965.

Allende proposed that immediate negotiations be held with the Radical party, with an eye towards merging the Socialists and Radicals on a platform that would be acceptable to both but would not completely reflect the position of either. The old Socialist prejudice against the Radicals was too strong, however, and Allende's suggestion was rejected out of hand. For some time thereafter, Allende retired from an active role in the leadership of the Socialist party.[3]

Ever since the reunification of the Socialists in the late 1950s, the party organization had been dominated by Senator Raúl Ampuero, leader of the Partido Socialista Popular. Ampuero had sought to impose upon that party the principles of Leninist "democratic centralism" and had persuaded the PSP to declare itself to be Marxist-Leninist. Within the reunited Partido Socialista, Ampuero had also tried to impose an unaccustomed degree of party discipline. His success was very relative.

A few months before the 1964 election, Ampuero had had to squash a serious rebellion against his control in the party's congress of February 1964. This revolt was headed by Clodomiro Almeyda, leader of the party's Santiago regional organization and at that time a protagonist of the Socialists' establishing a clear identification with the Chinese Communist party. Ampuero was able to stifle the Almeyda forces by interpreting the principles of democratic centralism in such a way as to refuse the Santiago regional group the right to elect its own delegates to the national party convention.[4]

Only about a year later, Ampuero was faced with a more serious rebellion, provoked by discontent over the defeat of Salvador Allende in the 1964 presidential election and by the magnitude of that defeat. At a party congress held in Linares, Ampuero was not reelected secretary general; he was replaced by Aniceto Rodríguez, who not long before had been one of his closest collaborators. Thereafter, relations between Ampuero and the new party leadership deteriorated further. In July 1967, the former secretary general was expelled from the Socialist party, along with Senator Tomás Chadwick and a number of other supporters. They thereupon set up their own party, which took the name Unión Socialista Popular.[5]

The fall of Ampuero reflected widespread discontent with his autocratic rule of the party. It also reflected the difficulty, if not impossibility, of developing monolithic unity within the Socialist party, which had traditionally included the most varied elements—democratic Socialists, proto-Trotskyites, Leninists of various sorts, and, in the years just preceding Ampuero's exit, Titoist, Maoist, and Fidelista factions or currents. At the time of his ouster as secretary general, Ampuero seems to have been the victim of an alliance of the most disparate groups, ranging from moderate reformists to the most ardent advocates of guerrilla warfare. They agreed on little else except the desire to rid the party of Raúl Ampuero's domination.

Although the defection of the Ampuero group did not constitute a major split in the Socialist party, it did weaken the Socialists. This was true in relation to the Communist and the Radical parties which at that time were comparable to the Socialist party in size and influence. As an illustration, in the congressional elections of 1969, the Socialist party received about 12.3 percent of the total popular vote, whereas the Unión Socialista Popular got 2.2 percent. Together they would have had 14.5 percent, which would have made the Socialist party the third largest of the opposition groups, after the Partido Nacional and the Communists, who won 15.3 percent of the total votes in that election. As it was, the Socialist party came in fourth, trailing the Radicals by 0.6 percent.[6]

The Socialists continued to be riven by factional disputes. They also maintained their rivalry with the Communist party in the labor movement and in the politics of the far Left. From time to time, the Socialist and Communist leadership engaged in bitter polemics, particularly in July and August 1968 when there was an exchange of open letters between the two parties. The Socialists continued to be suspicious of the Communists, fearing that in one way or another their allies were trying to reduce the influence and following of the Socialist party.

During the Frei administration, the Socialist party had greater funds than in the past, and they were able to maintain a considerably larger paid staff, particularly for work in the trade unions. However, they continued to be secondary to the Communists in the labor movement.

THE COMMUNIST PARTY

Throughout the Frei administration, the Communist party continued to be the best organized, most diciplined, and largest single element in the far left of Chilean politics. It had major influence in the labor movement, and it shared with the Socialists control of that part of the new peasant movement which was affiliated with the Central Única de Trabajadores de Chile.

The Communist party continued to be exceedingly loyal to Moscow in the internecine struggles within the Communist world. During the early 1960s, it engaged in strong polemics with the leadership of the Chinese party, and during the Frei period, when the Castro leadership in Cuba was antagonistic towards the Soviet Union, the Chilean Communists had open controversies with Fidel Castro and other Cuban Communist leaders. The Chilean Communist party demonstrated its pro-Moscow position clearly in August 1968. Immediately after the Soviet invasion of Czechoslovakia, the Chilean party announced its support of the U.S.S.R's action, even though the invasion was very unpopular in Chile. In so doing, it exposed the Chilean Communist party to charges of subordinating itself to the Soviet Union and the Communist Party of the Soviet Union.

Throughout the Christian Democratic regime, the Communist party sought to broaden FRAP into a more inclusive coalition, an effort opposed by the Socialists. For instance, in October 1968 a plenum of the Communist party supported the alliance of FRAP with the Radical party and with left-wing elements, particularly the *Rebeldes,* of the Christian Democratic party.[7] Undoubtedly, the Communists were principally responsible for the formation of the Unidad Popular coalition for the presidential election of 1970.

The Communists gained ground during the Frei administration both in the labor movement and in the general political scene. Within organized labor, Communist influence in the rank-and-file organizations of the labor movement expanded, and the party came to have the largest single following of any political group in the unions.

The Communists' political progress was reflected in the elections of the 1960s. Whereas in the 1961 congressional elections, the Communists had received only 11.4 percent of the total vote cast, four years later they had increased their share modestly to 12.4 percent. In the municipal contest of 1967, on the other hand, they enjoyed a considerable rise to 14.8 percent of the total vote, and by the 1969 congressional poll, they received 16.6 percent of all votes cast.[8] In the 1969 election, the Communists received 380,721 votes, electing four senators and twenty-two deputies. They thus surpassed the Radicals by almost 75,000 votes (although as a result of electoral pacts, the Radicals elected more senators and deputies than the Communists) and received almost 90,000 more votes than their Socialist competitors and allies.[9]

THE EMERGENCE OF THE MIR

One of the most important developments on the extreme left during the Frei years was the emergence of the Movimiento de Izquierda Revolucionaria (MIR). This group was formed in 1965 by several small factions, including an offshoot of the Socialist party led by Oscar Waiss who had been expelled from the Partido Socialista in 1961 on Raúl Ampuero's instigation; and one of the country's several Trotskyite factions, led by Luis Vitale.

Soon after its establishment, the MIR moved quickly to the extreme left of the Chilean political spectrum. With the call of the Castroite Organización Latino Americana de Solidaridad (OLAS) for guerrilla wars throughout Latin America at its founding congress in Havana in mid-1967, the MIR enthusiastically endorsed this position. Early in 1969, it went underground and launched a series of urban guerrilla activities. It remained underground until after the inauguration of President Salvador Allende. Meanwhile, it was abandoned by some of its older leaders, including Oscar Waiss who did not agree with the terrorist and guerrilla orientation adopted by the party.[10]

The MIR's chief activists were middle- and upper-class elements. Its only obviously significant support was in the University of Concepción, where it controlled the University Student Federation after 1967. Its efforts to organize groups among peasants and workers were of no importance until after Allende came to power.

In 1969 and 1970, the MIR engaged in a number of terrorist activities, including robberies of a large supermarket and of a branch of the Bank of London and South America, as well as the waylaying of a pickup truck of the Banco Continental containing a substantial amount of money. These events took place in and around Santiago. The MIR was also said to have carried out a raid on a small police post in the region of Copiapó, several hundred miles north of the capital.

In a police raid following the first holdups by MIR members, the authorities announced their discovery of a detailed outline showing the MIR's five-stage plan of operations: (1) to gather money through robberies of banks and other institutions, (2) to commit a series of assassinations of political figures and of raids on public utilities, (3) to launch rural guerrilla war, (4) to provoke an open confrontation with the national armed forces, and (5) to organize a political structure to take over the rule of the country.[11]

The government reacted swiftly to this outbreak of criminal activities under the guise of politics. Its most spectacular move took place in June 1969, when the Carabineros and plainclothes detectives raided the campus of the University of Concepción, the first such police raid on a university in fifty years. The move was made on the orders of a local judge, after hearing testimony by a journalist of the Concepción newspaper *Noticias de la Tarde,* Hernan Osses Santa María, who said that he had been kidnapped by a MIR group headed by Luciano Cruz, former MIR head of the Concepción University Students' Federation. According to Osses, the MIRistas had beaten him and taken pictures of him in the nude.[12]

Robberies and other urban guerrilla activities by the MIR occurred from time to time during the rest of the Frei administration. Meanwhile, other elements of the far Left reacted to the outbreak of MIRista violence. The Communist party expressed its strong opposition to the MIR and to its line, going so far as to say that "with its ultra left and ultra revolutionary line it is seeking to carry on the struggle in favor of imperialism,"[13] that is, that the MIR was acting as an agent provocateur. Elements of the Socialist party, on the other hand, expressed sympathy for the MIR. Thus, Edmundo Serani, one of the leaders of the Socialist youth, stated in August 1969 that "we consider that the MIR represents something, because it has clarity in its positions. The Socialist Youth has no discrepancies with the MIR and doesn't accept allegations that it is acting irresponsibly."[14]

These divergent points of view among other far left elements were to continue long after the Christian Democrats had left office and were to constitute a point of weakness in the subsequent regime of President Salvador Allende.

For some MIR members, the group's theory and activities were not sufficiently revolutionary. Thus, several tiny groups of MIRistas broke away to form even more extremist organizations. Two of these were the Movimiento Revolucionario Manuel Rodríguez, usually called MR-2; and the Vanguardia Organizada del Pueblo (Organized Vanguard of the People—VOP). These split from the MIR in 1968 and were to continue in existence for several years; the VOP gained notoriety for its terrorist activities during the first year of the Allende regime.[15]

THE RADICALS

During the Frei administration, the Radical party moved increasingly to the Left, finally allying itself fully with the far Left opponents of the Christian Democratic regime. At the same time, this evolution underscored the heterogeneous nature of the Radical party, since it provoked a major split in the already weakened group, assuring the Radicals' final decline to the status of a minor party.

In 1968 the Radical party decided to affiliate with the Socialist International, into which it was accepted as an "observer member." At the same time, its youth branch joined the International Union of Socialist Youth (IUSY), and in January 1969, the Juventud Radical played host to the First International Seminar of Social Democratic Youth of Europe and Latin America.[16] However, there was a bitter struggle over what position the Radicals should adopt in internal Chilean politics. This became clear in the 1967 convention of the party, where the first serious effort was made to align it with the Socialists and Communists in a common front against the Christian Democrats on the one hand and the new Partido.Nacional on the other.

Although the 1967 convention did not take a clear position on this new alignment, it elected a new National Executive Committee (CEN) which was committed to such a regrouping for the 1970 election. As the next convention approached (the party's twenty-fifth, which was to take a definitive position with regard to the presidential election), the internal crisis within the party ranks deepened.[17] This convention met in June 1969. At that time, it adopted a clear position in favor of joining with the Socialists, Communists, and smaller groups to support a joint candidate for the 1970 presidential election. It also expelled nine of its leaders who were most strongly opposed to that position.[18]

Clearly, the Radicals were hoping that the 1970 election would be a repeat of the Popular Front experience of 1938. The party convention nominated Alberto Baltra as its candidate and issued a call to "all popular and left parties and movements" to rally behind him.[19] No such support came, however. The Socialists were absolutely opposed to a Radical as the candidate of the new Unidad Popular (UP) coalition, and as a result, all efforts to agree on a candidate failed for some time. A meeting of the leaders of all UP parties on December 31, 1969, for the purpose of choosing a nominee broke up in deadlock.

The crisis threatening the continuation of the Unidad Popular was finally broken when Alberto Baltra, obviously after consultation with the CEN, submitted his "indeclinable resignation" as candidate, on January 19, 1970. Although the Radicals announced that they would support Rafael Tarud, the only non-Marxist-Leninist candidate still in the race for the UP candidacy, this proved to be little more than a gesture, since within forty-eight hours there was agreement that Salvador Allende, the Socialist, would be the presidential nominee of the Unidad Popular.[20]

Meanwhile, a serious split had taken place within the Radical ranks. As a result of the June 1969 convention's expulsion of a number of dissident leaders, including the 1964 presidential candidate Julio Durán, many other leading figures in the party resigned. These included a number of ex-presidents of the party such as Angel Faivovich, Marcial Mora, and Ulises Correa; ex-vice-presidents of the republic such as Alfredo Duhalde and Alfonso Quintana; and various current and former senators and deputies.[21] The dissidents formed a new party, the Partido de la Democracia Radical (PDR). It held its first convention in November 1969, attended by approximately 900 delegates from all over the country. The new party was legally recognized shortly after this meeting.[22] The PDR threw its support to Jorge Alessandri in the 1970 presidential election.

This was probably the Radicals' most serious division in their long history, which was marked by many splits. It came at a time when the Radical party had already suffered a severe decline in popular support, and it ended the role of the Radicals as a major factor in national politics.

OTHER OPPOSITION GROUPS

Other small opposition groups emerged during the Frei administration. One consisted of a faction of the sadly diminished Partido Democrático. That party, the first avowedly Socialist party in Chile, dating from the late 1880s, had been reduced to minor proportions by the 1960s. It had split during the 1964 elections, one faction backing Frei and the other Allende. Subsequently, the pro-Frei group reorganized as the Partido Democrático Nacional (PADENA) and continued to be aligned with the Christian Democratic government. During the last two years of the Frei administration, one member of PADENA was in the president's cabinet. The group aligned with FRAP took the name Partido Social Demócrata (PSD). As such, it was an official member of FRAP, along with the Communists and Socialists. As the 1970 presidential election approached, it became part of the Unidad Popular.

That neither of these parties was any longer a serious force in national politics was amply demonstrated in the 1969 congressional elections. In that contest, the PADENA received 44,564 votes, or 1.9 percent of the total, whereas the PSD got only 20,485 votes, or 0.9 percent. Neither of the parties elected any senators or deputies.[23]

In the closing phases of the Frei administration, two other small parties appeared. One was the MAPU, formed by Christian Democratic dissidents who resigned from or were thrown out of the party in the middle of 1969. This new group, which was soon wracked by its own internal dissension, immediately aligned itself with the emerging Unidad Popular and supported Allende in the 1970 race.

The other new party was the Acción Popular Independiente (API), a heterogeneous group including people who had belonged to various other parties at one time or another. Its two most important figures were Senator Rafael Tarud, who had been president of the Partido Agrario Laborista and a minister of President Carlos Ibáñez in the 1950s; and Lisandro de la Cruz, once an important figure in the Socialist party. During the 1970 presidential campaign, API attempted to win support for the Allende candidacy among small businessmen and other lower middle-class groups. Tarud continued to be its only member of Congress.

FREI AND THE OPPOSITION

Although during most of the first four years of his administration, President Frei enjoyed a parliamentary majority in the Chamber of Deputies, throughout this period he was faced with an opposition majority in the Senate. As a result, he had to maneuver considerably with both the Right and the Left opposition in order to get his legislative program through Congress. By and large, he was successful in his maneuvering, although it delayed passage of much of his reform legislation. As noted earlier, the most important laws he and his party supported were not passed until the administration was about half over.

Given the heterogeneity of the oppositon, Frei was able to get support from the Left for some measures and from the Right for other laws. The Left, for example, was highly critical of the details of the Agrarian Reform Law but finally supported it. Similarly the Right backed the legislation for Chileanization of the mining industry, even though it was not happy with it.

Splits between one or another of the opposition groups sometimes favored the administration. A case in point was the Readjustment Law of 1968 whereby, following a custom established some years earlier, Congress enacted a general wage increase for the whole country. The Socialists were strongly opposed to the terms of the law proposed by the administration at the beginning of 1968. However, with the support of the Communist senators, it was finally passed, more or less as requested by Frei.[24]

Some of the legislation failed passage more because of dissidence within the PDC than because of resistance from the opposition. This was true, for instance, of the project for thorough revision of the Labor Code, presented by Frei's first minister of labor, William Thayer. It never got out of committee.

Not infrequently, the opposition groups felt frustrated by Frei's ability to play one of them off against another. This frustration found somewhat ridiculous expression in January 1967, when Congress refused to grant the president permission to make a trip to the United States. According to the 1925 Constitution, the president of Chile could not leave the country without such permission, and so the trip had to be canceled.[25] Although the congressional action was then widely interpreted as a gesture against the United States, it was more likely intended as a kind of "revenge" on the president

—this being one matter of no major importance on which both the Right and Left in Congress could agree. It was embarrassing but not crucial to the president.

CONCLUSION

The opposition during the Frei administration played the normal role which an opposition plays in a democratic system. It exercised vigilance over the party in power, it forced some modifications in the legislation proposed by the executive, and it sometimes severely criticized the administration.

Probably the most important development with regard to the role of the opposition during this period was a growing polarization in national politics. For one thing, the rise of the Partido Nacional signified the resurrection of a strong conservative group, resistant to all significant change. The Partido Nacional differed from earlier Rightist factions in that its base was among middle-class rather than upper-class economic and social interests.

Second, the Christian Democratic period witnessed a decline in the power and influence of the center-Left in national politics, as reflected in the poor showing of both the Christian Democrats and the Radicals in the 1969 elections; the evolution of the Radicals as a junior partner in a coalition dominated by Marxist-Leninists; and the alignment of a dissident Radical group with the Right.

The most disturbing trend of all was the rise at both political extremes of groups hostile to the democratic system itself. Both the Patria y Libertad on the Right and the MIR on the Left believed primarily in the use of force to achieve their ends, rejected democratic constitutionalism, and sought violent confrontation.

These trends helped to prepare the way for The Tragedy of Chile.

9
Military and Constitutional Issues During the Frei Regime

Serious constitutional issues arose during the Christian Democratic regime. For the first time in many years, discontent within the military resulted in an abortive attempt at a coup d'etat, once again bringing into question the armed forces' role within Chile's constitutional democracy. On the other hand, on the initiative of the Frei government, certain modifications were made in the Constitution itself in an attempt to make it more responsive to the popular will and to try to avoid future deadlocks between the executive and legislative branches of government. (One of the major controversies of the next administration was to be over the failure of President Salvador Allende to make use of the most important of the constitutional changes enacted during the Frei regime, that is, the resort to a plebiscite to resolve deadlocked issues.)

CAUSES OF MILITARY GRIEVANCES

Two basic grievances of the armed forces—unhappiness over the quality and quantity of military equipment and discontent over military pay—finally resulted in the attempted coup d'etat of October 22, 1969. The same salary complaint had motivated the young officers' mutiny which in September 1924 had ushered in the only other instance of active military intervention into Chilean politics in the twentieth century.

Unhappiness over military equipment surfaced at least as early as 1966, when the Frei government sought to equip the Carabineros who served as frontier guards with mortars and light artillery. This move was thwarted when the army protested against providing such equipment to the militarized police so long as the army's own equipment was not improved. At that time, the army complained that its weapons were not only inadequate in quantity but were also of such ancient vintage and heterogeneous origins that getting replacement parts and munitions would be very difficult.[1]

President Frei was not anxious to expend large sums on reequipping the armed forces. Part of his rationale was made clear during an official visit to Brazil in September 1966 when he warned publicly against the possible dangers of an armaments race in Latin America, which he commented "would be fatal for Latin America and for my country." He added that "I have similar opinions from other Governments."[2] On various other occasions, too, Frei voiced his conviction that the countries of Latin America had to come to agreements to avoid an arms race.

In the 1966 speech given in Brazil, Frei implied another reason for not enlarging expenditures on the armed forces. He commented that "an armaments race is unacceptable in the light of economic and social development plans, and the utmost must be done to avoid it." Here he was probably referring to the increased government expenditures, particularly for agrarian reform and education.

With regard to the pay issue, during the Frei government military salaries tended to lag behind those of other public service branches and of private industry. Even the cash pay of military officers and noncoms was not exorbitant, although they also received perquisites in addition to their base salaries. In 1969, a captain reportedly received the equivalent of $110 a month, plus an orderly, free rent, and "generally a rations allowance" for "him and a wife and three children." At the same time, a sergeant received $80 a month, a housing allowance, and a family food ration.[3] Unlike the officers of many other Latin American armies, Chilean officers seldom had second jobs in the civilian bureaucracy to supplement their military pay.

The long-standing discontent over salaries contributed to the growing tension between the Christian Democratic government and some elements of the armed forces, which broke into the open in the last months of 1969.

THE MILITARY AND POLITICS

Military officers came under attack from elements of the Left opposition to the Frei administration. For example, at a meeting of the commanders-in-chief of American armies in Rio de Janeiro in October 1968, the Left registered considerable objection to Chile's representation there by General Sergio Castillo. General Castillo defended his attendance by noting that he had frequently been in the minority at the session "exactly because of maintaining points of view of strict support for constitutionalism and the non-deliberative role of the Armed Forces."[4]

The armed forces came under particularly bitter attack in June 1969 when during a press conference the minister of national defense, General Tulio Marambio, condemned the guerrilla activities then going on in Chile. According to *El Mercurio*, this statement "produced a violent reaction in the Socialist Party, a group which has engaged in continuous attacks on the Armed Forces." The newspaper added that "in a more moderate tone the spokesman for the Communist Party has also criticized the Minister for demanding that secondary students spend more time at their studies."[5]

THE VIAUX COUP

Military discontent culminated in the attempted coup d'etat of October 21, 1969. The immediate antecedents to this action were the dismissal of Brigadier General Roberto Viaux as commander of the First Division of the Chilean Army a week earlier, combined with his premature retirement from the armed forces; and a protest against these steps on the part of some of the officers under his command. General Viaux himself attributed his dismissal to the fact that "I had too much support from the officers and troops, that I was a leader."[6]

Subsequently, a prolonged special cabinet meeting was held on the night of October 20 "to analyze the economic and institutional problem of the Armed Forces." The meeting lasted until 3:00 A.M. Two hours later, Major Arturo Marshall and Captain Nierad went to the headquarters of the Yungay regiment in San Felipe, thirty miles north of Santiago, with the apparent intention of arousing that unit to rebellion. Instead, they were arrested.

In the Tacna tank regiment stationed near the center of Santiago, the result was different. There at 6:00 A.M. on October 21, according to *El Mercurio,* "Captain Mora seized command of the Tacna Regiment and turned it over to General Roberto Viaux."[7]

President Frei declared a state of siege throughout the country, and loyal units were mobilized for possible conflict with General Viaux's regiment. At the same time, there was an outpouring of civilians to demonstrate their opposition to a military coup; the CUTCh called a general strike in support of the continuance of the constitutional regime; and the presidential palace of La Moneda was inundated with groups who came to express their support of the government and their opposition to any military takeover.

No actual conflict took place. After seven hours of negotiations, General Viaux and his supporters surrendered to the military commander of Santiago, General Alfredo Mahn. They were arrested, and were subsequently tried and convicted of sedition. Viaux remained in jail until after the military coup of September 1973, when he was allowed to go into exile.

Both during and after the mutiny, General Viaux insisted that his intention was not to overthrow the government. In a statement issued at the end of the incident, he expressed

our absolute loyalty to Your Excellency the President of the Republic and our obedience to the constituted authorities. . . . Our purely military aspirations were to achieve
solution of the institutional problems which weigh so heavily in material and human
terms: to obtain pay which is dignified and in accordance with the importance of the
function fulfilled by the members of the institution, and to reestablish the command
function to the fullness of its prerogatives and creative dynamic action.

Earlier in the day, in a press conference held at the headquarters of the
Tacna regiment, Viaux had summarized the objectives of the mutiny in
somewhat different terms. "Our attitude," he said, "is not political. We
merely seek to demand, or less than that, to bring pressure to remedy the
situation of the Army, both with regard to materiel and emoluments."[8]

The unanswered question concerning the October 1969 mutiny of the
Tacna regiment centered on what agreements were reached as the condition
for the submission of the rebels. Subsequent events hinted that Minister of
Defense Marambio's removal was one part of the agreement, since he was
soon replaced by Sergio de la Ossa, while the government quickly drew up
a bill providing for substantial increases in military pay scales.

The military situation did not approach normalcy again until several
weeks later. Almost a month after the attempted coup, on November 20,
President Frei found it necessary to reassure the military forces that they
would quickly receive the pay increases promised them, while at the same
time stating that any further subversive movements in the armed forces
would be severely repressed. On December 3, the Parisian daily *Le Monde*
was still reporting that "fears that the Chilean Army might be planning a
coup to overthrow Dr. Eduardo Frei's Christian Democrat government
were gaining ground in political and diplomatic quarters in Santiago last
week."[9]

No further serious trouble with the military erupted during the remainder
of the Christian Democratic regime. Even the assassination of Army Commander René Schneider a few weeks before the end of Frei's term did not
provoke any movement within the armed forces, as it was obviously intended
to do by the right-wing terrorists who carried it out. However, there is little
doubt that the events of October 21, 1969, and the unsettled situation for
some time after that date, represented a serious blow to the tradition of
military subordination to civilian authority.

THE CONSTITUTIONAL ISSUE

Military insubordination during the Frei administration thus constituted
something of a threat to the continued functioning of Chilean constitutional
democracy. During this period, too, long-standing discontent with the
country's constitutional system found expression in the Christian Democratic
government's move to enact substantial revisions of the Constitution itself.

For many years, leaders of differing political tendencies had felt the need for some major reforms in the Constitution of 1925. Several of Frei's predecessors in the presidency had complained about the slowness of the legislative process and of their inability to get projects and programs through Congress with reasonable dispatch.

Although in the past Eduardo Frei had been skeptical about making any major changes in the balance of power between the executive and Congress, as president he shared the complaints of his predecessors. Soon after taking office in 1964, he tentatively suggested significant modifications of the Constitution but dropped the matter for about four years. It was not until early 1969 that he again sent to Congress a series of proposed reforms in the Constitution, which after almost a year of controversy were finally enacted, at least in part.

The general thrust of Frei's proposed amendments, and of that part of them which was finally accepted by Congress, was to strengthen the power of the president vis-à-vis the Congress in the Chilean constitutional system. As in other regimes in which the presidency and Congress are autonomous of one another, Chile's presidential system as established in the 1925 Constitution often resulted in struggles between the executive and the legislature. Deadlock between the two powers sometimes engendered feelings of frustration on both sides. Frei's proposed constitutional amendments tended to shift the balance of power considerably in favor of the president and to provide means of breaking deadlocks. Even though not all of his suggestions were finally enacted, the changes made had these two effects.

These proposals for constitutional alterations aroused strong criticism from the far Left, whose position was in favor of the power of the Congress. They accused Frei and the Christian Democrats of trying to impose "political Caesarism" on the country.[10] This charge seems quite ironic in view of the violent attacks the Socialists and Communists later made upon Congress in the Allende administration. At that time, the legislature sought to block some of the president's actions, and the president refused to make use of the powers the Frei constitutional reforms had given him for ending his deadlock with the Congress.

THE CONSTITUTIONAL AMENDMENTS

President Frei sent Congress at least eleven major proposals on the Constitution. Only two of these—and among the most important—were not acted upon favorably by Congress.

The first proposal was the rather novel one that within the first six months of his term of office the president decree elements of the social and economic program upon which he had been elected. It was proposed that if Congress did not act upon this request within ninety days, the president should be free to issue such decree-laws without congressional authorization. Congress could reject the president's request, however, if it did so within ninety days of the time in which it was submitted. This proposal aroused strong opposition, not only from the parties aligned against the government, but also within the Christian Democratic party itself. (Again the resistance of the Socialists and Communists to this idea is ironic, since if it had been incorporated in the Constitution, President Allende might well have been able to enact most of his social and economic program by presidential decree within his first six months in office.) After furious debate, Congress rejected the proposal.

Frei's second major suggestion was that the president be authorized to dissolve Congress once during his term of six years, and to call new elections for the legislative branch. This proposal was designed to end any deadlock between the president and Congress over particular issues, although if the Congress resulting from such dissolution and new elections were still dominated by the opposition, the president would be in an anomalous position. Again, this proposal aroused great opposition and was finally defeated.

Another suggestion for resolving legislative-executive deadlocks was accepted and was incorporated in the Constitution. This was Frei's proposal that the president be entitled to call a plebiscite over specific issues on which he and the Congress were in disagreement. There were extensive provisions for drafting the issues on which a plebiscite might be held and for giving equal access to the media to proponents and opponents of a proposition that might be submitted to the voters. (It was this amendment to the Constitution, which was passed, which President Salvador Allende subsequently refused to use to resolve the bitter issues between himself and the opposition-dominated Congress.)

Another method to resolve controversies between the executive and other branches of the government was also incorporated in the Constitution by the 1969 reforms. This was the establishment of a constitutional tribunal, made up of three members named by the president of the republic and two members of the Supreme Court, chosen by all members of the Court. The amendment provided that if Congress or the comptroller general of the republic should challenge the constitutionality of an act of the president, or if the executive or the comptroller general should challenge an act of Congress, the issue should be presented to this tribunal. This body was used on various occasions during the Allende administration.

Several of the amendments which were adopted strengthened the powers of the president. One of these was a provision giving the president the right to introduce legislation on a wide range of subjects. Another was a considerable extension of the president's right to declare that action on a particular piece of proposed legislation was "urgent," thus forcing Congress to act on it within a given period of time. A third was a proposal giving the president wide powers over the organization and reorganization of the public administration, including the establishment of "departments," the administrative subdivisions of the Chilean government. Two other proposals granted the president and ministers permission to leave the country for short periods of time without having to petition the Congress.

Two measures were designed to limit the powers of Congress and to make it more efficient. One forbade the addition of riders to bills, and the second was a proposal that would streamline congressional consideration of legislation.

Finally, an amendment that had general support, and was in fact the culmination of at least a fifty-year struggle, was the proposal that the voting age be dropped to eighteen years and that all literacy requirements be dropped for the franchise. However, literacy was still required for election to the Senate or Chamber of Deputies.[11]

FINAL ENACTMENT OF THE CONSTITUTIONAL REFORMS

Debate on the constitutional changes suggested by President Eduardo Frei continued throughout most of 1969. Although, as we have noted, two of his major proposals were rejected by Congress, the others were passed through both houses of the legislature. The final step of their adoption by a joint session of the two houses took place on December 28, 1969. The amendments passed with the support of the Christian Democrats and the Partido Nacional, and the opposition of the Socialists, Communists, Radicals, and members of MAPU.

10
Rural Reform

The strongest impact of the "Revolution in Liberty" was felt in rural Chile. Aside from the expansion of the educational system in the countryside (which we shall discuss later in this chapter), the reforming zeal of the Christian Democratic government was evidenced in the rural sector by the establishment of legal unionism and collective bargaining, and by the agrarian reform.

ANTECEDENTS OF RURAL UNIONISM[1]

In order to understand what happened in the area of rural unionism during the Christian Democrat regime, it is necessary to examine the ebbs and flows of rural unionism in earlier times.

A few organizations of rural workers apparently began to appear in the midst of the social ferment preceding Arturo Alessandri's first election to the presidency in 1920. These unions had no legal authorization, and they seem to have been primarily under anarchosyndicalist influence. Relatively few groups of workers in the areas adjacent to the major cities appear to have been affected by this development.

During the turbulent situation following the "Rattle of the Sabres" in September 1924, further efforts were made to extend unionization to rural areas. During the few months in which the possibility existed, little progress was made in organizing the rural workers, and when legal unions began to be recognized under Ibáñez's first administration, few if any organizations of agricultural workers received recognition.

It was not until the advent of the Socialist Republic of 1932 that another drive to unionize the rural workers was undertaken. This move was very shortlived, and with Carlos Dávila cracking down on supporters of the now exiled Colonel Marmaduque Grove, it was quickly curtailed.

The issue again arose at the end of 1938, when the Popular Front regime of President Pedro Aguirre Cerda took power. In the opening months of the Aguirre Cerda administration, the Ministry of Labor for the first time began a wide processing of rural unions' applications for legal recognition, and in a few cases it did in fact extend such recognition. Some of these organizations survived during the next quarter of a century. However, in May 1939, fearful of the right wing's reaction to any large-scale attempt to union ize the rural work force, Aguirre Cerda issued an order that no more such unions be given recognition.

Thus, another seven and a half years were to pass before another short period of rural unionization took place. This time it was a result of the accession to power of Gabriel González Videla, in whose first cabinet the Communists had representation. The Communist party undertook an intensive campaign of rural unionization, and some unions were legalized. Under Communist auspices, the first federation or agricultural workers, the Federación Campesina was established. The Socialists also succeeded in organizing a handful of rural unions. However, with the break between González Videla and the Communists, the government curtailed all efforts in the rural areas.

In 1948, the González Videla regime passed the first law specifically dealing with the unionization of rural workers, although it was designed more to prevent than to facilitate their organization. The law required that unions be established on individual *fundos* (farms), thus making it relatively simple for landholders to prevent unionization of their workers, who were not in a position to mobilize support of the workers on other *fundos*. Unionization was limited to those *fundos* with twenty-five workers, the minimum number required to form a union. The law also required that all officers of the rural workers' unions be literate and that a high proportion of their members also be able to read and write. In view of the widespread illiteracy in the countryside, this provision guaranteed that few unions could meet the requirements for recognition.

In fact, almost no rural workers belonged to legal unions in the period preceding the inauguration of the Christian Democratic government. Julio César Jobet has indicated that of the 222,870 members of legally recognized unions in 1960, only 1,870 were members of unions of agricultural workers.[2]

ANTECEDENTS OF CHRISTIAN DEMOCRATIC RURAL WORKERS' UNIONS

For more than a decade before Eduardo Frei came to power, Christian Democratic and allied groups had been active in laying the basis for extensive organization of the rural workers: the Unión de Campesinos Cristianos (UCC) and the Asociación Nacional de Organizaciones Campesinas (ANOC).

UCC had its origin in a small trade union confederation under Catholic auspices, Acción Sindical Chilena (ASICH). It had its first success in rural organization in 1953, when it unionized a substantial number of vineyard workers in the province of Talca. Of course, these organizations did not have legal recognition, and they were not officially supposed to engage in collective bargaining with the landowners. However, when the employers proved recalcitrant, and the government showed little interest in supporting the workers, the ASICH organized a march on Santiago by these rural workers, which received a great deal of publicity. Although it did not gain legal authorization for the organization of the vineyard workers, it did strengthen the prestige of the "unlegal" unions. These unions continued to exist in the Talca region and were able to enter into collective bargaining on an informal basis with some landowners in the area.

In 1960, the ASICH formally organized its rural affiliates into the Unión de Campesinos Cristianos, which began to extend beyond the confines of Talca. It gained several thousand adherents by the 1964 election, in which the members of the UCC played an active part on behalf of Eduardo Frei.

ANOC had its roots among the alumni of the Instituto de Educación Rural. This institute was a small organization with some support from the Catholic hierarchy, which sought to train leaders for a future rural labor movement. Although legal unions of rural workers were not yet possible, the churchmen involved saw that the time was not far off when they would come into existence, and they felt the need to have a corps of trained peasants who might assume leadership of the new groups. The Asociación Nacional de Organizaciones Campesinas sought to organize not only agricultural laborers, but also small landowners.

Although they developed independently, UCC and ANOC sometimes cooperated. One instance was the 1961 congress of the Central Única de Trabajadores. Both groups sent delegates, and had they been seated, the Christian Democrats might have taken over the leadership of the CUTCh. The peasant delegates were not seated, however. They organized their own "convention," which got a good deal of publicity but did not result in any permanent unification of the two groups at that point.

Two other Christian Democratically oriented peasant groups were active in the period just before the election of 1964. One was the Movimiento Campesino Independiente, considerably smaller than UCC and ANOC, and like ANOC was largely headed by graduates of the Instituto de Educación Rural. During the election campaign, the Christian Democrats also organized the Movimiento Nacional de Liberación Campesina as a purely political group for winning votes among the peasantry. After the election, it was converted into the Peasant Department of the Partido Demócrata Cristiano.

THE LEY DE SINDICACIÓN CAMPESINA

One of the most important elements in the program of the Christian Democratic party in the 1964 election was enactment of a new law covering legalization of unions of rural workers and their engaging in collective bargaining. This law, called the Ley de Sindicación Campesina, Law. No. 16,625, was finally passed on April 29, 1967, half way through the Frei regime. The "regulation" to put it into effect did not appear until September 21, 1967.

The Ley de Sindicación Campesina contained a number of innovations in Chilean labor legislation which Frei and Minister of Labor William Thayer would have liked to have extended to the urban sector as well, although they were not able to do so. These innovations were designed to give rural workers' organizations a degree of independence from outside political groups which the urban workers generally did not have.[3]

One significant change was the provision that the basic agricultural workers' unions should not consist only of workers of a single *fundo,* but rather should be organized on the basis of the municipality or *comuna.* In comparison with the old law of González Videla, this provision had several advantages for the workers. First, in allowing workers of all the *fundos* in a given *comuna* to come together to form a union, it made it possible for those on a *fundo* on which the union was strong to bring pressure on a recalcitrant employer in the municipality, who was resisting unionization. He could not destroy the union of the *comuna* by discharging those workers on his farm who belonged to the union.

In the second place, the communal basis for organization removed another major handicap to rural unionization under the González Videla law. This was the requirement that a base union have at least twenty-five members on a *fundo.* Only a minority of relatively large landholders employed as many as twenty-five heads of families, but it was not at all difficult to get together in a *comuna* twenty-five eligible workers to establish a union.

Another innovation in the Ley de Sindicación Campesina was the provision that there could be more than one base union or *sindicato* in each *comuna.* Indeed, the agricultural workers in a municipality could form as many *sindicatos* as they wished, so long as each had the requisite number of members. This made it possible for unions of several different political orientations to be formed in any given area.

In contrast to the provisions of the Labor Code, agricultural workers' unions were allowed to pay their officers for work done for the union. Thus, the rural sindicato leaders were not forced to do their union work after their hours of regular employment on their *fundo,* but could carry it out at any time, so long as the union paid their wage and compensated the employer for the social security payments he continued to have to make for the union leader. This meant that the local unions were not going to have to depend on people from outside the legalized labor movement to intervene in disputes with the employers, to present cases to the Ministry of Labor, and the like, as was often, if not usually, the case with the unions organized under the old Labor Code.

Finally, the Ley de Sindicación Campesina differed from the Labor Code in legalizing regional federations of rural unions and national confederations made up of a certain number of regional federations. These organizations higher up in the union hierarchy, like the communal *sindicatos,* were to receive funds originating from a 2 percent levy on rural payrolls. The Ministry of Labor was designated to administer the fund and distribute it on a pro rata basis to the federations and confederations in proportion to their total number of members. This provision, of course, meant that the higher echelon rural labor organizations did not have to depend upon outside agencies for their financing and manpower.

The Ley de Sindicación Campesina also provided for establishment of legal organizations of agricultural employers and for collective bargaining between them and the workers' organizations. Collective agreements could be on a municipal, provincial, or even national basis between *sindicatos,* federations, or confederations of workers and employers. As in the urban areas, boards of conciliation and arbitration, functioning under the aegis of the Ministry of Labor, were to try to seek agreement between the two sides. Similarly, the labor inspectors of the Ministry were to help settle grievances that could not be negotiated on a direct basis between a *sindicato* and an employer or group of employers.

This law was of fundamental importance for rural Chile. It marked an end to the era when employers could treat their agricultural workers as children, or worse. It meant that for the first time the rural workers would have organizations of their own which could defend their interests through both governmental administrative machinery and direct action, that is, the strike. It meant, too, that large numbers of workers had their first experience with a grass roots kind of democracy in their unions, and that they could not only defend their economic interests but also maintain their dignity as human beings. Rural unions also had great political significance, for they provided a potential power base for those parties that could obtain the support of the peasants, and a position of leadership among them. The peasants were now free to enter into political activity on their own behalf instead of as useful tools of their landlords.

SPREAD OF RURAL UNION ORGANIZATION

During the Frei administration, the Ley de Sindicación Campesina had a more direct effect on a much larger proportion of the rural population than did the agrarian reform. A large part of the rural work force was brought into the unions and experienced the impact of unionization in terms of a modification, if not elimination, of the old paternalistic relationship of employers to workers, and in terms of specific economic benefits, in the form of higher wages and fringe benefits.

Three major peasant union confederations were formed during the Frei administration. One was under the political influence of Communists and Socialists and belonged to the CUTCh; the other two were predominantly under Christian Democratic influence. (A fourth, much smaller, group of peasant unions was also under PDC orientation.)

The CUTCh's peasant affiliate, the Confederación Campesina y Indígena Ranquil, had its origins in the Federación Campesina organized by the Communists during the early part of the González Videla regime. In the 1950s, it became known as the Federación Campesina e Indígena Ranquil, a name change signifying the organization's particular effort among Indian groups and commemorating a massacre of unionized peasants some years before. During the PDC administration, this federation grew in size with renewed organizing activity among the peasants. Its principal centers of strength were in Santiago province and in the provinces immediately south of the capital city, and among Indian tenants and smallholders in the area around the city of Temuco in the southern part of central Chile.

With the enactment of the Ley de Sindicación Campesina, the unions belonging to the Federación were reorganized and received legal recognition, while regional federations of unions were also formed. In May 1968, the Federación was finally renamed Confederación Campesina e Indígena Ranquil and received recognition. During the Frei administration, its membership tended to be smaller than that of the two Christian Democratic confederations.

The largest peasant union confederation during the Frei period was the Confederación Campesina El Triunfo Campesino whose origin and early growth can be ascribed directly to the Christian Democratic government. The Instituto de Desarrollo Agropecuario (INDAP), an organization which until 1964 had been engaged in giving credit and technical assistance to farmers, took upon itself the added task of stimulating the organization of peasant unions. INDAP officials did organizational work among the tenants and agricultural laborers, helped them obtain recognition after the Ley de Sindicación Campesina was passed, and assisted them in negotiations with employers and officials of the Ministry of Labor. In most provinces, the headquarters of the federations belonging to El Triunfo Campesino were in the offices of INDAP during much of the Frei period. As a result of this strong encouragement, the Confederación El Triunfo Campesino became the largest national peasant group in the country during the Frei administration.

The third confederation was formed from the earlier groups of peasants and smallholders established under Christian Democratic auspices before 1964. Soon after Frei's election, the Unión de Campesinos Cristianos and the Asociación Nacional de Organizaciones Campesinas merged to establish the Confederación Nacional Campesina (CNC), without formally dissolving either of the older groups. The CNC became a kind of umbrella group under which organizing activities among agricultural laborers and tenants, as well as smallholders, was organized. The CNC ran extensive training courses for leaders of the new peasant unions and sent out organizers to help establish new unions and to service those already in existence. During its lifetime, the CNC received substantial financial help from the U.S. government's foreign aid program.

With the passage of the Ley de Sindicación Campesina, the unions associated with the CNC were reorganized to conform to the law, and federations were established in a number of provinces. The CNC itself was displaced in the middle of 1968 by a new Confederación Nacional Sindical Campesina "Libertad."

The smallest Christian Democratic-oriented peasant group, the Movimiento Campesino Independiente, participated in the negotiations leading to the formation of the Confederación Nacional Campesina. However, it did not join forces with the CNC; it remained quite small, with almost all of its membership concentrated in the province of Santiago. It finally died, and its local unions joined one of the PDC-oriented peasant union groups.

One other peasant union during this period was the Confederación Nacional de Pequeños Agricultores which consisted of small landholders. It was originally established with the help of Acción Sindical Chilena and was loosely associated with the CNC. However, it had no legal standing under the Ley de Sindicación Campesina, and its members' interests were quite distinct from those of the tenants and agricultural laborers. Years later, it merged with the Confederación de Sindicatos de Empleadores Agricolas, which was organized as the principal employers' group under the Ley de Sindicación Campesina.

As was traditional in Chilean labor legislation, the Ley de Sindicación Campesina provided for the organization of employers' unions as well as workers' unions, and for the federation and confederation of these employers' unions along worker union lines. As a result, the rural employers organized local *sindicatos* under this law, formed provincial federations, and in the middle of 1968 established the Confederación de Sindicatos de Empleadores Agrícolas. Thereafter, the local sindicatos and federations of this group usually negotiated collective agreements with the peasant unions and federations.

THE IMPACT OF RURAL UNIONISM

Rural unionization had a profound impact on life in the countryside. It marked the demise of a social and economic system that had existed for hundreds of years, giving a heretofore inert group participation in national life.

Wherever an agricultural workers' union was formed, the landlord could no longer treat his tenants and workers as his servants. For the first time, he had to meet them, or at least their representatives, on a nearly equal plane. The degree to which the master-servant relationship was reversed naturally varied considerably, depending on the relative power and influence of the individual landowner and of the union involved.

The landowner could no longer unilaterally decide the wages he would pay or the benefits he would give, nor could he arbitrarily decide how many and which of his workers he would dismiss at any given time. And, too, it was now more difficult for him to avoid paying social security taxes on his employees. Once a rural union became established, all of these matters became subject to collective bargaining or to the vigilance of the union. Paternalism gave way to an apportionment of power and of income on the *fundo* through a process of negotiation between the workers as a group and the owner of the land.

All of these changes did not, of course, take place overnight. The effect of unionization and collective bargaining varied widely from *fundo* to *fundo* and *comuna* to *comuna*. In some cases, the workers continued to have an exaggerated respect for the *patrón* and to approach him as union representatives with only a little less reticence than before. In other instances, the workers fully asserted their newly gained rights; they met with employers who were willing to respect these rights—although the employers were not always certain about what this willingness entailed.

Things changed in other ways. Collective bargaining brought immediate and substantial material benefits for unionized workers. In parts of the country where the unions were strongest, real wages went up as much as 100 percent between 1964 and 1968. In other areas, the improvements were less spectacular, but wherever rural unionization had progressed the workers' living levels had correspondingly advanced.

The new unions became a kind of training ground for the workers in many respects. For the first time they were involved on a personal level in the workings of democracy. They learned to conduct union meetings, to elect officers, to speak in public, to decide on issues. At the same time, they began to learn how to manipulate the political government. They became more exigent in their demands upon the public authorities, whether those of the Ministry of Labor, the Ministry of Education, the Ministry of Health, or local officials. They began to actively play the role of citizens, one that had always been denied them. Even more important, their participation in public and civic affairs was now on their own behalf. They did not participate because of their landlords' "gracious permission" but because it was their right, and they now had organizations and spokesmen who were willing and able to defend this right. So the peasants increasingly spoke for themselves as citizens, and not for their employers as agents of their employers, as in the past.

Although the process of change which rural unionization set in motion was not completed during the Christian Democratic period—and indeed had not even begun in all sections of the country—it had come to involve a large segment of the rural population before President Frei went out of office in November 1970.

THE AGRARIAN REFORM LAW

During the 1964 presidential election campaign, the Christian Democrats promised a law for redistribution of rural landholdings. Candidate Eduardo Frei talked about distributing land to 100,000 rural families during his hoped-for six years in office. Although his administration came nowhere near to the achievement of this goal, it did initiate a profound agrarian reform program which, by the time Frei went out of office, had progressed so far that no successor civilian regime could easily have stopped or reversed the process.

The Agrarian Reform Law provoked bitter fights in Congress. Both the Right and the Left opposed it, though for different reasons, while the Christian Democratic party itself was unable to reach a consensus as to the form the Agrarian Reform Law should take. As a result of these problems, the new law, Law 16,640, was not passed until June 1967. It went into effect on July 29, 1967.

The Agrarian Reform Law of 1967 remained in effect during the succeeding Allende administration and (in theory at least) in the military regime that followed that. It is a very long and complicated law, consisting of 357 articles and running to 160 pages, but its principal provisions can easily be summarized.

Law 16,640 allowed the state to expropriate all landholdings in excess of a basic unit of 80 hectares (approximately 200 acres) of irrigated land. Larger maximums were established for naturally watered land and for holdings used for grazing. Although in most cases the landholders were to be left with the maximum acreage stated in the law, they could lose all of their *fundo* if it was badly cultivated or abandoned, or if they were guilty of maltreating their workers. This last provision became a useful weapon for rural union leaders, for it got recalcitrant employers to deal with the unions.

Landlords who lost land were compensated for it on the basis of the land's declared value for tax purposes, plus improvements that had been made after the declaration of value had been made. They could be compensated partly in cash and partly in government bonds which would run for no longer than thirty years. This provision was exceedingly important, since in the earlier Agrarian Reform Law of the Jorge Alessandri administration the requirement of cash compensation had been an effective deterrent to the application of that law. The new legislation of the Frei government included a constitutional amendment ending the need for full payment in cash.

Land expropriated from the landlords was to be organized into *asentamientos agrarios* (agrarian settlements), which were transitional institutions designed to provide a period of experience and training for the peasant beneficiaries, as well as a period of substantial investment in the areas taken over. At the end of three to five years, the residents of the *asentamientos* would decide what form the final distribution of land should take—individual family plots, cooperatives, or a combination of the two.

A pamphlet issued by the Christian Democrats while the Agrarian Reform Law was being considered in Congress explained the *asentamiento* in the following terms:

The system accelerates the process of Agrarian Reform, because it has not been necessary to wait as before, and to the disadvantage of production, the division of the land and the water in order to continue the work of a divided landholding. Without disorganizing the fundo, the asentamiento permits in the short time that it exists—two years, in exceptional cases up to three—:

To train the peasants to maintain the organization of agricultural labor without being subject to an employer's system;

To train them to work on their own lands, perfecting their sense of responsibility;

To select them on the basis of number of days worked, of their efficacy as workers, and their dedication to the work;

To create a spirit of community which will crystalize in the creation of a Cooperative.[4]

In choosing people to become part of the *asentamientos,* those who had been permanent tenants on the expropriated landholding were to have first priority; after them, those who had been *aforinos* or part-time workers on the *fundo* were to have precedence; and finally, the Corporación de Reforma Agraria (CORA) could bring in workers who had had no previous association with the particular landholding if it deemed that there was sufficient land.

The general administration of the agrarian reform program was assigned to the Corporación de Reforma Agraria whose council consisted of representatives of several government ministries and peasant organizations. CORA decided which *fundos* should be expropriated and under what circumstances, and it was in charge of the *asentamientos* during their existence. INDAP also had a significant role in the *asentamientos* through the granting of credit and technical assistance to the *asentados*.[5]

EXTENT OF LAND REDISTRIBUTION UNDER FREI

The Christian Democratic government did not wait for the enactment of the new Agrarian Reform Law to begin the process of land redistribution. Under the threat of the ultimate passage of the new law, many landlords began to negotiate with CORA, in the hope of obtaining somewhat better conditions than they might get once the law was enacted. As a result, between January 1965 and the passage of the new law, CORA was able to take over by negotiation some 478 estates, covering 1 million hectares.[6]

By July 1970, less than four months before the Frei government went out of office, it had expropriated 1,319 landholdings, with a total area of about 3.5 million hectares (8.75 million acres), of which about one-third was in the three central provinces of Santiago, Valparaiso, and Aconcagua. Some 29,000 peasant families formed 910 *asentamientos* on 3 million hectares of land. By August 1, 1970, *asentamientos* with some 500,000 hectares had been distributed to 5,568 settlers, some of whom received cooperative titles, and others family ones.[7]

Establishing and finally distributing land to the peasants went slowly because the process was a very expensive one. The government's policy was not merely to distribute land, but also to train the peasants who received it in how to administer their new holdings, and to give them adequate capital equipment and other inputs. These aspects of the Frei agrarian reform policies help explain why the *asentamiento* was established as a provisional organizational form for land taken from the large holders. The *asentamientos* were run by peasant committees together with officials of CORA, while CORA, INDAP, and frequently the Ministry of Education and other government organizations cooperated in improving the land and helping peasants learn how best to use it.

The *asentamientos* characteristically brought into cultivation substantially more land than had been used before. This fact, as well as the extensive investment in the *asentamientos,* partially explain the increase in the agricultural production rate (3.8 percent per annum) during the Frei administration.[8]

Considerable controversy arose over how costly the agrarian reform was. There are indications that it may have been as high as $10,000 per family.

Joseph Thome, writing in 1970, has commented that "it cannot yet be said that Chile is in the process of a massive or substantial agrarian reform. On the other hand, it is certainly much more than a mere colonization program or one of token expropriation and redistribution."[9] It should be noted, however, that the process of actually granting titles to peasants did not get started until the last year of the Frei administration. Nonetheless, the Christian Democratic government made agrarian reform an integral part of public policy. As suggested earlier, it would have been very difficult, if not impossible, for any elected government after that of the Christian Democrats to have halted the program of land redistribution.

OTHER RURAL PROGRAMS

Although rural unionization and agrarian reform were the cornerstones of the Christian Democratic government's program in the rural areas, several other elements were also significant. These included encouragement of small landholders, expansion of rural education, and extension of the community development movement to the countryside. Small family-farm owners were on balance given considerable encouragement during the Frei administration, despite controversy among the Christian Democrats as to their role in the future of Chilean agriculture. In June 1968, CORA issued a regulation permitting small farmers to join together to buy a large landholding, and ultimately divide it among themselves; this was done on some scale during the rest of the PDC government. Meanwhile, INDAP was quite active in granting loans to small holders, both for financing their crops and for capital investment in their holdings.

The position of the small landholders was strengthened by the establishment in April 1967 of the Confederación de Pequeños Agricultores to represent this group. About a year later, it claimed some 30,000 small farmers in its ranks. In many instances, it and its regional federations represented the smallholders in negotiations with CORA, INDAP, and other government organizations, and it was active in stimulating the organization of consumers' and buying cooperatives among its members.[10]

During the first part of the Frei administration, a special effort was made to expand the school system. Since educational institutions were most deficient in the rural parts of the country, this crash program was of particular importance to agricultural workers and their children. In his Fifth Annual Message to Congress, President Frei noted that "in 1965 efforts were concentrated on incorporation into the educational system of all of the children of school age, and in this same year 95% of the children were in school, a level which has only been achieved in the most highly developed countries. Since then this percentage has been maintained."[11] As a result of these efforts, primary school enrollment increased from 1,689,000 in 1964 to 2,204,405 in 1968.[12] At the same time, the construction of school buildings increased by 132 percent during the first three years of the Frei administration, compared with the last three years of that of Jorge Alessandri.[13]

In a speech in November 1967, President Frei listed a number of other features of the government's education program in its first three years. Among these were:

Increase of more than 100 thousand students between 1964 and 1966 in secondary education.

Increase of more than 50 thousand students between 1964 and 1966 in technical education.

Establishment of the Instituto Nacional de Capacitación Profesional (INACAP) for adults, with 20,125 workers in 1966 and 25 thousand in 1967.

Creation of 58 evening schools for workers in 20 provinces.

Educational Reform which prolongs primary studies from six to eight years and a new structure of 4 years on the secondary level.

Extraordinary increases in school furniture, free texts, scholarships, dental care, vacation colonies, office equipment, cloakrooms etc.

Extraordinary increase of school lunches and breakfasts, 600 thousand and 800 thousand respectively in 1966.

National Program of Improvement of Teaching for more than 14 thousand teachers.

Creation and construction of the National Center for Pedagogic Improvement, Experimentation and Research.[14]

The author was able to observe a little of these educational efforts on the spot in 1968. In several rural areas of the country which were visited, many new schools (many of them made of prefabricated materials) had been built since the advent of the Frei government. The peasants exhibited great pride in finally having school facilities and teachers available for their children, and were very solicitous about maintaining the buildings and ensuring their offspring's regular attendance.

The spread of community development institutions to the rural areas can also be credited to the Christian Democrats. This program had been begun by the party even before their advent to power and was intensified thereafter. These institutions included the so-called *juntas de vecinos* and *centros de madres* as well as cooperatives and other organizations that helped the peasants to help themselves. The community development groups were often closely associated with a rural workers' union or with an *asentamiento agrario*.

POLITICAL CHANGES IN THE COUNTRYSIDE

The profound changes in rural Chile during the Christian Democratic period were reflected in local politics. The nationwide municipal elections held in early 1967 demonstrated the peasants' intensified political interest and their determination to have a major, if not decisive, role in local government.

In the middle of 1968, a striking pattern could be observed in the municipal councils of many rural areas in central Chile. As a result of the elections of 1967, most of the rural municipalities had Christian Democratic majorities in their communal councils. Almost without exception, the Christian Democrats who sat on these bodies were peasants or agricultural workers. Where there were minority members from the Radical, Socialist, or Communist parties, these generally were professional people—lawyers and teachers predominating. In most cases, there was one representative of the Partido Nacional, who was usually a landlord or the son of a landlord.

11
Economic Policies of the Christian Democratic Government

President Eduardo Frei and his associates understood intuitively what steps were necessary to get the process of Chilean economic development going again after more than a decade of virtual stagnation. They launched a number of programs designed to deal with this problem. Unfortunately for the administration, these programs required some painful redistribution of income, and therefore certain short-run sacrifices by some elements of the population. The benefits of the Frei government policies, on the other hand, could not become evident until after Frei's term in office expired.

Had these programs and policies been continued through one more administration, they would have begun to pay off substantially in terms of increasing national income, rising living standards for most of the population, and increased stability for the Chilean economy in terms of its relationship with the rest of the world. However, during Frei's six-year term they proved to be politically counterproductive and contributed, to at least some degree, to the defeat of the Christian Democrats in the 1970 election.

CHILE'S POST-IMPORT SUBSTITUTION CRISIS

The possibilities of maintaining sustained economic development on the basis of import substitution had largely expired in the early 1950s. The two administrations in office between 1952 and 1964 had no clear view of this fact and no clear set of policies to move the economy into a new stage of development and growth.

With the expiration of import substitution as a motor force for Chilean economic development, further economic progress came to depend largely upon the possibilities of expanding the market for the country's goods and services. This meant that it was necessary to amplify the internal market and to develop new kinds of export markets—with the country exporting new types of products and expanding the range of its customers.

Between 1952 and 1964, little was done to foster development by expanding markets. The rural sector of the economy remained backward, with most rural workers receiving so little money income that they could not constitute a substantial market for the country's manufacturing or service sectors. The income of the urban working population was increasing at best in exceedingly slow fashion. Little was done to develop new types of exports or to seek out new foreign customers for the products the country had to sell abroad.

The policies of the Frei administration were designed to further economic growth and development, although not exactly in the frame of reference posed here. At the same time, they were designed to deal with at least two other problems: the knotty issue of foreign control of strategic elements of the national economy and the possibility of expanding the country's traditional exports.

In terms of expanding the internal Chilean market, the single most important move by the Frei government was the series of agrarian policies it developed, as discussed in the previous chapter. Both the rural unionization program and the land redistribution policies were introduced (at least in part) to provide higher incomes for the million or more Chileans who still worked in agriculture and who until then had participated only marginally in the money economy. Simultaneously, the government's substantial investments in the *asentamientos agrarios* established under the agrarian reform program were intended to make Chilean agriculture more productive, and therefore better able to meet the growing demand for food, and to provide greater purchasing power for the rural sector of the economy. These new expenditures in the rural segment created new burdens on the government's treasury. The Frei administration sought to shoulder these new burdens by increases in taxation, which served to redistribute income from the urban to the rural sector, but this approach was politically unpopular.

The Christian Democratic government also moved energetically to expand traditional exports—combining this with the move to "Chileanize" the ownership of the mining industry—and to develop the export of new manufactured goods. Simultaneously, it sought to develop substantial new foreign markets by taking the lead in establishing the so-called Andean Bloc.

As indicated earlier, all of these were middle- and long-range development programs whose burdens were felt during the Frei period but whose benefits were not generally scheduled to accrue until at least the next administration. As a result, the inflation problem continued to plague the Christian Democratic administration, as it had plagued its predecessors. After some success in curtailing price increases in the first years of his government, Frei found it increasingly difficult to do so in the second half of his administration.

The rest of this chapter will deal with all the Frei economic policies except those in the rural sector, which have already been discussed.

THE CHILEANIZATION PROGRAM

It is not generally recognized that the Frei administration effectively nationalized the country's mining industry. Although it did so through a progressive rather than a precipitous process, it could be argued that the Frei government's actions in this area made the subsequent nationalization measures of the Allende regime superfluous. This is true in spite of the banner of "patriotism" with which the Allende regime wrapped its own moves in this area.[1]

Before coming to office, the Christian Democrats had toyed with the idea of outright nationalization of the copper and nitrate mines. By the time they won the 1964 election, however, they had come to believe that that would be counterproductive. Instead, they felt the government should attempt to obtain majority stock ownership in the mining companies. They strove for eventual total state ownership and continued cooperation of the foreign mining companies in the process of expanding the productive capacity of the mines, particularly the copper mines.

In his Third Annual Message to Congress, President Frei sketched his government's objectives with regard to mining:

This program seeks as its fundamental objectives the duplication of the production of copper in the country; substantial increase in refining in Chile; participation of the state in the exploitation of the mines; direction of international trade in copper; exploitation of mining discoveries and development; intensification of purchase of merchandise and inputs produced by national industry, a program which should be carried out within five or six years and which will signify for the country an explosive increase in foreign exchange and government income; the creation of thousands of new jobs, construction of about 6,000 houses and conversion of the country into the largest individual producer of copper in the world.[2]

Two basic laws laid the basis for the government's program. These laws authorized the assumption of majority government ownership of the mining companies, the incorporation of these companies under Chilean law, and the establishment of an overall state firm, the Corporación del Cobre (CODELCO) to supervise the copper mining industry. By the second anniversary of the Frei government, these laws and the appropriate regulations applying them had been enacted.[3]

The fulfillment of Chileanization required protracted negotiations with foreign firms that had subsidiaries in Chile, that is, Kennecott, Anaconda, and Cerro de Pasco. In the case of the first company, agreement had been reached by early 1966. Kennecott's former Braden Copper Company was converted into the Chilean-incorporated Sociedad Minera El Teniente S.A., in which the Chilean government held 51 percent of the stock and Kennecott continued to hold 49 percent, with the Chileans holding majority representation on the board of directors of the new firm.

The agreement with Kennecott provided for increasing the capacity of the El Teniente mine from production of 180,000 tons a year to 280,000; ending the mining camp at El Teniente through construction of housing in the nearby city of Rancagua; and building a modern highway from Rancagua to the mine. These would be financed by U.S. Export-Import Bank loans of $110 million to the Sociedad Minera El Teniente and $80 million to the Braden Copper Company, and an Eximbank loan of $23 million to the Sociedad Minera El Teniente.

The agreement also provided that while the mine's capacity was being amplified, and for six years thereafter (by which time the debts incurred would presumably be repaid) the Braden Copper Company would have a management contract with the Sociedad Minera El Teniente. Thereafter, as President Frei reported in his 1967 Annual Message to Congress, "El Teniente will have increased its production to more than 280,000 metric tons a year; the government's payments will have been amortized; the costs of expansion will have been totally met, and Chile will have 51% of the capital of the firm."[4]

Reaching an agreement with Anaconda proved more difficult; an accord was not reached until June 1969. According to Marcel Niedergang, the Latin American correspondent of *Le Monde* in Paris, Anaconda was forced to an agreement when spokesmen of the supposedly right-wing Partido Nacional suggested that the company's holdings would be expropriated and that if the Nacionales won the 1970 election and no agreement had been reached by that time, their government would unilaterally take over the Anaconda properties.[5]

The Chuquicamata mine, the largest surface mining copper operation in the world, and the relatively new El Salvador mine were involved in the Anaconda negotiations. The government's Corporación del Cobre (CODELCO) gave promissory notes (guaranteed by the Chilean Development Corporation) to Anaconda for $174.5 million in payment for 51 percent of the shares of the two Anaconda subsidiaries operating these mines, payable in semiannual installments extending over twelve years at 6 percent interest on the unpaid balance. The policies of the companies were to be determined by their boards of directors, on which the Chileans would have a majority, although Anaconda was to provide management services for at least three years for 1 percent of the gross sales plus expenses. It was agreed that the Chilean government would acquire the remaining 49 percent of the companies' stock sometime between 1972 and 1981.[6]

The Anaconda agreement also involved considerable further investment in expansion of copper production. By the middle of 1970, over $116 million had been authorized for this purpose.[7] As was true in the case of the ex-Kennecott properties, these funds were to be acquired through borrowing from foreign sources. In the case of Chuquicamata, the expansion program was designed to increase production from 281,000 tons to 350,000 tons per year.[8]

Two new copper mines were developed during the Frei administration. One was the Rio Blanco mine near Los Andes, for the exploitation of which the Compañía Minera Andina S.A. was established. By the time the mine began operations in July 1970—ten months ahead of schedule—30 percent of the company was owned by the government firm CODELCO and 70 percent by the Cerro de Pasco Corporation. The Sumitomo Metal Mining Company of Japan had helped to finance the project and had signed contracts to buy 70 percent of its first five years' production. The Export-Import Bank had also given a loan of $56.4 million to the Cia. Minera Andina.[9]

The second new copper mine was the Compañía Minera Exótica. The state had a 25 percent interest in this company, and as President Frei reported, "between taxes and dividends the State will obtain 55.37% of the profits of this firm."[10]

The extension of Chilean government control over the copper industry also involved intervention in the sale of the country's copper abroad. CODELCO, according to President Frei, "participated directly in the campaign of sales of copper in Europe in the months of September, October and part of November" 1966.[11]

The Frei government also sought to help stabilize the world price of Chile's major export. To this end, it joined with Zambia, Zaire, and Peru which produced 70 percent of the world's copper exports, in the Conference of Lusaka in June 1967. This meeting established the Intergovernmental Council of Copper Exporting Countries, patterned after the Organization of Petroleum Exporting Countries (OPEC). It was the first major step towards setting up a copper producers' cartel to bargain on a more or less equal basis with the copper consuming nations.[12]

Both foreign and domestic critics of the Frei government's Chileanization program have argued that the copper companies got more out of this policy than the Chilean government did. For instance, Gary MacEoin contends that the benefits of the Chileanization process from the Chilean point of view were "more apparent than real." He states that the Frei government agreed to pay too much for the 51 percent of the foreign firms it acquired, and he claims that net return to the Chilean government after the assumption of majority ownership was less than before this transaction.[13]

Such criticisms overlook certain facts. For example, the Chileanization move was designed to be only the first step in the total transfer of these mines to Chilean government ownership, a move provided for in the agreements with the foreign companies. After Chileanization, the Chilean government had majority control of the companies, which were then Chilean-incorporated enterprises instead of firms incorporated in Delaware or New Jersey. Another example is that the substantial expansion of copper output was an integral part of the Chileanization process. If the procedures begun under Frei had been continued to their planned conclusion, by the early 1980s Chile would have been the full owner of its copper mines, the productive capacity of which would have almost doubled from that of the 1960s.[14]

Chileanization was also applied to the nitrate industry, the country's second most important exporter of mineral products, through a process extending over several years. After negotiations between the government and the principal foreign nitrate company, the Cia. Salitrera Anglo-Lautaro, agreement was reached early in 1968 to establish a new mixed firm, Sociedad Química Minera de Chile (SQM), in which the Corporación de Fomento would have 37.5 percent of the stock and Anglo-Lautaro the other 62.5 percent. However, two years later, on July 1, 1970, the Chilean government's Corporación de Fomento acquired 51 percent of the stock.[15]

By the end of the Frei administration, only two important mining operations remained completely in private hands. These were the iron mines near Coquimbo, which belonged to the Bethlehem Steel Corporation, and the coal mines near Concepción, which were the property of several private Chilean companies.

TAXATION CHANGES

While the Frei administration increased taxes substantially, it did reduce some taxes, particularly on lower income groups. The net effect of the government's fiscal measures was to establish a more progressive tax system.

In his 1967 Annual Message to Congress, President Frei noted: "Between the years 1964 and 1966, tax income increased from 1,615,648,100 escudos to 4,005,675,700. This represents a nominal increase of 147.9% and a real increase, discounting for inflation, of 56.1%."[16] Nearly 250 million escudos of this increase in taxation came from increases in the income tax; another 221 million from more efficient collection of previously existing taxes; and 215 million from higher taxes on the large copper companies.[17]

Frei sketched the tax reductions on some of the poorer taxpayers in his 1967 Annual Message:

"All those who were owners of property producing an income of less than 5,000 escudos in the year 1965 were exempted from property taxes. This exemption favored

300,000 modest proprietors out of a total of 1,200,000 with another 200,000 able to obtain exemption if they request it.

Small and medium sized industrialists and merchants were given an increase in their deduction for personal income from one to three minimum wages, which has meant in the year 1967 an overall decrease of approximately 12,000,000 escudos. This measure has favored 28,129 small and medium industrialists and merchants.[18]

EXPANSION OF EXPORT POTENTIALITIES

The continued growth of the Chilean economy required the expansion of the kinds of goods exported, as well as of the countries to which Chile sent its products. The Frei administration sought to attain both objectives.

The industrial sectors with the greatest potential for providing new exports were the steel industry, petrochemicals, forest products, and fishing. The Frei administration made major efforts to expand the production of all four of these sectors. In his final message to Congress, on May 21, 1970, in which he presented a progress report on these efforts, Frei reported that the Huachipato steel firm near Concepción had received $150 million to finance an expansion from its then current capacity of 620,000 tons to 1 million tons. Plans had also been prepared for a second expansion stage, which would provide an annual output of 1.5 million tons a year, much of which would be destined for foreign markets.[19]

Investments amounting to about $200 million were made in the petrochemical industry, much of which was in the government-owned oil firm ENAP (Empresa Nacional de Petroleo). As a result, by the end of 1970 an ethylene plant belonging to ENAP as well as six other plants in the Concepción area, had begun operations. Construction had been started on eleven other plants in the petrochemical field.

Expansion plans were also pushed vigorously in the pulp and paper industry, with the establishment of several new firms to compete with the Cia. de Papeles y Cartones, which had had a virtual monopoly in the field until the PDC administration. As a result, Frei's expansion program resulted in a growth of cellulose output from 87,000 tons in 1965 to 243,000 tons in 1969. Programs underway at the end of Frei's government should have further expanded output to 550,000 tons by 1972, by which time two new plants were planned to be in operation. These were capable of bringing the government an additional export income of some $30 million a year.

The fishing industry, under the direct stimulus and orientation of the government's Corporación de Fomento, was rationalized and considerably expanded during the Christian Democratic regime. Although the number of firms operating in the sector was considerably reduced, production of frozen fish products rose from 1,484 tons in 1964 to 11,717 tons in 1968, and output of fishmeal and fish oil also increased substantially.[20]

A number of other industrial projects, designed at least in the short run more for the domestic market than for exports, were undertaken during the Frei administration. The electronics industry expanded production of television sets by 600 percent and of radios by 300 percent; sugar beet production rose 88 percent; and a processing plant with the capacity of increasing sugar production from 4,800 tons a day to 10,500 tons a day was established. The growth of the auto industry (a manufacturing branch which admittedly had dubious justification in the relatively small Chilean economy) was also substantial, with production of cars rising from 7,813 in 1964 to 22,069 in 1969.[21]

THE FREI GOVERNMENT AND THE GRUPO ANDINO

While working to promote the expansion of industries with export possibilities, the Frei administration also assumed a major role in developing new markets, particularly among Chile's neighbors. Frei was acutely aware of the smallness of Chile's internal market and of the need to attract foreign buyers for Chile's products. A major step in this direction was the Frei government's participation in establishing the Andean Group. In his 1967 Annual Message to Congress, Frei noted the origins of this effort:

With clear vision of the historic moment of Latin America, the President of Colombia, Carlos Lleras Restrepo invited the Presidents of Ecuador, Peru, Venezuela and Chile to meet in Bogota in August of last year. The object of the meeting was to discuss the possibilities of coordinating the efforts of these five countries to create new conditions for our economies.

The results were precise and positive and have had a profound repercussion on subsequent international events. It was agreed there to go forward with the creation of a subregional common market among countries of a similar level of development as an important and practical step for advancing those countries towards the goal of Latin American economic integration.[22]

The political context of this meeting is important. In August 1966, democratically elected, reformist governments were in power in Venezuela (President Raúl Leoni), Colombia (President Lleras Restrepo), Peru (President Fernando Belaunde), and Chile (Frei), and a civilian provisional government was in office in Ecuador following the recent overthrow of a military dictatorship. The common political interests and objectives of the regimes greatly facilitated the task of laying the groundwork for economic unity among these nations. In spite of much subsequent political turbulence in several of these countries—especially in Bolivia, which subsequently joined the Grupo Andino—the movement towards economic unity did not falter until the Chilean military dictatorship withdrew in 1976.

In his 1968 Annual Message to Congress, Frei reported on the steps Chile had taken to carry out the Bogotá accords of 1966:

With the integration efforts, the bilateral relations of Chile with the other countries of the Grupo Andino have had special emphasis, giving rise to new forms of relationships, expressed in permanent contacts, common decisions, increase of trade and communications. It is worth noting, in this regard, our participation in complementary accords, particularly with Venezuela and Colombia, with regard to industries which are vital to our economies, among others those of automobiles, electronics and petrochemicals. Also, the bringing together of Chilean and Ecuadorian capital and technical knowhow to establish the mixed company Acerias de Ecuador, the Protocol of Agreement on Cellulose and sugar signed with Colombia; and the co-operation with Peru with regard to production and commercialization of copper; and with that country and Ecuador for the protection of deep-sea resources; our support for the increase of transportation and transit facilities for Bolivian products, etc. reveal the rapid advance with which we have stimulated regional integration.[23]

Thus, in addition to efforts in the agrarian sector, the Frei administration attempted to expand foreign markets for the nation's products. In the face of what seemed to be a long-run growing demand for the traditional export, copper, the government sponsored a program for nearly doubling the country's shipments of that product. At the same time, it sought to create or expand nontraditional exports, especially in the iron and steel, petrochemical, pulp and paper, and fishing products industries. Accompanying these policies were its intensive efforts to expand the range of countries with which Chile conducted substantial trade, giving special attention to the neighboring Andean countries of South America.

In foreign trade and balance-of-payments terms, the Frei administration was very successful during its term of office, although much of this success was more the function of buoyant prices for copper than of its programs. Thus, exports for the 1965-1969 period, which were approximately $890 million, were 75 percent higher than the average for the previous five-year span. At the same time, between 1965 and 1969, the country had an average annual balance-of-payments surplus of $101 million. As Frei stated at the time, "This situation has enabled Chile to import the largest volume of capital goods ever purchased, as well as to continue to uphold her international credit rating by regular service of the foreign debt and to reach a level of foreign reserves highly satisfactory for the needs of the country."[24]

For the full value of these policies to be felt, the Frei administration had to be succeeded by one that would continue them—an eventuality that did not come to pass.

THE INFLATION PROBLEM

The administration's most pressing short-run problem was that of inflation. Although it had some initial success in slowing down the rise in the general price level, on balance it lost the inflation battle. This failure was largely responsible for the defeat of the Christian Democrats in the 1970 election.

In his 1969 Annual Message to Congress, President Frei admitted that inflation had plagued his administration most of his period in office. As he observed, "The rate of inflation, which thanks to the application of a series of other anti-inflationary measures was diminishing in 1965 and 1966, began to rise in 1967, and in 1968 and 1969, in spite of my renewed efforts, again demonstrated its virulence with increasing force, to which are now added the effects of the drought."[25]

The continued rapid increase in prices in the last two years of the administration was the result of "imported" inflation—the higher prices Chile had to pay for goods brought in from the outside; the continued unsatisfactory performance of agriculture, which barely (if at all) had begun to be improved by the heavy investments of the Frei administration; the administration's tax increase program, some of the new taxes directly raising prices and others causing entrepreneurs to boost the prices of their goods; and the terrible drought of 1968—the worst in the 100 years since records began to be kept on the subject—which not only restricted agricultural output but also limited the availability of electricity. The long history of inflation, which led to the expectation that prices would go up, as well as certain built-in institutional factors, also contributed to the continuing rise in prices. The system by which all wages were increased at one time by act of Congress after considerable debate gave employers ample time to adjust their prices in anticipation of wage rises. This was one of the most important institutional elements in inflation.

Whatever its causes, inflation damaged the Christian Democrats' political prospects. During the last year of the Frei regime, the rate of inflation was approximately 35 percent, one of the highest in the decade. With the exception of newly unionized agricultural workers, few groups of wage-earners were able to keep up with the inflation. At the same time, some of the middle-class elements—white-collar workers, small businessmen, and the like—to whom the Christian Democrats had appealed with success in 1964 and 1965 were alienated by the continued rise in prices and began to desert the party.

12

Labor and Communal Issues

The Christian Democratic administration followed a hesitant and sometimes confusing labor policy, which in the end hurt it badly. Its lack of sure direction and consistency resulted largely from internal controversies within the Partido Demócrata Cristiano over the principal questions at issue. These questions involved the project to revise the country's Labor Code; and the problem of whether the Christian Democrats should sponsor the establishment of a rival to the Central Única de Trabajadores de Chile.

PROBLEMS WITH THE LABOR CODE

The principal elements of the Chilean Labor Code had been laid down in 1924, and the existing body of legislation had been formally brought together in a Labor Code seven years later. By the middle 1960s, it had grown into an exceedingly complex series of laws, in itself a good reason for streamlining it. Many Christian Democrats believed that the Code should be revised for some strictly political reasons. These centered on the forms of trade union organization authorized by the Labor Code. These forms had not been changed since the original legislation of September 8, 1924.

The Labor Code provided for two kinds of workers' unions. One was called the *sindicato industrial,* an organization of twenty-five or more manual workers of one particular factory or mine or workshop. Once a majority of the workers in such a unit had decided to form a *sindicato industrial,* all manual workers employed in it were thereafter members. Their dues were automatically deducted from their wages, and these dues were indirectly passed to the union. The *sindicato industrial* had the right to share in the profits of the employing firm, and the funds it received from dues, profit sharing, and anything else could be used only for social welfare and cooperative activities.

The other kind of union was the *sindicato profesional,* an organization composed of white collar workers; of manual workers employed in several workshops, none of which had as many as twenty-five employees; or of specialized manual workers who wanted their own organization in addition to the *sindicato industrial* to which they perforce belonged. Although it also had the dues checkoff, the *sindicato profesional* did not have the right to profit sharing.

The Labor Code contained no effective provision for organizations above this local level. Hence, national industrial or trade unions were not provided for, and it was exceedingly difficult, if not impossible, to obtain legal recognition of a central labor body on a local, regional, or national level.

Other serious restrictions were imposed on the unions, particularly with regard to the expenditure of their funds. It was not legal for an officially recognized union to have paid officials. Members of the executive committee of a *sindicato industrial* or a *sindicato profesional* had to work their regular eight-hour day before conducting their union business. As a practical matter, some employers allowed the officials of their unions to take longer or shorter periods of time off to conduct union business and still gave them their full wage or salary, but this was not provided for in the Labor Code.

Furthermore, legally recognized unions could not use any funds to pay dues to unrecognized national industrial or trade unions or to a central labor body. Hence, the national unions and central labor groups that did in fact exist had few financial resources of their own.

Finally, unions were specifically forbidden to collect strike funds. This restriction seriously weakened them in negotiations with employers and made the unions dependent on outside sources for any financial help their members might need if a strike occurred.

As noted earlier, these provisions had for many years played principally into the hands of the Communist party. It was the only political group with sufficient financial resources to maintain on a full-time basis a sizable group of functionaries who could deal with trade union affairs. In most national industrial unions, the full-time officials were members of the Communist party or people who were closely cooperating with the Communists. The same was true of the central labor bodies to which the Communist-controlled unions belonged.

There were a few exceptions to this situation. After passage of new legislation in 1955, the Copper Miners Confederation, the national industrial union in that field, was able legally to pay its officers to do at least part-time union work. The Railroad Workers Federation (FIFCh), which was not legally recognized, nonetheless had arrangements with the State Railroads which permitted dues deduction from the payroll and allowed some of the dues to be paid to the FIFCh and its three subsidiary organizations covering locomotive workers, other manual workers, and white collar employees.[1]

REFORMS PROPOSED BY WILLIAM THAYER

President Frei's first minister of labor, William Thayer, sought to remedy most of the weaknesses of the Labor Code. Although his proposals were never enacted, the changes he wanted were incorporated in the Ley de Sindicación Campesina, the special law passed for unionization of rural workers. In a book which Thayer wrote at the end of his ministerial stint, he cited the provisions of this law as synthesizing the changes he thought should be enacted in the general Labor Code.[2]

Since we have already reviewed the major provisions of the Ley de Sindicación Campesina, suffice it to state here that that law provided for legal recognition of provincial federations of peasants, as well as local unions; that it allowed union officials to be paid while doing work for their organizations; and that it permitted the formation of parallel unions, federations, and confederations.

Throughout the Frei administration, it was expected that the Labor Code would be revised considerably. As a result, the Labor Relations Institute of the University of Chile, in conjunction with the leadership of the CUTCh, undertook a study of the problem and drew up their own suggestions for changes.

The revisions of the Labor Code were never enacted under Frei largely because of the opposition of those elements within the Christian Democratic party which wanted to work with the Socialists and Communists both within the labor movement and in the general political arena. They understandably fought a measure which would undermine the trade union influence of the far Left, particularly the Communist party, and which, for that reason, would be strongly opposed by the parties that ultimately formed the Popular Unity coalition.

This opposition within the PDC came mainly from the *Rebeldes,* which, so long as they remained in the party, tended to control the Trade Union Bureau of the PDC. The *Rebeldes* were able to give the impression that the opposition to the legislation came from the Christian Democratic party's own trade unionists—even though the more important trade union leaders of the party had little influence in or even much contact with the Trade Union Bureau, which was manned largely by students or young professionals.

Even after the *Rebeldes* left the party in the middle of 1969 it was not possible to push forward with the revisions of the Labor Code. The PDC's presidential nominee in 1970, Radomiro Tomic, also favored an alliance with the far Left during the campaign; those elements most closely associated with him continued to oppose any legislation that might alienate the Communists and Socialists.

President Frei himself was apparently not willing to push very hard for Thayer's program. Even after he succeeded in ousting the combined *Rebelde-Tercerista* group from control of the party leadership in January 1968 and in installing a group of *Oficialistas* he made no serious effort, at least publicly, to get the legislation enacted. By the middle of 1968, Minister of Labor Thayer, despairing of getting the Labor Code changes passed, retired from his cabinet post to become rector of Southern University (Universidad Austral) in Valdivia.

THE QUESTION OF TRADE UNION UNITY

One of the basic ideas behind the legislation suggested by William Thayer was to have a framework within which two or more legally recognized trade union movements might be established. It would have allowed the Ministry of Labor to recognize as many industrial and trade federations and as many central labor bodies as the workers' organizations might have wanted to form. The Communist and Socialist parties' virtual monopoly over the top echelons of the labor movement might then have been upset, with the possible establishment of a Christian Democratic-oriented central labor body and industrial federations parallel to those dominated by Socialists and Communists.

Of course, passage of the Thayer legislation was not essential for the Christian Democrats to have launched their own central labor body and subsidiary organizations. They might have established their own "nonlegal" groups parallel to those controlled by the far Left. However, they did not do so.

The question of whether the Christian Democrats should work within the CUTCh had been debated since the Central Única was established in 1952. The predominant element among the Christian Democratic trade unionists during most of this time had continued to participate in the CUTCh, but a minority element had maintained a rival group, Acción Sindical Chilena, which had a handful of unions affiliated with it until the advent of the Frei administration. With the launching of the Christian Democratic unionists' drive to organize the agricultural workers after the 1964 electoral victory, one of the groups involved in this campaign worked under the aegis of Acción Sindical Chilena.

By the middle and late 1960s, the Christian Democrats had substantial support in the labor movement. They had control of numerous *sindicatos industriales* and *sindicatos profesionales,* and they dominated the Maritime Workers Confederation, as well as several smaller national industrial unions.

With organization of agricultural workers after 1964, they controlled the two national confederations which throughout the Frei period continued to be the largest groups of rural workers' unions.

It is not clear how much of the labor movement that was under their control the Christian Democrats might have been able to induce to join in a breakaway effort to form a rival to the CUTCh. No serious effort to do so was made until it was too late, and that attempt was torpedoed from within the ranks of the PDC itself.

A bitter struggle developed among various political elements during the 1966 congress of the CUTCh. As a result, both the Christian Democrats and the Radicals were frozen out of the national leadership of the CUTCh, whose Executive Committee consisted only of Communists and Socialists in the period thereafter. At that congress, as at the previous one in 1962, Christian Democratic union leaders claimed that the credentials committee had deprived them of a sufficiently large number of delegates to take away any real decision-making power they could have in the proceedings of the meeting and the selection of a national CUTCh leadership.

Not surprisingly, then, there was considerable resistance within the Christian Democratic union ranks to participation in the next congress of the CUTCh, held late in 1968. Some argued against attendance at the congress, and others advocated that they split away and form a rival central labor group if they were not given substantial representation in the leadership of the CUTCh.

An attempt to establish a rival to the CUTCh was made in the middle of 1968, but failed completely. Under the leadership of Hector Alarcón, one of the top figures in the Central Nacional Campesina, a group of some 120 trade unionists met at the beginning of July to discuss launching a rival to the CUTCh. Those in attendence included Christian Democrats as well as Radicals and independents. At the meeting they decided to set up a provisional organization under the name Unión de Trabajadores de Chile (UTRACh). It was agreed that several of those in attendance would travel to various parts of the country to discuss with local unionists and with leaders of some of the national industrial federations the possibility of cooperating in launching UTRACh. The move had the support of a substantial element within the Christian Democratic party and the discreet backing of President Frei. It was officially endorsed by the Partido Democrático Nacional, which was then a partner in the PDC government, and it also had the backing of some elements in the Radical party.

The initial plan was to form the UTRACh out of elements that did not belong to the CUTCh. It was hoped that, once it got well established, UTRACh would be able to attract some of the unions that were members of CUTCh. The founding congress of UTRACh was scheduled to be held sometime in September 1968.[3]

Alarcón and UTRACh were subjected to immediate attack by the Communist and Socialist press. They were also strongly criticized by the newspaper *El Diario Ilustrado,* which was aligned with the Partido Nacional. Other newspapers, including the government daily *La Nación*, were reticent about carrying news about UTRACh.

The Communists attacked Alarcón scurrilously, repeating the kind of charges levied many years earlier against Bernardo Ibáñez and other Socialist trade union leaders who had fought the Communists. *El Siglo* accused Alarcón of being a CIA agent and a businessman. The latter charge was based on his having signed the incorporation papers for a housing cooperative, Congrevi, formed principally by Christian Democratic peasant leaders. *El Siglo* falsely insisted that Congrevi was a private business.[4]

The attacks by the Communists and Socialists, combined with the indecisiveness of the Christian Democratic party on the issue, proved fatal to UTRACh. The PDC's Peasant Department, which was controlled by the *Rebelde* faction of the party, officially asked for Alarcón's expulsion from the PDC. No such expulsion occurred, but those within the party who favored the establishment of UTRACh were not willing to go very far in supporting the proposed new organization. The only apparent effect of this effort to expel Alarcón was to postpone the CUTCh congress, which had originally been scheduled for October 1968, for two months. The president of the CUTCh, Luis Figueroa, announced that the postponement was "for the purpose of developing greater contacts with organizations which are studying their return to the CUTCh."[5]

UTRACh proved to be stillborn. Its failure considerably strengthened the CUTCh, and hence Communist and Socialist control over the labor movement, as shown by the CUTCh congress and the events that immediately followed it.

The 1968, CUTCh congress met from November 20 to 24, with some 2,950 delegates in attendance. One of the resolutions it passed sought "to avert trade union fragmentation and fight for united industrial unions." In voting for the new Executive Committee, each delegate cast a number of votes which reflected the total membership of his organization. The Communist party slate received 134,250 votes; the Socialists, 63,818; the Christian Democrats, 40,165; the Radical party, 23,825; the Unión Socialista Popular, 11,511; and the MIR 4,667.[6] In an editorial, the conservative daily *El Mercurio* commented that "the indisputable victory belonged to the Communists."[7]

The degree to which the move to form a rival to the CUTCh had collapsed was illustrated soon after the CUTCh congress, when the Confederación de Empleados Particulares de Chile (CEPCh) decided to join the CUTCh. CEPCh was one of the largest independent union organizations.[8]

About a year after the CUTCh congress, the prestige of the organization was reinforced by the Christian Democratic government itself. On December 3, 1969, Minister of Interior Patricio Rojas and Minister of Finance Andrés Zaldívar signed an agreement with the top leaders of the CUTCh, setting forth the terms of the annual wage increase law to be sent to Congress. By this action, the government practically made the CUTCh the national collective bargaining agent for all of Chile's workers.[9]

LACK OF A DECISIVE LABOR POLICY

The Frei government could not formulate a decisive labor policy for the obvious reason that the Christian Democrats were divided on the issue. Another major reason was that Frei and the other PDC and government leaders paid relatively little attention to labor problems. Their main concerns were with agriculture, education, general economic policy, and the political problems involved in getting desired legislation through Congress.

One explanation for their relative disinterest in labor was the fact that few, if any, trade union figures were high in the echelons of the PDC. The nearest approach to such a figure was William Thayer, who had been a leading labor lawyer for a decade or more, but was not himself a trade unionist. (He left the administration two-thirds through its tenure.) Another possible explanation is that Frei and other PDC leaders were apparently misled by their party's victories of 1964 and 1965, in which the party won great support in traditionally Socialist-Communist working-class areas. Accordingly, Frei may well have thought that, if necessary, he would be able to appeal over the heads of Socialist and Communist leaders of the labor movement to the rank and file, as he had done in 1964 and his party in 1965. Hence, there was no great urgency about trying to weaken Marxist-Leninist control over the unions.

This was a misconception. In strictly labor and trade union matters, the rank-and-file workers tended to follow the lead of the heads of their organizations, which continued to be dominated by the PDC's left-wing opponents. The continuing inflation did not strengthen Frei's hand in this regard: it tended to undermine political support for the PDC among the urban workers.

LABOR CONFLICTS

The success of the government's efforts to undermine Communist and Socialist control of organized labor might well have depended upon its ability to push through legislation favorable to urban organized labor and/or to help labor to make substantial advances through collective bargaining. Given the already extensive labor and social legislation and the economic circumstances of the period, neither of these possibilities was very great.

Unlike the case of their rural counterparts, the urban workers' situation did not change markedly during the Frei regime. However, many labor conflicts erupted during the Frei years, a few of which the Left-wing opposition was able to exploit to the detriment of the Frei government.

The number of collective conflicts—of which only a few reached the stage of an actual strike or lockout—rose considerably in the early years of the Frei government. In fact, in nearly every year of the administration a new record was set for the number of labor controversies. President Frei commented on this phenomenon in his penultimate Annual Message to Congress:

The number of conflicts in 1964 was 1939 and in the year 1968 was 3441, that is to say in four years there was an increase of 77.4%. The average number of workers involved in conflicts in the period 1960-64 was 177,960, and in the period 1965-1968 reached 293, 133. These figures demonstrate that today the workers better know and exercise their rights and interests, which indicates the efficacy of the Government.[10]

Frei went on to note that the percentage of conflicts resulting in strikes had declined greatly from 1967 to 1968. Although there was a marginal decrease in the number of legal walkouts, illegal walkouts declined by more than 50 percent during this period.

President Frei's optimistic tone notwithstanding, serious strikes occurred during his administration. Probably the most important one was the copper mine strike in El Salvador in April 1966 in which army soldiers fired on strikers, killing eight and wounding others.[11] The far-Left opposition to the Christian Democratic government used incidents such as the El Salvador strike to undermine the prestige of PDC in the eyes of the trade unionists. They pictured the Frei regime as having no different attitudes towards the workers than the conservative regimes of the past.

GROWTH OF THE COMMUNAL ORGANIZATIONS

Although the Frei government tended to underestimate the importance of the trade union movement, except in the rural areas, it instituted important programs designed to touch the lives of most of the country's workers, organized and unorganized. These programs were in the community development field.

In the years before the 1964 elections, the Christian Democratic party had carried out active campaigns in working-class and slum areas to develop self-help groups under Christian Democratic direction. In the process, the PDC hoped to develop loyalty towards the Christian Democratic party. Once the party was in power, it sought to expand the network of these organizations and to give them official status.

This effort was in conformity with the Christian Democratic ideology. The core of "communitarianism," which in many other respects remained a somewhat amorphous concept, was the idea that individuals and small groups in society should take their destiny into their own hands to the greatest degree possible. Community development, and the establishment of communal organizations was an integral part of the government's effort to make self-reliance and self-help possible.

Three kinds of communal organizations were established in both urban and rural areas during the Frei administration: the so-called *juntas de vecinos* (neighborhood councils), *centros de madres"* (mothers' centers), and youth groups. The *juntas de vecinos* consisted of heads of families whose functions were to organize self-help projects, including educational programs for their members, and to act as pressure groups on the local public authorities. The *centros de madres* were originally organized as centers of education and training for the women involved, and later as social centers and organizers of community activities centering on family needs. The youth groups organized sports, recreational, and educational activities for youngsters.

The Christian Democrats saw these groups as grass roots democratic organizations, where members could gain experience in conducting their own affairs, participating in meetings and projects; and as organizations from which grass roots leaders would emerge. At the same time, they believed that some of the powers of the municipalities and of local government in general would ultimately devolve to these neighborhood organizations.

President Frei commented on these communal organizations in his Annual Messages to Congress. For instance, in his 1968 Annual Message, he noted that more than 15,000 communal groups were then in existence. Of these, 8,500 were *centros de madres,* to which some 400,000 women belonged. According to Frei, these women

have encountered there shops where they can work; courses where they can acquire education, and above all, a place for social intercourse, which in many cases has transformed their formerly humble, obscure and abandoned lives. These Centers represent one of the greatest of human projects, and the mothers who make them up, one of the major forces in the country.

Frei also stated that members of the communal organizations had constructed more than 500 buildings to house their groups; and that 150,000 leaders of the *juntas de vecinos* had been given training on what the official role of these groups would be once the government's bill on the subject had passed in Congress.[12]

In his next Annual Message, Frei outlined the new official status which the administration's bill would give the communal groups. The bill had passed in the Chamber of Deputies, but was still pending in the Senate. Frei specified the most important purposes of the measure:

To amplify the concept of the Junta de Vecinos, recognizing it as an expression of solidarity and organization of the people in a local area and as collaborators in the authority of the State and the Municipalities.

To recognize and grant legal personality not only to the Juntas de Vecinos, but to the other communal organizations, which are the genuine functional expression of the community.

To give wide powers to the Juntas de Vecinos, in urban affairs and social promotion and in representing the neighbors in everything concerning the regulation of their property, obtaining credits for construction and civic improvements, collaboration in price control and in public health, inspection of public transportation, promotion of and participation in programs of training, etc.[13]

The law on community organizations was the last major measure of the Christian Democratic government's program to pass Congress. It did not get through until after the PDC setback in the 1969 congressional elections. In its final form, the new law only gave the *juntas de vecinos* and other communal organizations advisory powers, rather than the right to both voice and vote in purely neighborhood affairs which the government had at first proposed.

13
The 1970 Election

The presidential election of 1970 ended the Christian Democratic "Revolution in Liberty" and opened the door for a three-year experience with "The Chilean Road to Socialism," which in turn led to the culmination of the tragedy of Chile: the military regime that seized power on September 11, 1973.

The electoral results of September 1970 were markedly different from those of six years before for several reasons: the Right wing had a strong candidate; the Christian Democratic government had numerous weaknesses and committed many errors; the PDC candidate was not very able; and the Left put together a broader coalition, at least in terms of parties involved, than it had been able to do in 1964.

THE PHENOMENON OF JORGE ALESSANDRI

One major difference between the 1964 and 1970 campaign was the presence of ex-President Jorge Alessandri as one of the three contenders. He provided a rallying point for those elements in the citizenry who were either opposed to or frightened by the basic social and economic changes that both the Christian Democrats and the Left-wing Unidad Popular were advocating.

Jorge Alessandri was a "phenomenon," as was frequently noted in the press and in conversation during these months. The ex-president bore an exceedingly illustrious family name. His father, Arturo Alessandri, had twice been president, and two generations before had been the great popular idol; his brothers were also distinguished politicians who had been deputies, senators, and presidential candidates in their own right. Jorge Alessandri had something even beyond these associations which worked in his favor: he had an ability to cut across class loyalties. He had a long experience as an industrial manager and had acquired a reputation as a very good employer. He was also reputedly something of a financial and economic wizard. He had behaved with great dignity and authority during his earlier term as president of the republic. His personal characteristics—he was a kind of father figure—gave him the appeal of an Eisenhower in the United States or a De Gaulle in France.

Early in the 1970 campaign, the Communist daily *El Siglo* posed the question of what gave Alessandri his broad appeal. It summed up very well the widely accepted picture of the ex-president: "The image of a don Jorge Alessandri, austere, straightforward, gentlemanly, disinterested, patriotic, a doer, solitary, generous, without ambitions."[1]

Alessandri made it possible for the elements of the economic and political Right to run a strong campaign on their own behalf and that of Alessandri —rather than having to accept a "lesser evil," as they had had to do in the 1964 election. Alessandri was an enthusiastic candidate. Among his many motives for running for the presidency again was his deep resentment of what he considered the unfair image given him by the Christian Democrats and the far Left—that of a plutocrat, presiding over the largest private "monopoly" in Chile, the paper company. He was particularly bitter at the Christian Democrats, whom he thought had especially maligned him and whom he viewed as only slightly less dangerous for Chile than the parties of the far Left.

A second motivation was his desire to show that he could undo the mess in Chile which he felt had been caused by the Christian Democratic regime and to demonstrate that he could get the process of economic development going again, in a way he felt the Christian Democrats had not done.

Alessandri's presence in the race tended to polarize politics further. Elements of the political and economic Right, who had come to dislike the Christian Democrats as much or perhaps more than they did the Socialists and Communists, hoped that with Alessandri's reelection they could reverse all the changes made by the Christian Democrats and in a sense, "get revenge" on the Christian Democrats for seriously trying to carry out the platform on which they had been elected—and which the Right had grudgingly supported six years earlier.

HANDICAPS AND ERRORS OF THE FREI ADMINISTRATION

The Frei administration's inability to deal adequately with the problem of inflation was one of its most vulnerable points in the election. During the last year of the PDC regime, the rate of price increases was about 35 percent. The Christian Democrats' failure to control inflation weakened them among the middle class, their major constituency, and even more among those portions of the manual working class who had been temporarily attracted to the Christian Democrats in 1964 and 1965.

Policy errors, particularly with regard to the labor movement, also hurt the Christian Democrats in the 1970 election. If the Frei administration had made fundamental reforms in the Labor Code freeing the organized labor movement from excessive reliance on the well-financed Communist and Socialist parties, a larger segment of the unions would likely have supported the Christian Democrats in 1970. Also, if the Frei government had aided trade unionists of the Christian Democratic party and of other groups in their efforts to organize a rival to the CUTCh, the PDC would have been in a stronger position in the election. As it was, the labor movement was almost entirely in the Salvador Allende camp, and Allende's supporters were able to use it to strengthen their nominee's position.

THE CAMPAIGN OF RADOMIRO TOMIC

Even with their errors of omission and commission and with the presence of Jorge Alessandri in the race, the Christian Democrats might have won. But their defeat was ensured by their candidate, Radomiro Tomic.

From the beginning of the Falange Nacional in the late 1930s Tomic had been one of the principal leaders of the Chilean Christian Democracy. He was generally recognized as the second most important figure in the party. In 1964, he had stepped aside in order to assure Eduardo Frei the undisputed party nomination in that campaign.

During the first half of the Frei administration, Tomic was Chilean ambassador to Washington, a position that kept him out of the day-to-day controversies within the Christian Democratic party. However, it may have influenced his thinking as the 1970 campaign approached. As ambassador to the United States he was open to the charge (which was made by the far Left upon occasion) of being a servant of the "Yanquis," of not adequately defending Chilean interests. His felt need to refute this charge may have helped determine Tomic's stance as the Christian Democratic candidate.

When serious discussion of the 1970 campaign began at midpoint in the Frei administration, it was generally taken for granted that Tomic would be the party's nominee. Nevertheless, he was not easily nominated by the party. Tomic's position was that "popular unity"—an alliance with the forces of the far Left against the expected candidacy of Jorge Alessandri—was needed in 1970. At one point, he formally withdrew his name from consideration as the PDC candidate on the grounds that "without popular unity, there is no Tomic candidacy."[2] However, he later relented.

On August 15, 1969, Tomic was officially proclaimed candidate for president by the Christian Democratic party's National Board of more than 500 members. His nomination was unanimous, although it was apparently preceded by considerable hard bargaining between Tomic and party leaders who were more closely associated with Eduardo Frei, involving changes in the national leadership of the PDC.[3]

In his acceptance speech, Tomic warmly praised "the first Christian Democratic administration" and promised to follow in its footsteps in "the second Christian Democratic administration." He did not maintain this line during much of his campaign, however. Many of his PDC colleagues felt that as the campaign developed, Tomic increasingly sought to disassociate himself from the Frei regime and to picture the administration he hoped to lead as being much more profoundly "revolutionary" than Frei's. Some critics within the PDC argued that once the Unidad Popular candidate, Salvador Allende, had been chosen and his campaign for "The Chilean Road to Socialism" had been launched, Tomic tried to portray himself as an advocate of even more radical changes than those Allende was proposing.

It was not possible to out-Allende Allende, however. Those who wanted a "Chilean Road to Socialism" were certain to vote for the candidate who for three decades had been one of the principal leaders of the Socialist party, and who was supported by the Communist party as well as his own. They would not likely switch to the candidate of the Christian Democratic party, a party whose non-Socialist orientation had been made clear during the Frei administration. On the other hand, those who feared the changes the Unidad Popular would likely bring about were not prone to cast their votes for someone who was trying to seem even more radical than the Unidad Popular candidate. Finally, Frei remained personally very popular, and Tomic could gain little from disassociating himself from the president.

Only in the last few weeks of the campaign did Tomic again associate himself closely with the outgoing administration. By then, it was too late to win back those middle-of-the road voters who had been alienated by Tomic's use of far Left rhetoric and who in fact probably ended up voting for Jorge Alessandri.

THE UNIDAD POPULAR CANDIDACY

Salvador Allende, running for the presidency for the fourth time, was this time the nominee of a new coalition, Unidad Popular. In terms of the parties involved, the Unidad Popular was broader than the coalition that had supported Allende's previous presidential bids.

Neither the formation of the Unidad Popular nor the naming of its candidate was achieved without a great deal of maneuvering and negotiation. There was considerable opposition, particularly within the Socialist party, to forming the kind of broad alliance that the Unidad Popular represented.

Although the Radical party was much less powerful and important in 1970 than it had been at the time of the Popular Front a generation before, the Socialists did not again want to be in a position where the Radicals and Communists would be allied against them within a new coalition. The Socialists, therefore, demanded that before the Unidad Popular was formally established, with the inclusion of the Radicals, previous agreement be made that the presidential candidate come from the parties which had formed the Frente de Acción Popular. The candidate would then be a Socialist, since a Communist party leader had no chance of being elected president of Chile at that point.[4]

After much negotiation, the Unidad Popular was formally launched. It included not only the Socialist and Communist parties, which had been the major elements in FRAP, but also four smaller parties: the Partido Radical, the Partido Social Demócrata, the schismatic Christian Democratic group MAPU, and the Acción Popular Independiente (API).

The Partido Radical did not enter the Unidad Popular before suffering a serious split (as noted earlier). The Partido Social Demócrata, a small group with only a handful of deputies, was a sad remnant of the once important Partido Democrático. The MAPU, whose members sought to guide the PDC towards an alignment with the far Left, announced their support for such an alliance immediately after forming their own party. This group had distinguished leaders, but a very limited rank and file. The API was a kind of catchall, consisting of people who had left or been thrown out of several other parties; it was led by Senator Rafael Tarud, one-time minister of Carlos Ibáñez in the 1950s.

In an attempt to achieve unity on the basis of principles all parties could back, the Unidad Popular first drew up an electoral program and then decided on a candidate. (This program will be described in more detail later in this chapter.)

It proved more difficult to agree on a candidate than to reach accord on a platform. As a preliminary step, each party put forward its own nominee. The Radicals suggested Senator Alberto Baltra, the API and Partido Social Demócrata named Rafael Tarud, the MAPU suggested Jacques Chonchol, and the Communists nominated the poet Pablo Neruda.[5] The Socialists' contribution to this list was once again Salvador Allende. He did not gain his party's support easily, since a sizable part of the Socialist leadership was opposed to naming him a fourth time. This opposition to Allende was motivated in part by disagreements with him in internal Socialist politics and in part by the feeling that a three-time loser was not a very good bet as a candidate. As a result, he was first named by the party's Central Committee in a vote in which opponents of his candidacy and those who abstained outnumbered those who voted for him. Under these circumstances, Allende refused to run. Thereupon, a new vote took place in which Allende won the strong backing of his party's Central Committee.[6]

Once Allende was nominated by the Socialists, his becoming the Unidad Popular candidate was all but assured. Pablo Neruda was at best a token nominee, although if the UP coalition had fallen apart, he might well have continued in the race, to test the Communist party's electoral strength. The Socialists would under no circumstances have agreed to support a Radical candidate of the coalition. Although the Communists might have preferred a candidate who did not come from the Socialist party, their most important rival among working-class voters, they were not disposed to push very hard for a nominee from outside Socialist ranks, whose designation almost certainly would have alienated the Socialists from the Unidad Popular.

THE UP PROGRAM

The program on which Allende ran for president in 1970 was adopted by the parties of the Unidad Popular on December 22, 1969. It proclaimed that "through a process of democratization on all levels and of an organized mobilization of the masses there will be constructed from the bottom a new structure of power." The program then outlined this "new structure of power" in detail.

The UP program called for drastic changes in the political structure of the republic, suggesting among other things that the two-house legislature be replaced by a single-chambered Assembly of the People. As it proclaimed: "The Assembly of the People will be a single Chamber which will express nationally the popular sovereignty. In it will be represented and be manifested the various currents of opinion." In addition, the Supreme Court would be transformed from a body of professional judges with lifetime tenure into one "whose components will be designated by the Assembly of the People without any other limitation than that which its members decide upon. This tribunal will freely determine the internal powers, individually or jointly, of the judicial system."

Concerning "the New Economy," the UP program provided for establishment of three distinct sectors: social, mixed, and private. With regard to the social, it stated:

The process of transformation of our economy begins with a policy destined to construct a dominant state sector, formed by those firms which the State presently possesses plus the firms which are to be expropriated. As a first step, there will be nationalized those basic riches which, like the copper mining industry, iron, nitrates and others, are in the power of foreign capital and of internal monopolies. Thus, the sector of nationalized activities will consist of the following:

1) Large copper mining, nitrates, iodine, iron and coal.
2) The financial system of the country, particularly private banking and insurance.
3) Foreign trade.

4) The large firms and monopolies in the field of distribution.

5) The strategic industrial monopolies.

6) In general, those activities which condition the economic and social development of the country, such as production and distribution of electric energy; railroad, air and maritime transport; communications, production, refining and distribution of petroleum and its derivatives, including liquid gas; iron and steel; cement, petrochemicals and heavy chemicals, cellulose, paper.

With regard to the private sector of the economy, the UP program said that it would include "those sectors of industry, mining, agriculture and services in which private enterprise will continue." According to the program, this sector would benefit from government planning and would be guaranteed adequate credit and other requirements.

The mixed area "will be mixed because it will consist of enterprises which combine State capital and that of private individuals." In the case of firms in which the government was a creditor, the program called for the debts owed to it to become shares in the enterprises.

The program called for a "deepening and extension of the agrarian reform," maintaining that "the expropriated land will be organized preferentially in cooperative forms of production. The peasants will have personal property titles to their houses and gardens, and in some instances agricultural land will be assigned to peasants as individual property, but with encouragement to the organization of work and of the sale of the products on the basis of mutual cooperation." In some instances, too, state-owned agricultural enterprises would be established.

In the area of education, the UP program promised an extensive program of building additional schools, providing scholarships for students, and, on the university level, a "reorientation of the academic functions of teaching, research and extension in terms of national problems," and elimination of "class privileges which will make possible the entry of sons of workers in the university and will also permit adults through special scholarships and work study programs to enjoy higher education."

The foreign policy part of the program denounced the Organization of American States as "an instrument and agency of North American imperialism" and called for establishment of a separate regional organization of Latin American countries. It also expressed hostility towards U.S. policy in Vietnam, strong solidarity with Cuba, refusal of all foreign aid "with political conditions or which imply . . . conditions which violate our sovereignty." It also called for renunciation of various treaties with the United States, particularly "mutual aid pacts and other pacts."[7]

While the UP program did not proclaim the objective of following "The Chilean Road to Socialism," during the campaign this became one of the principal slogans of Allende and the Unidad Popular.[8]

THE RESULTS OF THE POPULAR ELECTION

As the election campaign progressed, it became obvious that the race would be a close one. Any one of the three candidates appeared to have a chance to win a plurality, but it appeared increasingly unlikely that any of them would get the absolute majority of the popular vote which the Constitution required for a clear winner to emerge. It therefore appeared certain that the final decision would rest with Congress.

The results of the popular vote were indeed very close. Salvador Allende received 1,075,616 votes, or 36.3 percent of the total; Jorge Alessandri came in second, with 1,036,278 votes, or 34.9 percent; and Radomiro Tomic received 824,849 votes, or 27.8 percent. Although Allende had come in first this time, he received a smaller proportion of the total vote than he had gotten in 1964, when he polled almost 39 percent of the popular votes.

The election showed a considerable difference between the preferences of men and women, who under Chilean electoral law voted in separate booths and whose votes were counted separately. Allende and Tomic each received about 30 percent of the woman's vote, while Jorge Alessandri got 40 percent. On the other hand, Allende had a substantial lead among the male voters, receiving about 41 percent of their votes.[10]

The early returns from Santiago showed Alessandri leading Allende by 30,000 votes. Allende is reported to have joked with some friends with whom he was listening to the election results that it looked as if in 1976 he would be for the fifth time the bourgeois presidential candidate of the Chilean revolutionary parties.[11]

PRESSURES FOLLOWING THE POPULAR ELECTION

As many predicted, the close results of the popular vote on September 4 threw the presidential succession issue into Congress. There, according to the Constitution of 1925, the members of both houses meeting together had to make a decision between the two candidates with the most votes—Salvador Allende and Jorge Alessandri.

Precedent dictated that Allende, as the nominee who had received the highest popular vote, be elected. However, his election was by no means certain, and the decision basically lay with the Christian Democrats, who could cast the balance in favor of either of the remaining rivals. In spite of rumors that Tomic had signed an agreement with Allende before the election to the effect that either would throw his support behind the other in case only one of them was among the two leading candidates,[12] the PDC was not officially committed to either Allende or Alessandri.

The period of nearly two months between the popular election and the decision of Congress was marked by great tension and uncertainty. There were innumerable rumors that "deals" were being worked out in Congress—all of which proved false. One of the most persistent rumors was that the Christian Democrats had agreed to support Alessandri and that he in turn had agreed to resign after a short time in office, thus requiring a new presidential election in which Eduardo Frei would be eligible, since (in accordance with the Constitution) another president would have served between his two terms. Anyone conversant with the Christian Democratic leaders' thinking or aware of Jorge Alessandri's hostility towards the Christian Democrats should have been able to reject this story.

Considerable pressure was placed on Congress and on the Christian Democrats. Some of Allende's more extreme supporters threatened violence and political chaos if his victory was not confirmed. On the other hand, as later revelations disclosed, the CIA spent large amounts of money in an effort to "buy" votes for ex-President Alessandri—an effort that not only reflected strong ethnocentric biases in the extreme, but also was stupid and insulting to the Chilean political leadership.

THE ASSASSINATION OF GENERAL SCHNEIDER

The most serious move of this disturbing period was an attempt made to convince the armed forces to intervene in the presidential selection process. General René Schneider, the commander of the army, had made it clear that the presidency was none of the military's business and that the armed forces would simply support the constituted authorities, whoever they were or might be in the future.

On October 22, 1970, General Schneider was assassinated by a group of young men who blocked his car while he was being driven from his home to his office. A week later, General Roberto Viaux, the leader of the abortive[13] military mutiny of late 1969, was arrested for his alleged implication in Schneider's murder.

The immediate popular reaction, that this act had been committed by far rightest elements determined to block Allende's candidacy, was borne out by later investigation. Testimony offered several years later before an investigating committee of the U.S. Senate also indicated that the CIA had participated in a plot to kidnap General Schneider, although it was said that the CIA had withdrawn from the plot before it was executed and had had no direct role in General Schneider's ultimate fate.[14] Aniceto Rodriguez, secretary general of the Socialist party, had charged soon after Schneider's murder that the assassins had been "trained" by the CIA.[15]

The Schneider assassination proved to be counterproductive. It reinforced the determination of the leaders of the armed forces not to intervene in the electoral process, but rather to leave the decision up to those whom the Constitution gave the right to make it.

THE FINAL ELECTION OF ALLENDE

The decision as to who should be elected president of Chile was not determined by threats, bribes, or any other such consideration. It was determined by agreement between Salvador Allende and the Christian Democrats, with regard to certain conditions which the Christian Democrats laid down as the price of their support for the UP candidate. While the Christian Democrats were predisposed to accept Allende under certain conditions, they had a number of grave reservations concerning the ultimate objectives which the UP parties—if not Allende personally—would have once they came to power. As a result, they sought agreements from Allende which they hoped would assure that a Unidad Popular government would not subvert the democratic constitutional system of Chile.

The demands the Christian Democrats made on Allende were summed up in a document they submitted to him almost three weeks after the popular vote. They were stated in terms of things which "interested" the PDC. These included:

We are interested in maintenance of political pluralism and constitutional guarantees.
    We are interested in the full maintenance of the rule of Law.
    We are interested that the Armed Forces and the Carabineros continue being guarantors of our system of democratic tolerance.
    We are interested in having education remain independent of all official ideological orientation and that the autonomy of the universities be respected.
    We are interested in the free existence of trade union and social organizations.[16]

Each of these points was elaborated in the Christian Democratic document. Under the heading democatic pluralism, they demanded the free maintenance of political parties, and freedom of the press and other means of communication. Under the demand for maintenance of the rule of law, they insisted that the autonomy of the three branches of government—executive, legislative, and judicial—be maintained. With regard to the armed forces, they demanded that "the organic structures and hierarchy of the Armed Forces and Carabineros, the systems of selection, and disciplinary norms" be preserved and that no "armed organizations parallel to the Armed Forces and Carabineros" be created. In the labor field, they demanded the continuance of the free functioning of unions and of the Law on Agrarian Unionization and the continued recognition of the right to strike.

For several more weeks, negotiations continued between Allende and the Christian Democrats. The final result was that a Statute of Constitutional

Guarantees, providing for the PDC's demands as its price for supporting Allende, was finally passed by Congress, with the support of Allende and the Christian Democrats. The new changes in the Constitution also provided for establishment of Constitutional Tribunal made up of representatives of the president, Congress and the Supreme Court, with the executive nominees having a majority. The function of the tribunal was to pass on government actions that involved issues of constitutional interpretation.[17]

As a result of this agreement and the passing of the Statute, Salvador Allende was elected constitutional president of Chile by joint session of Congress on October 24, 1970, with the votes of the deputies and senators of the Christian Democratic party as well as those of the parties making up the Unidad Popular. He was inaugurated on November 3, 1970.

PART THREE:
THE CHILEAN ROAD TO SOCIALISM

14

The Nature of "The Chilean Road to Socialism"

Exactly what was "The Chilean Road to Socialism?"* What was the nature of the "socialism" towards which this "road" was supposedly leading? An attempt to provide an answer to these two questions must be a starting point for any assessment of Chile's experience during the almost three years of Salvador Allende's presidency.

Most of those who have discussed the Allende regime have tended to ignore one or the other of these two questions. Apologists for the Unidad Popular government have stressed the democratic nature of the processes used by the Allende government, but have not gone on to ask what the ultimate objective of that government was. Thus, Gary MacEoin, in his book *No Peaceful Way,* has noted that Allende had a "mandate to lead his country to socialism by constitutional means" (p. 1) but at no point bothers to raise any questions concerning the nature of the "socialism" towards which Allende was leading "his country." The nearest he comes to defining the matter consists of such a phrase as "a new experiment in man's long search for a better society" (p. 1) or "a new road to economic and social well-being" (p. 2).

On the other hand, many critics of the Allende regime have presumed that its objective was the implantation of totalitarianism. On the basis of this presumption, they have taken for granted that it actually destroyed basic civil liberties during its tenure in power. They have been so fixed on the nature of the "socialism" which they took for granted that Allende was trying to implant that they have paid little attention to the facts concerning the "road" the regime was actually using to get there.

Both of these interpretations are incomplete and inaccurate, and lead to false portrayals of the Allende regime. In this chapter, both the "road" and the "socialism" involved in the "Chilean Road to Socialism" are assessed.

* The phrase "Chilean Road to Socialism" was often used by those describing what was happening in Chile during the Unidad Popular regime. President Allende himself used the phrase in his First Annual Message to Congress.

DIVERSITY OF ACTORS AND OBJECTIVES

The objectives of the Unidad Popular government, as well as its proposals and methods for obtaining these objectives, are not easily understood. One reason is the heterogeneous nature of the Unidad Popular as a political coalition. Another is the fact that the leading figures in the UP usually preferred to speak of the immediate problems rather than the ultimate objectives of the regime. When they did speak of long-range goals, they usually resorted to vague general terms or euphemisms.

These complications are, as we shall see, the easier ones to resolve. Much more difficult is the fact that the political leaders of the UP, and even of the UP and the MIR together, did not completely control the events set in motion by the presidential inauguration of Salvador Allende in November 1970. More or less spontaneous movements developed, particularly among the industrial workers in and around Santiago, which did not necessarily follow the leadership of any political group. These movements were not closely coordinated, and their ultimate objectives were very confused, even to the actual participants.

Finally, the question of the objectives of the individual leaders of the Unidad Popular regime, particularly Allende himself, is perhaps the unclearest aspect of all with respect to an understanding of the objectives of the Unidad Popular government.

Certain facts are clear, however—namely, the declared objectives of the major partners in the Allende government; and their own explanations of the process through which they were trying to carry out these ultimate ends.

Here the primary focus should be on the positions of the Communist and Socialist parties, since they were the largest members of the UP coalition and had the major responsibility in the government. Throughout most of the Allende regime, the Communists controlled the principal economic ministries as well as the Ministry of Labor. On the other hand, the president of the republic was a member of the Socialist Party. It also controlled key ministries, as well as the Corporación de Reforma Agraria throughout the Allende government.

Before turning to a more extensive study of the views of the Communist and Socialist parties, a word must be said about the junior partners in the Unidad Popular. Throughout the Allende period, the Radical party continued to proclaim itself a democratic Socialist party. It was in fact affiliated with the Socialist International. Privately, its leaders insisted that if they felt that the government was moving in any but the democratic direction, they would not hesitate to leave it. Nonetheless, they remained in the administration and the UP coalition until the end, and in the last months of the regime they took as extreme and absolutist a position as any other group in the inner councils of the Unidad Popular.

The two Christian parties, MAPU and Izquierda Cristiana, were somewhat different. In the beginning, MAPU proclaimed its allegiance to traditional Christian Democratic principles and criticized the PDC for not being vigorous enough in applying these principles. By the second year of the Allende government, however, MAPU had been converted, by its own proclamation, into a Marxist-Leninist party, largely losing any connection with even far Left Catholic social ideas. Its place as the spokesman for Left-wing Christian Democracy within the Allende coalition was taken by Izquierda Cristiana, formed in the middle of 1971. It continued to believe in a somewhat vague philosophy of communitarianism and in political democracy, according to the statements of its leaders.

The other small parties associated with the Unidad Popular were in no sense revolutionary or totalitarian. The base of the Acción Popular Independiente was among small businessmen and professional people, and its leadership was composed of ex-members of various democratic parties of the 1940s and 1950s. The Partido Social Demócrata, a remnant of the traditionally democratic Partido Democrático, merged with the Partido Radical in early 1972.

With the exception of MAPU after 1971, the smaller partners in the Unidad Popular were proclaimed believers in political democracy, were not in favor of the violent overthrow of the status quo, and were more reformist than revolutionary. However, their political weight within the Unidad Popular was small at the inception of the Allende government and with time tended to decline substantially. They had little ability to resist the policies and actions of the Communists and Socialists.

THE COMMUNIST PARTY'S ULTIMATE OBJECTIVES

The Communist party of Chile was (and remains) probably the most orthodox party of its type in all of Latin America. There has been no taint of the kind of "revisionism" characteristic of the Italian, Yugoslav, and even French Communist parties in that of Chile. It has remained absolutely loyal to the principles of Marxism-Leninism, including democratic centralism and the dictatorship of the proletariat. It has remained unquestioningly loyal to Moscow.

A clear picture of the Chilean Communist party's ultimate objectives during the period of the Unidad Popular government can be obtained from a pamphlet *Que es el Comunismo?* (originally issued by the Novosti Agency). This pamphlet was used by the party as a basic text in its training school, the Instituto de Investigaciones Marxistas. In a kind of catechism form, this pamphlet asks and answers a variety of questions about the party and about the Soviet Union, which is the major example used in the book to illustrate the kind of society the Chilean Communists are seeking.

One section of the Communist pamphlet answers the question "Why do the Communists advocate the dictatorship of the proletariat and what do they mean by this?'' The answer begins:

The Communists propose the dictatorship of the proletariat because they consider it the political instrument necessary to transform social relations in conformity with the principles of scientific socialism. The dictatorship of the proletariat represents the political power of the workers, the nucleus of which is the direction of the State by the working class and its party (pp. 46-47).

The pamphlet then states:

The tasks of such a State are clearly defined: it must be the political tool to eliminate capitalist social relations and establish socialist ones, that is, to destroy the social and national yoke and to preserve and strengthen the incipient socialist structures. After completing these objectives, the dictatorship of the proletariat will be transformed— as in the Soviet Union—into the Socialist State of the Whole people (pp. 47-48).

The author of *Que es el Comunismo?* then discusses terror under the dictatorship of the proletariat. He notes that ''if the reactionary classes do not voluntarily abandon the historical stage, if they appeal to armed violence, to terror, to uprisings, to reconquer their lost power, the new power (the State of the dictatorship of the proletariat) will have the full right to respond to violence with violence, to terror with terror'' (p. 48).

The case for the dictatorship of the proletariat is summed up as follows: ''Consequently, with their notion of the 'dictatorship of the proletariat,' the Communists mean the class essence of the State necessary to organize the transition from capitalism to socialism'' (p. 49).

Another section of the Communist pamphlet deals with the question ''For What Reason Does the Party Direct the Soviet People?'' It starts with the comment that ''No one will deny that in every society, no matter what its structure, there must exist a sector of men who rule public life. At least that has been true until now'' (p. 43). On the basis of that idea, the author of *Que es el Comunismo?* argues that ''bringing together the politically most active and most competent, the party can with certainty of what it is doing make judgments about all facets of Soviet society and effectively channel its development, becoming aware in time of its contradictions and taking adequate measures to resolve them'' (p. 44).

The pamphlet admits that even Communists can make mistakes, but adds that the party can be

immunized against these errors if there is the possibility of creating an environment in which error can be avoided in time and the noxious consequences of this or that mistaken decision can be reduced to a minimum. . . . This environment, experience teaches, can be achieved through the full exercise of internal party democracy and the consequent fulfillment of the principle of collective leadership. Means to this end are consecrated in the Program and in the Statues of the PCUS. Their execution consolidates even more the prestige of the party, raising its role and ascension in Soviet society (p. 46).

Another authoritative source for the ultimate objectives of the Communist party appeared during the Unidad Popular regime. This was a book written by Sergio Ramos, member of the Technical Commission of the Communist party, entitled *Chile: Una Economia de Transición*? published in 1971. In this volume, Ramos wrote that

taking into account all of its peculiarities the transition to socialism in Chile must necessarily pass to (and be inaugurated by) the dictatorship of the proletariat, independent of the form which it may assume. This signifies that the Leninist thesis of the necessity to destroy the apparatus of the State of the bourgeoisie in order to create a new one, that is to say, to change radically the class content of the system of domination is as valid in Chile today, as in Russia of 1917 for the construction of the socialist society.[1]

THE COMMUNIST VIEW OF "THE CHILEAN ROAD TO SOCIALISM"

It would be hard to find a clearer statement than that which *Que es el Comunismo?* gives concerning the ultimate objectives being sought by the Chilean Communist Party during the Unidad Popular period. However, the question still remains concerning the Communists' view of the nature of "The Chilean Road to Socialism."

Some indication of this view can also be garnered from *Que es el Comunismo?* In the discussion of the Communist advocacy of the dictatorship of the proletariat, the writer explains that "certainly in other circumstances the dictatorship of the proletariat will present different aspects. Thus, in the pacific development of the socialist revolution, the use of Parliament for the passage to socialism will offer other forms of the dictatorship of the proletariat (p. 49).

For the Communists, the use of constitutionalism and electoral democracy was clearly a means, not an end. However, in assessing the Chilean Communists' view of this means, it is necessary to keep in mind that the Communist party of Chile was a loyal member of the bloc of Communist parties under the leadership and tutelage of the Communist party of the Soviet Union. Its horizons went far beyond just what was occurring in Chile, and its assessment of desirable strategy and tactics was profoundly influenced by this fact.

In conversations with me during the Allende period, Communist leaders freely conceded not only that there would be free elections at the end of the Allende period, but also that if the Unidad Popular were defeated in those elections, it would leave power. At least some of the top Socialist leaders were not willing to make any such concessions.

This perspective of the Communists can be understood in terms of two factors. First, the Chilean Communists were looking at what was going on in their country in terms of what was good for the pro-Moscow Communist movement internationally. European Communists, especially those of Italy and France, were keeping a close eye on the Unidad Popular experiment in Chile. The Chilean comrades were probably willing to stick to the niceties of parliamentary democracy, including even the possibility of being voted out of office, not because they really believed in such practices, but because of the good effect such behavior would have on the much more important Communist parties of France and Italy.

In both Italy and France, the Communist parties have for some time been seeking an alliance with Socialists—and in Italy's case, even with Christian Democrats—which would permit them to return to the government of those countries, at least as junior partners. Their efforts have been plagued by lingering doubts among the leaders of the non-Communist Left in those two countries about whether the Communists, once in government, would ever be willing to allow themselves to be defeated and hence removed from the government. In this context, the demonstration that the Chilean Communist party was indeed willing to allow itself to be voted out of office could be expected to have a favorable impact on their becoming at least junior partners in their respective governments.

Luis Corvalan, the secretary general of the Chilean Communist party, frankly admitted the international importance of the Unidad Popular experiment for the Italian Communists. After a visit to Europe early in 1971, in an interview with the Santiago leftist weekly *PLAN*, he commented on his reception and observations in Italy:

No, it certainly was not for us—as individuals—that the Italians went crazy at our presence. It was due to what we signified and I could feel in all its importance the international dimension of our experience and of the triumph of the UP. . . .

What interested the comrades of the Italian left was that we explain the ways our popular forces used to arrive at unity in such a dynamic way as the UP has done. . . . However, it was not a matter of asking for recipes; this curiosity is explained by a coincidence of the situation, because there is no reason why the force of arms must be the only way in which the people gain power.[2]

A second factor important for the Chilean Communists was that they have always had a long-run perspective. Only once (during their participation in the administration of President Gabriel González Videla in 1946-1947) had they shown themselves too eager to exploit power before it was firmly in their hands. They had learned well the bitter lessons of that experience which had resulted in their being outlawed by the same President González Videla. They may well have seen the Allende administration as an opportunity to entrench themselves firmly in the public administration and to get a strong grip on some of the less conspicuous levers of power, with the hope that they could hold on to most of the positions gained through this experience, even if the Unidad Popular was voted out of power. If they could do so, the next time they came into a position of power, they could conceivably be the senior rather than the junior partners.

Thus, during the Allende administration, the Communists generally played a moderating role. They sought to restrain the excessive revolutionary enthusiasm of some of their Socialist partners, and they tried to get agreements with the opposition which would assure that President Allende would be able to serve out his constitutional six-year term. They were even willing to contemplate the defeat of the UP after that period, hoping that they would emerge from the experience stronger than when they had gone into it. This moderation during the Allende years did not mean that the Communist party of Chile had given up its ultimate objectives. These objectives were to achieve full power for themselves and to establish the dictatorship of the proletariat, which as they themselves spelled it out, meant the dictatorship of themselves, on the model of the Communist party of the Soviet Union.

ULTIMATE OBJECTIVES OF THE SOCIALISTS

It is more difficult to present a single set of objectives of the Socialist party of Chile insofar as the Unidad Popular experience is concerned. The PSCh has always been a party of many quarreling factions, with different ideologies and different concepts of strategy and tactics. This was no less the case during than before the Allende administration.

The Chilean Socialist party had always included one element that might best be described as Social Democrats. This element sincerely believed in political democracy, with its party pluralism and the traditional democratic principles of freedom of speech, press, assembly, and thought. The party also included an element that was committed to the concepts of Leninism, which believed in the establishment of a single-party regime and did not believe in the rules and procedures of political democracy. The Partido Socialista Popular, under the leadership of Raúl Ampuero in the 1950s, was such a Marxist-Leninist group; after the reunification of the Socialists in 1957, their party as a whole tended to be committed to the principles of Marxism-Leninism.

During the 1950s and 1960s, the leading elements in the Socialist party were attracted to the Communist regimes that deviated from the Soviet model. Oscar Waiss, who during the UP government was to be editor of the government newspaper *La Nacion,* was a particular admirer of the Tito regime in Yugoslavia.[3] During the early 1960s, Clodomiro Almeyda, who was later Allende's foreign minister, was the leader of a pro-Chinese Communist faction within the party, which was narrowly defeated by the then dominant party leader, Raúl Ampuero.[4]

The one political element on the Left with which the Chilean Socialists rather stridently did not associate themselves was the Social Democratic parties of the Socialist International. They steadfastly refused to join the International or to maintain any kind of formal relations with it throughout the 1950s and 1960s. They disparaged it for its Social Democratic proclivities, which were not in conformity with the "revolutionary" stance of the Chilean Socialist party.

Shortly after Allende assumed the presidency, control of the Socialist party passed to its more extremist elements, who were unabashedly in favor of Marxism-Leninism and the dictatorship of the proletariat. A manifesto issued by the new Socialist Central Committee right after the party's January 1971 congress made clear the context in which the Socialist leadership saw "The Chilean Road to Socialism." Julio Cesar Jobet has observed that the manifesto "indicates the process of social revolution in the contemporary world, from the Russian revolution and that of China to the struggle for the liberation of the countries of the third world and the overwhelming Cuban experience." Jobet then cites the resolution as indication that "in this historic and ideological context is the Socialist Party of Chile."[5]

In various statements and documents issued during the Unidad Popular period, the leadership of the Socialist party made clear that its ultimate objective—which it sought sooner rather than later—was the dictatorship of the proletariat. For instance, in June 1971, the Agrarian Commission of the Socialist party issued a critique of the march of the agrarian reform program. In setting forth what it thought the objectives of this program should be, it stated: "The Government of the Unidad Popular must be transformed into an instrument of support to the struggles which the workers of the countryside are carrying out, and carry forward the tactic of strangulation of, the definitive destruction of the power of the bourgeoisie, and in this way pave the way for the installation of the dictatorship of the proletariat."[6]

This position of the party leadership headed by the secretary general, Senator Carlos Altamirano, was also emphasized by a declaration of a plenum of the Socialist party's Central Committee in March 1972. As this statement proclaimed:

To construct Socialism, the Chilean workers must exercise their political domination over the bourgeoisie, must conquer all Power and gradually take from them all capital. This is what is called "the dictatorship of the proletariat." That has not been set forth in the program of the Unidad Popular, but the Socialist Party has not repudiated this Leninist-historic position.[7]

That a totalitarian regime, patterned after those in Communist party-controlled states, was the ultimate objective of the dominant group in the Socialist party was borne out by discussions I had with leaders of this group during the Allende period. On one occasion, when he was asked what would happen if the UP were defeated in the election of 1976, one leading member of the Secretariat of the Socialist party replied, "*Perhaps* there will be elections in 1976." At another time, this same Socialist leader, when asked what kind of socialism lay at the end of the Chilean Road, replied "Something like what exists in Eastern Europe."[8]

Clearly, then, the dominant element in the Chilean Socialist party shared the ultimate Marxist-Leninist goals of their Communist comrades, including the establishment of the dictatorship of the proletariat, that is, a dictatorship of their own party. They differed with the Communists on the latter's subservience to the Soviet Union, and on matters of tactics and strategy, but not on their concept of the nature of the socialism towards which the Chilean Road was leading.

ALLENDE'S OBJECTIVES

The kind of society which Salvador Allende saw himself as trying to build is not so clear as that sought by the Communists and by the dominant element in his own Socialist party. Allende's own history would seem to offer contradictory evidence.

In the 1940s, Allende had been a leading Socialist opponent of the Communist party. He had become secretary general of the Socialist party, representing those elements opposed to unity of action and ultimate merger with the Communists. He spoke and acted like a Social Democrat, at least until the presidential campaign of 1952. Allende's position at that time is illustrated in the following excerpts from a speech he made in the Senate on June 18, 1948:

The Chilean Socialists recognize fully many of the achievements in Soviet Russia; we reject its political organization, which has brought the existence of only one party, the Communist Party. We do not accept either a multitude of laws which limit and curtail individual liberty in that country and proscribe rights which we deem inalienable to the human personality.[9]

On a personal basis, throughout his career in the Senate Allende maintained friendly relations with leaders of the democratic parties, particularly the Christian Democrats. He was considered an expert at parliamentary debate and maneuver. Certainly his political opponents in Congress did not consider him to be a man of totalitarian convictions, as is borne out by a statement by Pedro Ibáñez, one of the most conservative figures in the Partido Nacional, written after Allende's downfall and death.

Allende was an old-style politician, but one who, knowing human weaknesses only too well, knew how to manipulate them. It cannot be said that at any time in his long political career he ever achieved great popularity as a political leader. His style and his character resembled very closely those of a radical socialist of the Fourth French Republic. Ambitious and tenacious, while not absolutely scrupulous, he was definitely a man who was loyal to all those who gave him their political support.

In his public appearances he was arrogant, and looked like a patent leather dandy; while in private he was unaffected and nice. He was a skillful political manipulator. In the forty years that I knew him, and in spite of the intensity of our political battles, I never saw him act with deliberate ill will, or become the slave of hatred or incurable resentments. . . .

How and when the moment came, I do not know, but at some point, powerful circumstances or pressures converted Allende into an unquestioning and effective servant of perhaps the most treasonous conspiracy against Chile in all its history. I do not believe that he had this as his purpose, or that he was aware of such a thing when he put forth his candidacy, or when he took office as President. But the course of political events, his licentious manner of living, the desperate corner into which he found himself driven soon after he assumed the Presidency were factors, taken separately or as a whole, that led him to become the figurehead for a policy, and to participate in heinous crimes for the condemnation of which the proper words do not exist.[10]

Whatever judgment one may have of Ibáñez's ideas of "conspiracy" and "heinous crimes," it is clear that his conservative opponent and long-time fellow senator did not believe Allende wanted ultimately to establish any kind of dictatorship. There is other evidence for this conclusion. For example, Allende did not accept oversimplified views of the opposition. Thus, after the 1964 victory of the Christian Democrats, he rejected the notion proffered by his Socialist colleagues that the PDC was "the left wing of reaction." At that time, as mentioned earlier, he urged the formation of a new party through the merger of Socialists, Radicals, and some smaller groups, to present a viable alternative to both the Christian Democrats and the Communists.

On the other hand, Allende had worked fairly closely with the Communists since 1952. During the 1960s, he had closely associated himself politically and in the public eye with Fidel Castro, in doing so he had sacrificed his long friendships with Democratic left groups in other Latin American countries, such as the leaders of Acción Democrática in Venezuela. He had attended the founding and only congress of the Organización Latino Americana de Solidaridad (OLAS), the sort of mini-Comintern that Castro sought to establish as the center of Marxist-Leninist elements in Latin America which were under his influence. Allende was the head of the Chilean branch of OLAS, although many of his colleagues in that effort accused him of dilatoriness in transforming it into an effective organization.

With regard to Allende's attitude toward the opposition during the period of his presidency, there is contradictory evidence. He sought to "buy off" the MIR, whose extremist Marxist-Leninist credentials are unchallenged, and he rejected all suggestions until nearly the last moment to break with the extremist Altamirano faction of his own party. His reluctance to break with the frankly totalitarian MIR and with Socialist elements allied with it was probably influenced by his own situation within the Socialist party. He had never had a sizable personal following among the secondary party leadership, nor had he been the head of a well-defined faction within the party (except in 1952 when he was followed by a small group who quit the PSP over the issue of backing the candidacy of Carlos Ibáñez). In this, he differed from Marmaduque Grove, Bernardo Ibáñez, Raúl Ampuero, Clodomiro Almeyda, and Carlos Altamirano, who at one time or another during the party's history had had such factional leadership.

After his first candidacy for the presidency in 1952, Allende had had wide popularity with the Socialist rank and file, was the most prestigious Socialist, and was perhaps better liked and more trusted by his political opponents outside of the party than any other leading Socialist. During his presidency, Allende undisputably had the backing of the great majority of the Socialist rank and file, and any party leader who had broken with him would have done so at great peril to his own political future. Unfortunately, Allende does not seem to have recognized his own strength within his party.

The spectre of the González Videla experience may also have influenced Allende to maintain his alliance with elements which in all likelihood he probably did not agree with. On various occasions during his presidency, he commented to friends that he "would not be another González Videla," that is, he would not turn against elements to his Left that had helped to make him president.

Some of Allende's critics have cited the evidence of Régis Debray to indicate that Allende was seeking to establish a dictatorial regime. Throughout his book, *Conversations with Allende,* Debray portrays Allende as a convinced Marxist-Leninist who was using political democracy only with the ultimate objective of subverting it. However, this book contains so many factual errors and outlandish attributions of statements by the Chilean president (for example, Allende is reported to have lamented the "assassination in 1961 of Brazilian President Janio Quadros"[11]—who in fact died in 1976 of normal causes) that Debray's evidence can be called suspect at best.

ALLENDE'S PROFESSIONS OF DEMOCRATIC BELIEF

Before and throughout his administration, Allende professed his belief in a democratic society. For instance, during his campaign, when he was asked whether future elections would be abolished if he became president, he replied: "It is stupid to think that way. They will continue to be held. There is nothing Chileans like more than elections. If the next ones go against us, then we will put out our candles and leave."[12]

Typical of Allende's democratic pronouncements as president was one made in a speech which he delivered in the National Stadium in Santiago soon after his inauguration. In describing how Chile was "going to overcome its under development," he commented:

In general terms we shall tread a path dictated by our experience. It will be the path backed by the people in the elections and the one pointed out in the program of Popular Unity: a road to socialism, with democracy, with pluralism and liberty. . . . The theorists of Marxism have never claimed, nor has history proved, that the process of transition towards socialism requires only one party. . . . Chile will now, on the basis of its traditions, endeavor to create the mechanisms that will make possible—within the pluralism supported by the great majority of the people—radical transformation of our political system. This is the great legacy of our history.[13]

President Allende gave one of his clearest definitions of his view of the Chilean Road to Socialism in his First Annual Message to Congress.

The circumstances of Russia in the year 17 and of Chile in the present are very different. However, the historical challenge is similar. . . . Russia of the year 17 took the decisions which most affected contemporary history. There they came to think that backward Europe could face up to advanced Europe, that the first socialist revolution did not necessarily have to take place in industrial powers. There the challenge was accepted and there was built one of the forms for the construction of socialist society, that is, the dictatorship of the proletariat. . . . As Russia then, Chile is faced with the need of starting a new way of constructing the socialist society: our revolutionary way, the pluralist way, anticipated by the classics of Marxism, but never before carried out. Social thinkers have supposed that the first to take it would be the most developed nations, probably Italy and France, with their powerful workers parties of Marxist definition.

Allende then reemphasized the special nature of the Chilean experience: "However, once more history permits a break with the past and the construction of a new model of society, not only where it was theoretically foreseen, but where there are created the concrete conditions most favorable to its achievement. Chile is today the first nation of the earth called upon to develop the second model of transition to the socialist society."[14]

Later in the same speech, Allende said that "it is important to note that for us, representatives of the popular forces, political liberties are a conquest of the people on the painful road to their emancipation. They are part of what is positive in the historical era we have left behind. Therefore, they must remain."[15]

A year and half later, in his Second Annual Message to Congress, Allende again asserted his commitment to policital democracy: "In the vigor of political democracy we have one of the most important instruments for assuring regular development of the revolutionary process. To strengthen it and to amplify the bases on which it rests is one of the most important tasks of the Government.[16]

ALLENDE'S OBJECTIVES: CONCLUSIONS

Allende, who had run for the presidency four times, naturally wanted to finish out his term of office, and so he did not consciously seek a confrontation that would risk the downfall of his government. His failure to hold in check those in the Unidad Popular and to the Left of it who were seeking such a confrontation—believing that they could win it—did not reflect any desire on Allende's part to establish a dictatorship of the proletariat or of any other kind, but rather his confidence in his ability to maneuver among conflicting interests and forces.

Salvador Allende may have been a believer in democracy, but he was also an opportunist. In this he was not an atypical Chilean politician. As a leading figure in the Socialist party since its inception in 1933, he had had long experience with maneuvering in PSCh politics. Although he himself was not a convinced Marxist-Leninist, he had long been able to keep his balance among the various schools of Marxist-Leninists which existed from time to time within his party. Likewise, he had associated himself with Fidel Castro at the start of the Cuban Revolution, when nearly everyone in Latin American politics except people of the extreme Right were doing the same thing. In the light of Socialist politics in Chile, he subsequently found it impolitic to change his allegiance, even when Castro went headlong in a Marxist-Leninist direction after 1960. Allende may also have been flattered by his close association with Castro in the Chilean public mind during the 1960s.

In a sense, Allende allowed himself to be a prisoner of his allies, particularly those in his own party. He refused to break with those who disdained democracy and hoped for an apocalyptic confrontation, until it was too late. No doubt, he feared undermining the political base of his administration and was determined "not to be a González Videla." These factors, together with the economic and political problems of his regime, made it rather irrelevant what Allende's personal convictions and objectives were. His government's policies and the actions of many of the politicians associated with it led almost remorselessly towards a polarization of society and politics and a confrontation that would almost inevitably lead only to some kind of dictatorship—of Left or Right.

FINAL OBSERVATIONS

The Chilean Road to Socialism was not as pictured either by the apologists for the Allende regime or by many of its critics. As we shall see later, in its three years in power the Allende regime left civil liberties largely intact. It was not, however, dedicated to the use of democratic means to implant a democratic regime. Its major parties were not simply seeking to profoundly alter economic, social, and political institutions and destroy existing power relationships, but also to do away with Chile's traditional freedoms of speech, press, organization, and elections. Whatever Allende's own objective may have been, the two major parties in the Unidad Popular coalition were dedicated to the ultimate establishment of a so-called dictatorship of the proletariat, which in plain English means a dictatorship of themselves.

The experience of the Unidad Popular cannot be judged apart from its ultimate ends. Democratic elements of the opposition were motivated largely by their fear of the Allende government's longer run objectives. Rightly or wrongly, the Christian Democrats, the opposition Radicals, and some elements of the Nacionales saw the Allende regime as seeking to supplant democracy with totalitarianism. They interpreted many of its policies as well as its denunciations of the opposition, of Congress, the Supreme Court, and the comptroller general as steps towards establishing the dictatorship of the proletariat. They were fully aware that this was the declared objective of both the Communists and the Socialist leaders. The government's failure to curb illegal activities of the Movimiento de Izquierda Revolucionaria and of certain elements in the Socialist party was interpreted in the same light.

15
Nationalization

Fundamental to the Allende government's program of paving the way for a "socialist" economy and society was its effort to nationalize most of the important means of production and distribution. By the time Allende was overthrown, the whole mining industry, all of the banking system, a large segment of manufacturing, and some key elements in wholesale distribution were in the hands of the national government.

The first steps towards nationalization were taken with relative ease and a minimum of resistance. In time, however, objections became intense, especially when nationalization went far beyond anything the Unidad Popular program had suggested. Two confrontations with the trucking industry played an important role in disorganizing the economy and polarizing the country's political life, thus creating the conditions leading to the fall of the Allende government.

STATE CONTROL BEFORE ALLENDE

Chile did not have a free enterprise economy before the Unidad Popular regime; in fact, large parts of the national economy were already in the hands of the state before Allende became president. Most of the railroads had been built by and belonged to the government. Most electric power outside of the Santiago-Valparaíso region was provided by the government firm Empresa Nacional de Electricidad S.A. (ENDESA). The exploitation of oil and some of its processing were in the hands of the state. A major part of mass transport in Santiago and other major cities was provided by companies belonging to the government. The national steel firm had been built by the government. The state, through the Corporación de Fomento de la

Producción, was a large stockholder in a wide range of manufacturing enterprises.

During Frei's Christian Democratic administration, the state's role in the economy had expanded considerably. At that time, the government became the majority stockholder in the larger part of the copper mining industry and in the nitrate mining firms, and a minority stockholder in other copper enterprises. It also took over the Chile Electric Company, providing the power needs of the capital and the major port city. The agrarian reform program had given the state a substantial part of the country's agricultural land, although as land redistribution proceeded, the peasants and agricultural workers would ultimately get this land. The government was made a partner in several new industrial concerns, notably in the paper manufacturing industry, which were started during the Frei regime.

Nonetheless, a major sector of the national economy remained in private hands. Most of manufacturing, all of banking except the Central Bank, the State Bank, and the Corporación de Fomento, most of wholesale and retail trade, most services, and the major part of agriculture constituted the private sector when Allende became president of the republic.[1]

THE ALLENDE REGIME'S "AREA" APPROACH

When it came to power, the Unidad Popular government sought to expand the sector of the economy that was under state ownership, as part of its wider attempt to reorganize the economy into three "areas": the social, mixed, and private. The social area was to consist of firms that were completely under state ownership. It was to include not only the enterprises already owned by the government in 1970, but also mining, banking, most manufacturing, and the wholesale trade. The mixed area was to be made up principally of manufacturing firms that hitherto had been subsidiaries or branches of foreign firms, and that required continuous access to the technological skills and trade secrets of the foreign enterprises. The government was to become the senior partner in such enterprises, controlling a majority of the stock, but the former owners were to remain as minority stockholders so as to make their technological resources available to the new mixed company. The private area was to contain, in a numerical sense, the largest part of the economy. However, all the firms in this area were small enterprises, including most of retail trade, some of agriculture, artisan shops, and even small family-run manufacturing enterprises. Allende professed to want to encourage, rather than discourage, the progress of firms in the private area.

The support for this reordering of the economy went beyond the ranks of the Unidad Popular. The Christian Democrats were willing to accept the idea of such a realignment of the nation's business enterprises, but they strongly objected to the transfer of certain firms to the social area, as well as to the government's organization plans for the enterprises in the social area. The Christian Democrats' most strenuous objection was to the methods the Unidad Popular government was using to bring about the transfer of firms. The Allende regime's nationalization policy contributed greatly to the polarization of the country's political life and the hardening of the attitude of the opposition to the Unidad Popular government.

NATIONALIZATION OF MINING

Allende moved almost immediately to carry out his campaign promise to fully nationalize the large mining industry, usually referred to in Chile as *La Gran Minería*. He submitted a proposal to Congress for a constitutional amendment proclaiming that henceforth *La Gran Minería* would be a monopoly of the state. Included in the measure were the larger copper mines, the nitrate mines, and the iron and coal mines.

The provisions of the mining nationalization measure, as summarized by Eric Baklanoff, are as follows:

1. Compensation of properties taken, excluding mineral resources on the basis of book value as determined by the comptroller general. Payment to be made in 30-year bonds at no less than three percent per annum.

2. Authority to the president to make a series of deductions from value of compensation including "excess profits" earned by the U.S. companies between 1955-70. (This provision, however, was permissive rather than obligatory.)

3. Debts of the mixed enterprises guaranteed by the Chilean government during President Frei's administration not to be assumed unless the proceeds were deemed to be "invested usefully" in the judgment of President Allende.

4. Appeal of the comptroller general's decision within a period of 15 days before a five-man Special Copper Tribunal set up for this purpose, constituted of two jurists and three government officials appointed by President Allende.[2]

This measure aroused virtually no political opposition. It went through Congress with little debate, and in the final joint session of the legislature, which was the last step in enacting the constitutional amendment, not a single vote was cast against the measure. Clearly, the Allende government had succeeded in picturing the nationalization of the large, principally foreign-owned, mining enterprises as a patriotic act which no self-respecting politician could refuse to support.

Proceeding on the basis of this legislative enactment, President Allende approached each segment of the mining industry somewhat differently. The constitutional amendment had provided, other things being equal, that compensation would be paid to the expropriated firms.

This provision was not always given uniform interpretation. In some cases, there were no problems. For example, the country's iron mines were the property of the Bethlehem Steel Corporation, and the Allende government reached an agreement with Bethlehem to buy out its interests for approximately $30 million.[3] In a similar fashion, although somewhat later, the nitrate firms and the coal industry, the latter being owned by Chilean firms, were also able to make settlements with the government for compensation over a period of years.

The story in the copper mining industry was markedly different. Although an agreement on compensation was reached between the Allende government and the Cerro de Pasco Mining Corporation, whose new Exótica mine had not yet entered fully into production, the same was not true with the older foreign firms, the Anaconda Corporation and the Kennecott Corporation.

The comptroller general, after a survey of the issue, decided that the book value of the holdings of the two U.S. companies was $333 million. However, President Allende asserted that Anaconda and Kennecott had made "excess profits" under the copper legislation of 1955 to the amount of $774 million. Therefore, the government concluded, the Chilean government not only owed the two companies nothing, but the companies were in debt to it to the tune of $224 million.[4] The rationale for the "excess profits" charge was given in Article 7 of Decree 92 of the Ministry of Mines, which said that the president could "deduct excess profits obtained by the foreign companies as a way to restitute to the nation, the legitimate participation which it should have received from these natural resources." Article 8 also stated that in making his calculations, the president should particularly consider "the spiritual and the historical-political inspiration" of the nationalization amendment.[5]

Anaconda and Kennecott refused to accept this judgment, demanding that the U.S. government help them obtain what they felt they had coming to them from the government of Chile. In addition, Kennecott took steps to try to harass the Allende regime. Kennecott sought in the courts of several European countries to have embargoes placed on the unloading of copper originating from mines that had formerly belonged to them, on the grounds that this ore had been illegally taken from them. Although these suits caused some embarrassment to the Chilean government for some months, they were not successful.

DIFFICULTIES IN ADMINISTERING THE COPPER MINES

The controversy over nationalization and compensation was not the only difficulty the Allende regime encountered in the copper mining industry;

they also had extensive problems with the managerial and technical staff in the mines. Early in the administration, the government accused the supervisory personnel of the copper mines of "sabotaging" the government's efforts to maintain and increase production. Threats were voiced that some of those accused would be tried for their alleged crimes, but such trials never took place.

One action of the Allende administration did severely reduce the size and efficiency of the managerial and technical force in the industry. This was the government's decision to change the basis for paying salaries to this personnel.

Many managerial and technical employees of the Anaconda and Kennecott companies, both foreigners and Chileans, traditionally received part or all their pay in U.S. dollars instead of Chilean currency. Some of these employees had some of their dollar payments deposited in U.S. banks, and the rest they exchanged for Chilean currency in the country's "grey market" for foreign exchange, where the rate was usually considerably higher than the official one.[6] The Allende administration decided to end this practice. It translated the rates of pay of all managerial and technical personnel into Chilean currency at the official rate of exchange—which throughout the Allende administration became increasingly out of line with the unofficial, or illegal, rate. Thus, a substantial real salary decrease was imposed on the personnel involved.

When the head of the Corporación del Cobre, the government holding company for the copper industry, was asked why this action was taken, he replied that the government had acted in terms of social justice. It was not fair, he explained, for the better paid employees of the copper industry to continue to be able to deal in the currency black market with that part of their salaries which they received in dollars, when the rank-and-file employees were being paid in Chilean escudos. No government dedicated to taking Chile down the road to socialism could continue to tolerate such a situation, he added.[7] While this argument was a cogent one, it might be termed a triumph of ideology over common sense—particularly in view of the brusqueness with which the action was taken and the failure to award any additional compensation in terms of escudos to the people involved, even on a temporary basis.

This action caused a substantial part of the managerial and technical personnel of the copper mines to abandon their jobs. It was widely reported at the time that they were encouraged to quit by the dispossessed foreign companies, which offered those who wanted them jobs in their mining operations in other parts of the world.

Norman Gall, who visited Chuquicamata during the Allende period, described other difficulties in the management of that mine at that time. He noted that "the professional or supervisory payroll was swollen by swarms of new nontechnical personnel, such as a sociologists and psychologists and public relations men who plunged into political work on behalf of Unidad Popular or infantile rivalries among themselves.'' Gall quotes David Silverman, the Communist manager put in charge of Chuquicamata by the Allende regime, as saying: "There are few people who know about copper and have the government's confidence."[8]

Throughout the Allende regime, the copper industry continued to suffer from this situation. The government sought to ameliorate it by bringing in foreign technicians and managerial people, particularly from the Soviet Union, but this was no solution. The opposition questioned the quality of the Soviet personnel involved. Thus, a charge was made in the Chilean Senate that "since the Russians wish to prepare their technicians for the Siberian mines Udekan, they send them to Chile to learn and to obtain industrial secrets, camouflaging this as technical assistance, paid for, of course, in dollars."[9]

In addition to the government's difficulties with the managerial and technical personnel, it had severe labor problems with the rank-and-file manual and white collar employees. (These problems are discussed more extensively in Chapter 18.)

Because of the UP government's difficulties in administering the copper industry, the large increases in copper production which the Frei administration had projected for the early 1970s did not materialize. The falloff was especially noticeable in the older mines—El Teniente (ex-Kennecott), and Chuquicamata and El Salvador (ex-Anaconda). Production increases in these mines fell drastically behind what had been planned in the first part of the Allende period, and overall production began to decline in the last year of the regime. The entry into production of the new Exótica mine resulted in a continued increase in total output during most of the time the Unidad Popular was in power, but total production did not increase anywhere near the amount forecast several years earlier. We shall discuss this problem more fully in a later chapter.

NATIONALIZATION OF THE BANKS

Those banking institutions which were Chilean owned were acquired by the government through the open purchase of their stock; those firms which were foreign owned were taken over by the regime as the result of negotiations with the foreign principals.

Before 1970, there was a substantial number of Chilean-owned private banks, the largest of which was the Banco de Chile. In addition, Chile had several foreign financial institutions, including branches of the First National City Bank, the Banco do Brasil, the Bank of London and South

America, the Banco Francés-Italiano de America del Sud, and the Bank of America.

On December 20, 1970, President Allende accounced that he was going to send Congress a bill providing for nationalization of all banks, and at the same time that within the next forty days the government would buy the shares which any bank stockholders wished to offer it.[10] Such a bill was never in fact sent to Congress, and the government kept its offer to buy bank shares open indefinitely. The nationalization of the banks was thus carried out entirely by administrative action, without any authorization by the legislature.

On January 5, Minister of Finance Américo Zorilla noted that the government was offering very favorable terms to bank stockholders. He added: "The explanation . . . of this incentive, so to speak, is very clear: to encourage the shareholders of the banks to sell their shares to the State without awaiting the termination of action on the proposals which within a few days will be sent to Parliament."[11]

The process of buying out the private banks went forward rapidly. By May 3, 1971, ten such institutions had come under government control.[12] By March 13, 1972, only three banks remained in private hands—the Banco Yugoslavo, the Banco de Constitución, and the Banco de Chile.[13]

On September 20, 1971, after considerable opposition protest to the government's slowness in sending a bank nationalization bill to Congress, the administration announced that it controlled 57.2 percent of all the stock of the private banks, and that it was therefore no longer necessary to send a bill to Congress. The announcement added: "We shall continue buying stock. We don't need a law to buy stock."[14] The Allende government never sought from Congress any budgetary allocations for those stock purchases or for any other purchases made in connection with its nationalization program.

Some stockholders resisted being bought out by the government, but considerable pressure was brought to bear on the private banks and on their owners to force the stockholders to sell. For example, on February 2, 1971, the Corporación de Fomento ordered all of its affiliated companies to withdrew all funds from private banks.[15]

Some foreign banks were also reluctant to turn their operations over to the government. Although some of the foreign enterprises voluntarily agreed to turn over their Chilean branches, the First National City Bank, the last foreign firm to reach agreement with the government, only did so under great pressure and when its officials became convinced that they had no alternative.[16]

The question of the rightness or wrongness of nationalization aside, the Allende government made an unwise move when it forced out all the foreign-owned banks at the time it did so. This may be called another triumph of ideology over common sense. Some of Allende's own supporters advised him and Minister of Economy Pedro Vuskevic of the difficulties the country and the government might face if the foreign banks were forced out of business in Chile and urged that no such step be taken immediately. These warnings proved to be very sound.

The "home" institutions of the foreign banks with branches in Chile had customarily made available to their Chilean affiliates considerable lines of credit, which were used to finance imports on a comparatively short-term basis. Once they were forced to close their Chilean branches, the foreign banks had little interest or incentive to keep open these lines of credit, which were reported to amount to as much as $250 million. This drying up of short-term credit seriously complicated Chile's balance-of-payments problem. It constituted one of the major elements in the "blockade" to which Allende, his supporters, and apologists insisted Chile was subject during the UP period.

OTHER EXAMPLES OF NATIONALIZATION THROUGH PURCHASE

The Allende government bought out other kinds of private firms, most of which were foreign enterprises they wanted to transfer to the mixed area of the economy. In a few instances the government also purchased the stock of Chilean-owned private enterprises.

Among the foreign firms in which the Corporación de Fomento bought a majority share of the stock were the Radio Corporation of America (RCA) subsidiary, and the INSA tire plant, in which CORFO was already a partner of the General Tire Corporation. Among other private firms in which CORFO bought a majority or a substantial share of the stock were Refractarías Lota Green S.A. (ceramics), Alimentos y Fideos Carozzi S.A. (pasta), Cristalerias de Chile (glass), Manufacturas de Cobre S.A. (copper products), Refinería de Azúcar de Vina del Mar S.A. (sugar refinery), and Astilleros Las Mabas (ship repair).[17] CORFO also purchased a majority interest in the two national shipping concerns Compañía Interoceanica de Navigación and Cia. Sud Americana de Vapores. In the latter case, the management initially resisted registering the CORFO purchases but subsequently yielded.[18] Some of these firms became part of the social area and others part of the mixed area of the economy. In practice, all became subsidiaries of the Corporación de Fomento.

The Allende government's program of purchasing private firms through CORFO and other state enterprises aroused considerable opposition. For one thing, no budgetary appropriations were ever made authorizing such purchases, and for another, it was not known where CORFO obtained the funds for such operations. The opposition claimed that a great deal of illegitimate pressure was exerted on stockholders to force them to sell.

Understandably, private industrialists strongly opposed the government's nationalization program. Owners or managers of firms made use not only of statements to the press, but also of paid advertisements, in those papers that would accept them, to proclaim their opposition to the nationalization policy as applied to their own enterprises.

During most of this period, the Sociedad de Fomento Fabril, the principal organization of private industrialists, was headed by Orlando Saenz. He was young and aggressive, and his public statements on the Allende government became increasingly hostile. He issued many calls for solidarity upon the part of the private enterprise groups.[19]

In one government reply to such criticisms, an editorial in *Puro Chile* on July 1, 1972, quoted the executive vice-president of CORFO, José Rodríguez Elizondo, as denying that CORFO was bringing any pressure on stockholders. They were free to sell or not to sell, Rodríguez Elizondo said. The editorial added:

The criticisms which are formulated, supposedly inspired in the Law, are provoked by inconfessable political objectives. They are trying to avoid by any means, the changes which the country requires, to provoke, with this closed obstinacy, confrontations between the workers and enterprises. They are trying to close the road to peaceful transformation and open the road to violence.

REQUISITIONS AND INTERVENTIONS

Most of the firms the state took over during the Allende administration were acquired neither by legislation nor by purchase; the great majority were put under government control through "requisition" or "intervention." The difference between these two procedures was largely technical, and the result was much the same: the firm involved came under government control without formal title to the property passing to the state.

One of the most important firms to be intervened was the Cia. de Teléfonos de Chile, a subsidiary of the International Telephone and Telegraph Company (ITT). Soon after coming into office, Allende authorized the beginning of negotiations for the purchase of this public utility. By late September 1971, these negotiations were not making satisfactory progress, and so the president signed a decree, countersigned by his ministers of interior and defense, which provided that the government take over the administration of the enterprise and that an interventor be named to manage it, pending the ultimate settlement between the government and the firm.[20]

The intervention in the telephone company was carried out in conformity with general laws governing public utilities. Although this was not stated in the decree, intervention was not intended to be a substitute for ultimate agreement with ITT concerning terms upon which the Chilean state would obtain permanent title to ITT's Chilean subsidiary.

The situation was different with regard to most of the other firms taken over. The great majority of these were seized under the terms of a decree-law of August 1932. This law had been enacted by the de facto government of the Socialist Republic of 1932, headed by President Carlos Dávila, and had been designed to deal with the situation created by the Great Depression.[21] This decree-law provided that in case an enterprise closed down (presumably as a result of the economic crisis gripping Chile in mid-1932), the government could "requisition" it, that is, take it over and run it so that the workers could continue to be employed and the firm's products would still be turned out. Government seizure under these conditions was deemed to be temporary and did not involve passing on the title to the property to the state.

This legislation was given a new twist by Allende's government. Starting in the early months of 1971, a procedure developed whereby either a strike would be declared by the workers of a company destined for government takeover, or such a firm would be "occupied," that is, seized by force, whether by its own employees or by outsiders. In either case, the firm would be closed down, thus providing the government with an excuse to "requisition" it under the Dávila decree-law.

By June 1972, the government had taken over some 264 industrial, transport, and service companies. Table 1 shows the sectors of the economy of which these enterprises were a part, as well as the number of companies whose title had passed to the state, and those that had been taken over as a result of requisition or intervention.

TABLE 1
Takeover of Firms by the Allende Regime

Sector	Number of Pre-1970 State Firms	New State Firms	Firms Intervened or Requisitioned
Foodstuffs	7	20	24
Textiles	—	2	30
Wood	6	—	16
Paper and printing	5	1	4
Chemicals	4	3	11
Nonmetallic products	—	4	7
Metallic products	2	10	17
Transport	4	3	6
Services	5	30	15
Miscellaneous	—	2	59
Total	33	75	189

SOURCE: Adapted from *El Mercurio,* June 22, 1972.

In the remaining fifteen months of the Allende regime, after June 1972, the state took over many more enterprises. Obviously, the number of companies the government acquired was vastly in excess of the 91 companies the Unidad Popular had originally listed as eligible for being passed to the social area of the economy. *El Mercurio* noted in its June 22 article that of the 205 firms listed, 169 were not on the famous list of 91, while only 36 were on that list. (The list of 91 firms can be found in Appendix 1.)

CONTROVERSY OVER REQUISITIONS AND INTERVENTIONS

The Allende government's interventions and requisitions aroused a great deal more opposition than did its outright purchase of enterprises. It brought the administration into direct conflict with two other branches of the government; the comptroller general and the courts.

Under the Chilean Constitution, all presidential and ministerial decrees had to be submitted for registration to the comptroller general of the republic. If the comptroller general found such decrees to be unconstitutional or illegal, he could refuse to register them. They would then be legally null and void unless the president issued a "decree of urgency," countersigned by all his ministers. In that case, the comptroller general had to register the decrees in question, but if in subsequent court proceedings his original judgment concerning their illegality was upheld, the president and ministers would be personally liable in a financial sense for any damages resulting to anyone as a result of the decrees, and might also be subject to criminal action.

In pursuance of his prerogatives, the comptroller general, Humberto Humeres, frequently declared the Allende government's decrees of requisition and intervention to be illegal. For instance, as early as July 1971, he rejected the requisition of six Arab-owned textile plants by the Dirección de Industria y Comercio.[22] In November 1972, he rejected the requisition of the Ferriloza ceramics plant,[23] and on February 2, 1973, he declared illegal the requisition of the Gas Company of Concepción.[24] The comptroller general's most sweeping decision was that of April 1973, which rejected requisitions by the government of over forty firms that had closed down during the month-long truckers' strike of October 1972. Some of these had been closed as a result of sympathy strikes by workers, and others by action of the owners.[25]

In virtually all of these cases, President Allende responded by sending decrees of urgency, whereupon the comptroller general had to register the decrees that he had previously rejected. Some of the cases were taken to the courts, and on some occasions, the Supreme Court ordered the nullification of the requisitions. Such was the case with the metal firm FENSA.[26] The president paid little heed to the decisions of the courts, and very few of the seized firms were ever returned to their owners during his administration.

The opposition press regularly attacked the government's requisitions and interventions. With equal regularity, the press supporting the government, and the administration itself, defended the government's actions. For example, in the July 1, 1972, issue of the Communist paper *El Siglo* there was a full-page advertisement of the interventor of the Pfizer pharmaceutical company. It justified the seizure of that firm on the grounds that it had been holding much of its product off the legal market and had been selling that part of its output on the black market. On July 4, 1971, in discussing the case of the Yarur textile plant, an article in *El Siglo* argued that the workers' increased output and more efficient management of the plant than its owners constituted justification of the government's takeover. On July 14, 1972, Communist Senator Luis Valente Rossi was reported by *El Siglo* as generally defending the government's program of taking over industries by arguing that "basically the Unidad Popular is recovering for the State, for the social area of the economy, all those firms which, organized and financed by CORFO between 1940 and 1960, were taken away from the State by monopolistic private groups. He explained that the majority of the 91 firms were in that situation."

COMMERCIAL ASPECTS OF THE NATIONALIZATION PROGRAM

As part of the general, if uncoordinated, drive of the Allende regime to nationalize the country's strategic means of production and distribution, the government created several important state commercial enterprises covering various sectors of the economy. If the regime had remained in power, most of the country's distributive apparatus would have belonged to the state.

The Empresa de Comercio Agrícola, a preexisting government firm, was given a monopoly over importing agricultural products. Its field included both farm and grazing products.

The Empresa Nacional de Distribución y Comercialización (DINAC) was set up to operate in the wholesale field. At the same time, a number of the largest private wholesale enterprises, including Agencias Graham, Williams-Balfour, and Gibbs, were acquired by the government through purchase or intervention, and were placed under the control of DINAC. Industrial firms taken over by the government channeled all of their sales through DINAC and its subsidiaries, rather than through private wholesale enterprises.

A firm established before the UP came to power, the Sociedad Comercializadora de la Reforma Agraria, was given a monopoly of the distribution of grazing products produced in the country. It intervened in private markets through which meat had previously been distributed.

The firm known as ENADI was created to have a monopoly of the distribution of liquid gas. The companies producing this product had been nationalized by the Allende regime.

Finally, the Empresa Nacional Avicola (ENAVI), organized on the basis of the Purina firm, which was one of the earliest to be intervened, was established to control production and distribution of chicken feed, as well as to get control over the commercialization of fowl.

In the early months of the regime, there was extensive discussion of organizing government control over retail distribution as well. DINAC presented a proposal for establishing a network of supermarkets under its control. However, the government finally opted for the Juntas de Abastacimiento Popular (JAPs).[27]

EFFICACY OF GOVERNMENT ADMINISTRATION OF FIRMS

One of the most hotly disputed aspects of the whole program of the Allende government was its administration of firms once they had passed to the social area. In the first place, the appointment of interventors to run the requisitioned or intervened plants was made on a strictly partisan political basis rather than on the basis of competence. The author saw confirmation of this fact at a Socialist party meeting which he attended in the Teatro Caupolican in Santiago on July 9, 1972, at which a number of "our interventors" (meaning those of the Party) were presented proudly to the audience.

Second, the production records of the seized plants varied a great deal from plant to plant. In quite a few of them, the workers were very enthusiastic about the seizure of the plant, with the result that they put themselves out to have a good production record. Indeed, industrial production continued to grow until a few months before the fall of the Allende government.

Third, the financial administration of the seized firms left a great deal to be desired. Although the full story will perhaps never be known, it is clear that a large percentage of the plants that were taken over incurred large deficits. For example, between January and April 1973, some 43.2 percent of the total currency emission of the Central Bank was for loans to cover deficits of government-administered firms.[28] In at least a few cases, the losses were large enough that the owners of the firms involved were unwilling, after the fall of Allende, to take back their plants, since they would also have to shoulder the debts that had been run up during the period of state control. These debts were so large as to make the profitable management of the firm unlikely.

The state met the deficits of the requisitioned and intervened firms, thus contributing in a major way to the rampant inflation of Allende's last two years, which had reached runaway proportions by the end of the regime. (The inflationary problem is discussed in Chapter 17.)

THE QUESTION OF OWNERSHIP

Legally, requisition or intervention of a firm did not give the government title to it, but the administration had no intention of returning any but a minute proportion of the enterprises it had seized. In conversations I had with officials of CORFO in mid-1973, it was plain that CORFO regarded those firms it controlled through requisition or intervention to definitively belong to CORFO.

This government point of view is further confirmed by decisions of the administration's Economic Committee in Janury 1973, as announced on January 12:

The Ministry of Interior submitted this afternoon the following document with the most recent decisions taken by the Economic Committee.

With regard to the formation of the Area of Social Property, the Economic Committee of the government has agreed to the following:

1. To send a bill to Parliament authorizing the President of the Republic to expropriate the enterprises included in the following groups:

a) Firms requisitioned or intervened, belonging to the list of 91 submitted by the Government.

b) Some requisitioned or intervened firms not included in the mentioned list and which are strategic for the national economy.

2. In those firms which have been definitely passed to the State the requisition or intervention will be ended.

3. For those firms included in the bill mentioned in point one, and in which there are conflicts, it is proposed that there be an integrated administration. This integrated administration will be transitory and will be applied in those cases in which the proprietors are ready to negotiate the passing of their property to the State.

4. Simultaneously with the sending of the bill, administrative measures will be taken for the adequate definiton of the social area. Among such measures are included the reopening of purchases and the creation of negotiation and other commissions.

5. Those requisitioned and intervened firms which are not strategic to the economy will be studied by a commission of special cases depending upon the Ministry of Labor. This commission will have for its mission the resolution of problems which might arise from raising the requisition or intervention now applying to them.

6. There will be established a permanent commission of negotiation which will centralize the decisions to acquire firms which are decided upon. This comnission will depend upon the Ministry of Economy and will have the following subcommissions:

a) A subcommission charged with negotiating with foreign investors.

b) A subcommission charged with negotiation with national and resident foreign proprietors.

7. There will be created a permanent commission to resolve problems arising from requisitions, interventions and expropriations of agricultural properties. This commission will depend upon the Ministry of Agriculture.[29]

Needless to say, no bill such as was mentioned in this press release was ever passed by Congress.

IMPACT OF ALLENDE GOVERNMENT'S NATIONALIZATION PROGRAM

The Allende government put under state ownership and/or control a substantial part of the Chilean economy that had been privately owned before it came into office. The regime was ingenious in its selection of legal justifications for taking over a large proportion of the firms over which it assumed control; these justifications were challenged by the comptroller general and the courts, as well as by the political opposition.

That the Allende regime went far beyond the original 91 firms which it had proposed to transfer to the social area of the economy cannot be disputed. Nor can it be argued that the administration did not intend to have most of these firms remain indefinitely in the social area.

The excessive nationalization of the Allende regime was very damaging to the administration. On the one hand, virtually all private entrepreneurs became fearful that no matter how small or how ''unstrategic'' their firms might be, the government would find some way of seizing them. Hence, there was practically no private investment during Allende's three years in office. In addition, financial mismanagement of a large percentage of the seized firms contributed immensely to the inflation which undermined the stability of the Unidad Popular government.

16

The Agrarian Revolution

The Unidad Popular government came into office committed to completing the agrarian reform started under Frei. It also was committed to favoring collectivized agriculture over the individual peasant holding and to pushing the establishment of state farms "in some instances."

The Allende regime carried out all three pledges and went considerably beyond them. While proposing to Congress that the maximum amount of land which a private holder would be allowed to keep be reduced by 50 percent, it used the administrative apparatus of the Corporación de la Reforma Agraria (CORA) to bring about a de facto reduction of the size of private landholdings. At the same time, it sought to undermine, and if possible destroy, those peasant organizations that did not agree with its program of socialization of agriculture, while doing very little to interfere with the considerable number of illegal land seizures that were being carried out by elements of the far Left, particularly the MIR and the more extreme elements of the Socialist party.

The agrarian program as carried out by the Allende government brought the regime into open conflict not only with the large landowners whose holdings were subject to the law, but also with the small landholders whose farms theoretically were not subject to the agrarian reform and with the landless peasantry who wanted land for themselves, not for the state. The economic effects of the land reform program were disastrous and contributed to the economic crisis that beset the regime.

COMPLETION OF THE FREI AGRARIAN REFORM LAW

The Allende government rapidly completed the expropriation of large landholdings provided for in the Agrarian Reform Law passed during the

Frei administration. In this sense, the Unidad Popular regime completed the process of agrarian reform during its first year and a half in power.

About fourteen months after the Allende government came into office, the pro-UP Santiago newspaper *Clarín* summed up the work done up to that point by the Corporación de la Reforma Agraria in terms of expropriating landholdings. It noted that during the Frei government, some 1408 *fundos* had been taken over, covering 3,585,553.2 hectares and involving 20,976 peasant families. In contrast, in only one year the Allende government had taken over 1,378 holdings, including 2,549,319.6 hectares on which were living 16,317 families. In addition, "There have been expropriated 471,000 irrigated hectares, which means that in a few months there has passed to the reformed sector 50 percent of all of the irrigated land in the country, which amounts to 1,300,000 hectares."[1]

The anti-UP newspaper *El Mercurio* also attested to the rapidity with which the Allende regime had carried out the expropriation provisions of the Frei Agrarian Reform Law. It concluded in February 1972: "Therefore, we can say that the Agrarian Reform has practically concluded its stage of expropriation as provided in Law 16,640. In synthesis, Chilean agriculture is based on small and medium proprietors and asentamientos."[2]

In some cases, CORA completely liquidated the *latifundia* in a particular province in a very short period. For example, in the province of Aysén during June 1972, it took over all twelve landholdings in that province which surpassed the legal limit of 80 hectares.[3]

Early in July 1972, the Council of the Corporación de la Reforma Agraria held a meeting in the southern city of Osorno during which it approved the expropriation of some fifty landholdings, principally in the provinces of Linares, Osorno, and Valdivia. The Communist newspaper *El Siglo* observed that "they marked one of the last steps in the death of latifundia in the country. The popular Government has expropriated in only 18 months, 3,500 properties."[4]

COLLECTIVE AND STATE AGRICULTURE

By expropriating land from the large landholders, the Allende regime did not intend to turn the land over to the peasants themselves. Rather, it sought to establish collective and state agriculture as the principal forms of landholding in Chile.

The Allende regime clearly enunciated its objectives in this regard. From the beginning, Minister of Agriculture Jacques Chonchol announced that the government would make no grant of land to individuals.[5] Subsequently, a pamphlet on the basic program of the government stated: "The expropriated lands will be organized preferentially in cooperative forms of property. The peasants will have property titles for their house and garden, and corresponding rights to the cooperative.''[6] In addition, the Public Relations Department of CORA published a small brochure entitled *ABC de la Reforma Agraria*, which constituted a short catechism on the subject. In response to the question "What are the objectives of the agrarian reform?" the brochure stated, "Principally to give the peasants property in the land in a cooperative form, to establish a social organization of production in the countryside and to thus produce the bread which Chile needs, place Chilean agriculture on a level equal to the best in the world."[7]

An authoritative statement of the organizational objectives of the agrarian reform under Allende was made by David Baytleman, the executive vice-president of CORA, to the Fourth Inter-American Meeting on Agrarian Reform Objectives in May 1972: "The transitory organizations are the asentamientos and the centros de reforma agraria. The definitive ones are the centers of production or state haciendas and the assigned cooperatives."[8]

Baytleman commented on each of the "definitive" forms. "The Centers of Production," he said, "are limited to the great firms in Magallanes, the large forest enterprises, the few haciendas which are highly capitalized or from which are obtained selected products such as seeds or fine reproductive animals, and to some areas in which the peasants really freely decide." Insofar as the "assigned cooperatives" (*cooperativas asignatorias*) were concerned, Baytleman stated:

In the Cooperativa Asignatoria, the peasants receive two types of titles of ownership: one individual for the house and garden, and the other collective for the rest of the land, and payment for these is in cash over thirty years, with two years of grace. Many of the old Asentamientos are being assigned by the Government and the program which exists for the year 1972 contemplates the assignment of the land to four hundred fifty of them.[9]

In practice, only a few state farms and collective farms were established during the Allende regime. One state farm was set up as early as December 31, 1970, when CORA expropriated what was said to be the largest land-holding in the world, the grazing area of the Sociedad Ganadera de Tierra del Fuego in the extreme southern part of the country. This covered an area of 528,000 hectares—in addition to some 265,000 which had been expropriated previously. According to *Clarín*, "The enormous area of superlatifundia which is now incorporated will be transformed into a modern industrial-grazing complex, in which Centers of Production have already been established."[10]

Near the end of the Allende regime, it was announced that the country's vineyards would be organized as *centros de producción*. All of the peasant organizations, including those aligned with the government, opposed this move. In a meeting at which all such groups were said to have been represented, they unanimously agreed on opposition and proposed instead that the peasants take over the vineyards and operate them on a cooperative basis.[11] The ultimate decision on this proposal was still pending when Allende was overthrown.

During the Allende regime, CORA attempted to have the *centros de reforma agraria* supersede the *asentamientos* as the primary transitional form of organization of the expropriated rural enterprise. David Baytleman, in the document already cited, gave one explanation for this effort:

The asentamientos are a legacy from the previous government, and their fundamental defect is in the closed nature of their structure. Based on a false concept of potential capacity, of a static character from the point of view of technical and capital investment, they not only limit the number of peasants who could be benefited by being members, but in almost all cases they have produced unemployment, reducing the original number of peasants that existed there at the moment of expropriation.

In many asentamientos there exists the fact that as output increased through intensification of production, a need for a larger permanent labor force gave rise to a wage-earning group, which in fact brought about the creation of a privileged group of peasants. If this situation were to persist it would leave the agricultural sector in a blind alley, in a frustrated and highly conflictive agrarian reform.

Therefore the Popular Government of Chile, in consultation with various groups of peasant organizations, especially those not yet benefitted by the previous agrarian reform, has felt itself obliged to invoke existing legal provisions in the Law of Agrarian Reform to create Centers of Agrarian Reform. These, in addition to being open and permitting the entry of new peasants, insofar as the needs for permanent labor require it, create conditions of greater internal democracy through the participation of women who don't work in production and of all men and women over sixteen years of age in the election, through secret vote, of General and Social Welfare Committees. The Production Committee is elected exclusively by the men and women who work there on a permanent or seasonable basis.[12]

This explanation would ring truer if the Socialist and Communist parties had not been committed as a matter of principle to collectivized agriculture, and if the Unidad Popular had not pledged to reorganize agriculture on the basis of collective and state farms. The least that can be said is that the ideological commitment of the dominant government parties made the administration predisposed to use collectivized agriculture as a way out of difficulties that were real enough.

The *centros de reforma agraria* were designed as organizations in which the peasants would receive training and experience on a collective farm, as demonstrated in the way work was organized there. According to an official CORA description of the *centros*, the members were to be organized as production groups (*equipose de producción*): "With the objective of assuring efficiency in the work and accentuating the unity of the peasants, these will be organized in Production Groups, according to the nature of their functions and/or the physical area in which they work within the area of the

CENTRO.'' Permanent leaders of the production groups would be named, although individual workers might be shifted from one to another according to requirements of the work.[13]

Three other developments presaged the establishment of a pattern of collective and state farming. The first was the establishment of the equivalent of Soviet "machine tractor stations," pools in each region of the country to "operate, repair and maintain" agricultural machinery and make it available to the collective farms in the vicinity.[14] This contrasted with the Frei government's more expensive procedure of having each *asentamiento* have the machinery it required.

The second development was the establishment of the government-owned Entidad Commercial Agrícola (ECA) which, as Barahona Zuleta affirmed, "until now has had no appreciable participation in the regulation of the agricultural and grazing market, [and] had been transformed into a fundamental element." Subsidiaries of the ECA were established to handle particular kinds of agricultural output. The ECA and its affiliates were authorized to extend credit to peasant groups to finance their crop; the repayment of this credit would come from the sale of the output, which would be handled by the ECA. Within the general context of the government's agrarian policy, this was a major step in making the state the sole buyer of agricultural products.

The third innovation was the establishment of "peasant councils." President Allende himself described these in his Second Annual Message to Congress in May 1972:

In agriculture have been organized the National Peasant Council and twenty Provincial ones. They have been created also in the municipalities, covering 80% of them in 1971. In the Communal Councils popular participation has been achieved on a democratic level never before known in the country. They consist of all the peasants, men and women, whatever their condition. Present are wage earners, renters, sharecroppers, small proprietors, members of asentamientos, casual laborers, unemployed, cooperative members, members of the Centros de Reforma Agraria. Their functions include planning, executing and controlling agricultural measures and include political matters which in some way affect them.[15]

Opposition peasant leaders interpreted the peasant councils rather differently from the way Allende saw them. They believed the councils were being used on a local basis to coerce peasants who were opposed to the regime and who belonged to peasant unions not under Unidad Popular control.

If one puts together the various elements of the UP rural program, the result is a picture of a drive to reorganize Chilean agriculture basically along the lines of the model of the Soviet Union of Stalin's day. Collective and state farms as the basic productive units, machine tractor stations as the source of machinery for the collective farms, state monopoly of purchase of agricultural products, all fit into this pattern. Indeed, there was no indication of any agreement even to permit the one exception to the socialized agricultural pattern of Stalin's Soviet Union, the peasant market.

The attempt to impose collective and state-owned agricultural patterns brought the Allende government into conflict with a substantial proportion of the peasantry. It is difficult to say how large a proportion resisted this effort. It is clear, however, that the two peasant confederations that continued to be under Christian Democratic influence during the Allende regime were strongly opposed to the *centros de reforma agraria*. The fact that relatively few *centros de reforma agraria* were actually established also reflects the resistance to them. Probably no more than fifty were set up throughout the country. Vastly more *asentamientos* than *Centros* were organized in this period, despite the government's commitment to the concept of the *centro de reforma agraria*.

The government's insistence on collective and state farming as its immediate program constitutes another example of the triumph of doctrine over common sense. This policy placed the government in conflict with elements of the rural population with which it might otherwise have had the closest cooperation and from which it might have drawn the strongest support. Had the Unidad Popular government been satisfied (as the Frei government ultimately was) to let the peasants themselves decide how to organize the expropriated landholdings, the peasants' aspirations for land for themselves would have been satisfied. And, too, in many cases where the peasants themselves realized that the family farm was impractical, as in vineyards and grazing areas, the peasants would have opted for cooperative farming.

Indeed, it appears that if the execution of agrarian policy had been more completely in the hands of the more pragmatic Communist party, a more cautious approach to the rural question might have been adopted. The policy of the Allende government between 1970 and 1973 ran counter to the experience both of the Bolshevik regime in Russia and the Communist governments in Eastern Europe after World War II. In both of these instances, the regimes had allowed the peasantry to take the land for themselves during the period in which the Communists were consolidating their power and had taken the land away from the peasants again, collectivizing and making it state property, only after such consolidation had been secured. The Allende government, as events proved, was never able to achieve consolidation, and part of the reason was that even from a Marxist-Leninist point of view their attempt to impose ideological purity on the countryside was premature.

THE ATTEMPT TO REDUCE MAXIMUM
PRIVATE LANDHOLDINGS

The government's drive to reduce the size of private landholdings, which were assured by law, caused unnecessary turbulence in rural areas and, ultimately, a steep decline in agricultural production. The Frei legislation provided that private landlords could hold on to 80 hectares and that only amounts in excess of that limit would be subject to expropriation. Almost from the beginning, the Allende regime sought to have this limit reduced to 40 hectares, and where possible, to have no limit at all.

In many cases during the Allende period, the Corporación de la Reforma Agraria did not respect the legal right of landowners to keep 80 hectares. As Jacques Chonchol, minister of agriculture until November 1972, explained in January 1972: "I know that many times conflicts occur between peasants and expropriated landlords, and in some cases where the landlords are entitled to keep a reserve, the peasants oppose this and violent conflicts result. . . . In many cases, when the conflict is insolvable, we have conversed with the proprietors to get them to renounce their reserves, in more favorable conditions than the law permits. There are various alternatives for this."[16]

The process went considerably beyond mere persuasion. In June 1972, the Colegio de Abogados (Bar Association) denounced CORA's policy of not granting landlords the reserves to which they were entitled.[17] As Robert Moss has reported, "The small landlords soon discovered that there existed at least fifty legal pretexts which could be used by the functionaries of CORA to take over a fundo without taking into account its physical size."[18]

The parties of Unidad Popular, as well as the MIR, advocated a drastic reduction of the legal limit of rural private holdings. For instance, the Socialist party and Izquierda Cristiana officially proposed reduction to 20 hectares, while MIR argued that the maximum legal private holdings should be set at only 5 hectares.[19]

Both the government and the Christian Democrats presented legislative proposals for reducing the legal amount of land that would not be subject to agrarian reform and that a landlord who had less than this amount would be able to keep. A proposal was finally passed by both houses of Congress as a constitutional amendment, but it apparently lapsed before the coup of September 1973. The amendment, which passed both houses with the votes of the opposition parties but with the legislators of Unidad Popular voting in the negative, reduced the amount of inalienable land from 80 hectares to 40 hectares. It provided that peasants must be given titles to expropriated land within two years. It also stipulated that any small or medium-sized landowner from whom land was taken under the state's right of eminent domain for public uses had to be compensated beforehand in cash for what was taken. Finally, it put into the Constitution "the freedom of commerce and transport." Opposition deputies and senators voted for all four provisions, while Unidad Popular members voted against all of them.[20]

Two proposals presented by the Allende administration were rejected by the Senate. One provided that the government could place in the social or mixed areas of the economy any landholding "which the Government considered productive units of preeminent importance for agriculture, as well as those on which the workers solicited the incorporation in one of these two areas." The second proposal was that not only land should be expropriated, but all "improvements, installations, utensils, equipment, machinery, houses, buildings and animals."[21] In fact, many landowners expected that the maximum limit they would be allowed to hold would be lowered, and some took steps to get rid of all of the land they owned in excess of 40 hectares. One who did so was ex-Senator Eduardo Alessandri, son of the late President Arturo Alessandri and brother of ex-President Jorge Alessandri, who after losing all of his holdings over 80 hectares, later sold all in excess of 20 hectares, since he expected that the legal limit would ultimately be reduced to that level.[22]

THE TOMAS

Instability in rural areas during the Allende regime was also fostered by its series of illegal seizures of land (popularly called *tomas*), generally under the leadership of the MIR and its rural affiliate, the Movimiento de Campesinos Revolucionarios (MCR), and not infrequently supported by left-wing elements in the Unidad Popular. Although CORA officials with whom I talked during the Allende regime insisted that the number of such seizures was greatly exaggerated by the hostile segments of the press, they were prevalent enough to cause great uneasiness among small and medium-sized landowners as well as those who possessed *latifundia* (who in any case had largely disappeared by the middle of 1972, as we have noted). In some parts of the country, illegal seizures were sufficiently widespread to involve a substantial proportion of the landholdings in those areas.

Reports of illegal land seizure were published throughout the Allende period. Typical was a notice in *El Mercurio* on March 23, 1972, concerning the situation in the region of Chillan: "Numerous agricultural properties joined today those which previously had been illegally occupied, while in others the strike called by the Isabel Riquelme and Pedro Aguirre Cerda Peasant Federations continued." In addition, some foreign correspondents visited areas in which land seizures were widespread. James Goodsell of the *Christian Science Monitor* reported extensively on such a visit in early 1972.[23] The Paris newspaper *Le Monde* described the illegal seizures in September 1971, noting that "the occupation campaign is being organized chiefly by the MIR. . . . whose leaders have adopted an attitude of 'tactical support' with respect to the government."[24]

Many of the seized holdings were not large enough to be legally expropriated under the Agrarian Reform Law. In November 1971, a list of seized properties was published by the landowners' confederation. Most of those listed were in the province of Cautin, and in all 131 *fundos* were named. They included one of 1,500 hectares and another of 1,400 hectares, as well as holdings as small as 2.5 hectares. Only thirty-seven of those listed had areas of more than 80 hectares.[25]

Although it will probably never be known exactly how many landholdings were seized illegally during the Allende period, Robert Moss reports that there were 2,000 such occupations during the first two years of the Allende government.[26]

In some cases, agrarian reform officials reportedly participated in or cooperated with illegal land seizures. Such participation was charged by the landowners' federation of the province of Bio-Bio in February 1972. It denounced "the sectarianism of those functionaries who while receiving and 'negotiating' with the farmers, during the night dedicate themselves to organizing land seizures to bring pressure and to intimidate."[27]

Robert Moss describes the role of CORA official Gabriel Coll in aiding illegal land seizures:

It is proven that the CORA and the functionaries of Unidad Popular worked in collusion with the extremists. The record of Gabriel Coll, at one time chief of CORA in the province of Linares, is a notorious example. Coll supported openly the illegal seizures and was one of many functionaries of CORA who formally expropriated fundos which had been seized by force from their owners. After the local agriculturalists had assembled an extensive archive of his activities, the government was obliged to suspend him from his functions. In October 1971 he was surprised in Valdivia driving a government automobile loaded with firearms.[28]

Illegal land seizures sometimes aroused protests even from elements of the Unidad Popular itself. In March 1972, Raúl David Lebon of Acción Popular Independiente protested the activities of the MCR which he said "are publicly known, such as seizures. . . . We are studying the way to overcome these differences. Negotiations for this end will be held."[29]

The illegal land seizures created a situation in which no agriculturalist could be sure that his property was safe. They also helped to convert many of the small landowners, who might otherwise have been allies of the Allende government, into enemies of the regime.

THE ALLENDE GOVERNMENT AND THE
PEASANT ORGANIZATIONS

The Allende government's relations with the existing peasant organizations were turbulent. Although some peasant groups were controlled by Unidad Popular parties, and they generally supported the programs of the Allende government, these same programs tended to alienate the non-UP peasant groups.

At the time the Allende government came to power, there were five principal peasant organizations: the Confederación Campesina Ranquil, which was affiliated with CUTCh and controlled by Communists and Socialists; the Confederación Campesina El Triunfo Campesino and the Confederación La Libertad, both of which were Christian Democratic in orientation and consisted of workers on still private *fundos*; the Confederación Nacional de Asentamientos, made up of peasants on agrarian reform settlements; and the Confederación Nacional de Pequeños Agricultores, consisting of small and medium-sized landowners.

Soon after the inauguration of the Unidad Popular government, the Confederación Campesina El Triunfo Campesino was split. A group of peasants led by elements of MAPU and Izquierda Cristiana, the two splinter groups from the Christian Democratic party, broke away to form the Confederación Unitaria de Campesinos.

The Allende government was openly hostile to the peasant organizations that were not controlled by the Unidad Popular parties. It refused to pay the Confederación El Triunfo and the Confederación La Libertad the dues of the members of their affiliated unions which were deducted by the rural employers and turned over to the Ministry of Labor, and which in accordance with the Law of Rural Unionization of 1967 were supposed to be paid by the Ministry to the confederations. "Technical" problems were constantly given as explanations for this failure to obey the law, but the Allende government was unwilling to solve these technical problems. Naturally, the lack of financial resources resulting from this failure to receive the monies due them severely hampered the two confederations in their efforts to service their member unions.[30]

The peasant organizations other than the Ranquil and Unitaria groups strongly opposed the establishment of *centros de reforma agraria*, the general policy of establishing collective farms, and state farms. They frequently demonstrated their disagreement with government policy. They especially opposed efforts to impose collectivization. Thus, the Confederación Campesina La Libertad argued that "the peasants do not wish to be wage workers for anyone, neither the reactionary landowners, nor for the State, whose only visible representatives are bureaucrats and public functionaries."[31]

The small landholders shared the other peasants' skepticism about the intentions of the Allende regime. The president of the Confederación de Pequeños Agricultores complained: "The declaration of the Government and of the Unidad Popular, in the sense that the small and medium agriculturalists have nothing to fear are pure words. The reality is that some functionaries have transformed themselves into a supergovernment, adopting arbitrary measures against this large sector of the peasantry. They are expropriating us as well as the large landholdings."[32]

On several occasions, peasant groups held mass demonstrations against the government's agrarian policies. On September 1, 1971, several thousand peasants marched to Santiago to protest the establishment of *centros de reforma agraria*. The police prevented many of the marchers from getting to the capital.[33] In January 1972, the Libertad and Triunfo confederations, together with the Confederación de Asentamientos and several regional peasant groups, organized a demonstration consisting of a six-hour general strike. At the same time, they blocked a number of highways in the rural areas. *El Mercurio* reported that this strike was a demonstration "against the Government, Minister Chonchol, the Centers of Agrarian Reform, persecution of their leaders and political prices set for their products."[34]

In many instances, small landholders were threatened not only by the possibility that their land might be illegally expropriated, but also by illegal seizures by the MIR and its allies. Robert Moss states that "the rage and the frustration of the middle sized farmers, converted into the principal butt of the MIR and the reform organizations, carried on violent resistance in the South, where they established various vigilante groups."[35]

Thus, a many-sided conflict occurred in the countryside during the Allende administration. Large landholders, small and medium-sized landlords, agricultural laborers and tenants, *asentamiento* dwellers, officials of CORA, groups of students, and other outsiders were all in conflict with each other, and there were often clashes within these groups. Basic, however, was the alignment of large segments of the smallholders, laborers, tenants, and *asentamiento* dwellers against the government and its policies. One peasant leader in July 1973 described the situation to me as one of "virtual civil war between the peasants and the government."

DECREASE IN OUTPUT

One effect of the turbulence which swept the countryside during the Allende period was a drastic decline in agricultural output. Although Unidad Popular leaders boasted during the first year of the regime that the intensification of the agrarian reform was resulting in a marked increase in production, it became clear during the last year that the output of agricultural products had fallen substantially from pre-Allende levels.

The fall in agricultural output was reflected in the dramatic increase in imports of agricultural products. In 1970, some $217 million were spent on importing such goods; in 1971, this figure rose to $295 million, and in 1972, to $400 million. Allende's second minister of agriculture, Rolando Calderón, predicted that the total for 1973 would be $480 million.

Only part of the increase in imports of agricultural goods could be attributed to a decrease in Chile's output of these products. Another factor was the increase in consumption of foodstuffs during the Allende period, particularly during the first two years. The real income of a large part of the urban working class increased during the 1971-1972 period, and given the high proportion of the average worker's budget spent on food, this income rise was reflected in an increased demand for foodstuffs. It has been estimated that the consumption of food rose by about 25 percent during the first two years of the Allende regime.[36]

In addition to the increase in consumption of foodstuffs in Chile, however, there was a marked decline in food production during the Allende years. Robert Moss estimates that between 1970 and 1972 overall production fell by about 12 percent and that in 1973 it dropped by an additional 10 percent. At the same time, wheat output fell from 1,360,000 tons to 700,000 tons, while production of meat fell by as much as 60 percent.[37]

THE ISSUE OF "SABOTAGE"

The Unidad Popular and its apololgists abroad frequently charged that the Allende government's problems in the countryside were the result of deliberate "sabotage" by the landowning classes. It was argued that those hurt by the agrarian reform were trying to undermine the government economically and politically, and that since these activities were creating shortages and higher prices, they bordered on treason.[38]

What were the real facts of the matter? The landholders, knowing that much of their land would soon be taken by the agrarian reform, could not be expected to invest new sums in capital development, or even to invest much in taking in a harvest which in all likelihood would not belong to them. Such an attitude might well be interpreted as an exercise in economic rationality rather than as "sabotage." Moreover, many smallholders in areas where *tomas* were widespread were hesitant to invest either their efforts or funds in activities that might make their farms appear prosperous enough to attract the attention of those organizing illegal land seizures. The *tomas* themselves undoubtedly directly disrupted production. If any "sabotage" was involved in this situation, it was committed by the alleged "revolutionaries" who were taking land to which they had no right.

This period also witnessed a struggle over whether land taken over under the agrarian reform should be organized as *asentamientos* or *centros de reforma agraria*. Often, because of conflicting views of peasants and CORA officials, it took a considerable amount of time to reach a decision, and one can presume that this uncertainty must have had a negative impact on production.

Another important factor was the Allende administration's decision early in its period in office to end the Frei government's policy of investing heavily in the *asentamientos* set up by CORA. As we have seen, the administration's emphasis was on establishing machine tractor stations rather than on providing each *asentamiento* with its own machinery and equipment. However, this new system was barely organized during the Allende period.

In addition, foreign exchange shortages soon made it increasingly difficult to import agricultural equipment from the United States. Although this problem was somewhat offset by machinery imports from the Soviet Union, the quantity of such equipment was limited and its quality left a great deal to be desired. Moreover, few replacement parts were imported with Soviet machinery.

As a result of all these factors, economic and social conditions in the countryside grew increasingly bad during the Allende years. Under Frei declines in production in areas eligible for agrarian reform but not yet subjected to it had been offset by greater output in the new *asentamientos,* but there were no such countervailing circumstances under Allende.

Neither the state farms nor the *centros de reforma agraria* proved successful from a productivity point of view. Luis Corvalán, secretary general of the Communist party, reported to a meeting of the Agrarian Committee of his party in August 1972 that the state farms were marked by ''lack of labor incentives, bureaucratic inefficiency, robberies and petty corruption.'' With regard to the *centros de reforma agraria* and the *asentamientos*, he complained of alcoholism, absenteeism, and corruption.[39]

One cause of this situation was the heavy hand which patronage exerted over state-controlled or -influenced agricultural units. As was true with factories seized by the government, administrative officials in state farms, *centros de reforma agraria*, and *asentamientos* were appointed on the basis of party affiliation, each party receiving a given number of such posts.

Given all of these circumstances, the apologists for the Allende regime have to ignore the obvious facts of the situation in order to explain the substantial decline in agricultural production during the Allende period in terms of ''sabotage.'' Lowered output and productivity were natural results of the government's policies in the rural sector of the economy.

17

Economic Policies and Problems of the Unidad Popular Government

The Allende government's economic policies were an almost unmitigated disaster. With the exception of an interesting and positive experiment made during the first year of the administration, these policies were negative and generated Chile's worst economic crisis in its entire history as an independent country.

The economic disaster was multidimensional. Before the end of the regime, production was declining precipitously, investments were severely curtailed, savings were all but nonexistent, levels of living of the masses were as low as or lower than they had been when Allende took office, shortages were all but universal. Most striking of all, inflation had become completely uncontrollable, running at more than 300 percent a year, with the prices increasing more and more each day.

The political consequences of the economic situation were equally disastrous. The economic catastrophe further polarized the population and created a widespread atmosphere of desperation. As we shall see, the economic failure did not itself bring down the Allende government, but it helped create a "prerevolutionary" atmosphere which strained Chile's hitherto sturdy political democracy to the breaking point.

The question arises as to whether the economic chaos of the last part of the Allende regime was deliberate government policy, or whether it was the result of bad judgment, incompetence, and political pressures. The following pages will attempt to answer this query.

THE EXPERIMENT OF 1971

The most positive aspect of the government's economic policy was the experiment it carried out during 1971. In itself, this experiment was worthy of study by other Latin American countries and of possible adaptation by some of them.

During its first months in office, the Unidad Popular regime attempted a massive redistribution of income in favor of the lower classes. As a one-shot effort, this was highly successful. Early in 1971, when the annual wage and salary readjustment law was enacted, the administration got through Congress a bill providing for an increase somewhat in excess of the rise in prices during 1970—35 percent. In practice, however, the law sometimes permitted adjustments considerably in excess of 35 percent and in some instances as high as 50 percent. Alberto Baltra estimates the overall wage increase at about 45 percent.[1]

At the same time, the Allende government decreed that prices would not be allowed to rise, at least for some time. During the first nine months of 1971, the administration was quite successful in preventing price increases, and throughout the year, it proved possible to limit price rises to only 22.1 percent, according to official figures. This was the third lowest annual price increase in a decade, outstripped only by the 17 percent of 1966 and the 21.5 percent of 1967.[2] These actions resulted in a substantial redistribution of income. Thus, the part of the national income going to wage and salary earners rose from 45.3 percent in 1970 to 61.6 percent in 1971.[3]

In the short run, this policy of reactivating the national economy was very effective. Whereas the gross national product had increased only 3.4 percent or 1 percent per capita in 1970, it shot up to 8.3 percent in 1971, the largest rise in a decade, the only comparable year being 1966 when a 7 percent increase was achieved.[4] Industrial production rose by 12.1 percent, and within that sector, the output of basic metallurgical industries went up 6.7 percent, while the mechanical and metallurgical segment's production rose 5.1 percent.[5]

During this period, unemployment fell. In December 1970, the rate of unemployment was 8.3 percent, decreasing to 5.3 percent by June 1971 and to 3.8 percent by December.[6] Not all of this decline can be attributed to the income redistribution program of 1971. The increased demand for goods produced by privately owned industries during the year was not reflected proportionately in increased employment. As a result of a law passed in the Frei administration making it difficult to lay off workers, many employers chose to pay overtime pay to their already employed workers rather than to take on new ones for additional shifts. Their rationale was that if and when demand sloughed off again, it would be difficult to dismiss workers who had been hired in response to the increased demand in 1971.

Much of the increased employment in 1971 was in the social area, that controlled by the government. Many, if not most, of the workers hired then and afterwards by state-owned and -controlled industries were employed because of political reasons rather than because of production demands.

Thus, the El Teniente copper mine added 4,000 white collar workers during 1971 to the 8,000 they already employed; the Sumar textile mill took on 1,000 additional workers to the 2,500 employed before 1971; and the brewery Cervecerías Unidas more then doubled the number of its workers after it was nationalized in 1971.[7]

The government planning organization, the Oficina de Planeamiento (ODEPLAN), in its annual report of 1971, cautiously recognized the nature of much of the increased employment during the year. It commented that the reduction of unemployment "does not imply the elimination of the problem, given the important part of the inactive labor force which would like to work," as well as noting "the high proportion of underemployment which is hidden among those who are working."[8]

The wage-price program of 1971 was profitable for many of the firms in the private sector of the economy, and by itself would likely have generated a positive response from those industrialists and merchants. In most cases, the large increase in the quantity of consumer goods sold more than offset the increase in labor costs resulting from the wage increases given in the 1971 Ley de Reajuste.

I was in Chile in the middle of the year for several weeks and was surprised to find that there was little complaint from businessmen that they were being squeezed by wage increases and forced stabilization of prices of their goods. One well-informed foreign observer resident in Chile, who must remain anonymous, was convinced that most industrialists and merchants handling consumer goods were benefiting substantially from the situation.

THE TEMPORARY NATURE OF THE
1971 ECONOMIC SUCCESS

The success of the Allende government's economic policies during 1971 proved to be very shortlived. By the end of the year, the tide had already turned, and during 1972 and the first eight months of 1973, the first year's apparent success in price stabilization was completely reversed.

One reason for the only temporary success was the special circumstances in which the wage-price program of 1971 was undertaken. According to Alberto Baltra:

Through the redistribution of income the attempt was made to increase demand, which would act as a pressure on supply, which for the purpose of responding had large stocks of raw materials and finished goods, idle industrial capacity, unemployed manpower, agricultural and grazing production at normal levels, and profit margins sufficient so that the private entrepreneur could absorb the readjustments in wages without translating them into price increases."[9]

Allende apparently hoped that the success of his government's income redistribution program in 1971 would be continued. In his May Day speech of that year, he called upon the workers to help make this goal a reality: "The purchasing power that you have now has increased sales like never before. However, that signifies that adequate supply must be maintained. It is necessary to produce in the fields, in the industries. The workers have the responsibility. It depends upon you that we gain the great battle of production."[10]

The circumstances that made the government's economic program a success in 1971 had changed by the latter months of the year. Inventories had been depleted, idle capacity no longer existed, problems had begun to appear in agriculture, and there was virtually full employment—albeit many of those newly placed on the payrolls had relatively little work to do.

For the process which had worked in 1971 to have continued during the following and subsequent years, it would have been necessary for the considerable increase in demand for consumer goods in 1971 to have been accompanied by at least the beginning of a large rise in productive capacity. For this, extensive investment would have been required; substantial import of machinery and equipment, as well as of replacement parts for existing installations, would also have been necessary. None of these things happened, however. Instead of increasing, investments fell in 1971. The importation of capital goods declined by almost 17 percent during that year. Thus, the productive capacity of the Chilean economy, in spite of the spur provided by the greatly increased demand for consumer goods in 1971, did not respond as might have been expected, "other things being equal."

The problem was, of course, that other things did not remain equal during 1971. Other actions of the Allende government—and perhaps even more decisively, inactions of the Unidad Popular regime—were discouraging investments by the private sector of the economy. Already in 1971 the government was seizing large segments of industry through "requisitions" and "interventions." Even more significantly, enterprises were being seized illegally, and the government was doing little or nothing to discourage these actions—in fact, in many cases it was giving them its blessing by itself taking over the seized firms.

Thus, private entrepreneurs, uncertain as to when their properties would be taken over by government decree or by force, were little inclined to invest in expanding the capacity of their factories or workshops. Furthermore, the social area itself made few investments, so that the decline in investment in the private sector was not offset by an increase in the government-controlled part of the economy.

Therefore, it was not possible to repeat the performance of 1971 in subsequent years. Massive wage increases, coming at a time when there was full use of existing capacity and no new capacity was being added, could result only in inflation. This was particularly the case when shortages of repair parts and raw materials were becoming increasingly intense and labor productivity was markedly declining.

One other factor favoring the success of the government's wage-price program in 1971 was reversed in subsequent years. This was the proclivity of many middle- and upper-class people to hold money during 1971. According to Alberto Baltra, "In general, with the increase in liquidity, the private businessman sought to defend himself against unforeseen negative developments" during 1971.[11] A study of the Chilean economy in 1971 by the Institute of Economics of the University of Chile, as quoted by Baltra, explains that

on the one hand this reflects the concrete effect of policy measures changing the regular method of financing private activity. . . . on the other hand, it shows the *answer* of one part of the community, particularly the private entrepreneur, to the political model of 1971. In this last sense, the greater retention of liquidity is reflecting a primary mechanism of defense put into effect by this entrepreneurial class in a situation deemed risky, through which they reduce their financial commitments in a possibly adverse situation, and which simultaneously permits them to obtain means for resisting the degree of control in the model for orienting private activity included in the short term policy of 1971.[12]

Baltra states that a large part of the liquid funds was used to purchase foreign exchange. He argues that such a tendency "is intensified when a man contemplates, among other possible alternatives, abandoning the country which he inhabits."[13]

In any case, before the end of 1971, the apparent success of the government's economic policy in the first part of the year was already beginning to be reversed. By the end of 1972, the redistribution of income of the previous year had also been turned around. The Department of Economics of the University of Chile estimated that by the end of 1972 the share of labor in the national income had reached levels lower than those of 1970, and that during the first months of 1973 it fell to a level below that of 1965-1966.[14] After the fall of Allende, it was reported that real wages had fallen by September 1973 to only 50 percent of what they had been in 1970.[15] While such a large figure seems dubious, there is little question that real wages had declined massively by that time.

The trends which were to continue for the last two years of the regime were already making their appearance by the end of 1971. We shall now turn to those tendencies and to the policies accompanying them.

THE PRODUCTION RECORD

As mentioned earlier, nearly all aspects of the Allende government's handling of the economy were disastrous, particularly during the last two years and certainly with regard to production. As we shall see, by the end of the period production was falling in almost all sectors of the economy, while at the same time, productivity was declining even more.

We have noted that industrial production increased 12 percent during 1971. In 1972, the rate of increase had slowed to 2.8 percent, according to the National Statistical Institute, or to 2.5 percent as recorded by the industrialists' Sociedad de Fomento Fabril. This 2.5 percent increase is somewhat misleading, since throughout 1972 there was a declining rate of increase, and in the last four months of the year there was in fact a decrease in output as compared to the previous year. This tendency continued through five of the first seven months of 1973.

Table 2 presents increases or decreases in industrial production for 1972 and 1973, as compared with output during the same month in the previous year.

TABLE 2

Monthly Industrial Production

Month	Pct. Increase or Decrease Compared to Previous Year
January 1972	19.9
February	19.3
March	12.8
April	14.6
May	6.1
June	4.6
July	2.9
August	1.0
September	− 8.8
October	− 8.3
November	− 8.8
December	− 6.2
January 1973	− 2.3
February	1.4
March	3.1
April	− 7.7
May	− 6.2
June	− 8.7
July	− 9.3

SOURCE: Alberto Baltra Cortes: *Gestion Economica del Gobierno de la Unidad Popular*, pp. 79-80.

Within the industrial sector, substantial declines in production occurred during 1972. Thus, food products fell 7.5 percent; leather, 5.9 percent; furniture and accessories, 4.1 percent; paper, 3.1 percent; petroleum derivatives, 1.9 percent; basic iron and steel, 5.8 percent; electronic equipment, 25.5 percent; domestic electric apparatuses, 5.9 percent; and professional and scientific equipment, 11.6 percent.[16]

It is perhaps surprising that industrial production did not fall earlier and more rapidly. Alberto Baltra has described the conditions of manufacturing beginning in 1972:

On the one hand, idle industrial capacity was exhausted and there were no investments to increase it, one being able to presume with reason that that capacity was reduced by the lack of investments in repairs. On the other hand, the firms encountered growing difficulties in importing replacement parts and other inputs, due to the precarious position of the balance of payments, aggravated by the need for importing increasing volumes of food, as a result of the agricultural disaster. Furthermore, there existed uncertainty, lack of confidence and fear in the private area and absence of direction and planning in the social area.[17]

Agriculture suffered an even greater decline in output than did manufacturing. In 1972, the fall was about 6.7 percent, and it is estimated that the further decline in 1973 was 16.8 percent.[18] The falloff in output of specific crops was especially striking. For instance, the output of wheat fell almost 50 percent, that of barley by more than a 25 percent, oats by 12.4 percent, and rice by almost 30 percent. Similar declines were to be noted in almost all of the other product areas.[19]

The decline in agricultural output was in stark contrast to the government's hoped-for increases. A pamphlet issued by the president's office early in 1971 had stated: "The goal is to increase by five percent the production of the previous year and thus end the expenditure of 200 million dollars which leaves the country annually to import food which our soils could produce."[20]

Agricultural output undoubtedly declined because of diminution in the amount of land under cultivation. In the three years of the Allende regime, this total fell by about 22.4 percent, a figure comparable to that of the Depression years of 1929-1933.[21] A "secret" report of the Socialist party in 1972 admitted that almost half of the land the Allende government had taken over in the agrarian reform was not being cultivated.[22]

Again, other reasons for the decline are not hard to find. The decrease in rural output was largely the result of the government's own policies, both active and passive. The insistence of leading CORA officials that the maximum private landholding be reduced from 80 hectares to at most 40 hectares, and CORA's actions in many instances in forcing landowners to give up more land than the law required, created a great deal of uncertainty among the old landowners and an understandable reticence to invest in land. The widespread and completely unlawful *tomas* of land, in most cases from small and middle-sized farmers, by the MIR and left-wing Socialists had the same effect.

In addition, the government's insistence on establishing a form of collectivized agriculture as the general pattern of the agrarian reform brought open conflict with many of the peasants and discouraged them from making the land more productive. The peasants' efforts in this direction were also discouraged by the government's suspension of its predecessor's program of investing substantially in the *asentamientos agrarios.*

Apologists of the Allende regime have treated the reaction of much of the rural population in terms of a "plot," conceived clandestinely and carried out subversively, with the purpose of bringing down the government. A more reasonable explanation of the disaster in the Chilean countryside is that the private landowners—large, medium, and small—who felt that they had no security of tenure, and peasants who saw the state taking the lands that had been promised to them under the agrarian reform, did not have the incentive to invest much more than their own labor—if that—in cultivating and harvesting their crops.

One small branch of the economy which progressed during the Allende period was fishing. In this sector, the regime had help from the Soviet Union and Cuba. The *World Affairs Report* revealed that "the USSR has rented five modern trawlers to Arauco, the national fishing company. They have Soviet crews and some Cubans, possibly serving as intermediaries between the Russians and the Chilean trainees (captains). . . . Thanks to the Soviet ships, the Chilean fish catch has risen 44 percent."[23]

Elsewhere we have noted the production record of the copper mining industry. Here it is sufficient to state that there were also serious production declines in other branches of mining. In 1972, there was a 12 percent decrease in coal production, 15 percent in nitrates, 18 percent in iodine production, and 23 percent in iron output.[24]

The decline in sectoral output was reflected in figures on the total production of the economy. Thus, whereas the gross domestic product grew by 8.3 percent in 1971, it increased only 1.4 percent in the following year, which meant that the per capita gross domestic product decreased by 0.9 percent in 1972. When these global figures are disaggregated, they show that the income of the agricultural sector decreased by 6.7 percent in 1972, while the income of mining fell by 1.1 percent and construction dipped by 10 percent. At the same time, income of industry rose by 2.5 percent and that of services by 3.3 percent. Within the industrial sector, the income generated by producing traditional consumer goods fell by 1.1 percent and consumer durables income declined by 9.1 percent.[25]

Investments and labor productivity also declined. Investment figures during this period vary according to the source, but they all agree that investments fell during those years. During 1960-1970, the average investment coefficient of the Chilean economy was 17.4 percent. President Allende, in his last Annual Message to Congress in May 1973, reported that in the two previous years, this coefficient had been only 14 percent.[26] On the other hand, the Department of Economics of the University of Chile maintains that the rate of investment in 1971 was only 13.3 percent, while that of 1972 was only 12.4 percent.[27]

Official and unofficial estimates of what happened to investments during this period also disagree in percentage terms, but they do agree that investment declined. ODEPLAN at various times gave different figures for the decline in investments during 1971, ranging from 4.2 to 16 percent. The Department of Economics of the University of Chile, on the other hand, insisted that the decline in Allende's first full year had been 24 percent.[28]

Labor productivity also fell during the Allende regime. Thus, in the larger copper mining enterprises, output per man-day fell from 39 tons during 1966-1970 to 29 tons during 1971-1972.[29] The Economics Department of the University of Chile estimated that in the first six months of 1973, general labor productivity decreased by 6.1 percent as compared with the previous year, labor output in the production of goods, 9.1 percent, and the service sector, 3.6 percent.[30]

THE BALANCE-OF-PAYMENTS PROBLEM

The decrease in output contributed to the complete depletion of the country's foreign exchange reserves, as the result of a large increase in the value of the nation's imports and a substantial decrease in the income from exports. This balance-of-payments crisis in turn, contributed to the extensive shortages of goods during the last year of the regime.

Table 3 presents an overall view of the balance-of-payments situation from 1970 to 1973. During most of 1970, the Frei government was still in office, thus presenting a comparison with what occurred subsequently. The Allende regime was in power during almost three quarters of 1973.

TABLE 3

Overall Balance-of-Payments Situation (in millions of dollars)

Item	1970	1971	1972	1973
Exports of goods and services	1,254.7	1,086.0	963.7	1,194.5
Imports of goods and services	1,177.9	1,198.8	1,463.0	1,632.4
Commercial balance	78.3	− 110.4	− 497.8	− 436.4
Payments from abroad (invisibles)	57.0	35.9	24.2	10.0
Payments made abroad (invisibles)	211.2	125.7	141.0	39.4
Balance on current account	− 75.9	− 200.2	− 614.6	− 465.8
Net entry of autonomous capital	248.4	− 108.8	295.7	205.7
Balance of payments	155.3	− 309.0	− 318.9	− 260.1

SOURCE: Alberto Baltra Cortes, pp. 97, 100, 103.

These figures show that the major balance-of-payments problems during the first full year of the Allende regime, 1971, were the decline in export earnings and the substantial exit of capital. The decline in export earnings is explained by a fall in earnings from mineral exports-overall about 13.3 percent. Although about 23 percent of this fall can be attributed to a decline in copper prices, the declines are also noticeable in iron exports and amounted to 50 percent in nitrates and iodine exports. Industrial exports, mainly fish meal and fish oil, increased, and agricultural exports declined.[31] The figures on invisible payments to and from abroad reflect the flight of capital which took place during the first year of the regime. They also reflect the beginning of the reduction of amounts of short-term credit extended to the country by private foreign banks.

Total imports rose modestly during this first year, by only about $20 million. However, there was a dramatic shift in the nature of imports. Food products brought into the country rose by 117.5 percent during 1971, while machinery and equipment imports declined by 16.8 percent.[32]

During 1971, the main cause of the increase in food imports was likely the income redistribution program of the Allende regime. Since lower income groups in Chile still spend a great proportion of what they earn on food, their larger revenues resulted in their demanding more food, which under the circumstances, had largely to be purchased abroad. A big decrease in domestic agricultural production did not begin until the following year.

During the whole of the Allende regime, the agricultural situation undoubtedly contributed greatly to the country's balance-of-payments problem. Table 4 presents the decline in the percentage of consumption of various agricultural products which was met by Chilean agriculture in 1970 and 1973.

TABLE 4
Percentage of Consumption of Agricultural
Products Met by Internal Production

Product	Percent of Consumption Provided by Chilean Agriculture	
	1970	1973
Wheat	82	45
Rice	69	46
Corn	46	29
Potatoes	93	73
Refined oil	57	22
Sugar	55	37
Beef	75	57
Pork	93	57
Milk products	83	59

SOURCE: Alberto Baltra Cortes, p. 84.

The net result of the run on foreign exchange reserves during 1971 was to reduce them to only $32.3 million by December of that year. This was about one-tenth of the reserves left by the Frei government when it went out of office.[33]

In 1972, Chile's balance on current account deteriorated seriously. Exports fell 11.3 percent during the year; the additional decline of 1.5 percent in the price of copper during the year was responsible for only a small part of this decline. Export income from agricultural and industrial exports declined about one-third in each case, and the total value of mineral exports fell by 8.6 percent.

Simultaneously, there was an increase of 22 percent in imports. Most of this rise was accounted for by increases in agricultural products, transport equipment, and agricultural raw materials, such as cotton, leather, and wool. By this time, the decline in agricultural output was beginning to be seriously felt. Most of the imports of transport equipment were accounted for by material for the Santiago subway which was then under construction, as well as by buses and cars imported on credit from Brazil and Argentina. Industrial raw material imports declined by 12 percent, fuel by 7.6 percent, and replacement parts by 6.7 percent.[34]

Quite notable in the balance-of-payments picture for 1972 is the increase in autonomous capital. This reflects the postponement of payments to the Paris Club of $165 million, the payments agreement reached with U.S. private banks early in the year, and commercial credits extended by the Soviet Union and other countries.[35]

The figures for 1973 probably reflect the recovery in the price of copper during the early months of that year, as well as further credits the government obtained from a variety of different sources. Industrial exports continued to fall, by about 24 percent.[36]

Overall, Chile's balance-of-payments picture during the Allende period was one of large increases in foreign exchange expenditures on food and a significant decline in such expenditures on replacement parts and on manufactured goods. It also shows an overall decline in the value of goods and service exports, caused in part by a decline in copper prices in the first two years. Also responsible were the failure of the program launched by the Frei government to increase the volume of copper production to meet its targets, and a fall in the amounts and value of agricultural and manufactured exports. Within the first year, the period also saw a complete exhaustion of the country's foreign exchange reserves. Finally, during its last two years, the regime was making no payments of profits to foreign ex-owners of the copper mines or on the dollar debt to the United States.

SHORTAGES

Increases in the real income of lower income groups, production problems, and balance-of-payments difficulties all contributed to the development of acute shortages. Already noticeable by the middle of 1972, they had become notorious by the following year. These shortages created economic problems and intensified political conflicts.

There were shortages of all kinds. One of the first areas in which they became obvious was that of heavy consumer goods. By early 1972, the stores selling radios, television sets, refrigerators, and similar household appliances had virtually no inventories, their shelves and showrooms were empty, and customers seeking such goods were told that they would have to wait at least several months to receive delivery. By the middle of 1972, there were shortages of food, clothing, tobacco products, and most other light consumer goods. These shortages were dramatized by long lines outside of stores, or even in front of kiosks which received limited quantities of such goods from time to time.

It became necessary for housewives to stand long hours in line seeking the goods they needed for their families. It became a commonplace for a person to stock up on a product, even though he had a considerable amount on hand, in fear that when family reserves had been liquidated the product would no longer be available. People of all walks of life would buy larger or smaller amounts of their daily requirements from black marketeers who proliferated during the last part of the regime.

Much controversy has arisen concerning just who the black marketeers were. Supporters of the Unidad Popular insisted that they were principally businessmen who had lost their enterprises and who thus turned to the black market to earn a living—or even industrialists and merchants who still had their businesses, but refused to sell except at black market prices. On the other hand, the opposition insisted that the black market was organized largely by supporters of the government, having control as they did, through the Dirección de Industria y Comercio (DIRINCO) and other channels, of most of what was produced in and imported into Chile. There may be truth in both charges.

A particularly annoying shortage was that of replacement parts for motor vehicles, a shortage that idled a sizable part of the fleets of buses which served Santiago and other cities, as well as a large percentage of the country's taxis. As a result, the normally hectic task of getting from one part of the capital city to another became even more difficult.

Thus, shortages were general throughout the Chilean economy. A survey made by one chain of cooperative stores operating mainly in the poorer neighborhoods reported that at the end of 1972, about 2,500 of some 3,000 products for the home which were normally kept in stock could no longer be obtained.[37]

RATIONING

In the face of these shortages, President Allende was very reticent about establishing an open and formal system of rationing. Over and over, he insisted that he would never impose rationing on the citizenry. To the end he denied that there was a system of rationing. In fact, during at least the last year of the government a de facto rationing system did exist. It operated on at least two levels, that of the working-class areas and that of the middle- and upper-class parts of the cities.

By early 1972, the government's DIRINCO had control of a sizable part of the goods sold to the general public. Several of the major private whole-saling agencies were taken over by the regime, and DIRINCO thus had a major role in distributing not only imported goods but also nationally produced goods. Early in 1972, DIRINCO undertook to establish neighbor-hood committees, the so-called Juntas de Abastecimiento y Precios (JAP), the declared functions of which were "to assure adequate supplies, supervise price controls and struggle against speculation and monopolies." By the end of 1972, 1,500 of them were said to be in existence.[38]

Although no legislation was ever passed authorizing or even referring to the JAPs, they came to be regarded by the government as an integral part of the public administration. This was indicated quite early by President Allende, in his Second Annual Message to Congress in May 1972: "We are stimulat-ing the Juntas de Abastecimiento y Precios to collaborate with functionaries in the control of official prices and to assure supplies. These came into existence as a necessity among the masses to defend them from price goug-ing, from bad distribution, and from hoarding. It is an obligation of the Government to cooperate in their formation and development."[39]

Subsequently, the organization and coordination of the JAPs was of-ficially made part of the work of the Consejería Nacional de Desarrollo Social, the body in charge of the community organizations (neighborhood boards, mothers' clubs, and youth groups) originally organized during the Frei regime. Thus, a publication issued by the Public Relations Department of the Consejería described *abastecimiento* (supply) as one of the "areas" in which it functioned.

With the large tasks of change confronted by the Government of the Unidad Popular, an inescapable one is the problem of supply. For it, there are joined the forces of the institutions associated with economic and social development (Empresa Nacional de Distribución y Comercialización (DINAC), Direccion de Industria y Comercio and Consejería Nacional de Desarrollo Social and of the organized people.

There are two fundamental aspects of mobilization of the workers to participate in the creation of the Juntas de Abastecimiento y Precios (JAP) in the communities, and the creation of Centers of Supply.

The first will permit the assurance of a just distribution of consumers goods in terms of quality and official prices, and the second the creation of warehouses where they don't exist.

To the CNDS is allotted the role of mobilizing the masses (organizing, training, and publicizing the Program) for overcoming the problem.[40]

The JAPs operated primarily in working-class neighborhoods. They were firmly under the control of the Unidad Popular, and the popular belief at the time was that most of them were managed by the Communist party. They became the informal rationing instrument among the poorer sectors of the population. Through them families on the JAP lists were assured of a "market basket" of essential goods each week at controlled prices. The nature of the "market basket" rationing of the JAPs was indicated in January 1973 by Minister of Finance Fernando Flores. He stated that it consisted of "a quota of products necessary for the family. . . . which will be composed of sugar, rice, coffee, meat, coming to a total of about thirty products."[41]

The JAPs were among the instruments of the Allende government most feared by the opposition. There were frequent complaints that they were being managed politically, that families which did not support the Unidad Popular were not receiving the weekly allotments from JAPs. Most of the opposition was firmly convinced that the Unidad Popular intended to use the JAPs as a means of coercing the considerable element of the working class which did not support the Unidad Popular into switching its allegiance.

In the middle-and upper-class sections of Santiago and other cities, other informal rationing devices appeared. Many of these areas were served by consumer cooperatives, and starting in 1972 these generally closed their rolls to new members. At the same time, they sought to provide their members with a "market basket" similar to that provided by the JAPs, consisting of essential foodstuffs and other items at a reasonable price. Some private stores adopted similar measures.

Thus, although the Allende government never officially adopted rationing, with its concomitant books of coupons and other paraphernalia, de facto rationing did exist during the last year or more of the regime. This informal rationing system contributed to the political polarization in Chile.

THE INFLATION PROBLEM

The most spectacular aspect of the economic crisis was the inflation characterizing the last two years of the administration. Prices rose so rapidly during that period that Chile won the dubious honor of having the world's most rampant inflation.

As we have already noted, the rate of price increases was kept relatively under control during the first year of the regime. Thereafter it began to gather momentum, and during the last few months it was completely out of control.

September 1971 was the last month in which the rate of inflation declined. From then on, it gained speed with each passing time period. In contrast to the increase of only 22.1 percent in 1971, the rise in the price level in the following year was 163.4 percent, which was greatly in excess of the situation in the worst inflationary years in the past—1954 and 1955—when prices had gone up 72.2 percent and 76.2 percent respectively. Between January and August 1973, prices rose 150.5 percent, whereas between August 1972 and August 1973, they rose by 303.6 percent. While Allende was still in office, the Central Bank authorities estimated that the rate of inflation for the whole year 1973 would surpass 500 percent.[42] No other country in the world had in recent years had a comparable rate of increase in the general price level.

As Alberto Baltra has correctly pointed out, the official figures for the inflation rate tell only part of the story. They reflect "official" prices. However, during the last months of the Allende government, and in the face of the shortages rampant at the time, most Chileans bought on the black market a larger or smaller part of the goods they purchased. According to an estimate of the Department of Economics of the University of Chile, as cited by Baltra, black market prices were at least 30 percent higher than official ones.[43]

The government had no program at all to deal with the inflation problem. Why did such a high rate of price increase occur? Why didn't the government try to do something about it? The pages that follow will examine these two issues.

THE ROOTS OF INFLATION UNDER ALLENDE

The rapidly increasing government deficit and annual legal wage increases resulted in an increase in demand in the economy, while the decline in national output and the balance-of-payments situation reduced the supply of goals and services available in the economy.

Although government deficits had been chronic in Chile for several decades, during the Allende administration the budget deficit increased substantially, mainly as a result of the government's policies. During 1971, when the regime was buying out most of the country's banks and a variety of other enterprises, and paying cash for them, the government advanced large sums to the Corporación de Fomento and the Central Bank for this purpose. CORFO was reported to have spent 12 billion escudos in 1971 and 1972 and 170 billion escudos in 1973 on such purchases.[44] Once a large part of the economy had been taken over by the government, the firms involved generally lost money. Although quite a few of these enterprises had good production records, almost all of them had a disastrous financial history.

The deficits of the firms in the social area were financed by the national government through subsidies from the Central Bank. In 1972, the accumulated deficits of the social area amounted to 21,871 million escudos. In the following year, these deficits came to 175,600 million escudos, or almost nine times as much. This quantity compares with the regular government deficit of 148,400 million escudos.[45] Put another way, the total deficit of the firms in the social area by the end of the Allende regime (in terms of the exchange rate prevalent at the time Allende was overthrown) amounted to some $5 billion. This was equal to seven years' production of Chilean copper, at an average price of the years 1971-1973.[46]

In global terms, government expenditures rose from 22,100 million escudos in 1970 to 277,800 million escudos in 1973. The government deficit rose from 13 out of every 100 escudos spent in 1970, to 34 escudos of every 100 in 1971, to 40 per 100 in 1972, and finally was running at the rate of 53 escudos for every 100 spent by the time Allende was ousted.[47]

The spread of graft and corruption in the Allende years aggravated the situation. We have no exact figures, but there were widespread rumors of misuse of funds for personal gain by "interventors" in firms taken over by the regime and in other government dependencies. These rumors were not completely without foundation.

Another important factor in the inflation was the *reajuste*, or readjustment, of wages which was made at the beginning of 1972 and 1973. Wage increases in 1971 had relatively little inflationary effect because there existed a large amount of unused capacity which could be brought into production, thus increasing supply along with the rise in demand for products. This was not the case later, however. With full use of the available capacity, further wage increases pushed prices up instead of raising output.

The vastly increased government deficits and the officially granted wage increases greatly augmented the amount of money in circulation. Table 5 indicates the increase in the money supply during the Allende period.

TABLE 5

Increase in Money Supply (in millions of escudos)

Money Category	1970	1971	1972	June 1973
Total money supply	21,114	25,838	70,484	126,570
Money in private sector	10,068	21,487	54,111	92,185
Currency in circulation	7,928	21,213	57,002	120,101

Alberto Baltra (p. 70) defines these categories as follows: "The words *total money supply* include banknotes and coinage in free circulation, demand deposits of the private sector and current bank deposits of the public sector. The expression *money in private sector* includes the same items as the total money supply, minus the current bank deposits of the public sector. Increase in *currency in circulation* measures the fabrication of new currency, whether notes or metallic money."

SOURCE: Baltra, p. 69.

As the figures in Table 5 show, the total money supply increased 133.3 percent during 1971. The inflationary effect of this increase was mitigated by (1) a substantial increase in goods and services available during the year; and (2) a tendency, particularly on the part of the upper and middle classes and of some political opponents of the Allende regime, to hoard currency. These people did not spend what they hoarded on goods and services; many of them bought foreign currency, which helps explain the drain on foreign exchange in 1971.

The situation was far different in 1972. By that time, increases in goods and services had practically come to a halt, while the inflation itself discouraged people from holding money—instead encouraging them to get rid of it as quickly as possible. These tendencies intensified greatly during 1973, thereby stimulating an even greater increase in the general price level.

MOTIVATIONS OF THE ALLENDE REGIME

Some critics of the Allende regime have suggested that the inflation of that period was the result of a deliberate government policy. They argue that the government allowed prices to rise out of control in order to destroy the propertied class and effectively liquidate the capitalist system. There appears to be a better explanation, however, of why the Allende regime did so little about the problem. This explanation is to be found in the former associations of the people responsible for the government's economic policy.

Pedro Vuskevic, Allende's first minister of economy and the president's chief economic adviser throughout his years in office, had long worked for the Economic Commission for Latin America (ECLA). He belonged to the structuralist school of economics, which had largely originated in ECLA. A number of Vuskevic's associates in the Allende government had also worked with ECLA. The basic thesis of the structualist economists is that the economies of the Latin American countries require basic structural changes, such as agrarian reform. Furthermore, they believe that the problem of inflation, which is chronic in many Latin American countries, cannot be resolved without such structural changes.

In the mid-1960s, I discussed the problem of Brazil's inflation, which in 1964 was approaching 100 percent, with a number of Brazilian structuralists. These economists were very critical of the measures of the military government, and of its Minister of Planning Roberto Campos, to limit the inflation through "monetary" policies (i.e., cutting the government's budget, restricting credit, limiting wage increases). They offered me no immediate alternative to the Campos program, however. They unanimously argued that Brazil's inflation could not be curtailed until basic institutional changes had been made and therefore, would probably continue as it was for five or six more years.

Hence, the structuralist bias of Allende's economic advisers and policy may have caused them to discount inflation as a problem that could be dealt with in the short run. This thesis is reinforced by the fact that some of Vuskevic's friends, strong supporters of the Allende regime, tried to convince him of the need to bring price increases under control, but found him completely unreceptive. He insisted that inflation was a short-run problem that would disappear with the economic changes being created by the administration.

Apparently, some of the Allende regime's foreign economic advisers also warned about the danger of the mounting inflation. For instance, Edward Boorstein, an American economist of Marxist inclinations who had worked for the Castro regime in the early 1960s and who in 1973 was associated with the Chilean Central Bank, wrote a letter to the manager of the Central Bank, Jaime Barrios, in which he stated: "Apparently there are persons who think that there is something non-revolutionary about taking inflation seriously; that the monetary factor is not real, etc. But what will happen if we inundate the country with money will be very real. Something in the economy must give way." Boorstein's suggestions for counteracting inflation and the adverse balance of payments included cutting down the expenditures of Chileans sent abroad on government business; discrimination in the granting of periodic wage increases; and cutting the deficits of the firms in the social area. Boorstein ended his letter with the following advice: "The fight against inflation will be difficult. But, it is very important to conduct it to prevent inflation from making distribution difficult for us, causing us to lose control of the economy, or reversing the redistribution of income already achieved."[48]

LACK OF CENTRAL PLANNING

The Allende government made no serious effort to introduce economic planning, despite the fact that the Unidad Popular (and certainly the two major parties of the coalition) was pledged to the ultimate establishment of a so-called command economy, a system which substitutes a central plan for the market.

Alberto Baltra has described the lack of planning in the Allende period:

Even though it appears incredible, under the Government of the Unidad Popular the social area did not work in a planned fashion. There were planning and planners, but the plan remained on paper. The firms of the area were not submitted, therefore, to an authentic social decision, but functioned according to the knowledge and understanding of the *interventors*, lacking in knowledge and experience. There was no decision by society with regard to the proportion of resources which should be destined for investment, nor concerning the concrete forms the investment should take to achieve the objectives of development. As a consequence, there was lacking one of the basic elements of a definition of socialism: A social area without planning is like a capitalist enterprise without a management, or a person devoid of his will. It is confusion and chaos. Each interventor acted on the basis of his individual judgment, and in general, was anxious to fully use the benefits and advantages which fortune had given him. It is therefore not strange that efficiency and productivity fell vertically, to the prejudice of the country and of the consumers.[49]

The lack of central planning appears even more strange because the government had available the basic elements necessary for establishing an appropriate planning apparatus. ODEPLAN, the government's planning office, already existed when Allende took office. CORFO became a kind of holding company for the firms the government took over, except the banks and the copper mines, which were subject to the control of the Central Bank and the Corporación del Cobre (CODELCO), respectively. Furthermore, among the personnel of the Allende government were people with considerable experience with the techniques—if not the successful operation —of planning. Max Nolf, executive vice-president of CODELCO; Vladimir Arellano, director of the budget; Alberto Martínez, head of DIRINCO; and Jaime Barrios, director general of the Central Bank, had all worked for the Castro regime, as had Jacques Chonchol, the minister of agriculture. Both Vuskevic and his successor as minister of economy, Carlos Martus, had worked at length for ECLA, which had long advocated planning—although of a different kind from that attempted by the Castro government, to be sure.[50]

President Allende himself was aware of the need for planning and was committed to establishing it. In his First Annual Message to Congress, he emphasized "the urgency of establishing a system of planning which allots the economic surpluses to distinct productive tasks." He then sketched what the government was doing in that direction:

This year we have begun to structure this system, creating Advisory Organs such as the National and Regional Councils of Development; the 1971 Annual Plan has been formulated and during the rest of the year the planning organisms will elaborate the National Economic Plan 71-76. It is our intention that no investment project will be carried forward if it is not included in the plans that the Government will centrally approve. Thus we shall put an end to improvisation and we shall be organizing socialist planning, in fulfillment of the Unidad Popular program.[51]

Why then did the Unidad Popular make no serious efforts to institute general planning of the Chilean economy? Certainly one factor was the uncoordinated way in which the nationalization of the economy was proceeding. Very frequently, the government seized plants in response to pressure groups rather than in pursuance of a planned policy. Similarly, in agriculture the government's efforts to reorganize the rural sector in collective farms was to a large degree frustrated by the peasants' resistance, creating a diverse patchwork pattern in that part of the economy.

A second reason was the fact that the administration of enterprises seized by the state was apportioned on a political basis among the Unidad Popular parties. A species of fiefdom thus originated in the manufacturing and commercial parts of the economy, and each party's fiefdom was jealously guarded from encroachment by other parties. In some cases, workers of a plant—with or without outside advice and leadership—took over management of a particular firm. In any case, those in control of a state-owned enterprise were very loath to submit to any kind of "coordination" or direction from ODEPLAN, CORFO, or any other centralizing body.

The polarization of the political system during the Allende period may have been another reason. Polarization deprived the government of the services of economists and other technicians who under other circumstances might have been interested in establishing a planning apparatus.

In addition, the government was unwilling or unable to recruit planning experts from the Communist-controlled countries. In contrast, the Castro regime in the early 1960s relied very heavily on East European, particularly Czech, experts, as well as a number from Latin America.

The growing economic and political crisis itself made planning increasingly difficult. The scarcity of immediately available foreign exchange, the rampant inflation, declining productivity, together with the regime's failure at that time to crush the still militant political opposition, were hardly conducive to planning. Conditions changed so rapidly from one day to the next that it was almost impossible to lay down guidelines, let alone establish the kind of tightly administered central plan in which the left-wing Socialists and the Communist party believed.

Finally, the government's conflicting objectives contributed to the difficulties of introducing planning. The administration had started out with a massive redistribution of income, which from its point of view had positive political effects, as demonstrated in the municipal elections of April 1972. It was anxious to continue this redistribution process and did so in the *reajustes* of 1972 and 1973. At the same time, it wanted to increase production and productivity of the economy, and at various times it called upon the workers to sacrifice, in terms of working extra periods without pay and doing "voluntary" labor. There was a basic contradiction between these two objectives, but given the relatively free political atmosphere, the government was in no position to resolve this contradiction by imposing sacrifices in place of redistribution and enforcing the change by massive coercion —as Castro had been able to do in Cuba in the early 1960s. As a result, the workers, who for many decades had been schooled in the class struggle philosophy of the Socialists and Communists continued this struggle, even though, in theory at least, the mines, factories, and other enterprises were now "theirs." This situation led to declines in output and inflationary pressures, and impeded the effort to plan.

Similarly, in the countryside, the regime was caught in the contradiction between its desire to impose a collective pattern on agriculture and its promise to "give the land to those who till it." Again, the regime was in no position politically to forget completely its promise of land to the peasants, and to force them to accept collectivization as Castro had done in the previous decade.

ECONOMIC AND POLITICAL EFFECTS OF ALLENDE'S ECONOMIC POLICIES

After apparent successes during its first months, the UP government's management of the economy created the worst economic crisis in Chile's history. By the last months of its tenure, production was falling drastically in nearly every sector, foreign exchange reserves were all but exhausted (although in time the loans offered by foreign powers might have altered that situation), labor productivity was markedly down, and the country was in the grip of an inflation unmatched in the nation's history.

This crisis was not the result of deliberate administration policy. Rather, it was the result of the chaotic and often illegal way in which private enterprises were being shifted to the social area; the total discouragement of investment in, and even maintenance of, the property still held by private firms and individuals; the conflicting government objectives to redistribute income and expand the economy in which the economy was largely sacrificed to income redistribution; the decline in output caused by social conflict and mismanagement; and the increasingly convulsed political situation resulting from the government's unwillingness to compromise with the still majority opposition.

Whatever the causes of the economic crisis, its political effects proved catastrophic. The economic situation, particularly the shortages and the uncontrolled inflation, helped create the "prerevolutionary" atmosphere of the last weeks and months of the Unidad Popular government.

18

Organized Labor During the Allende Regime

The Allende regime considered itself to be a workers' government, the first such regime to have come to power in Chile. It pictured its programs as being peculiarly in the interest of the workers and as being designed especially for their benefit. It tended to characterize any attacks on its program or behavior as attacks on the workers themselves.

Unquestionably, the Unidad Popular regime's major support did come from the urban manual working class and one of the most powerful institutions backing the regime was the Central Única de Trabajadores, the country's chief central labor organization. The organized workers, however, did not unanimously support the government. The Christian Democrats had substantial influence in the unions belonging to CUTCh, and their influence was growing in the latter part of the Allende period. The Christian Democrats continued to have a larger following than the Unidad Popular among the rural organized workers.

The Unidad Popular's working-class constituency caused it many problems. The Allende regime had not been able to convince the workers that their position had improved to such a degree that they no longer needed their unions and the strike weapon. Nor was the labor movement led by the Unidad Popular able to exert the kind of leadership and discipline that might have given firm direction, particularly in some of the industrial areas of Santiago, to those workers in the last phases of the regime who had seized control of the plants in which they worked.

As a result, there was some chaos in the labor field, especially in the last months of the Allende period. Although the Movimiento de Izquierda Revolucionaria capitalized on the situation somewhat, the period was frequently characterized by an aimless spontaneity. Many groups of workers had a new feeling of importance and power, but they were unsure of what to do with this power and had no government direction on how to channel their energies and enthusiasms.

THE SIXTH CUTCH CONGRESS

One of the major labor events of the Allende period was the Sixth Congress of the CUTCh, held in December 1971. It met in Santiago and was attended by 2,500 delegates, claiming to represent 1,700 affiliated unions.[1] Also present were fraternal delegates from union groups in the USSR, Cuba, Rumania, Czechoslovakia, East Germany, Uruguay, France, Peru, and Venezuela.[2]

Luis Figueroa, the president of CUTCh, Hernan del Canto, its secretary general, and Serafín Aliaga, a representative of the World Federation of Trade Unions (WFTU), addressed the opening session. The main speaker was President Salvador Allende who gave an extensive defense of his administration, emphasizing that the firms the government had taken over and would take over for the social area would never be returned and that they would be operated for the benefit of the workers. He called for strong cooperation by the workers, in their own interest, and reiterated his government's intention of following a peaceful, democratic course. He also warned that if the opposition resorted to violence, the regime would respond not only with the law, but also with "revolutionary violence."[3]

The congress was completely dominated by parties of the Unidad Popular, particularly the Communists and Socialists, as was clear not only from the choice of speakers for the opening session, but also from the heavy representation of fraternal delegates from trade union groups of the Communist-controlled countries. Many delegates belonging to non-UP parties attended, as was shown when 400 delegates belonging to the Partido Demócrata Cristiano temporarily withdrew from the session. Other delegates belonged to far-Left groups outside the Unidad Popular. Some of their activities provoked Edgardo Rojas, vice-president of CUTCh, to comment that "in some of the plenary sessions there were frankly provocative and divisionist expressions by some declassed elements who seek to make difficult the process of unity of the workers." These elements, whom he identified as belonging to the Maoist Partido Comunista Revolucionario, "were definitively repudiated because the working class and people know that they have been working against the people in all of the battles that it has gained. For us, these elements are objectively counter-revolutionary and must be confronted, isolated and defeated by the people."[4]

While some delegates were openly hostile to the Unidad Popular in speeches and actions, the overwhelming tone of the congress was one of strong support for the government. Certainly this demonstration of support was one of the most important aspects of the congress.

Aside from its general expressions of support, the congress made two important decisions. One was to endorse the CUTCh leadership's agreement with the government concerning the annual wage readjustment to be granted early the following year. The second was that for the first time CUTCh officials would be chosen by a national election in which all dues-paying members would be free to participate. Previously, leaders had been elected at the congresses of the organization.[5]

CUTCH ELECTIONS

In conformity with the decision of the Sixth Congress, general elections were held within the central labor body to choose its new officials. Although they were first scheduled to be completed on May 30-31, 1972, the balloting actually was extended several days beyond May 31.[6]

The management of the election and the counting of the votes were in the hands of the National Electoral Commission, chosen on a political party basis. Seven groups were represented on this body. There were six members each from the Communist and Socialist parties, three each from MAPU, Partido Radical, and the Christian Democrats, and one each from the Izquierda Cristiana and the Frente de Trabajadores Revolucionarios, the trade union grouping of the far-Left Movimiento de Izquierda Revolucionaria. Six of the thirteen political parties which had lists of candidates in the poll were not represented.[7] Among these were the Unión Socialista Popular, the Partido Izquierda Radical, and the Partido Nacional.

The results of the CUTCh elections were not announced until a month and a half after the ballots were cast. This delay gave rise to many rumors. Various versions of the results were circulated, although it was generally agreed that the Communists, Socialists, and Christian Democrats had together polled over three quarters of the total votes cast and that at most a few thousand votes separated the standing of the three leading parties.

During these weeks, different tentative results were published. On July 1, 1972, the Christian Democratic newspaper *La Prensa* carried an editorial which said in part: "Nonetheless, as the recount of the votes progressed in the unofficial but trustworthy way which is usual in these cases, it began to be clear from the first instant that the Christian Democrats had triumphed in the person of their leader Ernesto Vogel." The Communists gave out a different version of the results. As early as the first week of June, they announced that they had received 31.5 percent of the votes, that the Socialists had gotten 26.6 percent, and that the Christian Democrats had received 26.3 percent.[8]

The results of the election were probably not announced early because of conflicts between Communist and Socialist members of the National Electoral Commission. Rumors were rife at the time that the Communists were willing to recognize the Christian Democrats as having come in second in the poll, which would have assured them the second post in the organization, that is, the secretary generalship. The Socialists, quite naturally, were not inclined to make any such concession.

The official results were finally made known on July 15. The official recount gave the Communists approximately 170,000 votes, the Socialists, 145,000, and the Christian Democrats, 144,000. Several other parties were reported to have received 25,000 each, and the MIR was credited with 10,000.[9] As a result, the Communist deputy Luis Figueroa was reelected president of CUTCh, the Socialist Hernan del Canto was chosen as secretary general, and the Christian Democrats received the first vice-presidency.[10] About half of the claimed 1 million members of CUTCh had not voted.[11]

Whatever negotiations may have preceded the announcement of the results, it was impossible to ignore the fact that the Christian Democrats had made a surprisingly good showing. They were conceded to have won a plurality in the CUTCh in Santiago, with 67,117 votes compared with the Communists' 54,042 and the Socialists' 53,756.[12] As a result of this victory, Christian Democratic trade unionist Manuel Rodriguez was chosen head of the Santiago Provincial CUTCh, and the Executive Council of the Santiago group was made up of twenty-seven Christian Democrats and fifteen opposed to the PDC.[13]

LEGALIZATION OF THE CUTCH

The CUTCh elections assumed more than usual importance because the Allende administration had been able to carry out its electoral promise to have legal recognition extended to the Central Única de Trabajadores. It was one of the few pieces of legislation the Allende administration was able to get through Congress; its passage was accomplished through the support of the PDC and even the Nacionales. Before passage of this legislation, the Chilean Labor Code had had little or no provision for legal recognition of labor organizations above the level of the local union. Thus, the law that was finally passed late in December 1971 represented a major modification of the Labor Code.

The issue of legal recognition for the CUTCh aroused little debate in itself, but it did provoke a number of controversies about related subjects. The Christian Democrats suggested (as they had not when they were in power) that the occasion be used for a general revision of the Labor Code. In addition to recognizing the CUTCh, they advocated recognition of other trade union groups—regional industrial unions, provincial federations of these unions, and national confederations by industry. They also urged that the law recognize the right of different groups of workers to establish competing unions on all levels of the hierarchy.[14] None of these proposals was ever passed as law.

There was considerable debate over the financing of the CUTCh. The original bill sent to Congress by President Allende provided for a checkoff system of dues for members of all organizations belonging to the CUTCh, with these dues being paid directly by the employers to the CUTCh, which would then distribute them on a pro rata basis to the affiliated organizations. The opposition rejected this part of the bill. They expressed fear that the CUTCh leadership would distribute the sizable funds that would accrue to it under such legislation in a politically partisan manner. At the same time, both government and opposition deputies rejected a Senate provision which would establish dues at from two-to five-tenths or 1 percent of a worker's wage, payable to the CUTCh, but permitting any CUTCh affiliate to exempt its members from payment of these dues. Luis Figueroa, Communist deputy and CUTCh president, argued that this provision would sow dissension in the unions, with affiliates opting out of paying dues to the CUTCh any time they were unhappy with its leadership.[15]

The government took other steps that did not require changes in the law. These included extending *personería juridica* (legal recognition) to two unions of government employees, the Agrupación Nacional de Trabajadores Semifiscales and the Agrupación Nacional de Empleados Fiscales. The same was done with two national organizations of white collar workers, the Confederación de Empleados de Industria y Comercio and the Confederación de Empleados Particulares.[16]

INTERNATIONAL RELATIONS OF THE CUTCH

As we have noted, the CUTCh was very close to the trade union movements of the Communist-controlled countries and to trade union groups in Latin America that were under Communist party influence. This relationship was indicated by the foreign delegations that attended the Sixth CUTCh Congress in December 1971. It was also demonstrated by the "trade union commercial agreement" signed by the largest white collar workers' organization, the Confederación de Empleados Particulares de Chile with the Union of Workers of State Commerce and Consumers Cooperatives of the Soviet Union early in 1973. This agreement was reportedly made in order "to develop fully international workers solidarity and to develop and apply to the maximum friendship and collaboration between the two national organizations."[17]

The CUTCh sought an even wider range of international relationships during the Allende period. For example, on the invitation of the CUTCh, a World Trade Union Assembly was convened in April 1973 in Santiago. It was reported that all three world trade union groups, the World Federation of Trade Unions (predominantly Communist), the World Confederation of Labor (Catholic), and the International Confederation of Free Trade Unions (Socialist-neutral-U.S. labor), had been invited, but only the first two had accepted the invitations. The opening session of the assembly was addressed by President Allende, who on the following day received the group at La Moneda. Other speakers at the inaugural meeting were Luis Figueroa, then serving as minister of labor, and Ernesto Vogel, the Christian Democrat who was then acting president of the CUTCh.[18] This meeting was called in order to raise the international prestige of the CUTCh and to rally wide international labor support for the Allende regime.

CUTCH FUNCTIONS IN THE ALLENDE PERIOD

The basic function of the CUTCh during the Unidad Popular regime was political, in a partisan sense, inasmuch as the central labor body performed a role that was more that of a political party or group of political parties than of a labor group. At the same time, it ignored the economic function it might have been expected to play.

The CUTCh was the principal institution used for mobilizing public displays of support for the Allende government, not simply on holidays like May Day, but whenever the regime found itself in a crisis—as when Christian Democratic leader Edmundo Pérez Zujovic was assassinated, or after the suppression of the *tancazo* revolt in late June 1973. On such occasions, the CUTCh and its constituent unions were called upon to mobilize their members and to assure their presence at meetings organized to demonstrate for the government. One might have expected that the Unidad Popular parties supporting the government would have been responsible for such activity, but the Unidad Popular never developed the necessary machinery to mobilize its members quickly for public purposes. Apparently, the Committees of the Unidad Popular, organized throughout Chile in connection with the presidential campaign in 1970, were originally intended to function in this capacity, but they withered away in the months following Allende's victory.

The CUTCh was used relatively little to mobilize workers on the economic level. It mounted no noticeable campaign among union members to convince the workers that they should modify their economic demands in order to give the government a chance to deal with its massive economic problems. Although there were fitful attempts to organize "productivity" campaigns, consisting of having union members work overtime or on weekends without extra pay, the CUTCh made no major effort along these lines. Indeed, such efforts received their principal backing from the Communist party; the Socialists and other groups represented in the CUTCh had little enthusiasm for them.

WORKERS' PARTICIPATION

One of the most interesting and important developments in the labor field during this period was the move to give the workers a voice in managing Chilean firms, particularly those in the social area. The Unidad Popular had promised worker participation during the 1970 campaign, and it became the subject of a great deal of discussion and action during the Allende period.

The first step in initiating a system of workers' participation was the signing in December 1970 of an agreement between the government and the CUTCh, which included the establishment of participation in the enterprises in the social and mixed areas. As a result of the agreement, a CUTCh-Government Working Committee was set up, which submitted a provisional document on the subject to the specially called Ninth National Conference of the CUTCh. The conference approved the Working Committee's document in general terms, after which it was forwarded to the individual CUTCh unions for their discussion and revision. By June 1971, a final agreement had been reached by the Working Committee and was submitted to President Allende and to the Executive Committee of the CUTCh. Both approved it. The Working Committee was then converted into an executive body, charged with putting the workers' participation mechanism into effect.[19]

The original Working Committee consisted of four members named by the CUTCh and five members representing the government. The government members were from the Ministry of Economy, Ministry of Labor, ODEPLAN and the government's vocational training program center (known by its initials as INACAP), as well as Pedro Gugliemetti, representing the Ministry of Economy and long-time head of the Labor Relations Institute of the University of Chile.[20]

During discussions preceding the official adoption of the plan for workers' participation, the role the trade unions should play in workers' representation was the most important subject of debate. The Communists maintained that the trade unions should become the organs of workers' participation and that the union leaders should sit on the bodies involved in the process. The Christian Democrats strongly opposed this idea, arguing that the trade unions should remain independent and that it should be incompatible for the same individual to hold a union post and a position on any of the organs of workers' participation. The Socialists supported this point of view.[21] The final document represented something of a compromise, since it provided that union officials could not sit on workers' participation bodies, but gave the unions a substantial role in organizing and maintaining the workers' participation structure.

The final document of the Working Committee, which served as the basis for the subsequent organization of workers' participation, was entitled *Normas Básicas de Participación de los Trabajadores en la Administración de las Empresas del Area Social y Mixta*. In its preamble, it noted that co-participation by workers in management of the economy had to go forward on two bases: participation in general decisions concerning management of the national economy, and participation on an enterprise level in decisions concerning management of the individual firm. The *Normas Básicas* contained provisions for both, although it dealt in most detail with co-participation on the enterprise level.

Each firm was to have workers' participation on two levels: the board of directors and the departments or sections into which a firm was naturally divided. The role of workers' representatives was to be substantially different on these two levels. It was provided that the board of directors should consist of five representatives elected by the workers and five named by the president of the republic or by the government institution to which the enterprise was subordinate, with a presiding officer also named by the president or the appropriate governmental organization (in most cases, CORFO). Each member was to have a voice and a vote. The board of directors was to have ultimate control of the enterprise, although the *Normas Básicas* indicated that it was expected to operate in conformity with the government's general plan for the economy. This last provision proved superfluous, since by the time it was overthrown, the Allende regime had not as yet developed any coherent national economic plan.

In the subdivisions of the enterprise, the *Normas Básicas* called for Production Committees to be chosen by the workers of that section. These committees were only to advise management rather than give actual direction.

The basic organ of co-participation was to be the Workers Assembly, "composed of the totality of the workers of the firm and . . . to be convoked and presided over by the Directorate of the union." In cases where more than one union existed in the firm, the assembly was to be called and be presided over by a delegation from the several unions.[22]

The Workers Assembly was to elect the workers' representatives on the board of directors, by "direct and secret vote" (p. 17); to control, censure, and if necessary recall those workers' representatives (p. 18); and to seek to resolve any disputes that might arise in the conduct of the enterprise. Three workers' representatives were to be manual workers, one an administrative worker, and one a technical-professional worker.

A Coordinating Committee of the workers of the firm was also set up. It was to consist of the five workers' representatives on the board of directors, the executive of the union, and a representative of each Production Committee. Its role was defined as "a) To give instructions to the workers representatives in the Board of Directors, in accord with the decisions of the Workers Assembly of the Enterprise; b) To propose ways to solve problems presented by representatives of the Production Committees, and c) To instruct these representatives to obtain better functioning of the Production Committees and their unity of action" (pp. 10-11).

Where a firm had more than one plant, there were provisions for similar organizations as those already described, in each plant, as well as organizations for the firm as a whole.

The role of the union within this structure of co-participation was spelled out, albeit in somewhat vague terms. It was provided that "the trade union organization of the firm has the responsibility for directing and orienting in an organized, effective and creative way, the participation of all the workers of the firm, as the fundamental condition for assuring the revolutionary transformations which will open for us the road to the establishment of socialism in Chile" (p. 19).

With regard to participation of the workers in general planning and management of the economy, the *Normas Básicas* stated:

To make this power effective, the workers are integrated through the representatives of the Central Única de Trabajadores and of the Federations and Confederations, in the higher organs of national, regional and sectoral planning and development Councils, the Regional Development Councils, ODEPLAN, Sectoral Development Committees, Ministries and others. There the workers make known their positions, which represent the general interests of all the workers of the country, participation in a real and effective form in the planning of development, which subsequently will be applied in the firms in the form of production plans and programs (p. 2).

The *Normas Básicas* made transitory provisions for the establishment of workers' participation. The first step was to set up in each enterprise a Joint Committee of workers and management which would draw up the Internal Regulations of the Enterprise. Only after such regulations had been agreed upon would the various organs of co-participation be established.

ESTABLISHMENT AND PROGRESS OF WORKERS' PARTICIPATION

By the end of 1971, considerable progress had been made in establishing workers' participation in the firms under government control. The National Government-CUTCh Committee on Workers' Participation reported that the system had been fully established in virtually all the seized textile plants. In only a few other enterprises, in mining, the metal industry, and chemicals had the process been fully completed, although it was underway in all other state-controlled firms.[23] By the end of the Allende regime, the system had been established in almost all government-controlled enterprises.

The process of establishing and implementing the system of workers' participation did not go entirely smoothly. It was extensively criticized by workers and by outside observers, particularly by those to the Left of the UP. One example of such criticism is given by two U.S. left-wing observers, James and Eva Cockroft, in their comments on the operation of co-participation in the Fabrilana textile plant, previously part of the Yarur enterprises:

In practice, Fabrilana workers found there were many faults in this system of workers' participation. Each production committee tended merely to raise demands relevant to its own action, without considering the need for national planning and coordination. Some union and government representatives tended to have a top-down attitude that merely confronted production committees with production norms, that is, incorporating the workers into a battle of production without genuine worker participation at the section level in the decision making process. Fabrilana workers found that it was at the level of the Coordination Committee of Workers where these problems had to be hammered out—and were.[24]

Another example comes from the May 23, 1972, issue of the far-Left Chilean weekly *Punto Final.* It quotes the comments of Hugo Vicencio, a worker in the SUMAR textile plant and a member of MAPU, on the positive and negative aspects of workers' participation:

The positive is to understand that we can direct industry. And that was what they told us when the intervention took place. But it isn't so. The organs of participation don't fulfill the function which they have on paper. There is a sensation of frustration in the plant, we all have it. We are asking loudly for direct workers' control in this plant. Here we only know that we must produce, but we don't know how sales are conducted, what is distributed, what is done with the profits.

A third example involves a striking group of while collar workers in the Hirmas textile plant. The leader of their union demanded "real participation" and explained that in spite of the presence of five workers on the board of directors, "here in this textile plant, there is always a tie and the one that decides finally is the interventor named by the Government. Therefore, we have no way effectively of presenting our positions."[25]

Andy Zimbalist and Barbara Stallings, writing in the *Monthly Review* of October 1973, have given an interesting assessment of the workers' participation program:

There is a clear tendency for those factories with PC [Communist party] administrators (the administrators are appointed by the government according to a party quota system) to be more rigid and top-down in their management and to be less developed with respect to workers participation. As a broad estimation, it would seem that of the 320-odd state firms, the formal participation structure is functioning in approximately 170, and a genuine workers involvement and consciousness in decision-making is present in some 35 enterprises.[26]

CAUSES OF DIFFICULTIES WITH WORKERS' PARTICIPATION

Problems arose with workers' participation first because of the high degree of politicization of the situation in the government-operated enterprises. Second, in many cases the workers did not have the feeling that the firms were now "theirs." These two factors were undoubtedly interrelated, but for analytical purposes they can be dealt with separately.

Elsewhere in this book it is noted that the Allende government apportioned the post of interventor in intervened or requisitioned factories on a partisan political basis, assigning a given number of such posts to each of the parties in the Unidad Popular coalition. Given the intense rivalry and competition among these parties, workers of particular party affiliations were frequently unhappy with the interventor in their plant because he belonged to a different party. This situation was intensified when jobs in intervened plants were also made available on a party-line basis. For instance, *Punto Final* reported that one of the sources of unhappiness of workers in the SUMAR Algodon textile plant was this system of assigning jobs. It noted that 350 new workers had been taken on after the government seized the plant and that these had been selected on a party quota basis. The magazine quoted Hugo Vicencio, a MAPU-affiliated worker in the plant, as saying: "We want to end the quota. Not only members of the Unidad Popular have the right to work. This cannot continue in this way."[27]

It can also be supposed that in cases where the workers' representatives belonged to parties of the opposition (most often the Christian Democratic party), they might be on guard against attempts by the UP-controlled management to discriminate against them in favor of their opponents. This may well have been the root cause of at least some of the difficulties in the country's largest copper mine, Chuquicamata. There the PDC had four of the six posts on the workers' side of the Joint Committee which established the co-participation program, the other two being a member of the Partido Nacional and of the Partido Izquierda Radical.[28]

Furthermore, to be effective, workers' participation had to create a sense among the workers involved that they really did have a major input into the decision-making process of the enterprise. *Punto Final* reporter Lucia Sepúlveda's interview with the interventor in SUMAR Algodon, Jaime Cre, a member of MAPU, suggests at least two reasons why such a sense had been slow to develop in the plant he had taken over three weeks before. Cre suggests that co-participation had produced too little a change in the attitude of the plant's administrative personnel. "Here," he said, "there reigns a paternalistic pattern. All problems end up in the office of the administrator, because the rank and file have no power. The bureaucracy functions on the same system. To solve this, participation must become part of the system. Experience has also shown that pressure hastens solutions."

As another aspect of the problem, Cre cited the workers' lack of preparation for co-participation. After noting that the Production Committees often tried to give orders to the administrators instead of advising them, he stated: "All that took place because there was no training of the workers for participation, they weren't given the information. A worker gets nothing from being on the board of directors if he doesn't even know what a balance sheet is. Then he can go there only to listen."[29]

THE WORKERS' ENTERPRISES

As an alternative to the workers' participation scheme, the Christian Democrats suggested a proposal labeled "Workers' Enterprises," which would turn over full control to the workers in state-controlled firms. The idea was elaborated in a pamphlet published by the Trade Union Department of the Christian Democratic party in April 1972. Senator Renán Fuentealba, then the PDC president, summed up the idea by saying that in the social area of the economy "the use and enjoyment of the property—regardless for this purpose of whose property it is—belongs to the workers, who have the administration and are owners of the profits, although paying interest or rent on the capital."[30]

The possibility of establishing such Workers' Enterprises was a major subject of discussion between the Christian Democrats and President Allende and other UP leaders at the time of the negotiations between the two sides in June 1972. Early in these negotiations, President Allende was reported by the Christian Democrats to be favorably disposed to the idea.[31] However, no final agreement was reached in these negotiations, and so the issue remained in abeyance.

The UP leaders were very critical of the Workers' Enterprise concept. The basis of their criticism was presented in the June 16, 1972, issue of *Chile Hoy*, a pro-Unidad Popular magazine.

Now Unidad Popular doesn't attempt only to statize; it doesn't attempt to transform the State into the employer. If this had been its intention it would have been enough that the expropriated firms pass into the hands of the State. Unidad Popular wishes the workers of the social area to run their enterprises, but not in the function of the particular interests of the group but in function of the interests of all society and in accordance with a general planning of the economy. The CUT has insisted that the workers must have the role of protagonist in this process, not only in direction of enterprises, but also in economic and political direction of the country. However, we must recognize with honesty that, as the song says, between what is said and what is done there is a wide chasm. The process of workers participation has not been carried out with sufficient vigor, audacity and necessary creative initiative. And this weakness of ours has served as the basis for the weeping of the Christian Democracy and its propaganda against the government (p. 15).

ROLE OF THE LABOR MOVEMENT

One of administration's most serious errors of judgment was its failure to use the CUTCh, and the labor movement in general, to obtain the economic backing it needed. It might have been expected that the Communist and Socialist leaders of the CUTCh would have concentrated on changing the attitude of the workers, particularly in the nationalized enterprises. Although for decades these parties, and the trade union movement in general, had had an "economistic" attitude towards workers' demands, the Communists, Socialists, and other Unidad Popular labor leaders should have tried to tone down such demands under the Allende government.

Only a few attempts in this direction were made. For instance, in May 1971 the National Directive Council of CUTCh issued a widely distributed pamphlet entitled *Call of the CUT to the Workers*, which sought to alter workers' attitudes. The pamphlet called on the workers "to study the installed capacity of each firm and propose new shifts of workers where that is necessary, so as to incorporate more workers in industries, and to absorb unemployed workers." It also urged that "the elaboration of Lists of Demands, study ahead of time the financial capacity of each firm: production, sales, cost of the demands and the consumer price index in the year of the renovation of the collective agreement."[32]

The labor leadership, however, seems to have made little sustained effort to persuade the workers to follow this advice. The Communists did conduct propaganda in favor of workers trying to get greater productivity, but the Socialists tended to be hostile to such ideas, and the Communists were not willing to take serious political risks in attempting to change worker attitudes.

Hence, the labor movement was of little help to the administration in controlling the increasingly difficult economic situation. Its contribution to taking the country down "the Chilean Road to Socialism" was largely limited to the political arena.

LABOR CONFLICTS UNDER ALLENDE

Many strikes were called during the Allende administration, despite the regime's wide base of support among the organized workers. Or perhaps it was true *because* of that support, with workers insisting that the government treat them better than they thought they had been treated by previous administrations.

The walkouts of the Allende years can be divided into two types: (1) strikes whose real purpose was to provide the government with an excuse to intervene the enterprise involved; and (2) strikes that were economically motivated and that mostly occurred in firms which had already been nationalized. It is the latter with which we are dealing here.

Although at least one of the economic walkouts was of major political importance, and many of them were a severe inconvenience to the administration, there was no instance of large-scale clashes of striking workers with police and soldiers such as had taken place in virtually every previous government. This was undoubtedly the result of Allende's policy of not using the police or armed forces to end strikes or even seriously curtailing or controlling most of them.

Walkouts occurred in the most varied sectors of the economy. A few took place in the intervened textile enterprises. Other strikes of some significance included the following: coal miners in July 1971;[33] maintenance-of-way workers on the railroads, out for almost two months in mid-1971;[34] merchant marine captains, January 1972;[35] workers in Mapocho railroad station in Santiago, July 1972;[36] employees of the General Directorate of Commerce and Industry, September 1972;[37] mechanics of LAN-Chile airline, September 1972;[38] medical and technical personnel of Curicó hospital, November 1972;[39] construction workers building the Santiago Metro, December 1972;[40] and workers of Petrodow Chemical Company, October-December 1972.[41]

Most serious, however, were the frequent strikes in the copper mining industry. Most of these walkouts were carried out by groups of workers in one part or another of the major mines, without necessarily stopping all production of the enterprises. But some of the strikes did involve the complete closing down of one or another of the large mines. Again, we may give a few examples, which by no means exhaust the list of major walkouts in the copper mining industry: in August 1971, a walkout over wage issues in the El Salvador mine, the country's third largest;[42] and Chuquicamata, the largest mine, struck in May 1972 when workers demanded, among other things, "real participation" in management.[43]

In October 1972, President Allende announced that there had been thirty-two work stoppages in Chuquicamata alone in the previous two years and that these had cost the country over $14 million in copper exports. He pleaded for the workers to be more conscientious.[44] Several months later, an incoming minister of mines, Pedro Felipe Ramírez of the Izquierda Cristiana, announced his intention of imposing "new discipline" on the workers in the copper mines.[45]

None of the exhortations, and even threats, of the government really changed the labor situation in the copper industry. The most serious strike of all in that industry took place less than six months before the end of the Allende government and further undermined the political position of the regime. This was the walkout of the miners of El Teniente, the second largest mine, near the city of Rancagua, some sixty-five miles south of Santiago. The question at issue in this strike, which began in April 1973 and lasted for more than two months, was that of wages.

The El Teniente strike was called because of the annual wage readjustment law of 1973, passed in October 1972. That law had provided for a wage increase equivalent to the cost of living rise in the previous year. It also contained a clause providing that any increases workers had won through collective bargaining during the year should be deducted from the general wage rise. For about three decades, the El Teniente miners had had a clause in the collective contract which provided for monthly wage adjustments in conformity with the rise in the cost of living. They argued that the October 1972 law was not intended to negate their long-standing *conquista*. When the government interpreted it as doing so and gave them a wage rise that took into consideration what they had received through their contract, the workers struck.[46]

This walkout presented the Allende government with a crisis. The union involved was led largely by Socialists, so it could not be claimed that it was part of a subversive movement. On the other hand, the strikers were adamant and sent a delegation to Santiago to confer with the president. The delegation was given a lively and friendly reception by the opposition, which took every advantage of using the incident to "prove" the infidelity of the Allende government to its claims of working for labor.

The walkout was finally settled by a compromise. The government conceded the wage increase which the El Teniente strikers were demanding. For their part, the miners agreed that this was a one-time concession and that, henceforward, their collective agreement would have to conform to overall government economic policy.[47]

19

Foreign Relations of the Allende Regime

The relations of the Allende regime with the United States were difficult (as will be discussed in Chapter 20), and so the UP government sought to strengthen Chile's association with other nations of the hemisphere. It also extended diplomatic and other contacts with Communist-dominated regimes in Europe, Asia, and America, and cultivated close relations with Western Europe, particularly countries with Social Democratic governments.

RELATIONS WITH OTHER LATIN AMERICAN COUNTRIES

Contrary to all expectations, Chile's first Marxist-Leninist regime had surprisingly good relations with most of the other Latin American republics, regardless of their ideologies.

When the Allende regime came to power, there was some fear that its existence might imperil the Andean Group, the bloc formed in the late 1960s by Venezuela, Colombia, Ecuador, Peru, Bolivia, and Chile to establish a common market within fifteen years. Progress towards this goal would inevitably involve limitations on the national sovereignty of the co-operating countries, which some felt the Allende regime would interpret as a limit on its program to alter the Chilean economy.

Such a break in the Andean Group never occurred. The Peruvian government, a military dictatorship headed by General Juan Velasco, was itself conducting a vast reform program and felt a kinship with the Allende regime. Although several other governments of the Andean Group had reservations about Chile's UP government, they were careful not to allow such reservations to interfere with their relations with the Allende regime.

Allende supported the objectives of the Andean Bloc, as he made clear in his introduction speech to the Third Meeting of the United Nations Conference on Trade and Development in April 1972: "The Andean Pact, authentically Latin American, is of vital importance not only because of the technical pragmatism with which we are tackling problems as they arise, but also because we are conducting an autochthonous experiment in integration, based on the most absolute respect for ideological pluralism and for each nation's legitimate right to adopt whatever internal structures it may deem appropriate."[1]

The Allende government's representatives participated in drawing up two important new agreements elaborating on the basic Andean Pact. One was an accord on double taxation, known as Decision No. 40, and the other was the highly controversial Decision No. 24, covering the question of a joint policy on foreign investment.

According to the *Alliance for Progress Weekly Newsletter* of January 17, 1972, the double taxation accord, Decision No. 40, provided for the following: "The signatory governments will levy taxes on individuals and corporations on that part of their income that is actually generated within a given territory. Any other income—from profits, capital gains, interests, salaries, wages, dividends, participation sales—originating in another country of the Group will be taxable where such income is collected or paid out."

Decision No. 24, negotiated within a few weeks after the Allende government came to power, imposed severe limitations on the conditions under which foreign firms might invest in the Andean Group countries, forbidding such investments entirely in a number of sectors.[2]

Allende made personal contact with most of the leaders of the Andean Group countries. During his trip outside the country in December 1972, he made short stops in Peru, Ecuador, and Colombia.

In February 1973, President Rafael Caldera of Venezuela, a Christian Democrat, stopped briefly in Chile during a swing through Latin America. He was met at the Pudahuel Airport by President Allende, who was accompanied by leading figures of the Unidad Popular as well as by ex-President Eduardo Frei and other Christian Democratic leaders. Allende and Caldera conferred at some length in the Presidential Suite at the airport. In an interview with Chilean and foreign journalists, Caldera affirmed that "I wanted in the name of Venezuela to express my solidarity with Chile in whatever situation or circumstances."[3]

Relations were particularly close between the Allende regime and that of President Luis Echeverría of Mexico. Echeverría attended the United Nations Conference on Trade and Development (UNCTAD) in Santiago in April 1972, and in his address to that meeting he praised Chile's nationalization of copper, comparing it with Mexico's nationalization of the oil industry in 1938. Before leaving, the Mexican president signed a joint communique with Allende "calling for closer relations between Mexico and the Andean Group, reaffirming the right of nations to control their natural resources and condemning economic or political pressures by any nation to prevent another from transforming its own internal structures."[4]

Several months later, during his trip abroad at the end of 1972, President Allende made a special point to visit Mexico. He was received by President Echeverría and expressed his thanks both for the solidarity Mexico had demonstrated towards his regime and for the economic help it had offered.[5]

Relations with the government of Bolivia changed during the Allende regime. From the time Allende took office until August 1971, Bolivia's President was General Juan José Torres, who was closely allied with the far Left, including Moscow and Maoist Communists, Trotskyites, and other extremist groups. The Torres and Allende regimes had good relations. However, in August 1971 General Torres was overthrown by a civilian-military coup led by Colonel Hugo Banzer, supported by the country's two major parties, the Movimiento Nacionalista Revolucionario and Falange Socialista Boliviana. General Torres took temporary refuge in Chile, and later went to Peru; a number of other figures prominent in the Torres regime stayed in Chile.

Tupamaro guerrillas from Uruguay and leftist figures from Brazil also sought sanctuary in Chile during the Allende regime. Not all of those who sought refuge in Chile were extremists, however.

After Allende was overthrown, there was much adverse comment about the large number of political refugees that had gathered in Chile during the UP government. Whatever violence and subversion a small percentage of these exiles may have engaged in, however, the Allende government was not violating Chilean tradition in opening the frontiers to political exiles from neighboring countries. From the middle of the nineteenth century, when Domingo Sarmiento and Alberdi took refuge in Chile from the oppression of the Rosas regime in Buenos Aires, Chile had been hospitable to those fleeing from tyranny in other Latin American countries.

Allende also sought, and obtained, good relations with nonreformist regimes. Particularly notable was his friendship with the military president of Argentina, General Alejandro Lanusse, who came into office early in 1971. On July 23 and 24, 1971, Allende met Lanusse in the Argentine city of Salta. This was the first time Allende had left Chile since becoming president. The occasion for the Salta meeting was the ratification of a recently completed agreement to settle a long-standing border dispute. This dispute had plagued relations between the two countries for almost seventy-five years and had sometimes led to armed conflicts. The agreement, dealing with the Beagle Channel, provided the basis of arbitration by the queen of Great Britain.[6] Further negotiations resulted in an accord in April 1972 to submit any pending disagreements to the International Court.[7] The Lanusse government later extended credits to the Allende government amounting to $100 million.[8]

After the fall of Allende, there were extensive rumors that the military regime of Brazil had been involved in the plotting that led to his overthrow. If this was indeed true, it was very strange behavior, for the Brazilian regime had given Allende substantial economic aid. On June 14, 1972, the Chilean government announced that it had received credits of $108 million from Brazil, Mexico, Colombia, and Peru, with Brazil making the largest contribution.[9]

RELATIONS WITH THE COMMUNIST COUNTRIES

In its program, the Unidad Popular had promised to establish relations with "all countries," which in the context meant particularly those Communist regimes with which Chile did not then exchange diplomatic missions. The Allende government carried out this promise.

On January 5, 1971, the Chilean government announced establishment of diplomatic relations with the People's Republic of China. On June 1, 1972, relations were also established with the governments of North Korea and North Vietnam. Later, China and North Korea extended substantial economic aid to Chile.[10] On September 11, 1971, diplomatic relations were established with Albania,[11] and on November 12, 1970, diplomatic ties were also renewed with the Castro government of Cuba.[12]

The Unidad Popular government made extensive efforts to extend its contacts with the Communist regimes considerably beyond mere diplomatic recognition and exchange of embassies. A mission headed by Foreign Minister Clodomiro Almeyda visited the Soviet Union and Eastern Europe in May 1971 to express solidarity with the regimes there and to seek economic help from those countries.[13] In December 1972, President Allende himself visited Moscow, where he was received by Communist party Secretary Leonid Brezhnev, as well as by President Podgorny and Prime Minister Kosygin. After Allende's departure, the Soviet leadership promised continuing support of the Allende regime.[14]

In January 1973, Foreign Minister Almeyda, who in the early 1960s had been the leader of a pro-Maoist faction in the Socialist party, made a visit to China. On this occasion, the Chilean Ministry of Foreign Affairs issued a communique, which said in part:

The presence of Foreign Minister Almeyda in the Peoples Republic of China has a double purpose. On the one hand, this official visit is designed to give evidence of the existing consensus between both countries on various political matters. Chile has the honor of having been the pioneer country within the Latin American system to establish diplomatic relations with the Peoples Republic of China, in an act which marked the independent character of the foreign policy of the present Government. Also, our country maintained with special energy the need to admit the Peoples Republic of China to the United Nations to give that world organization an effective representation which contributes to strengthening real dialogue. On the other hand, it has sought to increase existing commercial relations, using to the maximum the existing instruments of economic contact between the two countries.[15]

Relations with North Korea were said to be particularly close. Visits were exchanged between various groups in the two countries. The North Korean visitors entered into contact not only with the Chilean government, but also with the major parties participating in it. On one occasion, a group of North Koreans visited the headquarters of the Socialist party and was received by the party's secretary general and other leaders.

RELATIONS WITH THE CASTRO REGIME

The government with which the Allende regime probably had the closest relations was that of Castro. Allende had been an early and persevering supporter of Castro. He had made various trips to Cuba; he had sacrificed his long-time friendships with leaders of the democratic Left in Latin America to maintain that with Castro; and he had been the president of the Chilean national committee of the "little Comintern" which Castro had organized in 1967, the Organización Latino Americana de Solidaridad (OLAS).

The Unidad Popular had pledged to reestablish diplomatic relations with the Castro regime and to contribute as much as possible to ending the embargo on Cuba imposed by the Organization of American States. Allende moved quickly after taking office to carry out these pledges, recognizing the Cuban government on November 12, 1970, and pushing within the OAS for an end to the embargo. During the nearly three years of the Allende government, modest trade relations developed between Chile and Cuba. Visits were even exchanged between their military leaders.

A high point in relations was Castro's visit to Chile in November-December 1971. Castro arrived on November 10, 1971, accompanied by Armando Hart, organizing secretary of the Cuban Communist party; Pedro Miret, Cuban minister of mining; and Major Arnaldo Ochoa, army commander of Havana. He was received by President Allende, accompanied by the comptroller general of the republic, the commanders of the three armed services and of the Carabineros, the cardinal archbishop of Santiago, and representatives of the Unidad Popular parties.[17]

Castro stayed in Chile for almost a month. He first traveled to the north, visiting the city of Antofagasta and the copper and nitrate mining centers.

He then went with President Allende on an extended trip to the southern part of the country, visiting not only the cities of the Central Valley, but also Patagonia and Tierra del Fuego in the far south.

The Castro visit was remarkable for its length. The opposition newspaper *El Mercurio* reported that "the international practice is a period of two or three days for offical visits of Chiefs of State or Chiefs of Government, aside from the possibility that the guests may continue their visit on a private basis for purposes of rest."[18] Castro got little rest during his stay in Chile: he was traveling and speaking almost every day.

Certainly, Castro's prime motivation for his visit to Chile was to demonstrate to the rest of Latin America and to the world in general that the boycott of Cuba and the isolation of the Castro regime in the Western Hemisphere had been broken. However, a few days' stay would have been time aplenty to make this clear.

From Allende's point of view, Castro's visit would lend political support to Allende himself. Such a demonstration of backing was much more important in terms of its impact on those to the Left of the Unidad Popular and on the more restless members of the UP itself than on the opposition. The importance of this aspect of Castro's visit was underscored by *Intercontinental Press*, a Trotskyite New York periodical, which was highly critical of what it deemed to be the timidity and "reformism" of the Allende regime.

Castro's position is extremely delicate. He is caught between his need to expand his relations with the Unidad Popular government and the risk of disavowing his most fervent supporters, in this case the MIR.

From reading his initial statements, it seems that the "Comandante en Jefe" has made a decision. His declarations about "superrevolutionary impatience," his appeals to the workers in the Maria Elena saltpeter mine to "moderate" their wage demands, his statements in the Chuquicamata copper mine, calling on the workers to put the national interest first and not block expanding production by untimely work stoppages, are quite clear. They are appeals for discipline and unity behind the Allende government, and for the demobilization of economic movements outside the framework of the Unidad Popular organizations.[19]

On one or two occasions, Castro had public discussions with MIR representatives, particularly at the University of Concepción. He urged them to support the Allende regime, and not to cause it problems, and he constantly reiterated his support for the Allende government. Thus, during his visit to Antofagasta early in his trip, he commented: "We like the Chilean process. We have never had contradictions with the Chilean government. This doesn't mean that our policy has changed. We arrive at socialism by different paths, but the final objective is the same."[20]

There is little evidence that Castro succeeded in modifying the policies of the MIR and other extreme Left groups. They certainly did not desist from their illegal occupations of land, buildings, and other properties, and they only modestly, if at all, modified their criticisms of the Allende administration.

From some points of view, Castro overstayed his welcome in Chile. Although during the first few days of his visit, large crowds would turn out to see the legendary leader of the Cuban Revolution, during the last part of his stay his presence was hardly noticed by those who were not directly involved in his activities. He was no longer a novelty. Only 20,000 people turned out for his final speech in the National Stadium in spite of intensive efforts to turn out a large crowd.[21] The stadium had a capacity of 80,000.[22]

Rank-and-file Chileans, even some who generally supported the Allende regime, resented Castro's frequent comments on the Chilean situation, as well as his frank and frequent advice to Allende and the UP. A similar resentment had been engendered twenty years earlier when President Juan Perón had made a visit and had undertaken to give advice to President Carlos Ibáñez and his followers.

In December 1972, Allende returned Castro's visit, stopping for four days in Havana on his way back from the Soviet Union.[23]

RELATIONS WITH WESTERN EUROPE

President Allende, and at least some of his supporters, sought to gain the sympathy and support of the West European countries. Early in the regime, an economic mission dispatched to that part of the world to seek financial aid had considerable success.

Allende also sought political and diplomatic support in Western Europe. He especially desired the backing of the Social Democratic and Labor parties, an effort facilitated by the fact that his party was called the Socialist party and that the West Europeans knew little if anything about Latin American or Chilean politics.

An official invitation to Allende's inauguration was sent to the Socialist International, an organization that includes the Socialist and Labor parties of Western Europe, as well as affiliates in Canada, the United States, Jamaica, and several countries of Asia. Hans Janutschek, the secretary of the Socialist International, headed an official delegation which took part in the celebration of Allende's accession to power.[24] Subsequently, Janutschek consistently published articles in the International's periodical picturing Allende and his government as Chilean counterparts of the democratic Socialist parties and governments of Western Europe.

The Swedish Social Democratic government of Olav Palme was very well disposed towards the Allende regime. The Palme government made two economic aid agreements with the Allende government, which, unlike many of the other aid programs given the Chileans, were not tied to specific projects. Rather, money was given to be freely spent as the Allende government saw fit.[25]

The democratic Socialist and liberal opinion in Europe generally accepted the version of his regime which Allende gave them. This to a large degree explains the subsequent mistaken portrayal of Allende as a martyr to an attempt to carry out democratic reforms leading to a democratic economy, society, and polity.

THE UNCTAD MEETING

One of the highpoints of the regime's foreign relations was the holding of the Third Meeting of the United Nations Conference on Trade and Development in Santiago in April 1972. The first two meetings of UNCTAD had been held during the 1960s in Geneva and New Delhi respectively.

The Allende government made extensive preparations for the meeting. With financial help from the government of The Netherlands, it constructed a new skyscraper on the main street of Santiago, the Alameda, a few blocks from the presidential palace, to serve as headquarters for the meeting. It was later converted into a government office building, and after September 1973, when the presidential palace La Moneda was partly destroyed during the coup against Allende, it became the seat of the presidency.

The UNCTAD session began on April 13, 1972. President Allende delivered the opening speech, at considerable length, in which he called for unity of the so-called Third World, denounced foreign investment as seriously hampering the development of the underdeveloped countries, praised the progress of the Andean Group, and outlined his program for Chile.[26]

20

The "Boycott," the CIA, and Other Yankee Activities

It is widely believed that most of the Allende regime's problems were caused by the actions of the U.S. government and certain U.S. private firms. It has been argued, or at least implied, that had it not been for the position assumed by the United States, Chile would have prospered economically under Allende, political stability would have been maintained in the country, and the Chilean military would not have moved against the Unidad Popular regime.

Perhaps the most explicit statement of this line of reasoning is that given by Gabriel García Márquez in an article in *Harper's Magazine* in March 1974. There it is argued that the overthrow of Allende was planned in a meeting between Chilean military men and representatives of the Pentagon, held in a suburb of Washington, D.C., several weeks before the election of September 4, 1970. Interestingly, the writer does not make it entirely clear how he, a left-wing Colombian novelist, was made privy to a highly secret meeting between military officers of Chile and the United States, or why the execution of this plan was postponed for more than three years.

Most other commentators have been more circumspect than García Márquez. They have confined themselves to spelling out the activities of the CIA, the plotting of some U.S. companies, particularly the International Telephone and Telegraph Corporation (ITT), the activities of U.S. military personnel, and the U.S. government's reduction of its own aid and its blocking of aid to Chile from international lending agencies. All such discussions tend to lead to the conclusion that the U.S. role was indeed of major importance in undermining and bringing down the Allende government.[1]

While the facts surrounding the U.S. role are generally incontrovertible, the *conclusions* drawn from these facts are gravely in error. Whatever the

ITT did or did not do, whatever the CIA did or did not do, whatever certain U.S. military personnel did or did not do, whatever economic policies the United States followed or did not follow with regard to Chile—all of these factors had only the most marginal impact in generating the economic and political crisis of the Allende regime in its final months. And they had nothing to do with the Chilean military leaders' decision to oust the Unidad Popular regime.

Many of the U.S. government's policies towards Chile under Allende were very wrong. The U.S. representatives in the international lending agencies followed policies towards Chile which at best were questionable, and CIA personnel engaged in unpardonable activities in Chile. The top echelons of the Nixon administration evinced a hostility towards the Allende government which was both deplorable and counterproductive.

In addition to being wrong, these activities and postures were stupid. Without having any really important impact on the situation developing in Chile, they made it possible for the errors, abuses, and scarcely hidden objectives of the Allende regime and of its supporters to be obscured. The United States' position made it possible for it to be blamed for something which in the last analysis it had had very little to do with.

Discussions of the relations between the Allende regime and the United States tend to center on four issues: (1) the so-called blockade, that is, the supposed prevention by the U.S. government and certain private U.S. firms of economic aid going to the Allende government; (2) the activities of the Central Intelligence Agency in Chile during the Allende period; (3) the activities of some U.S. military personnel, particularly in the last phase of the Unidad Popular government; and (4) the Nixon administration's overall unfriendly attitude towards the Allende administration.

THE "BLOCKADE"

It has been frequently maintained that during the Allende years the U.S. government imposed a "blockade," which effectively prevented the UP government from receiving economic and financial aid from abroad. This, it is said, gravely undermined the economic and financial situation of the Allende administration and was largely responsible for its balance-of-payments problems.

President Allende himself frequently referred to a "blockade" against his regime. In his speech at the United Nations in December 1972, he said:

From the very day of our electoral triumph on the 4th of September 1970, we have felt the effects of a large-scale external pressure against us which tried to prevent the inauguration of a Government freely elected by the people, and has attempted to bring it down ever since, an action that has tried to cut us off from the world, to strangle our economy and paralyze trade in our principal export, copper, and to deprive us of access to sources of international financing.

We are aware of the fact that, when we denounce the financial and economic blockade applied against us, it is somewhat difficult for world public opinion, and even for some of our fellow citizens, to understand what we mean. This aggression is not overt and has been openly declared to the world; on the contrary, it is an oblique, underhanded, indirect form of aggression, although this does not make it any less damaging to Chile.[2]

The facts do not support such allegations. The international lending agencies did not completely refuse to provide aid to Chile during the Allende administration. To be sure, the U.S. government's Export-Import Bank made no loans to Chile during the Allende regime—but it had made virtually none during the last two years of the Frei administration either. The private U.S. banks sharply reduced their short-term lines of credit to Chile during the period—but for business reasons having nothing to do with an organized and deliberate "blockade." Finally, whatever efforts it may have made in that direction, the United States was utterly ineffective in preventing aid from being offered by other governments; in fact, the Allende regime received more economic help and promises of help then any previous Chilean government had ever gotten in a three-year period.

THE INTERGOVERNMENTAL AGENCIES

The U.S. government has strong influence in three intergovernmental institutions, and if it had wanted to do so, it could probably have completely blocked the disbursal of funds to the Allende government. These are the Inter American Development Bank, the International Bank for Reconstruction and Development (or World Bank), and the International Monetary Fund (IMF).

In the case of the Inter American Development Bank, two loans were provided to Chile in 1971, for the Catholic University of Santiago and the Universidad Austral of Valdivia, for a total of $11.6 million.[3] The then U.S. ambassador to Chile, Edward Korry, has claimed that he urged the bank to provide these funds.[4] Three other proposals were never acted upon by the Board of the Inter American Development Bank: one submitted by the Frei administration for $30 million for a petrochemical complex, and two smaller ones for the Catholic University of Valparaíso and the Universidad del Norte, submitted by the Allende administration. Professor Paul Sigmund of Princeton University, who has studied this question at some length, has made the following assessment of the role of the United States with regard to the Inter American Development Bank in the Allende period:

It appears almost certain that U.S. influence was exercised to delay the submission of Chilean projects to the Bank board, on which the United States controlled 40 percent of the votes, sufficient to block approval at least of the university loans under Bank rules requiring a two-thirds affirmative vote for this lending category. On the other hand, non-U.S. Bank officals now assert that by the time of the coup the two university projects were well on the way to being financed by the Bank using Norwegian resources, and that very substantial political pressures from member-nations were building up for some kind of loan to Chile before the next annual meeting of the IDB, scheduled for Santiago in early 1974. What the U.S. position would have been by that time can only be speculated.[5]

In the case of the World Bank, three loan requests came up for decision during the Allende years. One was for money for an electric power loan, which the bank ceased to consider when the Allende government refused to raise electric rates as advised by the bank. The World Bank was prone to giving advice of this nature to any government when, according to its criteria, such a suggestion was justified, and as such was not necessarily displaying any particular prejudice against the Allende government.

With regard to the second World Bank case, Professor Sigmund explains that "consideration of the second stage of a cattle breading program was postponed in April 1971, when it was discovered that there were sufficient funds in an earlier loan to last at least another year." He also maintains that the third project, for the development of orchards and vineyards, "moved rapidly through the preparation and appraisal stages so that by September it was nearly ready to be considered by the Bank's board of directors."[6]

It should also be observed, however, that a mission of the bank sent to Chile in 1971 reported in October of that year that from the bank's point of view, there were serious questions posed by the decision not to pay any compensation to the copper companies, as well as by the sharp decline in investment, the growth of strong inflationary pressures, and the very rapid drain of foreign exchange reserves. Although the president of the Chilean Central Bank accused the World Bank at the bank's annual meeting of September 1972 of being "manifestly precipitate and prejudiced" in its assessment of the situation in his country, the history of the World Bank would seem to contradict this assertion. From its inception, the World Bank has shown a marked concern about the ability of its borrowers to pay back their loans, and Chile was far from being the first country to express annoyance at this concern.

Although the World Bank granted no new loans to Chile during the Allende administration, Chile did continue to receive funds pending from previous loans. Professor Sigmund has pointed out that between July 1, 1970, and June 30, 1973, the World Bank made more than $45 million available to Chile.[7]

The International Monetary Fund made two three-to-five year loans available to Chile during the Allende period. The first was in the amount of

$39.5 million, granted in December 1971, and the second was for $42.8 million, extended in December 1972. With regard to these two loans, Professor Sigmund comments that "the Fund's willingness to aid Chile doubtless reflected the fact that it is not a bank but a mechanism to assist member-countries with foreign exchange difficulties; moreover, since the Fund had clear authority to make compensatory loans for this type of foreign exchange shortfall, the United States did not object." He adds that the IMF did refuse to enter into a so-called stand-by agreement with Chile because that country would not conform to certain austerity measures which it insisted on.[8] Again, this attitude did not differ from the IMF's traditional position. While its attitude may or may not be correct, its application to Chile did not constitute special adverse treatment of the Allende government.

During the Allende period, then, the international lending agencies provided the Chilean government with $139.9 million in loans. By no means can this be considered conclusive evidence that the United States was relentlessly using its influence in these organizations to choke off all help to the Allende regime.

THE EXPORT-IMPORT BANK AND OTHER U.S. AGENCIES

There is perhaps a better case for a blockade with regard to the Export-Import Bank and the Agency for International Development (AID), both of which are U.S. government institutions. President Allende made charges against the AID in his speech to the United Nations. "In the last decade," he said, "Chile was granted loans worth $50 million by the Agency for International Development of the United States Government. We do not expect that these loans will be continued. The United States, in its sovereignty, may grant or withhold loans in respect of any country it chooses. We only wish to point out that the drastic elimination of these credits has resulted in sharp restrictions in our balance of payments."[9]

Here too, some questions can be raised. The facts do not bear out Allende's claim that the reduction of U.S. government aid to Chile during his tenure had any significant impact on the country's balance of payments. It is true that no loans were given to Chile by the Export-Import Bank or AID during the Allende period. One loan which had already been negotiated before Allende came to power, for $21 million to purchase three Boeing jets for the LAN-Chile airlines, was "deferred" shortly after the Allende government's decision not to compensate the copper companies. The *New York Times* reported a State Department official as saying that this decision was "basically political" and had been "made at the White House level." After Chile's declaration of a moratorium of further debt payments, the Chilean government was officially notified by the United States that no further loans would be extended to it.[10]

Two additional comments concerning U.S. government aid to Chile during the Allende administration are in order. The first is that although the Export-Import Bank did not make any new loans to Chile during the 1970-1973 period, that did not mean that economic aid ceased entirely. For one thing, disbursements on old Export-Import Bank loans continued until June 1972. For another, different kinds of aid continued: technical assistance grants averaged about $200,000 a year; Peace Corps volunteers continued to work in Chile on the specific request of President Allende; and Food for Peace grants between November 1970 and September 1973 were worth a total of about $10 million, and in fact rose slightly during the Allende years. Concerning this last form of aid, Professor Sigmund explains that "ironically a part of this assistance was used to fulfill an Allende campaign promise: 10,738,000 pounds of powdered milk, delivered in 1971, helped President Allende to carry out his pledge to give a free daily pint of milk to every school child."[11]

The second comment is that massive U.S. aid to Chile had ceased considerably before Allende's election. Although during the first three and a half years of the Frei administration, such aid amounted to approximately $310 million, no new loans were given Chile after the middle of 1969. In part, at least, this cutoff occurred because by that time the Frei administration had accumulated substantial foreign exchange reserves.[12]

DEBT MORATORIUM AND DEBT RENEGOTIATION

Any discussion of a "blockade" as the cause of the economic difficulties of the Allende regime must include some consideration of how that regime handled the interest payments and amortization of the country's preexisting foreign debt. What occurred in this area represented a substantial reduction in the amount of foreign exchange allocated to debt service.

Professor Sigmund says that "By early 1972, it was clear that Chile was indeed no longer credit-worthy. . . . Yet despite all this a total collapse of Chilean international credit was somehow avoided."[13] This was made possible largely by a process of renegotiation of the debt with Chile's foreign creditors.

In November 1971, the Allende government declared a moratorium on the payment of interest and principal on most of the country's foreign debt, public and private. This action provoked a series of negotiations with those to whom the debt was owed. Rather quickly, by January 1972, an agreement was reached between the Central Bank of Chile and private foreign banks to which money was owed. This agreement called for rescheduling the private debt over a number of years and for payments of only $5 million in 1972 and 1973—payments which the minister of finance called "symbolic."[14]

Three months later, in April 1972, an agreement was reached with the Club of Paris, consisting of the United States, Canada, Japan, and Chile's West European creditors, on rescheduling the portion of the Chilean debt owed in 1972. According to this agreement, 70 percent of what was owed in 1972 would not fall due until 1975. It was also agreed that further negotiations concerning the debts coming due in 1973 would be conducted at the end of 1972—which bargaining had not yet been completed when the Allende government fell.[15]

The net result of these negotiations was to reduce greatly the amount Chile had to pay on its foreign private and public debt during the last two Allende years.[16] The actual reduction was a great deal more than what had been provided for in the January and April 1972 accords inasmuch as (1) no agreement whatever was reached concerning repaying debts due in 1973, as a result of which nothing was paid on those debts; and (2) no supplemental agreement, such as was called for by the Club of Paris-Chile Pact of April 1972, was ever reached between Chile and the United States. As a result of this latter situation, the Allende government paid nothing in either interest or principal on its public debts to the United States after 1971.

In a perverse sort of way, this constituted one of the United States' largest foreign aid programs during the early 1970s. Since the debts owed to the United States accounted for the great majority of all Chilean debts during that period, the result of the continuance of the moratorium insofar as the debts to the United States were concerned was that the United States (quite unwillingly, to be sure) was freeing for current uses large amounts of foreign exchange which Chile earned.

CHANGES IN COPPER PRICES

Some might argue that the drop in copper prices which took place soon after the Allende administration came to power also constituted part of the "boycott."[17] However, not only was this fall quite clearly explainable in market terms, but it was also reversed during the last year of the Allende regime.

Copper prices have been notoriously unstable since World War II, regardless of what regime has been in power in Chile. They have been subject to sudden upward and downward lurches, sometimes of extreme severity. The situation was no different in the Allende years. During its first two years the prices of Chile's major export product were substantially below what they had been during the last part of the Frei administration, thus reducing Chile's income from copper exports. They fell from averages of 60 cents and 70 cents a pound in 1969 and 1970 to an average of 46 cents a pound in 1971.[18] The situation once again reversed itself during the early months of

1973, when copper prices rose from 48.5 cents to 68 cents a pound during the first quarter of 1973.[19] By that time it was too late for the Allende regime to benefit fully from this rise, as it might otherwise have done, because the country's output had dropped substantially as a result of the variety of problems in the nationalized mines.

Such rapid and extensive alteration in the international price of copper did not originate during the Allende regime. It was virtually endemic. Nor was the price decline at the beginning of the Allende period any more the result of some hidden ''blockade'' of Chile than was the price increase in the last year of the regime the result of lifting such a ''blockade.''

THE LINES OF CREDIT OF FOREIGN PRIVATE BANKS

More important than restriction of lending by the international agencies (particularly in view of the limited number of loan requests made to these agencies by the Allende government in any case) was the curtailment of short-term lines of credit by private foreign banks. Such curtailment occurred particularly during the second and third years of the Allende government, but it would be rather difficult to interpret it as part of a coordinated ''blockade'' of Chile during this period.

By November 1972, short-term credit from U.S. banks had been reduced from $219 million to $32 million, according to Minister of Finance Orlando Millas. It is likely that other foreign banks which customarily made short-term advances to Chilean affiliates or correspondents had also curtailed their lending, although no exact data on this possibility are available.[20]

Almost certainly private foreign banks began to limit credit simply because the Unidad Popular regime had forced all such banks out of the country. It had been customary for the home institutions to extend lines of credit to their Chilean affiliates, and it was reasonable to suppose that once those affiliates no longer existed, the foreign banks would be less inclined to extend credit to their successors. This was indeed foreseen by some of Allende's supporters, who strongly advised him not to force the foreign banks to sell out, at least not in the short run. This advice was ignored.

It can be presumed that the nationalization of the foreign banks was one factor in bringing about the curtailment of short-term lines of credit to the Chilean banking system. Another was the deteriorating economic situation within Chile. As we have noted, the Allende government suspended all payments on its foreign debt as of November 1971, a measure not designed to engender confidence among foreign private bankers. Within a little more than a year, the Allende regime had depleted virtually all of the substantial foreign exchange reserves accumulated by its predecessor. Under these circumstances, good banking practice is enough to explain why foreign banks would become increasingly cautious in extending loans to their Chilean correspondents; it is not necessary to suggest a "blockade" as an explanation.

Professor Sigmund cites the specific behavior of three U.S. banks during this period. He reports that the Bank of America (one of those bought out by the Allende regime) continued to lend on the 1970 level until December 1971, after the date of the debt moratorium, when it extended loans "on a lower level with selected borrowers."[21] In the case of Chase Manhattan, according to a Chase spokesman, lines of credit were reduced "because of our own appraisal of the deteriorating economic conditions in Chile," from $31.9 million in the first quarter of 1971 to $5 million in the last quarter.[22] Finally, the Manufacturers Hanover representative is quoted as saying that his bank "cancelled lines or withdrew little by little over a period of a year and a half. . . . The first cancellation occurred in early 1971, and the last ones in early 1973."[23]

ECONOMIC AID FROM NON-U.S. SOURCES

Whatever curtailment of commercial loans from U.S. banks, from the U.S. government, and from international institutions in which the United States had great influence occurred during the Allende years, Chile received an unprecedented amount of help from other countries during that period. Minister of Finance Orlando Millas announced in November 1972 that Chile had obtained short-term credits amounting to $250 million from Canada, Argentina, Mexico, Australia, and Western Europe, and $103 million from the U.S.S.R. He also noted that the country had gotten $446 million in long-term aid from the Soviet Union, Eastern Europe, and China, and $70 million in such help from other Latin American countries.[24] It even received some grants from West European countries, notably from Sweden, whose help was used largely to import machinery, including mining machinery from the United States.[25]

The Allende government prided itself on having greatly diversified the country's access to help from abroad. On November 15, 1972, Millas made the following report to the Mixed Budget Commission of Congress:

Decisive changes have been achieved in the structure of foreign financing. The high concentration of short term financing, reflected in the fact that that coming from the United States represented 78.4% of the total at the beginning of this Government, has today been transformed into a much more diversified structure with the United States for example providing only 6.6% of the total. The volume of lines of credit now available amounts to $490 million, with a high degree of diversification. It is worth noting particularly the cases of the Soviet Union with $103 million, Australia with $29 million, West Germany and France with $28 and $26 million respectively, Spain with $15 million, Italy with $52 million, Canada with $11 million, Argentina with $56 million and Mexico with $26 million.[26]

More aid came to the Allende regime subsequent to Millas' speech. For instance, in July 1973 the Franco government of Spain made a loan of $45 million.[27]

Millas expressed assurance and pride in the ability of the Allende government to obtain long-term financing from many different countries.

In long term financing, also, objectives of enormous significance have been obtained, increasing their amount and diversification in a very important way. Outstanding are the establishment of agreements with Brazil ($10 million), Mexico ($20 million), Peru and Argentina, in which cases global financing agreements for a period of more than eight and a half years have been reached, which have made possible the acquisition of machinery and equipment worth more than $40 million. Specific financing agreements of great importance have been reached with countries of Western Europe such as France, Spain and others. Chile appreciates particularly, because of their special provisions, the credits offered by Sweden, Holland and Finland. Insofar as financing of investments coming from the socialist countries is concerned, a great step forward has been taken. Credits amounting to $446 million have been agreed upon, with periods of amortization fluctuating from 5 to 20 years. With the Soviet Union for $259 million, with Peoples Republic of China for $55.5 million, Poland for $35 million, Bulgaria for $25 million, Hungary for $22 million, the Democratic Republic of Germany $20 million, Rumania for $20 million, Czechoslovakia for $5 million, the Peoples Republic of Korea for $5 million.[28]

Alberto Baltra has calculated that in less than three years the Allende government received some $822.7 million in foreign credits. He also notes that more than 75 percent of this total came from non-Communist countries.[29]

This amount of aid proffered to and accepted by the Allende government greatly surpasses any amount received by any previous administration. During the whole six years of the Frei administration, that government was granted $310 million by the U.S. government.[30] President Frei reported in his last Annual Message to Congress that the country's total foreign debt had risen an average of $91 million a year during the previous six years (May 1964-1970), or a total of $546 million.[31]

THE CIA AND THE ALLENDE REGIME

Beyond dispute, the Central Intelligence Agency conducted a variety of activities in Chile, first in order to try to prevent Allende's election, and then to seek to undermine his regime. From any point of view these activities were despicable, and most of them were puerile in addition. The real question at issue in this discussion, however, is whether they contributed to any significant degree to the ultimate fate of the Allende government.

The staff report of the so-called Church Committee of the U.S. Senate indicates that U.S. government policy, executed through the CIA, was not to support any specific candidate in the 1970 election, but rather to conduct a "spoiling" campaign against Salvador Allende. "In all," the report notes, "the CIA spent from $800,000 to $1,000,000 on covert action to effect the outcome of the 1970 Presidential election. Of this amount, about half was for major efforts approved by the 40 Committee. . . . By CIA estimates, the Cubans provided about $350,000 to Allende's campaign, with the Soviets adding an additional undetermined amount."[32]

According to the staff report, the objectives of the 1970 CIA efforts were "(1) undermining communist efforts to bring about a coalition of leftist forces which could gain control of the presidency in 1970; and (2) strengthening non-Marxist political leaders and forces in Chile in order to develop an effective alternative to the Popular Unity coalition in preparation for the 1970 presidential election."[33] With regard to fulfilling these objectives the report stated:

In working toward these objectives, the CIA made use of half a dozen covert action projects. These projects were focused into an intensive propaganda campaign which made use of virtually all media within Chile and which played and replayed items in the international press as well. Propaganda placements were achieved through subsidizing right-wing women's and "civic action" groups. . . . In addition to the massive propaganda campaign, the CIA's effort prior to the election included political action aimed at splintering the non-Marxist Radical Party.[34]

The report contends that while the CIA did not accept an offer of $1 million from ITT to subsidize the candidacy of Jorge Alessandri, it did give advice to ITT on how to place money which ITT had given to the Alessandri campaign. The ITT spent $350,000 on this effort according to the staff report, and other U.S. companies gave an additional $350,000.[35]

Subsequent to the September 1970 election, the U.S. government sought to prevent congressional confirmation of Allende's victory. According to the staff report of the Church Committee, it carried out two programs with this in mind, which the report dubs Track I and Track II.

Track I consisted of political efforts to block Allende's victory. One of these efforts was the appropriation of $250,000 for the CIA "to bribe Chilean Congressmen to vote for Alessandri." "That," the report says, "quickly was seen to be unworkable, and the $250,000 was never spent." Another effort was to try to persuade Eduardo Frei to agree to Christian Democratic support for Alessandri's election, after which Alessandri would resign, paving the way for new elections, which Frei could then win. The report comments that "Frei refused to interfere with the constitutional process and the re-election gambit died."

The staff report recounts in some detail the CIA's propaganda activities during the period between the September election and the congressional choice of Allende. "These efforts included: support for an underground press; placement of individual news items through agents; financing a small newspaper; indirect subsidy of Patria y Libertad . . . and the direct mailing of foreign news articles to Frei, his wife, selected leaders and the Chilean domestic press."[36]

Track II was more sinister. It "was initiated by President Nixon on September 15, when he instructed the CIA to play a direct role in organizing a military coup d'etat in Chile. The Agency was to take this action without coordination with the Department of State or Defense and without informing the U.S. Ambassador."[37] To this end, "Between October 5 and October 20, 1970, the CIA made 21 contacts with key military and Carabinero (police) officials in Chile. Those Chileans who were inclined to stage a coup were given assurances of strong support at the highest levels of the U.S. Government both before and after a coup."[38] The staff report notes that these activities also failed: "Despite these efforts, Track II proved to be no more successful than Track I in preventing Allende's assumption of office. Although certain elements within the Chilean army were actively involved in coup plotting, the plans of the dissident Chileans never got off the ground. A rather disorganized coup attempt did begin on October 22, but aborted following the shooting of General Schneider."[39]

With regard to the murder of General Schneider the staff report provides information concerning possible CIA connection: "The CIA knew that the plans of all groups of plotters began with the abduction of the constitutionalist Chief of Staff of the Chilean Army, General René Schneider. . . . On October 22, one group of plotters attempted to kidnap Schneider. Schneider resisted, was shot, and subsequently died. The CIA had been in touch with that group of plotters but a week earlier had withdrawn its support for the group's specific plans."[40]

The CIA continued to be active in Chile throughout the Allende administration:

Of the total authorized by the 40 Committee, over six million dollars was spent during the Allende presidency, and $84,000 was expended shortly thereafter for commitments made before the coup. The total amount spent on covert action in Chile during 1970-73 was approximately $7 million, including project funds not requiring 40 Committee approval. . . . More then half of the 40 Committee-approved funds supported the opposition political parties: the Christian Democratic Party (PDC), the National Party (PN), and several splinter groups. . . . All opposition parties were passed money prior to the April 1971 municipal elections and a congressional by-election in July.

. . . Besides funding political parties, the 40 Committee approved large amounts to sustain opposition media and thus to maintain a hard-hitting propaganda campaign. The CIA spent $1.5 million in support of *El Mercurio,* the country's largest newspaper and the most important channel for anti-Allende propaganda. . . . The 40 Committee approvals in 1971 and early 1972 for subsidizing *El Mercurio* were based on reports that the Chilean government was trying to close the *El Mercurio* chain.[41]

The claim that the CIA had subsidized *El Mercurio* during the Allende administration was strongly denied by representatives of the newspaper two days after it was made public.[42] It is doubtful that CIA subsidies were needed to make *El Mercurio* oppose the Allende government, in view of the paper's long tradition of being strongly anti-Allende. The subsidy charge seems even more doubtful in light of the fact that the firm publishing the newspaper was one of the largest and most prosperous enterprises in Chile.

More serious than the charge that the CIA financed some of the opposition press is the claim that it largely financed the two truck owners' strikes, which played a major part in the crisis leading to the fall of the Allende government. The Church Committee's staff report presents the following assessment:

With regard to the truckers' strike, two facts are undisputed. First, the 40 Committee did not approve any funds to be given directly to the strikers. Second, all observers agree that the two lengthy strikes (the second lasted from July 13, 1973 until the September 11 coup) could not have been maintained on the basis of union funds. It remains unclear whether or to what extent CIA funds passed to opposition parties may have been siphoned off to support strikers. It is clear that the anti-government strikers were actively supported by several of the private sector organizations and the groups which coordinated and implemented the strikes. In November 1972 the CIA learned that one private sector group had passed $2,800 directly to strikers, contrary to the Agency's ground rules. The CIA rebuked the group but nevertheless passed it additional money the next month.[43]

Belief that CIA money was responsible for the success of the truckers' shutdowns requires an act of faith. The facts are that the needs of the truck drivers were relatively modest and that the strikers received widespread help within Chile to meet these needs. The longer of the two strikes lasted about eight weeks, the other about half as long. During these periods, the principal needs of the strikers were for food. Certainly, the walkouts did not last long enough to provide those truckdrivers who didn't own their own homes with a crisis with their landlords. They could postpone purchases of clothing and incidentals.

The Confederation of Truck Owners received large-scale contributions from broad sectors of the population—both from humble citizens and from the wealthy. Conversations both with participants in the trucking strikes and with people who themselves contributed or helped to raise contributions for the strikers leave little doubt that large amounts of food were collected in the headquarters of the confederation and its affiliates. These would be enough to tide the truck drivers and their families over during the strikes.

The truckers' magazine *El Camionero*, in its issue of November 1972, described the aid they had received during their first waikout: "Caravans composed of automobiles, station wagons, and other private vehicles, brought food to the headquarters of the Confederación Nacional de Dueños de Camiones, collected house to house, sector by sector, by women and students of good will which thus contributed to the efforts of those who were sacrificing in the national stoppage."

Information which I received subsequently from both truckers and people who raised aid for them bears out this picture.

It thus seems unlikely that the truck drivers needed funds from the CIA to maintain their walkouts. Certainly, CIA funds were not responsible for whatever damage the truck drivers did to the Allende regime.

The question remains concerning possibility of CIA influence in the coup of September 11, 1973. The Church Committee staff report makes the following judgment:

There is no hard evidence of direct U.S. assistance to the coup, despite frequent allegations of such aid. Rather the United States—by its previous actions during Track II, its existing general posture of opposition to Allende, and the nature of its contacts with the Chilean military—probably gave the impression that it would not look with disfavor on a military coup. And U.S. officials in the years before 1973 may not always have succeeded in walking the thin line between monitoring indigenous coup plotting and actually stimulating it.[45]

In conclusion, several statements can be made. First, CIA operations did indeed exist in Chile and were designed to cause difficulties for the UP government and to bring it down if possible. Such activities were unconscionable and cannot be justified. They constitute a violation of nonintervention in the internal affairs of Latin American states to which the U.S. government is committed by several international agreements, notably the Charter of the Organization of American States.

Second, the CIA's activities in Chile just before and during the Allende regime reflect an ethnocentricity, a contempt for Chilean political and military leaders, and a remarkable lack of understanding of Chilean political life. The attempts to bribe Chilean politicians and journalists were puerile as well as unpardonable.

Third, the staff report of the Church Committee makes no suggestion that most of the recipients of CIA funds, particularly the political parties involved, were aware of the source of these funds. Nor does it indicate that the CIA had any influence in the decision making of opposition groups during the Allende period. Indeed, there is ample evidence that the CIA was unable to influence such decision making in the weeks before Allende's inauguration.

Fourth, the CIA's activities, whatever they were, were of little or no importance in determining the ultimate fate of the Allende regime. They failed to prevent the election of Allende as president, they at most made only marginal contributions to the campaigns against the Unidad Popular government, and they had nothing to do with the final decision of the military leaders to oust Allende.

Fifth, the fact that the CIA did conduct a maladroit campaign against the Allende regime left the United States open to the charge that it was responsible for that regime's overthrow. The CIA's activities provide those who want one with a red herring to divert attention from the policies and actions of the Allende government which were primarily responsible for the crisis leading to its ouster by the military. The CIA thus greatly confused the issues surrounding the process and end of "the Chilean Road to Socialism." Their efforts were of relatively little importance in Chile, but were highly counterproductive for the United States.

THE U.S. MILITARY AND THE ALLENDE REGIME

The U.S. military is also alleged to have played a key role in the ouster of Allende. Two concrete charges are made, and implications are drawn not only from them, but from a number of other less clearly defined events.

One charge is that military aid to Chile continued, though on a very modest scale, throughout the Allende years. Gary MacEoin cites the amount of such aid as being "$6 million in 1971, over $12 million in 1972, and a similar amount projected in 1973."[46] Paul Sigmund implies that the amount was somewhat smaller:

U.S. aid to the Chilean military forces, under the Military Assistance Program in operation since the early 1950's, continued throughout the Allende regime. In June 1971 a new $5 million credit for the purchase of C-130 transport planes and paratrooper equipment was approved. U.S. military advisers remained in Chile, the Chilean navy continued to lease U.S. naval vessels, and Chile continued to participate in the Inter American Defense Board. In May 1972 . . . another $10-million loan to the Chilean military was approved.[47]

Tad Szulc has noted that on June 5, 1973, the United States agreed to sell F-5E fighters to Chile.[48]

The Church Committee staff report also discusses the relations between the U.S. and Chilean military during the Allende period:

Close personal and professional cooperation between Chilean and U.S. officers was a tradition of long standing. The American military presence in Chile was substantial, consisting both of military attaches, the Embassy, and members of the Military Group who provided training and assistance to the Chilean armed services. In the late 1960's the Military Group numbered over fifty; by the Allende period, it was reduced to a dozen or so, for reasons which had primarily to do with U.S. budget-cutting.[49]

The same staff report elaborates further on the supposed role of U.S. military personnel in Chile during the Unidad Popular period: "Throughout the Allende years, the U.S. maintained close contact with the Chilean armed forces, both through the CIA and through U.S. military attaches. The basic purpose of these contacts was the gathering of intelligence, to detect any inclination within the Chilean armed forces to intervene."[50]

It is thus clear that during the UP government the United States continued to provide very modest aid to Chile's armed forces. However, those who seek to read something sinister into this fact seem to overlook that the United States did not force this aid upon the Chilean government. Allende's government requested it, Allende decided to continue the participation in the Inter American Defense Board, the Allende government decided to continue the presence of the U.S. military mission in Chile. And when the Allende government requested the closing down of a U.S. air force ionospheric research station on Easter Island, the United States complied.[51]

The second charge against the U.S. military is that the overthrow took place during the so-called Operation Unitas, joint maneuvers of the U.S. navy with those of the West Coast countries of South America. The Chilean navy was supposed to be a participant in these maneuvers, but after ostensibly taking off to take part in them, it turned around and returned to Valparaíso to start the uprising against Allende.

It is not entirely clear how these facts constitute complicity in the coup. Certainly, Operation Unitas, a war game which had been planned several years in advance and which was part of a regular series of such maneuvers, was not undertaken for the purpose of ousting Allende. Certainly, even the presence of some U.S. officers on the Chilean ships which were to participate in the operation would be explainable in terms of their being liaison personnel who might well be expected to be there for such a maneuver.

Gary MacEoin cites other U.S. military activities at this time which he considers highly suspicious and indicative of U.S. participation in the coup. One of these consisted of four flights of a U.S. air force WB57 plane based in Mendoza, Argentina, which he describes as "the weather model of the spy plane RB57." He observes that these flights took place between September 7 and September 12. Violation of Chilean air space by this plane, he says, "would not be necessary to perform the function of coordinating communications between the various air force, army and navy bases in Chile."[52]

MacEoin names another incident which leads him to conclude that U.S.

armed forces personnel were implicated in the revolt of September 11, 1973. He notes the presence in Valparaíso on September 10 of Charles Horman, a U.S. citizen who had been in Chile for some months making a documentary film.

At the Miramar Hotel, where he stayed, Horman met some Americans, and he later told his wife that some of them had spoken frankly and perhaps carelessly to him about their reasons for being where they were. They included a Captain Ray E. Davis, U.S. Navy, Lieutenant Colonel Patrick Ryan, U.S. Army, both attached to the United States Embassy in Santiago, and a retired naval engineer named Arthur Crater. Ryan, who had been nine months in Chile after three tours in Vietnam, told Horman he had taken a Chilean naval officer to the United States on a million-dollar shopping spree for equipment the previous month. . . . Crater was a little less specific about his concerns. All that he confided was that he arrived from Panama on September 5 "to do a job with the navy." Horman suspected he knew what that job was when several United States naval officers and other military personnel who were also in the hotel boasted to him of "the smooth operaton" which the revolt proved to be.[53]

None of this, however, proves that the U.S. military had a role in the overthrow of Allende.

The issue goes far beyond the weakness of the evidence available to prove that the U.S. military had a part in Allende's overthrow. In order to believe that such was the case, one must accept certain preconceptions about the Chilean military which either reflect a degree of ethnocentricity and disdain for Chileans—to which most of those making the argument would not wish to admit—or a description of the situation existing in September 1973 which is contrary to the facts.

Any important participation of the U.S. military in a move against Allende would require the acquiescence and collaboration of their Chilean counterparts. Such acquiescence and collaboration presumes that the Chilean military would permit such a degree of foreign interference in their own internal affairs and those of their country. This is difficult to believe.

The Chilean army and navy are institutions with a very strong esprits de corps. They have a high opinion of their own professional capacity. They consider themselves the defenders par excellence of the national sovereignty and national dignity of Chile. Recognizing their inability to obtain within Chile the modern equipment (and the training necessary to use it), they have been willing and anxious to get these from abroad. But this willingness does not mean that they are naive souls who can be "convinced" by their foreign advisers or colleagues to overthrow their country's constituted government. Nor, once they committed themselves to a coup, does it seem likely that they would have sought foreign involvement in the enterprise; such involvement would run counter to their own view of their role in national society.

It might be presumed that the Chilean military might involve foreign officers in their internal affairs only if they conceived their own and their country's position to be so desperate that it could only be saved with out-side help. There is no evidence, however, that the Chilean military leaders felt any such desperation.

Thus, there is little to indicate that the U.S. military was engaged in doing anything in Chile beyond the legitimate duties connected with long-established aid programs to equip and train the Chilean army, navy, and air force, and with long-planned maneuvers in which both the Chilean and U.S. navies were participating. Nor is there any indication that President Allende or his administration sought to end the military cooperation programs that had existed for two decades. Finally, there is no evidence that the Chilean mili-tary moved against Allende because American military officers had con-vinced them of the need to do so, and it seems highly unlikely that they would have been willing to accept this kind of foreign interference in their own affairs.

GENERAL HOSTILITY BETWEEN THE NIXON AND ALLENDE ADMINISTRATIONS

The general atmosphere of hostility that developed between the Allende and Nixon administrations originated in Washington. Soon after Allende took office, rumors spread in Santiago that he had received a letter from Fidel Castro, advising him not to take a position of open hostility towards the United States, as Castro had mistakenly done. Whether or not Castro ever gave such advice, Allende did act as Castro reportedly suggested.

During his years in office, Allende often insisted that he did not wish a confrontation with the United States. In his First Annual Message to Con-gress, for example, he declared:

It is the intention of my Government to maintain with the United States of America friendly and cooperative relations. We have attempted to create conditions for com-prehension of our reality, which will impede the generation of conflicts and avoid unessential questions which interfere with this intention, creating obstacles for the negotiated and friendly solution of problems that might arise. We believe that this realistic and objective conduct will be reciprocated by the people and Government of the United States.[54]

Even when he appeared before the United Nations General Assembly to protest against the "blockade" against his regime, he did so more in terms of injured innocence than of militant defiance. He usually insisted that there was no reason for the hostility the United States was demonstrating towards his government.

From the beginning, the Nixon administration made clear its hostility towards Allende and his government. It subjected the Unidad Popular re-gime to a series of insults, which although not very damaging in themselves, underscored the basic attitude of the Nixon government. Only two weeks after Allende received a plurality in the popular poll, Henry Kissinger made the first overt attack on Allende. Giving "background" to reporters, in his capacity as national security advisor to Nixon, he asserted that if Allende won, the United States would be faced with "massive problems."

I have yet to meet somebody who firmly believes that if Allende wins, there is likely to be another free election in Chile. . . . Now it is fairly easy for one to predict that if Allende wins, there is a good chance that he will establish over a period of years some sort of Communist Government; in that case, we would have one not on an island off the coast which has not a traditional relationship and impact in Latin America, but in a major Latin-American country you would have a Communist Government, joining for example, Argentina . . . Peru . . . and Bolivia . . . So I don't think we should delude ourselves that an Allende take-over would not present massive problems for us, and for the democratic forces and for pro-U.S. forces in Latin America, and indeed in the whole Western Hemisphere.[55]

A few weeks later, President Nixon himself offered an overt insult to President-Elect Allende. Nixon was one of the few chiefs of state who did not offer Allende congratulations upon his final choice by the Chilean Congress.

The same kind of insult was offered a few months after Allende became president. This was Nixon's refusal to allow a U.S. naval vessel that was making a "good will" tour of South American countries to visit Chile, in spite of Allende's request that the ship put in at Valparaíso.[56]

These and similar insults were symbolic. In addition, the Nixon administration took more practical steps to hurt the Allende regime. Some of these, involving U.S. economic policy and CIA's activities, are discussed earlier in this chapter.

At least one other Nixon administration position was designed to damage the Allende government. This was Nixon's public policy statement in January 1972 to the effect that (as Professor Sigmund paraphrases it) "unless there were 'major factors' to the contrary, the United States would not itself extend new bilateral economic benefits, and would oppose multilateral loans, to countries expropriating significant U.S. interests without taking 'reasonable steps' toward compensation."[57] This statement was aimed directly at Chile.

SUMMARY OF U.S.–CHILEAN RELATIONS DURING ALLENDE PERIOD

In view of the frequency of allegations of U.S. responsibility for the fall of the Allende government, and the confusion such allegations make for an understanding of the real causes for the demise of the U.P. regime, it is worthwhile to summarize the principal elements involved in U.S.-Chilean relations during that period:

1. The Allende regime did not want a confrontation with the United States. In essence, then, although it did not hesitate to take such measures as confiscating the interests of Anaconda and Kennicott companies in the Chilean copper industry, which were essential parts of its program, it would not engage in public polemics with the U.S. government if such could be avoided.

2. In contrast, the Nixon administration made no secret of its strong dislike of the Allende government.

3. The United States gave only very limited economic aid—food, Peace Corps volunteers, goods in the pipeline from loans made before 1970—to the Allende government. It blocked consideration of loans by the World Bank and Inter American Development Bank (except for two small ones from the latter institution), although this attitude may well have been largely symbolic since the Allende regime made few requests to either organization. The United States did not block IMF loans. None of these measures was effective in preventing foreign aid from going to the Allende regime, which got more aid than any of its predecessors had.

4. The CIA conducted activities in Chile hostile to the Allende government. Given the publicity these activities have received, they were surprisingly limited, involving expenditure of $400,000 during the 1970 campaign on propaganda against Allende's candidacy, and of $7 million to "destabilize" the Chilean economy, apparently through subsidizing opposition publications and perhaps helping indirectly, and only to a very minor degree, to finance the two truck drivers' strikes of 1972 and 1973. These activities (even the most outrageous of all, the plot to kidnap General Schneider in 1970) were on balance of little significance in generating the crisis culminating in the fall of the Allende government.

5. Rumors and suppositions notwithstanding, as of now at least, there is little concrete evidence that U.S. officers in Chile did anything beyond their prescribed professional duties as technical advisers and trainers of the Chilean military.

6. The Nixon administration attitude and policies towards the Chilean regime between 1970 and 1973 were more often than not either morally wrong or simply mistaken. The operations of the CIA were certainly wrong, being a violation of international agreements. The economic policies and public declarations of hostility were exceedingly ill advised, since all they accomplished was the generation of anti-Yankee sentiment in Chile, strengthening the hands of extremists inside the Unidad Popular and to its Left.

7. The Nixon administration's hostility to the Allende government, and the measures it took against the Unidad Popular regime, were of no real importance in creating the problems that increasingly plagued the Allende regime. Their only major effect was to convince those who wished to believe that U.S. policies rather than those of the Allende government generated the difficulties that led to Allende's overthrow.

21

Freedom of the Press, and Other Constitutional Issues

One of the charges most frequently leveled against the Allende administration both before and after its overthrow has been that it was in the process of destroying freedom of the press and other constitutional guarantees. Those who overthrew the government, have cited this alleged effort as a prime motivation and justification of their actions. Allende's supporters and apologists have denied all such accusations.

Typical of their blanket denial of all charges that the regime was undermining the democratic structure of Chile is a statement by none other than Fidel Castro, in an interview with the American television newsman, Dan Rather. Castro told Rather that

actually, Allende was very respectful of parliament. He was very respectful of the opposition parties, and was very respectful of the opposition press and of the constitution and of the laws. It is absolutely false and absolutely baseless that Allende tried to establish a single party, that Allende tried to destroy the opposition parties, that Allende tried to destroy parliament. I knew Allende very well, and I can assure you that Allende scrupulously respected the law, the constitution and the institutions of Chile.[1]

Any discussion of this issue must deal with (1) the nature of the ultimate objectives of the principal Unidad Popular leaders and (2) the actual situation which existed during Allende's tenure. Considerably different conclusions will emerge with regard to these two aspects of the problem.

The charge that the Allende government was destroying the democratic nature of Chilean political life involves several specific kinds of activity, and an additional one which at first glance may not seem to be directly related. These aspects of the problem include at least the following: freedom of the press and other mass media, including special reference to the effort to nationalize the country's principal source of newsprint; the question of establishing "popular tribunals"; the role of the Juntas de Abastecimiento Popular (JAPs); and abuses of power of the executive in its relations with the legislative and judicial branches of government. The more general question concerns the political objectives of the government's nationalization program. Each of these aspects will be dealt with separately in this chapter.

THE QUESTION OF FREEDOM OF THE PRESS
AND OTHER MASS MEDIA

With regard to freedom of the press and other mass media during the Allende period, an extremely wide variety of newspapers and magazines, representing practically every shade of public opinion, continued to be published. However, the range of opinion reflected in the nation's television stations was drastically reduced. There was considerable harassment of both newspapers and television and radio stations which were opposed to the government. Moreover, the domestic movie industry was unabashedly converted into a Unidad Popular propaganda tool, while at the same time, film imports from non-Communist countries were severely restricted and those from Communist countries greatly expanded.

During the Allende period, there were eleven daily newspapers in Santiago —some of which were sold widely throughout the country. These dailies included *El Siglo*, the official organ of the Communist party, and *Puro Chile*, an afternoon paper of pro-Communist inclinations; other pro-UP papers such as the Socialists' afternoon tabloid *Última Hora* and *Clarín*, of general UP orientation; and the official government daily *La Nación*. There were also various publications aligned with the opposition, which included not only the three papers belonging to the El Mercurio chain, that is, *El Mercurio, La Segunda*, and *Últimas Noticias,* but also *La Tribuna*, owned by leading figures of the Partido Nacional, and *La Prensa*, belonging to the Partido Demócrata Cristiano. *La Prensa* appeared first in October 1970, when the PDC bought out the bankrupt ex-Conservative newspaper *El Diario Ilustrado* and renamed it, while making it the official Christian Democratic organ.

A wide variety of weekly or monthly papers, magazines, and reviews also appeared. These included, on the Left, *Punto Final*, controlled by MIRistas and left-wing Socialists; *Chile Hoy*, a magazine appealing mostly to intellectuals; *PLAN*, concerned with Latin American problems; the left-wing news weekly *Ahora*, and the pro-Communist party *Vistazo*, as well as the monthly "theoretical" publication of the Communist party, *Principios*; and a similar periodical, *Posición,* of the Socialist party.

On the other hand, many such publications were hostile to or very critical of the Unidad Popular government. These included the old weekly news magazine *Ercilla*, more or less pro-PDC; the frankly pro-Christian Democratic *Política e Espiritu*; and the Jesuit monthly *Mensaje*. Much more militant than these were *P.E.C.*, which was very conservative and as critical of the PDC as of the Unidad Popular; and *Impacto* and its sister journal *Sepa* (both were closed down on several occasions), which were extreme rightwing journals of opinion. The news magazine *¿Que Pasa?* was unfriendly to the regime in power. Most strident of all were *Tacna* (only a few issues of which appeared, but which were continuing to be displayed a year or more after the paper was apparently suspended), *Tizona*, and *Patria y Libertad*. These extremist periodicals did not hesitate to reveal their editors' belief that the armed forces ought to depose the Allende government.

Although book publishing also continued to reflect the widest range of opinion, one fundamental change occurred in this area. Within a couple of months after Allende assumed office, a tripartite arbitration panel, made up of representatives of management, unions, and government officials, and presided over by a Communist official of the Ministry of Labor, rendered an award with regard to a labor dispute in the Zig-Zag publishing firm. It gave the workers a 65 percent wage increase, more than twice the previous year's cost of living rise. This decree forced the company into bankruptcy, whereupon the government bought the plant and machinery as well as some of the copyrights of the bankrupt firm. These properties were reorganized as the Empresa Nacional Quimantú.

Throughout the remainder of the Allende regime, Quimantú published an exceedingly large number of books, as well as a wide range of magazines, including a very pro-government news magazine, *Mayoría*. The books brought out by the firm included extensive editions of Marx, Engels, Lenin, as well as books on the history of the Socialist party, the labor movement, and other similar items, virtually all from the Marxist or Marxist-Leninist point of view. Some publications were frankly doctrinary tracts.[2]

Editorial Quimantú had its own problems of freedom of the press. The publisher, Socialist ex-deputy Alejandro Chelen Rojas, insisted on publishing Leon Trotsky's *History of the Russian Revolution*, in spite of vigorous protests from the Communists, protests which reportedly reached the highest councils of the Unidad Popular.

HARASSMENT OF THE OPPOSITION PRESS

A great deal has been made by opponents of the Allende regime of the harassment of the opposition press by the president and by various organs of the government. There was such harassment, but some of what was alleged to be persecution of the opposition press was in fact little more than partisan polemicism which had long been a characteristic of Chilean politics.

This was particularly the case with the relations between President Allende and the newspaper *El Mercurio*. Allende had long had a personal political feud with this newspaper, the largest publishing enterprise in the country. This somewhat sedate "newspaper of record" was quite openly opposed to the UP and its government and had historically been closely associated with the Liberal party, one of the right-wing groups which joined in 1965 to form the Partido Nacional.

Throughout his regime, Allende was annoyed by items published either in *El Mercurio* itself or in one of the other two newspapers it put out. He made his unhappiness known in interviews with reporters, and sometimes wrote long letters to the editor of *El Mercurio*, which were published *in extenso* in the paper in a prominent position. Both in his comments at news conferences and in his letters, Allende charged the paper with being reactionary, unfair in its criticisms of his regime, and a "monopoly" (a word very loosely used by all of the Left in Chile), and he rhetorically asked why the owner of the newspaper, Agustín Edwards, had left the country soon after the Unidad Popular victory.[3]

Some of Allende's charges were themselves unfair and grossly exaggerated, but they were never accompanied by threats to close down the publication, or even by hints that someone else ought to close it down. They were the give and take of democratic politics, and in and of themselves could hardly be called persecution of the nation's largest and most prosperous newspaper. Indeed, they probably were helpful from a circulation point of view.

More accurately described as harassment, and even persecution, were other actions. Perhaps in this category was an inspection of the finances of *El Mercurio* ordered by the Allende government, in connection with alleged tax evasion by the firm (an inspection which exonerated *El Mercurio*). Also in this category were frequent charges brought by the government and its adherents against newspapers and magazines under certain parts of the Law for the Security of the State and the Penal and Military Justice Codes. These moves were made in spite of a Unidad Popular campaign promise to eliminate these particular pieces of legislation, a promise that was never kept.

One of the principal victims of this kind of harassment was the newspaper *La Tribuna*. By the end of 1972, forty-seven suits had been brought against this daily. Its editor, Raúl González Alfaro, had been jailed for short periods more than once. The courts had thrown out almost all of the suits, which were lodged by the government, individual ministers, UP deputies, and various government functionaries. On at least one occasion, the paper was not allowed to publish as reprisal for having printed something "offensive to the armed forces."[4] Also, on one occasion, the government ordered the *La Tribuna* building sold at auction, supposedly for payment of social security contributions which it owed. After a crowd gathered in front of the paper and physically prevented the auction, the government relented and a settlement of the debt was arrived at.[5]

The magazine *Sepa* was also subjected to government lawsuits. By late 1972, seventeen suits had been entered against it. Almost all of these cases were decided in favor of the newspaper by the courts, although on three occasions, short suspensions of publication were ordered.[6] Fifteen cases were brought against the papers published by the El Mercurio firm, and twelve of these were quashed by the courts.[7]

These lawsuits, demanding criminal punishment for individuals, suspension of publication, and other retribution, did indeed constitute harassment of the press. No similar charges were brought against publications friendly to the government. However, it is important to emphasize that although in previous administrations such cases had been few in number, they had by no means been completely unknown.

In a number of instances, especially in the provinces, Unidad Popular elements took violent action against some of the opposition press. In some cases, newspapers were seized by MIRistas and members of the Unidad Popular. These seizures sometimes prevented publication of news items that those involved felt were unfavorable to them. However, in no case were the usurpers allowed to keep control of such periodicals, and in only one case, that of *La Mañana* of Talca, was the incident used as an excuse for the government to take over the paper.[8]

THE QUESTION OF LA PAPELERA

The most bitterly fought and probably most significant battle over freedom of the press involved the issue of nationalizing the Compañía Manufacturera de Papeles y Cartones, popularly known as La Papelera. This was the country's first and largest producer of paper, particularly newsprint. It had added symbolic importance because its head was ex-President Jorge Alessandri.

The opposition was absolutely and unalterably opposed to nationalization of the firm. Such a move would give the government an absolute monopoly on production of paper, since CORFO already had a controlling interest in the other two paper firms. There was great fear, which bordered on absolute conviction, that once the government got a monopoly of paper, it would squeeze out of existence the newspapers, periodicals, and book publishing firms that were not politically aligned with the Unidad Popular. There was a well-known and -remembered example of this kind of operation across the mountains in Perón's Argentina. This precedent was frequently cited.

Certain Unidad Popular elements, particularly the Altamirano wing of the Socialist party, were equally determined to bring about the nationalization of the enterprise. It was widely believed that the two negotiations between the government and the Christian Democratic party in 1972 had foundered because of the insistence of Altamirano and his associates that La Papelera be one of the firms to be placed in the social area of the economy.

Throughout the period of Allende's presidency, the administration used various strategies to get control of La Papelera. There were negotiations with Jorge Alessandri, who was willing to pass to the government some of the firm's operations but was not willing to turn over newsprint production. There were unsuccessful efforts to get the company's workers to go on strike, so as to present the possibility to "intervene" or "requisition" the firm, but these failed.

The Corporación de Fomento made a determined effort to buy up a controlling interest in the shares of the company. Although the stock of the firm was comparatively widely held, CORFO was never able to acquire as much as 10 percent of the total—even though it offered a price far above that which had existed in the stock market before CORFO began to buy. A counter fund, which its originators dubbed the Liberty Fund, was set up to purchase shares from small stockholders who wished to sell, but not to the government.

The final tool used against La Papelera was a refusal to allow the prices of its products to keep up with the rise in the general price level. Although President Allende frequently stated that he had no intention of using price controls to force firms into bankruptcy so that they could be easily acquired by the government, his actions in this case seemed to contradict his statements. The firm made an application for a substantial rise in prices in January 1972. However, it was only granted such an increase by President Allende in August, and that rise was only 19.6 percent. Between January and August, the firm claimed to have lost 230 million escudos, and prices of most other products had risen from 30 to 100 percent. The prices of all but one of the inputs used by the company had increased by more than 35 percent during these eight months, and most of them had risen by more than 50 percent.[9]

None of the regime's methods succeeded in getting it control over La Papelera. The fears of what the Unidad Popular government might have done with an absolute monopoly of newsprint were therefore never tested.

THE SITUATION OF THE TELEVISION STATIONS

A much stronger case that the Allende government was trying to curb freedom of expression in the mass media can be made for that of the country's television stations. One of the three existing television outlets was used completely to express the government's point of view; a second was almost totally so used; and the position of a third outlet was increasingly precarious.

Television had developed in Chile in a somewhat different way from that of most other countries. In Santiago there were three television channels in 1970, one belonging to the Catholic University, one to the University of Chile, and the third, the National Channel, belonging directly to the government. Only the National Channel had relays, so that its programs were heard all over the country. Valparaíso had an additional channel, that of the Catholic University of that city.

Shortly before the Unidad Popular came to power, a new general law regulating television was passed. This statute, Law No. 17,377 of October 21, 1970, contained two clauses that have special relevance to the present discussion: "University television is to be the free pluralist expression of the critical conscience and creative thought," and "Television will not be at the service of any particular ideology and will maintain respect for all tendencies which express the thought of sectors of the Chilean people."[10]

As might have been expected, the National Council which ran the National Television Enterprise and controlled the National Channel, was given a Unidad Popular majority of four to two soon after the Allende government came to power. José Miguel Varas, a member of the Communist party, was made news director of the National Council.

Almost from the beginning of the Allende regime, the opposition strenuously criticized the National Channel's slanting of the news in favor of the Unidad Popular. Having heard it myself on various occasions, I can personally testify that these complaints were well grounded.

Even more significant was the suppression of the "Meet the Press" kind of program that had been established in the last months of the Frei administration, under the title "Three Bands." During the election campaign, and for some time thereafter, representatives of the three political currents represented by the three 1970 presidential candidates exchanged ideas and arguments on this program. After their victory, Unidad Popular elements became increasingly hostile to "Three Bands." They first objected that it was unfairly loaded with opponents of the Allende regime, since one Christian Democrat, one member of the Partido Nacional, and one representative of the Unidad Popular appeared regularly on it. They demanded changes, and the formula of two UP, one PDC and one Partido Nacional representative was established.

This concession did not satisfy the Unidad Popular members of the Council of the National Channel. Arguing that the program caused "tensions" among its listeners, they demanded that "Three Bands" be suspended. This finally occurred, in August 1972, by a four to two vote of the National Council. From that time on, the National Channel almost exclusively presented the Unidad Popular point of view. Virtually the only exception was a court-imposed requirement that once a week, for a twenty-minute period, each party represented in Congress have the right to present its point of view on the National Channel.

In the case of the television channel of the University of Chile, the same kind of situation arose. The news section of the channel was firmly in the hands of Unidad Popular elements. These people decided to suppress two of the three programs carried by the station which brought elements of the government and the opposition face to face. (Rector Eduardo Boeninger of the University of Chile canceled the decision with regard to one of these programs, and it continued to be broadcast.) Although the University of Chile was controlled by elements opposed to the Unidad Popular, a majority of the workers in the university's television station were government supporters, and they carried on a continuous campaign to limit the expression of elements of the opposition.

The Catholic University was strongly anti-Unidad Popular. Here again, however, the press department of the television channel was headed by a Unidad Popular supporter. At one point, he decreed an "internal regulation" in the press department, providing that the Workers Assembly of the channel should have control over what the department should put out over the air, and also stating that this assembly should elect a Directive Council, which would discipline any member of the work force who was deemed to be acting "contrary to the interests of the workers." These regulations were rejected by a majority of the workers themselves, as well as by the faculty and students of the university. When efforts were made to dismiss the news director, however, work stoppages were provoked in the station, which as a result was off the air about a week.

President Allende vetoed a law that would have permitted the two university stations to have their programs relayed throughout the country. However, the Catholic University channel in Santiago did extend its coverage to three cities outside of Santiago, while that of the Catholic University of Valparaíso also extended its broadcasts to two other areas.

On balance, the net effect of the Allende administration, insofar as "pluralism" of ideas on television was concerned, was negative. There was serious restriction of diversity of expression, particularly on the National Channel, and less serious curbs on the other two channels. At the same time, both the government and Unidad Popular elements sought to restrict the extension outside of the capital and Valparaíso of any television channel that was not strictly under their control.[11]

THE RADIO STATIONS

Unidad Popular's control over radio stations expanded considerably during the Allende administration, while radio stations controlled by or sympathetic to the opposition suffered from a variety of difficulties inspired by the government or Unidad Popular elements. These included reduction of revenue, much increased costs as a result of collective labor agreements applied only to opposition stations, and forceful seizures of longer or shorter duration.

By late 1972, the Socialist, Communist, and Radical parties had bought twenty existing radio stations and had obtained government permission to establish five additional ones. By that time, there had been at least ten forceful takeovers of anti-UP stations by supporters of the Unidad Popular and MIR, and three of these remained in the hands of those who had seized them. By late 1972, some 170 radio stations were licensed throughout Chile.

The government attempted to cripple the resources of opposition radio stations by markedly reducing government advertising over them. As the regime took over increasingly large numbers of industries, these, too, ceased to advertise over anti-UP radio stations as they had previously done.

At the end of 1971, the Radio Controllers Union, headed by a Communist party member, made extensive demands on antigovernment radio stations for wage increases, refusing to accept an offered raise of 50 percent. The government then named an "intervertor" to settle the problem, and he decreed a wage increase reported to be three times the rise in cost of living since the previous contract, and equally greater than the wage rise generally established for the economy by a government-CUTCh agreement. The intervertor also insisted that from then on each of the stations involved must provide, without charge, one half-hour's time every two weeks to the Radio Controllers Union to present whatever it wished. This last provision was in violation of the law regulating radio emissions.

Radio Balmaceda, which had been purchased in 1969 by the Partido Demócrata Cristiano, suffered particular difficulties. The government refused to renew its waveband, announcing that it wanted to turn that band over to the CUTCh station, Radio Luis Emilio Recabarren. Before the matter had been definitively settled, a station calling itself Luis E. Recabarren began broadcasting on the Radio Balmaceda wavelength. Two months later, an engineer of the government Department of Telecommunications removed the condenser from Radio Balmaceda, thus effectively driving it off the air. Finally, Radio Balmaceda was given a new wavelength, and in May 1972, it received a thirty-year concession to use it. However, it continued to suffer minor harassments.[12]

LONG-RUN UP OBJECTIVES WITH REGARD TO THE MASS MEDIA

Freedom of expression through the mass media was not destroyed during the Allende regime. As much is admitted by Tomás MacHale, a strong opponent of the UP government and author of a study of the problem of the mass media under Allende, published while the Unidad Popular regime was still in power. According to MacHale, "To avoid possible misunderstand-ings, the author affirms immediately that in Chile there still exists that free-dom, in spite of numerous attempts to do away with it, through coercion and subtle means, shown in the pages which follow."[13] Although MacHale wrote late in 1972, he might have said much the same thing on September 10, 1973.

The picture of the mass media under the Allende regime would not be complete without some notice of the avowed ultimate objectives of the Unidad Popular and its leaders with regard to this question. Evidence here is somewhat contradictory.

President Allende and others in his administration often reiterated their desire to maintain complete freedom of expression in the printed and spoken word. For instance, while still a senator, Allende explained his vote in favor of the Statute of Constitutional Guarantees, which pledged his forthcoming government not to tamper with freedom of the press: "I have come to say that these dispositions must be understood not only as principles consecrated in the Constitution, but as a moral promise made to my own conscience and before history."[14] Similarly, Minister of Interior José Toha, speaking in November 1970 before a meeting of pro-UP journalists, commented: "It will not be the Government which through pressure, menaces or coercive action tries to orient, direct or dominate the organs of the press." At about the same time, Foreign Minister Clodomiro Almeyda stated in an interview with an Argentine newspaper: "The press constitutes a bulwark which will always be able to count upon the respect of the government, whatever its tendency. More than praise, we need criticism, when it is in a constructive and well intentioned spirit."[15]

It is not the province of this book to judge the real beliefs and intentions of President Allende and his ministers with regard to this problem. How-ever, it must be noted that the statements cited here conflict sharply with others made by responsible leaders and organizations associated with the Allende regime.

The fundamental document of the UP, its program, adopted on Decem-ber 17, 1969, presents the following notion:

These means of communication (radio, publishing houses, television, press, movies) are fundamental for aiding the formation of a new culture and a new man. For that reason, they must be given an educational orientation, and they must be freed from their commercial character, adopting measures so that social organizations can get control of these means, eliminating from them the nefarious presence of monopolies.

Communist deputy Luis Figueroa, president of the CUTCh, in speaking to a meeting called by the Regional Council of Journalists to discuss "Social Responsibility of the Means of Communication," was somewhat less vague than the UP about the issue when he noted that "only in a society in which the means of mass communication are social property can there be guarantee of authentic freedom of expression." A UP sociologist, Patricio Saavedra was even clearer when he spoke to this same meeting. Tomás MacHale paraphrases Saavedra's ideas as follows: "He affirmed that the ideal in the field is the Soviet Union, where news is given when the public is mature enough to receive it; thus it ceases to be merchandise, being transformed into an instrument of political education."[16]

The Unidad Popular committee backing a slate of candidates in the Santiago Regional Council of Journalists in January 1972 maintained in its election statement that:

the journalists who support this candidacy, among whom are professionals of all of the ideological currents of the Left, sustain the position that a real freedom of the press can only be achieved in Chile when the means of mass communication form part of the social area. The press, radio, television and movies must be instruments at the service of the liberation of our peoples and not a private business, an ideological weapon of the national and foreign minority, as it is at the present time.[17]

In April 1971, the Unidad Popular organized the First Assembly of Left Journalists. In its final resolution this meeting maintained "that a journalist is only truly objective who identifies with the great revolutionary, historical process, which these days agitates the world, and which is raising its victorious bulwark in our fatherland."[18] One of the principal speakers at this meeting proclaimed that the "absolute expropriation of the means of information must be considered the final objective of a process and the victorious result of the confrontation with the bourgeoisie."[19]

CONCLUSIONS WITH REGARD TO FREEDOM OF MASS MEDIA

Freedom of the press, which in its broadest sense encompasses the broadcast spoken word as well as the printed page, continued to exist during the Unidad Popular period. There was very wide diversity of newspapers and magazines, and also extensive political variety in the radio stations at the time that Allende fell. More restrictions were imposed on television stations. In general, however, such ill treatment as the press received at the hands of the UP government was at most harassment and could hardly be called persecution, and even less suppression.

In this regard, one must conclude that this tolerance to the opposition press was a phase, a tactic. It was not a matter of principle; rather, it was dictated primarily by the fact that by September 1973 the Unidad Popular had not yet obtained the "total power" of which their leading spokesmen talked so often. The statements noted in this section indicate that the ultimate objective with regard to the organs of public expression was strict conformity with the UP in the name of "real" freedom of the press. Certainly, the dictatorship of the proletariat, which was the declared objective of both the Communist and Socialist parties, could have resulted in nothing short of complete conformity with the regime. "The Chilean Road to Socialism" involved a short detour through freedom of the press, but the ultimate socialism towards which this road supposedly led had no room for such a "bourgeois" institution.

THE ISSUE OF *TRIBUNALES POPULARES*

Within a few weeks after taking office, President Allende announced that he would soon be sending Congress a bill providing for the setting up of "popular tribunals" (*tribunales populares*). He subsequently changed his mind, and little more was heard of the question during the rest of the regime.

The popular tribunals were conceived of as supplements to the existing judicial system, which was itself to be fundamentally transformed. They were to be neighborhood courts, elected within each local area and with broad but vague jurisdictions. Among other things, they were to have control over petty crimes, as well as dealing with family problems.[20]

President Allende actually sent a bill to Congress early in his administration to set up the *tribunales populares*. The opposition in Congress unanimously declared that it would not approve the bill, and within a few weeks of having been sent to the legislature, it was withdrawn by President Allende. The widespread rumor at the time was that the president had withdrawn the bill not so much because of congressional opposition, as because public opinion surveys in working-class areas, conducted for the government, indicated very strong opposition to the measure among the administration's own rank-and-file supporters.

PROPOSED CONSTITUTIONAL CHANGES

The Allende administration proposed two other fundamental changes in the structure of the Chilean government, although neither was formally presented to Congress for action. These dealt with the general judiciary system and with the legislative branch of the government.

From the beginning of the regime, the president and other leaders denounced the court system as a bulwark of reaction and a roadblock on the "Chilean Road to Socialism." Particularly during the last year of the regime, there were increasingly bitter conflicts between the courts and the administration, culminating in the declaration by the Supreme Court that the Allende government was behaving "unconstitutionally."

The principal suggestion of the UP with regard to the courts was that the system of life tenure of judges be abolished. Under the existing system, young lawyers entered upon a career in the judiciary soon after graduation; they were advanced in their careers as vacancies appeared and by the decision of the members of the higher level courts. Unless guilty of grave offenses, they could not be removed from the judicial system. Members of the Supreme Court were nominated by the president of the republic from among lower ranking members of the judiciary and had life tenure.

The Unidad Popular's proposal was fundamentally to alter this system. The Supreme Court was to have a term coterminous with that of the president and was to be chosen by the members of the legislature, which itself was to have an entirely different character from that of the traditional Congress.[21] Allende never sent Congress a proposal for this change. However, it was widely discussed and advocated by Unidad Popular leaders during the administration. There was little doubt that the Unidad Popular intended to make the courts subordinate to the political authorities in control of the state.

Another institution which was obviously a stumbling block on the "Chilean Road to Socialism" was the Congress. Although it was unable to offer any effective resistance to the government's program for nationalizing the economy and otherwise fundamentally altering Chilean institutions, Congress was constantly denounced by the pro-government forces. From the beginning of his term, Allende made it clear that he wanted to bring about a fundamental change in the nature of the Congress. Although he promised to submit to Congress a constitutional reform bill that would substitute a popular assembly (*asamblea popular*) for the existing legislature, he never in fact did so. Nor did he carry out his oft-repeated threat to submit the issue to a plebiscite.

Sentiment in favor of modifying the existing legislature was not confined to the ranks of the Unidad Popular. It was widely felt that the Congress, as established under the Constitution of 1925, was a somewhat unwieldy and very slow-moving body. There was even some sentiment in the oppositon ranks for substituting a single-house legislature for the Senate and Chamber of Deputies.

Perhaps understandably, there was widespread suspicion in the ranks of the opposition concerning the kind of change Allende and the Unidad Popular wanted to make in the legislative branch of the Chilean government. The president remained vague concerning the characteristics of the single-house legislature he wished to substitute for the existing Congress.

There appears to have been considerable justification for the skepticism of the opposition. In the middle of 1971, when the issue was one of the major subjects of discussion in political circles, President Allende had lunch with a foreigner who was a mutual friend of his and mine. In the conversation which ensued, Allende sketched the nature of the *asamblea popular* which he indicated he would submit to a plebiscite before the end of the year. As he outlined it, this new legislature would be very similar to the Supreme Soviet of the U.S.S.R., being very large, meeting only for short periods of time, and being so organized as to leave most of its work to a small presidium. Of course, a proposal of this kind would have met the unanimous resistance of Allende's opposition. In any case, the idea was never submitted to the popular vote, which Allende frequently said he would like to call. However, the changes Allende and the Unidad Popular wanted to make in the judicial and legislative branches helped engender the conviction among the oppositon and many outside observers that the "Chilean Road to Socialism" was in fact a road towards a totalitarian dictatorship.

22

The Politics of the Unidad Popular and Its Allies

Coalition politics plagued the Unidad Popular throughout the period in which the Allende government was in power. The governing group remained an alliance of two major parties and several smaller ones, the number of the latter changing several times. During most of the period, all these groups were represented in the cabinet, and throughout it they shared jobs in the public administration and in the direction of state-controlled firms.

With time, the role of the minor parties became less important within the Unidad Popular and the government itself. Their diminishing role only made the relations between the two major groups in the coalition—the Socialists and Communists—more tense. Although, as indicated earlier, their basic differences were not over questions of long-range objectives (except insofar as each of the parties saw itself as the one exercising power in the ultimate dictatorship of the proletariat), they did differ profoundly over issues of strategy and tactics. Furthermore, in the last months of the regime, as the situation became increasingly taut, polarized, and violent, both of the major parties found themselves forced into extreme positions.

The fundamental differences between the Socialists and Communists—and the smaller parties allied with one or the other of them—centered on the rapidity with which the process of transforming Chilean society, economy, and polity should proceed. As corollaries to this basic argument, they disagreed over relations of the UP and the government with the groups further Left, particularly the MIR; over relations with the opposition, especially the Christian Democrats; and over how to deal with the armed forces. At least until shortly before Allende's fall from power, the Communists tended to take a more moderate position on these issues and the Socialists a more radical stance.

In addition to the parties in the Unidad Popular, there were groups to the

Left of the coalition which in a sense were of the government without being in it. The Movimiento de Izquierda Revolucionaria in particular gave "critical support" to the Allende regime, had close relations with elements of the president's own Socialist party, and probably were given some jobs on the public payroll, including the president's bodyguard, the Grupo de Amigos del Presidente (GAP). Any discussion of the politics of the government supporters must include an account of them.

GENERAL POLITICAL DEVELOPMENT
DURING THE ALLENDE YEARS

Before analyzing the parties of the Unidad Popular and of those to its Left, it is useful to sketch the major political events during the Allende years. The parties involved frequently reacted differently towards those events, depending upon their basic stances and views of the situation.

The first major political development after Allende took office was the municipal election of April 1971. It proved surprisingly favorable to the Unidad Popular, which, if all votes cast are taken into consideration, received slightly less than 50 percent, and if the votes declared null and void are dropped, received almost exactly 50 percent.[1]

This good electoral showing was followed within the next year by three substantial defeats. One was in a by-election for a seat in the Chamber of Deputies from Valparaíso in July 1971;[2] the other defeats were in two by-elections for a Senate seat and a Chamber seat in January 1972.[3] The second of these events was followed by a kind of "retreat" for several days, in which the leaders of all the UP parties met with President Allende on an estate outside of Santiago to plan further strategy. This meeting gave rise to strong differences of opinion among Unidad Popular parties.

Meanwhile, in the middle months of 1971, both government and opposition forces suffered minor splits, which just about canceled one another out in terms of their net impact on the balance of forces. The Christian Democrats suffered a new schism, with formation of the Izquierda Cristiana, while the Radical party underwent a further division with formation of the Partido Izquierda Radical (PIR), which stayed in the Unidad Popular for about six months and finally joined the opposition early in 1972.

On February 19, 1972, Congress passed the Hamilton-Fuentealba amendment to the Constitution, defining the areas of the economy and ending the right of the president to decree nationalization of any firm without previous approval of Congress.[4] President Allende vetoed part of this measure, and his veto was overridden by a majority of Congress. A deadlock developed, however, over the question of whether a simple majority was sufficient to override a veto of a constitutional amendment, as the opposition insisted, or whether a two-thirds vote was required, as was maintained by President Allende and the Unidad Popular.[5]

During 1972, the President made two efforts to negotiate this issue with the Christian Democrats. One occurred in March, when PIR Minister of Justice Manuel Sanhueza met with PDC leaders on behalf of Allende and reached an agreement, which was then repudiated by the president, with the result that the PIR moved into the opposition.[6] The second effort took place in June and was also on the verge of agreement, but foundered over the issue of whether La Papelera should be nationalized.[7]

In October 1972, the first nationwide strike of truckers, backed by small retailers and some groups of professionals, took place. The strike was ended only when three military men were brought into the government, and General Carlos Prats was made minister of interior.

For the following five months, attention was largely centered on the congressional elections of March 1973. Two blocs were formed, composed of the Unidad Popular parties, with some support from the MIR on the one hand and the opposition parties on the other. The opposition hoped for a two-thirds majority in Congress, which would have made possible the constitutional impeachment of President Allende; the UP hoped to hold its own, getting as large a percentage of the vote as Allende had received in 1970.

The results of the election were something of a triumph for Allende and the Unidad Popular. The government forces received almost 44 percent of the total vote, blocking the attainment of the two-thirds required by the opposition to impeach the president and improving the Unidad Popular's showing in the 1970 presidential election. However, the results were inconclusive, since the opposition won a majority and the deadlock between the executive and legislative branches of the government remained.

The last six months of the Allende regime were marked by the exit of the military from the government, growing and rapid polarization of opinion, an unsuccessful coup on June 29, considerable arming of civilians, the declaration by both Congress and the Supreme Court that the president had acted unconstitutionally, and a second truckers' strike, this time backed by a large number of middle-class people in commerce, the professions, and even offices. Once again frantic efforts were made to bring the military back into the government and to reach an agreement with the Christian Democrats, but these proved fruitless. When it was already too late, President Allende decided to break with the extremists within and outside his own camp. On September 11, 1973, the regime fell in coordinated moves by the three armed forces and the Carabineros.

The events of the last eleven months of the Allende regime will be dealt with at greater length in two later chapters. Here they will simply be outlined as a background for the discussion of the political activities and stances of the various parties in the Unidad Popular and more or less allied to it.

IMPACT OF CONFLICTS IN THE LEFT

Disagreements on policies and tactics among the Unidad Popular parties were a major difficulty facing the Allende government. The fact was well recognized by President Allende himself. In his Second Annual Message to Congress in May 1972, the president noted that "it is not possible to accept that the judgments, differing basically in terms of tactics, among the political forces which support us, can come to be obstacles in the path we have taken towards the integral fulfillment of our Program." After observing that such differences were "always overcome in the leadership," Allende stated that "they flourish sometimes in the organs of administration or of economic policy, or in the base organizations of the labor movement or politics. It is the unavoidable duty of everyone of the parties and movements which make up the Government to continue all our efforts—day by day—to eliminate such divergences within the limits of ideological pluralism."

Continuing with this subject, the president argued that the top leadership of UP "has been able to push with success the realization of the program of the Government." But he added that "there are still deficiencies which retard or interfere with decisions, preventing their being carried out as promptly and efficaciously as is demanded by the reality in which we live."[8]

Allende also recognized in this same Annual Message that patronage difficulties among the components of the Unidad Popular were hampering the regime. "Repeatedly," he said, "popular forces have condemned party exclusiveness as a factor interfering with the government's work. Party differences will never be a just cause for defending inefficiency or for tolerating slackness in the management of public affairs. The people themselves, and especially the workers, must force the end of such practices."[9]

THE RADICALS AND OTHER MINOR PARTIES

The Socialists had been hesitant about entering the Unidad Popular because they feared that, as in the days of the Popular Front of the late 1930s and early 1940s, they would be outflanked by an alliance of the Communists and the Radicals. However, they need not have had such a fear. The Radical party largely disintegrated during the Unidad Popular period. It had already split in the early months of the 1970 presidential campaign, and it split once again in mid-1971.

The 1971 division, which gave rise to the establishment of the Partido Izquierda Radical, was brought about by changes in the party constitution and declaration of principles enacted by its Twenty-fifth National Convention. The new program of the party declared that "only outside of the capitalist system is there a possibility for a solution for the working class." It also declared that "the Radical Party is socialist, and its struggle is directed towards the construction of a socialist society." Finally, the new declaration of principles stated the necessity of accepting "historical materialism and the idea of the class struggle as the means of interpreting reality."[10]

The twenty-fifth convention also sought to reorganize the structure of the Radical party. In place of the Asamblea Radical, which had been at one and the same time a political group and a social club, the convention decided to organize as the basic units of the party groups that were more purely political and more highly disciplined.

A dissident group, headed by many of the party's best known leaders, rejected both innovations. They declared that the Radical party had never been a Marxist organization and that they were opposed to its becoming one; they also rejected the proposed reorganization of the structure of the party.

The breakaway of the Partido Izquierda Radical reduced what remained of the Partido Radical within the Unidad Popular to very small proportions. Instead of the country's largest party, which it had still been a decade before, the Partido Radical was reduced to the status of one of several minor parties which collaborated with the Socialists and Communists in the UP.

President Allende was careful, however, to keep Radicals in his government and to give them the benefit of considerable patronage. He indicated the importance they had for the Unidad Popular, as representatives of the middle class, in his speech to the Radical party congress in July 1971: "I therefore wish to point out once again the higher responsibility of radicalism as the most qualified interpreter of the sectors of the petty and middle bourgeoisie, the employees, teachers, technicians, the small merchants, industrialists and farmers. We require these social groups to understand that they have and shall have a decisive influence in the building of the new society."[11]

In spite of such presidential statements, the Radicals did not have a major voice in determining the policies of the Unidad Popular or the government. They could hardly be expected to do so in view of their sharply declining strength, the schisms among them, and the fact that they no longer represented a major proportion of the middle class, whom they were supposed to speak for in the Unidad Popular coalition.

Most of the other parties in the Unidad Popular were even more insignificant than the Radicals. The Partido Social Democrático, one of the two small vestiges of the country's first Socialist party, the Partido Democrático, lacked either any outstanding leaders or much in the way of a rank and file. It finally merged with the rump of the Partido Radical early in 1973.

Acción Popular Independiente (API) never had much weight in the councils of the Unidad Popular. It was formed for the purposes of the 1970 election, designed to bring together the independents who wanted to support the UP candidate and to give the semblance of a middle-class voice in UP affairs. Its appeal was to small businessmen, but they largely turned against the UP and the government, particularly during the last year of the regime.

Of somewhat more significance were the two left-Catholic parties. The Movimiento Acción Popular Unido (MAPU), formed by the *Rebeldes* of the Christian Democrats who broke away from the PDC in 1969, moved rapidly to the Left and became increasingly Marxist-Leninist in its philosophy. This preoccupied the party's principal leaders, and when a new split away from the PDC took place in mid-1971, giving rise to Izquierda Cristiana, most of the better known leaders of MAPU joined the Izquierda Cristiana.

Thereafter, MAPU took its place on the far Left of the Unidad Popular coalition, allied with the left-wing Socialists and the MIR. This drift to extremism proved too much for some of the MAPU leaders, and in March 1973, a split occurred within the group, with two different parties emerging, both of whom used the name MAPU.[12] The more moderate was headed by Jaime Gazmuri, one-time head of INDAP during the Frei administration; the other, more closely aligned with the MIR, was headed by Oscar Garretón.

Meanwhile, Izquierda Cristiana brought together those within the Left-Catholic political ranks who still remained loyal to the principles of Social Catholicism. However, it, like the MAPU, tended to align itself with the more radical wing of the Unidad Popular, that is, with those who were less willing to take Lenin's advice to "take one step backward so as to take two steps forward." They demonstrated this attitude in early November 1972, when they refused to remain in the cabinet because three military chiefs were brought into it.[13]

THE COMMUNIST PARTY

The Communist party remained the best organized party in the Unidad Popular, and perhaps in all of Chile, throughout the Allende period. It increased its membership substantially. Perhaps because of Socialist President Allende's personal prestige, however, it proved to have less strength among the voters than its colleague and competitor, the Socialist party.

A four-point strategy was followed by the Communist party during the Unidad Popular regime: (1) to channel the process of change exclusively through the Unidad Popular and the government; (2) to neutralize and, if possible, split the Christian Democratic party; (3) to avoid a military coup against the Allende government; and (4) to strengthen the position of the Communist party itself throughout the public administration.

As indicated in an earlier chapter, the Communist party's perspective was considerably different from that of the Socialists and the other tactically more radical groups inside and outside the Unidad Popular. The Communists, more accustomed to long-term planning, were less anxious than their partners to achieve all of their objectives in the short run. They were more conscious than the Socialist or MIR leadership of the risks involved in the Unidad Popular experiment. Furthermore, they were much more concerned than their partners with the international implications of the "Chilean Road to Socialism" and did not want to make any false steps which might weaken the worldwide position of the group of pro-Moscow Communist parties, particularly those of Western Europe. All this meant that the Communists generally adopted a cautious attitude, making them the most "moderate" element on the Chilean Left. This stance led some of the more exalted souls in the Chilean Left and among the UP's sympathizers abroad to accuse them of "betraying" the cause of the Revolution. In reality, the Communists' tactics merely reflected the fact that they were more realistic and less prone to take great risks than were the more impatient elements inside and outside the Allende government coalition.

CHANNELING CHANGE

Part of the Communist's basic tactics and strategy during the Allende years was to keep the process of change under the control of the government and of the Unidad Popular parties. They wanted the agrarian reform to be carried out by the Corporación de la Reforma Agraria and other governmental bodies, as authorized by the Agrarian Reform Law of 1967. They wanted nationalization to be executed by the government, under the various stratagems worked out by President Allende's legal advisers. They wanted a governmental structure established to administer rationing, a structure that could be tightly controlled, particularly by them. They were not opposed to the widest possible interpretation of the law to justify the policies the government wanted to follow and the acts it wanted to carry out. However, having a considerable grasp on the machinery of the state, they wanted to use the state as the vehicle for carrying through the Revolution, and for imposing the social, economic, and political structure that was their objective.

This attitude meant that the Communists were generally opposed to allegedly "spontaneous" actions by groups outside the direct control of the state and of the Unidad Popular parties. This position quite naturally brought them into frequent conflict with the MIR, the more radical elements of the Socialist party, and some of the minor Unidad Popular parties that were trying to hasten the process of change by taking actions outside the law (no matter how widely interpreted), actions that were not initiated by the state machinery.

The Communists made their position clear throughout the Allende period. In an interview with the Belgian Communist paper *Le Drapeau Rouge*, which appeared on January 1, 1971, Luis Corvalán, secretary general of the Communist party, defined the party's attitude: "There is nothing more revolutionary than to contribute to the success of the people's government presided over by Comrade Allende; there is nothing more revolutionary than carrying out his program, widening the support of the people's government and . . . consolidating the influence of the Communist Party."[14]

One of the most lucid presentations of the Communist party's position favoring channeling change through the government was an article by Orlando Millas which appeared in *Punto Final* on June 20, 1972:

Lamentably, the indiscipline and voluntarism which in the agrarian field has transgressed the Basic Program of Government of Unidad Popular, alienating from us great masses of peasants and small agriculturalists, is also observable in industry and commerce. . . . This gives the monopolists the support of a great mass of petty and medium bourgeoisie and even a wide percentage of petty bourgeoisie and even white collar workers and functionaries or professionals.

. . . Those have caused great harm who have thought it easier to propose incorporation of whatever firm by hook or crook into the social area, instead of sustaining coordinated and efficient trade union, social, political, economic and administrative action which assures the rights of the workers, takes care of their demands, and wins over the entrepreneurs for the development of production, constraining speculative and sabotaging activities.[15]

COMMUNIST ATTACKS ON THE MIR

The Communist party position throughout most of the Allende regime brought it into frequent conflict with rasher elements within and outside the Unidad Popular. This was particularly the case with the MIR, of which the Communists were sharply critical throughout most of this period.

For example, as early as June 1971, Gladys Marín, secretary general of the Communist Youth, in reporting to the Ninth National Conference of the Youth, expounded on the Communists' conception of the role of the Allende government and launched a polemic against the MIR. She criticized Nelson Gutierrez, a MIR leader, who had argued that the importance of the UP government was that "it opens new perspectives to the popular movement, which creates new conditions for developing the struggles of the exploited classes and for their advance towards the taking of power." Gladys Marín stated that "this definition implies a grave underestimation of what the people have actually gained by the possibility of generating a popular, antiimperialist government, constructing in Chile a socialist society." Gutierrez' view, in contrast, was "to situate the government above classes and as arbitrator of confrontation." Gladys Marín ended this part of her discussion by saying "we alert you today against these tendencies, and we say that nothing could be more dangerous today than the generation of an attitude of lack of confidence among any sector of the youth in the revolutionary government which today directs the destinies of our fatherland, and which is, as we have said, the work and pride of the people of Chile."[16]

Earlier in June 1971, upon the occasion of the murder of Christian Democratic leader Edmundo Pérez Zújovic by left-wing extremists, the Political Commission of the Communist party welcomed the MIR's repudiation of that crime. But it cautioned that "although the MIR has evolved in its political position, it continues to maintain attitudes which, such as the indiscriminate seizures of fundos and of industries, and its calls to armed struggle, favor the creation of a climate that facilitates the plans of internal and external reaction."[17]

A plenum of the Communists' Central Committee at the end of June 1971 was the occasion for several attacks on the MIR, its ideas and its activities. Thus, Claudio Alemany, speaking for the party's Trade Union Commission, attacked

the action of the ultras of all kinds who push the workers to make mistakes and take prejudicial positions. . . . Thus we have "the seizure of factories," many of them without any significance in the process of the development of the economic liberation of the country. Thus, for example, in Valparaíso, they went so far as to seize a children's clothing factory which had 16 workers. They seized a City Service laundry, and in Concepción they took a bakery, obliging the government to intervene in it.[18]

At this same meeting, Deputy José Cademartori insisted on the existence of "a unanimous consensus in the UP that the seizure of small factories or small fundos, the seizure of fundos and industries where there are social conflicts, does not aid the Chilean revolution. The methods and the forms of struggle of the working masses change with the changes produced in the country. Much of what yesterday was just, today no longer is."[19]

After the by-election defeats of early 1972, when the Unidad Popular parties separately and together went through a period of soul searching to determine what was wrong with the situation, the Political Commission of the Communist party drew up a report giving its conclusions. Among many other points, this report again attacked the more impatient elements inside and outside the Unidad Popular:

The ultraLeft is without any doubt one of the factors which has contributed to the deterioration of the Government's position, and seeks to find in the electoral defeat arguments to reinforce its positions. Its spokesmen, such as Manuel Cabieses in "Ultima Hora," have begun their analysis, labelling as fascists all opponents of the Government, without exception. In commenting on the electoral result they have said, "Fascism took a step forward."

The ultraLeft presents as antagonistic the efforts to gain support for the Goverment among the petty bourgeoisie, and the petty and middle bourgeoisie, and the growth of that support in the proletariat. A similar idea has been put forth by comrade Carlos Altamirano. . . .

With regard to the treatment of the middle groups, we must keep in mind the real character of the revolutionary tasks which we must accomplish at this time. We work with the perspective of building socialism. But today the tasks are fundamentally anti-imperialist and anti-oligarchical.

In conformity with this, with regard to the present stage of the Chilean revolutionary process, we must respect the petty and middle bourgeoisie.[20]

Later in this document, the Political Commission noted: "Some negative effects have been produced in the Socialist Party as a result of the electoral results. There are indications of an offensive of ultraLeft sectors, of bitter internal discussion which require strong political work on our part." This section of the document concluded that "the battle with the ultraLeft must be reinforced."

In this same period, the Communist party launched a strong verbal attack on the MIR by name. In an article published in *El Siglo*, the party claimed that "the MIR presents the peasants with a mirage." It added:

Deliberately or unconsciously it attempts to involve them in an adventure. . . . The MIR doesn't defend the landless peasants, as it claims, but attempts to strengthen that group of farmers who obtain incomes of nearly one hundred thousand escudos a month. . . . The definitive and positive solutions in the countryside will not be the product of the feverish demands of the MIR but of the faithful application of the Program of Unidad Popular and will depend certainly on the conditions which are being created by the Chilean revolutionary forces, and will depend upon the greater or smaller accumulation of forces in the countryside.[21]

Later in 1972, the Communists returned to the attack against the MIR. In a plenum of the party's Central Committee in April, Senator Volodia Teitelboim commented with regard to the "ultraLeft": "Incapable of overcoming their dogmatism, they help the major enemies find allies in the middle classes, thrown into their arms by the revolutionary verbiage which fails to see the difference between imperialism and the large bourgeoisie and the small and middle proprietors who could and should make an important contribution to the success of economic development of the country."[22]

This same theme was sounded by Mario Zamorano, the party's organization secretary, in summing up the results of the plenum. "The gravest thing about the ultraLeft," he said, "is that through every one of their actions they help to give a majority to the ultraRight and leave those who support the Government in a minority. All of the actions of the ultraLeft alienate the middle sectors, which in Chile are considerable, and give victory to the side which they attack, in this case the Right."[23]

As late as April 1973, the Communists were sounding the same warning. A document which the party's Central Control Commission sent to its regional organizations was published by the opposition periodical *El Mercurio*, which had also published the earlier February 1972 document of the Political Commission. The Communists here questioned the validity of the document published by *El Mercurio*, but the MIR regarded it as authentic enough to justify their answering it. The Central Control Commission document set forth the party position in the following terms:

The situation of the ultraleftist positions has reached an intolerable limit in the parties of the UP. This commission recommends that drastic and urgent methods be taken; we will not elaborate details which are fully known by the party and on which we gave information in the meeting where we studied the facts and documents of the adventurist actions of the ultraLeft. The touchstone of our action is the resistance to the project of Comrade Millas for political consolidation of the area of social property. This project has aroused all the anti-Communist elements which have infiltrated the MAPU, the SP, and the RP (especially the Radical Youth) and even organizations like the API.[24]

The document urged "our allies of the MAPU to initiate the purge of anti-Communists and adventurers as soon as possible" and to support the Socialist party groups associated with Allende, Clodomiro Almeyda, and other moderate elements. A new note was sounded in this document with the comment that

the splitting of some of the allied parties is inevitable, the fractional work of the ultraLeft has taken on professional characteristics. Only one fact held us back until now, the elections of March. But the frankly good results for the party cannot further hold us back. It is necessary to prepare the party for a definite offensive against the elements of the ultraLeft. This includes within our own party. Concerning that, the Political Commission, on the basis of evidence of the Central Control Commission, has decided that it is good to purge the party of ultraLeftist elements and opportunists. In a separate document we shall inform you of the method to follow.

COMMUNIST ATTITUDE TOWARDS THE CHRISTIAN DEMOCRATS

Throughout the Allende period, the Communists sought to neutralize and, insofar as possible, split the Christian Democratic party. They realized better than the other Unidad Popular parties did that the Christian Democrats were supported by a large core of workers and the middle class. They were also willing to admit, to a degree that the other parties were not, that the Christian Democrats were not reactionaries, that they favored some kind of reform.

During the first part of the Allende administration, therefore, the Communists sought to prevent the formation of an alliance between the Christian Democrats and the rest of the opposition, particularly the Partido Nacional. At the same time, throughout the Unidad Popular government, they sought to draw distinctions among currents within the PDC and, to the degree that that might be possible, to exploit such divisions to split and weaken the Christian Democrats.

In his report to the June 1971 plenum of the Communist party, José Cademartori described its attitude toward the PDC in some detail. He noted that at the convention in Cartagena which nominated Radomiro Tomic for president, the Christian Democrats had declared themselves "for the revolution and for socialism." He stated that they were nonetheless increasingly critical of the UP government on various grounds, each of which he rejected as invalid.

Cademartori, noting the government's parliamentary initiatives designed to suppress terrorism and augment the Carabineros, commented: "If these measures and others do not materialize, the responsibility lies not with the Government but with the Christian Democracy, which instead of showing attitudes of collaboration in accord with its own resolutions, shows a desire to embark on a Holy Alliance with the Right to try to block the Popular Government."

The Communist deputy then touched on the other aspect of his party's approach to the Christian Democrats, that is, encouraging division within their ranks: "The warning of the Christian Democratic Youth and the thinking of not a few leaders and members of that party who look with distaste at the path of reactionary confabulation, show that the plans of the Freist sector are encountering difficulties in the ranks of his own party." Cademartori then concluded:

The Christian Democracy is faced today with the question of fulfilling or throwing in the wastebasket the agreements of Cartagena; to follow or abandon the program of the candidacy of Tomic; to contribute from their own positions to social change or to dedicate themselves to placing obstacles in its way. . . . The Communist Party makes clear its invariable position favorable to an understanding with all social and political sectors favoring revolutionary transformations. If the people defeat the policy of "deals" and the PDC changes, our Party will consider that conditions have been created for a dialogue and an agreement on matters of common interest.[25]

A year later, Communist party Sub-secretary Victor Díaz, speaking to another plenum of the party, returned to the theme of relations with the Christian Democrats, once more expressing hope for cooperation with them, while at the same time stressing divisions within the PDC. After saying that *El Mercurio* was becoming as ferocious in its attacks on the Christian Democrats as on the UP, Díaz mentioned that he did not know whether negotiations then under way between the two groups with regard to the Hamilton-Fuentealba amendment would be successful. "Many obstacles," he added, "must still be overcome. To the reactionary pressure there has been added the maneuver of the right wing sector of Christian Democracy, which through señor Moreno and señor Zaldivar, attempts to create an unbreathable atmosphere which frustrates the dialogue, using the daily *El Mercurio* to present a projected constitutional reform which brings a confrontation of Christian Democracy and Popular Unity."[26]

Mario Zamorano, in his summation speech at this same Plenum, was more optimistic: "In recent days the heavy atmosphere of hatred which threatened to poison seriously national politics, has tended to be corrected. The way has been opened to dialogue and the possibility of developing a language which if not common is at least convergent, between Unidad Popular and the Christian Democracy."[27]

COMMUNIST EFFORTS TO AVOID A COUP

The Communists' denunciation of and struggles against illegal activities of the MIR and other extreme Leftists, as well as their efforts to get as much support as possible for the UP government from the Christian Democratic ranks, evidenced their desire to avoid the kind of polarization and confrontation that might provoke military intervention and a coup. Their efforts in this direction went beyond these two positions.

These efforts were reflected in the Communist insistence on the need for labor discipline. For example, they organized "voluntary" labor projects in which workers did special tasks on their free time, particularly in the social area of the economy. Typical of the Communist efforts in this direction was a report of a party plenum in 1971. *El Siglo* recounted a speech by Mario Zamorano to this plenum: "With respect to the multiple forms that the workers' new attitude toward their plants, production and work discipline must take, Compañero Zamorano recommended a broad and creative spirit to promote production. A concrete way to do this is through the spirit of emulation that can be manifested in a thousand ways.'" Zamorano urged that voluntary work "has to be encouraged through dialogue, persuasion, and intense propaganda," especially voluntary work "performed within the worker's own company or service."[28]

The Communists' desire to avoid too great polarization and confrontation was also shown by the fact that they, almost alone among the elements making up the Unidad Popular, showed genuine concern about the degree to which inflation was weakening the regime. For instance, Orlando Millas, reporting to a Central Committee plenum in March 1972, stated: "It is a matter of life or death not to permit the repetition of the inflationary cycles to which the bourgeois governments have been accustomed, to reduce severely the emission of money, to improve the health of the economy of the country."[29]

The Communists' desire to avoid a violent confrontation, particularly with the armed forces, was also demonstrated by their support of certain policies. They strongly backed the three efforts to reach agreement with the Christian Democrats on a definition of the three areas of the economy. They likewise, supported bringing the military into the cabinet on all three occasions on which this was done.

At the same time, the Communists tended to go out of their way not to attack the military, and even to praise them. This effort was recognized by the very anti-Communist *El Mercurio* two days before the September 11 coup, when in an editorial it said of the Communist party that "its leaders outdid one another in rendering tribute to these institutions and in recognizing their valuable participation in the cabinets of President Allende."[30]

Typical of the public attitude of the Communist party towards the armed forces was a statement by Luis Corvalán in his interview with *Le Drapeau Rouge* in January 1971. He remarked that any move to form paramilitary groups was "equivalent to showing distrust in the army" and that the Chilean army "is not invulnerable to the new winds blowing in Latin America and penetrating everywhere."[31]

Less than three months before the coup, Corvalán was quoted in *Chile Hoy* as saying that the reactionaries "are claiming that we have an orientation towards replacing the professional army. No sir, we continue and will continue to support keeping our armed institutions strictly professional."[32]

Finally, there is some evidence that the Communists were in fact more cautious than other elements in the UP about forming paramilitary groups that would provoke the military into action against the government. Although the Communist Youth had for some time had special units known as Ramona Parra Brigades, it appears that these groups were not armed until well into 1973.[33]

The Communists did finally establish their own paramilitary formations, not so much because they wished to but because they had largely lost control of the situation. During the last months of the Allende regime, there was little the Communists could do to save the situation.

COMMUNIST EFFORTS TO STRENGTHEN
THEIR PARTY

Throughout the Allende period, the Communists sought to take advantage of the situation to strengthen their own position. They held key ministries during all of the UP's nearly three years in power. Perhaps even more important, they held subsecretariats in other ministries. Probably the most significant of these was the subsecretariat of interior, held throughout the period by Daniel Vergara.

The Communists were also given their share of other jobs in the public administration. These included positions as managers of government-owned firms, which were apportioned on a party basis. From time to time, they were very critical of some of the plant managers of the other Unidad Popular parties, perhaps indicating that they were paving the way for these people's removal if the time became opportune.

As the economy worsened and the prospect of rationing arose, the Communists prepared to turn this situation to their own benefit. They took the lead in forming the so-called Juntas de Abastecimiento Popular, a network of committees throughout the country, whose ostensible function in the beginning was to see to it that the local merchants in working-class areas did not gouge their customers. When rationing became a reality in 1973, the JAPs became the organizations responsible for distributing basic commodities to working-class neighborhoods. The opposition frequently charged that the JAPs were used to coerce those workers who did not support the Unidad Popular. Under the control of the Communists, they could in time have become a tool for exerting pressure on other elements of the regime as well as on opposition groups. However, the Unidad Popular's grip on power never became firm enough, or the relative strength of the Communists within the regime great enough, for the Communists to make a bid for power at the expense of their coalition partners.

Thus, throughout most of the Allende government the Communists sought to have the Unidad Popular regime move towards its objectives as deliberately and in the most organized way possible. It attempted to keep the process of change carried out by the regime under as strict control of the government and of the top leadership of the Unidad Popular as possible. Hence, the Communists came into almost constant conflict with the MIR and into frequent clashes with the Left wing of the Socialist party, both of which were less cautious, less deliberate, and more impatient than the Communists.

SOCIALIST PARTY FACTIONALISM

Unlike the Communists, the Socialists were not a rigidly disciplined, highly centralized party. On the contrary, the Partido Socialista had been plagued with continuous factionalism from its inception. This continued to be true during the Allende regime.

During the period of the Unidad Popular, four factional groups existed within the Socialist party. One was the element that controlled the party at the time of Allende's victory in 1970. This group was led by Aniceto Rodríguez, who had succeeded Raúl Ampuero as secretary general of the party, when Ampuero was expelled from the leadership and from the party itself in 1967. The Rodríguez section of the Socialist party generally shared Raúl Ampuero's belief in Marxism-Leninism and, after Eduardo Frei's victory, had come to the conclusion that a victory for the Revolution was only possible through violence. Nevertheless, it had been willing to participate in the Unidad Popular experiment, albeit with skepticism.

Important to the Socialist situation during the Allende years was the fact that Aniceto Rodríguez had himself been a serious rival of Allende for the Socialists' nomination as UP candidate for the presidency in 1970. The party leadership, under the control of Rodríguez, had nominated Allende only with great reluctance. As a result, Allende did not like Rodríguez, and vice versa. It was thus very difficult for Allende as president to form a close alliance with the Rodríguez faction, as a result of which he more or less became the logical ally of the other major organized group within the Socialist ranks.

The principal competitor of the Rodríguez faction was that led by Senator Carlos Altamirano. Altamirano was a scion of the Chilean aristocracy, but had gained fame during the 1960s for being an activist extremist within the Socialist party. At one point, because of the violence of his personal attacks on President Frei, he was arrested and was threatened with losing his seat in the Senate.

Altamirano was even more convinced than the Rodríguez group that violence was the only road to "total power." In accordance with this position, he and his faction had developed a close working relationship with the MIR. This association continued throughout the Allende government. Altamirano had particularly strong support among the Socialist Youth and generally among the younger members of the party.

The third element in the Socialist party might be called its Social Democrats. They were not Leninists; they believed in political democracy in principle, and not just as a tool for achieving a dictatorship. Rather than being organized as a faction, they were dispersed throughout the party. They were perhaps strongest among its trade unionists. In the 1940s, they had tended to be predominant in the party but had lost out in later decades. During the Allende government, they had little or no influence within the Socialist party hierarchy.

A fourth group, very amorphous in nature, might be found within the Socialist Party. This element, much stronger in the rank and file than in the leadership, might be labeled "the friends of the president." Although Allende had not usually aligned with any faction and had no faction of his own, he was widely popular within the rank and file of the party. If he had had a showdown with any of the competing factions of his party, he would likely have had the strong backing of the majority of the Socialist militants. One of the tragedies of the political situation, as it developed between 1970 and 1973, was that Allende never put his widespread popularity to the test. There were a few leaders who perhaps belong in this category of presidential friends; Clodomiro Almeyda and José Toha, members of virtually all of Allende's cabinets, were most outstanding in this regard.

THE ASCENSION OF CARLOS ALTAMIRANO

When Allende became president, the Aniceto Rodríguez faction still controlled the Socialist party. At the end of January 1971, at the party's Twenty-third Ordinary Congress, Rodríguez was deposed as secretary general, and with President Allende's support a new Central Committee, largely composed of Altamirano's backers, proceeded to elect Carlos Altamirano as secretary general. The party machinery was completely in the hands of Altamirano and his associates for the duration of the Allende government.

Julio Cesar Jobet has said of the Altamirano group at the January 1971 convention that "it aspired to change the leadership and open it to a large number of young people, desirous of giving more dynamism to the UP, accentuating its theoretical and political role as the axis of the government and the political party of the Chief of State."[34]

The Central Committee membership of the party was increased at this convention from twenty-eight to forty-five. Most of the new people elected were in their twenties and early thirties; and only nine of the twenty-eight members of the former Central Committee were reelected.[35] The only member of the new Central Committee who had been in a top leadership position at the time of the reunification of the Socialists in 1957 was Clodomiro Almeyda.[36] Thus, the leadership of the Socialist party after January 1971 was not only representative of the far Left elements, but it was also exceedingly young, lacked much political experience, and had few among its number who would hold back from a policy of adventurism and confrontation, such as that which was put forward by Secretary General Altamirano.

The positions adopted by the Twenty-third Congress of the Socialist party, and by its new Central Committee and secretary general soon afterwards, indicate important differences from those of the Communist party. For example, the section of the political resolution of the Congress dealing with the Christian Democrats read as follows:

At the present time, the bourgeoisie is grouped around the Christian Democracy and secondarily around the Partido National and the Radical Democracy. The so-called "left of the Christian Democracy" with its continuation in that party and with its indecision, is serving as a shield for the Right and the reactionary sectors which participate in the great conspiracy against the government of Comrade Salvador Allende and against the workers. Only a policy of profound transformations and growing acceleration of the revolutionary process will force a definition upon the groups of Christian Democratic workers.[37]

This line of reasoning was in sharp contrast to the Communists' stated desire to get as much cooperation as possible from the Christian Democrats for the fulfillment of the Unidad Popular program, and to wean away as large a segment of the Christian Democrats as possible from the influence of the PDC leadership. It reflected the Socialist leadership's feeling of great urgency in bringing about the Revolution, which was again in sharp contrast with the Communists' willingness to move steadily but cautiously, even to make partial retreats from time to time if that was necessary to consolidate gains already made.

The perspective of the Socialists was set forth in its political resolution at the January 1971 congress:

The conjunction of measures taken and initiated by the government reinforces objectively the revolutionary potential of the situation, and sharpens the polarization of classes. . . . The contradiction between the growing forces of the masses and the power of the bourgeoisie defines this stage as an essential transitory period. Our objective, therefore, must be that of strengthening the government, making more dynamic the action of the masses, crushing the resistance of the enemies and converting the present process into an irreversible march towards socialism. . . . We recognize self-critically that some of the actions of the workers have gone beyond the political direction of the Unidad Popular and are raising, in fact, the question of power.[38]

In contrast to the Communists' emphasis on winning over to the government, or at least neutralizing, as much of the lower middle class and even middle middle class as possible, at least in the short run, the Socialists declared open war on all elements of the bourgeoisie. Their political resolution stated that the Socialist party "postulates the class independence of the workers vis-a-vis the Chilean bourgeoisie, which as the class which maintains the present order constitutes together with imperialism an irreversibly counter-revolutionary force. Alliances and permanent agreements with it have brought defeats and postponements to the camp of the exploited."[39]

Finally, although paying homage to the need for maintaining the unity of the Socialists and Communists within UP and the government, the Socialists' political resolution took a very different attitude from that of the Communists towards the revolutionary groups outside of the UP. It noted that differences between the Socialists and Communists "must be overcome in action and through ideological discussion," and that "equally, the relations of the Socialist and Communist parties with other Marxist movements must be defined in action, establishing political alliances which are necessary as a function of the process of the Chilean revolution.''[40] Although this passage does not mention the MIR by name, it certainly refers to it in the mention of ''other Marxist movements.'' In so doing, it differs markedly from the Communists' position, which did not recognize any ''Marxist groups'' except the Communist party and (somewhat grudgingly, for tactical purposes) the Socialist party.

Carlos Altamirano remained secretary general of the Socialist party throughout the Allende regime. In May 1973, a party conference, which was interpreted by some as a ''decisive defeat'' for Altamirano, replaced the two under secretaries of the party with people allied with Allende against Altamirano, but Altamirano remained in charge of the party apparatus.[41] Allende did not then or later undertake a break with Altamirano or bring his own great power to bear within the party to remove the secretary general.

STRENGTH AND INFLUENCE OF THE SOCIALIST PARTY

The significance of the Altamirano faction's triumph within the Socialist party early in the Allende regime was heightened by the fact that the Socialists quickly emerged as the largest and most popular of the Unidad Popular parties. For more than twenty years before Allende's victory, the Socialists had been inferior to the Communists in popularity and voting strength; now this situation was reversed.

The shift in the fortunes of the Socialist and Communist parties was shown in the municipal elections of April 4, 1971. In this poll, the Socialists emerged as the second largest party in the country in terms of votes, trailing only the Christian Democrats, and they considerably surpassed their Communist colleagues and rivals.

The Socialists had received only 12.2 percent of the popular vote in the 1969 congressional elections, the last previous vote in which a meaningful comparison is possible. However, in the April 1971 municipal elections, they got 22.38 percent of the total, being outdone only by the 25.62 percent showing of the Christian Democrats. The Communists, on the other hand, who had received 15.9 percent in 1969, only moved up one percentage point to 16.9 percent in 1971. Thus, the Socialists received in the municipal elections almost half again as many votes as the Communists.[42]

Unquestionably, Allende was primarily responsible for this change in the fortunes of the Socialist party. His personal popularity was at perhaps an all-time high at the time of the municipal elections, and those without any particular party affiliation who wanted to show their support for the president and his administration were more frequently than not inclined to vote for the party to which he belonged.

In the 1973 congressional elections, the Socialists still surpassed the Communists in the popular vote, although by nowhere near as wide a margin as they had done two years earlier. In March 1973, Socialists received 18.66 percent of the total vote, and the Communists got 16.22 percent. The Communists had thus lost only about half a percentage point, whereas the Socialists' vote had fallen by almost 4 percent.[43]

The area in which the Socialists did not make as notable gains in popular support was in the organized labor movement. The elections in the CUTCh in mid-1972 seemed to indicate that the Unidad Popular as a whole lost ground to the Christian Democrats and that much of this loss may have been at the expense of the Socialists. There seemed to be relatively little discussion about the Communists' receiving more votes than any other group, and the Socialists were finally recognized as having obtained a few thousand more votes than the Christian Democrats. However, the fact that it took six weeks of counting before the position of the Socialists was recognized would seem to cast some doubt as to whether, in fact, they were the second force in the CUTCh.

ALLENDE AND THE SOCIALIST LEADERSHIP

Although Allende supported the Altamirano triumph over the Aniceto Rodríguez faction in the January 1971 congress of the Socialist party, he felt increasingly uncomfortable in his relationship with the Altamirano leadership.

Since no split took place in the Socialist party during Allende's regime, and since I was privy neither to internal publications of the Socialist party nor to those of the presidency of the republic, it is not possible to document in any detail controversies and conflicts between Allende and the Altamirano faction. However, based on discussions with friends and acquaintances in the Socialist, Communist, and Radical parties, as well as with Christian Democrats and other members of the opposition, both during and after the Unidad Popular period, as well as scanty published speculation, mainly in the anti-UP press, it is possible to make some educated guesses as to the nature of these arguments.

Allende and Altamirano disagreed on at least five issues: the nature and rapidity of the process of change; relations with the MIR and with its illegal activities; negotiations with the Christian Democrats to get an agreement on the "areas" of the economy and other issues; the presence of military men in the cabinet; and conspiracy by Altamirano and others within the armed forces.

From time to time, the Socialist party leadership was highly critical of what they conceived to be the government's "slowness" in carrying out the Unidad Popular program. These complaints were sometimes made public, as in June 1971 when the Agrarian Commission of the Socialist party strongly criticized the government's conduct of the agrarian reform program. Among other things, it noted, that "it is incomprehensible to the masses that there are negotiations with the landlord concerning his reserve, when in the program of the UP it is set forth that expropriation will take place 'without the owner having any preferential right to choose his reserve.'" This same document also stated a point of view which, judging from his repeated public statements, President Allende rejected. It said that "we must think that it will not be possible to produce a change through a gradual transition which is not accompanied by violence."[44]

One of the most difficult problems between the president and his party was that of relations between the Socialist party and the MIR. As the political resolution of the 1971 party congress indicated, Altamirano and his colleagues favored working with the MIR, even though it was not part of the Unidad Popular and was frequently very critical of the Allende regime. Cooperation on a local level not infrequently meant that Socialists, sometimes including those holding patronage jobs with the government, collaborated with MIRistas in seizing landholdings, houses, and other property. Allende at various times announced his objection to such illegal activities, and Altamirano himself occasionally observed that they were unwise. Nonetheless, little was done to discipline Socialists who worked with MIRistas in such illegal seizures. Nor was much done about the fact that some younger Socialists held dual membership in the MIR. At one point, such dual membership was declared incompatible,[45] but in only a handful of cases was action taken against Socialists who also held membership in the MIR.

The Altamirano leadership of the Socialist party did its utmost-and successfully—to thwart Allende's attempts to reach agreement with the Christian Democrats. Both in March and in June 1972, agreements were in fact reached between PDC negotiators and those speaking for the president. Altamirano himself is authority for the assertion that the Socialist party leadership thwarted the ratification of these agreements.[46]

At the time of the June 1972 negotiations, the Christian Democratic newspaper *La Prensa* commented on this attitude of the Socialist leadership: "The Central Committee of the Socialist Party attempted to create obstacles until the last moment to the Government's seeking to compromise with the Christian Democracy, and yesterday, at the time of the closing of this edition, the Political Commission was studying the implications of the agreement which seems to have been reached between the PDC and the Government."[47]

The Socialist party leadership officially and publicly opposed another attempt at compromise, which involved an initiative by Communist Minister of Economy Orlando Millas but no direct negotiations with the PDC. This was the bill Millas introduced in January 1973 to define the three areas of the economy. The Socialist Political Commission's formal objection to the Millas proposal provoked a letter from President Allende supporting Millas' initiative and reminding the Socialists that Millas' move was in conformity with the Unidad Popular position.[48]

There is also some evidence that Altamirano originally opposed the entry of the military into the government at the beginning of November 1972. Soon after the formation of the UP-military cabinet, a plenum of the Central Committee of the Socialist party was held to discuss the issue. The opposition press reported at the time that President Allende himself attended the meeting and that it was only after he delivered an impassioned plea that the plenum overrode objections to the presence of the military in the administration.[49]

Altamirano's treatment of Allende often seemed to border on the insolent. An example is in a letter he wrote to the president, dated June 4, 1973. After discoursing at some length on the Socialist party leadership's demand for changes in the top ranks of the Carabineros, Altamirano wrote: "Frankly we don't understand this attitude of yours in circumstances which demand more than ever an attitude of firmness, decision and loyalty among the forces of the revolution. Even less, the clear deceit surrounding a matter of this kind, in dealing with the principal force of the Government to which you yourself belong." Altamirano then announced that the party was ordering the resignation of the minister of interior and the *intendente* of Santiago, both members of the Socialist party.[50]

It is certain that Allende was very upset by and very much opposed to the conspiratorial activities of Altamirano and his associates in the military. These activities became public in August 1973, at a time when the president was trying desperately to get the cooperation of the military in facing the crisis provoked by the second truckers' strike.

After the elections of March 1973, Allende and his supporters moved to limit Altamirano's influence within the Socialist party. A plenum of the Central Committee resulted in the naming of a new Political Commission of the party. Three men who were regarded by the opposition to be close supporters of Allende—Clodomiro Almeyda, Hernan del Canto (ex-minister of interior and ex-secretary general of the government), and Rolando Calderon (ex-minister of agriculture), were named to the Political Committee. *El Mercurio* commented on this change: "In Socialist spheres it is felt that Almeyda in a few weeks or months will be the one who takes the reins of the political group in favor of an orientation in the direction of moderation, to which Altamirano doesn't want to adhere.[51]

Although Allende moved to curb Altamirano's influence, he did not act —at least not until it was too late—to break with the party secretary general and oust him from his post. Although close friends and political associates continually urged Allende to take this step, he held back. His rationale was that if Altamirano and his followers were to quit the Socialist party and join forces with the MIR and other extremist groups, they could for the first time create a major force of opposition to the Left of the government. He feared that this would seriously weaken the position of the regime and that it was better to keep the Altamirano group within the Socialist party where they could be "controlled." He realized too late that Altamirano and his associates had already escaped all "control" by Allende and that the continuation of Altamirano as the principal spokesman for the president's own Socialist party had weakened the government among the only group that was really in a position to overthrow the regime—the armed forces.

THE MIR

The Movimiento de Izquierda Revolucionaria was not part of the Unidad Popular coalition. In fact, the Unidad Popular victory in the 1970 presidential election was a major defeat for the MIR, sowing doubt among its own members and its sympathizers as to the Movimiento's thesis that the Revolution could only be brought about in Chile through guerrilla war.

The MIR leadership recognized the impact of the UP victory. The National Secretariat of the MIR issued a statement soon after September 4, 1970, in which it admitted that "the electoral majority obtained by the Left has brought some confusion into the ranks of the Revolutionary Left, especially among its youngest militants and in the periphery."[52]

This same statement elucidated the doctrinal position which the MIR maintained throughout the Unidad Popular period. It made clear the divergence of the MIR from the Unidad Popular, and particularly from the Communists: "We will declare that the defense of the triumph lies on the level of mass mobilization more than on possible institutional supports. We shall try to displace the center of decision-making from the Moneda and the corridors of Congress to the mobilized mass fronts. We shall raise slogans such as 'Allende to the Moneda, Power to the People.'"[53]

The MIR statement also indicated that the organization had by no means given up its insurrectionary orientation. It insisted that "because the *Left's electoral majority* only produced an impasse between the classes in Chile, a *left-wing government,* with the state apparatus and the system of exploitation in the towns and countryside of Chile still untouched, can only mean that the Left occupies posts in the executive; and the goal remains the struggle for the *seizure of power by the workers,* which inevitably involves an armed confrontation, sooner or later."[54] [Emphasis in the original.]

On the basis of this early statement, the MIR adopted a flexible policy. Although expressing its critical support of the Unidad Popular government, it followed a policy of taking advantage of the tolerance of that regime to expand its insurrectional activities, in the form of armed seizures of agricultural land, apartment buildings, and other "bourgeois" property holdings.

Allende's strategy in handling the MIR and other smaller extremist groups was in effect to buy them off. He hoped that by legalizing their parties and groups, exhorting them to cooperate with the revolutionary program of the UP regime, giving them some patronage, and forbidding the Carabineros to interfere with their illegal activities, except in cases where they were caught *in flagrante delicto* and it could not be avoided, he could win the tolerance of the extremists and ensure that they would not try to launch a guerrilla conflict against his government.

President Allende demonstrated his tolerance of the MIR almost immediately after taking office. He freed all MIR members and other extremists who had been jailed for bank robberies, supermarket stickups, and other "guerrilla" activities committed during the Frei administration. In doing so, Allende announced that they were "young idealists, who have a different and distinct tactic, who act erroneously, but inspired by a superior desire for social transformation." He declared his freeing of the MIRistas as being "destined precisely to eliminate and eradicate violence definitively."[55]

It was widely believed that MIRistas were given some of the positions in the presidential bodyguard, the so-called Grupo de Amigos del Presidente (GAP). This group, which included between fifty and one hundred members at any one time, consisted of young men who accompanied the president wherever he went and also supplemented the Carabineros guarding the presidential palace La Moneda and the presidential residence at Tomás Moro.

The great majority of GAP—the turnover of which was substantial during Allende's thirty-four months in power—were probably members of the Socialist Youth. Some of them may also have held membership in the MIR.

Allende's overtures to the extremist groups were imperilled early in June 1971, when Christian Democratic ex-Minister of Interior Edmundo Pérez Zujovic was assassinated. This act was committed by members of the Vanguardia Organizada del Pueblo (Organized Vanguard of the People—VOP), a splitoff from the MIR, which had been established a couple of years before Allende came to power.

The Allende regime moved very quickly to crack down on the VOP. Nearly all of those implicated in the murder of Pérez Zujovic were themselves killed within a few days of the assassination. Part of the opposition press accused the government of getting rid of the VOPistas "because they knew too much" and implied that Eduardo Paredes, the head of the secret police and a member of the Socialist party's Central Committee, was implicated in the murder.[56] However, in spite of its virtual annihilation of the VOP, the Allende administration made no move against the MIR. The

Movimiento itself condemned the assassination of Pérez Zujovic, thus justifying continued tolerance by the government.

From time to time, Allende issued mild chastisements of the MIR and other left-wing groups outside the Unidad Popular. Thus, in his Second Annual Message to Congress, Allende asserted: "If tactical differences flourish on occasion within Unidad Popular, even greater are those which are manifested in other revolutionary groups which, by their actions, put themselves in a potentially conflictive position with the Government and the Parties which form it. This requires reflection. If the opponent is not in the Left, the enemy must never be there."[57]

MIR ACTIVITIES

Throughout the Allende regime, the MIR carried on an extensive campaign to "arouse the revolutionary consciousness" of the workers and peasants. The campaign involved not only a great deal of propaganda but also a long series of illegal seizures of property both in the countryside and in the cities. The strategy of the MIR during this period was summed up by Miguel Enriquez, the major leader of the Movimiento, when he reportedly said that "we must be above bourgeois legality. It is necessary to dissolve Parliament, take over the industries and fundos without paying compensation."[58]

The MIR conducted extensive activities in the province of Cautín, centering on the city of Temuco, some 300 miles south of Santiago. The Movimiento was especially active among the Mapuche Indians, a poverty-stricken group making up a substantial part of the population of that province. Living on the equivalent of reservations where they had tiny plots of land, they were exceedingly poor and had largely been ignored during previous administrations. Many of the land seizures organized by the MIR were carried out by the Mapuches. In some cases, they took over large *fundos* by force, but the landholdings seized usually consisted of only a few acres.

As good followers of Fidel Castro, the MIRistas hoped to expand their rural activities to the point of establishing *focos*, areas of the country over which they, rather than the government, held effective control. In some isolated areas, they succeeded, but they were not able to take the next step of organizing a guerrilla army on the basis of such areas of control.[59]

The MIR property seizures resulted in some casualties. One source hostile to the Allende government estimated the number of such deaths at 122. Other sources estimated a considerably higher number.

The MIR organized subsidiary organizations among various segments of the population. They set up the Movimiento de Campesinos Revolucionarios (MCR) in rural areas, and the Frente de Trabajadores Revolucionarios (FTR) among urban workers. They also had an organization among the country's university students.

In terms of size, the MIR organizations never were of particular importance. The FTR received a very small vote in the CUTCh elections of 1972.
The MIR peasant groups did not seek or obtain legal recognition, and there
are no official records of their membership totals. Clearly, however, they
could not compete in size with either the UP- or PDC-controlled peasant
groups.

The MIR had considerable strength only among the students. The Movimiento had originated among student leaders of the Socialist Youth in the
mid-1960s and continued to have an appreciable following among university
students. Although they controlled the student organization of the University
of Concepción during the first two years of the Allende government, they
lost this position to the forces of the Unidad Popular.[60] In Santiago, Valparaíso, and other university centers, the MIR represented a small minority.

The MIR continued to be a thorn in the side of the Allende regime so long
as the UP remained in power. Although Allende voiced his opposition to
the land seizures and other illegal activities of the MIR, the MIR was not
deterred. Allende seldom went beyond statements. One of the few occasions
on which he did so was on April 3, 1973, when he was warned that the
MIRistas were about to try to seize private and state food-distributing agencies.
On April 4, when they actually did attack CEMADI, a private wholesaler,
they were driven off by the police, with thirty people arrested and ten injured.
The MIR denounced this action as "police repression" and said that they
were merely helping the people " to defend themselves against inflation and
the shortage of essential articles" through their raids. They called for formation of "commando groups in each factory, farm village and school" to
combat "government repression."[61]

To an increasing degree, left-wing elements of the Socialist party cooperated with the MIR. Shortly before the overthrow of the Allende government,
this cooperation was underscored when it was revealed that Socialist Secretary General Carlos Altamirano himself had joined with MIR Secretary
General Miguel Enriquez and Oscar Garretón of MAPU in conspiring with
enlisted men of the navy to undermine the discipline in that military institution.[62] Altamirano not only did not deny such activity, but boasted of it
only two days before Allende's fall.[63]

SUMMARY AND CONCLUSION

There were strong tensions within the Unidad Popular throughout the
Allende administration. The Communist party and the dominant group in
the Socialist party had very different perspectives of the situation. The
Communists favored a policy of caution, seeking to reduce the civilian
opposition to the regime, split the largest party opposed to the UP, and

prevent any situation that might provoke the intervention of the armed forces. The Socialist leadership, on the other hand, was convinced that the Allende regime was only a transitional government, paving the way for a confrontation, which was the only way to assure "full power" for the forces of the Revolution. They therefore sought to emphasize and deepen the polarization of classes within the civilian population, and to prepare militarily—within the existing armed forces and outside of them—for the armed crisis they foresaw as inevitable.

As a result of these different perspectives, the policies they advocated and followed were strikingly different. The Communists sought to develop as wide support for the regime as possible, focusing especially on the middle class, and to neutralize and split the opposition, particularly the Christian Democrats. They opposed as long as they could any moves to undermine the discipline of the armed forces or to create paramilitary groups to fight against them.

In contrast, the Socialist leadership saw the middle class as inevitable enemies of the Unidad Popular regime. They saw no hope of substantially splitting the PDC. They therefore sought to intensify class divisions in the country and to prepare for the inevitable armed confrontation, while working with the MIRistas who were of the same general orientation, and even participating with them in some of their illegal "guerrilla" activities.

Allende's view of the situation was closer to that of the Communist party than to that of the Altamirano leadership of the Socialist party. However, he feared a split with the Altamirano faction more than he feared the results of that faction's policies. He decided too late to break with Altamirano; by the time he made the decision, the fate of his regime had been sealed.

23
The Politics of the Opposition

The lines dividing the government from the opposition became increasingly taut as the Allende administration progressed. With respect to the opposition, with time this meant increasing cooperation among the major political forces aligned against the Unidad Popular regime, in spite of continuing sharp ideological and strategic differences among them.

The polarization of forces resulted in two other important trends. On the one hand, there were relatively minor splits in both camps, with elements from the Partido Demócrata Cristiano joining the pro-government alliance, and with a part of the government Radical party breaking away to join forces with the opposition. At the same time, there developed a small but vociferous element among the opponents of the regime which sought to use terrorism and other illegal methods against the government in power.

Throughout the Allende period the two major parties in the opposition continued to be the country's largest party, the Partido Demócrata Cristiano, and the right-wing Partido Nacional. Closely associated with the Partido Nacional was the Partido de la Democracia Radical (PDR), a splitoff from the Radicals which had taken shape during the 1970 election campaign and had supported Jorge Alessandri. Similarly, aligned with the PDC were the Partido Izquierda Radical, the group that split off from the Radicals in 1971, and the by-then minute Partido Democrático Nacional.

In most of the elections of this period, the opposition presented a united front. An exception was the municipal poll of April 1971, but it was true in several congressional by-elections and in the general congressional election of March 1973. Nonetheless, divergences between the PDC and its closest allies on the one hand, and the Partido Nacional and its ally on the other, continued. Almost until the last moment, the PDC group sought a basis for cooperation with President Allende, a strategy that the Partido Nacional consistently rejected. Factions within the two major opposition parties also continued, with some elements taking a "harder" line than others against the government in power.

THE OPPOSITION RADICALS

Throughout the Allende period, the Partido de la Democracia Radical, headed by Julio Durán and other former leaders of the united Radical party, was counted among the opposition to the government. During these years, it continued to align itself with its 1970 election partners. In the April 1973 congressional elections, it formed a federation with the Partido Nacional, which then joined with the PDC and its allies to establish a Confederación Democrática to offer joint candidates in the congressional races throughout the country.

The alliance of the Partido Democracia Radical with the Partido Nacional well reflected the point of view of the Radical faction. The PDR was made up of the relatively conservative and anti-Socialist element that had existed within the Radical party ranks since the early years of the twentieth century. It tended to be quite "hard line" in its relationships with the Allende regime.

A recruit to the opposition of some significance and considerable ideological interest was the new Partido Izquierda Radical (PIR), established in August 1971. This group broke away from the so-called CEN Radical party, which was a partner in the Unidad Popular. It included five senators and eight deputies, who disagreed with the decisions of the party's twenty-fifth National Convention to declare the party Marxist and to substitute new Committees of Radical Action, purely political organizations, for the traditional Radical Assembly (a social/political club) as the basic local unit of the party.[1]

The dissident leaders—among whom were many of the best known figures in the party, including its nominee for the UP presidential candidacy in 1970, Senator Alberto Baltra, and a former candidate for president, Senator Luis Bossay—immediately formed the Movimiento Radical Independiente.[2] Late in the year, a convention of the new party met and gave it the name Partido Izquierda Radical.

Meanwhile, serious questions had arisen concerning the relationship of the PIR to the Unidad Popular. The Unidad Popular named a committee headed by President Allende himself, and consisting of members of the Communist party, the MAPU, and the Partido Social Demócrata, to try to bring about a reunification of Radical ranks. This move failed early in October 1971.[3]

From the beginning the PIR expressed its intention of staying in the Unidad Popular and of supporting the Allende government. Its leaders met with the president several times to indicate their support for him. Allende encountered some difficulty, however, in bringing the dissident Radical group into his government because of opposition from the Partido Radical. It was not until January 1972 that a new cabinet reorganization gave him the chance to do so.

Relations became increasingly difficult between the PIR and the government. At the end of March, the PIR issued a statement characterizing the government's economic policies as "leading us to disaster."[4] The final break came a little more than a week later, on April 6, when President Allende repudiated an agreement which PIR Minister of Justice Manuel Sanhueza had reached with the Christian Democrats over the issue of the Hamilton-Fuentealba constitutional amendment. Thereupon, the PIR withdrew both from the government and from membership in the Unidad Popular, passing formally into the opposition.[5]

Its leaders considered the Izquierda Radical to be a party of the Democratic Left. It sought contacts with such parties as the Venezuelan Acción Democrática and proclaimed itself to be a democratic Socialist party. It also agreed with the position espoused by some National Revolutionary and Christian Democratic party leaders in several Latin American countries, that the logical alliance in these countries was between the National Revolutionaries and the Christian Democrats against conservative and authoritarian elements to their Right and totalitarian elements to their Left. Thus, too late, they formed the Radical-Christian Democratic alliance which, had it been established half a decade earlier, might well have saved Chilean democracy.

Neither Radical group constituted a major element within the ranks of those aligned against the Allende government. Each, however, was a useful ally to the major party with which it was allied, and both Radical groups served in a sense as buffers between the two principal political groups of the opposition.

Towards the end of the Allende regime, active negotiations were initiated with the purpose of unifying the two opposition Radical parties. Whether such unification would have been possible if the catastrophe of September 11, 1973, had not occurred, no one can say. Although both groups had their origins in the old Radical party, they were separated by important ideological and strategic differences, and any unity they might have achieved would probably have been highly unstable.

PATRIA Y LIBERTAD AND OTHER FRINGE GROUPS

On the fringes of the opposition, with undoubtedly some contacts with elements of the Partido Nacional, was the organization known as Patria y Libertad. Consisting of young people of the upper and middle classes, it preached armed opposition to the Allende government. There was a wide-spread belief both in government and opposition circles that Patria y Libertad had been involved in the murder of General Schneider in the weeks preceding the final election of Allende as president. They were definitely involved in the abortive military revolt of June 1973; their major leaders sought refuge in foreign embassies and went into exile for the short period before the final overthrow of the Unidad Popular regime.

Patria y Libertad specialized in painting provocative signs on the walls of buildings in Santiago and other cities and towns. Some of these called on the army to do its "patriotic duty" and oust Allende. The group also probably organized small paramilitary groups, looking towards an ultimate armed showdown with the left-wing government. It likewise had a role during the last months of the regime in organizing a neighborhood-type militia in the middle-class and wealthier *barrios* of Santiago. The ostensible purpose of this militia was to defend these areas against possible "invasions" by people from the squatter colonies located near many of the "better" sections of the city. Patria y Libertad may well have viewed such local groups as potentially useful in a violent showdown with the regime.

The group sporadically issued a periodical, *Patria y Libertad*, during the Allende regime. This publication was particularly strident in its suggestions of the need for the military to intervene in the political situation.

Patria y Libertad probably never had more than a few hundred members. However, it had personal contacts with more respectable elements of the opposition, particularly among upper-class economic groups and perhaps with some leaders of the Partido Nacional. It contributed substantially to the polarization in the country as the Allende regime went on.

There is no indication that Patria y Libertad played any role when the final military showdown with the Allende government did take place. For one thing, most of its leaders were either in exile or refugees in foreign embassies at that time. For another, the overthrow of Allende was almost completely the work of the military, with no participation by Patria y Libertad or any other organized civilian group.

Other small fringe groups with extremist proclivities were also in the ranks of the opposition and principally centered on a periodical. One of these was the group that put out the weekly newspaper *P.E.C.* (an acronym derived from Politics, Economics, Culture), edited by Jorge Rogers Sotomayor, a former Christian Democratic deputy who had long since broken with the PDC. This periodical was very extreme in its condemnation of the Allende regime, preaching the lesson that there was no hope of compromise with it or with any constituent part of the government forces.

Another small group centered on the newspaper *Tacna*, named after the Tacna regiment, which had followed General Roberto Viaux in his mutiny against the Frei government. It made clear its belief that ouster by the military was the only solution to the problem of the Allende regime. Although copies of the newspaper continued to be sold until shortly after the September 1973 coup, these were old copies, and no new ones seem to have appeared in the year or so before the coup.

THE PARTIDO NACIONAL

In spite of the noise made by Patria y Libertad and other extremist right-wing groups, the bulk of the conservative opposition to the Allende regime came from the ranks of the Partido Nacional. This party had the support of the most important landowning and business interests of the country, as well as of many white collar workers and other middle-class elements.

The Partido Nacional consistently continued to represent about 20 percent of the electorate. The Christian Democrats feared that the Nacionales might make serious inroads into their own middle-class following, as lines hardened between the government and its opponents.

The Nacionales were absolutely unwilling to make any "deals" with the Allende regime. Although even their deputies and senators voted in favor of nationalization of the copper mines in July 1971, they strongly opposed the idea of authorizing the Allende government to proceed with extensive nationalization of Chilean-owned enterprises. Undoubtedly, if the Christian Democrats had succeeded in reaching an agreement with Allende on a list of such firms and had supported their nationalization in Congress, the Nacionales would have held out and voted against such a measure.

Some of the Nacionales were more strident than others in their condemnation of the government. One of their principal editorial mouthpieces was the afternoon newspaper *La Tribuna*. It was a "popular" periodical in the sense that it tended to publish sensational and even scandalous information, particularly about the government and its leaders. It was a frequent butt of attack by the government, as we have noted in an earlier chapter.

The chief political figure to emerge within the Nacionales' ranks during the Allende period was Sergio Onofre Jarpa. He had been a leader of the youth movement of the pro-Ibáñez Partido Agrario Laborista in the 1950s and was a relatively new face in Chilean politics. He emerged as the principal spokesman for the Nacionales and gave the appearance of being their major political strategist. By early 1973, Jarpa was being discussed as a possible candidate of the Partido Nacional (which was rather lacking in attractive national leaders) in the presidential election of 1976. However, he suffered something of a setback in the March 1973 election, when he ran far behind Eduardo Frei in their joint race for the Senate, representing the province of Santiago.

At least until shortly before the coup of September 1973, the Nacionales advocated constitutional rather than violent opposition to the regime. Most of their important leaders probably feared the results of a coup that would place power in the hands of the military. Veterans of decades of democratic politics, they favored continuing the constitutional regime if at all possible.

PUBLIC DEMONSTRATIONS AGAINST THE REGIME

Sizable public demonstrations were sporadically staged against the Allende regime. The most colorful of these was the so-called March of the Pots which took place on the day Fidel Castro left Chile early in December 1971. The marchers were mostly women from the middle- and upper-class sections of Santiago, but also included many lower-class women from the poorer parts of the city. They brought with them pots and pans and other noise-makers which they used vigorously as they walked towards the center of the city. They paraded down the Alameda past the presidential palace.

Although young men of the opposition accompanied the marchers to protect them, some attacks were made on the paraders by young government supporters. However, no major incidents of violence took place.[6]

This incident received considerable publicity abroad and was also used widely as a propaganda weapon by the opposition. Subsequently, there were other street demonstrations against the regime, including student riots in its last weeks. In addition, frequent meetings were held in the Teatro Caupolican and other closed meeting places by the opposition parties and groups throughout the regime.

SPLIT IN THE CHRISTIAN DEMOCRATS

Throughout the Allende years, the Christian Democratic party remained the largest element of the opposition and the largest party in the country. Although it suffered a small split early in the Unidad Popular period, its strength was not affected. It opposed the Allende regime throughout the administration, but the nature of this opposition changed somewhat over the years.

The process of separating the various groups or factions making up the Christian Democracy during most of the time it was in power was completed in the middle of 1971, a little more than six months after Allende took office. The first step in this process of disaggregation had been the splitaway in 1969 of the so-called *Rebeldes*, along with a few of the *Terceristas*, to form the Movimiento Acción Popular Unida (MAPU). The second schism two years later separated most of the *Terceristas* from the party.

The issue which brought the *Terceristas*' discontent with the PDC leadership to a head was the by-election for a seat in the Chamber of Deputies from Valparaíso. The Christian Democrats named Dr. Marín as their nominee, and he was supported by the other parties of the opposition, that is, the Partido Nacional, Partido de la Democracia Radical, and Partido Democrático Nacional. The *Terceristas* interpreted the PDC's acceptance of support of the two right-wing parties as being an alliance with the Right, which they opposed. Dr. Marín won the election.

About a month after the Valparaíso by-election, during the last week in July, there began a series of resignations from the Partido Demócrata Cristiano. Those quitting included the president of the Christian Democratic Youth, Luis Badilla, as well as two vice-presidents and several lesser officials of that group. They were followed by ex-Deputy Bosco Parra, and finally on July 30, by six Christian Democratic members of the Chamber of Deputies. These were Fernando Buzeta, Jaime Concha, Pedro Uraas, Luis Maira, Alberto Jaramillo, and Pedro Videla.[7]

Subsequently, most of the leading figures who had established MAPU in 1969 resigned from that party and joined the new Movimiento de Izquierda Cristiana, established by the *Terceristas* on leaving the PDC. The MAPUistas who joined Izquierda Cristiana included Senator Alberto Jeréz, Deputy Vicente Soler, and Jacques Chonchol, the most important figure in MAPU.

Izquierda Cristiana held its founding convention as a political party at the end of October 1971. At that meeting, it declared its support of the Allende government and its willingness to enter the Unidad Popular and the government if certain conditions were met.[8] At the end of February 1972, Izquierda Cristiana was formally registered as a political party, having submitted a petition with more than 10,000 signatures.[9] By that time, the party was a member of the Unidad Popular and had representatives in the Allende government.

After the exit of the elements forming Izquierda Cristiana, the PDC remained united. Different currents of opinion within the party leadership and rank and file continued, however, and tension among them became somewhat more acute in the last months of the Allende regime.

The differences of opinion within the PDC did not involve matters of doctrine, but rather different appreciations of how to deal with the UP administration. A relatively hard-line group, for whom Senator José Musalem was perhaps the chief spokesman, saw little or no hope in trying to reach agreement with the Allende government and the Unidad Popular. The most sanguine group in the party, in terms of the possibility of an accord with the UP, was headed by Senator Renán Fuentealba, who had been president of the party during the middle months of the Allende period. The great bulk of the party, centered on ex-President Eduardo Frei, was willing to seek an accord with the Allende regime if possible, but grew increasingly skeptical about the possibility of doing so.

These differences of opinion, which found expression in private conversations and internal meetings of the party rather than in public pronouncements, did not result in any further division in the party's ranks. In the face of its opponents to the Left and Right, the party remained united.

PDC ATTEMPTS AT NEGOTIATION

On three different occasions, the Christian Democrats entered into negotiations with President Allende or his representatives, in efforts to reach agreement on legislation that could be mutually supported by the PDC and the Unidad Popular. The Christian Democrats were willing to accept nationalization of most of the firms on the famous list of 91 which the Unidad Popular had drawn up and to aid in passing legislation authorizing such nationalization. Two of the negotiation efforts centered on this issue. The third, shortly before the fall of Allende, dealt with an effort to maintain the stability of the constitutional regime.

The first two sets of negotiations took place during 1972 and centered on the so-called Hamilton-Fuentealba constitutional amendment, introduced in October 1971 and passed by Congress in February 1972. This measure involved a proposed change in the Constitution, introduced by the two Christian Democratic senators, Juan Hamilton and Renán Fuentealba, which sought to limit and regularize the government's nationalization efforts. Robert Moss has described the essence of this amendment:

Its principal points were that no new requisitions of private firms could be carried out without specific legislation of Congress; the government would be permitted to intervene in a business (in conformity with Decree-Law 520) only if production had been interfered with for more than twenty days and if it could be proved that the administration was incompetent; and the purchase of shares by the government after October 14 [1971] would be declared null and void. Naturally, the result of this amendment would have been to deprive the government of a large part of its power which it had used to expand its control over the private sector of the economy.[10]

President Allende proceeded to veto the key parts of this amendment, giving rise to a bitter controversy between him and the congressional majority. The legislators maintained that the president had no right to veto a constitutional amendment and that the Constitutional Tribunal established at the beginning of the Allende period had no jurisdiction over the issue. President Allende, on the other hand, contended that his veto was valid unless overridden by a two-thirds majority of both houses of Congress—something which was patently impossible for the opposition to achieve, given the political makeup of the legislature.

This issue remained pending for the rest of the Allende administration.

However, the 1972 negotiations between the Christian Democrats and Allende's representatives centered around the possibility of agreement on modifications of the Hamilton-Fuentealba amendment which would be mutually acceptable and which therefore could get through Congress and would be approved by the President.

President Allende was moved to seek negotiations with the Christian Democrats for the first time by the defeat of government candidates in a by-election for the Chamber of Deputies in Linares and for the Senate in O'Higgins and Colchagua. In these races, the Christian Democrats ran Rafael Moreno, head of the Corporación de la Reforma Agraria under Frei, for the Senate, with Partido Nacional support; the Partido Nacional ran Sergio Diez for the deputy post, with backing from the Christian Democrats. Moreno won with 52.7 percent of the votes; Diez got 58 percent of the votes in his race.[11]

As a result of these defeats, President Allende authorized Minister of Justice Manuel Sanhueza, a member of the Izquierda Radical, to negotiate on his behalf with the Christian Democrats. The minister reached an agreement on a list of firms that would be nationalized. He felt that he had Allende's authorization to sign this agreement, but "when other members of the government (especially the Socialists) objected violently to the idea of restricting the powers of the executive to requisition private firms,"[12] Allende repudiated the accord. The immediate effect was the retirement of the PIR from the cabinet and soon afterwards its joining ranks with the opposition.

This situation provoked President Allende to a discourse in which he violently attacked the opposition, and threatened to dissolve Congress and submit a new constitution to a popular referendum. Since the result of such a referendum was unlikely to be favorable from his point of view, Allende backed down and some weeks later authorized further negotiations with the opposition.

Robert Moss notes that Renán Fuentealba, as president of the Partido Demócrata Cristiano, authorized Tomás Pablo and Felipe Amunátegui to deal with the president's representatives on behalf of the PDC. Several other leading figures of the party were also involved in these negotiations, including Bernardo Leighton.[13]

There was a certain time urgency involved, since a by-election for a seat in the Chamber of Deputies from Coquimbo was about to take place, and Fuentealba felt that the negotiations had to be completed before this election date. He argued that it was impolitic to be negotiating with the government when an election campaign in which the government and opposition were bitterly attacking one another was fully under way.[14]

These negotiations were no more fruitful than the previous ones. Robert Moss correctly states why: "It became clear that Allende was not prepared to give guarantees for the survival of La Papelera, or of four private banks which the Christian Democrats had originally desired to be converted into workers cooperatives."[15]

The third set of negotiations between the Christian Democrats and the government took place in August 1973 through the intermediary of Cardinal Silva. They proved to be very shortlived. The polarization of opinion and suspicions on both sides were so great that it would have required a miracle for them to have been successful. (We shall deal more extensively with these negotiations in our discussion of the final denouement of the Allende regime.)

Much controversy has raged over who was to blame for the failure of the negotiations between the Christian Democrats and Allende's representatives. The pro-Allende forces have generally tended to place the blame on the Christian Democrats, while most Christian Democrats have argued that Allende was unwilling to back up agreements reached but opposed by his more extreme supporters. Fuentealba has attributed the failure to rightwing elements outside the Christian Democratic party and to extremists, particularly in the Socialist party, in Allende's camp.[16]

Perhaps the last word on who bore the principal responsibility can be left to Carlos Altamirano. Speaking two days before the coup against Allende, he "warned the Government that the SP decided not to accept dialogues and it would only fight at its [the government's] side if it loyally fulfilled the program which says that there must be created the Popular Power, which will be given to the workers and peasants."

Altamirano emphasized that the Socialist party was against any dialogue. He said that two attempts had been made in spite of the Socialist party and that these had failed. The Socialist secretary general concluded, "The SP has said that there can be no dialogue with terrorists, with those responsible for so much misery. The Right can only be defeated with the invincible force of the people, enlisted men, noncoms, and officers united with the constituted government."[17]

Altamirano's speech suggests that the major force thwarting an agreement between the Allende government and the Christian Democratic part of the opposition was the leadership of the Socialist party. They were definitely not interested in any arrangement between the president and the PDC which might limit and regulate the nationalization of the private segments of the economy. Such agreement would have slowed down, if not frustrated, the objective of Altamirano and his associates to establish the dictatorship of the proletariat. The ultimate result of the failure of negotiations was the consolidation of the situation which made the culmination of the tragedy of Chile all but inevitable.

24

Allende and the Military

It was the military who ultimately overthrew Salvador Allende and the Unidad Popular regime. From the beginning of his term of office, Allende was aware of the possibility of such an event and sought to head it off. At the same time, he was anxious to use the prestige and supposedly "apolitical" nature of the Chilean armed forces to strengthen his regime politically, a move that may have been his second most serious political miscalculation, surpassed only by his refusal to break with Altamirano and the extreme Left. Any attempt to understand the ultimate fate of the Allende regime requires a careful analysis of the development of the relationship between the administration and the Chilean armed forces.

TRADITIONS AND ATTITUDES OF THE CHILEAN MILITARY

The Chilean military had certain characteristics that differentiated it from the armed forces of many other Latin American countries. In the light of what happened on September 11, 1973, and subsequently, many observers have tended to engage in a kind of "revisionism" by denying these differences. Such revisionists debunk the picture of the Chilean armed forces that had been widely accepted—even by President Allende—before that fateful September 11. As is the case with many revisionist movements in historiography, a kernel of truth is vastly inflated, to the point of obscuring the real nature of the situation under discussion. The fact is that in political terms the history of the Chilean armed forces was sustantially different from that of most other Latin American countries.

An understanding of the Chilean military requires a discussion of (1) the self-image of the Chilean armed forces; (2) their record with regard to intervention in overt political activity; (3) the social background of the military leaders; and (4) the civilian population's view of the armed forces.

The Chilean armed forces were very proud of their institutional past. Although they had not engaged in a foreign war for almost a century, they had won all the wars they fought in the nineteenth century—against Spain, Peru, and Bolivia. They had a high regard for their sense of discipline and confidence in their ability to conduct a war.

Compared to the military in other Latin countries, the Chilean military had a clean record of keeping out of overt political activity. Since the 1830s, the Chilean armed forces had taken an active part in making and unmaking governments in only two periods: 1890-1891 and 1924-1932. In the first case, there was a civil war, in which the navy was on the victorious side and the army on the losing side. The result was the overthrow and suicide of President José Manuel Balmaceda. Once the war was over, however, the military quickly returned to relatively free elections. Although the first elected president was the admiral who had been the principal leader of the rebel forces in the civil war, all of his successors for the next thirty years were civilians, freely chosen by the civilian electorate.

The second instance was of longer duration. It began with the culmination of the crisis that had started with the election of a reformist president, Arturo Alessandri, in 1920 and continued during almost four years of Alessandri's term in office. Military intervention began in September 1924, with the armed forces' insistence on very rapid passage of reform laws; moved on to forcing President Alessandri out of office, and then to his recall by a countercoup early in 1925. In the second phase of this Alessandri administration, as we have noted earlier, a new constitution was adopted and other fundamental changes were made, but President Alessandri was again forced out of office by the overweening ambitions of Colonel Carlos Ibáñez, who a year and a half later, in May 1927, had himself elected president. Ibáñez presided over the one dictatorship of the twentieth century before that which is presently in power, and his overthrow was succeeded by a year and a half of changing governments, alternately installed and ousted by the armed forces. This period of military intervention was brought to an end by President Arturo Alessandri, elected once again at the end of 1932. Thereafter, until September 1973, there were some military conspiracies and attempted coups, but there was no successful effort by the military to overthrow the constituted government.

Thus, in spite of recent attempts to reinterpret Chilean history, the fact is that the degree to which the Chilean military abstained from intervention is remarkable within the Latin American context. Indeed, the constitutional stability of Chile, with regularly elected government succeeding regularly elected government, is highly unusual—a record matched only by a few nations in any part of the world.

In judging the role of the military during the Allende regime, one must consider the question of the social antecedents of the members of the armed forces. This has differed somewhat for enlisted men and officers.

Chile has had conscription for decades. A certain number of young men —as many as 20,000—are called up annually for one year's service in the army. Although theoretically draftees include youths of all classes, it is to be presumed that in Chile, as in most other countries, a much higher proportion of them come from the lower economic and social groups than from the higher ones—particularly in view of the fact that the number of draftees needed each year is very much less than the number available in the 20-year age group, and it is therefore possible for youths with acceptable justification to get exempted from service.

All enlisted men in the navy and air force are volunteers. The same is true of the Carabineros, the militarized national police force, which in 1969 had some 23,000 officers and men. These national police have tended to make their careers in the service, the disciplinary standards of which are strict.[1]

For many decades, the officer corps of the armed forces, especially the army, has been drawn largely from the lower middle classes, particularly from the sons of public employees and other white collar workers. There is evidence that these officers have regarded their careers as a means of attaining social mobility.[2] Another important element among the officers consists of members of "military families," that is, those whose fathers were also military officers.

In the past, considering the lower middle-class origins of the officer corps, there was strong support in the military for social reform movements. This was most noticeable in the 1924-1932 period, and perhaps for a few years thereafter. Presumably, many of the officers, especially the younger ones, who were active in the 1970-1973 period were also sympathetic to the cause of Chile's poorer classes. This attitude may have been reinforced by the longstanding discontent within the military over their own living and working conditions, a discontent that had found expression in the abortive military coup late in 1969. It is likely that the officers generally looked with sympathy on the efforts of President Allende to improve their situation.

The social origins of the officers may have made them dubious however, about one other aspect of the Allende regime. This was the emphasis the president and his whole administration placed on portraying their regime as representative particularly of "the workers," which was usually interpreted as meaning the manual workers. The evident hostility of many elements in the Allende coalition towards the middle class, even the lower middle class, did not generate sympathy among officers who came from that group.

Even more important, however, was the officers' concern for the armed forces as an institution. The conditions of life in the armed forces, military discipline, and the special role the officers saw their institution as fulfilling within Chilean society made the preservation of the military institution the first priority for many of them. No matter how much they may have been willing to allow the civilians to run the civilian economy and society, they were certain to resist any moves that might destroy the cohesion and unity of the armed forces themselves.

With regard to the average Chilean civilian's attitude toward the armed forces, it may be generalized that unlike the situation in many other Latin American countries, the Chilean civilians did not have a strong dislike for their armed forces. To the contrary, they tended to be proud of them and to have a high regard for them, perhaps, because in spite of their recent history, they tended to regard their nation as one with military prowess. The respect and regard for the army, navy and air force also had something to do with the very fact that they were not constantly engaged in ousting governments and putting in new ones.

The Carabineros, on the other hand, did not enjoy such a high opinion among the Chilean masses. This militarized national police force had too often been used to help break strikes and to enforce unpopular laws. Furthermore, the Carabineros were always visible. They were feared even in the most humble parts of the cities and in the countryside, whereas the three senior armed forces were seldom put into a situation of confrontation with groups of civilians.

ALLENDE'S PROMISES WITH REGARD TO THE MILITARY

When Allende and the Unidad Popular administration came to power, the Christian Democrats' great fear was that they would try to convert the armed forces into their own partisan political tools. During negotiations leading up to the Christian Democrats' support for Allende in Congress, this question immediately loomed in importance.

Part of the agreement between Allende and the Christian Democrats which was converted into law dealt with the armed forces. It provided that "the organic structures and hierarchies of the Armed Forces and Carabineros be respected, the systems of selection, perquisites, and disciplinary norms now existing; that these groups be assured of adequate equipment for their mission as watchmen of the national security, and that their work on national development not be used to change their specific functions, nor compromise their budgets, nor create armed organizations parallel to the Armed Forces and Carabineros."[3] The PDC regarded this pledge as a rather secure guarantee that the Unidad Popular government would not be able to "colonize" the top ranks of the armed forces by giving preferential treatment to people politically sympathetic to it. The PDC reasoned that even if, as commander-in-chief, Allende chose what he considered the most politically desirable officers among those eligible for promotion to the highest ranks, it would take longer than one presidential term to develop a group at the top who would be pledged specifically to the political policies of the Unidad Popular.

Allende did not violate this agreement insofar as treatment of the armed forces was concerned. He did not seek to manipulate the hierarchy of the four services so as to favor his political allies. However, Allende did not fulfill the last part of the agreement, to prevent the creation of "armed organizations parallel to the Armed Forces and Carabineros." His failure to do so proved fatal to him and his regime.

ALLENDE'S GENERAL ATTITUDE TOWARDS THE ARMED FORCES

As president, Allende sought to maintain friendly relations with the armed forces and their leaders. He made it a policy to "show the flag," so to speak, as commander-in-chief. Allende went out of his way to attend military ceremonies, personally award honors, and take part in patriotic and other celebrations of the military. He wanted to give them a feeling that he had a concern for them, for their welfare, and for their role as defenders of the national sovereignty.

Allende also demonstrated his confidence in the military officers by appointing many of them to posts in the civilian administration for which their technical training qualified them. Such appointments were not unusual for a Chilean president. With regard to this aspect of Allende's policy, Gary MacEoin states that "a general was named head of the Chuquicamata Copper Company, and representatives of the three services were put on the national production boards of the copper, iron and nitrate companies, and also on the National Planning Organization."[4] A military man was also put in charge of the increasingly difficult and pressing problem of allocating consumer goods during the last half of the administration.

There are indications, too, that Allende met frequently with the military high command. He is reported to have had lengthy discussions with them at least fourteen times during his first seven months in office. At one point, he explained that he discussed with the military leaders "the future of national institutions."[5] In April 1971, the president was reported to have met with 1,600 officers and noncoms at a stadium in Santiago. He addressed them for two hours, although no official version of what he had discussed with them was ever released.[6]

Furthermore, Allende showed a genuine confidence in the loyalty of many top officers of the armed forces. He had a high opinion of the loyalty of General Carlos Prats, and of Prats' successor, General Augusto Pinochet.

Similarly, Allende had full confidence in the top officers of the Carabineros, whom he felt would remain loyal even if the army, navy, and air force deserted him.

Allende frequently gave public expression to his faith in the armed forces, as for example, in his First Annual Message to Congress, on May 21, 1971:

I have absolute confidence in the armed forces' loyalty. . . . Our forces are professional forces at the service of the state, of the people. The Chilean Armed Forces and the Carabineros, faithful to their duty and to their tradition of non-intervention in the political process, will support a social organization which corresponds to the will of the people as expressed in the terms of the established Constitution. . . . The difficulties we face are not in this field.[7]

Allende probably had too much confidence that the Chilean armed forces would remain attached to their forty-year tradition of supporting the constituted regime. Also, he obviously had misplaced belief in the loyalty of certain top officers—for instance, in Augusto Pinochet, who, unbeknownst to Allende, was one of the leading figures in the plotting against him; or the top Carabinero officers in whom he placed his confidence, who were unwilling to defend him and instead gave way to the seventh man in the police hierarchy, who was one of the conspirators against the regime.[8]

Finally, Allende showed his desire to get along with the armed forces leaders by his agreement to their continuing to get aid from the United States. The loans granted by the United States for military purchases, and agreements to allow the military to buy other U.S. equipment on their own, would not have been possible without Allende's support.

Even bitter opponents of the Allende regime grudgingly paid tribute to his concern for the prestige and material welfare of the armed forces. *El Mercurio* recognized Allende's regard for the military in an editorial:

Insofar as the Armed Forces are concerned, it is just to recognize that this Government adopted a policy of paying greater attention to the most urgent needs of these institutions.

It is certain that this new treatment of the military branches of the State has permitted the men under arms to recover little by little the position which they formerly had in Chilean society, thus overcoming a state of relative alienation which occurred because the limits of the constitutional obedience of the Armed Forces were never clarified, nor were the limits of the patience in supporting with heroism the grave risks of slow professional deterioration due to lack of indispensable requirements.[9]

While paying respect to the armed forces, Allende also respected the hierarchy of the military, as he had promised to do before becoming president. Thus, his first choices for commanders of the military branches were General Carlos Prats, who was a holdover from the Frei government, for the army; Vice-Admiral Raúl Montero Cornejo, the second-ranking officer in the navy; and General César Ruíz Danyau, the third-ranking officer of the air force. None of these choices basically interfered with the chain of command.[10] These appointments set the pattern for the rest of his administration.

There were only two important premature retirements of officers for political reasons until the last weeks of the regime. One was Rear Admiral Victor Bunster del Solar, naval attache in Washington, who was accused of close relations with the CIA. The other was Colonel Alberto Labbe Troncoso, secretary general of the army and commandant of the Military School. He was summarily retired after sudden mass "illness" overtook the cadets of the school when Fidel Castro was scheduled to visit it.[11]

ALLENDE'S INVOLVEMENT OF THE MILITARY IN THE GOVERNMENT

Quite early in his administration, Allende began to put military officers in cabinet positions where they necessarily assumed political responsibility for government decisions. In April 1962, when the Partido Izquierda Radical withdrew from the government and the Unidad Popular, Allende brought a military man into his cabinet for the first time. This was Army Brigadier General Pedro Palacios, who became minister of mines. In this instance, military participation in the cabinet did not last very long. With a new cabinet crisis in June 1972, General Palacios withdrew from the government. According to an important opposition leader who was presumably in a position to know, the general retired from his ministerial post because the principal military chiefs had come to think that it compromised the armed forces for one of their number to have to sign "decrees of insistence" legalizing seizures of private enterprises.[12]

The second military appointment to the cabinet was made during the first truckers' strike early in November 1972. This time three military men, representing the army, navy, and air force, respectively, became ministers. Most important of all, the head of the army, General Carlos Prats, assumed the quasi-prime ministerial post of minister of interior. At the same time, Admiral Ismael Huerta became minister of public works, and Air Force Brigadier General Claudio Sepúlveda was made minister of mining. The officers' cabinet colleagues included four Socialists, three Communists, two Radicals, one member of MAPU, and two "independent Leftists."[13] The Izquierda Cristiana refused to have its members serve alongside military men in the cabinet.[14]

The UP-military cabinet had two basic purposes: to reestablish social stability after the trauma of the truckers' strike, and to guarantee that the

March 1973 congressional elections would be held in a peaceful and honest manner. As a result, it left office soon after the elections, and the military retired from political participation in the regime.

The armed forces leaders were brought into the Allende government for the third and last time during the last weeks of the regime, when the situation of the administration and of the constitutional system itself was desperate. On August 10, a "cabinet of national security" was established.[15] Four officers of the armed forces, this time including the Carabineros, entered the government. General Carlos Prats became minister of defense; General José María Sepúlveda, chief of the Carabineros, became minister of lands and colonization; Air Force General César Ruíz Danyau was named minister of public works and transport; and Admiral Raúl Montero Cornejo was put in the ministry of finance. Members of the UP parties made up the rest of the cabinet.[16]

This cabinet was of short duration. It disintegrated rather than resigning as a body. Only nine days after it took office, President Allende demanded the resignation of General Ruíz as minister, which he got immediately, and as chief of the air force, which he did not receive until the night of August 20.[17] Another military-UP cabinet was then installed, in which only Carabinero General Sepúlveda was a ranking officer.[18]

Meanwhile, on August 23, General Prats had been forced by his fellow generals to resign as minister and as commander of the army.[19] He was succeeded as army chief by General Augusto Pinochet, in whom President Allende had full confidence.

THE MILITARY AND THE OCTOBER 1972 CRISIS

The loyalty of the armed forces to the Allende government was of key importance in bringing the regime safely through the crisis provoked by the first truckers' strike in October-November 1972. Indeed, the military leaders' behavior at that time aroused considerable criticism from some of the political opposition.

At the time of the crisis, the military were assigned a major role. A state of emergency was declared in the Santiago region, and General Hector Bravo was placed in command to administer this virtual martial law.[20] He established a curfew between the hours of midnight and 6:00 A.M., which remained in force until November 5.[21] Thirteen other provinces were also put under martial law.[22]

The military also sought to curtail the propaganda against the regime which accompanied the truckers' strike, particularly radio propaganda. To this end, they decreed that all radio stations, for the time being, had to join a "national network" and that everything broadcast on that network would be subject to previous censorship by military authorities. Several opposition radio stations refused to conform to these regulations and as a result were temporarily forced off the air.[23]

Even though the opposition resented these activities of the military during the crisis, opponents of the Allende regime generally welcomed the entry of the armed forces leaders into the government at its end.

THE CASE OF GENERAL PRATS

General Carlos Prats was the most outstanding military leader to resist any attempt by his colleagues to subvert the constitutional regime. His name became practically synonymous with a policy of using the influence of the military to modify the policies of the Allende government rather than to overthrow it. His final removal from top command all but assured the success of those officers who had finally decided that they had to depose the Unidad Popular government.

General Prats had succeeded General René Schneider as commander-in-chief of the army, when Schneider was assassinated shortly before Allende's coming to power. Allende confirmed him in his post and kept him there until about three weeks before his own fall.

On the first anniversary of assuming office, Prats issued a special declaration, which he gave to the press and also addressed to all units of the army. In this declaration, after recounting the circumstances under which he had come to the top army post, Prats set forth his philosophy, which he insisted guided his actions as head of the army:

The tradition of command which has guided my endeavors has been that of guaranteeing the nation the most vigorous cohesion of its armed services, honoring their tradition of apolitical and legalist professionalism, the basic condition which makes the Army an unsubstitutable instrument of force, which does not deliberate.

The discipline, professional vocation, and loyalty of my subordinates, on all levels, have been essential factors in my indicating today to all of Chile my satisfaction at having this patriotic objective, in spite of constant attempts of extremists to involve the institution or its members in political affairs, or to interfere in its internal affairs. My work, then, has been especially difficult and delicate, corresponding to a new historical period of national development, different from the traditional evolution which I myself have known throughout my military career.

This opportunity is appropriate for issuing a fervent call to all Chileans, asking them to respect the serene professionalist position which—uncompromisingly—the Army has had and will have, in order to maintain itself separated from daily political matters.[24]

As we have seen, General Prats became minister of interior when the armed forces leaders entered the government in November 1972. During the next month, when President Allende went abroad on official visits and to address the United Nations General Assembly, Prats became vice-president, serving in conformity with the constitution as chief executive during Allende's absence.

Prats' experience as Chile's temporary chief executive aroused a great deal of speculation among the politicians. After Prats left the vice-presidency, rumors circulated that he had very much enjoyed the experience and would not be loath to repeat it. There were even rumors that he might be considered the Unidad Popular candidate for president in the 1976 election.

The possibility of such a candidacy coming to pass was not remote. At that time the Unidad Popular had no figure who came close to Salvador Allende in popularity and general influence. In contrast, the opposition had Eduardo Frei, who until the end of the Allende government continued to maintain a wide base of popular support. The Communists and other more moderate elements in the Unidad Popular might therefore have been willing to accept a candidacy such as that of General Prats. He might also have been expected to receive the disciplined support of the UP parties, while at the same time attracting the backing of elements who would not have voted for a nominee drawn from any of the UP parties.

There is little proof that Prats had presidential ambitions. However, such speculation was engaged in by the politicians of the opposition, as well as elements of the military who were hostile towards, or at least doubtful of, the Unidad Popular.

CHALLENGES TO THE MILITARY'S MONOPOLY OF FORCE

Of particular concern to the military during the Allende years were the large-scale arming of civilians with weapons, which for the most part were smuggled into the country; and some evidence of attempts to destroy the unity and discipline of the armed forces themselves. Together, these developments would deprive the armed forces of the monopoly of force which under the Constitution, and in their own minds, belonged to the military. They thus felt that the basic role and cohesion of the armed forces were being threatened.

Quite early in the Allende administration, fears were expressed, particularly by the opposition, concerning the existence of armed civilian groups. After the assassination of Christian Democratic leader Edmunto Pérez Zújovic in June 1971, Minister of Defense Alejandro Ríos Valdivia sought to allay such worries. He told reporters that "it is the decision of the Government to dissolve all armed groups. . . . as soon as they are discovered." At the same time, however, he insisted that the government had received little or no direct evidence of the existence of such groups.[25]

Nevertheless, Valdivia's protestation was, at the least, somewhat disingenuous. For one thing, the MIR had for years proclaimed its belief in the violent road to power, and in the last years of the Frei regime had carried out a number of armed robberies, resulting in jail terms for some of the perpetrators. Hence, it would not be expected that the MIR groups involved would have given up their arms or would cease to try to get more.

In the second place, foreign journalists, opposition politicians, and so presumably Allende's government, knew that armed groups principally associated with the MIR, were seizing landholdings of all sizes around the city of Temuco. But the government made only occasional efforts to do anything about them. The MIR made no secret of these activities—indeed they boasted about them and justified them.

These actions by armed groups of the MIR continued throughout the Allende period. In addition, large numbers of arms were imported from early in the regime, at least some of them with the tolerance, if not the support, of the government.

One case of suspected arms imports gained very wide publicity. This was in March 1972, when an unscheduled Cuban Airlines plane arrived at the Santiago airport. Eduardo Paredes, head of the secret police, was returning on this plane from a visit to Castro. Unloaded from it were thirteen very large packages, which the then Minister of Interior Hernan del Canto rushed onto trucks without their passing through customs. Subsequently, Allende and others circulated many conflicting stories as to the contents of those parcels—personal effects of Paredes, art objects for an exhibit in Santiago, gifts to the mothers' centers of Santiago from mothers of Cuba. The opposition maintained that the real content of the bundles was arms.[26] After Allende's downfall, the new regime claimed that among Paredes' possessions it had discovered a list of the contents of the mysterious packages, and that these were arms and ammunition, including automatic pistols, a great variety of cartridges, and even some rockets.[27]

A definitive explanation for what the famous "Cuban airplane" was actually bringing to Chile will perhaps never be given. At any rate, the incident, which soon became public knowledge, aroused widespread suspicion that arms were being smuggled into the country with the connivance of the Allende government, or at least of high officials of the regime.

During the last year or so of the Allende government, the arming of civilians intensified. Not only the MIR, but also the Socialist and Communist parties had paramilitary groups functioning during this period. On the other side, the rabidly right-wing Patria y Libertad was also smuggling arms and had its paramilitary formations. Even beyond that, distribution of arms, on an almost haphazard basis, among civilians who were not part of any organized political paramilitary group became widespread. In visits to Chile during this period, and after the coup of September 11, I heard well-confirmed first-hand stories that bordered on the bizarre concerning the proliferation of arms among rank-and-file citizens during the last months of Allende's government.

Elements of the Socialist party, including some government officials, were involved in these activities. On one occasion, a traffic accident in the city of San Felipe, involving a Chevrolet stationwagon belonging to the Directorate of Social Assistance of the presidency of the republic, resulted in the arrest of two men, when it was discovered that they were carrying machine gun ammunition, hand grenades, as well as guerrilla war manuals and plans showing disposition of military units in the provinces of Valparaíso and Rancagua.[28]

The problem of illicit arms provoked passage of Law no. 17,798 on October 21, 1972, the so-called Arms Control Law. President Allende largely accepted this law, seeking to veto only one article, which veto was overridden by Congress. The law prohibited the formation of any private militia or paramilitary groups. It absolutely prohibited possession of submachine guns, machine guns, and heavier types of weapons by anyone except members of the armed forces, the Carabineros, the secret police, or prison guards, and provided for licensing the use of weapons of smaller calibre. Appropriate penalties were provided for violation of these sections of the law.

The operative sections of Law no. 17,798 turned over to the Ministry of National Defense the task of searching for illegal arms. Such searches could be initiated at the request of the minister of interior, the minister of defense, legal advisers (*fiscales*) of the Supreme Court and of the Appeals Court, provincial chiefs (*intendentes*), the director general of recruitment, garrison commanders, prefects of Carabineros, and mayors and councilmen of municipalities which were county seats. President Allende vetoed the granting of such power to the last two categories, but the provision was passed over his veto. The law also provided that cases involving violations should be tried before military courts.[29]

Following passage of this law, the armed forces began actively to search for hidden arms. This search assumed growing intensity during the last months of the Allende regime.

At the same time, leaders of the military became increasingly worried about attempts by extremist elements in the Unidad Popular and to its Left to conspire within the armed forces themselves. Evidence presented before and after the coup of September 11, 1973, indicates that such activities were particularly under way in the air force and the navy. A public trial in the middle of 1974 revealed that a considerable organization, involving both junior officers and enlisted men, had been established, before September 1973 in the air force.

Plotting in the navy was brought to light and given much publicity, during the last weeks of the Allende regime. Periodicals friendly to the administration claimed that sailors who had been arrested in connection with the plot had been tortured and otherwise mistreated by those investigating the affair.[30]

Among the evidence developed in connection with this naval plot (which seems to have been confined to enlisted men), was the fact that Carlos Altamirano and Miguel Enriquez, leader of the MIR, had been among those who had been meeting with the navy men involved. Not only did Altamirano not deny such activities, but in the speech he gave two days before the coup, he boasted about his participation. He said he would continue such activities, which he claimed were designed to block any attempts by navy leaders to move against the Allende regime.[31]

STRENGTHS AND WEAKNESSES OF ALLENDE'S HANDLING OF THE MILITARY

Allende sought to maintain good relations with leaders of the country's armed forces. Not only did he demonstrate his support in symbolic ways, such as frequent appearances at military ceremonies, but he also helped improve the military's material situation and facilitated modernization of their equipment.

Allende believed in the loyalty of the top military officers and of the armed forces in general until the end. He apparently believed that their tradition of noninterference in politics, together with his favorable disposition towards them, would dissuade them from moving against his regime.

He undermined his own position vis-à-vis the military. On the one hand, he gave them political responsibility in his government to a degree that was resented by the leadership of the armed forces. On the other, his fear of forcing the left wing of his own party and the MIR into open confrontation with his administration restrained him from taking any serious steps to prevent large-scale arming of civilians and conspiracy by the far left within the military ranks—two things that he, as an experienced politician, should have known the military would not tolerate. He did not survive the disaster which these two errors of judgment brought to his regime.

25

Onset of the Fatal Crisis: October 1972-June 29, 1973

In retrospect, the events of October 1972 to September 1973 seem almost to have been preordained. Each move Allende made, seemed destined to weaken his position and to seal his fate. Every effort made by those who sought to avoid the final catastrophe seemed doomed to failure before it started. Allende's "friends" were in fact his worst enemies, but he was unable or unwilling to reach out to those who might have been able to save the situation.

The final and fatal crisis which led to Allende's fall, and to at least the temporary end of the constitutional system of Chile, can be traced to the first truckers' strike of October 1972. This event brought about the massive entry of the military on the political scene for the first time and worsened the already acute economic crisis. It also intensified the polarization of classes and political groups, thus narrowing the margin for compromise. All of these tendencies were reinforced during the following ten months.

In addition to the truckers' strike, the period of October 1972 to September 1973 witnessed the species of truce before the March 1973 elections, the elections themselves, the dismissal of the military from the government, the *tancazo* of June 29, 1973, and the rapid intensification of the crisis after that date. In the end, the economy was barely functioning, the government was all but powerless, and plotting was going on from several directions. The tragic result was September 11, 1973.

BACKGROUND OF THE FIRST TRUCKERS' STRIKE

The onset of the crisis of the regime can be traced to the first indications that state control over the economy was to be extended into the trucking industry. Such an action had not been provided for in the Unidad Popular program, and trucking was an industry that by no stretch of the imagination could be classified as a "monopoly." The first moves to bring the trucking industry under state control also ran counter to promises made by President Allende himself. For instance, in his Second Annual Message to Congress, delivered only four months before the crisis of October 1972, he had said, "We guarantee that there does not exist nor will there exist any menace to the merchants, artisans, small industrialists or miners, small independent enterprises, because of the extraordinary importance of thousands of private family enterprises as an area of production of goods and services, which employ a much larger number of workers than the large monopolistic enterprises."[1]

Trucking was a small businessman's field par excellence in Chile. There were 52,000 members of the official truckers' organization, most of whom owned one or two vehicles. Altogether, they owned some 62,000 trucks. The largest firm in the industry had eighty-two vehicles.[2]

In recent decades, trucking had become more important to the national economy. With the building of good highways and connecting roads, motor vehicles had taken over the transport of many commodities that had formerly been handled by the railroads. Altogether, the trucking firms had come to have a strategic position in the national economy, but no one of them by itself was big enough to significantly influence the market.

On the other hand, the truckers did have powerful organizations. These were *sindicatos* covering owners in a given geographical area, which were grouped on a national basis into the Confederación Nacional de Dueños de Camiones. These organizations conducted cooperative activities on behalf of their members, such as purchasing spare parts and other requirements; they engaged in collective bargaining, generally on a regional level; and they acted as public spokesmen for the trucking industry.

There also existed some truck drivers' *sindicatos* consisting of workers employed by the truck owners. However, labor relations in the industry in recent years had been relatively peaceful, and in the events of October-November 1972, the workers' organizations expressed their solidarity with the truck owners.[3]

During the Allende period, the spokesman for the truckers was León Vilarín, president of the Confederación Nacional de Dueños de Camiones. He was a man with a checkered political career, having been in the 1930s and 1940s a member successively of the Communist, Trotskyite, and Socialist parties. He had supported Allende in his first presidential campaign in 1952. By the early 1970s, his political philosophy had altered again, and his chief concern now was the organization and representation of the truck owners.

THE OCTOBER 1972 CRISIS

The crisis of October-November 1972 was set off by the announcement by the Aysén provincial office of the Corporación de Fomento that the government was going to establish a state enterprise to control all land, maritime, and air transport firms in the southern part of the country. Vilarín characterized this decision as constituting "in reality a plan to liquidate all privately owned means of transport, beginning in Aysén and ending in Arica."[4] This government move was the last straw in a long-standing struggle between the truck drivers and the Allende regime. As a result, the Confederación Nacional de Dueños de Camiones declared a general work stoppage through most of Chile on October 9.

The menace the truck owners saw in the government's move in Aysén, and the reasons this action provoked the strike, were expressed in the editorial in the Truck Owners' Confederation periodical *El Camionero* of November 1972, after the walkout had ended.

The strike of our *gremio* which began on October 1 in Coyhaique, as a virile expression of opposition of the truckers and of all the *gremios* of that southern region to the unfortunate initiative of CORFO-Aysén to create a state enterprise which in practice implied a monopoly of all transport activity towards, from, and in that region, and also signified the beginning there of a PILOT PLAN to end private activity in our field, was suspended on the 5th of the present month.[5]

The truckers' strike soon mushroomed into a general showdown between the Allende government and its supporters on the one hand, and the economic and social groups and political parties opposed to the regime on the other. Within a few days, the Confederation of Retail Commerce and Small Industry, the Federation of Taxi Chauffeurs' Unions, the Confederation of Production and Commerce, and the National Confederation of Small Industry and Artisans agreed to close down all activities. Lawyers, some doctors, secondary school students, and several other groups also joined the movement, as did some peasant organizations. The groups involved soon formed a joint body which they called the Comando Nacional de Defensa Gremial.

Most of the participants in the movement, which became known as *the gremios*, kept their ranks solid. Three weeks after the movement began, its proponents claimed that the truckers were still 100 percent idle and that 99 percent of the retail merchants had closed down in the provinces and 91 percent in Santiago. It was also claimed that some 400,000 peasants were still supporting the movement.[6]

Although they had had little or nothing to do with launching the movement, the opposition political parties soon expressed their support for it. Ex-President Frei, Christian Democratic party president Renán Fuentealba, and Partido Nacional President Sergio Onofre Jarpa were among those who appeared on television to express this support.[7]

The government forces rallied their supporters in opposition to the strikes. The Central Unica de Trabajadores mobilized workers to stay on the job, and in a number of cases they volunteered to do special work to show their loyalty to the regime.[8] When the opposition declared a "day of silence" as a protest, the Unidad Popular parties mobilized their followers to inundate the center of Santiago and other cities with shouting partisans of the government.[9]

The government itself made a variety of moves against the *gremios* movement. Leaders of the truckers, the retail merchants, and other groups were arrested. Several hundred trucks were requisitioned, and President Allende threatened they would never be returned to their owners.

Allende denounced the *gremios* as "subversive," implying that the whole movement was an attempt to destroy the government. At the same time, it was decreed that all radio stations had to form a single network throughout the country for the duration of the emergency and could broadcast only what the government permitted. Several stations which refused this arrangement were temporarily closed down. A curfew was declared in Santiago.

The degree to which the crisis initiated by the truckers' strike developed into a general showdown between the government and the opposition was shown by the "Petition of Chile," which was submitted to President Allende by the Comando de Defensa Gremial. It went far beyond the issues that had given immediate cause for the movement and included most of the major grievances Allende's opponents had against the administration's policies.

Among the demands in the Petition of Chile were the reinstatement of workers fired for political reasons from the SUMAR textile plant, and of administrative personnel dismissed from the mines; reopening of Radio Agricultura of Los Andes, suspended by the government; and granting permission to the university television stations to establish broadcasting facilities outside of Santiago; promulgation of the Hamilton-Fuentealba constitutional amendment; changes in banking policy to end political discrimination in its administration; strict fulfillment of the provisions of the Agrarian Reform Law of 1967; strict conformity with judicial decisions; and promulgation of the law recently passed by Congress limiting the carrying of arms largely to the military and police.[10]

While there were some negotiations between the *gremios* and the government, they proved fruitless, in large part because the president rejected the Petition of Chile as not being directly connected with the issues of the truckers' strike.[11]

Events reached a climax in late October-early November. The opposition decided to use its control of Congress to impeach Jaime Suarez, minister of interior; Carlos Matús, minister of economy; Jacques Chonchol, minister of agriculture; and Aníbal Ponce, minister of education. Soon afterward, the whole cabinet decided to resign to give President Allende "freedom of action."[12] As a result, a new cabinet was appointed on November 2, headed by General Carlos Prats, commander-in-chief of the army, as minister of interior, and with Rear Admiral Ismael Huerta as minister of public works, with Air Force Brigadier General Claudio Sepúlveda as minister of mines. Their partners in the new cabinet included Luis Figueroa, Communist deputy and president of the CUTCh, as minister of labor; and Rolando Calderón, a young Left-wing Socialist leader and secretary general of the CUTCh, as minister of agriculture.[13]

General Prats quickly reopened conversations with the Comando de Defensa Gremial. An agreement was soon reached, providing that the government would not proceed with its plans for extending state control over the trucking industry, that no reprisals would be taken against those participating in the *gremios* movement, and that opposition radio stations which had been closed by the regime would be reopened. As a result of this agreement, the *gremios* called off their strikes on November 5.[14]

THE MILITARY IN THE GOVERNMENT

For almost five months after November 5, 1972, President Allende's cabinet continued as an unlikely coalition of top-ranking military officers and Socialist and Communist politicians. In spite of the fact that General Prats soon after taking office as minister of interior said that the presence of the military in the regime was "not a political commitment, but rather a patriotic collaboration to attain social peace,"[15] the new coalition did make the armed forces partners of the Unidad Popular. Inevitably, this had political repercussions in the Unidad Popular and in the opposition.

As noted earlier, elements within the Unidad Popular naturally resisted the presence of the military in the cabinet. The most open example of this resistance was the refusal of Jacques Chonchol, the leading figure of the Izquierda Cristiana, to continue to serve in the cabinet alongside the armed forces representatives. A large part of the Socialist party leadership was also exceedingly unhappy about the matter. On the other hand, the Communists supported the new arrangement wholeheartedly.

Insofar as the opposition was concerned, the leaders of the *gremios* had enough faith in the presence of the military men in the cabinet to be willing to call off their movement. They probably also feared an open confrontation with the armed forces partners in the Allende government if they did not do so.

Political opinion in the opposition remained divided, however. Some of its leaders saw the presence of the military in the government as a moderating force in the regime. Others feared that it might result in increasing commitment by leading armed forces figures to the political program which, as President Allende's cabinet ministers, they were supposed to carry out. At the very least, some opposition political leaders feared that the presence of the armed forces officers in the cabinet might lead to a deep split in the ranks of the military leadership.

Whatever doubts either side might have had, were attenuated in the months following the formation of the new cabinet. It was clear to all that the principal function of General Prats and his fellow officers was to assure the holding of free and democratic congressional elections in March 1973. The opposition felt that the armed forces' presence in the regime would largely assure the normalcy of the electoral process. Unidad Popular supporters of the new coalition felt it would serve to mitigate any charges the opposition might make concerning the holding of the March 1973 elections.

THE MARCH 1973 ELECTIONS

There was a truce between the government and the opposition during the months just preceding the March elections. Both sides put considerable stock in this test of public opinion; by all odds it constituted the most serious political challenge to the regime since Allende's election.

The Unidad Popular hoped to reverse a long series of electoral defeats, including not only defeats in congressional by-elections, but also in unions, student groups, and other private organizations during the previous two years. The opposition, on the other hand, hoped that they would be able to win a two-thirds majority in both houses of Congress, which would permit them to override any presidential vetoes, even of constitutional amendments, and would in effect make it possible to impeach the president.

For all practical purposes, the voters were offered a clear choice between the government and the opposition in these elections. To this end, traditional voting procedures had been modified in 1972. The Electoral Court had decided in the middle of 1972 that, although party coalitions were barred by the existing electoral law, nothing in it prevented the establishment of "federated" or "confederated" parties. As a result, both sides established such organizations, which were new to Chilean politics.

The six parties of the Unidad Popular—Communists, Socialists, Radicals, Izquierda Cristiana, MAPU, and API—established a new Partido Federado Unidad Popular (Popular Unity Federated Party). It then proceeded to allocate candidacies among the various elements of the government coalition.

The situation in the opposition was more complicated, reflecting the important ideological differences within its ranks. Two federated parties, one consisting of the Christian Democrats, Partido Izquierda Radical, and PADENA, and the other of the Partido Nacional and Partido de la Democracia Radical, were formed. These were then joined in a single confederated party. The groups in this coalition also allotted candidacies among their various members.

Virtually the only elements left out of these two coalitions were the Unión Socialista Popular of Raúl Ampuero, the MIR on the Left, and Patria y Libertad on the extreme Right. Unión Socialista Popular ran its own candidates in some constituencies, while the MIR endorsed a number of left-wing Socialist nominees. Patria y Libertad took no formal part in the election, although its members likely backed some of the more conservative nominees of the Partido Nacional.

Both sides hoped that the elections would be definitive, thus breaking the deadlock that had existed in national politics since Allende had taken office. This did not prove to be the case. Indeed, the March 4, 1973, elections gave both sides the chance to claim victory and did nothing to break the deadlock. The election confirmed that the government had the support of only a minority of the voters, but at the same time, this minority was shown to be larger than at the time of Allende's election—43.4 percent instead of 36.3 percent. The Unidad Popular gained 20 of the 50 Senate seats and 63 of the 150 Chamber of Deputies seats.

The opposition fell considerably short of winning the two-thirds for which it had been hoping; in fact, it received less support than the candidacies of Tomic and Alessandri had in 1970. But the opposition still emerged with a clear majority of the population: its candidates received 54.7 percent of the total vote.[16]

EXIT OF THE MILITARY FROM THE CABINET

Once the elections were over, President Allende was undoubtedly under severe pressure from his own ranks to end the military-UP coalition. For their part, the military, having resolved the crisis of October 1972 and having helped successfully to administer the election, seemed to have little reason to remain in the government. More clearly than in the pre-election period, to remain meant to cooperate with the president in carrying out the Unidad Popular program, which quite clearly had the support of less than a majority of the voters.

The political position of the military participants in the regime had become increasingly difficult. For example, on January 30, Minister of Education Jorge Tapia announced the government's intention of completely reorganizing the educational system and establishing a new Escuela Nacional

Unificada (Unified National School—ENU). The nature of this new educational institution was not precisely defined, but it seemed to bode the end of independent Catholic schools.[17] Tapia admitted that the government's model was the school system of East Germany.[18] The announcement opened a wide breach between the government and the Catholic Church and marked the Allende government's first open quarrel with the ecclesiastical establishment.

Another embarrassment for the military was the obvious impotence of the military men who had been given titular responsibility for organizing the distribution of essential foodstuffs and other basic household requirements. On January 22, President Allende had established by decree the National Secretariat of Commercialization and Distribution, to work under a newly established National Council of Distribution and Commercialization, presided over by the minister of economy, the Communist leader Orlando Millas. Allende had named Aviation General Alberto Bachelet Martínez head of the Secretariat.[19]

On February 16, General Bachelet publicly denounced a statement by Luis Inostroza, head of the nationalized wholesale distributor Agencias Graham, and presumably a subordinate of the general to the effect that a "popular market basket" of goods would henceforward be distributed regularly in the squatter colonies of Santiago. General Bachelet said that such a decision could only be taken by his Secretariat and that no such decision had been reached. When, on Bachelet's request, Inostroza was removed on February 22, a group of 500 demonstrators forced the removal of Inostroza's successor, Julio Stuardo, and the imposition of a left-wing Socialist, Sergio Juárez. The titular president of Agencias Graham, Navy Captain Alfonso Parodi, said nothing about these events.[20]

There was thus presure from several quarters for the military to leave the government. Finally, on March 27 the three military leaders resigned and were succeeded by three civilians of the Unidad Popular, Socialist ex-deputy Gerardo Espinoza Carillo taking the place of General Prats as minister of interior.[21]

PRELUDE TO THE *TANCAZO*

Three months passed between the resignation of the military ministers and the abortive coup of June 29, 1973, universally known as the *tancazo*. This period saw an intensification of the economic crisis, open disunity within the Unidad Popular, and a deepening of the gulf between the government and its supporters on the one side and the opposition on the other. Increasingly, there was an atmosphere of violence, stimulated by a long strike at the El Teniente copper mine.

During this period signs of the intensifying economic crisis appeared almost daily. In his May Day speech, President Allende noted that "a profession has been created, that of holding a place in line, and then selling it when one has reached the front."[22] On May 14, General Bachelet, secretary of national distribution, denounced the "veritable psychosis of scarcity."[23] On May 16, President Allende made a special plea to Mexican President Luis Echeverría for help in meeting an acute shortage of fuel.[24] On May 23, it was announced that 250 of the country's locomotives were out of use because of lack of replacement parts.[25] On June 19, it was announced that the amount of legal tender money in circulation had increased 274.3 percent since the beginning of the year.[26]

Allende was aware of the seriousness of the crisis. Thus, it was reported that his Third Annual Message to Congress "lacked the decisiveness and promise of action that marked his previous two state of the nation reports. So far from being a catalogue of future activity by the Unidad Popular government, congressmen heard Allende repeat his analysis of what was happening to Chile, and what the possible outcome would be. The President spared nobody's feelings in describing the present malaise, but offered no solutions either."[27]

Not only was the economy breaking down, but the political system was also being stretched close to its breaking point. Frictions within the Unidad Popular, particularly between the Communists and the MIR-left-wing Socialists were increasingly obvious. Relations between the government and the opposition had so deteriorated that no compromise seemed possible.

On April 3, an internal document of the Communist party was published by *El Mercurio*, which said in part: "We believe that our allies of MAPU should begin cleaning out as rapidly as possible the anti-Communists and adventurers; we are certain that decided action in the MAPU will bring about a rapid reform in the PS on the part of Allende, Almeyda and Calderón."[28] On April 22, a group of MIRistas and pro-Peking Communists seized the offices of the Ministry of Public Works, demanding employment there. President Allende himself went there to convince them to withdraw.[29]

On May 16, Luis Corvalán, speaking to a plenum of the Communist party, expressed fear that "a confrontation is inevitable." He also voiced his preoccupation over the attitude of President Allende, who, he said, had agreed on the need to suppress the MIR in order to improve relations with the army but then had "vacillated."[30] On May 29, Communist Deputy Mireya Baltra denounced the corruption among many heads of the state industries, and she was answered by Subsecretary of Transport Hernán Morales, a Socialist, who said, "I will not permit Comrade Baltra, in order to maintain her political party, to launch calumnious attacks."[31]

THE EL TENIENTE STRIKE

The most dramatic indication of problems within the government coalition was the strike of the miners of El Teniente. This movement, which lasted several weeks, also served to intensify the breach between the government and the opposition.

The copper miners of El Teniente had been under the control of the Socialists and Communists, and it was members of these parties who headed the unions there in 1973. Nevertheless, a strike was called by the El Teniente unions on April 19 over a wage dispute, the details of which have been given in an earlier chapter.[32] In the weeks that followed, this strike created considerable violence, both in the city of Rancagua, where most of the miners lived, and in Santiago. Both cities were declared "emergency zones" and were placed under modified martial law. Workers in several of the copper mines in the northern part of the country went on strike in solidarity with the El Teniente miners.

The two most violent clashes over the miners' strike took place on May 23 in Rancagua, and on June 14, 15, and 16 in Santiago. In the Rancagua incident, six people were wounded when a meeting in support of the strike was fired upon; the police laid the blame on local Socialist party leaders and raided their headquarters, where they seized arms and Molotov cocktails.[33] The officer in charge of the martial law in Rancagua was relieved of his duties for having ordered the raid.[34]

The disturbances in the capital began on June 14, when a "march on Santiago" of some 5,000 miners was met at the outskirts of the city by Intendente Julio Stuardo, together with three armored cars, some earthmoving equipment, and Carabineros. Tear gas was thrown at the miners, who dispersed but later got into the city.[35] On the following day, while President Allende was conferring in La Moneda with representatives of the miners, a demonstration of high school and university students in support of the strikers was attacked by paramilitary groups of the UP parties, as well as by Carabineros, outside Catholic University and the University of Chile. There were numerous wounded, who were given first aid in the two universities.[36]

On June 16, a meeting of miners in front of the National Telecommunications Company building on the Alameda was fired on by people hidden within that building. Some 218 people were reported as wounded. They were given first aid in the headquarters of the Christian Democratic party, across the street.[37] On the following day, President Allende sent a letter of congratulations to the CUTCh for breaking up the June 16 demonstration, saying "I wish to indicate through you to the workers of Santiago, the recognition of the Government and of the President of the Republic of their revolutionary attitude of yesterday."[38]

Violence not connected with the miners' strike was also widespread in various parts of the country. On April 4, a mob led by MIRistas attacked the warehouse of a cooperative wholesale firm, the Central Nacional de Distribución, but this time they were repelled by Carabineros.[39] A clash between pro-government and anti-government students on April 26 resulted in 120 wounded and hundreds arrested.[40] During a demonstration "to take control of the streets," ordered by the CUTCh on April 27, a Communist construction worker was killed and a right-wing journalist was very badly beaten.[41] On May 4, Mario Aguilar, a leader of the extreme rightist Patria y Libertad, was killed in the center of Santiago.[42] On May 5, attacks were made on opposition periodicals in Valdivia and Concepción.[43]

The growing wave of violence reflected the rapid deterioration of relations between the government and the opposition. President Allende pushed his "revolutionary" program ever more rapidly, partially relenting on only one point. For its part, the opposition for the first time raised the issue of the constitutional legitimacy of the regime. Both sides began talking about the possibility of civil war.

The only issue upon which Allende showed any willingness to compromise was that of the National Unified School. In the face of very strong opposition from the Church, Minister of Education Jorge Tapia announced on April 12 that this basic reorganization of the education system would be postponed "until there has been ample debate in the country on the proposal."[44]

The government persisted in other areas, however. On April 12, it was announced that, in open violation of the provisions of the Agrarian Reform Law, some, 2,500 rural properties ranging between 40 and 80 hectares in size, would be seized by the government.[45] On April 10, the president ordered the comptroller general of the republic to register all decrees requisitioning or intervening enterprises, thus resorting again to "decrees of insistence."[46] On May 15, President Allende signed a decree promulgating those parts of the Hamilton-Fuentealba amendment which he agreed with, but refused to put into effect those with which he did not agree.[47] This intensified the confrontation over the issue of how far and under what conditions nationalization of the economy should go forward. Allende steadfastly refused to submit the issue to a plebiscite, as he was authorized to do by the constitutional amendments of 1969.

THE ISSUE OF CONSTITUTIONALITY

During the months preceding the *tanzaco*, elements of the opposition for the first time openly questioned whether President Allende had so abused the Constitution that his government was no longer legitimate. On April 17, Senator Francisco Bulnes of the Partido Nacional asserted on a television program:

Since the first centuries of the Christian Era, jurists have established that a Government which is legitimate in its origin, falls into illegitimacy if it habitually abuses power. . . . This, unfortunately, is the case of the government of señor Allende. We citizens who wish to continue living in a democracy, cannot continue to ignore the illegitimacy of the Government or limit ourselves to considering it academically. We are obliged to employ against an illegitimate government, which marches straight towards the abolition of democracy, and which, furthermore, is destroying the economic patrimony of Chile whatever means are available and which do not involve a greater evil.[48]

During this period, the Christian Democrats did not go as far as Senator Bulnes, but at a meeting of the National Board of the PDC on May 13, it resolved that

the National Board of the PDC, in the face of the permanent campaign of the Government to concentrate in its hands all power, without caring that this breaks our juridical system, instructs the National Council of the Party to use all legitimate means to force respect for the Constitution and the laws, towards which the PDC will use all its parliamentary, municipal, trade union and neighborhood power.[49]

Fears began to be voiced that the situation might degenerate into a civil war. Thus, on May 8 an official Unidad Popular pronouncement proclaimed that "the fatherland is in danger" of a civil conflict.[50] On May 11, the Socialist party issued a statement that "we must keep track of the steps of the counter-revolution, unmasking the agents of civil war, opportunism and anarchy." This statement claimed that "rightists" were preparing to launch a civil war.[51] President Allende himself, in his Annual Message to Congress on May 21, argued that "Democracy and Civil Peace are in danger."[52] On May 27, the Political Committee of the Unidad Popular issued a statement that "forces of reaction, conspiring with elements which act abroad. . . . have passed 'from words to deeds,' in their proposal to overthrow the Constitutional Government, even at the cost of submitting the country to a bloody civil war."[53]

In some cases the opposition also touched on the theme. Thus, Senator Sergio Diez of the Partido Nacional remarked on June 3 that "Unidad Popular, which is accusing us of civil war, has it within itself, in its philosophy."[54]

Finally, there were disquieting signs that relations between the government and the armed forces were badly deteriorating. This was recognized on May 16 in a statement by Luis Corvalán, Communist party secretary general, to a party plenum.[55] And on May 25, the vice commander-in-chief of the army, General Augusto Pinochet, announced that the actions of the martial law commander in Rancagua, in ordering a raid on the Socialist party headquarters there, had had the full support of the army leaders, in spite of that officer's having been removed from office.[56] On June 19, there was an exchange of gunfire between members of the Communist party's paramilitary group, Brigada Ramona Parra, and Group 7 of the air force at the airport at Los Cerrillos.[57] Earlier, on May 28, the Corps of Retired Generals and Admirals wrote President Allende "to express to him the fears of the citizenry over the climate of insecurity and violence in which the country lives, as well as the evident disequilibrium in its development, which menaces national security."[58]

THE *TANCAZO*

At 8:55 on the morning of June 29, several tanks, and two trucks with forty men each, appeared in front of the presidential palace, La Moneda. Elements of the Second Armored Regiment, under the command of Colonel Roberto Souper, opened fire on the palace; the soldiers spread out in front of it and commenced firing towards the building also. They likewise opened fire on the nearby Ministry of Defense, in a vain attempt to gain the release of Captain Sergio Rocha Aros, who had been detained there four days earlier when another military plot had been discovered.

This action lasted two hours. At the end of that time, other elements of the Santiago garrison, led by General Carlos Prats, commander-in-chief of the army, appeared on the scene, and General Prats demanded the surrender of the insurrectionary troops. They finally gave up, but not until twenty-two civilians and military men had been killed and thirty-two more had been wounded. About fifty soldiers were arrested.

Meanwhile, President Allende, from his residence at Tomás Moro, broadcast a call for support over Radio Corporación. In part, he said, "I call upon the people to take over all the industries, all firms, to be alert; to come to the center of the city, but not to become victims; the people should come out into the streets, but not to be machinegunned, do it with prudence." He added, "If the moment comes, the people will have arms."[59] Allende's call to his supporters to occupy all the factories and workshops of Santiago was to have grave repercussions during the regime's remaining months. It proved to be an "emergency" measure which was hard to undo once the emergency was over.

On the evening of June 29, President Allende appeared on television flanked by the highest officers of the Chilean armed forces. He recounted what had happened earlier in the day and paid tribute to the military for their loyalty. These pictures were later broadcast throughout the world.[60]

After this abortive coup, President Allende sought to have Congress authorize him to proclaim a state of siege for six months in those parts of the country where he deemed it necessary. Both houses of the legislature rejected his request.[61] The agonizing final crisis of the regime continued.

26

Culmination of the Crisis: The Last Weeks of the Allende Regime

The weeks following the *tancazo* saw the climax of the first phase of Chile's tragedy. Almost inexorably the ultimate fate of the Allende regime was sealed. All further efforts to reach a compromise with the opposition failed. The economy was crippled once more by stoppages of truckers, merchants, and professionals. Attempts to strengthen the regime by again appointing the military to the cabinet proved fruitless. The distribution of arms among the civilian populace reached epidemic proportions. Finally, attempted subversion of the military by the far Left served only to snap the loyalty of the top leaders of the armed forces, who had rallied to President Allende's support on June 29. The result was the collapse not only of the Allende government, but of Chile's constitutional and democratic regime as well.

OCCUPATION OF THE FACTORIES AND THE *CORDONES INDUSTRIALES*

On the day of the *tancazo*, President Allende had urged the workers of Santiago to seize their places of employment. After the immediate crisis was over, he indicated that they should turn back their factories and workshops to their owners, private or public. In an interview with foreign journalists on July 6, he said, "I am a supporter of the return of many of them," but added, "But in a moment in which legality was broken, I told them to do what they did."[1]

During the weeks following the *tancazo*, the great majority of the workers who had taken over their workplaces on June 29 had still not returned them. Rather, many of these places were incorporated into the so-called *cordones industriales* (industrial cordons) in and near Santiago.

While the establishment of *cordones* had begun many months before June 29, it was in the weeks following that date that they assumed major importance, as virtual "soviets." Their prevalence was one evidence of the general breakdown of authority that took place in the weeks following the *tancazo*.

The *cordones industriales* took control of the manufacturing districts in and around Santiago. For the period after the *tancazo*, they became nearly autonomous governments. They not only took control of the factories, but of the neighborhoods surrounding them as well. Militia groups were organized in many of them. Police functions were undertaken by those in control of the *cordones*; the regular Carabineros and even the military were not allowed to enter these areas. Thus, when elements of the air force sought to conduct an arms search in the SUMAR textile plant, they were repelled by weapons fire, and they retreated from the area.[2]

The *cordones* also undertook to distribute basic commodities in the areas they controlled. In addition, some *cordones* purged the areas they encompassed of workers who were not in sympathy with the Unidad Popular or the MIR. Such purges were encouraged by Carlos Altamirano, who on July 12 called upon the *cordones* to "create a people's tribunal to judge the political and economic delinquents."[3]

All parties of the far Left participated in establishing and maintaining the *cordones*. Although until the *tancazo* they had been favored by the MIR and the left-wing Socialists, thereafter the Communists and other UP parties took a more or less active part in them also.

Even though the various parties participated in the *cordones*, it would not be correct to say that they controlled them. Whereas in a certain factory the union under the control of one or another of the parties might be able to maintain some kind of disciplined activity, other *cordones* were not so tightly dominated by any one group, and in general they lacked central coordination and direction.

The workers spent much of their time in those weeks attending meetings, participating in demonstrations, having rudimentary military drill, and other such activities. Few, if any, of them had a well-organized and coordinated program for organizing production of the factories involved, or otherwise guiding the workers' activities. There were cases in which well-meaning sympatizers attempted to help the *cordon* members establish community centers, organize educational and recreational activities, and encourage the workers to make the best use of their time, but finally they gave up in frustration.

Least of all were the *cordones* under the real control of the government. Although they were presumably established to strengthen the hand of the administration, the Allende governmemt did little, if anything, to try to organize and direct their activities. As a government, the UP regime had no more control over the *cordones* than did anyone else.

THE LAST ATTEMPT AT NEGOTIATION

Meanwhile, Allende's government was becoming increasingly isolated. The last bridges between it and the opposition were broken; it entered into open constitutional conflict with other branches of government; its relations with the military rapidly deteriorated.

On July 25, in a speech to a plenary meeting of the CUTCh, President Allende called for "an open dialogue, in the view of the people, with the sectors which wish to bring order to the process of changes and not with those who wish to return to a past which has definitively been surpassed." The implication of this statement was that the president was once again willing to conduct discussions with the Christian Democrats. The immediate reaction of the PDC was not very encouraging. Christian Democratic Senator Juan Hamilton argued that "in his extensive discourse, the president closed all possibility of establishing a dialogue. In effect, señor Allende not only fully rejected the prerequisites established by the PDC, but at the same time presented positions which were unacceptable for the great majority of the Chileans."

The reaction of Allende's own supporters to his call for negotiations was even more hostile. The Socialist party paper *Última Hora* commented that "the Secretary General of the PS, Senator Carlos Altamirano, proclaimed on July 12 that the Socialists would not accept dialogue with the Christian Democratic leadership, because it is participating in reactionary plans to overthrow the Popular Government." Izquierda Cristiana Senator Alberto Jeréz was even more categorical in commenting that "no one listens to anyone and, to continue on this route, dialogue would not only be between the deaf, but also between the blind, because no one wants to see the reality of things."[4]

These comments notwithstanding, negotiations did take place three days later. Patricio Aylwin, president of the PDC, together with Senator Osvaldo Olguín, met with President Allende, Interior Minister Carlos Briones, and Defense Minister Clodomiro Almeyda at 12:30 P.M. on July 30. They had two sessions, finally breaking up at 10:30 that evening.

The Christian Democrats presented the president and his advisers with five demands: (1) complete reestablishment of constitutional norms; (2) promulgation of the constitutional reforms passed by Congress; (3) return of industries seized on June 29 and thereafter; (4) intensification of efforts to disarm civilians; and (5) guarantee of the other four points by establishing a cabinet in which the military would be represented.

No agreement was reached, and when his visitors left, President Allende announced that no new meeting was scheduled. The Socialist party officially issued a statement, which was published the next day, to the effect that "the Socialist Party will never accept conciliation of the enemies of Chile, of the Popular Government, of the workers. At this time any formula of transaction with the Christian Democracy will serve to stimulate the seditious elements which operate in their midst, and the rest of the reaction, the only inalterable objective of which is to recuperate their power and their privileges."[5] The British weekly newspaper *Latin America* reported after the failure of these negotiations that "the country may have passed the point at which compromise is possible."[6]

Ever since these last futile efforts at compromise, it has been debated who was responsible for their failure. It appears that the major responsibility lays with the Socialist party and President Allende. Those in control of the Socialist party made it eminently clear that they were opposed to any negotiations and that they would do their best to sabotage any agreement the president might reach with the PDC. For his part, Allende was obviously unwilling to break with the left-wing elements that dominated his own party.

These negotiations were perhaps the last opportunity to reach a peaceful settlement of the crisis the country was facing. President Allende was being urged by many of his own supporters to break with the Altamirano wing of his party and with its allies, the MIR. However, he still continued to refuse to do so.

Thereafter, only one other move was made by Christian Democrats to find some constitutional—albeit highly unusual—way out of the morass. This was the party's suggestion only a few days before the coup of September 11 that both the president and all members of Congress resign, so as to give the people a chance in new elections to decide once and for all which way they wanted the country to go. It is doubtful that they thought the president would take this suggestion seriously.

CONFRONTATION WITH OTHER BRANCHES OF GOVERNMENT[7]

Meanwhile, President Allende had entered into open confrontation with the other branches of government—the legislature, the courts, and the comptroller general—all of which accused him of acting unconstitutionally. This confrontation was the culmination of a long-brewing series of disputes.

The clash with the comptroller general had begun on June 2. He refused to register the president's partial veto of the constitutional reforms passed by Congress on the basis that such a veto "does not conform to the norms of the Constitution, to which it must be subjected, because these provide that if the President's objections are rejected by Congress, the First Magistrate must convoke a plebiscite or promulgate the project approved by the National Congress and not just the part of it which he had not vetoed, as he has done here."[8]

Minister of Interior Carlos Briones responded a week later on behalf of the president. He asserted that "the Comptroller, in a surprising decision, has taken unto himself faculties which he does not constitutionally possess."[9]

The confrontation with Congress had more serious implications. On August 22, 1973, the Chamber of Deputies, by a vote of 81 to 45, resolved

to present to the President of the Republic and to the Ministers of State, members of the Armed Forces and of the Corps of Carabineros, the grave breakdown of constitutional and legal order in the Republic. . . . and to indicate to them, furthermore, that in view of their functions, of their oath of loyalty to the Constitution and the laws, and in the case of the Ministers, of the nature of the institutions of which they are high members, and the name of which they invoked upon becoming Ministers, it behooves them to put an immediate end to all of the de facto situations which infringe the Constitution and the laws, so as to conduct government action in legal channels and assure the constitutional order of our fatherland and the essential bases of democratic coexistence among Chileans."[10]

This document then listed a long series of specific constitutional violations by the Allende government. The first charge read: "It has usurped from Congress its fundamental function, which is to legislate, by adopting a series of measures of great importance for the economic and social life of the country, which are indisputably matters of law, through decrees of insistence which have been abused, or by simple administrative resolutions based on *legal devices.*" [Emphasis in original.]

The document accused Allende of having violated the watchdog functions of Congress, by "depriving of *real effect*" its impeachment of cabinet members, and it added, "and—which is most extraordinarily grave—has made tabula rasa of the high function that Congress has as the Constituent Power, in refusing to promulgate the constitutional reform on the three areas of the economy."[10] [Emphasis in original.]

Yet another accusation was that the president had undermined the judiciary by conducting a campaign of infamy against the Supreme Court, refusing to enforce court decisions when they affected government supporters, refusing to enforce court orders which he didn't like, and in the face of objections by the Supreme Court, "the president of the Republic has gone to the unheard of extreme of arrogating to himself the right of *deciding on the merits* concerning judicial decisions and deciding when these should be enforced."[12] [Emphasis in original.]

The document also claimed the government had violated basic constitutional principles, including those of equality before the law; freedom of speech, particularly with regard to radio stations and to its attempts to establish a government newsprint monopoly; university autonomy; the right of assembly; freedom of education; and "the constitutional guarantee of property through permitting and protecting more than 1500 illegal seizures of rural holdings and promoting hundreds of seizures of industrial and commercial establishments."[13]

After criticizing Allende's political manipulation of the military presence in his cabinet, the Chamber of Deputies resolution declared that

the Armed Forces and the Corps of Carabineros are and must be, by their very nature, guarantees for all Chileans and not only for a sector of the nation or for a political combination. Consequently, their presence in the Government cannot be used to cover a given partisan and minority policy, but must be directed towards re-establishing the conditions of full rule of the Constitution and the laws, and of the democratic coexistence indispensable to guarantee to Chile its institutional stability, civil peace, security and development.[14]

CONFRONTATION WITH THE SUPREME COURT

The confrontation of the Allende administration with the Supreme Court actually reached a climax just before the *tancazo*. Even so, it contributed heavily to widening the breach with the opposition in the weeks following June 29.

The Supreme Court had been unhappy for some time about the president's failure to execute court orders, particularly with regard to illegal seizures of land and industries, and to returning to their owners some enterprises which the administration had "requisitioned" or "intervened." This annoyance was reflected once again in a short note the Supreme Court dispatched to the president on May 26, 1973. After citing the government's failure to execute an order of a court in Rancagua, the justices noted that "this Supreme Court wishes to call to Your Excellency's attention for the Nth time the illegal attitude of the administrative authorities in illicit intromission in judicial affairs."[15]

Allende replied to this message from the Supreme Court with a long letter dated June 12, 1973. Early in this epistle, the president asserted the chief executive's right to decide which court orders to enforce. His position was stated as follows:

However, in virtue of universally accepted principles and of various constitutional and legal provisions, the authorities of the Government, guarantors of peace and public order, cannot proceed without knowing previously the facts which permit them, in each case, to foresee the consequences of a personal, family or social nature which the execution of a judicial decision might produce in the moment involved. It is consequently inadmissible to sustain that these authorities must lend police support in a totally indiscriminate way, since this might lead to situations which precisely imperil social peace and public order which they are called upon to guard. Thus, these administrative and political authorities see themselves constrained frequently to judge the merit or the opportuneness of the use of the police.[16]

The president then complained about a number of the Court's actions. Allende accused the judiciary of "subverting its inherent powers" and "transforming them into a means for interfering with the legitimate exercise of authority," saying that this had been done with regard to a number of industries that had been requisitioned or intervened.[17] Similarly, he said, the courts had abused their powers in interfering with the temporary closing of several radio stations.[18]

Allende also accused the Supreme Court of failing to behave correctly in cases involving libels against administrative authorities, including the president, and in particular a court's holding for trial two ministers and the secretary general of the government who were involved in suppressing such insulting behavior. He argued that the Supreme Court's actions under previous administrations had been very different.[19]

After citing several other complaints, Allende leveled a general indictment against the judiciary:

It is clear from what has been said that there is a manifest failure on the part of some sectors of the Judiciary, particularly the Higher Courts, to understand the process of transformation in which the country is living, and which expresses the long-postponed aspirations for social justice of the great masses, which in practice means that the law as well as judicial procedures are put at the service of interests affected by these transformations, to the damage of the institutional regime and of pacific and regular coexistence of the various hierarchies and authorities."[20]

The Supreme Court delivered what can only be labeled a scathing answer to Allende, in a letter dated June 25, 1973. It began by saying that "this Tribunal wishes to inform Your Excellency that it has understood your letter as an attempt to submit the free criteria of the Judiciary to the political needs of the Government, through seeking for forced interpretations of the precepts of the Constitution and the laws. So long as the Judicial Power has not been erased as such from the Constitution, its independence will never be abrogated."[21]

The Court accused the president of taking part in a systematic campaign against the judiciary carried on by his supporters. It then commented that "the outstanding position of the Supreme Chief of the Nation signifies a guarantee, even though relative and apparent, of the correct functioning of the judicial institutions; but the guarantee has disappeared now when the President accepts the erroneous innovations of his presumed collaborators and assumes full partisan militancy in the offensive unleashed against a branch of government which without diverting itself from its duty, cannot submit itself to the exigencies and desires of any other branch of the State."[22]

The judges then refuted Allende's claim that the administrative branch of the government had the right to choose which judicial decisions to enforce.

After citing appropriate constitutional provisions, the justices said that they had always respected the powers of the president and expected him to respect theirs. The Court "claims the right to judge any case between parties which is submitted to it through legal channels, and in case of judgment, the administration is subject to the decision and must respect what is decided in that particular case."[23]

The Court responded in detail to each of Allende's complaints in his letter. With regard to his claim that the courts were not conscious of the changes then under way in society, the Court asked: "Does the letter of Your Excellency suggest that the courts forget the law, put aside all principles and [act] in the name of a social justice without law, arbitrary, accommodating and even criminal . . . ?"[24]

THE SECOND TRUCKERS' STRIKE

The breach between Allende and the opposition, and between the executive and the other branches of government, expanded further after July 25 when a new truckers' strike was called. The strike quickly took on the aspects of a general passive rebellion of the Chilean middle class. On that day, at midnight, the Confederación de Sindicatos de Dueños de Camiones issued a call to its members to cease activities.

This new movement of the truck owners had been foreshadowed for some time. Their confederation insisted that the agreements that had been made to end the 1972 stoppage had not been fulfilled by the government. For instance, an editorial in the March-May 1973 issue of the confederation's journal *El Camionero* complained that the government had instituted reprisals against the truckers, in violation of the November 1972 accord. The editorial said "our *gremio* and all the *gremios* that supported us in October know that, so far, our problems HAVE NOT BEEN RESOLVED, on the contrary, they have been made worse and reprisals continued to be carried out in spite of the declarations and promises of General Carlos Prats, whose conduct, in our judgment, does not add to the prestige of the Armed Forces in our country."[25] [Emphasis in original.]

León Vilarín, head of the confederation, explained the new walkout:

The 198 sindicatos which constitute the Confederación have voluntarily suspended their activities in the face of the reiterated failure of the government to fulfill the promises which it made in September [sic] 1972. It is false that we are on strike. Simply, we have temporarily suspended our activities because it is materially impossible to continue them, because the Government has not fulfilled its promise to sell us vehicles directly, or to provide tires, and for fourteen months we have been seeking fulfillment of a promise to fix a national price list for our activity, or else to readjust those prices every 50 days because of the violent inflation."[26]

The walkout continued until after the fall of the Allende government. Allende named Jaime Faivovich, the subsecretary of transport, intervenor, authorizing him to seize the trucks involved and get them rolling again. Numerous attempts were made to take over the vehicles which the truckers had placed in huge parking lots in and around Santiago, and several of these attempts resulted in considerable violence. Nonetheless, Faivovich was unable to break the walkout or to get most of the vehicles operating again.

The truckers' strike was the beginning of a much broader movement. On August 3, all other private commercial transport ceased to operate.[27] On September 3, the Confederation of Professionals of Chile declared a general walkout, and it was reported that in seventeen southern provinces, there was an almost complete cessation of commercial, professional, industrial, and artisan activities. On the following day, it was estimated that as many as one million people were on strike.[28]

The cessation of trucking, the closing of retail establishments, and the refusal of professional people to continue their activities resulted in a chaotic economic situation. Symptomatic was President Allende's announcement on September 6 that "we don't have the most minimal stock of flour. At most enough for three or four days."[29]

THE QUESTION OF ARMS

The situation was full of tragic implications in the last weeks of the Allende regime. But even the near total break with the opposition, the confrontations with the legislature and the judiciary, and the chaos provoked by the truckers and associated groups might not have brought down Allende and the regime if it had not been for one other factor: the challenge to the armed forces by left-wing elements inside and outside Unidad Popular.

This challenge to the military took two forms in the last weeks of the Allende regime: widespread distribution of arms, and attempts to subvert the branches of the armed forces. These developments finally pushed the top military leaders into a state of open rebellion against the regime.

Although it was difficult to document most of the stories about distribution of arms after the *tancazo*, some accidents which occurred in this period presented evidence to the press. For example, on July 8 two youth leaders of the Socialist party had an accident in a station wagon belonging to CORA, in which were found arms, munitions, and bombs. The Carabineros who investigated the incident found a list on the two young men naming people to whom the machine guns and pistols were to be distributed, and information on the placing of 150 Mauser pistols, 150 hand grenades, 300 Molotov cocktails, and 6 machine guns.[30]

During this period, the military was very active in searching for arms, in conformity with the new Law on Control of Arms, which had passed Congress and been approved by Allende in October 1972.[31] The Central Cemetery of Santiago, churches, private houses, and various other places all had cachés of arms. The military's searches aroused considerable protest from some elements of the Unidad Popular.

Only a small proportion of the armaments which were then in civilian hands was in fact discovered by the armed forces. Substantial quantities had been distributed among the residents of the *cordones industriales*, which for the most part the police and the military did not enter during those weeks. On the other hand, large quantities of pistols, revolvers, and even rifles had been acquired by residents of middle-class and upper-class areas of Santiago, where there were some cases of attacks on houses by residents of nearby squatter colonies. It was feared that in the event general violence erupted, there would be intensive attacks on the "better" neighborhoods by the squatter colony residents.

These developments in the middle- and upper-class areas further demonstrated the general institutional breakdown during the last weeks of the Allende regime. The residents of these areas no longer felt they could count on the regular police to protect them and their property, and so they resorted to measures of self-protection. Not only did they purchase arms, but they also widely organized a neighborhood militia. Every night the streets of these areas were patrolled regularly by armed men from the neighborhood, whose task included keeping track of any hint of a disturbance and issuing a general warning in case their fears of a general attack materialized. Large numbers of the adult men of the middle-and upper-class sections of the cities were in these neighborhood vigilante groups.

REENTRY OF THE MILITARY IN THE CABINET

Meanwhile, President Allende made one more effort to fortify his regime by bringing the leaders of the armed forces into his cabinet. He undoubtedly felt that this move would discourage both the armed forces and his civilian opponents from any plans to overthrow his government.

On August 9, Allende swore in a new cabinet, in which General Prats held the post of minister of defense; Admiral Raúl Montero, commander-in-chief of the navy, became minister of finance; the commander-in-chief of the air force, General César Ruíz, took over the post of minister of public works; and the director general of the Carabineros, General José María Sepulveda became minister of lands and colonization. Upon swearing in the new ministers, Allende commented that "this is the last opportunity," and he reiterated an earlier warning that "Chile is in danger."[32]

Allende was most anxious to have the military share responsibility for ending the truckers' strike. This task fell largely to General César Ruíz as minister of public works. Allende's efforts failed, however, and on August 17, the truckers issued a statement saying that Ruíz "has not had the ample powers which would have permitted him to overcome the various difficulties which were presented by other parts of the Government."

On August 10, General Ruíz resigned not only as minister, but also as air force commander-in-chief. He announced that "I presented my resignation because I could not fulfill the goals which I had set myself." Soon afterwards, the president's office announced that "General of the Air César Ruíz Danyou, Commander-in-Chief of the Air Force of Chile and Minister of Public Works and Transport, presented to the Chief of State his resignation of the posts of Commander-in-Chief and of Minister of the post indicated, which were accepted by the President of the Republic."[33]

General Ruíz was succeeded as commander-in-chief of the air force by General Gustavo Leigh Guzmán.[34] This choice proved to be a fateful shift in command insofar as the Allende regime was concerned.

General Prats was the next military minister to leave. When he and Admiral Montero first presented their resignations, on the day following the exit of General Ruíz, Allende rejected them.[35] However, on August 21, 300 wives of officers waited upon Prats, presenting him with a letter to his wife, in which they expressed their distress at her husband's serving in a "Marxist government." Two days later, the general announced that "I cannot break with the Army. The President has accepted my resignation." Like General Ruíz, he resigned both his cabinet and his military position.[36]

In noting General Prats' resignation as head of the army, the British publication *Latin America* very ironically (as it turned out) observed that "the new commander-in-chief, General Augusto Pinochet Ugarte, formerly head of the Estado Mayor, is regarded as a 'friend' and 'pupil' of General Prats, but he will have his work cut out to avoid conspiracies among senior officers and insubordination in the ranks."[37]

On the day after Prats' resignation, President Allende refused to accept that of Admiral Montero as head of the navy, although he did accept his withdrawal from the Ministry of Finance. On August 31, Montero again offered his resignation, which Allende once more rejected on September 3, saying that he could not ask the admiral to stay on indefinitely, but adding that "I insisted to him that Chile must count upon his valuable cooperation in these hours."[38] Montero was not replaced until shortly before the September 11 coup.

On August 28, President Allende swore in his last cabinet, once again headed by Carlos Briones and with only one military member, Air Force Brigadier Hector Lacrampette Calderón. In the speech he gave upon swearing in the new ministers, Allende asserted that he "would not hesitate for a moment to resign if the workers, the peasants, the technicians and the professionals of Chile asked it or suggested it.''[39] But this was no indication that the president intended in fact to resign.

SUBVERSION IN THE ARMED FORCES

Perhaps more serious than the arming of the civilians, from the point of view of the chiefs of the Chilean armed forces, were the efforts by far Left elements to subvert the military. These efforts became overt in the weeks following the *tancazo*.

On August 10, the air force issued a communique announcing that ''in various parts of the country, there have been discovered extremists dressed in uniforms of the Armed Forces.'' It added that ''the Air Force of Chile and the Aviation Justice will punish those who, using illegally the uniform. . . .''[40]

Meanwhile, the MIR was conducting a concerted campaign urging enlisted men of the armed forces to mutiny against their officers. For example, on July 18 some MIRistas were arrested near the Coraceros Cavalry regiment of Viña del Mar, while putting up posters urging, ''Soldiers, don't die for the employers. Live struggling together with the people.'' Similar posters were placed in other cities.[41]

The left-wing Socialists carried on a similar campaign against the leadership of the military. Secretary General Carlos Altamirano was reported to have ''exhorted soldiers, sailors and aviators to disobey the orders of officers who revolt against the Government.''[42]

A particular campaign was conducted against General Manuel Torres de la Cruz, commander of the Fifth Division of the army in Punta Arenas, as the result of an arms search in Punta Arenas in which a Communist party member was killed. The CUTCh, the Socialists, as well as the MIR, demanded the removal of General Torres.[43]

The far Left activities with regard to the military were not confined to propaganda. On August 7, the command of the navy announced that a conspiracy had been discovered on the cruiser *Almirante Latorre* and the cruiser *Blanco Escalada*, which it said was ''supported by extremist elements foreign to the institution.''[44] About a week later, the MIR claimed that this denunciation by the navy leadership

has served the reactionary naval officers to hide the truth to the people, to accuse the anti-coup sailors of ''subversive attempts'' and of ''connections with the ultra-Left''. . . . The only ''crime'' of the anti-coup sailors of the Navy was to prepare themselves to resist and disobey the incitations to a coup which have been carried out in an increasingly frequent and open way towards their subordinates by this sector of the reactionary officer group.[45]

On August 23, the naval authorities specifically accused Carlos Altamirano, MAPU leader Oscar Garretón, and MIR leader Miguel Enríquez of conspiring with plotting sailors. They described the three politicians as being ''the brains of the subversive plan which contemplated the death of officers and of guards who wouldn't obey them in getting control of fighting units of the Navy.'' On the following day, it was reported that sailors involved had received orders from the three left-wing politicians to bombard a navy housing development near the Naval Academy.[46]

On August 30, Vice-Admiral José Toribio Merino, commander of the First Naval District, in his capacity as a navy judge, requested Congress to remove the congressional immunity of Altamirano and Garretón, thereby allowing their trial for conspiratorial activities.[47]

CARLOS ALTAMIRANO'S CHALLENGE

The penultimate scene in the tragedy of Salvador Allende and of Chilean democracy was a speech Altamirano delivered to the closing session of a plenum of his party's Central Committee held in the Chilean Stadium on Sunday, September 9, 1973, two days before the coup d'etat. In his speech, Altamirano made two basic points.

First, the Socialist secretary general proudly stated that he had attended ''a meeting to which he was invited to listen to denunciations of noncommissioned officers and some sailors against the subversive acts supposedly perpetrated by officers of that institution, and I shall be present anytime that they invite me to denounce actions against the constitutional Government of Salvador Allende.'' Later in the speech, Altamirano defied the authorities who had brought charges against him for his contacts with navy personnel and had asked for removal of his congressional immunity. ''This class justice,'' he maintained ''will secure nothing by removing my immunity because the truth, comrades, is that I was meeting with these sailors, with some of them.''

Altamirano's second major point was that he and his friends were opposed to any compromise with any part of the opposition. The press reported that ''he warned the Government that the PS decided not to accept dialogues and that they would only struggle combatting at its side if the government fully carried out the program which he said would create the Popular Power, and give it to the workers and the peasants.''[48]

This last public speech by Carlos Altamirano was in effect a declaration of war on the armed forces leadership. At the same time, it was an act of defiance of President Allende, warning him that Altamirano and his followers would no longer support the president if Allende did not conform to the intransigent policies upon which the extremists insisted.

At least two questions are raised by this speech: what motivated him to make it, and what was Allende's reaction to it? Some kind of answer is needed to fully understand what occurred on September 11.

The only rational explanation for Altamirano's behavior was that he wanted a final confrontation and was convinced that the forces of which he was a part, and of whom he was one of the leaders, would win out in such a showdown. There are various indications that this was precisely his thinking.

One piece of evidence elucidating Altamirano's attitude is a statement issued by the Socialist party leadership on July 21:

The Socialist Party is in a state of emergency throughout the national territory. Every member must remain in uninterrupted contact with the ruling groups of the party. . . . Take control of all enterprises. . . . Mount guard, defense committees, armed with whatever is available. . . . Inform your defense committee about any suspicious meeting or movement of the fascists or reactionaries. Closely watch the reactionaries and keep constantly on guard.[49]

An even better indication is a speech which Altamirano gave on August 14 at the Cobre Cerrillos factory.

We have aroused the people and we have aroused it to action, and nothing and nobody can detain its gigantic strides. When it passes, all those who wish to thwart it or frustrate it turn pale. The obscure political jealousies; the pertinacious and demagogic obstruction of Parliament; the arbitrariness of the judiciary; the promoters of sedition and civil war; the lamentable economic errors of the Government; the indiscipline and irresponsibility of some groups of workers; certain spontaneous and voluntarist actions of the masses; excessive impatience and indolence; the corruption of some interventors, functionaries and leaders of Unidad Popular; all of this, in spite of its gravity, is subsidiary and secondary in the face of the grandness and magnitude of this social torrent, and nothing can depreciate it."[50]

Whatever Altamirano's views on the outcome of a violent confrontation between the revolutionaries and their opponents, President Allende did not share his view, as demonstrated by Allende's reaction to Altamirano's speech.

The president did not attend the meeting which Altamirano addressed in the Chilean Stadium, but he did hear his speech over the radio, and it infuriated him. He fully understood the subversive nature of the Socialist secretary general's admission that he had been conspiring within the military and that he had been essential in preventing any kind of understanding with the opposition.

Allende was outraged. He listened to the speech from his home in Tomás Moro, together with a few of his cabinet members and other close associates. Those present were anxious to have the president break with the left-wing leadership of his party, and Altamirano's speech finally convinced him of the need to do so.

Altamirano's speech also decided Allende, finally, to submit the major issues pending between him and the opposition to a national plebiscite. He instructed one of his cabinet members to draw up the terms of the questions to be submitted to the people, and also to draft the speech in which Allende would announce his decision to the general public. The speech was scheduled to be delivered on the afternoon of Tuesday, September 11, 1973.

Allende went to bed soon after midnight, September 9–10. His associates left the presidential residence sometime after 2:00 A.M. Because of the tardiness of their departure, it was late on the following day before those who had been at Tomás Moro were back in action. As a result, the speech the president was supposed to give on September 11 was never completely finished.

As it turned out, it didn't matter. President Allende's decision to break with his left-wing "allies" and to submit the country's major issues of controversy to the decision of the electorate came too late. He was dead by the time he was scheduled to announce these decisions.

PART FOUR:
THE CULMINATION OF
THE TRAGEDY OF CHILE

27
The Coup

On September 11, 1973, the government of President Salvador Allende was overthrown by the Chilean armed forces. The president was killed and with him died the constitutional government that had existed with only two interruptions for 140 years.

DETAILS OF THE COUP

The military movement to overthrow the Allende regime got under way in the early hours of September 11. At that time, the bulk of the Chilean navy returned to its home bases. The day before it had left the ports of Valparaíso and Talcahuano, ostensibly to take part in Operation Unitas, a joint maneuver with elements of the fleets of all the Pacific countries of South America and that of the United States. The navy occupied Valparaíso, and took control of Talcahuano and the Concepción area virtually without firing a shot.

The leaders of the military movement were not certain where President Allende was spending the night. By monitoring a phone call from the Valparaíso commander of the Carabineros, they discovered that he was at his home at Tomás Moro. The commander, loyal to the president, had called him to inform him of the return to port of the navy and of events in Valparaíso.

Meanwhile, the armed forces throughout the country had begun to seize control of the respective cities and towns in which they were garrisoned. Apart from Santiago, the main centers of resistance were encountered in Linares and Antofagasta.

About 7:30 A.M., President Allende, by then aware that a movement against the regime was under way, arrived at La Moneda. He was soon joined by a group of friends and supporters. These included Minister of Defense Orlando Letelier, Minister of Interior Carlos Briones, Secretary General of the Government Fernando Flores, Minister of Agriculture Jaime Toha, ex-Minister of Defense José Toha, the journalist Augusto Olivares, ex-head of the secret police Eduardo Olivares, and Allende's doctor, Patricio Guijón. Allende was accompanied from Tomás Moro by a contingent of Carabineros, and this police guard remained in place until about 9:00 A.M. At that hour, the proclamation of the military commanders' seizure of power was read over a radio network, whereupon the Carabineros withdrew from La Moneda.

At about the same time, the presidential palace was surrounded by tanks, and the president was given an ultimatum: to surrender or to have La Moneda bombed from the air. He was given an hour to consider the matter; this time limit was later extended twice by one hour each time.

Upon receipt of the ultimatum, there ensued a lively discussion among the group in La Moneda concerning whether or not to resist. Minister of Interior Carlos Briones was reported to have been among those who urged the president to surrender. After a number of secretaries, Allende's two daughters, various detectives, and other people, including his three military aides—who had urged the president not to resist—had left La Moneda, the decision was made not to surrender.

Thereafter, there was considerable exchange of gunfire between the soldiers in the streets and plazas outside La Moneda and the defenders of the palace, principally some forty members of Allende's personal guard, GAP. The president himself was among those who fired at the besieging troops. The soldiers were also being fired upon by people located in, and on the roofs of, a number of buildings in the vicinity of La Moneda.

Shortly before noon, three people emerged from La Moneda under a flag of truce—Subsecretary of Interior Daniel Vergara, Osvaldo Puccio, Allende's private secretary, and Secretary General of the Government Fernando Flores. They went to the Ministry of Defense, where there was a discussion of the possible terms of Allende's surrender. It was subsequently reported that it had been agreed to send a jeep to pick up the president, but that the jeep was held up by sniper fire from nearby buildings and did not get to La Moneda before the aerial bombardment of the presidential palace began.

At noon, La Moneda was attacked by Hawker Hunter airplanes of the Chilean air force. The north side of the building, facing the government newspaper *La Nación* across a small plaza, was particularly badly damaged; a fire was started which ultimately burned out all of that side of the building, which included the presidential offices and those of the Interior Ministry.

After the bombardment, President Allende indicated a willingness to resign, according to the official version of events given out afterwards. A number of those remaining in the building did in fact leave. President Allende was not among them. He was dead.[1]

By about 2:00 P.M., the presidential palace was in the hands of the rebels. Although some fighting continued with snipers in neighboring buildings, most of the battle in the center of the city was for all practical purposes over shortly afterwards. However, it continued in some of the industrial centers and other centers of resistance in the capital.

On September 13, the new Military Junta issued its Edict No. 26, in which it listed the principal military actions that had taken place in the Santiago area in the process of the coup, some of which were still in process at 4:00 P.M. on September 12.

Occupation of the Government Palace, with the capture of a great quantity of explosives.

Occupation of the presidential residence of Tomás Moro with the capture of great quantities of arms and explosives.

Occupation and search of Industria Hirmas.

Occupation and search of Cristalerías Chile.

Occupation and search of the ex-Yarur industry, without opposition of the workers.

Occupation and search of the SUMAR industry, in face of resistance from armed extremists.

Occupation and search of the Banco de Chile, capturing armed extemists.

Occupation of the Central Bank, capturing armed extremists and arms.

Occupation of the Banco del Estado, defeating extremists and permitting the peaceful withdrawal of the employees.

Occupation and search of the Banco Nacional del Trabajo.

Occupation and search of the building of the Ministry of Public Works, defeating armed extremists.

Defeat of extremists in O'Higgins Park.

Occupation and defeat of extremists in the principal building of the Social Security Service.

Defeat of extremists and occupation of the newspaper *Clarín*.

Defeat of extremists and occupation of the magazine *Punto Final*.

Defeat of armed extremists and occupation of Pizarreño, Viña Santa Carolina and Cristalerías Chile industries.

Search of the clandestine arsenal in Teatro Septiembre.

Occupation and search of the Universidad Técnica del Estado, after armed resistance, with surrender of about 600 people and capture of great quantity of arms and foreigners.

Detention of numerous armed foreign extremists.

Occupation and search of Quimantú publishing house.

Occupation and search of the El Arrayán (presidential) residence.

Search of the CORFO warehouse.

Surrender of 150 Cuban extremists and capture of great quantity of arms.[2]

For some time after the coup, it was rumored, particularly abroad, that important military units had offered resistance to the coup. At one point, it was even suggested that General Carlos Prats was leading army units to the south of Santiago, which were preparing to march on the capital. From all the information I have been able to gather in two visits to Chile since the coup, it does not appear that there is any substance to these rumors. The most severe resistance to the coup took place in Santiago, and it was largely overcome within twenty-four hours, although a few of the factories mentioned above did hold out for several days, finally being reduced by hunger and exhaustion of ammunition rather than by force.

This judgment is borne out by some far Left sources. For example, Eduardo Creus, an Argentine Trotskyite who was in Chile at the time of the coup and was arrested by the military but was later released and escaped from the country, was asked some time later, "How extensive was the resistance to the coup?" His answer was:

There was no organized resistance. The workers wanted to fight. But in the absence of a genuinely revolutionary organization there could be no organized resistance. There was some resistance by snipers. There was some resistance by groups besieged in places like the Instituto Pedagógico, but they were slaughtered. They tried to put up a fight in the Universidad Técnica, but they were massacred. There was resistance in the shantytown of La Legua, but there was a massacre there.[3]

In my two visits to Chile in 1974 and 1975, I discovered no confirmation of *Latin America*'s claim in its issue of November 9, 1973, that "much of the fighting during the first three days after the coup was said to be among units of the armed forces."[4] The support for the coup among the military was very strong. Virtually all of those who had doubts about it failed to offer resistance to it.

THE PLOT AGAINST THE ALLENDE REGIME

The move to oust the Unidad Popular government by armed force was undertaken by most of the top leaders of the Chilean military. Almost a year after the event, General Augusto Pinochet revealed that discussions about the possibility of overthrowing the regime had begun among key military leaders shortly after the March 1973 elections.[5] It is not likely, however, that they took concrete form until at most a few weeks before the coup of September 11.

The Junta of Commanders of the Armed Forces and Carabineros, in whose name the movement of September 11 was carried out, consisted of General Augusto Pinochet, commander-in-chief of the army; General Gustavo Leigh, commander-in-chief of the air forces; Admiral José Torribio Merino, commander-in-chief of the navy; and General César Mendoza, director general of the Carabineros. As I have noted in an earlier chapter, Generals Pinochet and Leigh had taken over those posts less than a month before the coup. Admiral Torribio Merino took control of the navy with the outbreak of the coup, his predecessor Admiral Raúl Montero having sought to resign a few weeks earlier, but his resignation not having been accepted by President Allende. Admiral Torribio Merino was the effective commander of the naval forces in Valparaíso before the coup and was the second-ranking man in the navy.

The plot against the Allende government was thus mounted primarily by the leadership of the army which succeeded the resignation of General Prats, the leadership of the air force which took over at the end of August, and those just under the top commander of the navy. It would appear that the Carabineros were brought into the movement only days, and perhaps hours, before it took place.

General César Mendoza, who appeared on September 11 as director general of the Carabineros, had been in fact the seventh man in the hierarchy of the national police the day before the coup. Most of his six superior officers were with President Allende in La Moneda early on the morning of September 11. However, they did nothing to stop the movement against the president, and when the Carabinero guard at the presidential palace withdrew at about 9:00 A.M., they withdrew with it.[6]

There is at least some reason to believe that Carlos Altamirano's speech of September 9 was decisive in convincing the top leaders of the Carabineros either to join the movement against the regime or, at the very least, not to offer any resistance to it. One important and well-informed figure in the Allende regime revealed that until the Socialist party secretary general's open proclamation that he was conspiring in the armed forces, the top leaders of the national police were ready to oppose any move to oust the Allende regime. The speech of September 9 changed their minds.

Had the Carabineros remained loyal to Allende, it might have made a very considerable difference. At the time of the coup, they were a corps of some 35,000 professionals—unlike the ranks of the army which consisted mostly of conscripts. They were relatively well armed and highly disciplined, and had posts in many parts of the country where there were no garrisons of the regular armed forces. At the very least, if the Carabineros had stayed with Allende, the coup of September 11 might have been converted into a civil war. It is even possible that in the face of the loyalty of the Carabineros, important elements of the army might not have gone along with the coup.

REASONS FOR THE COUP

Proponents and opponents of the succeeding military regime have offered the greatest variety of explanations as to the motivations of the military leaders who overthrew President Allende. The opponents have suggested that the military chiefs took over with the intention of establishing a "fascist" regime, that they did so for the purpose of protecting the country's upper classes, who were losing their economic, social, and political power under Allende. Some have even suggested that the military acted on the urging of the Christian Democrats, who hoped that conditions would then be created which would quickly bring them back to power.

In contrast, supporters of the Junta Militar have tended to insist that the military acted because they were convinced that elements of the far Left, with or without Allende's acquiescence, were planning their own coup. After September 11, members of the Junta themselves expanded considerably on a so-called Plan Z, which they claimed was to be put into effect by MIRistas, left Socialists, and others on September 18, with the assassination *en masse* of the military leaders and the principal figures in the opposition. However, the famous Plan Z seems to be a rather dubious "discovery," made after the fact, and not a justification for their actions at the time the military launched the coup.[7]

Upon taking power, the military leaders issued their own explanation of their move. This is Edict No. 5, the full text of which lists fourteen reasons why the military moved against the Allende regime. In summary, these reasons were that the Allende government had made itself illegitimate by violating the Constitution and the laws of the republic; that it had fomented class hatred and destroyed the basis of coexistence of the citizenry; that it had sought an abusive accumulation of "all political and economic power"; that it had gravely undermined the economy; and that it had placed in jeopardy "the internal and external security of the country."

The subsequent behavior of the Military Junta itself may raise questions concerning the importance in the thinking of the military leaders of many of the factors cited in Edict No. 5. Probably some of them played a part in the armed forces chiefs' decision to oust Allende, with different officers undoubtedly regarding different factors as important.

In discussions with a number of military officers, including those near the top of the regime, and with several civilian advisers of the Junta Militar, I concluded that the overwhelming factor in the military's final decision was their conviction that the armed forces were being undermined and destroyed by the Allende government. They feared that unless the arming of civilians and the plotting within the ranks of the military were brought to a halt the result would be civil war. The Allende government was either unwilling or unable to bring these activities to a halt, and so the military chiefs acted.

THE DEATH OF ALLENDE

Another controversial aspect of the coup was how President Allende died. The official version of the Junta Militar was that he had committed suicide with a gun given him by Fidel Castro. Allende's widow apparently accepted this story at first, but she later concluded that he had been killed by the military. Her second version is the one that most of Allende's supporters have maintained.

There is evidence for both versions. "The Scene from Within the Moneda," by Luis Renato González Córdoba, a chapter in Laurence Birns' *The End of Chilean Democracy*, gives one version of Allende's death:

Once we had retreated to other combat positions, we encountered a group of fascists under the command of Captain Mayor, in the halls near the Red Room. He shouted: "Surrender, Señor Allende." Our compañero said, "Never. It is better to leave dead than surrender." When he finished we heard a shot from the military. It hit the Doctor. They opened machine gun fire, and we fired against them. Twelve of our compañeros fell dead at the side of President Allende. Our firing became more intense. The officer and six soldiers fell. We approached the President's body. He was mortally wounded. He told us, "A leader must fall, but still there is a cause. America will be free." It was 1:50 P.M. when compañero Allende fell, assassinated by the bullets of the fascists and traitors. He had been hit by about six bullets; four in the neck and two in the thorax.[8]

The official version of the Military Junta was published on September 13.

1. At 13:50 o'clock on Tuesday, September 11, through Fernando Flores and Daniel Vergara, Salvador Allende offered to surrender unconditionally to the military forces.

2. To this end it was agreed to send a patrol immediately, the arrival of which at the Moneda Palace was interfered with by the fire of franc-tireurs particularly in the Ministry of Public Works, who attempted to intercept it.

3. When the patrol entered La Moneda it found in one of the rooms the body of Señor Allende.

4. A commission of the Medical Department of the Armed Forces and Carabineros and a forensic doctor attested to his death.

5. At noon on Wednesday, September 12, a private funeral, attended by his family, was held.*[9]

On a visit to Chile in August 1974, I was able to obtain independent evidence concerning Allende's death. I talked to the first fireman who entered the burning presidential palace, and he asserted that he had seen Allende's body in a chair, with a gun under his chin, the gun having gone off and destroyed a good part of his head. On the basis of this account, it therefore seems likely that Allende committed suicide rather than having been killed in the fight.

---

*This version obviously conflicts with newspaper accounts of the events of that day. *El Mercurio* reported Vergara and Flores as leaving La Moneda before the noontide bombardment, not at 1:50 P.M.

Additional considerations point to the probability of suicide. Suicide makes sense in the light of Allende's career and his historical view of himself. He sought the presidency for almost twenty years before finally succeeding in 1970. After he became president, he asserted numerous times that he would not leave office before the expiration of his term, unless he was taken dead from La Moneda.

Furthermore, Allende had upon occasion compared his role with that of Balmaceda, who had been overthrown in 1891; during the Allende regime there developed something of a cult of Balmaceda among government supporters. Allende saw himself, as he saw Balmaceda, as fighting for the interests of the humbler citizenry of the republic. The fact is, of course, that Balmaceda committed suicide. It would therefore be consistent for Allende, seeing himself ousted by the armed forces—as Balmaceda had been—also to have killed himself. That would make the historical parallel complete, in his eyes.

The manner of Allende's death is not that important; he is a martyr to whatever cause he believed in, in any case. However Allende perished, constitutional government perished with him, and whether and when it will be revived are still pending questions. In the final chapters of this book, we shall try to present some of the evidence relevant to answering these queries, information about the military regime, and their actions since taking power —which in turn might give some hint as to its future and that of the country over which it has ruled since September 11, 1973.

28
The Politics of
the Military Junta

The coup of September 11, 1973, gave Chile the most completely military government in its history. This regime was in marked contrast to that which took over the government after the civil war of 1891, when a largely civilian cabinet was installed by Admiral Jorge Montt, the new president; and to the situation during the military dictatorship of General Carlos Ibáñez from 1927 to 1931, in which most of the office holders were established civilian politicians.

As mentioned in Chapter 27, full power was assumed on September 11 by a Military Junta consisting of Army General Augusto Pinochet, Air Force General Gustavo Leigh, Admiral José Torribio Merino, and Carabinero Director General César Mendoza. Four years after the coup, the Junta still remained in control.

The Junta's first official act was to issue Decree-Law No. 1, dated the day of the coup, giving it "legal" standing. This document, after a preamble stating reasons for the Junta's overthrow of President Allende, made the following provisions in the name of the four military chiefs:

1. On this date they constitute a Junta of Government and assume Supreme Command of the Nation, with the patriotic promise to restore Chilean nationality, and the broken justice and institutions, conscious that this is the only way of being loyal to the national traditions, the legacy of the Fathers of the Country and to the History of Chile, and of permitting the evolution and progress of the country to be vigorously channeled in the direction that the dynamic of the times demands of Chile within the international community of which it forms a part.

2. They designate General of the Army Augusto Pinochet Ugarte as President of the Junta, who on this date assumes this post.

3. They declare that the Junta, in carrying out its mission, will guarantee the full operation of the Judicial Authority, and that it will respect the Constitution and the

laws of the Republic insofar as the present situation of the country permits, thus to best carry out the postulates which it sets forth.[1]

It is to be noted that Decree-Law No. 1 did not promise to respect the rights and position of the elected Congress, although it did say it would respect the courts. In fact, on September 13, the Junta issued its Edict No. 29, which provided that "the National Congress is dissolved, and the posts of all those holding parliamentary positions are declared vacant."[2] This automatically meant that the Junta government was taking into its own hands full power to legislate, as well as to enforce the laws.

The first cabinet announced by the Junta underscored the military domination of the regime. It included the following ministers:[3]

Interior, Major General Oscar Bonilla Bradanovic
Foreign Affairs, Rear Admiral Ismael Huerta Díez
Economy, Major General Rolando González Acevedo
Finance, Rear Admiral Lorenzo Gotusso Rolando
Justice, Gonzalo Prieto Gandara, lawyer
Defense, Vice-Admiral Patricio Carvajal Prado
Public Works, Air Force Brigadier General Sergio Gutiérrez Figueroa
Agriculture, Retired Air Force Colonel Sergio Crespo Montero
Education, José Navarro Tobar, professor
Lands and Colonization, Retired Carabinero General Diego Harbad
    Valdés
Labor and Social Security, Carabinero General Mario MacKay
    Jaraquemada
Health, Air Force Medical Colonel Alberto Spoerer Covarrubias
Mining, Carabinero General Arturo Vovane Zuñiga
Housing and Urban Affairs, Brigadier General Arturo Vivero Avila
Secretary General of Government, Army Colonel Pedro Jovín

Military men were also named to head a number of other government dependencies. These included the Central Bank, the Development Corporation, the Mining Corporation, and the secret police. The Junta also resorted extensively to the list of high-ranking retired officers of the various services to fill a substantial percentage of the country's ambassadorial posts. Also, virtually all positions as *intendentes* (in charge of administration of provinces) were given to active or retired military personnel.

During more than a year and a half after the coup, this heavily military complexion of the regime was modified in only one respect. Within a few weeks of their assuming power, the Junta largely turned over to civilians the management of the country's economic problems. Raúl Sáez, an economist and one-time Christian Democrat, became the Junta's major economic adviser, and a team drawn from the managerial group of the newspaper *El Mercurio*, and from economists of both the University of Chile and the Catholic University of Santiago, took over direction of economic policy. In this field, at least, the military men admitted that they lacked competence. Although the "economic team" changed several times in subsequent years, it continued to be made up of civilians.

As time went on, civilians were given other posts. By March 1976, there were eight civilians in the fourteen-man cabinet.[4]

POLITICS OF THE MILITARY

During its first four years in power, the military regime succeeded in keeping an outward appearance of unity. Whatever differences of opinion existed were debated behind closed doors, and the public was not informed of them in any great detail. However, after the second year there were many rumors of disagreements among the military chiefs.

The coup itself strengthened the cohesion of the military leadership. Those officers, active and retired, who did not support the ouster of the Allende regime were eliminated from any posts in which they might have had influence. Most notable was the case of General Carlos Prats. After being erroneously reported as leading an armed move in the south against the new regime, General Prats appeared on national television to deny the report and to urge the citizenry to cooperate with the new government. Some television viewers claimed that General Prats was handcuffed while making this speech. What is certain is that he was almost immediately deported to Argentina, and a few months later was assassinated there.

The six Carabinero generals who had been General César Mendoza's superiors on September 10 and who had remained "neutral" during the events of the following day were retired from active service. A certain number of high-ranking army, navy, and air force officers were arrested, although in the nature of the case exact details are impossible to obtain.

A very extensive purge was not necessary, however. The great majority of the leadership of the four armed forces either supported the coup or did not actively oppose it. The country's military chiefs presented a picture of wide solidarity in the wake of the coup.

The military sought to avoid the development of any kind of *caudillo* from their midst. Their reticence on this score was shown by the fact that, in the beginning, General Pinochet did not assume the title of president of the republic, but rather that of president of the Junta de Gobierno. There were at least some indications that that title might rotate among the various members of the Junta.

Given the realities of the military situation, the army is by far the most powerful of the armed services. This fact was finally recognized on June 26, 1974, when General Pinochet's title was changed to president of the republic, and it was announced that he would continue to hold the post until the end of the military regime.[5]

The military leaders had differences of opinion on both the short-run policies and the regime's longer term program for "reconstructing" Chile. At least three important political currents have been identified.

One current consisted of generals described by *Latin America Political Report* as being "hostile to General Augusto Pinochet and broadly sympathetic to the Christian Democrats." Three generals were identified as leaders of this group: General Oscar Bonilla, the Junta's first minister of interior; General Sergio Arellano Stark, who during most of 1975 was army chief; and General Javier Palacios Ruhmann, who was head of the army industrial enterprise Fabricaciones Militares until early 1977.

By the fourth anniversary of the coup, this element seemed to have been all but eliminated from positions of power within the military regime. General Bonilla died in March 1975 in a helicopter crash. General Arellano Stark was forced to resign and to retire late in 1976, and General Palacios was forced out of the army hierarchy in March 1977.[6]

After the removal of Bonilla, Arellano Stark and Palacios, only one figure remained who might be said to represent the "soft line" among the military leaders. This was General Hernán Brady, the defense minister. *Latin America Political Report* opined that he was "an inevitable choice for anyone looking for a change of face for the regime. . . . in the early days after the coup he made no secret of his distaste for some of his colleagues' excesses." The periodical concluded that "since then he has maintained an extremely low profile and resisted all invitations to conspire."[7]

A second current centered around General Gustavo Leigh, the air force member of the Junta. He was generally reputed to be a supporter of "corporativism," and in mid-August 1975 he issued a statement stressing the unforeseen high social costs of the government's economic program. At that time he also stated his opposition to an announced government plan to remove shantytown residents from land on which they had illegally set up their houses.[8]

Early in 1976, at a time when the economic situation seemed particularly difficult, and it was speculated that General Pinochet might be replaced as president, there were some rumors that his successor might be General Leigh. As *Latin America* commented at the time:

One possibility is that General Pinochet will be replaced by General Gustavo Leigh, an advocate of a more coherent, if more corporativist, economic policy. General Leigh, as an airman, would not normally be regarded as a candidate for the presidency. The airforce does not have enough troops on the ground to maintain control. But the situation demands unusual developments, and General Leigh is the most senior general who looks capable of effecting the basic changes in economic policy that will recover for the Junta some of the popularity that it has lost.[9]

No such changing of the guard took place. At the end of the fourth year of the Junta regime, General Augusto Pinochet remained president of Chile. He headed what might be called the center in Chilean military politics, the group that largely dominated the regime from the day it took power.

THE "FASCISM" OF THE JUNTA REGIME

The government which took over on September 11, 1973, has been widely accused of being "fascist." However, one is forced to conclude that when such accusations are made, the word "fascist" is being used more for vituperative than for descriptive purposes.

That the Junta government is oppressive is undoubtedly true. There is also no doubt that fascist regimes have generally been oppressive. However, it is also true that many different kinds of governments have been oppressive, including all of those under control of Communist parties, that of General Idi Amin in Uganda and those of various other African states, as well as a host of different governments in Latin America, none of which can be regarded as being fascist. Therefore, the fact that a regime does not respect civil liberties and governs autocratically is not sufficient for it to be labeled "fascist."

Fascist regimes have had certain peculiar characteristics, most of which have been lacking in the Chilean government that seized power on September 11, 1973. They have been one-party states, with distinct political and social philosophies, including belief in a "leadership principle," xenophobic nationalism, and reorganization of the economy along corporativist lines.

The regime of the Junta Militar in Chile has not fit this mold of a fascist state. There has been no one-party political system—indeed, there are no parties at all. There has been no expressed belief in a leadership principle; on the contrary, the regime's leaders have insisted on the collective nature of its leadership. There has been no more than the ordinary Latin American emphasis on nationalism in the Junta regime. Finally, there has been no commitment to any new organizing principle for the economy, such as corporativism, although one member of the Junta and some of its advisers are said to favor such a system. In fact, the economic policies of the regime have been largely those of extreme "free enterprise" rather than of any kind of governmental control over the economy.

Official statements concerning its objectives made by the Junta during its first four years in power did not indicate any clear ideology. Typical was President Pinochet's speech on the occasion of the Junta's first six months in power. Concerning the society the Junta was trying to establish, he said that "there will be constructed a society with responsibility on all levels and where the objectives will be fixed. All this will be within the harmony between economic development and social justice, which requires common ideals."

General Pinochet then stated the basic characteristics of the proposed new society:

1. It will have as its basis strong historical roots, which bring together and stimulate the Chilean people, and give it expressive continuity;

2. It will be a free society, where the individuals who make it up establish in realistic and not only legal terms the development of their personal possibilities and find in it and in the State a real support;

3. It will possess the capacity to provide its members a dynamic and convergent equality in terms of national values;

4. It will permit its components to live in liberty, not in an individualist sense but so that each citizen feels responsible for the needs and weaknesses of others, and in achieving their objectives will share their good fortune.[10]

Later in the same speech, Pinochet stated that "awarding merit, personal and collective achievement, will be all that receives stimulus in this new Chile, where there will be room only for honest workers and patriots."[11]

The Junta Militar regime, then, is not fascist. The best definition of it is that it is a repressive authoritarian government of the armed forces. It is conceivable that in time it might evolve into some kind of fascism, but certainly it had not done so by the time of its fourth anniversary in power.

REPRESSION

To say that the Junta Militar regime has not been fascist is not to assert that it is not tyrannical. It has been highly so. It has governed completely by decree; the general populace was not consulted even in a pro forma way during its first four years in power. It has outlawed all political parties, it has abolished freedom of the press and assembly, it has kept thousands of people in concentration camps for long periods of time, it has carried out arbitrary arrests and deportations, at least in some periods it has used torture extensively, and it has been more sanguinary than most people thought would be possible in Chile.

There was admittedly considerable exaggeration in some of the reports of repression and violence in the early days and weeks of the military regime. For instance, Peruvian Trotskyite leader Hugo Blanco was reported to have claimed that "there are reports that every fifteen minutes a body is cremated in Santiago. Many persons have seen bodies lying in the street. Murders have been seen in broad daylight. . . . Many persons have seen drug-crazed soldiers wandering around."[12]

The reality is bad enough without such exaggeration. During all of its first year in power, the Junta Militar insisted that the country was formally in a "state of war." It was never made entirely clear just whom it was at war with, or what the nature of the war was. However, since one of the avowed objectives of the regime was "to extirpate Marxism," defined as meaning all of the parties of the Unidad Popular, plus the MIR and other groups to the left of the Unidad Popular, the implication was clear.

On September 11, 1974, the Junta declared that the "state of war" was over, but it still kept the country under the more familiar "state of siege." This situation gave it more than ample justification to continue with most of the repressive measures it had used during the so-called state of war.

Exile, imprisonment, and arbitrary search and seizure continued to be used by the regime. During the first six months or so after the coup, several thousand citizens and an additional number of foreign residents were expelled from or left the country. By the middle of 1974, the number of people being forcibly sent abroad declined. Then, on September 11, 1974, President Pinochet announced that many of those being held for trial would be given the alternative of going into exile, and the stream abroad intensified once again.[13] By November 1976, 1,226 prisoners had asked to be sent into exile, and of these, 669 had actually left the country.[14]

At the time of the coup, several thousand people had sought refuge in embassies in Santiago. Other thousands of foreigners had been located in centers run by the United Nations High Commissioner for Refugees in and around the capital. The Junta Militar gave exit visas to all of these people, with the exception for some time of those located in the Italian Embassy, who continued to stay for several months because the Italian government refused to extend formal recognition to the military regime.

Much larger numbers of people were kept in jails. Soon after the coup, the government announced that 4,000 people were being held in the National Stadium.[15] Subsequently, many of these were transferred to regular prisons, while others were sent to special camps established in the northern part of the country. People continued to be arrested for political reasons. Two years after the coup, those who were trying to help the families of the prisoners estimated that probably as many as 6,000 were still being held in these camps. In January 1975, the government officially put the number at 4,300.[16]

Those in the camps were for the most part lower ranking trade union and party officials and rank-and-file members of the Unidad Popular parties. The most prominent people of the deposed regime who were caught by the government were at first sent to Dawson Island, in the frigid far south of the country, where they were held for the better part of a year. Most of them were then brought back to the center of the country; some were released and went into exile, and others were kept in jail pending trial. The most famous of those continuing in jail until late 1976 was Luis Corvalán, secretary general of the Communist party.

Although most of the prominent prisoners who were released were allowed to go into exile, some were immediately rearrested on new charges. This was the case in September 1975 with Pedro Felipe Ramírez and Anibal Palma, both of whom had served in Allende's cabinet; they were released on orders of President Pinochet but were promptly rejailed and taken to Valparaíso to stand trial there.[17]

By late 1976, it was reported that some 1,400 political prisoners were still being held by the government. Of these, "755 have been tried (after a fashion) and sentenced, 362 are being tried and 283 are being held without charges."[18]

At the time of the exchange of Communist ex-Senator Jorge Montes for eleven East German political prisoners in June 1977, the Chilean government claimed that it was no longer holding any political prisoners. Hernán Bejares, President Pinochet's chief of staff, was quoted at the time as saying that "at this moment no one is detained in Chile under the state of siege law."[19] However, doubt continued to be cast on this statement because of the problem of those political prisoners who had allegedly "disappeared."

At least some prisoners were tortured. Although I have not talked with anyone who underwent torture, I heard enough rumors about tortures, some of them from people who were strong supporters of the regime, during my visits to Chile in mid-1974 and mid-1975, to believe that there was at least some truth in these reports. Furthermore, Jeff Gaynor and Lawrence Pratt, strong supporters of the Junta, admit the prevalence of torture and say that the only issue is whether it was authorized by the Junta. They think not.[20]

More or less official statements by international bodies that have looked into the matter during the years since the coup also bear out the charges of the use of torture. Thus, at the end of 1974, the Inter American Commission of Human Rights reported to the OAS that there had been "extremely serious violations" of human rights in Chile and that many of the prisoners the commission members interviewed reported that they had been tortured. The report said that these people had "brutally visible marks remaining" from their tortures. They identified five torture centers.[21] Early in 1977, Amnesty International published a document giving details on three such installations controlled by the new intelligence organization, the Dirección de Investigaciones Nacionales (DINA).[22]

Considerable numbers of people, including both civilians and military men, were put on trial for their activities during the Allende period. During the first months, various death sentences were handed out by the military courts conducting these trials. However, this was ended in May 1974, when Interior Minister Oscar Bonilla commuted the death sentences imposed on five local Socialist leaders in San Fernando, accused of participating in guerrilla-type activities.[23] Long prison terms continued to be meted out to many of those found guilty of similar charges.

During the first year of the Junta regime, most of those jailed were people who had had some connection with the Unidad Popular. Anyone who had been active in the UP lived under considerable apprehension, even if they had been opposed to many of the policies of the Allende regime. There were enough cases of raids on private houses by police in the middle of the night to create an atmosphere of fear and insecurity.

After the first year, the government also began to take reprisals against many who had not been in the Unidad Popular at all. For instance, it forbade Christian Democratic leader Bernardo Leighton to return to Chile. Then, in November 1974, Renán Fuentealba, who as president of the Christian Democratic party had been exceedingly critical of the Allende government, was suddenly arrested and deported.[24]

Symbolic of the rigidity of the Junta was its maintenance of the curfew in Santiago. Four years after the coup, the curfew was still imposed during the early hours of each morning, and citizens were subject to arrest or even death for violating its provisions.

During the second year of the Junta regime, an extensive espionage network was established throughout the country. This network was organized by DINA, in which members of all four armed services participated. An Amnesty International document noted that Decree-Law No. 521 of July 18, 1974, establishing DINA, gave it "complete control over all security matters and the power to make arrests and to keep persons in detention without warrants or any formal order. DINA was made responsible only to the president of the republic of Chile. This of course meant that no authority, not even the commanders of the different military zones of the country, had access to detention centers under the control of DINA."[25]

DINA generated a widespread atmosphere of fear, sometimes sowing distrust even among friends, who became apprehensive that conversations might be reported back to DINA.[26] Apparently, even military leaders of the regime objected to the activities of DINA, which was responsible directly to President Pinochet.

In mid-1977, upon the occasion of a visit to Chile by the U.S. assistant secretary of state for Latin American affairs, DINA was officially dissolved. Another organization with a different name was immediately created, and so, rather than being abolished, the dreaded secret police organization was merely rechristened.

DEATHS AND DISAPPEARANCES

As mentioned earlier, the military regime was bloodier, particularly in the early weeks, than most people had thought possible in Chile. Although casualties in the actual fighting at the time of the coup were relatively small, there was an unknown but substantial number of people who were summarily executed in the weeks following the overthrow of the Allende government. Others were shot by firing squads after being court martialed.

It will never be known how many people actually were killed during the coup and in the weeks immediately following it. One source claims that 600 people died at the Universidad Técnica alone, although this number is probably a considerable exaggeration.[27] There were certainly several thousand casualties on and after September 11, however. A widely circulated estimate eleven months after the coup was that by that time close to 10,000 people had lost their lives, perhaps half of them as the result of curfew violations.

At least two of the prominent persons being held by the government died while in custody. On March 15, 1974, the regime announced that José Toha, former minister of interior, had committed suicide. It was known that he was dying of cancer, and friends doubted that he would have had the strength to hang himself. These suspicions were reinforced when the Cardinal Archbishop of Santiago, Raúl Silva Henríquez, celebrated a requiem mass for Toha, something which is never done for suicides. This mass was attended by Christian Democratic ex-Senator Tomás Pablo and other dignitaries.

Two days earlier, General Alberto Bachelet, the highest ranking military man held for trial, was officially reported to have died of a heart attack. *Le Monde* reported that Bachelet had been badly tortured.[28]

For some time after the coup, the government conducted mass raids in Santiago and other cities, which were reported in the press. Whole sections of Santiago were cordoned off, and hundreds, and on occasion thousands, of people were arrested. Most of these would be quickly released, although a few would be kept in prison, including both political suspects and people with records as common criminals. At least some of those arrested in these raids "disappeared" and were never heard of again.

The question of the "disappearance" of those arrested was a continuing preoccupation of those who were trying to aid the victims of the Junta's repression. In March 1974, a Catholic auxiliary archbishop of Santiago, the Lutheran bishop of Chile, and the chief rabbi of Santiago entered a habeus corpus plea on behalf of 131 people who had been arrested and whose whereabouts were unknown. By August of the same year, four of these people had been officially reported as having died, but no word had been received about the great majority of them.[29]

In May 1975, the Comité para La Paz officially requested the appointment of a special judge to investigate the disappearance of 119 people whose whereabouts were unknown. It presented eyewitness accounts of the arrest of 77 of these. However, in August the Supreme Court refused to appoint a special investigative judge. The 119 people listed in the Comité's petition represented about 10 percent of those of whose disappearance it had records.[30]

In the fourth year of the military regime, political opponents continued to "disappear" under very mysterious circumstances. The November 5, 1976, issue of *Latin America* (p. 338) discussed the reasons for the decline in the number of political prisoners officially held by the government.

The third and most sinister reason for the decrease in numbers is implicit. . . . in another set of figures, from the Vicaría de Solidaridad, on arrests and disappearances. These show that since January the percentage of "disappearances" among the detainees has risen from five percent (January) to 18 percent (April), 56 percent (June), 38 percent (July) and 57 percent (August). Although by themselves these figures might indicate only a temporary trend, there are other signs that the Chilean security forces, notably the DINA, are beginning to realize that named and numbered political prisoners are an embarrassment they can avoid by simply killing ("disappearing") those who cannot be released within a period of days. The number of prisoners in the "disappeared" category is now thought to be around 2,000, a total which has accumulated over the past three years, but which has grown notably in the last few months.

This same article cited several cases of those who had "disappeared." One of these was the following:

On 12 September a woman's body was discovered, strangled and half-naked, on a beach near La Ligua. The story was treated as a sensational *crime passionel* until the family of the woman identified her as Marta Ugarte Román, ex-secretary to Mireyra Baltra, a Communist party deputy during the Unidad Popular government, who had been arrested and disappeared in mid-August. The Valparaíso court has virtually been obliged to appoint a special commissioner to investigate her death.

Early in 1977, Amnesty International published a list of 236 people who had "disappeared" since September 1973. This document gave extensive details on a few of the cases and urged a worldwide letterwriting campaign to the Chilean government on behalf of those involved.[31]

RELATIONS WITH THE SUPREME COURT

At its inception, the Junta de Gobierno promised to respect the rights of the courts. It largely lived up to its promise. To do so has not been too difficult inasmuch as during the first three years the courts, particularly the Supreme Court, voiced little or no criticism of the military government, in sharp contrast to their behavior during the Allende regime.

Soon after the coup, the Supreme Court, in a "Declaration" signed by chief justice (president), Enrique Urrutia Manzano, gave explicit support to the new government. The Declaration, dated September 12, 1973, read:

The president of the Supreme Court, recognizing the proposal of the new Government to respect and enforce the decisions of the Judicial Branch without previous administrative examination of their legality, as is ordered by Article 11 of the Organic

Code of Courts, indicates publicly his most intimate approval of this in the name of the Administration of Justice of Chile, and hopes that the Judicial Branch fulfills its duty as it has done until now.[32]

Several weeks after the coup, General Pinochet paid an official visit to the Supreme Court, together with other members of the Junta. While there, he thanked the justices for the "moral support" they were giving the new regime.[33]

Many people, including leaders of the legal profession, felt that the courts did not subsequently "fulfill their duty," particularly with regard to the protection of civil liberties. Although under the terms of a state of siege, such as the Junta kept in effect, the courts could not constitutionally review the results of any courts martial or challenge the right of the military to keep people incarcerated, they were entitled to inquire into the treatment of prisoners and into the methods used to obtain testimony from them. However, so long as Urrutia Manzano remained chief justice, the courts did not make any such inquiries, in spite of persistent reports of torture and other mistreatment of prisoners. Nor did the courts act with any visible energy to inquire into the whereabouts of people who were "missing" after being arrested and were presumably either in jail or dead.

This attitude was in marked contrast to that of the Brazilian courts after the overthrow of President João Goulart by the military in 1964. It remains to be seen what long-run damage the attitude of the Chilean courts may do to their well-established reputation for honesty, nonpartisanship, and even-handed administration of justice.

The attitude of the Supreme Court changed somewhat with the accession of José María Eyzaguirre as chief justice in 1976, when it began to be more critical of the regime. Eyzaguirre's position was reflected in a vote of the Court late in 1976 on a request by the church's Vicaría de Solidaridad for an inquiry by the Court into the whereabouts of political prisoners who had allegedly "disappeared." Although the Court voted seven to five against conducting such an investigation, Eyzaguirre was aligned with the minority. He later paid a surprise visit to two concentration camps to observe conditions there.[34]

Several months later, in March 1977, Supreme Court President Eyzaguirre wrote a personal letter to President Pinochet, protesting the Interior Ministry's refusal to provide the Court with information on certain people who had "disappeared." Then, on April 2, the Court "announced the procedures to be followed in the case of a *recurso de protección* (a broader form of the old habeas corpus writ which covers a wide variety of individual and civil liberties), announcing at the same time that it regards this *recurso* as "generally applicable." Since it was specifically suspended under the state of emergency laws as amended at the end of January, this declaration seems to set the judiciary on a collision course with the military."[35] No such collision had occurred by the fourth anniversary of the regime, although the number of "disappearances" had declined substantially, a development that may have resulted in part from pressure from the Supreme Court.

DECLINING CIVILIAN SUPPORT OF THE REGIME

The continued repression of the military regime no doubt reduced its support among its original civilian adherents. In September 1973, much if not most of the middle class, as well as the industrial, landlord, and commercial elements of the upper class, and even some workers and peasants, greeted the coup with a sigh of relief. However, the economic disaster of the first four years of the regime, and its arbitrary and oppressive behavior politically, greatly weakened the popular base of the regime.

Given its general predisposition against the existing political parties, the Junta did not seek to organize its own political party. The only organization somewhat resembling a party which it established was the Movimiento de Unidad Nacional (MUN), which was set up in May 1975. President Pinochet explained some months later that the task of the MUN was to support the regime "with no privileges in return."[36]

Among the leaders of the MUN was Jaime Guzmán, widely credited as being the most influential civilian political adviser of the regime, and an authoritarian right-wing Catholic. Another important figure was Arturo Fontaine, who appeared to lead a faction opposed to Guzmán. Early in 1977, the anti-Guzmán group issued a statement denouncing "the concerted action of certain fascist groups" who were seeking to generate "a climate of fascism" in government circles. At the time of the suppression of the political parties in March 1977, the youth group of the MUN issued a general criticism of the policies of the government.

CONSTITUTIONAL ISSUES

The Junta did not officially suspend the existing Constitution. Indeed, in its first decree-law formally establishing itself in control of the government, it promised to obey the Constitution "insofar as the present situation of the country permits." However, it did initiate a process for writing a new basic document for the country.

General Gustavo Leigh announced on September 21, 1973, that the government was "studying the writing of a new constitution."[37] Shortly afterwards, the regime appointed a constitutional commission composed of some of the country's leading legal scholars. However, for many months thereafter, neither the commission nor the government seemed to be in any hurry to finish the work of drawing up a new constitution.

When I visited Chile in August 1974, a member of the constitutional commission explained the nature of the discussions within that body. At that time, it seemed clear that at least two fundamental changes would be made in the new Constitution, as compared with that of 1925. The first of these was the inclusion of a provision banning "undemocratic" parties, together with some kind of machinery for enforcing this ban. The second proposed change was the establishment of a mechanism whereby the armed forces would have an official role in governing the country, perhaps by giving the already existing National Security Council veto power over government actions. I was informed that there had been no discussion of writing a corporativist kind of Constitution.

Meanwhile, the military had used their control of the government to consolidate their power position in the long run. Thus, two important organizations formerly under the jurisdiction of the Ministry of Interior were transferred to the Ministry of Defense early in the regime. These were the Carabineros, the national militarized police force, and Investigaciones, the regular secret police. Thus, barring the unlikely possibility that the new Constitution should provide to the contrary, all coercive instruments of the Chilean government had been put under the control of the military hierarchy.[38]

Three members of the constitutional commission resigned in April 1977 in protest against the dissolution of the country's remaining political parties.[39]

THE "CONSTITUTIONAL ACTS"

Starting on December 31, 1975, the Junta began issuing documents which it called Constitutional Acts. The first of these established a so-called Council of State, set up so that the president could "obtain the recommendation or opinion of a high-ranking Consulting Council reflecting broad national representation and formed by highly qualified and experienced individuals of reputed integrity and prestige."[40] The makeup of this Council of State was designated in Article 2 of the decree:

The Council of State will be formed by former Presidents of the Republic, by own right, and the following individuals appointed by the President of the Republic:
   a) A former President of the Supreme Court;
   b) A former Comptroller General of the Republic;
   c) A former Commander-in-Chief of the Army;
   d) A former Commander-in-Chief of the Navy;
   e) A former Commander-in-Chief of the Air Force;
   f) A former General Director of Carabineros;

g) A former cabinet minister;

h) A former diplomat having held the category or rank of ambassador;

i) A former rector of one of the State or State-sponsored universities;

j) A professor or former professor of the Faculty of Juridical Sciences in any of the universities under the foregoing letter;

k) A professor or former professor of the Faculty of Economic Sciences in any of the universities under letter i;

l) A representative on behalf of professional associations;

m) A representative on behalf of entrepreneurial activities;

n) A worker, employee or laborer on behalf of labor activities;

o) A representative on behalf of women organizations; and

p) A representative on behalf of youth.[41]

The Council of State did not hold its first meeting until July 1976. Of its composition, *Latin America* commented at that time that:

most of its 18 members are ex-functionaries of one kind or another—retired heads of the armed forces, ex-heads of the Supreme Court and the university of Chile, and ex-Presidents Jorge Alessandri Rodriguez and Gabriel González Videla. (Ex-President Eduardo Frei has remained firm in his refusal to take part. . . .) Of the five currently active members, Julio Philippi Izquierdo for the professional associations and Pedro Ibáñez Ojeda, for the business community carry some weight, but the labor representative, Guillermo Medina Galvez of the copper workers union, is badly discredited even among those of his colleagues who support the regime for his totally uncritical position; the women and youth movement representatives appear to be nonentities.[42]

The total membership of the Council of State resigned in March 1977 at the time of a cabinet reshuffle.[43] Since Constitutional Act No. 1 provided that the members of the council would "remain in office for as long as they enjoy the favor of the President of the Republic,"[44] their mass resignation would seem to indicate that they had lost this favor.

On September 11, 1976, the third anniversary of the coup, the Junta issued three more Constitutional Acts. Constitutional Act No. 2, entitled "Essential Bases of Chilean Institutionality," seemed more a statement of principles and a brief for the military regime than a constitutional document. In its preamble, it listed five "essential values" on which the Chilean regime was based: "The Christian humanistic concept of the individual and society . . . the concept of national unity . . . the concept of a State of Law . . . the concept of a new and solid democracy . . . the existence of a unitary State."[45]

The act then declared that "sovereignty rests essentially in the Nation," that Chile was a republic, and that "all individuals, institutions or groups" were subject to the Constitution and the Constitutional Acts. Article 10 stated that "Chapter I and Articles 1, 2, 3 and 4 of the Political Constitution of the Republic are hereby revoked."[46] Chapter I of the 1925 Constitution, among other things, proclaimed Chile to have a unitary state and that its government was "republican, democratic and representative." Perhaps more significant, Article 4 provided that "no office holder, no person, no meeting of persons can attribute to itself, even on the pretext of extraordinary circumstances, other authority or rights than those which have been expressly granted by the laws. Every act in contravention of this article is null."[47]

Constitutional Act No. 3, entitled "Constitutional Rights and Duties," consisted of a thirteen-point preamble, four "chapters," and a total of nineteen articles. The tone for this document was set in the fourth and fifth points of the preamble. The fourth listed among the rights of the individual, "the right to individual life and integrity, legal protection of unborn life, equality of rights for men and women, legality of due process, right to defense and other rights that require to be invested with constitutional rank, inasmuch as they reaffirm the value of the individual as the basic cell of our society."

The fifth point of the preamble, however, then added that "on the other hand, lack of all consideration and respect for the private life of the individual, his family and honor, that featured the political period which preceded this government, requires that this constitutional guarantee be contemplated, subject to the protection procedures established by this Act."

The nature of "the protection procedures" contemplated by the act is shown by the sixth point of the preamble, which said that "freedom of opinion and information is one of the most significant freedoms in the world today," but then added that "it becomes necessary not only to consecrate it but, likewise, to enact essential provisions to avoid that abusive use thereof may attempt against the rights of the individual or those superior values which regulate community life."[48]

The Junta's judgment on what constitutes "abusive use" of freedom of opinion is shown in the twelfth point of the preamble: "As a way of protecting the fundamental values on which Chilean society rests, it is necessary to provide that any acts of individuals or groups thereof directed to circulate doctrines attempting against the family, promoting violence or a concept of society based on class struggle, or which are otherwise contrary to the established regime, will be declared illicit and contrary to the institutional system of the Republic."[49]

Through its Article 12 this Constitutional Act revoked Articles 10-20 of the 1925 Constitution which named individual rights and liberties on a much more extensive scale and much less equivocally than the Constitutional Act of the Junta.[50]

Constitutional Act No. 4, entitled "Emergency Regimes," presented a long list of states of emergency which henceforward would be at the disposal of the government. These included "a state of assembly," to be declared in case of external war, as well as states of "internal war or internal commotion, a state of siege; of latent subversion, a state of defense against subversion, and of public disaster, a state of catastrophe."[51] In contrast, there were only two cases of "exception" under the 1925 Constitution: the "state of assembly" in case of an external war, and the "state of siege" in case of "interior commotion." According to the Constitution, a state of siege could be proclaimed only if Congress was in session, and then only for six months. If Congress was not in session, the state of siege could last only until Congress met, when it had to be reviewed by that body.[52] In this connection, it is noteworthy that the state of siege declared by the Junta on September 11, 1973, was still in effect four years later.

THE DURATION OF THE DICTATORSHIP

The enactment of these Constitutional Acts was in no sense a step towards reestablishing a democratic and elected regime. On the contrary, as documents designed to delineate the general parameters within which the Junta intended to operate, they gave the distinct impression that the military intended to remain in power for an unlimited period.

After four years in power, the military government made no significant move to return to constitutional democratic government. The closest it came was vague talk about the possibility of creating a partly elected, partly appointed parliament by the mid-1980s.

The members of the military government have been very evasive about how long they intend to remain in power. This question of tenure came up frequently during the early months of the regime, and the answer usually given was that offered by General Pinochet, "We don't have a time table, we have goals."[53] The official statements that have been made concerning the military regime's goals have tended to be vague and sometimes even utopian.[54]

One leading figure in the military regime gave me a very ambitious set of goals, which would seem to imply a very long-term military regime. According to this officer, the military government had set itself the tasks of solving the country's major social problems, such as eliminating the squatter colonies of Santiago and other cities by giving the people in them permanent homes to replace their ramshackle ones; and solving the country's economic problems by getting economic development going again. Such goals might take many years, if not decades, to achieve.

By mid-1977, members of the Junta appeared to have sizable differences of opinion as to how long the military regime should last. This fact is underscored by statements made by President Pinochet and by Admiral José Torribio Merino, the naval member of the Junta, within a few days of one another. On May 23, 1977, President Pinochet announced that "we are entering the process of institutionalization." He explained that this was necessary because "we would have straightened out the country, the house, only then to put it back in the hands of those who would certainly bring us back to the same situation as that before 1973, that is to say, we would once again fall into demagoguery and petty politicking." He added that the government was obliged to build "a new Chile, and that is where we are going with the support of everyone, and today with the support of our brothers of the Navy."[55]

Only two days before, on May 21, Admiral Merino, after noting that the military had "achieved most of our goals," commented that "we are coming close to the moment when we are going to say: that's fine, no more. Everyone to the Identification Office to get a new identity card . . . then to the Electoral Register, and after that to vote. It will be a little bit longer, but that is the direction towards which we are marching."[56]

A few weeks later, on June 10, President Pinochet attempted to explain away the differences between his and Merino's points of view. He stated that Merino had mentioned that there would come a time to vote, but had not set a date; on previous occasions he, General Pinochet, had also said that there would ultimately be voting, but had not set a date either. So, he concluded, there was no fundamental difference between his point of view and that of the admiral.[57] Nonetheless, the basic contradiction remained. The question of how much longer the military regime would stay in power remained unresolved by the regime's fourth anniversary.

29
The Politics of the Opposition Under the Junta

The military government of Chile has made legal opposition to the regime practically impossible. Freedom of assembly has been nonexistent, freedom of the press has been very tightly circumscribed, and the exercise of freedom of speech, even on a personal and private level, has involved grave risks for those engaging in it. Political parties have been suppressed, and other important private organizations, such as the labor unions, have only been able to meet under police surveillance. Widespread espionage, the all-too-frequent "disappearance" of oppositionists, and the jailing and deportation of others have generated a general atmosphere of fear and even terror, which has severely hampered the opponents of the regime.

In spite of all of these factors, an opposition has continued to exist. Some of the political parties have remained more or less intact, and opponents have been quick to take advantage of whatever cracks may have appeared in the wall of oppression. The Catholic church has continued to be openly critical of the regime, although seeking to avoid an all-out confrontation with the men in uniform.

THE POLITICAL PARTIES

The Junta outlawed political parties in three stages. On September 22, 1973, General Pinochet announced that the "Marxist parties," defined as those of the Unidad Popular plus the MIR, were being outlawed "because they are the principal ones causing this chaos."[1] Five days later, the Junta Militar took its second step when it announced that all other parties were being declared "in recess." In explaining this measure, Federico Willoughby, press secretary to the Junta, explained that "the country was thrown into chaos, in large part, as a consequence of the excessive politicalization of national activities."[2]

While, the meaning of the outlawing of the UP parties and the MIR was clear enough, the exact significance of the "recess" imposed on other parties was not. In practice, it amounted to almost the same thing as outlawing the left-wing parties. Those groups in "recess" were not allowed to hold public meetings, maintain headquarters, have meetings of their local, regional, or national executives, or otherwise function as political parties. However, their property was not officially sequestered by the government.

This anomalous situation was "resolved" in 1977 when the Junta took its third step in extirpating the party opposition. Early in March, the government issued a decree dissolving the remaining political parties that until then had been "in recess." This involved seizure of the property of the four parties involved—the Christian Democrats, Nacionales, and the two Radical splinter groups, the Partido de la Democracia Radical and Partido Izquierda Radical.[3] As *Latin America Political Report* commented at the time, "This measure is aimed principally at the Christian Democratic Party."[4]

The real impact of the coup and its aftermath on the political parties that had existed on September 10, 1973, varied greatly. On the extreme Right, exiled leaders of Patria y Libertad soon returned home, but their organization gave little evidence of activity thereafter, although some of its leaders became acerbic critics of the regime. The Partido Nacional was splintered, some elements of the party (particularly conservative economic interests associated with it) giving uncritical support to the Junta de Gobierno. Many of the career politicians of the party, who had spent most of their adult lives in party activities or in Congress, were more hesitant about the regime. In any case, there is little evidence that the Partido Nacional continued to function as such after the government declared it to be "in recess."

The three Radical parties—Partido Radical, Partido de la Democracia Radical, and Partido Izquierda Radical—were largely destroyed by the coup. As a group, they had been severely undermined in the years preceding the coup, as a result of two major splits and bitter rivalry among the three factions. It seems unlikely that either the Partido Radical or the Democracia Radical continued to function as such after they were outlawed and "recessed." The status of the Izquierda Radical is not so clear, since by September 11, 1973, it had become closely aligned with the Christian Democrats.

Nothing was heard of Acción Popular Independiente after the coup. The two factions of MAPU were already severely weakened by their schism a few months before the fall of the Allende government, and although some of its members probably went underground, it is unlikely that the two organizations survived as national political parties, inside Chile at least. Much the same can be said of Izquierda Cristiana, most of whose important figures ultimately went into exile.

THE SOCIALIST PARTY AND THE MIR

The Socialist party was the most severely shattered of any of the major political groups in Chile as a result of the coup. It had little if any underground apparatus ready to go into operation once its public activities were banned. Although the still existing trade union leadership contained many people who had been elected as Socialists, the party was destroyed as a national organization. Because of its members' inexperience with underground activities, relatively large numbers of its secondary and tertiary leadership were arrested at the time of the coup or soon thereafter. In some parts of the country, the whole regional leadership of the party was executed on orders of officials of the new regime. The Socialist party will have to make a new beginning, if and when the opportunity arises.

The old divisions among the Socialist party leaders continued to be evident among those leaders in exile. Carlos Altamirano, after escaping to Europe, continued to talk in the name of the party there. He was widely accepted by European Socialist parties and was a major speaker at the first legal congress in the post-Franco era of the Spanish Socialist party. In that speech, he blamed the fall of the UP mainly on "Yankee imperialism," and he wrapped Allende's blanket of "martyrdom" around himself. He had seemingly forgotten both his hostility towards Allende in the months before the downfall of the Unidad Popular, and his own role in bringing about that downfall.[5]

Meanwhile, the anti-Altamirano faction, headed by Aniceto Rodríguez and Clodomiro Almeyda, made its headquarters in Caracas, Venezuela, and also spoke in the name of the Socialist party. It established contacts and had meetings with other exile groups, including some Christian Democrats, meetings from which the Altamirano faction was conspicuously absent. In May 1977, Almeyda made a trip to the United States and was received by the acting secretary of state.[6]

In the first weeks and months after the coup, the Movimiento de Izquierda Revolucionaria did considerably better than their Socialist friends. They had considerable experience with underground activities, and they had not abandoned their illegal apparatus when they had come out into the open during the Allende period. The new regime was particularly anxious about the MIR. As the result of shootouts with police and the military, however, many of MIR's top leaders were killed during the early months of the Junta. Among these was Miguel Henriquez, MIR secretary general, who was killed in a conflict with police in October 1974.[7] By the end of the first year of the military government, the MIR had probably been reduced at most to a few hundred people in scattered terrorist units. *Latin America* reported early in 1976 that the MIR "has invariably been thwarted by the efficacy of the military repression. Its principal leaders are dead or in exile."[8]

Rumors of a split in what remained of the MIR were reported late in 1975. The underground leadership was said to have expelled Nelson Gutierrez, Andrés Pascal Allende (nephew of the late president), Mary Ann Beausire, and María Elena Bachman, who were among its most important surviving leaders. The two men were said to have been condemned to death by their former comrades for having taken refuge in embassies in Santiago during the previous month.[9] This rumor was quickly denied by the "external committee" of the MIR, which had its headquarters in Havana.[10]

THE COMMUNISTS

The only two parties to survive largely intact were the Communists and the Christian Democrats. The Communists had had long experience with underground activities and had had an illegal organization parallel to their open party hierarchy in the years before the coup. The only important Communist leader to be captured by the new regime was Luis Corvalán; the others all succeeded in leaving the country or going into hiding. They maintained their base in the trade union movement and of all the UP parties were in the best shape to come out into the open again, if the opportunity presented itself.

The Communists made perhaps the most sober assessment [of any of the UP groups] of what had happened to the Unidad Popular. In October 1973, in its first public statement after the coup, the party stated:

The Communist Party is absolutely convinced that its policy of unconditional support of the Popular Unity government, its work to achieve mutual understanding with other democratic forces, especially at the grassroots level, its striving to inspire confidence in the middle strata of the population, its efforts to direct the main blows against the principal enemies—imperialism and internal reaction—its persistent labor to strengthen the alliance of the Communists and the Socialists, the unity of the workingclass and understanding among the Popular Unity parties, its efforts to increase production and raise the productivity of labor, to heighten the profitability of enterprises of the state sector, and to ensure strict observance of labor discipline, were all components of correct general policy.

The statement added that "the Communist Party feels that this is not the time to engage in debates about the mistakes committed by the government and the Popular Unity bloc as a whole and each of its political parties in particular."[11]

A few months later, however, the Chilean Communists were more willing to make a public assessment of what had happened between 1970 and 1973. The July 1974 issue of *World Marxist Review*, the organ of the international pro-Moscow Communist movement, carried an article by René Castillo, identified as "Member of the Leadership, CP of Chile," in which, after admitting that "the events in Chile are certainly a bitter, if temporary, defeat," he added that "a number of questions arise which revolutionaries must answer."[12] According to Castillo, "A factor that worked against united leadership was the ceaseless subversion of the ultra-Left elements against the Socialist-Communist alliance and the Popular Unity. Their aim was to create an avowedly anti-Communist 'revolutionary pole' to replace the 'reformist leadership' allegedly imposed by our Party. And their views met response among some Socialist Party members."[13]

Castillo also argued that "Right deviators" had contributed to the downfall of the Allende regime. He commented that "one of the most pronounced features of the Right deviation was the economism which sank deep roots among the more politically backward groups of working people." After alleging that the opponents of the regime engaged in encouraging the workers "to put forth excessive demands," Castillo observed that "all this affected the attitudes of these groups of workers in the battle for more production and higher productivity. And that was a battle the government had to win to strengthen its position and resolve the issue of power in its favor."[14]

Until his release and exile in December 1976, the Communists carried on a worldwide campaign on behalf of Luis Corvalán, the party's secretary general. He was arrested soon after the coup, was first sent to Dawson Island, and then was brought back to central Chile, where he was kept in several different prisons. The Communists, in their propaganda on his behalf, emphasized that his life was in danger, which may or may not have been the case.

President Pinochet long maintained that he would not release Corvalán until the Castro regime in Cuba released Hubert Matos, its most famous political prisoner.[15] In the end, the Chilean government permitted Corvalán to go into exile in return for the release and exiling of the Soviet dissident Vladimir Bukovsky.

Although the Chilean Communists were happy to see Corvalán released, they were reportedly not pleased with the circumstances surrounding his exile. *Latin America* reported soon after the event that "Corvalán himself had recently told a Danish journalist over the telephone from prison that the proposed exchange seemed to him very suspect, and he was prepared to stay in prison as long as he had to." It added that "the Chilean exile community in Moscow reacted first with disbelief at the news, and then with disapproval. They eventually put out a statement following the Soviet line, not mentioning the exchange and simply welcoming Corvalán's release as the fruit of international pressure."[16]

From his refuge in Moscow, Corvalán laid down the lines of Communist party strategy against the Pinochet dictatorship. Interviewed for British television, Corvalán was reported to have spoken "very much as the un-disputed party leader, and indeed said things that no other members of the party have spelt out before so explicitly."

The line of action which he enunciated conformed to what the Communist party was in fact doing, or trying to do, within the country. *Latin America Political Report* summed up his position: "His strategy is to re-form Popular Unity on the basis of the old Communist-Socialist alliance, along with the small social democratic Radical Party, and from that base enter into a firm alliance with the Christian Democrats." The British periodical also said that "Corvalán seems largely to be discounting the groups and parties to the left of the Communists (left-wing Socialists, Movimiento de Acción Popular Unitaria (MAPU), Movimiento de Izquierda Revolucionaria (MIR), and Izquierda Cristiana."

Finally, Corvalán indicated that he wanted the alliance with the Christian Democrats to be a relatively long one. He urged the two groups to "reach agreement on a common political project," which would ultimately include formation of a government "with the aim of reestablishing democratic rule."[17]

For at least two years earlier, the Communist actions in Chile had con-formed to the strategy Corvalán outlined. Within the labor movement, the Communists maintained quite cordial relations with the Christian Demo-crats—considerably more amicable in some cases than their relations with Socialist unionists. Communist trade unionists even showed a friendly attitude to some visiting labor people from the United States.

THE CHRISTIAN DEMOCRATS AND THE JUNTA REGIME

The attitude of the Christian Democrats towards the coup has been wide-ly debated and considerably—sometimes purposefully—misunderstood. Proponents of the fallen regime argue that the Christian Democrats cooper-ated with the coup, expecting that the soldiers would soon call elections, which could be won by Eduardo Frei, or that they would immediately turn power over to him as president of Congress. Perhaps the best answer to this charge is that given by one of the chief figures in the PDC, to the effect that the leaders of the party "may have been fools, but they weren't imbeciles," and that no rational person could have believed that the military, having gone to the extreme of revolting, would immediately pass power back to the civilians.

In essence, the Christian Democrats "accepted" the coup as a *fait accom-pli.* In the months following, however, their attitude towards the military government shifted considerably. They soon came to constitute the only opposition political group which was able to function in at least semi-legality.

Immediately after the coup, the Christian Democratic party issued a statement:

1) The situation through which Chile is living is the consequence of the economic disaster, institutional chaos, armed violence and moral crisis to which the deposed Government brought the country, which brought the Chilean people to pain and desperation.

2) The facts indicate that the Armed Forces and Carabineros did not seek power. Their institutional traditions and the republican history of our Fatherland inspires the confidence that as soon as they have fulfilled the tasks which they have assumed to avoid the grave dangers of destruction and totalitarianism which menaced the Chilean nation, they will return power to the sovereign people so that it can freely and democratically decide the destiny of our nation.

3) The proposals to reestablish institutional normalcy, peace and unity among the Chileans put forward by the Junta Militar de Gobierno interpret the general sentiment and merit the patriotic cooperation of all sectors. Their attainment require a just and unified action, respectful of the rights of the workers, together with a collective effort in the national task of constructing the future of Chile, distinct from the minority efforts of those who seek regressive models or those in conflict with the democratic tradition of our people.

4) The Christian Democracy laments what has occurred. Loyal to its principles, it exhausted all its efforts to find a solution through the political institutions and will not refuse to seek spiritual and physical disarmament. It seeks the pacification, the reconstruction of Chile and the return to institutional normality, postponing as always its partisan interests for the higher good of the fatherland.[18]

From the inception of the military regime, the party refused to have any official relationship with it. Any party members who accepted executive posts in the military government had to resign membership in the PDC. As time went on, the party became increasingly critical of the Junta regime. On January 18, 1974, a letter signed by the PDC's president and vice-president, Patricio Aylwin and Osvaldo Olguín, respectively, was handed to General Pinochet. It was simultaneously published in Buenos Aires. It informed the president that "a lasting order cannot be created on the basis of repression. Many Chileans have lost their jobs, been denied civil service promotions, been arrested, harassed, threatened or pressured in different forms without any evidence or concrete charge being brought against them." The letter also criticized the government's economic policy. It commented that "in view of the level of prices and the fact that the earnings of workers are insufficient to cover the cost of food and other vital items for their families, we feel it is no exaggeration to say that many of these people are simply going hungry."[19]

This letter produced a reply from Interior Minister General Bonilla, to the effect that since it was "in recess," the PDC had no right to speak out and should keep quiet. Subsequently, the PDC leadership made a number of other attacks on the regime, notably when the government deported former party President Renán Fuentealba in November 1975.[20]

In May 1975, Eduardo Frei gave a long interview to the magazine *Ercilla*, which strongly attacked the Junta regime and its policies. He censured at length the economic programs of the government, including the anti-inflation program, which he said was being borne mainly by "those who live from wages, salaries and pensions"; and the government's decision to sell to private interests firms that had been established by the Development Corporation between 1939 and 1970.[21]

Early in 1976, ex-President Frei published a small book entitled *El Mandato de la Historia y las Exigencias del Porvenir* consisting of a series of essays dealing with the contemporary situation of Chile. It severely criticized the economic policies of the regime and repeatedly called for the quickest possible return to political democracy.

One essay on the role of the military harshly criticized the armed forces' apparently unlimited continuance in power. Frei declared that "to submit the Armed Forces for a long period to the accelerated wear and tear produced by the management of a severe crisis; to connect its prestige and its name to particular economic formulas; to associate it with certain policies or have it carry out these policies itself, is fatal for its unity and prestige and dangerous for the country."[22]

Frei summed up his point of view in a kind of peroration at the end of the book:

Chile has also been characterized by historic tendencies which have given it its unique character. This country was cited as an example of political organization, of stability, of respect for juridical norms and impersonal authority and social advances, and its people have demonstrated maturity of judgment and a great sense of tolerance and mutual respect. These constant factors are not due to the action of one person, of a statesman or of accident; they reflect the profound character of a people which is manifested in all the forms of its existence. The current which emanates from this profound source cannot be extinguished and no circumstance can exhaust it. We are certain that it will reappear stronger and purer.[23]

CHRISTIAN DEMOCRATIC STRATEGY

The strategy of the Christian Democratic party has been to criticize the errors and misdeeds of the Junta government, while avoiding any confrontation with the regime that would bring about the total destruction of the party's semilegal (and after March 1977 completely illegal) organization. In this way, its leaders, as well as its rank and file, believe that the party can be kept alive, for the time when a democratic civilian regime can be restored.

This strategy has had the support of the overwhelming number of active party members. Two dissident currents within the leadership were headed by ex-Senator José Musalém, who favored a policy of cooperation with the regime; and by Renán Fuentealba until his deportation, who advocated a more militant attitude towards the military government. Both of these groups had only marginal followings within the party. Musalém and a few other PDC leaders were reported in November 1974 to have been suspended from the party for signing a statement widely interpreted as friendly to the regime.[24]

When Fuentealba went into exile, he suggested that the PDC join a coalition with the Unidad Popular parties to oppose the Junta. In a sharp public response, PDC President Patricio Aylwin completely rejected the idea, reminding Fuentealba of the totalitarian proclivities of the Communists, MAPU, MIR and the Altamirano wing of the Socialist party.[25]

Aylwin also repudiated a meeting of exiles that had been held a few weeks earlier in Caracas, under the patronage of the German Social Democratic party's Friedrich Ebert Foundation. Those attending this meeting included Leighton and Fuentealba of the Christian Democrats; Clodomiro Almeyda, Aniceto Rodríguez, and Carmen Lazo of the Socialists; Anselmo Sule, Hugo Miranda, and Carlos Morales of the Radicals; and Rafael Gumucio and Sergio Bitar of Izquierda Cristiana. As *Latin America* noted, "The Communists were conspicuous absentees, as were the wilder elements in the Partido Socialista associated with Carlos Altamirano." Bernardo Leighton stated that some of those present officially represented their parties and that "our hope is to strengthen the anti-junta current within the Christian Democratic party, which in practice is now virtually unanimous."[26]

During its first three years in power, the Junta de Gobierno seemed, like the PDC, to want to avoid a complete confrontation between the two. Unquestionably, however, the Christian Democrats were strongly disliked by many of those associated with the military regime. Among the government's civilian advisers were many who argued that the Christian Democrats had really started the crisis in Chilean institutions, that had it not been for them, Allende would never have come to power, and that they therefore were as responsible as he and the UP for what happened after 1970. These critics made no differentiation between the kind of program carried out by the Frei government and that pursued by the Allende regime.

Typical of such an attitude was a denunciation of the Christian Democrats' agrarian reform program by Junta member General César Mendoza. Interviewed by the newspaper *Últimas Noticias* of Santiago, he said that the Frei government program had been "demagogic" and was caused by "political motives." He claimed that it had opened the way for the Unidad Popular's "total destruction of the agrarian structure."[27]

Christian Democrats were subjected to increasing persecution by the Junta regime. Local and regional leaders of the party were frequently arrested, and in some cases those arrested were tortured in order to get them to reveal "subversive" activities by national PDC leaders. In addition, a number of Christian Democratic leaders were exiled. We have already noted the deportation of Renán Fuentealba. In August 1976, Jaime Castillo, generally regarded as the principal theoretician of the Frei wing of the party, was deported as "a danger to the security of the state."[28] Bernardo Leighton was not allowed to return from abroad, and on October 6, 1975, an attempt was made on his life, which the Italian police classified as an attempted political assassination.[29]

During the early months of 1977, relations between the Christian Democrats and the military regime became even more hostile. The formal outlawing of the four remaining political parties was justified by the government in terms of alleged "subversive" activities of the Christian Democrats, as demonstrated by letters from PDC president Andrés Zaldívar and PDC Executive Committee member Tomás Reyes which had been seized from the handbag of a party member at the Santiago airport. At the same time that the parties were outlawed, Radio Balmaceda, which had several times been suspended by the government, was finally confiscated. The grounds for the ban was that it belonged to the Christian Democratic party, which had no right to own a radio station since it no longer existed as far as the government was concerned.[30]

As the government intensified its persecution of the Christian Democrats, the party appeared to somewhat alter its political strategy in the direction of seeking a rapprochement with certain elements of the Unidad Popular. As early as September 1976, there were reports of informal consultations between Christian Democrats and the moderate factions of Izquierda Cristiana and MAPU, held in New York under the sponsorship of the National Council of Churches.[31] At the end of May 1977, both Eduardo Frei and the Socialist leader Clodomiro Almeyda were in Washington, where each conferred with leading officials of the Carter administration. There were rumors at the time that they may also have conferred with one another. Reports circulated of a tentative agreement between the PDC and UP elements about a possible transition government to be headed by Frei if and when the military regime retired or was overthrown.[32]

VIOLENT RESISTANCE

The military regime kept the country under a state of war or state of siege throughout its first four years in power. One explanation it offered was the danger of terrorist action by the MIR and elements of the deposed regime. In fact, available evidence would indicate that such armed resistance was relatively minor.

When I was in Santiago in August 1974, I was informed by a military source that the night before, a military patrol enforcing the curfew had been shot down by machine guns fired from a truck, and the occupants of the truck had then made their getaway. Other such incidents have probably occurred from time to time, although they seldom get reported in the press. One which did get reported was the assassination of an army captain in Talca in June 1975 by "extremists," who were not apprehended.[33] However, such incidents have been limited in number, and at most have merely been a nuisance, and not a serious threat, to the regime.

Armed resistance to the Military Junta has been limited primarily because in the first weeks the military so thoroughly broke up training centers and potential guerrilla bases that the MIR had established during the Allende period. Many of the most important guerrilla leaders were killed in fighting, and others were arrested and executed. As already mentioned, the most prominent leaders of the MIR itself were shot or went into exile.

RELATIONS WITH THE CATHOLIC CHURCH

The Roman Catholic church must be classified as part of the opposition to the Junta regime. It has consistently criticized the regime's policies, particularly its handling of the economy and its violations of human rights. It has on occasion provided "cover" for other, more political, elements that have had difficulty in getting publicity for their positions.

On the other hand, relations between the military government and the church have been cautious. Each has held the other somewhat at arm's length, and both sides have sought to avoid any sharp confrontation. While some of the actions of the church hierarchy have not pleased the military leaders, the regime has made no all-out attack on the church.

The September 11, 1973, coup itself had an important impact on the church. It eliminated the Catholic extreme left wing, grouped in an organization known as Christians for Socialism, to which a small but vocal group of priests had belonged under Allende. Those involved in Christians for Socialism either fled abroad or lapsed into silence. This is one reason why the church leaders may not have been entirely unhappy with the disappearance of the Allende regime. There are other reasons, too. In its last months, the Unidad Popular government had begun a major assault on Catholic education, an assault which, although temporarily suspended, was seen by the church as a real threat. Significantly, the cardinal archbishop of Santiago had not attended the 1973 May Day demonstration organized by the CUTCh, as he had those of 1971 and 1972.

While it may be true that the church hierarchy was not entirely unhappy to see the Allende regime disappear, it certainly did not like many of the things the new government was doing. In the early weeks of the military rule, the cardinal intervened on several occasions to prevent killings and to protect unions and other groups from arbitrary actions by the new authorities. The church hierarchy also took the lead in organizing the Comité de Cooperación para la Paz en Chile. An auxiliary bishop of Santiago was one of the sponsors and leaders of this group, together with Protestant and Jewish religious leaders. The Comité was established to aid the victims of the coup. It helped families of those imprisoned to keep in touch with their incarcerated relatives, and it gave material help to these families in the form of food, clothing, and money. It also organized work projects to employ some workers who had been summarily dismissed from their jobs by the new regime, and it frequently intervened to reinstate such workers in their jobs. Finally, it helped students who had been dismissed from the universities to gain admission to schools in other countries. The government tolerated the Comité activities for over two years largely because the church hierarchy was associated with it.

In November 1975, President Pinochet, in a letter to Cardinal Silva Henríquez, demanded the dissolution of the Comité para la Paz on the basis that "we have considered that the mentioned organization is a means used by the Marxist Leninists to create problems which upset the tranquility of the citizens and the necessary quietness which it is my principal duty as ruler to maintain."[34]

While Cardinal Silva Henríquez was on a trip abroad, the auxiliary bishops of Santiago announced that they and the leaders of the other religious groups participating in the Comité had agreed to its dissolution "to contribute at no little sacrifice to the strengthening of a positive relationship of reciprocal comprehension between the Government and the different religious creeds." At the same time, they insisted that the churches involved would continue to carry on the Comité's work, and they warned that the government's insistence on dissolving the Comité "will generate in all probability within and particularly outside of Chile greater damage than that which is being avoided."[35]

The work of the Comité para la Paz was continued by the Catholic church through the Vicaría de Solidaridad. This group was established in January 1976, under the leadership of Monsignor Christian Precht, who had been secretary of the Comité.[36]

Latin America reported that the Vicaría "took on most of the same work for the defense and aid of political prisoners and their families. It decided to limit its work in sending information abroad, which had laid the Committee for Peace open to charges of aiding Chile's enemies in the 'international Marxist conspiracy,' and to concentrate instead on informing public opinion inside the country." The periodical also noted that "the Vicaría itself has laid great stress on the continuity of its work with that of the Committee for Peace."[37]

Like the Comité para la Paz before it, the Vicaría de Solidaridad was subjected to considerable governmental harassment. In April 1976, one of its lawyers, José Fernando Zalaquett, was deported after he had briefed three visiting members of the U.S. Congress on the human rights situation in Chile.[38] A month later, the lawyer for the Vicaría, Hernán Montealegre, was arrested, first on charges of being a CIA agent and later of being a member of the Communist party.[39]

The Vicaría continued its predecessor's fight on behalf of people who had "disappeared." On August 20, 1976, it presented a petition to the Supreme Court, asking for the appointment of a special investigating judge to look into the cases of 383 such people. The Court turned down the request.[40]

The church hierarchy often warned the government publicly about the bad results of its economic, social, and political policies. While most such warnings were not couched in quite the sharp terms used by the Brazilian hierarchy in criticizing that nation's military regime, all the same they imparted the Church's strong disapproval of the Junta's actions.

On April 24, 1974, the majority of the Chilean bishops issued a declaration entitled "Reconciliation in Chile," which was distributed by the cardinal. The declaration conveyed the following concerns:

We are concerned in the first place, with the climate of insecurity and fear, whose roots we believe are found in accusations, false rumors and lack of participation and information. . . . We are also concerned with the social dimensions of the current economic situation . . . the increase in unemployment and job dismissals for arbitrary or ideological reasons.

It also attacked the Junta's educational policies as not allowing "enough participation by parents and the academic community." The bishops concluded their statement with the reassurance that they were not questioning the "righteous intention nor the good will of our governors. But as pastors, we see objective obstacles to reconciliation among Chileans. Such situations can be overcome only by the unrestricted respect for human rights as formulated by the United Nations and the Second Vatican Council."[41]

On May Day 1975, the cardinal organized a unique protest against the Junta and its policies. Several labor unions closely associated with the Junta organized a May Day meeting in Santiago's largest meeting hall, with the minister of labor as the main speaker. Cardinal Silva Henríquez scheduled a mass to be said at virtually the same time, in honor of Saint Peter, patron saint of workers, even though May 1 is not the name day of that saint. The mass was attended by a wide range of opponents of the regime, including many who had not been inside a church for years.[42] Two years later, on May 1, 1977, the cardinal again offered a special mass, when the government refused to authorize a meeting in the Teatro Caupolicán planned by leaders of the more independent union groups. Like the earlier event, it was attended by trade unionists of varied political and religious persuasions.[43]

In September 1975, Cardinal Silva Henríquez announced that the church would not participate in any ceremonies connected with the Junta's second anniversary, for "while there are those who hunger, who are ill, who have no work, and who live with no security, no Christian can feel himself comfortable, or unconcerned or satisfied with the world or the society in which he lives."[44]

The cardinal did attend the celebrations marking the third anniversary of the coup,[45] but his presence did not signify the end of church criticism of the military regime's actions. In March 1977, the bishops issued a new document entitled "Living Together as a Nation" which "criticized the government as unrepresentative and insisted that new constitutional laws would have to 'emerge as a result of the free and mature national consensus.'"[46] This document was characterized by *Latin America Political Report* as "perhaps the strongest, and certainly the most political, statement the Church has yet made."[47] The statement brought a blast from Minister of Justice Renato Damilano, who accused the bishops of being "useful fools getting themselves mixed up with politicians and Marxists," and "ambitious, ill-intentioned and resentful people." Interestingly, when the church vigorously protested the minister's statement, Damilano was forced to resign.[48]

Quite early in the military regime, the secretary of the Chilean Episcopal Conference, Bishop Carlos Camus, stated what continued to be the bases of the church's criticisms of the Junta government. In an interview published in the Italian weekly *Panorama*, he said that the church had three fundamental difficulties with the Junta: "1) the Church's obligation to denounce violations of human rights; 2) the economic policy of the government which victimizes the poorest classes; and 3) Church opposition to militarization of schools and universities, including intervention of the Catholic University."[49]

The Junta's relations with some of the Protestant groups, particularly the Lutherans, were also severely strained. The close cooperation of Lutheran Bishop Helmut Frenz with the Comité para la Paz first brought a split within the Lutheran church, apparently encouraged by the government. Then, in early October 1975, when Bishop Frenz was visiting Switzerland on church business, the government announced that he would not be allowed to return to Chile.[50] The Lutheran Church Synod of Chile defended Bishop Frenz against the attacks the government had made on him.[51]

30
The Foreign Policy
of the Junta Regime

The Chilean military government has suffered from a kind of international quarantine ever since its establishment in September 1973. Its many efforts to deal with this situation have more often than not intensified Chile's isolation. At the same time, in its mania for attaining full control over every facet of the public administration, the government has decimated the country's excellent foreign service, replacing its members for the most part with officers of the armed services whose ability for assuming extreme ideological postures far exceeds their capacity for diplomacy. Such new directions as the Junta regime has given to Chilean foreign policy have frequently been counterproductive.

PURGE OF THE FOREIGN SERVICE

With their penchant for inflicting long-run as well as short-run damage on their country, the Junta have all but destroyed the Chilean diplomatic corps, an institution long known as one of the best trained and most professional foreign services in the Western Hemisphere. In Latin America, it is perhaps surpassed only by the famous Brazilian foreign office known popularly as Itamaraty. The professional diplomatic corps has largely been replaced with members of the armed services, and in some instances with members of the extreme Right-wing civilian groups most closely identified with the regime.

From its inception, the Junta named active and retired members of the armed forces to posts as ambassadors, and even as consuls. By February 1977, 95 percent of all such posts were held by military men. On the top administrative level of the foreign ministry, most posts were also given to soldiers: Colonel Jaime Lavín was named director general of the foreign service; Colonel Carlos Derpsch was made head of the diplomatic academy; and Colonel Ernesto Videl was appointed chief of planning for the Foreign Ministry. A far Right civilian, José Manuel Casanueva, was named head of the economic section of the ministry, but the positions as head of the personnel and security sections of the ministry were given to a police major and a navy officer.

Meanwhile, the professionals in the foreign service were purged. Between November 1975 and early 1977, about 25 percent of them were dismissed and replaced with unconditional advocates of the regime, most of them military men and policemen, including some from the dreaded DINA. Forty of these new recruits were brought into the service in the last months of 1976, and forty more in the first half of 1977. Meanwhile, of the eighteen people graduating from the diplomatic academy in December 1976, twelve were members of the armed services, mostly of the rank of colonel.

Latin America Political Report has observed that "a world-defying, grandiloquent style characterizes the new diplomats. An anonymous critic from within the diplomatic service sums up his new colleagues thus: 'Most of their ideas date from before the last World War—or earlier. The most modern of them are still fighting the cold war.'"[1]

SENSITIVITY TO FOREIGN CRITICISM

From its inception, the Chilean military regime has been highly sensitive to criticism from abroad. During the first week after the coup, the newspaper *El Mercurio*, one of the two then being allowed to publish in Santiago and virtually a spokesman for the new regime, already was carrying an editorial entitled "False Image of Chile in the Exterior," in which it wrote that "information circulating abroad about Chilean events contains visible errors of fact and mistakes of interpretation."[2] Since then, *El Mercurio*, members of the Junta, and other figures in the regime have repeated these complaints. After a short time, they began to interpret the attacks made on the coup and on the regime emanating from it, in the press and other media abroad, as being a well-orchestrated campaign conducted by the Communists on a worldwide basis.[3]

One of the government's first reactions to the intense criticism it received was to invite anyone in Western Europe, the United States, or Latin America to come to Chile and see for themselves. Many different missions from many different organizations, official and unofficial, did in fact visit Chile. Some of these were given wide opportunities to talk with leaders of the new regime, to move around freely, and even to interview prisoners and people in the United Nations refugee centers.

When these moves failed to end the criticism abroad—since many of the visitors were horrified by what they saw—the Pinochet regime became less receptive to visiting foreigners and became increasingly convinced that criticism was being made in bad faith. By the time of the first anniversary of the military government, it had become an article of faith among supporters of the regime that Chile was purposefully being maligned abroad by the world Communist movement and that those critics who were not Communists were dupes of the Communists.

Foreign attacks on the Junta's handling of human rights were frequent. A typical one was the report of the strongly anti-Communist International Commission of Jurists in November 1974, which concluded that repression was "more systematic then ever" in Chile. In the same month, the United Nations General Assembly passed the first of its annual resolutions denouncing the situation in Chile. The resolution, which noted "flagrant violations of human rights in Chile," was passed by a vote of 63 to 9, with 21 abstaining. Only five Latin American countries voted against this resolution, and the United States and China abstained.[4]

One of the most flagrant instances of refusing foreign and international agencies permission to make further "investigation" was the government's sudden decision to ban entry of the delegation of the Human Rights Commission of the United Nations, which was scheduled to visit Chile early in July 1975. This decision was announced only a week before the group was scheduled to arrive. The Junta's decision caused serious strains in Chile's already somewhat precarious relations with the United States.[5]

Several observations may be offered with regard to the military regime's extreme sensitivity to foreign criticism. First, one must admit that there have been some grounds for this sensitivity. Both in Europe and the United States, there had been widespread misunderstanding of the Allende regime, with its fall widely interpreted as the frustration by the armed forces of an attempt to obtain a democratic Socialist society through democratic means —which was not the case.

The second observation is that the Communists, particularly those of the Moscow brand, have indeed carried on a worldwide campaign against the Chilean military regime. Characteristic of this campaign is a pamphlet published by the East German government, consisting of resolutions by the East German Socialist Unity party and trade unions, and statements by individuals in the German Democratic Republic praising the Allende regime and denouncing the Junta. The pamphlet was published in English and presumably in various other languages as well.[6]

Such Communist attacks are not surprising. However, this campaign by itself would not have generated the width and depth of the criticisms the coup and the military regime have received.

Third, some of the charges against the Junta have undoubtedly been exaggerated. For example, Neal MacDermot, secretary general of the International Commission of Jurists, came away from a visit to Chile claiming that the Junta government had set up "rehabilitation" camps to which 600,000 children of parents who had backed the Allende government were being sent.[7] In two visits to the country after the coup, I never even heard a rumor of such establishments, and I am convinced that nothing of the sort was set up by the military regime.

Hence, many of the Junta's claims with regard to its critics are justified. But what the Junta and its supporters have been quite unable to understand is that the executions, the massive rounding up of people in the National Stadium, the establishment of concentration camps, the "disappearance" of many hundreds of people, the almost complete suppression of freedom of the press, the outlawing of the political parties, and the suspension of most trade union activities have aroused profound disapproval among democratically minded people throughout the world. Furthermore, those in and around the Junta government have not been able to realize that in many respects the critics of the regime have evidenced a profound respect and admiration for the democratic tradition and the one-time democratic reality that had been Chile's. Many media and individuals abroad, like the Christian Democrats in Chile itself, "lament what has occurred" and even more have lamented the ferocity and violence with which the constitutional regime was disposed of—no matter that the overthrow of Allende was inevitable or that his regime provoked its own ouster. Moreover, democratic observers abroad have felt that nothing that the Allende regime had or had not done justified the ferocity, brutality, and tyranny of its military successor.

RELATIONS WITH THE COMMUNIST REGIMES

After the coup, Chile's international relations altered substantially. Nowhere was this change more marked than with regard to the Communist-controlled regimes. The most interesting aspect of this phase of Chilean foreign affairs was the different relations of the new regime with the Moscow-oriented Communist regimes and with the People's Republic of China.

The Junta did not have to break off relations with the Soviet Union and Bulgaria, since the governments of those two countries broke relations with the Junta regime soon after it took power. The government of East Germany also broke off with Chile; on September 21, 1973, it called in Ambassador Carlos Contreras Labarca (ironically, a former secretary general of the Chilean Communist party) to inform him of this break. Subsequently, it published a pamphlet in several languages, announcing its action and condemning the new Chilean regime.[8] The Junta took the initiative in ending diplomatic relations with Cuba and North Korea.[9]

Rumania was the only East European country that continued to maintain an embassy in Santiago.[10] This stance was consistent with Rumania's position of relative diplomatic independence from Moscow.

Even without diplomatic relations with East Europe, some trade between the East European countries and Chile did continue. For example, late in 1976 copper valued at three million marks was transhipped through Hamburg, destined for East Berlin. West German Communists were reported to have justified this shipment as payment for overdue debts owed to East Germany.[11]

Unlike the Soviet Union, the People's Republic of China has maintained normal diplomatic relations with Chile. This normalcy was underscored from time to time. Thus, *Peking Review* published General Pinochet's message to Premier Hua Kuo-feng on the occasion of the death of Chinese President Chu Teh in the summer of 1976: "On the grievous death of the distinguished personality Mr. Chu Teh, Chairman of the Standing Committee of the National People's Congress, I extend to Your Excellency my most profound condolences which are shared by the people and Government of Chile."[12]

When Mao Tse-tung died several months later, in September 1976, the Chilean president again sent a message to Hua Kuo-feng, which was published in *Peking Review*: "Please allow me, on behalf of the Chilean people and Government, and in my own name, to express to Your Excellency our sincere condolences on the unfortunate passing away of Mao Tsetung, an eminent statesman. The deceased leader who projected the road to prosperity and development for your country has left an illustrious image in the history of humanity. Your Excellency, please accept the feelings of my highest consideration."[13] The Chinese periodical also reported that Foreign Minister Admiral Patricio Carvajal and the naval aide-de-camp of the president, Commander Carlos Pinto Cáceres, "called at the Chinese Embassy in Santiago on the afternoon of September 9 to extend deep condolences on the passing of Chairman Mao Tsetung."[14] In Peking, Chile was one of the countries officially represented at the mourning ceremonies for Mao.[15]

At the time of the Tangshan earthquake, the Chileans offered to extend aid to the victims, and they received a message of "sincere thanks" from the Chinese regime. At this time, the director of communications of the Junta, Colonel Gastón Zuñiga, commented that relations with Peking "are good and are developing in an atmosphere of mutual respect."[16]

Apparently, the Chinese regime was urging those other Communist governments over which it had some influence to establish relations with the Chilean military government. Thus, in June 1976 the New China News Agency announced that the government of Cambodia had decided to establish diplomatic relations with Chile, as well as with Peru.[17] Some limits were placed on the Sino-Chilean friendship, however. For example, in early 1976 the Chinese Ambassador in Lima announced that rumors that China was planning to extend arms aid to the Chilean regime were false.[18]

RELATIONS WITH THE UNITED STATES

The Junta moved rapidly to try to mend relations with the United States, which had been severely strained during the Allende period. However, relations with the United States remained difficult throughout the first four years of the military government.

An important step in attempting to reestablish good relations with the United States was the military government's agreement to compensate the U.S. mining companies which had lost their properties as a result of the Allende regime's complete takeover of copper and nitrate enterprises. After extensive negotiations, agreements for compensation were reached with Anaconda, Kennecott and Cerro de Pasco. However, the mines remained in Chilean government hands.

The human rights issue proved to be the greatest stumbling block in achieving good relations with the United States. Until the advent of the Carter administration, the principal initiative within the U.S. government for bringing pressure on the Junta to modify its repression came from the U.S. Congress. One of the Congress's first moves was to add a proviso to the fiscal 1975 foreign aid appropriation law which would ban any further credits or grants to the Chilean government for purchasing arms in the United States.[19] This proviso did not interfere with arms shipments that were still "in the pipeline," or with the ability of the Chilean government to purchase arms with cash.

In early 1976, Congress threatened to go even further in its restrictions on arms aid to the Chilean regime. The so-called Kennedy amendment, sponsored by Senator Edward Kennedy, was added to the 1976 foreign aid bill in the Senate. It called for a complete ban even on cash purchase of arms by the Chileans in the United States. This amendment aroused anguished protests from the Chilean regime and its press. Thus, General Gustavo Leigh claimed that the amendment constituted "intervention in the internal affairs of Chile."[20] El Mercurio editorialized that the Kennedy amendment "implies a transgression of the system of continental defense."[21]

The House of Representatives did not go along with the Kennedy Amendment. As a result, the law as passed continued the prohibition on any grants or credit to Chile for arms, but it did allow Chile to continue to pay cash for arms bought within the United States.[22]

Another crisis in Chilean-U.S. relations occurred as the result of the Organization of American States' annual meeting held in Santiago in June 1976. As the price for the meeting being held in the Chilean capital, the United States demanded that the Junta release a number of political prisoners. Some weeks before the OAS session, Treasury Secretary William Simon went to Chile and at that time some prisoners were in fact released.[23]

One of the items of business at the OAS meeting was the report of the Human Rights Commission of the organization, which presented extremely damaging evidence that the Junta regime had violated civil liberties. During the discussion of this report, Secretary of State Henry Kissinger noted that "the conditions of human rights as assessed by the OAS human rights commission has impaired our relationship with Chile and will continue to do so."[24] This was the Republican administration's strongest formal condemnation of the political behavior of the Pinochet government. It was in sharp contrast to Secretary Kissinger's earlier reprimand to U.S. Ambassador David Popper for "lecturing the Chileans on political science," when the ambassador had protested certain human rights violations of the Junta.[25]

The administration of President Jimmy Carter, in accordance with its general policy of emphasizing human rights issues in its foreign policy, took a much sharper line with the Junta regime. This change had been feared by the Junta and its supporters. Thus, *El Mercurio*, in commenting on Carter's victory in the November 1976 election, reported: "Criticism of Chile was an attractive electoral theme and probably was made in those terms. Very different is the handling of that theme by Mr. Carter as President of the United States, taking into account the strategic interests of that country, the need for continental security and the requirements of world peace."[26]

The new thrust of the Carter administration's relations with the Junta became clear at the end of May 1977. Both ex-President Eduardo Frei and Clodomiro Almeyda were in Washington at that time. Frei was received by Vice-President Walter Mondale and by Zbigniew Brzezinski, the president's national security adviser, while Almeyda was received by Under Secretary of State (and Acting Secretary) Warren Christopher.[27] Although no details of these conversations were released, the reception of these two prominent leaders of the Chilean opposition indicated political support for them against the Junta government.

RELATIONS WITH WESTERN EUROPE

The military regime tried to maintain as good relations as possible with the West European countries, but as in the case of the United States, the Junta's repressive policies made friendly relations very difficult.

The first crisis with a West European country involved the Swedish ambassador, Harald Edelstam, who was declared persona non grata soon after the Junta took power. This step was taken on the grounds that he had illegally sought out people who were looking for diplomatic asylum and had brought them to his embassy—which in fact, he had been doing.[28]

Although this diplomatic crisis was overcome, Sweden and other Scandinavian countries continued to be exceedingly critical of the Junta regime. In December 1976, the Scandinavian representatives on the Governing Board of the World Bank first succeeded in getting consideration of a loan to Chile postponed[29] and then ultimately voted against it, although the loan was finally granted.[30] They had previously voted against World Bank loans to Chile in April 1974 and May 1975.[31]

West European nations generally took a critical position on Chile in international forums. Thus, in the 1975 United Nations General Assembly, West Germany and France joined the United States in voting to condemn Chile's violations of human rights. In 1976, France, West Germany, and the United States abstained. In December 1976, on a vote for a loan to Chile France, Italy, Belgium, Holland, and Britain all abstained in the Governing Board of the World Bank.

There were particular problems with Italy and Great Britain. For almost a year the Italian government refused to recognize the Junta regime. As a result, it was not until the end of 1974 that 221 refugees who had a sought asylum in the Italian Embassy in Santiago were finally given safe conduct to leave Chile.[33]

Late in 1975, a serious incident occurred with the British. As a result of allegedly giving medical aid to MIRistas who were hiding from the police, a British surgeon, Sheila Cassidy, was arrested and tortured by the Chilean police. The British lodged a formal protest with Chile over her arrest.[34] She was kept in jail until December 29, when she was finally allowed to return home. Although the British ambassador stayed to negotiate Dr. Cassidy's release, he left the country at the same time she did; *Latin America* noted that "he is unlikely to return."[35]

The Junta made particular efforts to establish a close association with Spain. Junta member Admiral Merino visited Spain in January 1975, at which time he had an interview with Francisco Franco, the Spanish dictator, and liberally distributed decorations among Franco's cabinet members.[36] Upon Franco's death in November 1975, President Pinochet announced that the passing of the Spanish dictator was "a great loss that the Government and people of Chile lament with mourning." He added a prayer, "Let God enlighten Spain so that it will not abandon its present path."[37]

Pinochet went to Spain for Franco's funeral. *El Mercurio* editorialized that "the presence of Chile in the funeral of the Caudillo and the investiture of the King Juan Carlos I, with the most high-ranking delegation headed by the President of the Republic, is a homage to the figure of Franco and his historical significance, but also is the way of expressing our best wishes for the Spain of yesterday, tomorrow and always.[38] Upon his return from Spain, where he had been received by King Juan Carlos, Pinochet reported on what he had seen: "I confirmed . . . the infamy and calumny of Marxist propaganda. This propaganda, which has for decades attacked Franco, claims that the people hated him. However, I could personally see that lines of 30 and 40 blocks waited to render posthumous homage to the Caudillo. The fervor and love the Spaniards had for Franco impressed me.''[39]

JUNTA CONTACTS WITH ARAB STATES AND SOUTH AFRICA

In its desperate search for friends, the Junta regime sought out the Arab states. The Chilean press played up apparently friendly comments by Arab diplomats towards the Chilean military regime. For instance, *El Mercurio* reported a statement by the ambassador of Jordan in which the ambassador described General Pinochet as ''a sincere man and a very agreeable and intelligent President of a Republic,'' and as ''a friendly President of a nation which is very nationalist and democratic and a friend of the Arab countries.''[40]

El Mercurio also recorded the comments of a newly arriving Egyptian ambassador. In March 1975, this dignitary stated: ''We were at the side of Chile when it was being unjustly accused in international organizations and in particular in the Commission of Human Rights. . . . There are some exceptions, but it appears to me that the favorable sentiment to Chile is notable in those Arab nations which have key influence in world affairs.'' These included Saudi Arabia and Kuwait, he added.[41]

In April 1976, Jorge Cauas, the minister of finance, made a visit to Kuwait, in an effort to reinforce relations with the Arab oil-producing countries.[42]

The Junta government also sought to establish relations with South Africa, with which Chile had had little contact in the past. The overtures to South Africa were the subject of denunciation at a ''Nonaligned Conference'' in August 1975.[43]

DIFFICULTIES WITH SOME LATIN AMERICAN COUNTRIES

The Pinochet regime made a concerted effort to establish strong relations with other Latin American countries; in fact, it sought to portray itself as a leader in the hemisphere. In a ''Message to Fellow Latin Americans,'' the Junta said that it ''hereby expresses to fellow Latin Americans the faith and confidence that the destinies of our countries shall never be controlled by Marxist totalitarianism, for the simple reason that its men, women and children repudiate all that the threat of slavery involves.'' Later in the statement, the Junta argued that ''it is thus that our example will serve to point out new and fruitful paths for the Latin American who will discover in his own native blood a reason for living and for remaining a free and true man, disdaining all foreign intervention.''[44]

The Junta's bid for Latin American leadership was not widely accepted in the area. Its most serious problem was with Mexico, which gave asylum to a large number of refugees from Chile, including President Allende's widow. At the same time, President Echeverría made no secret of his disapproval of the Chilean military government. Finally, in a variation from the traditional Mexican policy of nonintervention in the internal affairs of other Latin American countries—with the corollary of maintaining diplomatic relations with all Latin American nations, regardless of the nature of their governments—President Echeverría on November 29, 1974, broke formal diplomatic relations with the Pinochet government when Allende's sister was arrested.[45] Laura Allende was later released and went to Mexico, but the rupture between the two countries remained.[46]

The Chilean government and its supporters reacted bitterly to Mexico's action. *El Mercurio* ran an editorial entitled "A Rupture That Defines a Ruler," in which it pointed out that Echeverría had been the minister of interior responsible for the bloody incident in the Place of the Three Cultures in Mexico City in 1968, when police and soldiers fired point blank into a crowd, killing several hundred people. The Chilean newspaper added that "his subsequent demagogic actions, attempting to create a Leftist image, are only designed to erase those indelible stains of blood which mark his administration." It went on to say that a rupture of relations with Chile was additional evidence of this demagoguery.[47]

The Chilean Junta also had difficult relations with the democratic government of Venezuela. That country also gave refuge to many Chilean exiles, particularly those belonging to the Radical party and the moderate element of the Socialist party. The state of affairs with Venezuela sometimes reached public attention, as in mid-1975 when Army Chief of Staff General Arrelano Stark asked President Carlos Andrés Pérez to curb refugee activities in Venezuela and Pérez refused to do so. At about the same time, Pérez's offer to try to arrange a summit conference among the presidents of Chile, Bolivia, and Peru over the question of Bolivia's right to access to the sea was rejected by the Chilean government. *El Mercurio* denounced it as "interference in the internal affairs of other countries."[48]

Late in 1976, when Chile formally withdrew from the Andean Pact, the Venezuelans reacted strongly. Andrés Mercau, Venezuelan delegate to the pact, commented that "Chile has been a stumbling block for the advancement of the Andean Pact," and that "since Chile knows that there is no legal way to exclude it, it has abused the solidarity and patience of the other countries."[49]

Chile's withdrawal from the Andean Pact (which we shall discuss in more detail in a later chapter), was generally a disquieting element in her relations with the other members of the bloc—Bolivia, Peru, Ecuador, Colombia, and Venezuela.

THE JUNTA REGIME AND OTHER
MILITARY DICTATORSHIPS

The Junta sought to develop close relationships with other Latin American military dictatorships and claimed some success in this regard. In at least some cases, these regimes did not want to move too close to Chile or to share the general world isolation to which the Chilean Junta government was being subjected.

President Pinochet used personal diplomacy to strengthen relations with two nearby military dictatorships, those of Paraguay and Uruguay. In May 1974, he made a trip to Paraguay, where he was reported to have been "warmly received . . . by President Stroessner."[50] Pinochet went to the extreme of making President Stroessner a general in the Chilean army.[51]

In April 1976, President Pinochet made a five-day visit to Uruguay to visit President Juan María Bordaberry, the puppet civilian president of that country's military regime (who would be removed by the armed forces a few weeks later). Upon his return, General Pinochet pronounced the trip "very interesting. Both Presidents could exchange ideas with respect to our struggle against Marxism-Leninism and the way in which we were projecting our countries ahead towards a new democracy."[52]

The Junta dispatched lower ranking officials to some of the smaller military regimes. Thus, Junta member General César Mendoza made a special trip to visit the regime of General Anastasio Somoza in Nicaragua in December 1974. Upon his return he reported that "in Nicaragua there exists a very positive image of Chile. They are conscious that we succeeded in eradicating international Marxism. For that they admire Chile and the Chileans."[53]

In a few cases, the Chilean Junta even extended modest economic aid to other dictatorial regimes. For example, in March 1974 they loaned the government of Guatemala $5 million.[54]

Relations with the Brazilian military dictatorship, while friendly, were somewhat distant. When I was in Brazil in mid-1975, sources which were well-informed on Brazilian foreign policy assured me that the government there did not wish to be openly friendly towards the Pinochet government and that the Brazilian generals felt rather relieved that the great international attention on the human rights violations of the Chilean Junta had served to relieve much of the pressure formerly felt by the Brazilian regime.

From time to time, however, indications of friendliness between the two military regimes have appeared. Thus, in September 1976 Brazilian Army Minister General Silvio Frota attended Chilean Army Day celebrations and brought with him a message of congratulations from Brazilian President Geisel. He also presented Pinochet the decoration of the Grand Cross of the Order of Rio Branco.[55] A few months later, the Chilean government announced that because of President Carter's human rights policy it would henceforward increase its purchase of arms from Brazil.[56]

THE JUNTA'S RELATIONS WITH ARGENTINA

Since the advent of its own Junta regime, Argentina's attitude towards the Chilean Junta has changed.

Although President Juan Perón was willing to meet with Pinochet in May 1974, when the Chilean general made a "fueling stop" at Moron Air Base in Argentina on the way to his visit with Paraguayan dictator General Stroessner, Pinochet's reception was something less than overwhelming. *Latin America* reported that "as far as the Argentinians were concerned the visit was a non-event, best unrecorded. . . . There were no friendly *abrazos*, merely a formal handshake.[57]

With the advent of Argentina's new government of the armed forces in March 1976, relations between the two regimes became much friendlier. In November of that year, the Argentine chief executive made a visit to Santiago, which *El Mercurio* headlined "Argentine President General Videla Guest of the People of Chile for 4 Days." In an editorial, the paper proposed that "Chile and Argentina must unite to preserve their independence, their Christian Occidental culture and the dignity of their citizens, while at the same time pushing forward an ordered process of recuperation of the economy which has been submitted to ruinous experiments of Marxism."[58]

One major issue that had long been pending between Argentina and Chile came up for resolution after the Chilean Junta came to power. This was the question of the sovereignty of three islands (Picton, Nueva, and Lennox) in the Beagle Channel, the southernmost passageway through Tierra del Fuego, at the tip of South America, between the Atlantic and Pacific Oceans. Through arrangements made while Allende was president in 1971, the issue was to be arbitrated by five members of the International Court at the Hague (from Britain, the United States, France, Nigeria, and Sweden) who would pass on their decision to Queen Elizabeth II of Great Britain, who was the official arbitrator.[59]

The final decision was handed down early in 1977. It represented a diplomatic triumph for Chile, since it awarded all three islands to that country.[60] *Latin America Political Report* commented that the fourfold importance of the decisions was "first, that Chile now controls access to the Argentine naval base of Ushuaia, even though the decision gives Argentina territorial rights over the waters around the base. Secondly, it gives Chile status as a South Atlantic nation. . . . Thirdly, it will strengthen Chile's claim to the segment of Antarctica disputed with Argentina. . . . Fourthly, it will affect claims to drilling rights for offshore oil."[61] Argentina was given nine months to challenge the decision.

RELATIONS WITH PERU

Particularly critical were the relations of the Chilean military regime with that of Peru. During the Allende period, the reformist military government of Peru had been friendly with the Unidad Popular regime, which it regarded as sharing many common objectives. It was to be expected, therefore, that the Peruvian generals would denounce their Chilean counterparts' ouster of Allende. Instead, they quickly made it clear that they had no intention of intervening in the Chilean situation; they were very selective in granting asylum to Chilean refugees and made life difficult for those who were permitted entry.

One element in Chilean-Peruvian relations worried the Pinochet government, as well as many ordinary Chilean citizens. This was fear that the old border issue between the two countries—which presumably had been settled once and for all in 1929—might be reopened by the Peruvians. The approach of the first centenary of the War of the Pacific, which started in 1879, made many Chileans apprehensive that the Peruvians might seek to recover their lost provinces of Tarapacá and Arica before that date. These fears were enhanced in mid-1974, when the Peruvians received large shipments of arms, particularly tanks and rockets, from the Soviet Union and proudly paraded them in their Independence Day celebration.

The result was that war jitters were widely prevalent in Chile in 1974 and early 1975. There was much speculation about the possibility of a Peruvian *blitzkrieg* to recover their lost territory. This worry was reflected in the Chilean press's excessive coverage of statements of peaceful intentions by the Peruvian leaders; it was a case of "she doth protest too much" insofar as the Chilean papers were concerned.

THE CHILEAN JUNTA AND
BOLIVIAN ACCESS TO THE SEA

Relations with Peru were greatly complicated in December 1975 when Chile formally proposed to Bolivia that Bolivia be given a corridor of access to the Pacific Ocean through territory that had belonged to Peru before the War of the Pacific. According to the Chilean-Peruvian agreement of 1929, any such proposal had to have Peru's approval before it could be put into effect.

El Mercurio announced the Chilean offer to Bolivia in its issue of December 21, 1975 (p. 1), and provided considerable background on the document. It noted that as early as October 1973 Foreign Minister Admiral Ismael Huerta had said in La Paz that the Junta regime stood ready to discuss the Bolivian outlet to the sea. Some months later, President Pinochet had reiterated this willingness. This was followed in April 1974 by a meeting between Presidents Pinochet and Hugo Banzer in which it was agreed that diplomatic relations, which had been cut for a dozen years, would be reestablished as a preliminary to negotiations over the proposed Bolivian corridor to the Pacific. The Bolivians presented a memorandum to the Chilean government suggesting possible alternatives for the corridor.

Chile's offer made in December 1975 was a response to the earlier Bolivian memorandum. *El Mercurio* summed up the Chilean proposition:

It would accept the proposition to cede a corridor—with its southern limits parallel with the Arica-La Paz Railroad—the precise limits of which would be fixed by a mixed commission of technicians once the arrangements had been agreed to. It would provide that . . . the corridor would be extended to the 200 mile sea frontier. The total of the land and sea corridor would be taken as the basis for compensation which Bolivia would give in exchange for what Chile would concede. This compensation would consist of land along the frontier in which are lakes and streams which could possibly be used for irrigation and consumption of the population. Finally, the text of the Chilean memorandum said that as a result of these arrangements Bolivia would agree that the solution proposed would be recognized as a definitive solution of the problem of its landlocked status.

In the end, nothing came of Chile's proposal. Both Bolivia and Peru were unhappy over the Chilean offer. In March 1976, the Bolivian Foreign Ministry indicated that it could not agree to give Bolivian land in exchange for the proposed corridor, nor to turn over complete control of the River Lauca to Chile, nor to demilitarize the corridor, as the Chileans had proposed.[62]

The Peruvians further complicated the issue in November 1976 when they made their own counterproposal to the Chileans and Bolivians. It was summarized by *Latin America* as follows:

The principal novelty of the Peruvian proposal is that the area between the Pan-American highway and the sea, from the Peruvian frontier in the north to the northern city limits of Arica in the south, should be under the joint sovereignty of the three countries. Bolivia would be permitted to establish a port under its sole sovereignty in the trinational zone. The sea facing the zone would be Bolivia's territorial water. . . . The Peruvians have also demanded that a trinational port administration should be established for the port of Arica.[63]

The Chilean government lost no time in rejecting this proposal. They refused even to use it as the basis for further discussions. They argued that the Peruvian document dealt with matters which concerned Chilean sovereignty and had no relationship to the offer Chile had made to Bolivia.[64]

The issue of Bolivian access to the sea was still pending on the fourth anniversary of the Junta's seizure of power, and its resolution in the foreseeable future seemed remote.

31

The Cultural Blight of the Junta Regime*

For many decades, Chile had a degree of cultural freedom rare in Latin America—and in the world as a whole. Freedom of speech and press was carried almost to the point of liberatinism. Universities presented the widest scope of ideas, and academic freedom was widely respected. A flourishing publishing industry, of hemispheric reputation, included firms ranging from far Right to far Left. The clash of ideas, concepts, and theories was an integral part of the country's intellectual life, and it was not considered the right or function of the state to interfere with intellectual controversies or polemics.

As a result of all of these conditions, Chile had long had a highly sophisticated cultural life. Chilean intellectuals were *au courant* with the schools of thought and issues of controversy in other world capitals, and made significant contributions of their own in many fields. The country's social scientists had high repute, and some of them had attained international reputations. Chile's literary life was an exceedingly active one, and two Chileans had won the Nobel Prize for Literature, a remarkable achievement for such a small country.

Chilean universities contained a number of research organizations of top quality and international fame. Also, largely because of the intellectual freedom which had so long prevailed, Santiago had been chosen as the seat of such international organizations as the Economic Commission for Latin America (ECLA), the Facultad Latino Americana de Ciencias Sociales (FLACSO), and a variety of others; these groups, in turn, had contributed extensively to the intellectual life of Chile.

The military coup of September 11, 1973, put an end to all of this cultural excitement.

* An earlier version of this chapter originally appeared in the *Christian Science Monitor*. This chapter is adapted by permission of the *Christian Science Monitor* @ 1975 by the Christian Science Publishing Society. All rights reserved.

THE BRAIN DRAIN

A major disruptive factor in Chilean cultural affairs after the coup was the exodus of a large number of intellectuals. Particularly among the social scientists and literary people there were many activists in or sympathizers with the Unidad Popular. With the outbreak of the coup, some of these people sought refuge in embassies; others at first tried to continue their work under the new circumstances, but finding this impossible, they too ultimately sought work abroad.

This was the second time in the 1970s that Chile had suffered a "brain drain." With the advent of the Allende regime, several thousand people had left the country, and others had continued to go abroad throughout the UP period.

The nature of the exodus was very different in the two periods. During the Unidad Popular years, the expatriation was principally among entrepreneurs, managerial and technical people, and, to some degree, doctors. Their exodus was damaging to the national economy, but less so to the country's cultural life. Many of the emigrés of the UP period returned, their places abroad being taken after the coup by social scientists, literary and cultural leaders, as well as scientists and doctors.

Other important émigrés during the military government period were foreign intellectuals. For many decades Chile had been one of the two most hospitable countries (the other being Mexico) to political exiles in the hemisphere. Many of these exiles were intellectuals, some of whom had some international repute. After the coup, the military leaders complained about the number of foreign revolutionaries and terrorists who had been admitted under Allende, and vowed to rid the country of them. But many of those who had sought refuge in Chile, and who after September 11, 1973, found it impossible to continue to live there, were not terrorists or revolutionaries but intellectuals, artists, and other people whose exodus left Chile's cultural life much the poorer. In expelling refugee foreigners, the military regime made little distinction between terrorists and revolutionaries on the one hand and critical intellectuals on the other.

The brain drain continued through the fourth year of the military regime. In mid-1977, Incami, a Catholic organization concerned particularly with emigration, estimated that nearly one million people, approximately a tenth of the population, had left the country and that as many as 30 percent of Chile's professionals had emigrated. Both economic and political factors had stimulated this vast movement abroad. The United Nations High Commission for Refugees estimated at this same time that 18,500 Chilean political exiles were living in Europe.[1]

By 1977, the Junta regime had become worried by the brain drain. In March, General Fernando Matthei, the minister of health, reported that

12.3 percent of all the country's doctors had emigrated. He said that the whole brain drain phenomenon was difficult to deal with because its causes were not known. As *El Mercurio* stated, "The minister affirmed that one could only speculate, and thus one could say that if it was for political reasons or because some of those doctors were against the incumbent military regime, it would be necessary to change this regime in order to please them, and there is no solution to this." After observing that economic factors might also be cited as a cause of the brain drain, General Matthei added, "I personally think that all of those factors are real—but it is very difficult to weight them."[2]

El Mercurio also became worried about the brain drain. In an editorial in April 1977 devoted to the exodus of university faculty members, it noted that "the desertions have been taking place in successive sectors, beginning with the economists and administrators, followed by the agronomists and now the engineers and chemists. . . . That is to say, those deserting university teaching and research are those in the disciplines most indispensable for the future of the country." It attributed this exodus primarily to the low pay scales in the universities, and did not mention possible political causes.[3]

THE SITUATION OF THE UNIVERSITIES

The blow dealt by the military regime was perhaps felt most by the universities. All of the country's universities were put under *delegados-rectores*, military men, most of whom were retired from active service. Apparently, the government originally intended to appoint such officials only in the university with the greatest Leftist influence, but when some of the civilian rectors refused to serve if there were military interventors in other schools, the *delegados-rectores* were installed in all institutions of higher learning. The most distinguished university official to resign was Cardinal Raúl Silva Henríquez, who quit as rector of the Catholic University of Santiago.[4]

Purges of varying degrees were conducted in the faculties of all universities. At the Universidad Técnica del Estado in Santiago and at the University of Concepción, lists were published of expelled professors, without explanation or forewarning. These were the two institutions most completely under far Leftist influence before the coup.

At the University of Chile, on the other hand, the professors affiliated with the Unidad Popular parties were suspended (44 out of the 360 in the Law School, for instance)[5] and were then submitted to "trials" by bodies of their colleagues and administrators. Some were "acquitted," although the majority of those suspended were ultimately removed from their posts. At least some of those who were cleared were nonetheless not allowed to teach, although they continued for some time to receive their salaries.

Those professors who retained their jobs, unless they were of far Right points of view, labored under severe handicaps. They did not know what they could and could not say to their students without losing their jobs, or perhaps worse. There was no academic freedom after September 11, 1973. As a result, a number of faculty members who were not purged voluntarily resigned rather than continuing to teach under these conditions, thus causing further damage to the institutions of higher learning.

The social science faculties have been particularly hard hit by the purge of higher education. When I visited Chile in mid-1974, I was told that the Institute of Sociology at the University of Chile had all but ceased to exist. The United Nations-financed Facultad Latino Americana de Ciencias Sociales, with graduate-level programs in political science and economics, was forbidden to hold classes, and the few remaining faculty members and students were confined to innocuous research that could cause no problem with the military government. Even some of those who at first decided to stay in order to keep FLACSO in existence had decided to leave Chile by the end of the military regime's second year in power.

The university student population was also purged. Some 22,000 students —more than one-eighth of the student body—were dropped from the rolls of the country's eight universities.[6] Some 6,000 were reported expelled from the University of Concepción, 8,000 from the University of Chile, and 1,500 from the School of Fine Arts.[7]

The purging continued long after the coup. Thus, in August 1975 forty-four people were expelled from the eastern branch of the University of Chile. It was claimed that these people had been "proven to be participants in Marxist activities." Of the forty-four, twenty were administrators, twenty professors, and four students.[8]

Early in 1976, after Air Force Colonel Julio Tapia Falk was made rector-delegate of the University of Chile, he carried out a still more extensive purge.[9] When he took over, Colonel Tapia commented in an interview with *El Cronista* that "the two previous rectors, General Ruíz Danyau and General Rodríguez, began a purging process. But the infiltration and the destructive tendencies were so powerfully established that even their efforts were insufficient."[10]

LONG-RANGE PLANS FOR THE UNIVERSITIES

In addition to purging the universities and destroying academic freedom in the short run, the Junta did untold long-range damage to education, especially higher education. It reversed the process of university expansion which had been started under President Frei and ended the age-old system of virtually free higher education in state universities, thus confining access largely to youngsters of higher income groups.

In the name of "rationalizing" the country's university system, the Junta regime suppressed many faculties, as well as regional centers, of the universities. According to an extensive report by Minister of Education Admiral Arturo Troncoso Daroch in February 1976, the regional university centers which had been suppressed, or were about to be, included the following: units of the Technical University of the State in Arica, San Antonio, Los Angeles, Angol, Castro, Coyhaique, and Aysén; branches of the University of Concepción in Los Angeles and Coronel; the Iquique branch of the University of the North; the Concepción part of the University of Chile; and two faculties of the Southern University in La Unión.[11]

Even where whole regional units of universities were not abolished, particular faculties or departments were wiped out. Thus, at the Antofagasta branch of the University of Chile, eleven departments, with seventy faculty members, were suppressed in 1975.[12]

The suppression of faculties and university branches, particularly in provincial cities, made it more expensive and difficult for students of meager financial resources to get a university education. This same tendency is reflected in the Junta's insistence on imposing substantial tuition payments in the institutions of higher education. In mid-1976, Alfredo Prieto Befalluy, subsecretary of education, denied that the objective was to make the universities financially self-supporting. However, he added that "we only aspire to have students pay a part of the investments in education. Perhaps 70 percent of them. But the State will finance everything having to do with research, extension, communications, welfare and capital investments. All of these elements amount to considerably more than 50 percent of total university cost."[13]

The student payments in effect by the 1977 academic year provided for different rates in accordance with the students' financial resources. Four categories of students were established: those paying 1,900 pesos (about $100) per semester, those paying 1,300 pesos, those paying 700, and those paying nothing. It was estimated that about 59 percent of the students would pay full tuition, 9 percent would pay 1,300 pesos, 16 percent would pay 700 pesos, and 16 percent would be exempt from tuition payments. For some students, loans payable after graduation were available.[14]

While students were being called on to pay for their university education, government contributions to the universities declined drastically. Before the Junta came to power, the government paid about 90 percent of the income of the institutions of higher education; by 1976, the state contribution was down to 40 percent. *Latin America Political Report* noted that "from next year the universities are expected to be self-supporting. Student loans will replace grants, to be repaid over 15 years; the same policy also is to be applied to the second (optional) three-year period of secondary education.''[15]

BOOK BURNING

The most shocking aspect of the coup for foreigners of a democratic persuasion was a series of book burnings that reportedly took place during the early days of the new regime. Because of the parallels with the early days of the Nazi regime in Germany, these incidents likely did as much as any other single thing to give the Junta government the reputation abroad of being "fascist."

Book burning incidents did indeed occur. There were various cases in which police or soldiers raided the homes of people actually or allegedly associated with the fallen regime or the parties that had supported it, in the process of which private libraries were pilfered and "offending" books were burned or otherwise destroyed.

These events sometimes had ironic results. A friend of mine who has published a number of left-wing books was told by several of his friends in the weeks following the coup that they had themselves destroyed any books which, in case of a raid on their houses, might be regarded as "subversive." They confided to my friend, somewhat sheepishly, that among the books they had destroyed were several which he had written.

There is no reason to believe that such book burnings as took place were the result of a deliberate policy of the military regime. Rather, they were the efforts of overzealous lower ranking military men or police who took very seriously indeed the Junta's promise to "extirpate Marxism" and who saw the destruction of "Marxist" literature as one way of doing this. The regime never issued any orders to destroy books in private homes, or conducted any public ceremonial book burning such as the Nazi regime had done in 1933. Nevertheless, these incidents of the early weeks of the regime dealt Chile's reputation as a country of liberty and cultural freedom a severe blow.

THE PUBLISHING INDUSTRY

The military regime brought about a drastic change in the publishing industry. The government publishing house established by the Allende administration as Editora Nacional Quimantú was renamed Editorial Gabriela Mistral; its activities were severely curtailed, and, at least during the first year of the Pinochet government, most of its publications were pamphlets of speeches by one or another member of the governing junta, or other propaganda of the new regime.

In more general terms, the large stream of books on Chilean history and problems—together with Marxist-Leninist and even Trotskyite material—was cut off. Many books were withdrawn from circulation. The publishing houses of the Socialist and Communist parties were suppressed, and few new books from other publishers were issued. The only volumes on social problems or politics that were allowed were those discussing the reasons for the fall of Allende, written from a point of view friendly to the new administration.

Bookstores were closely censored. Their owners had to submit lists of the books they had on sale to the authorities, who reserved the right to tell them what they could and could not sell. In August 1974, I observed a truckload of "subversive" volumes, including books on psychology and sociology as well as works by Marx, Lenin, and Trotsky, and studies of Chilean history, being carted away from a bookshop in the center of Santiago.

One result of these restrictions was the development of a black market in books. Some bookstores kept quantities of proscribed volumes and sold them to customers whom they regarded as "trustworthy." Mimeographed lists of such available volumes, without identification of the bookstore involved, were circulating in Santiago by July 1975.

The Chilean military regime's attitude towards the publication and circulation of books was much more restrictive than that of the Brazilian military following their coup in 1964. Although the Brazilian authorities frequently censored newspapers and periodicals, they interfered relatively little with the printing and selling of books. Whether this difference in attitude demonstrates that the Chilean military had a higher opinion of the political importance of books than the Brazilians is difficult to say.

END OF FREEDOM OF THE PRESS

After the coup, there was complete censorship of newspapers and magazines. The daily newspapers of Santiago, which numbered eleven before September 11, 1973, and represented nearly all points of view, were narrowed down to five. Three of the remaining ones belonged to the El Mercurio publishing firm, whose former chief was minister of economy for more than a year in the military regime. A fourth was the government newspaper, the name of which was first changed from *La Nación*, which it had been called for more than fifty years, to *La Patria*, at the same time that it was reduced from full size to tabloid. Later, its name was changed yet again, to *El Cronista*.[16]

Newspapers associated with the left-wing parties were suppressed. The Christian Democratic paper *La Prensa* was allowed to disappear for financial reasons. Its owners and backers felt that there was little point in trying to raise funds to keep alive a newspaper that could do little more than publish government handouts and that would not be allowed to represent the Christian Democratic point of view.[17]

Newspapers that had been organs of the Unidad Popular or that, like *La Prensa*, might be expected to voice strong criticism of the military regime if they were allowed freedom were not the only victims of the press holocaust. Even *La Tribuna*, an exceedingly conservative newspaper that had been in constant battles with the Allende government, and whose editor had been jailed frequently by the UP regime, was suppressed.[18]

The government interfered with other right-wing dailies from time to time. Thus, in September 1975, Hernán López, assistant editor of *La Segunda*, was arrested because of something which appeared in his daily. He was released a day later.[19] In the same month, an issue of the Talca daily *La Mañana* was seized by the police.[20]

The casualty rate among the weekly and monthly periodicals which for many years had proliferated in Chile was as great, if not greater, than among the daily newspapers. Those which disappeared ranged from *Punto Final* on the extreme Left to *Tacna* and *P.E.C.* on the far Right. After the coup, however, virtually all of the country's politically oriented weeklies and monthlies disappeared. About the only journal of opinion that continued to appear was the Jesuit monthly magazine *Mensaje*, but it was reported to have been heavily censored. The weekly news magazine *Ercilla* continued to come out and in mid-1975 published a series of interviews with opponents of the regime, the first such material to be published legally after September 1973.

Because of its pro-PDC proclivities, *Ercilla* had difficulties with the Junta regime. In March 1976, an edition of the weekly was seized by the government, which led even *El Mercurio* to protest in an editorial.[21] The magazine was later purchased by a pro-Junta group.[22]

René Silva, editor of *El Mercurio,* defended the Junta's policy towards the press at the October 1973 meeting of the Inter American Press Association in Boston, Massachusetts. "Today," he said, "censorship is again in effect, but it is in the process of disappearing, in response to the constant democratic sentiments of the people. Censorship no longer exists in newspapers authorized to circulate, under editorial responsibility of their editors."[23] Three years after the coup, the situation mentioned by Silva had not in fact disappeared, and Silva had been removed as editor of *El Mercurio*, reportedly because he had become critical of the government's control of the press.

For one who had been in Chile many times before September 11, 1973, the transformation of the press was startling. Whereas before it had been extremely diversified, engaged in lively polemics, and was interesting and even exciting, after the coup it was exceedingly bland, with the news (still more ample in some papers than in others) much the same in all. It contained little comment except apologias for or praise of the military regime. This situation largely persisted four years after the coup.

The situation was much the same in the radio and television media. What had been a great variety in points of view and positions, particularly among the radio stations, became highly uniform, reflecting the regime's way of thinking.

The military regime did not remain satisfied with the limitations on freedom of the media represented by the disappearance of the Unidad Popular and Christian Democratic dailies, periodicals, and broadcast media. Late in 1975, it issued Decree 1281, which permitted local state of siege administrators to ban any national or international periodical they chose to. Both the Journalists Association[24] and the Radio Owners' Association protested this law.[25]

When the state of siege authorities in Santiago officially assumed the right to bar the entry of any foreign periodical and to suspend the right to publish of any Chilean periodical within their jurisdiction, the otherwise docile press protested vigorously. Even *El Mercurio* ran an editorial protesting this measure.[26]

THE STAGE AND SCREEN

The movie scene changed dramatically. During the Allende regime, the only U.S. films being shown were many years old. There were increasing numbers of films of Russian and East European origin, and many films from Western Europe, particularly France and Spain. After the coup, the movie theater offerings were once again dominated by U.S. films, with a sprinkling of Western European ones, while the Russian and East European offerings had disappeared.

After the coup, the Chilean government motion picture firm, Chilefilms, was reduced to producing short pieces and newsreels, and also served as an importer of some foreign offerings. In contrast, during the Allende period, Chilefilms had produced a number of full-length films, most of which had a Unidad Popular political message.

A decree-law issued in September 1974 set forth the military government's basis for censoring movies. Aside from establishing five categories of films, that is, "approved for all viewers, approved for those over eighteen, approved only for those over 21, approved as educational, and rejected," it provided that films would be rejected which "foment or propagate doctrines or ideas contrary to the fundamental bases of the Fatherland or of the Nation, such as Marxism and others, which offend States with which Chile maintains international relations, or which are contrary to public order, to morality or to good customs, and which lead to commission of anti-social or criminal actions.[27]

From time to time, the Junta interfered with the showing of foreign films. Thus, in 1974 they barred *Last Tango in Paris*,[28] and in the following year they suspended the showing of *The Day of the Jackal*.[29]

A limited number of theatrical productions continued to be given in Santiago and a few other cities. One of the most popular during the first year of the military regime was a version of "The Man of La Mancha." The large number of amateur theater companies, again organized by elements of the Unidad Popular during the Allende regime mainly for propaganda purposes, completely ceased to function.

Music perhaps suffered less from the change in regime than other aspects of cultural life. The National Symphony continued to hold its regular seasons and made special efforts to attract young people. A number of foreign musical groups, including the Chamber Orchestra of Cologne and the Vienna Boys Choir, gave performances in the months following the coup.

Even in music, however, there was a significant change. Under Allende most of the visiting foreign performers came from Eastern Europe. After the coup, soloists and ensembles were again mainly from Western Europe.

There were also some problems even in the musical field. In November 1974, the opera season in Santiago was suspended by the mayor of the city before it had been completed because of "lack of discipline."[30]

BALANCE OF MILITARY REGIME'S CULTURAL POLICIES

The establishment of a military dictatorship in Chile threatened to destroy the country's cultural life, which had given Chile distinction and greatness. It is as yet too early to know the long-term effects of the cultural blight that succeeded the coup of September 11, 1973. What is clear, however, is that the atmosphere in which ideas and theories can clash, and the intellectual search for that elusive thing, the truth, can be conducted without fear of economic and police reprisals, has ceased to exist. A cloud of conformity and coercion now hangs over Chilean cultural and intellectual life. If this change persists, Chile will have ceased permanently to be one of the world's great centers of intellectual freedom and creation. In this regard at least, it will possess little to distinguish it from any Central American banana republic in which the existence of an intellectual desert is taken for granted.

32

Economic Policies of the Junta Regime: The Shock Treatment

The Junta regime inherited an economic catastrophe. Inflation was totally out of control, production in practically all parts of the economy was declining, and scarcities of nearly all kinds of consumer goods created almost interminable queues. Furthermore, the country's international economic relations were in crisis: its balance of payments was adverse, there were few foreign exchange reserves left, and much of the nation's foreign debt was in default.

Obviously, the rehabilitation of the economy had to be a first priority for the new regime. Since the leaders of the Junta knew virtually nothing about economics, it was the one area of public affairs which they entrusted to civilians almost from the outset. There thus emerged in Chile, as in many other Latin American governments under military rule, an alliance of leaders of the armed forces and "technocrats."

THE ECONOMIC TEAM

The economic technocrats who were entrusted with management of the Chilean economy had a definite ideology. As a result, in addition to attacking immediate problems such as inflation, they were also trying to mold the future of the Chilean economy in conformity with this ideology.

The civilians in charge of economic policy for the Junta government were devotees of laissez-faire, as represented in the present day in the ideas of Professor Milton Friedman, late of the University of Chicago. Indeed, they were popularly known as "the Chicago Boys," since directly or indirectly they had acquired their ideas about economics from Professor Friedman. At the height of the economic crisis early in 1975, Friedman visited Chile to give some lectures and to talk with his pupils and their pupils who were then guiding Chile's economic destinies.

The Chicago Boys, as they often proclaimed, were trying to effect a fundamental shift in the policies which successive Chilean regimes had been following for half a century. They were determined to "destatize" the economy and to transform it into one in which the market would be as unhampered as possible by governmental restrictions or participation.

The military entrusted economic policy to this group first because they had all been decided and bitter opponents of the Unidad Popular regime. Second, their arguments undoubtedly seemed plausible to the economically untutored armed forces leaders who had taken over from a government that had been seeking to create the 180-degree opposite of laissez-faire, a totally state-controlled economy. In addition, the Chicago Boys were the only economists they could turn to. Chile's other economists had been closely associated either with the Unidad Popular or with the Christian Democrats, both of which were anathema to the military and their civilian political advisers. Furthermore, even if they had been invited to do so, it is doubtful whether most economists of those tendencies would have aligned themselves with the authoritarian Junta government. The devotees of "economic liberty" had no such compunctions about working with a politically repressive regime.

Although the leadership of the Junta's economic team changed several times during the first four years of the regime, its fundamental orientation did not alter with the shifts in its top personnel. Fernando Leniz, a leading figure in *El Mercurio*, was the first person placed in general charge of economic policy. Early in 1975, he was replaced by Jorge Cauas, who in his turn was "kicked upstairs" to be ambassador to Washington early in 1977. His place was taken by two men: Sergio de Castro, who had been subsecretary of economy, and Pablo Baraona, until then president of the Central Bank.

GENERAL OUTLINES OF JUNTA ECONOMIC POLICY

Several strains have consistently run through the economic policy of the Junta government. First, it applied the so-called shock treatment to the inflation problem, deliberately provoking the worst depression since the early 1930s. Second, the regime followed an extensive policy of "getting the government out of business," thus liquidating state control not only of most of the firms taken over under Allende, but also of most of those which the Corporación de Fomento had established since 1939. The regime also followed a consistent open door policy for foreign investment, an attitude that led to Chile's withdrawal from the Andean Pact.

The Junta paid special attention to stimulating exports, which involved it in controversies with other copper-exporting countries but at the same time encouraged the development of nontraditional exports. Finally, the Junta laissez-faire philosophy laid heavy emphasis on dismantling those parts of the economy which, by its standards, were deemed to be "inefficient."

In pursuing its goals, the Junta and its economic team were willing to extract from the people of Chile, particularly the lower income groups, a tremendously high price in terms of drastically reduced living standards and staggering unemployment. They also showed little or no concern that their policies were sharply polarizing classes and highly concentrating economic power in the private sector of the economy, thus reversing yet another trend of the previous half century. Finally, the Junta and the technocrats allied with it did not hesitate to vastly increase the dependence of the national economy on forces abroad over which Chile could have little or no control.

The rest of this chapter will examine the anti-inflation program and other short-run aspects of the Junta policy. The next chapter will deal with the long-run aspects.

THE RECORD ON INFLATION

Throughout the first three years of the Junta regime, Chile had the dubious distinction of having Latin America's (and probably the world's) highest rate of inflation. Chile did not fall into second place until 1976 when some modification of the pase of price increases occurred and Argentina was afflicted by galloping inflation.

By the time the Allende government was overthrown, the inflation rate was officially recognized as being over 300 percent. Supporters of the Junta regime argued that because the price index was based on official prices, and not black market prices, the actual inflation rate may have been as much as three times the official figure.

In any case, in April 1974, seven months after the Junta assumed power, the government recognized that prices were increasing at an annual rate of 746.2 percent.[1] The official report on price increases between May 1973 and May 1974 showed that they had gone up 670.3 percent. The rate of increase between May 1974 and May 1975 was 427.4 percent, and that between May 1975 and May 1976 was officially recorded as 231.9 percent.[2]

Failure in dealing adequately with the inflation was a major factor in the dismissal of the Junta's first civilian minister of economy, Fernando Leniz, early in 1975. With his removal and the entry of Jorge Cauas, the government adopted what it officially called shock treatment, which began to have a measurable effect on the inflation rate during the latter half of 1975. However, Orlando Saenz, former head of the Sociedad de Fomento Fabril, noted at the time that this decline was the result mainly of "the collapse, bankruptcy or simple paralysis of innumerable industries."[3]

In 1975, the annual increase in prices was 340.7 percent, and in the following year it had fallen to 174.3 percent.[4] The decrease continued during the first half of 1977. During the first five months, prices went up 29.3 percent; and in the twelve months from June 1976 through May 1977, the inflation was 109.0 percent, compared to 231.9 percent in the previous June-May period.[5]

THE NATURE OF THE ANTI-INFLATION POLICY

Initially, the Junta's economic policies greatly intensified the rise in the price level. Junta apologists have argued, with some reason, that part of this increase was more apparent than real because the inflation data of the Allende regime dealt with official prices "for articles which were, in fact, available only through the black market." Thus, these people maintain, the price increases of the first months of the Junta regime were "corrective."[6] However, much of the rise in the general price level was quite real, since working-class families were no longer assured of receiving certain basic necessities at relatively low prices, as had been the case in the last part of the Allende regime.

One of the first acts of the Junta was to free most goods from official price controls. At the time the military government took over, approximately 3,500 commodities were subject to price controls, a number which the government was physically incapable of handling. This effort to have official prices for almost everything had led to distortions and injustices, and to shortages and an extensive black market.

To deal with this situation, the Junta government adopted its own price policy. This was explained by the Junta's first minister of finance, Rear Admiral Lorenzo Gotuzzo, in the following terms:

1. Prices will be set so as to reflect real costs of production.

2. Prices of the monopolistic sector of the economy will be strictly controlled, with the establishment of a special list of products for this purpose. Furthermore, the Anti-monopoly Law will be modified so as to transform this legal instrument into a really operative mechanism.

3. With respect to articles in which there does not exist enough internal competition, the producers will fix their sales prices, but must justify their costs to DIRINCO. If there results an abusive price, drastic sanctions will be applied. Furthermore, in that case, DIRINCO will proceed to fix the price of such products and will use the mechanism of foreign trade to assure adequate supplies.

Agricultural prices will be regulated in accordance with the average price in the international market in recent years, thus providing incentive for rational production.[7]

The net result of this policy was that the number of items with prices fixed by the government was reduced within a few weeks from about 3,600 to about 60.[8]

While prices were being "freed," the government ended the Allende regime's system of informal rationing, by providing a minimal "market basket" of essential goods to people in the poorer areas. Economy Minister Fernando Leniz was reported to have referred to this distribution of basic commodities by the government as "laughable, political and demagogic."[9] The Juntas de Abastecimiento Popular, which had distributed these basic commodities to the working-class sections of Santiago and other cities, were abolished, and no substitutes for them were provided. Thereafter, any rationing was by price, not by direct government action. As a result, the cost of basic commodities to most working-class families skyrocketed, and the long queues of the Allende period disappeared almost immediately.

A completely free market was thus established for most goods and services sold in Chile. Even in the case of goods that were subject to government price regulation, the general policy was to allow them to increase at roughly the same rate as that of other goods in the free market. In some instances, the rise in prices of controlled goods was actually greater than in those on the free market—as in the middle months of 1975, when price-fixed goods rose 40 percent, while prices of free market goods went up only 10 percent.[10]

The only sectors in which the free market or its equivalent was not applied were those of labor and bank credit. Wages were rigidly controlled, and although the government periodically enacted substantial wage rises, these lagged far behind the increase in the cost of living. This policy is discussed at greater length in a later chapter. Bank credit, in conformity with the "monetarist" philosophy of the Chicago Boys, was kept under very close control, which results I shall note later in this chapter.

By the early months of 1975, the government was obviously dissatisfied with the progress made in the economic field. As a result, Fernando Leniz was replaced as minister of economy by Sergio de Castro, until then under secretary of that ministry, and Jorge Cauas beecame minister of finance.

With these changes, a new stringency in government economic policy was announced, in conformity with the stated belief that what was needed to deal effectively with the inflation was a "shock treatment." The new steps taken by the government included an immediate reduction of government expenditures by 15 to 20 percent, including virtually complete cessation of all public works programs; a 10 percent increase in the income tax; and a 10 percent tax on luxuries.[11] Drastic limitations on bank credit were also decreed, with the provision that 82 percent of all deposits in banks had to be kept with Central Bank as reserves.[12] Partially offsetting the expected increase in unemployment coming from these measures was a "make-work" program for a certain number of the unemployed.[13]

The "shock treatment" remained fully in force for about fifteen months. Only in mid-1976 did the government, arguing that the inflation was finally being brought under control, modify to a very modest degree some of the aspects of the policies launched in March 1975.

ECONOMIC EFFECTS OF THE ANTI-INFLATION POLICY

The effects of these economic policies were dramatic: they created an economic and social catastrophe as severe as the Great Depression of the 1930s.

Effective demand for goods and services was drastically reduced by the combination of rapid price increases, partly frozen wages, and almost non-existent bank credit. As a result, many of the country's important industries entered a severe crisis. According to figures of the Sociedad de Fomento Fabril, manufacturing firms on the average were working at 60 percent of capacity in mid-1975. Some of the important industries, including canning, textiles, shoes, and cement, were running at 50 percent or less.[14] In the case of one of the major cement plants, it was operating only two of its eight furnaces. The steel industry was said to be running at about 50 percent capacity.[15]

Smaller firms suffered most acutely. A perhaps typical example of which I was informed during a visit to Chile in July 1975 was that of a small shoe manufacturer, employing forty workers, who had not sold a single pair of shoes in two months, even though he had cut his prices by half.

A study of the Sociedad de Fomento Fabril issued in October 1975 reported that during the first half of the year industrial production had fallen by 21.7 percent compared with the same period in 1974, and sales had fallen by 19.5 percent. At about the same time, an article by ex-Finance Minister Sergio Molina in the Jesuit monthly *Mensaje* predicted that investment was likely to fall 60 percent in 1975, and "a substantial decline in the purchase of goods and services by state agencies" would result in a decline in state assistance to economic and social development, as well as in the quality of public services, to levels that it would be difficult to maintain for long.[16]

Early in 1977, in the process of praising the "recovery" of the Chilean economy during 1976, *El Mercurio* gave interesting information on just how serious the Depression was. It noted that, with the year 1969 as the index number of 100, total industrial production had fallen by September 1975 to only 75.4; that "production of various manufactured articles" had declined in the same month to 75; that output of intermediate goods for construction had fallen to 50.5; and that production of transport materials had fallen to 42.5. The article stated that on the basis of 1969 as 100, cargo handled by the railroad system had fallen to 55.3 by September 1975; that production of habitual consumer goods had fallen to 78 by the same month; and that production of consumer durables had fallen to 74.2 by September 1975 and to 64.6 by December of that year.[17]

Latin America Economic Report summed up a number of other effects of the Junta regime's "shock treatment" in 1975:

World Bank estimates show a fall of GDP [Gross Domestic Product] of 12-15%. Industrial production fell 24.1% compared with the previous year. The construction industry was down 40%. The only basic sectors to show any improvement were iron ore (8.4%) and coal (3.4%). However, 29% of last year's coal production was stockpiled, and unless there is a big improvement in sales this year production will decline. Industrial imports were down 56.9% and fuel and lubricants down 54.1%. Local oil production fell by 12%, and is now only enough to satisfy about 25% of Chile's requirements. Imports of capital goods fell only 9.6%, but intermediate goods fell 52.2%. The sharp reduction in the internal market was shown by the 30.2% rise in industrial exports. Exports of electrical appliances and metal products went up from US$7.3 million in 1974 to US$36.4 million. Non-copper exports went up by 36%.[18]

Agriculture also suffered from the "shock treatment." The production record was spotty, and official information on it was contradictory. Although official figures on the 1974-1975 crop year in comparison with that of 1973-1974 showed a substantial increase in output of some crops, including wheat, rice, sugar beets, and some other crops of less importance, they also showed large decreases in the output of corn and potatoes, and small decreases in oats, barley, and some other less important items. Furthermore, it was announced that "the country's agricultural surplus for export is going beyond previous estimates,"[19] indicating that much of such increase in output as there was would not go to the Chilean people.

The Junta government's figures on various branches of agricultural production were contradictory. For instance, with regard to wheat, the Instituto Nacional de Estadísticas announced in 1975 that the output of wheat in 1973-1974 had been about 940,000 tons, whereas the Office of Agricultural Planning put the figure at only 733,000 tons, slightly less than the production in the last full year of the Allende regime. For the 1974-1975 crop year, the contrast in the figures of various government agencies was even greater, insofar as wheat was concerned. The subsecretary of agriculture placed the output of wheat at 1.1 million tons, the Office of Agricultural Planning said that it was 1 million tons, but the Empresa de Comercio Agrícola, the government purchasing agency in the field, estimated output at only 600,000 tons.

Some indication of what happened to wheat production, at least during the first two years of the Junta regime, was given by Domingo Durán, president of the Confederation of Agricultural Producers, in January 1976. He referred to "the vertical decline of wheat production—which some agricultural sectors call 'the green earthquake,'" and noted that as a result of it, "it will not be possible even to cover costs of production."[20]

In the case of sugar beet production, government figures were again contradictory. The Instituto Nacional de Estadísticas insisted in February 1975 that in 1973-1974 the output had been 915,000 tons, but six months later raised this estimate to 1,025 million tons, whereas the Office of Agricultural Planning put the figure at only 830,000 tons.[21]

In 1976, the Instituto Nacional de Estadísticas estimated wheat production at 706,000 tons.[22] The Ministry of Agriculture announced that it was necessary that year to import between 600,000 and 650,000 tons, an increase of 150,000 tons in what had been planned, because of the poor Chilean harvest.[23]

One cause of agriculture's poor showing during the first years of the Junta government was the almost total absence of agricultural credit. A year after the coup, private banks had some credit available at an interest rate of 200 percent a year, while the Corporación de Fomento was making loans at 6 percent interest, but with the principal being regularly readjusted with the increase in the price level. Few farmers could avail themselves of this credit.[24]

The small farmers were in particularly dire straits. During the first three years of the regime, the Instituto de Desarrollo Agropecuario (INDAP), the organization whose primary role was the extension of credit and technical help to smallholders and agrarian reform beneficiaries, was close to being liquidated. The rationale for INDAP's inactivity was that it was a "discriminatory" agency, favoring smallholders over large landlords; all farmers should face the market on "equal" terms, the government argued.[25]

It was not entirely clear to what degree these exceedingly tight credit restrictions had been loosened by the 1977-1978 crop year. *El Mercurio* carried an article in March 1977 about the Central Bank's rules for agricultural credit for the coming crop season. It noted that the interest rate would be 16 percent a year, but with the amount of the farmer's debt being increased as the cost of living rose. It reported that bank credit could be extended to cover "purchase of seeds, pesticides and their application, fertilizer and veterinary products." Credits could run until one month after the harvest, and in any case not longer than a year.[26]

THE PROBLEM OF THE *FINANCIERAS*

One disastrous effect of the very severe credit restrictions on the regular banks was the mushrooming of so-called *financieras*, or investment companies. These were largely or completely outside the control of the regular banking system and the Central Bank until early 1977. Their operations led to three years of wild speculation, which collapsed in a financial scandal at the end of 1976.

I first heard of the operation of the *financieras* in mid-1975. At that time, I was told that the most important of them had first been established in the 1950s by a group of young men with access to borrowed funds who had begun to invest these funds in small industries and commercial houses. By 1970, they already controlled a substantial number of small enterprises. These entrepreneurs went abroad for the most part during the Unidad Popular period.

Upon their return after the coup, the *financiera* operators began to do a booming business. In 1975, they were reported to be borrowing money at 18 percent a month, whereas the regular banks were limited to paying 12 percent on deposits and were turning around and relending these funds to industrial and commercial enterprises at 22 percent a month or more. In at least some cases, they took stock of the firms to which they made loans as collateral, and as a result, by mid-1975 the largest entrepreneur of the *financiera* group was reported to have control of eighty-three corporations.[27]

By the end of 1976, it was reported of the *financeras* that there were "at least 65 known companies, financing some 680 enterprises."[28] According to an article in *Latin America Economic Report* early in 1977:

The financieras themselves fall into two categories, formal and informal. The formal companies have to comply with certain minimum legal requirements (capital holding, number of personnel employed and so on). In 1974 there were about 180 companies in this category; by mid-1976 they were down to about 25; a list in *El Mercurio* at the end of December gave only 12 names. The shrinkage is largely accounted for by problems in accumulating the necessary capital requirement. Undaunted, many of the aspiring formal companies have simply operated as informal companies (effectively simple brokers) offering no security whatever to investors, and commensurately high interest rates.[29]

This whole speculative bubble burst in December 1976. With the slowing down of inflation, the interest rates of the *financieras* became unrealistically high. Furthermore, as *Latin America Economic Report* noted, "Smaller borrowers and even many of the larger companies are facing serious cash flow problems, and as a result are quite unable to repay their loans to the financieras within the 30 days. Moreover, in the present depressed state of the economy there is no-one in Chile capable of buying them out, except perhaps the state."[30]

As a result of this situation, the *financieras* began to go bankrupt. The first to do so was the Manuel Rodriguez group, followed by various others. At the same time, some banks closely associated with some of the *financieras*, notably the Banco Osorno y La Unión and the Banco Español, were investigated by the government.[31] Ultimately, the Osorno bank was taken over by the Corporación de Fomento, and when efforts to auction off its stock brought unsatisfactory results, CORFO itself took over ownership of the institution, at least for the time being.[32] Subsequently, the Banco Chileno-

Yugoslavo was intervened by the government,[33] and several of its leading officials were brought to trial on charges brought against them by the University of Chile for misuse of the university's funds.[34]

The scandal surrounding the collapse of many of the more important *financieras* touched a number of the most important civilian advisers of the Junta government and some of the major economic conglomerates. One of the most important of the advisers was Jaime Guzmán, implicated in the collapse of the La Familia *financiera*, who for a short while was forbidden to leave the country.[35] The most important conglomerate affected was the so-called Fluxa group.[36]

In the wake of the scandal over the *financieras*, the Junta enacted new legislation concerning them, requiring "all financieras to have a minimum capital (75% of the requirement for a commercial bank), to be accumulated within two years, and the plans for which are to be presented within 60 days from 30 December. Any company which does not comply within the specified period will be automatically dissolved. Further, there are strict prohibitions against any form of advertising of or for loans by unauthorised bodies."[37]

THE SOCIAL COST OF THE SHOCK TREATMENT

The social costs of the Chicago Boys' experiment with the Chilean economy were immense: massive unemployment, drastic reduction of living standards, and probably slow starvation for at least a part of the population.

In August 1975, the government officially admitted unemployment to be at 14.5 percent in Greater Santiago,[38] whereas the Economics Department of the University of Chile claimed the figure for June of that year to have been 16.1 percent.[39] Both estimates were almost certainly drastic understatements. For example, the government, regarded anyone who had worked one hour a week as employed. A more realistic estimate which I received from foreign observers of the scene in July 1975 was that unemployment was running at about 25 percent of the total work force of Santiago.

In addition to open unemployment, there was a large amount of hidden unemployment. For instance, in mid-August 1975, the country's coal mines closed down to give their workers a two-weeks unpaid "vacation."[40] Furthermore, many industrial and commercial firms were keeping workers on their payrolls, although they had only enough work to keep them busy two to four of the eight hours they were on the job. Firms followed this policy not only because of sympathy for the fate of their workers if they became unemployed, but also because if they were to dismiss the workers, they would have to give them dismissal pay which they could not afford and which might well drive them into bankruptcy.

Unemployment continued to be an exceedingly serious problem. According to the figures of the University of Chile Economics Department, it reached a high point of 19.8 percent in Greater Santiago in March 1976. After more than a year of supposed economic "recovery," *El Mercurio* predicted that "in spite of this, several years will pass before the country can recover the levels of employment which were registered in the previous decade, as a result of which this will constitute one of the principal preoccupations of the country in the future." The article claimed that the unemployment level in March 1977 was 13.9 percent compared to 13.3 percent in March 1975 "when the rectification of the economy began." It also noted that, although total employment had risen 7.9 percent in the previous two years, employment in the production of goods had fallen by 26,000 people, including 20,000 in construction. Hence, it concluded that all of the increase in employment had been concentrated in the services.[41]

Several observations on the *El Mercurio* article are apropos. The first is the point raised previously, that official estimates of unemployment almost certainly understate its extent. The second is whether or not the supposed reduction in unemployment is in fact not specious, accounted for by the employment of workers on special government emergency work programs. Finally, the decrease in relatively high-paid employment in industry and construction, and the increase in low-paying service jobs have obvious implications for the living levels of those who still can claim to have employment.

To somewhat soften the political impact of massive unemployment, the government began a "minimum employment program" in 1975. By the end of that year, it was taking care of 126,765 workers, and by January 1977 it had 206,465 on its rolls. Although about one-third of the work force of Chile is concentrated in Greater Santiago, only about one-fifth of those in the minimum employment program were in that area.

Latin America Economic Report described the kind of work performed by those in the government's program: "The workers . . . are employed by the municipal authorities on road-sweeping, tidying public gardens and similar 'non-fundamental' tasks." It added that "the wage is 660 pesos a month; the minimum basic wage is now 1,190 pesos (about US$65). The cost to the state in 1976 was 2.5% of the total budget."[42]

In addition to creating massive unemployment, the Junta's shock treatment policy drastically lowered the living standards of a large part of the population. Although the situation of the unemployed was tragic, that of the employed was only relatively better.

A well-informed Chilean economist provided the following analysis of the situation of the employed workers in mid-1975. The minimum wage was at that time 130,000 escudos, and it was estimated that about 20 percent or more of those employed actually received only the minimum wage. However, if one calculated the average wage as being 200,000 escudos a month, one could understand the plight of a working-class household. A kilo of bread was selling at 1,500 escudos, and bread had largely taken the place of more expensive starches in the average diet; hence, a family would be likely to use two kilos a day, costing 3,000 escudos each day, or about 90,000 a month. If they also ate rice and used some vegetable oil, these would cost some 25,000 escudos a month. Thus, about 115,000 escudos, or more than half of an average wage, would be used for three basic diet items.

Even if one considers that the basic wage was not all the income an average employed worker would receive (he also had monthly allowances of a few thousand escudos for each of his children, and for transportation and lunches at work), it is clear that a working-class family would spend virtually all of its income on food. At that time, shoes cost about 20,000 escudos a pair, and shirts about 40,000 escudos each.

The drastically reduced real income of employed workers, and the lack of any money income at all for the unemployed, radically altered social customs. Although no precise figures are available, tens of thousands of people, and perhaps even more, were no longer able to pay rent on their houses or apartments, and so moved in with relatives or friends, thus adding to an already difficult housing situation.

Thus, throughout most of the first four years of the Junta regime, a substantial part of the working-class population of Chile had no visible means of income whatsoever. Even those who were employed or were being provided with work relief had drastically reduced incomes which, if they were lucky, barely provided them and their families enough to eat. There can be little doubt that malnutrition and even, in many cases slow starvation was the fate of large parts of the working class. The efforts of the church and other organizations to provide "soup kitchens," to supply at least one meal a day to small children, only very minimally offset this situation.

It was not only the manual workers who were suffering from the economic crisis. The middle class was being rapidly proletarianized. In July 1975, relatively well-off professional people were spending half or more of their income for food alone. There was little room in their budgets to purchase household appliances or automobiles, or to finance vacations and all the things most middle-class Chileans had become accustomed to in previous decades.

Apparently, by the fourth anniversary of the Junta regime, in spite of a modest economic recovery, this situation had not fundamentally changed.

BALANCE-OF-PAYMENTS PROBLEMS

Upon coming to power, the Junta regime was faced with a catastrophic balance-of-payments situation. The Allende government had left practically no foreign exchange reserves, and the country was faced with staggering payments on its foreign debt coming due in the middle years of the 1970s.

By the fourth anniversary of the coup, this aspect of the country's economic situation had improved a gread deal, although one can question how the improvement had been brought about.

The Junta was faced with the repayment of $1,010 million of foreign debts in 1974, $720 million in 1975, $400 million in 1976, and $400 million in 1977.[43] As a result, one of the government's first moves was to try to reschedule its debts. The Junta succeeded, with considerable difficulty, in bringing about a rescheduling of the debts coming due in 1974.

Negotiations with the Paris Club were not so successful in 1975. A meeting scheduled for March 1975 between Chilean and Paris Club representatives did not take place, when the British government refused to attend in protest against the repressive political policies of the Junta regime. Thereafter, the United States, West Germany, and Spain reached bilateral agreements with Chile on rescheduling their parts of the 1975 debt. No such agreements were reached with Great Britain, the Netherlands, and Sweden, however.[44]

After 1975, the Junta undertook to pay the full amount coming due each year on its foreign debt. As a result, some $800 million was spent on this during 1976.[45] The amount to be paid in the following year was approximately $1 billion, consisting of $649 million for amortization, $251 million for interest, and $104 million on short- and medium-term payments.[46] Debt repayment accounted for 20 percent of the value of Chilean exports in 1974, 36 percent in 1975, and 47 percent in 1976.[47]

Another factor complicating the Chilean balance-of-payments problem during the first years of the Junta regime was the erratic behavior of the price of copper, the country's major export. While this was by no means a new phenomenon in Chilean history, at least some of the problem in the 1973-1977 period can be attributed to policies of the Junta government.

At the time of the overthrow of the Allende regime, the price of copper was rising, and it continued to do so for a few months after the Junta came to power. It reached a high point of $1.40 a pound in mid-1974 and then began to decline. By late 1976, it had fallen to 65 cents a pound.[48] By May 1977, it was "dangerously near the 60 cents a pound figure on which the budget calculations are based."[49]

One reason for the slipping price of copper in these years was the ineffectiveness of the Intergovernmental Council of Copper Exporters (CIPEC), for which the Chilean Junta was to a large degree responsible. In November 1974, soon after the price began to slip, CIPEC agreed on a 10 percent cutback of production. A year later, it raised this figure to 15 percent. However, a few months later, the Chilean government announced that it was not going to abide by the CIPEC decision and was resuming full production. When an emergency meeting of CIPEC was held in June 1976, Chile refused to change its position, and for all practical purposes, CIPEC's attempt to maintain copper prices collapsed.[50]

There are indications that the Junta's attitude towards CIPEC was partly a reflection of the laissez-faire/free trade ideology of the regime. *Latin America Commodities Report* recounted the November 1976 CIPEC meeting:

In pre-conference statements, the Chileans clearly laid out their policy, which conflicts strongly with what some other members wanted. Colonel Rubén Schindler, undersecretary of the Chilean copper commission, reportedly spoke out against any restrictive policy, favoring instead "the free play of supply and demand." Admitting that the international market did not favor producers, he still thought it "the best system."

The periodical suggested another possible motivation for the Chilean government's policy—in "the understanding the Chilean junta has with United States copper mining transnationals." It went on to say that "unrestricted production by the primary producers only strengthens the position of copper transnationals such as Kennecott and Anaconda. Last week's domestic price cuts to US$.65 from US$.70 a lb. by at least four major United States copper refiners reflected their belief that this was necessary in view of the poor demand."[51]

The varying price of copper is reflected in Chile's foreign exchange income from the product. In 1973, it received $1,025.6 million for copper, which rose to $1,653.5 in 1974, fell to $890.4 million in 1975, and rose again to $1,246.5 million in 1976. Significantly, in 1976, copper represented only 60 percent of the country's export income, instead of the more traditional 80 percent.

This decline in the relative importance of copper exports in the overall balance of trade during the Junta period was in part the result of the rise of nontraditional exports, on which the government placed great emphasis. The exports of agricultural, grazing, forestry, and fishing products rose from $25.5 million in 1973 to $118.9 million in 1976, whereas industrial products rose from $44.7 million in 1973 to $328.7 million in 1976.

At least some of the increases in nontraditional exports reflected the fulfillment of development programs begun during the Christian Democratic administration. This was probably the case with paper exports, which rose from $12 million in 1973 to $61.1 million in 1976, and cellulose exports, which climbed from $7 million in 1973 to $33.1 million three years later.

Other increases almost certainly reflected the depressed state of the domestic market, resulting in the sale abroad of products which, had domestic effective demand not been drastically reduced, would otherwise have been sold in Chile. This was probably the case with processed food products, the export of which climbed from $9.3 million in 1973 to $72.8 million in 1975 and $48.9 million in 1976. It also probably was true with metal, mechanical, and electric products, which accounted for only $3.4 million in export income in 1973 but rose to $52.6 million by 1976.[52]

In addition to exporting more nontraditional products, the Junta put emphasis on expanding trade with nontraditional customers. One of those countries with which trade expanded was the People's Republic of China, as the result of a special trade mission sent there in mid-1975.[53]

Another factor which helped the Chilean balance of payments during the Junta years was the large-scale financial credits which the regime received. By early 1976, Chile was reported to have gotten "more than 2,000 million dollars in external assistance since the coup in 1973." Of this, "$729 million had come from international agencies, $295 from credits from individual foreign governments, including the United States, Brazil and Argentina; $275 million was in the form of suppliers credit, and $700 million had come from foreign banks."[54]

In April 1977, ex-Economy Minister Jorge Cauas (by then ambassador to Washington) boasted that "the financial situation of Chile abroad couldn't be better," and he added that "I can point out that the support of private financial institutions in the United States is extraordinarily important. Insofar as the multilateral organizations such as the Inter American Bank and the World Bank, there are no problems and very fluid credits are coming from them."[55]

One of the more interesting foreign credits received by the Junta regime was a loan of $62 million from the Chinese People's Republic. It was given "free of interest and without any additional condition or privilege," in April 1977.[56]

Chile's improved balance-of-payments situation was indicated by the fact that by the end of 1976 foreign exchange reserves of the Central Bank amounted to some $720 million.[57] This figure was approximately twice the reserves at the end of the Frei administration.

THE "ECONOMIC RECOVERY"

During the fourth year of the Junta regime, government leaders from President Pinochet on down boasted frequently of the "recovery" the economy was experiencing. These claims were based on the decline in the inflation rate, the improved balance-of-payments situation, and the turnaround in production in a number of sectors of the economy.

We have noted earlier in this chapter that the inflation began slowing down in mid-1975. After 1975, production also recovered substantially. *El Mercurio*, on the basis of statistics from the Sociedad de Fomento Fabril, claimed in April 1977 that by December 1976 overall industrial production had reached an index number of 107.7, using 1969 as the base year of 100. It showed that the output of "various manufactured articles" had reached a level of 86.6 compared to 1969 output of 100; production of intermediary goods for construction had risen from a low of 50.4 in September 1975 to

89.8 by December 1976. Production of transport materials was back by December 1976 to an index number of 70.2, railroad car loadings were back to 91.9, goods for "habitual consumption" were at the level of 108.2, production of intermediate goods for industry had reached 144.9, and production of consumer durable goods was at 83.3—in all cases using the output level of 1969 as 100.[58]

The pro-Junta periodical *Chilegram*, distributed by the Chilean Embassy in Washington, sought to emphasize the importance of the 1976 recovery in terms of the national income. It reported that the Gross Domestic Product, using the 1960 level as the index number of 100, had reached a high point of 167.0 in 1974, then had fallen to 145.0 in 1975, but had recovered to 150 during 1976. The Chilean per capita income had risen from the 1960 equivalent of $776.2 to a high point of $1,028.2 in 1971, and then reached a level of $832.8 in 1975, but had recovered to $850.4 in 1976.[59]

By the beginning of 1977, the government felt that the recovery had made sufficient progress to justify a mild relaxation in the shock treatment. Thus, Minister Sergio de Castro announced in March that legal bank reserves would be reduced from 83 to 75 percent, and some other credit terms, particularly for exporters, would also be relaxed. He also announced that the Corporación de Fomento and the Banco del Estado would make modest sums available for importation of capital goods and other investments.[60]

A month and a half later, President Pinochet announced some other measures which he said were designed to stimulate the recovery. These included increases in salaries of government employees and modest reductions in direct taxes. Rather counterproductively, they also included advancing the date for proposed reductions in tariffs by two months.[61]

Although the recovery in 1976 and the first months of 1977 was real, if one compares the situation with the depth of the Junta-created Depression in mid-1975, there are certain obvious reservations concerning the nature of the recovery. First, only a small dent, if any, had been made in unemployment by the fourth anniversary of the coup. Second, the recovery was principally export-oriented. It had done little to stimulate effective demand within the domestic economy, a fact which was underscored by the continuing bankruptcies among those firms oriented mainly to national consumption (which we shall note in the next chapter). By the Junta's fourth anniversary, then, Chile was still in the grip of the worst economic crisis since the 1930s.

33

Economic Policies of the Junta Regime: Long-Run Effects

The Junta and the Chicago Boys were not interested solely in curbing the inflation and getting the Chilean economy moving again. They were perhaps even more concerned with effecting fundamental changes in the organization of the Chilean economy and in altering the direction of its development.

The drive of the Junta government and its economic team to establish as complete a laissez-faire economy as possible in Chile had numerous long-run implications. One was the attempt to reduce drastically the government-owned sector of the economy, that is, denationalize the economy. A perhaps unintended result of denationalization was the increased concentration of control of the private sector in the hands of a limited number of groups and private individuals. This tendency was notable both in the industrial field and in agriculture.

Another effect of the long-range program of the Chicago Boys was the strong stimulation of foreign investment. This part of the Junta government policy meant a reversal of the tendency over the previous generation or more to bring the national economy under Chilean control.

One of the results of the drive for foreign investment was the withdrawal of Chile from the Andean Pact. Although Chile specifically rejected the pact's limitations on foreign investment, the objections of the Junta's economic team went beyond that. They sought to free Chile from what they conceived to be the Andean Pact's limitation on Chile's ability to follow the policy of free trade.

Finally, the Chicago Boys put almost manic emphasis on making the Chilean economy "efficient." In this case, "efficiency" was interpreted as the ability of sectors of the Chilean economy to confront foreign competition. In effect, the emphasis on "efficiency" was a policy of opposition to industrialization, or at least to much of the industrialization that had taken place during more than forty years before the Junta seized power. It meant deliberately condemning to death a substantial number of existing industrial concerns.

DENATIONALIZATION

An avowed objective of the Junta was to remove the state as much as possible from participation in the economy. Accordingly, the Junta government sought to divest the state of ownership not only of most of the industrial and commercial firms that had been taken over by the Allende regime, but also of most of the enterprises established by the Corporación de Fomento since its establishment in 1939.

One of the early acts of the Junta government was to announce its willingness to turn back to private owners those firms that had been "intervened" by the Allende government, that is, those enterprises that had been seized but had not actually become the property of the state. At the same time, the government announced that the former owners, upon receiving their companies back, would have to assume any debts those companies had acquired during the Unidad Popular period. In at least a few cases, the debts were so large that the former owners decided not to ask for the return of their firms. However, by the end of the first year of the Junta government, the great majority of the intervened companies were back in the hands of their former private owners.

In the case of firms that had actually been purchased by the government during the Allende period, the Junta did not immediately sell all of them back to their former proprietors. Thus, it was more than two years before the government began to divest itself of the banks taken over under Allende. By the beginning of November 1975, CORFO had begun to dispose of the shares of bank stock which it held.[1]

Although the Junta did not immediately divest itself of some of the firms taken over under Allende, in pursuance of its general attempt to establish a "free enterprise" economy and laissez-faire, the regime undertook to get rid of most of the industrial and infrastructure enterprises that had been brought into existence by CORFO between 1939 and the advent of the Allende regime. It was reported in 1975 that the government was planning to sell some 200 such enterprises to private owners.[2]

In October 1976, Colonel Luis Danus Covián, executive vice-president of CORFO, outlined to *El Mercurio* what the CORFO had done and was going to do with regard to state-owned enterprises. He noted that when the Junta took over, CORFO controlled more than 500 enterprises. The 295 which were merely "intervened" had been returned to their owners in 1973 and 1974, he said. In addition, 200 firms had been "passed to the private sector," and 32 more were in the process of being disposed of. CORFO would continue to own a majority interest in only 23 firms. "These are the ones considered strategic or of national interest, such as the electric, telephone, steel, coal, petroleum and nitrate industries. . . . Also in this list are some new ones created during the present Administration."[3]

Latin America Economic Report related in March 1976 that "the sale of public companies has been surrounded with secrecy, and details, particularly concerning the purchasers, are hard to come by." It cited a CORFO report to the effect that "nationalized companies have been sold to 6,400 individuals, 80 cooperatives and about 20 companies," and added that "few of the purchasers are known."[4]

Colonel Danus Covián reported that the government had received $335 million for the firms it had sold by October 1976.[5]

In some instances, the government's zeal for denationalization seemed to be almost macabre. For instance, in mid-1975 it was announced that the General Cemetery of Santiago, which had been run by the government since its establishment almost a century before, would be turned over to a private firm.[6]

Some of the government's supporters did not think that its denationalization program was going far enough. Thus, Domingo Arteaga, head of the Sociedad de Fomento Fabril, complained that the government still owned more than half the stock in sixteen of the largest companies in the country. He urged the regime to sell, among others, the airline LAN-Chile, the sugar refining industry, and nitrate and coal mining.[7]

CONCENTRATION OF CONTROL IN THE PRIVATE SECTOR

Although the Junta and the Chicago Boys were very anxious to divest the government of ownership of economic enterprises, they seemed completely unconcerned about the high concentration of control that was resulting in the private sector. This tendency was notable both in the urban economy and agriculture.

Ever since Chile's industrialization got seriously under way during the Great Depression, a relatively small number of economic groups have controlled some of the country's more important privately owned industries and commercial enterprises. Although it is difficult to get firm information on who bought up the CORFO companies as the corporation divested itself of them, the indications are that these private "conglomerates" acquired the lion's share. *Latin America Economic Report* has described what took place. It observed the existence of

the twenty or so picturesquely named conglomerates—which are disputing the carcass of Chile's dismembered economy. . . . Each of these groups is a kind of economic clan, with family links, originally centred around particular industries or interests. . . . Each group, among the first ten at least, aims to have a slice of the action in the main profitable areas of the economy, or the most developed areas of industry (fishing, mining, banking—including banks and financieras—agro-industry, consumer durables), and there is cut-throat competition among them. . . . Much of their attention has been concentrated on buying up the denationalized companies which the government has sold off, often at absurdly low prices.[8]

The government's dogmatic emphasis on industry's need for "efficiency," as well as its shock treatment anti-inflation program, have further concentrated economic power in the hands of a very small number of powerful groups. The emphasis on efficiency favors larger firms over smaller firms inasmuch as larger firms can compete in international markets and smaller firms might be concerned principally with the domestic market. The shock treatment has already dispensed with many small and middle-sized firms that had less resources than the conglomerates to resist its impact and that in any case the Junta and Chicago Boys regarded as "inefficient."

RURAL RECONCENTRATION AND JUNTA AGRARIAN POLICY

The tendency of Junta economic policy to lead to a high degree of concentration of wealth and economic power in the private sector is also reflected in agriculture since during its first four years the Junta undid much of the agrarian reform carried out in the previous decade.

Early in the regime, the Junta issued a widely distributed pamphlet, ostensibly directed to state functionaries in the agrarian field, in which they stated the general agrarian policy of the regime. The core of the pamphlet stated that "as a General Policy: Individual Property Titles will be given to the expropriated holdings to the Peasants who work them, except where technical reasons require assigning them to an Agricultural Society also made up of Peasants. On the other hand, JUST AS LATIFUNDIA IS CONSIDERED NEGATIVE, MINIFUNDIA IS CONSIDERED MORE NEGATIVE." [Emphasis in the original.] The pamphlet also affirmed that "the peasants will be able to establish the organizations that they wish, since they will be free," and that the "social objective" of the Junta policy would be "to transform the peasant into a farmer."[9]

In August 1975, the government paper *La Patria* proclaimed the government's agrarian policy to be "the land for those who cultivate it."[10]

There is a good deal of evidence that the Junta's agrarian policies not only involved granting individual property titles to small farmers, but also returning much of the land taken under the earlier agrarian reform program. Although the Junta and the newspapers have from time to time given publicity to land grants being given to the peasants, they have been quite reticent about publicizing the return of land to the large landholders.

Nevertheless, *El Mercurio* did so in a report on the current status of the agrarian reform in February 1977. It said that between 1965 and 1973 some 5,800 landholdings, containing about 10 million hectares, had been expropriated. By November 1976, "as part of the program of regularization" of the agrarian situation, 25 percent of those landholdings had been totally returned to their former owners. These accounted for 21 percent of the total land that had been expropriated. In addition, some 2,142 holdings, or 37 percent of those originally taken over by the government, had been partially restored to their former owners. "The land affected in these cases represents 6.7% of the total in terms of physical hectares, and 12% if 'hectares of basic irrigation' are calculated." A total of 2.75 million hectares had been restored, nearly 28 percent of the total that had been taken over by CORA.

In addition, the government had plans for granting 60,000 parcels of land to peasants, and according to *El Mercurio* this process was to be completed by the end of 1977. By October 31, 1976, some 30,576 parcels had already been granted, amounting to 1.25 million hectares.[11]

Certainly the most serious aspect of these statistics, with regard to undoing the land redistribution provided for under the Frei government's Agrarian Reform Law, is the landholdings that were totally restored to their former owners. Although under Allende larger amounts of land were taken from many landlords than the law provided for, there were few instances in which total *fundos* were expropriated illegally by CORA.

In addition to returning much land to former landowners, the Junta made the financial situation for the agrarian reform beneficiaries more difficult. According to *Latin America Economic Report*, "A new formula has been developed to determine compensation payments for expropriated land. Whereas before compensation was based on the value stated in the expropriation agreement, it now uses the usually higher evaluation agreement that includes improvements. . . . The new formula may be applied retroactively to 28 July 1967, in cases where the expropriation agreement was not accepted by the owner."[12]

The partial liquidation of the agrarian reform did not simply involve the return of land to large landowners by the government. Liquidation was also stimulated by the general economic orientation of the regime. During its first three years, the Junta government refused to give any special consideration in terms of credit and technical assistance to the agrarian reform beneficiaries and other small landholders, on the grounds that such help would constitute "discrimination."

By its fourth year, the regime had begun to modify this policy somewhat. In 1977, the "Program for Integral Rural Development" was launched, and the Instituto de Desarrollo Agropecuario, of which nothing had been heard during the previous three years, was at least partially revitalized to administer it. The program was designed to provide 416 million pesos for small farmers, particularly those with less than 12 hectares of "basic irrigation" land.[13] At the same time, the Ministry of Agriculture indicated that it would finance 70 percent of the cost of technical assistance purchased by small farmers from private firms. It would only finance 20 percent of such purchases of large landholders.[14]

One reason for this at least temporary change in policy was the fact that many of those who had received land under the Agrarian Reform Law were losing it. Unable to obtain credit, technical assistance, and other requirements for successful use of their land, many agrarian reform beneficiaries were selling their land.

While no figures are available on how many such sales took place after 1973, *El Mercurio* noted in February 1977 that "for various reasons, among them deficiencies in cooperative policy and in programs of agricultural extension, sales of parcels by some new proprietors have taken place." The newspaper stated that, as a result, the government had issued Decree-Law 1800 of November 1976, providing that such sales could not be made henceforth without permission of the Corporación de Reforma Agraria and payment of any debts the peasant owed to CORA.[15]

Thus, in the rural as well as the urban sector, the economic policies of the Junta stimulated the concentration of private economic power. The large landholders were strengthened by their recovery of close to a third of the land that had been taken from them in the previous two administrations. They were also able to buy back at bargain prices an unspecified further amount of land from those who had received it under the agrarian reform but had been unable to hold on to it because of the Junta's policy (in the name of free enterprise and "efficiency") of refusing to make available to them the credit and technical assistance essential to make it an economic success. Even modest modification in the Junta regime's credit and technical assistance policies in the fourth year of the regime seemed unlikely to affect more than marginally this trend back towards *latifundia* in Chilean agriculture.

THE JUNTA AND FOREIGN INVESTMENT

Another trend of recent decades which the Junta reversed was that followed since the time of Arturo Alessandri, of reducing the importance of foreign firms in the control of the Chilean economy. The Junta and the Chicago Boys emphasized over and over again their desire to radically increase the amount of foreign investment in the country.

As a preliminary step in this direction, the Junta quickly settled the issue of compensation of foreign companies that had been taken over during the Allende regime. In the case of the three copper companies, Kennecott agreed to accept $68 million, Anaconda $253.2 million, and Cerro de Pasco some

$41.2 million. The International Telephone and Telegraph Company reached an agreement to accept $125.2 million in payment for its share of the Compañia de Teléfonos de Chile and "indebtedness and interest pending between the firm and ITT."[16]

Another move to stimulate foreign investment was the enactment of a new foreign investment law, the action that provoked Chile's break with the Andean Bloc. This decree-law, the final version of which was enacted by the Junta on March 18, 1977, was "designed to shorten investing process transactions, give foreign investors advantages equal to those enjoyed by Chilean companies and guarantee them the right to remit abroad all after-tax profits." It provided that foreign firms could buy foreign currency for remitting profits and could continue to import equipment and materials under whatever conditions existed when the investment was made, in spite of any changes in regulations controlling Chilean companies.

The decree-law also provided that foreign firms could choose either to pay a profit tax of 49.5 percent or the same taxes as those paid by Chilean companies. Foreign firms could also repatriate their investments after three years. Finally, conditions for approval of foreign investments were greatly simplified.[17]

Foreign investments were particularly welcomed in mining, although the firms taken over under Frei and Allende were kept in government hands, at least for the time being. Also, although extensive details are lacking, it is certain that a substantial number of CORFO firms were sold to foreign companies. Thus, the Arauco cellulose plant was sold to an American firm,[18] Chilefilms went to a mixed Chilean-U.S. enterprise,[19] and a tire company, IAMEA, was sold to Firestone.[20]

Early in 1976, it was announced that agreements had been signed during the previous year for $280 million in new foreign investments.[21]

The Junta's eagerness for foreign investment was shown by its agreement in 1975 to permit foreign firms to enter oil exploration and exploitation.[22] However, by June 1977 all but four of the forty-odd firms that had demonstrated interest in investing in Chilean oil had withdrawn.[23]

WITHDRAWAL FROM THE ANDEAN PACT

Chile's withdrawal from the Andean Pact was another fundamental change in long-run economic policy. It meant the abandonment of efforts started by the Frei regime to develop outlets for Chilean manufactured goods and other products in the other Andean countries of South America through the establishment among these six countries of a common market by the middle 1980s. Although provoked by one particular part of the Andean Pact, Chilean withdrawal reflected the laissez-faire, free trade bias of the

Junta and the Chicago Boys, who looked upon the Andean agreement as a limitation on free trade rather than as an expansion of unimpeded commerce among its six member countries.

The crisis in the Andean Bloc began with the enactment on July 13, 1974, of Decree-Law 600, the Foreign Investment Statute for Chile, predecessor of the revised law of March 1977.[24] That legislation brought protests from the other members of the Andean Group because it violated Bloc Decision 24 on the same subject.

The crisis over the Andean Pact came to a head in 1976, when several conferences were held to settle the Decision 24 problem and other issues that were endangering the continuation of the agreement. The CORFO periodical *Chile Economic News* stated Chile's position in these conferences: "The definite separation in Chile came about with the present Government. Chile's present economic philosophy differs diametrically from the philosophy previously held." It summed up these differences with the Andean Pact as follows:

the policy of substitution of imports has failed and the nation has to develop external markets in order to increase exports;

in order to export, fully enjoying comparative advantage, the country has to be ready to open up to imports from the exterior, substantially reducing their tariffs;

in any case, economic improvement demands the flow of foreign capital, which can only be achieved by creating attractive conditions for foreign investment; an adequate economic policy and a similar treatment of national investors;

state intervention in the economy was weighing heavily upon the population and hence the developing force has to come from private initiative.[25]

An emergency meeting of economy ministers held in Lima in April reportedly reached a compromise agreement. This accord, consisting of six new Group Decisions, was summarized by *Chile Economic News*:

Decision 96: which designates the new members of the Executive Board;

Decision 97: which authorizes Chile to sell CORFO industries to foreign investors, previously impossible under Decision 24;

Decision 98: which creates a special supportive program for Bolivia so that it may take advantage of the industries assigned to it in the sectorial programs;

Decision 99: which fixes the procedure for consideration of proposals about industrial development;

Decision 100: which postpones for two years the time limit for maintaining reserves of products which can be included in industrial planning and postpones, likewise, deliberations for agreements freeing tariffs. In this way another point of conflict is delayed;

Decision 101: which gives special treatment to Bolivia, a landlocked nation.[26]

Another meeting in October 1976 in Lima was the scene of a virtual ultimatum from the Chilean government. It demanded that in one way or another the Chileans be given the right to violate Decision 24 governing foreign investment. *Chile Economic News* noted that Economy Minister Sergio de Castro "also suggested that Chile would be amenable to an exception clause, opened only for itself for not more than three years, instead of for the entire Pact."[27]

The other five members of the Andean Pact refused Chile's ultimatum, and on October 30 Adelio Pipino, Chilean delegate to the pact, announced the withdrawal of his country. He also announced that Chile would continue to adhere to four of the agreements of the pact.[28]

As this is being written, it is still not known whether Chile's withdrawal from the Andean Group completely dooms that attempt to establish a common market among the western mountain countries of South America. It is clear, however, that the Junta ruled out the completely free access of Chilean industries and agriculture to a market that may soon approach 100 million people. In the other five Andean countries, as in all other nations, Chilean goods will have to get admission over whatever barriers—tariffs, quotas, embargoes, exchange controls—these countries decide to raise. Almost immediately after Chile's withdrawal from the Andean Pact, its former partners began raising barriers to Chilean imports. Thus, in February 1977, Colombia canceled all of the tariff privileges Chile had had under the Andean agreement.[29]

TAX REFORMS

A long-term policy of the Junta which nearly every Chilean felt almost immediately was its reform of the tax structure. The most important change was the introduction in 1975 of the Value Added Tax (known in Chile by its Spanish initials IVA). This is a tax, first introduced in France soon after World War II, whereby a levy is put on a product at each stage of its production and distribution.

Apparently, there was a considerable tendency in Chile to evade this new tax, particularly at the retail level. As a result, the regime instituted a system of rewards to informers who would alert the authorities to tax evaders.

Modifications were also made in other taxes, such as those on income and real property. In the case of real property, a system of an automatic increase in taxes in conformity with the increase in the cost of living was introduced, and the government carried out a general reassessment of all urban real estate. One tax, that on Chileans wishing to go abroad, was substantially reduced.[30]

The net effect of these tax changes was regressive; *El Mercurio* admitted as much in a February 1977 editorial.[31] The Value Added Tax is a kind of sales impost. The reduction of taxes on those traveling outside the country would almost solely benefit upper-income people.

THE EMPHASIS ON "EFFICIENCY"

A major aspect of the long-run economic program of the Junta and the Chicago Boys has been their insistence that Chilean industries either become "efficient" or go out of business. They define "efficiency" as the ability to stand up to foreign competition. It has been Junta policy that those industries which cannot meet foreign competition do not deserve to continue to exist and therefore must perish. To this end, the regime has largely eliminated tariffs and any other barriers that prevent the entry into Chile of goods produced in other countries.

El Mercurio, in an editorial commenting on a speech by Minister of Economy Sergio de Castro, underscored this aspect of the long-run economic policy: "There is under way in our country a true and profound change of the habits of the population, of the strategy of development and of the restrictions on liberty which the majority of the Chileans accepted consciously or unconsciously. The objective is to revindicate economic freedom, using this to achieve a more sustained and stable development." The editorial also observed that "the change that the Minister indicates is becoming evident with increasing intensity. The economy begins to grow with rapidity through exports and the development of those sectors which have competitive advantage. Simultaneously with that, the activity of those productive branches that were exaggeratedly protected are being restricted."[32]

The Junta regime took exceedingly drastic measures to eliminate the protectionism that had been characteristic of the Chilean economy since at least the second administration of President Arturo Alessandri in the early 1930s. It first abolished all embargoes and reduced all tariffs of over 200 percent to that figure, at the same time reducing all other tariffs by 10 to 20 percent. It then established a maximum tariff of 160 percent, and then reduced it still further to 140 percent. It announced that as of January 1977 the highest tariff for any product would be 60 percent.[33] In May 1974, the Central Bank announced that 2,400 articles were to be completely freed of tariffs. This move was said to be "designed to improve competition within the country and to favor the consumer."[34]

The program for reducing tariffs which was announced early in the regime was later expanded. The new goal was to make Chile's maximum tariff rate only 35 percent by the end of 1977. Reductions in rates early in May of that year brought the average tariff protection from 24.2 percent to 22.4 percent. The Central Bank announced at that time that of a total of 4,984 "tariff positions (locations on a scale of tariffs of the groups of products which are imported), 1000 had a rate of 25%, 1288 one of 20% and 960 one of 15%." Goods with an import tax of 45 percent had been reduced from 152 to 29, and those with a tariff rate of 40 percent, from 493 to 198. By May 1977, the tariff rate on twenty-five products which paid 55 percent duty and 89 percent of those with a 50 percent import tax had been reduced to 45 percent or less.[35]

Thus, the Junta government, adhering to the advice of its economic team, virtually decided that the great majority of the country's industries should henceforward not enjoy any kind of protection from foreign competition, and that existing industries which could not face such competition successfully had to disappear. Specific predictions concerning the long-run effects of such a free trade policy can only be made on the basis of a more intensive study than is offered here. However, it can be stated that a substantial part of the country's industries are not likely to survive foreign competition, if they are made to face it.

One authority for this assertion is Sergio de Castro, one of the major (and the most enduring) members of the Junta's economic team. In a conversation with me in 1974, he said that a study he had made before entering the government had indicated that at least one-third of the country's industries required substantial protection, and only one-third could certainly face up to imports from abroad. So, he agreed that two-thirds of the country's existing industries would either certainly or possibly perish if free trade policies were continued.[36]

As far as is known, there are no overall figures on how many Chilean industrial firms disappeared during the first four years of the Junta regime. In July 1976, Minister of Economy Sergio de Castro insisted that "in spite of the predictions made by the critics of the economic policy during the last year, the bankruptcies can be counted on the fingers of one hand."[37]

The minister's view appears to be excessively sanguine. *Latin America Economic Report* noted in October 1976 that among the firms which had recently failed were SIAM di Tella, a major producer of household appliances, and Ferriloza, the third largest firm in that field. It surmised that "most of the numerous small workshops and factories supplying parts and components must already have fallen by the wayside." The periodical also reported that the Federation of Metalurgical Unions estimated that the work force in the sector had fallen from 55,000 in 1973 to 15,000 three years later.

At the same time, the largest home products company in Chile, the CIT, or Compañia Tecno-Industrial, a merger of the former FENSA and MADEMSA firms, had drastically laid off personnel. In 1973, it had had 3,834 workers, and by 1976 this figure had fallen to 1,840. The unions in this firm were claiming that Rolf Luders, the president of CIT, was in fact planning to close down his company's operations in Chile (where, by the Junta government's criteria, it was "inefficient") and to transfer its activities to Bolivia, where Luders apparently felt that it could be "efficient."[38]

By early 1977, the collapse or near collapse of much of the home equipment industry was having an impact on firms that supplied the inputs for that industry. Thus, the steel products firm Aceros Andes S.A. went bankrupt early in January 1977.[39]

One might argue that the difficulties of these firms—which were devoted entirely to serving the internal Chilean market and which almost certainly needed protection in order to survive—derived from the Junta's shock treatment and that they would again become prosperous with a slowdown in inflation and general economic recovery. However, there are indications that such is not entirely the case.

It seems clear that producers of home appliances are among the sectors which the Junta and its economic team regard as "inefficient" and are therefore doomed to disappear. This is underscored by an article in *El Mercurio* in October 1976, devoted to a discussion of unused capacity in Chilean industry:

However, in some cases the apparent unused capacity is fictitious and not real. For example, among the durable consumers goods are "electric apparatus for domestic use," "electronic equipment," and "non-electric machinery," industries which, especially the first two, are not able to compete adequately in the present situation of opening to the exterior. The idle capacity is then only partially usable. The same is true in the case of transport material and some miscellaneous manufactured articles, which if manufactured would be more expensive than imports.[40]

Almost certainly, many other categories of products could not face up to foreign competition. For example, it seems likely that textiles produced in such places as Taiwan, the Philippines, Hong Kong, and other exceedingly low-wage areas could sell at lower prices than those manufactured in Chile.

The likely fate of the textile industry was indicated in November 1976, when it was announced that between January and October 1976 imports of textiles had increased by $8 million, or 115 percent, whereas exports of Chilean textiles had expanded in the same period by only $120,000, or 5.1 percent.[41]

The possible fate of Chilean industry in general was perhaps foreshadowed by what had happened to the Fluxa group, one of the important conglomerates, by mid-1977. It was reported that only five of the fourteen firms of the group, which had presumably gone bankrupt, were still operating. (No information was given out as to which ones had closed their doors.) The Fluxa group was probably the conglomerate most involved in the collapse of the *financieras* earlier in the year; even so, the fate of the group does not augur well for the future of Chilean industry.[42]

Thus, the Junta and its economic advisers have been committed to the decimation of Chilean industry as a long-run policy. Only manufacturing firms that can sell most or all of their output abroad will be allowed to continue in operation. Firms that serve only the domestic market and that cannot compete with imports will be allowed—one might even say "encouraged" —to perish.

If the policies of the Junta continue and a substantial number of Chilean manufacturing firms are allowed to disappear, the harm to the Chilean economy and to the people of Chile will be incalculable. It is highly unlikely that there will be alternative employment for the people who have worked in the disappearing industries. People thrown out of work will certainly not be employed in the mining sector, which has a very small work force and is highly "efficient." The could not be employed in agriculture, which is already overstaffed and which the Junta wants to mechanize, thus making much of the currently employed labor redundant. It is highly dubious that these workers will find employment in those Chilean industries which will be able not only to compete for the internal market but also to export. In a word, they will not be employed at all.

In deliberately sentencing a large part of the national work force to permanent unemployment by destroying their source of work in the name of an abstract principle of "efficiency," the Junta has been guilty of the same sin as the Allende regime—a triumph of ideology over common sense.

THE LONG-RUN SOCIOPOLITICAL CONSEQUENCES OF SHOCK TREATMENT

One can only speculate on the longer run social consequences of the economic crisis of the Junta regime and of the means used to deal with that crisis. Doctors in one of the major hospitals in the working-class section of Santiago reported in mid-1975 that the infant mortality rate in that area was back to the level it had been thirty years before. During at least the first two years of the Junta regime, slow starvation was the fate being faced by large segments of Chile's urban population.

Through its program of "make-work employment" and other measures in the third and fourth years of the regime, the Junta finally began to come to grips with these effects of its policy. Indeed, it claimed notable gains in depressing the national death rate, claims which, given the continuing depression of living levels of most of the country's population, cannot be taken seriously.

Other effects of the Junta's policy are likely to be disastrous in the long run. The elimination of the middle class in Chile as a result of the Junta's policies will mean the loss of the most stabilizing factor in Chilean society, a factor that was largely responsible for the kind of society and polity that had marked Chile for several generations. Whereas the Allende regime was threatening to destroy the middle class—with the result that the middle class reacted strongly against the Unidad Popular—the Junta regime did in fact largely destroy it and there was little that class could do when faced with a regime dominated by the military.

THE NATURE OF THE CHICAGO BOYS' "NEW ECONOMY"

The long-run effects of the Junta's economic policies are likely to be even more disastrous than the short-run impact of its shock treatment approach to inflation control. During the first four years of the military regime, the Junta and the Chicago Boys created fundamental changes in economic policies that had been followed for almost half a century. These changes, like many of the acts of the Allende regime, were dictated by ideological considerations and in defiance of common sense.

The Junta regime sought to convert an economy in which the state had long had the decisive role into a free enterprise system. It not only returned firms which had been seized under Allende, but it also sold to private interests most of those which CORFO had developed between 1939 and 1970. It also moved to put into effect the free trade principles that were an inherent part of the laissez-faire ideas of the economic team of the Junta. To this end, it totally abolished embargoes and quotas on imports, and it came close to abolishing all tariff protection for Chilean industries. These measures were taken with full determination that industries which the economic team did not consider to be "efficient" should perish.

By the end of the fourth year, the contours of the "new economy" which the Chicago Boys were fashioning for Chile were becoming clear. Such an economy would be peculiarly vulnerable to the ebbs and flows of foreign trade. The production of minerals, agricultural products that could be exported, and manufactured goods that could find markets abroad were to constitute the economy. The industries serving the home market, which had grown up during the previous generation behind a substantial wall of protection and had provided the bulk of the employment for workers engaged in manufacturing, were to be destroyed. Thus, the trend since the 1930s whereby the Chilean economy would be less vulnerable to variations in foreign economies was completely reversed.

At the same time, the "new economy" was to be one divorced from the economies of its neighbors. The efforts of the Frei regime to make Chile part of an Andean common market, in which much of Chilean industry and agriculture and some of its mining would have clear comparative advantage, were completely abandoned by the Junta.

The "new economy" was also to be one in which foreign firms would once again have a highly influential role. A new foreign mining sector was introduced, and foreign firms were allowed into petroleum, which previously had been developed only by the Chilean government and private entrepreneurs. A large number of firms that had originally been established by Chilean entrepreneurs and the Chilean government were deliberately turned over to foreign enterprises as a result of the denationalization program of the Junta. Thus, in this regard, too, control over the Chilean economy was transferred from the Chilean state and private businessmen to foreign interests.

The "new economy" was also to be one characterized by a higher degree of concentration of wealth in the private sector than had existed for several generations. Both through the denationalization policies and through the partial reversal of the agrarian reform, control over those parts of the economy not in the hands of foreigners, or not remaining in the hands of the state, was concentrated in the hands of private conglomerates. Whereas these conglomerates had always been a significant part of the national economy, the Junta's policies gave them domination of the private domestically owned sector.

The "new economy," too, meant the reversal of Chile's long-run tendency to be a middle-class society. Hundreds of small firms producing for the domestic market would no longer exist. The Frei government's attempt to create a prosperous class of middle-class farmers was largely reversed. Even the professional classes would become more dependent on foreign firms and domestic conglomerates than they had been for several generations.

Finally, the "new economy" would be one in which a larger or smaller part of the population would be deliberately deprived of the possibility of being gainfully employed. The destruction of the more labor-intensive industries, and the Junta's growing emphasis on the mechanization of agriculture, would, if continued, condemn a large part of the working class to unemployment—all in the name of "efficiency."

Thus, if the Junta and the Chicago Boys continue to have their way, the future economy of Chile promises to be one in which prosperity or deep depression will depend totally on the willingness of foreigners to buy Chilean goods; in which a relatively small number of workers in highly capital-intensive export industries and highly mechanized agriculture have relatively well-paid jobs; and in which the rest of the population ekes out a bare living (or doesn't, as the case may be) without any job or by providing menial services for their better off fellow citizens.

34
Labor Under the Junta Regime

The Allende regime had consistently pictured itself as a government "of the workers," and in fact, it had the solid support of the majority of the urban manual working class. The backers of the Allende government subsequently portrayed its overthrow as a move aimed basically against the workers and on behalf of the "monopolists and imperialists."

The earlier chapters of this book have presented enough information to raise serious doubts about both assertions. However, the Junta regime's policies with regard to the Chilean working class have served to give credence to the Unidad Popular's arguments in the eyes of many workers and will have an important bearing on the longer run effects of the coup and its aftermath.

PROTESTATIONS OF THE JUNTA LEADERS

From virtually the day the Allende government was overthrown, the leaders of the military regime have insisted that their action was not aimed against the workers. They pledged their determination to maintain intact the "conquests" which the Chilean workers had made over the process of nearly half a century.

One such statement was made by General Augusto Pinochet in an interview with reporters of Radio Luxemburg of Paris on September 17, 1973. He commented that "the Junta de Gobierno does not wish to go back on social gains. On the contrary, it wants to direct all social advances through legal channels, not illegal ones."[1] About a week later, General Gustavo Leigh noted that among the Junta's planned measures on behalf of the workers was one to have the "workers share in the profits of enterprises."[2]

A more comprehensive statement issued soon after the coup in the name of the whole Junta claimed that "the military Government will not be a return to the past, near or remote. The workers have waged long and difficult battles in defense of their legitimate interests. The Armed Forces are part of this noble people and never will betray those who, like themselves, join forces to return Chile to the place that history has reserved for it."[3] The statement then went on:

Chilean worker, the Armed Forces respect your rights. The participation of the workers in the management of large firms will cease to be a slogan and a pretext through which a caste of leaders obtains an absurd "total power."

No one needs to have fear who mistakenly had confidence in traitors who offered "a new fatherland," and only gave them hunger, hatred, beatings and injustice. Only national unity will save Chile from self destruction and will rescue its people from the degradation to which communism had reduced it. The Government will demonstrate with deeds its concept of sharing in management of firms. The workers will return to their work and trade union activities without fear, complexes or grudges in a united struggle for a common destiny of greatness and liberty.

During the fourth year of the Junta regime, its leaders continued to sound the same theme. Thus, in his May Day Message for 1977, President Pinochet proclaimed:

I wish the workers to know that they are the first preoccupation of the government. Furthermore, we have never said that we were going to change the rules of the game for the workers. I said this the first day that I assumed control of the country. I was in the Military School and they asked that and I said that what the workers had obtained will continue and will be maintained. There are no changes. . . . Nonetheless, because of the social security law which is under study some think that the rules of the game are going to be changed. What the workers have obtained will be kept in all its parts.[4]

These were indeed brave words. However, the military government's actual handling of the labor movement during the years following the coup fell considerably short of them, while, as we have already seen, the major weight of the readjustment of the Chilean economy was being placed on the workers, and their future was being further jeopardized by the long run economic program of the Junta.

IMMEDIATE IMPACT OF THE COUP ON LABOR

In the immediate wake of the coup, there were many casualties in the labor movement. A considerable but unknown number of labor leaders were shot, particularly in some of the mining areas. In some cases, rank-and-file workers were shot—as when ten at the San Bernardo railway workshops near Santiago were picked out at random and were executed, including rank and filers belonging to the MIR, Socialists, Communists, and Christian Democrats. Sizable numbers were also arrested, while some sought refuge in embassies and subsequently left the country, and others went into hiding. This kind of reaction subsided after the first few weeks, although some unionists continued to be picked up from time to time, with varying consequences to them.

One of the first actions of the Junta government was to officially dissolve the CUTCh. Decree No. 12 of the Junta, dated September 27, 1973, gave as its reason for dissolving the CUTCh that it "had been transformed into an organism of a political character, under the influence of tendencies which are foreign and alien to national sentiment."[5]

This move, in effect, decapitated the labor movement. Before the coup, there were three hierarchical levels within organized labor: the central labor body, CUTCh; the various national confederations and federations which grouped together workers of particular trades and industries; and the local unions.

In view of the political control of the CUTCh by the Communists and Socialists, and the Junta's move to illegalize those parties, the reason for the legal dissolution of the CUTCh is clear enough. What is not so clear—if the Junta meant what it said about its attitude towards organized labor—was why it did not permit the establishment of a substitute for the CUTCh.

The most important non-UP labor leaders attempted to organize such a substitute in December 1973, the Central Nacional Sindical (CNS). Although the military took no overt steps against the CNS, the organization expired for lack of financial resources, since there was no legal way that unions could contribute to the maintenance of the organization and since no party or other outside group was in a position to do so at that time. The government refused to give it even informal recognition.

In a conversation in July 1975 with the minister of labor of the Junta, General Nicanor Díaz Estrada, I was informed that the military regime would not provide for the formation of a legal central labor organization in the new Labor Code which it proposed to enact. The minister also indicated that the government would not permit the formation of any central labor body not authorized by law.[6]

At least one attempt seems to have been made to group together those union leaders who were unconditionally servants of the Junta. In December 1976, the formation of the Unión Nacional Laboral was announced. It was headed by Bernardino Castillo of the Copper Miners Confederation, who boasted that it would include fourteen union groups with one million members.[7] However, this effort does not appear to have borne any lasting fruit.

Although most of the important national industrial and craft union federations and confederations continued to exist, almost immediately after the coup substantial changes in their leadership were effected. In the Railroad Workers' Federation and several others, the Socialists and Communists who had been in control voluntarily resigned in order to give way to Christian Democratic and independent workers whom they felt would be less the butt of the new government's wrath. In a few cases, the pre-September 1973 leadership remained fully in control.

DECREE-LAW NO. 198

The Junta did not enact a general rule for the conduct of the unions until more than three months after the coup. The delay may have been caused by extensive discussion, and even controversy, among the Junta members and other officials of the regime concerning what to do with the labor movement. There was reported to be a strong element in the military government which wanted to suppress the unions entirely.

The general rule which finally emerged was Decree-Law No. 198 of December 29, 1973. Its major provisions dealt with union elections, the holding of union meetings, and collective bargaining. Specifically, it provided that no union elections were to be held until further notice and that those people holding union offices were to remain (unless removed by the Ministry of Labor) until the government decided to allow new elections. Meanwhile, vacancies in leadership were to be filled by placing the oldest member of the union in the vacant post. This provision of the decree-law was very unpopular with Chilean unionists. They felt that workers who were on the point of retirement were not likely to be very militant representatives of their fellows, not being anxious to do anything that might imperil their pensions.

The holding of union meetings was sharply circumscribed by Decree-Law No. 198. It provided that meetings could not be held without the approval of local police authorities at least forty-eight hours before the meeting was to take place. Furthermore, applications for permission had to be accompanied by an agenda for the meeting and by a description of those who were entitled to attend the meeting. In no case was a union session to discuss demands to be made on an employer or any political subject. Finally, every union meeting was to be attended by a police official, who was authorized to suspend the session if he found it talking about matters not on the agenda or being attended by people who were not authorized to be present. In practice, many union meetings were held without the presence of a recognized police officer, and people were sometimes present who were not officially authorized.

Decree-Law No. 198 also suspended all further collective bargaining over new contracts. Although the government proclaimed its intention of maintaining intact all "workers' conquests" obtained in collective bargaining or in legislation, it insisted that collective bargaining for new contracts was impossible so long as inflation was proceeding at such a breakneck pace. For the time being at least, wages would be determined by the government.[8]

This decree-law remained in effect at the time of the fourth anniversary of the coup. Under it, the function of trade union officials was limited largely to maintaining the bare existence of their organizations, doing such negotiating over grievances as employers would permit, and administering such social services as individual unions might have for their members.

As a result of the prohibition of union elections, it is estimated that about 75 percent of the union officials who were in power on September 10, 1973, were still in office a year later. Those who had been displaced consisted of a few who had died normal deaths and others who had been jailed, killed, gone into exile, or voluntarily resigned to protect their organizations from government harassment. In subsequent years, there was some turnover in union leadership, and some union officials were forced out by the government.

SITUATION IN THE PROVINCES

After the coup, the trade union situation was considerably worse in many of the provinces than in Santiago, other major cities, and the copper mining regions. On May 1, 1974, President Pinochet signed a decree-law establishing the post of labor delegate in each province. All labor delegates appointed were military men, who in effect superseded the authority of the regular labor inspector of the Ministry of Labor.

This change was particularly important in the processing of grievances. Traditionally, in Chilean labor relations, those grievances of local unions that could not be directly resolved with management were taken to the Labor Inspectorate for settlement. Procedures there were often slow, but they were in the hands of career officials who usually had considerable experience and a wide knowledge of the economic and labor conditions of their respective regions. More often than not, they gave a sympathetic ear to the workers' complaints. The military men who were superimposed on this system had no such experience and knowledge, and in many cases were suspicious of organized labor as being "subversive," if for no other reason, because of the political parties' influence in it. As a result, the processing of grievances in many of the provinces became much slower, and, at least in some instances, was brought virtually to a halt.

FOREIGN PROTESTS

Quite understandably, the situation of Chilean organized labor after the coup aroused a good deal of protest from the labor movement in other parts of the world. This protest not only arose from labor movements under Communist influence, but also from those belonging to the non-Communist International Confederation of Free Trade Unions and from the AFL-CIO of the United States.

International labor's reaction to the Chilean labor situation was very evident in the midmonths of 1974. At the annual meeting of the International Labor Organization (ILO) in Geneva in June, the Chilean situation was a subject of discussion, the result of which was the ILO's decision to send an investigating team to Chile to look into the state of things there. A few weeks later, delegates from Chilean unions which had long been affiliated with the International Transport Workers' Federation (ITF) were not seated at that organization's world congress in Stockholm.

After some hesitation, the Junta agreed to allow the ILO mission to come to Chile and to conduct a thorough investigation. The Junta apparently hoped, as it had in the case of other similar international groups that had come to look at the state of affairs under the military regime, that the ILO investigators would "understand" the situation as seen from the point of view of the regime and would give a favorable report.

The ILO mission was headed by Peruvian ex-President José Bustamante, long-time member of the International Court of Justice. The report which the mission rendered after returning to Geneva was highly critical of the curtailment of trade union rights under the military regime. The report was so critical that when the 1975 ILO conference decided to discuss it, the Chilean delegation withdrew from the meeting.[9]

The Junta also promised to allow a delegation from the ITF to come to Chile to investigate labor conditions there. However, when this group arrived on November 25, 1974, its members were informed that they would not be able to interview any Chilean labor leaders or to carry on any other form of investigation. On the grounds that their activities would interfere with the ILO study which was to be made shortly afterwards, they were not allowed to do what they had come to Chile for. The delegation protested to Labor Minister Nicanor Díaz and left the country on November 28.[10]

The labor movement of the United States also protested the treatment of organized labor by the Junta and sought to bring pressure for a change in the Chilean government's attitude and policies. The Chilean regime was anxious to get the approval of the AFL-CIO, and in March 1974 General Pinochet personally wrote George Meany inviting him to visit Chile or to send a delegation there. Meany replied that, although it was an honor to receive such an invitation, a visit "would only be possible when the rights of the workers have been restored."[11] At its August 1974 Executive Board meeting, the AFL-CIO adopted a resolution demanding the restoration of trade union rights in Chile and attacking the treatment of the unions there by the Junta government.[12]

The AFL-CIO continued to protest the Junta regime's treatment of organized labor and its general suppression of human rights. A letter written by George Meany to Minister of Labor Sergio Fernández, in reply to one from the minister, was widely publicized early in 1977. It said in part:

Referring specifically to the points raised in your letter, I am moved at the outset to say that our viewpoint vis-a-vis Chile is now, and always has been, marked by a singular objectivity: the defense of human rights and trade union freedom in that unfortunate nation. Our viewpoint is not the result of "Marxist propaganda" nor of "those who let themselves be influenced by it," as your letter states, but grows from painstaking interviews and research conducted by our representatives who have visited Chile and from Chilean trade unionists with whom we have maintained contact over the years. In that light, we have condemned the excesses of the Allende regime as well as those of the Pinochet regime as they have affected human rights and trade union freedoms in your country. I regret to say that we have seen precious little cause for rejoicing at the alleged efforts of the Pinochet regime to "safeguard such rights." Your reference to the anti-communist posture of the Chilean government that would disguise the consistent repressing of human rights and trade union freedoms in Chile is immediately transparent. The excesses committed by your government in the name of anti-communism are typical of the most tyrannical fascist regimes of our century.[13]

Some of the labor groups bringing pressure from abroad for an improvement of trade union conditions in Chile evidenced a lack of knowledge of, or even concern for, the actual situation under which the labor leaders were struggling in Chile. For instance, the International Confederation of Free Trade Unions (ICFTU), instead of throwing its support strongly behind those leaders inside the country who were trying to stand up to the government while at the same time seeking to preserve their unions, operated on the fiction that the CUTCh was still in existence in Chile and established an office for Luis Figueroa, the Communist ex-deputy who was the last president of the CUTCh, in its headquarters in Brussels.[14]

A change in the ICFTU's attitude was evidenced in mid-1977. At that time, it invited Eduardo Ríos and Tucapel Jiménez, two of the principal independent union leaders inside Chile, to go to Europe to explain the realities of the Chilean labor situation to officials of the ICFTU.

ATTITUDES OF UNION LEADERS

Those who remained union leaders, or accepted posts in the labor movement, after September 11, 1973, faced a peculiarly difficult task. They had to try to preserve their organizations intact, which meant that they could not afford open confrontations with the military regime. At the same time, they had to avoid any appearance of close collaboration with the government; otherwise they would be discredited in the eyes of rank-and-file members of their organizations.

As time passed, the positions of the major labor leaders evolved. During the first months after the coup, most of the leading unionists attempted to offer limited cooperation with the Junta in return for promises of an early return to normalcy for the trade union movement. When it became clear that the Junta had no intention of permitting an early reestablishment of trade union freedom, the unionists tended to split into two identifiable groups, one collaborating closely with the regime, and the other becoming increasingly open in its opposition to the Junta government.

On May Day 1974, several of the leading trade union figures cooperated with the government to the extent of participating in a meeting in the temporary government headquarters, the Diego Portales Building. Manuel Rodríguez, the Christian Democrat who had been elected head of the CUTCh in Santiago in 1972, was the principal speaker. On the platform with him were Federico Mujica, head of the major white collar workers' union, CEPCh; Osvaldo Martan of the electrical workers' union; Ermol Flores of the government employees' organization, ANEF; and Washington Sepúlveda of the social security workers. General Pinochet replied to Rodríguez' speech, stressing the government's desire to "depoliticize" the labor movement.[15]

In the following month, a group of major labor leaders, headed by Eduardo Rios of the Maritime Workers' Confederation, agreed to serve on the workers' delegation to the annual conference of the International Labor Organization. Rios and the others agreed to go to Geneva because the government promised that, upon the return of the ILO delegation, the Junta would issue a decree permitting new union elections and otherwise normalizing the functioning of the unions. It was after the government's failure to fulfill these promises that the most important segment of the trade union leadership refused any further cooperation with the regime.[16]

Thereafter, the Chilean labor leadership was divided into two well-defined groups. One was led by Rios and included the leaders of the CEPCh, the railroad workers, the government employees, the copper miners, and the largest of the peasant union organizations and several others. It adopted as critical an attitude towards the government as was consonant with maintaining their unions intact and keeping themselves out of jail. This group sought to maintain as close contacts as possible with their lower ranking leaders and rank-and-file members. They did this largely by holding "seminars" and "round tables" to train younger leaders and to report to their membership on problems facing the unions. The opening and closing ceremonies of these seminars and round tables were occasions for the principal labor figures who were standing up to the government to meet and be seen together in public, thus indicating their mutual solidarity in the face of the regime's repressive attitude towards the labor movement. In this job of educating their membership and keeping them informed, the Chilean labor leaders received invaluable help from the American Institute for Free Labor

Development (AIFLD), an organization directed by the AFL-CIO and largely financed by the U.S. government's Agency for International Development, which organized and administered many of these sessions.[17]

The government reacted to the continuance of these seminars with AIFLD backing by announcing the establishment of its own "trade union school." In March 1977, Ambrosio Rodríguez, head of the government's Division of Civil Organizations, announced that "the Government is attempting through this Trade Union School, to create the means for training labor leaders without the initial vice of politics, and to see that they don't receive prejudiced and tendentious information."[18]

The more militant trade union leaders exerted as much pressure on the government as possible in connection with the labor legislation the regime was preparing. They succeeded in getting some concessions from the government, particularly with regard to a proposed new Labor Code.

Although the more militant labor leaders had some contacts with the labor minister and other figures in the regime, for more than a year it was impossible for them to get appointments with General Pinochet or other Junta members in order to present them with the complaints and points of view of the more militant segment of the labor movement. It was not until late August 1975 that General Pinochet finally met with them. It was reported that after this session the Junta convened to discuss the arguments the labor leaders had presented to the president.[19]

Meanwhile, a much smaller group of labor officials, representing less significant unions than those of the more militant leaders, chose the path of close collaboration with the Junta. These included the heads of the Health Workers' Federation (social security workers), the bank clerks, and a small union of commercial and industrial white collar workers. At least some of the members of this group were widely reported as having adopted this position of collaboration after having been "broken" by severe torture while under arrest in the first period of the Junta government.[20] After 1974, these leaders supplied the members of workers' delegations to annual ILO conferences.

In a few cases, national unions were allowed to remain under Communist party control. This was so with the Construction Workers' Federation. *Latin America* explained this situation: "In their case they were not directly involved in political activities, in factory occupations or the like and they had also cultivated good relationships with the main construction companies, who are keen to see union organization of the workforce continue." The British periodical went on to say that "they have maintained their legal existence, but funds and union property have been expropriated, on the grounds that they were supplied by the Communist Party. The general secretary was arrested in May last year and detained for several months; he was released largely as a result of pressure from the construction companies."[21]

In April 1977, as part of a general drive against the established union leadership, the government formed a rival to the Construction Workers' Federation. The new federation immediately sent a letter of thanks to the government "for its concern for the workers."[22]

FACTORS AGAINST RELAXATION OF CONTROLS OVER UNIONS

In spite of extensive international pressure and growing passive resistance from Chilean labor leaders, the military government had not notably relaxed its controls over organized labor by the fourth anniversary of its advent to power. One factor responsible for its continued control was the continuing rapid inflation. So long as it was unable to reduce price increases to manageable levels, the regime was not willing to permit free collective bargaining. In addition, at least some of the military men and their civilian advisers continued to be deeply suspicious of the labor movement, because of the undoubtedly continuing influence of the political parties in the labor movement. It continued to be true that if free elections were allowed in the unions, members of the Socialist, Communist, and Christian Democratic parties would in all likelihood win most of the union leadership posts.

Finally, the government itself had not yet fully made up its mind as to the labor movement's future. One element in the regime favored some kind of "corporativist" regime for labor-management relations, in which collective bargaining would for practical purposes be outlawed; the role of whatever workers' organizations that would be permitted would be to "cooperate" with the government and employers' groups in establishing working conditions. Other elements wanted a return to collective bargaining, but some of them wanted less government support of unions and involvement in the collective bargaining process than had been customary in Chile. Virtually all of the government leaders dreamed of "depoliticizing" the labor movement.

The situation of those labor leaders who were trying to maintain freedom from government control became more difficult after Labor Minister Nicanor Díaz was replaced early in 1976 by a civilian, Sergio Fernández, who had close relations with the Patria y Libertad group. When the independent labor leader group sent a letter to Fernández in mid-June 1976, urging a relaxation of controls established in Decree-Law 198 of December 1973, he curtly replied that he would not discuss such matters with "a handful of unrepresentative unionists who neither knew nor understood the process going on in the country." Subsequently, he removed the leadership of the Copper Miners' Confederation—in obvious contradiction to the same Decree-Law 198—putting in a new executive committee headed by Guillermo Castillo, one of the few copper workers' leaders in the collaborationist camp.[23]

The persecution of the independent labor leaders continued in 1977. In May, the Ministry of Labor removed the Executive Committee of the Maritime Workers' Confederation, headed by Eduardo Ríos, the single most important figure in the independent union leadership. It also dissolved the Association of Retired Manual Workers, which also had associated itself with the independent union group.[24]

On May Day 1977, the independent union group planned for a meeting, supported by 120 different union groups, to be held in the Teatro Caupolican. At the same time, the government organized its own labor meeting at government headquarters in the Diego Portales building.[25] When the government refused to allow the Teatro Caupolican meeting to take place, the independent unionists repeated their maneuver of previous years and attended the special May Day mass organized by Cardinal Silva Henríquez.[26]

In spite of its general mistreatment of the labor movement, the Junta claimed that the number of unions and total union membership was growing. For example, one government spokesman alleged that between January and October 1976, "some 125 new unions have been legalized while 67 were annulled and 28 had their statutes reformed."[27] Another pro-government source claimed that between September 1973 and the beginning of 1977, the number of unions had increased by 10 percent and that by the latter date there were 1 million members of organized labor.[28] These figures do not seem plausible, given the almost complete inability of the unions during the Junta regime to accomplish anything on behalf of their members.

SOCIAL SECURITY PROGRAM OF JUNTA GOVERNMENT

By the end of its second year in power, the Junta government had begun to develop some long-run policies for the labor movement and for the workers who made it up. Three measures had been announced which were of particular importance: a new social security law, a "social enterprise" statute, and a new labor code.

The future of social security was apparently a matter of extensive debate within the Junta government. Some of this discussion very much reflected the extreme free enterprise outlook of some of the Junta's civilian advisers.

Minister of Finance Leniz, in an address before a meeting in July 1974 of the Confederation of White Collar Workers, made a proposal to change the retirement part of the social security system, a proposal that proved very disturbing to the trade union leaders. He suggested that the retirement funds of workers of each enterprise be drawn only from the savings of the workers of that enterprise, and that each worker be free to decide whether or not to contribute. According to Leniz' plan, these savings would be invested by a committee chosen by the workers involved. The state, he contended, would then have no responsibility insofar as workers' pensions were concerned. The social security system, as it had traditionally existed, would thus be abolished, with only the health insurance part of it remaining more or less intact.[29]

Understandably, the workers' organizations which were not unswervingly collaborating with the government were strongly opposed to this suggestion, on at least two grounds. First, it would omit employers' and state contributions from the pension system. Second, it would place the investment of the workers' pension funds in the hands of people with little experience or background in such matters.

Apparently, the government took the workers' protests on this issue seriously. A document issued by the regime in May 1975, entitled General Lines of Action, outlined a substantially different reorganization of the social security system. In expounding upon this document, the minister of labor, General Nicanor Díaz Estrada, said that the social security system was to be revised on the basis of "the principles of universality, integralness, uniformity, solidarity and sufficiency." In conformity with the first principle, Díaz Estrada noted, the system would be extended to all workers, regardless of sex or place of employment. The "integral" aspect of the new system would mean that it would pay "attention to all kinds of needs which are really justified." In terms of uniformity, the new system would give the same benefits and establish the same prerequisites for all members of the system. In terms of solidarity, it would provide for contributions in conformity with ability to pay and benefits in terms of need. Finally, the system would be "sufficient" in the sense of "giving everyone what he needs to maintain a dignified life, adequate to his needs, given the economic possibilities of the country."

Minister Díaz Estrada ended his discussion with the assertion that "the establishment of a system which substitutes for the present ones will not signify any change in rights already acquired or in the legitimate expectations of the workers."[30] This assertion was in marked contrast to Leniz's earlier proposals.

By the end of the Junta's fourth year, the new social security law still had not been issued, but an article in *Chile Economic News* of November 1976 had indicated the lines along which the government was by then proposing to reorganize the social security system. After affirming that the government wanted to establish a single system of old age pensions in place of the multiple funds, according to professions and industries which had been the pattern, the article stated:

Pensions in the new system will be calculated on a single base of 10% of disposable income, deposited monthly in the person's account. This money will be reinvested by financial groups in safe medium- and long-term returnables. At retirement, a person will be paid monthly a sum equal to their investment plus interest on the returnables. An average person, for example, who pays the fund for 40 years will receive two and one-half times what he deposited. These pensions will be paid regardless of years of service and will be collectable for age 60 for women and age 65 for men.

Leniz's basic idea, whereby only the workers would contribute to the social security retirement system and employer and state contributions would be abolished, thus persisted. The only modification in his suggestion was that the investing of the workers' forced savings would be done "by financial groups" instead of by workers' representatives.

The article also described the government's ideas for changing the health insurance aspect of social security: "Health care is also being changed, eliminating the differences between workers and employees. The nationalized medical plan will take the same amount from everyone. Payments will be made along specified rates. Any person will be allowed to opt for a private health plan."[31]

THE SOCIAL STATUTE OF THE ENTERPRISE

As mentioned above, the Junta leaders early spoke of their intention of allowing the workers some participation in the management of Chilean enterprises. This premise took form in the so-called Social Statute of the Enterprise, which was first announced by General Gustavo Leigh in January 1975. At that time, General Leigh stated the workers wanted: "1. To take part in management; 2. To obtain security, recognition and identity; and 3. To participate in the results. . . . These three objectives can be obtained without the workers necessarily being owners of the enterprise in which they work."[32]

The statute was formally promulgated on May Day 1975. It provided for an elected representative of the workers, with a voice but not a vote, on boards of directors of enterprises, including agricultural firms, and for establishment of an Enterprise Council, composed of workers' representatives. This council was to be largely an organ for passing information to the workers and, according to the law, was to receive complete information on the functioning of the firm, including its financial affairs, its production programs, and other relevant data. The statute also provided for the possible establishment of arbitration tribunals of workers and management in cases of disagreement over application of the statute.[33]

A NEW LABOR CODE

On the same day that the Social Statute of the Enterprise was promulgated, President Pinochet submitted a draft of a new labor code to an assembled group of collaborationist union leaders. A thorough revision of the Labor Code had been a subject of discussion for many years and had been promised by the Junta sometime before the draft was issued.

President Pinochet outlined some of the major features of the proposed new Labor Code:

The project puts an end to the legal differentiation between manual and white collar workers.

It authorizes the unionization of the public sector, with limitations which are inherent in the problem and in terms which are in accord with world wide legislation, giving precedence to the general interests of the nation over those of particular groups of individuals.

It also establishes mechanisms for collective bargaining, giving an effective mediating capacity to the State, recognizing the right to strike, and seeking solution for whatever conflicts might arise.[34]

Although the president's May Day speech made it appear that the proposed new Labor Code was designed to strengthen the unions, a careful reading of its provisions indicates that such was not the case. Those labor leaders who were not collaborators with the Junta were strongly opposed to some of the code's major provisions.

The draft legislation provided for a complete reorganization of the structure of the labor movement and changed the basic unit of local union organization from the plant or warehouse to a provincial union of workers of a "branch of economic activity." In exceptional cases, the proposed Labor Code provided that some plant unions could be established, but obviously these were meant to be legally recognized only in rare instances.

As a result of the proposed new union structure, all existing unions would lose their legal recognition. The work of rebuilding a legally authorized labor movement would have to begin all over again. In order to form a provincial union, at least 25 percent of the workers of a particular "branch of economic activity" in a province would have to participate. Apparently, more than one union of a particular jurisdiction could be formed in a province, as long as each of these had at least 25 percent of the total group.

The proposed code also allowed the organization of federations and confederations of provincial unions in a "branch of economic activity." To form a federation, 25 percent of the unions of a "branch of economic activity" had to participate; to form a national confederation, 25 percent of the legal federations in the jurisdiction had to participate. There was no provision for a legally recognized central labor organization.

The draft code also provided that there would be no compulsory unionism. This contrasted with the existing Labor Code, according to which all eligible workers in a factory which had an "industrial union" automatically were members of the union. The proposed code also provided for the legality of strikes, except in industries "which affect the health or social or economic conditions or damage the collectivity or part of it or affect the security of the country," in which case the government could suspend the right to strike. It would seem difficult to imagine a strike in which at least one of the enumerated conditions did not exist; hence, for all practical purposes, the draft code seemed to eliminate the right to strike.[35]

Trade union leaders who were not unconditional collaborators of the Junta strongly opposed the government's draft Labor Code. They felt that the establishment of provincial unions as the basic unit of organization would mean the disappearance of most of the country's unions. As they saw it, under the conditions of fear and uncertainty existing under the Junta, only in a small minority of cases would it be possible to get 25 percent of the eligible workers of an economic category in a province to join the unions that had to be formed within a year of the promulgation of the new Labor Code. They also felt that the elimination of the union shop arrangement that existed under the old Labor Code would also weaken even the few unions that could be formed in conformity with the proposed new law.

Some employer elements also joined the opposition to the draft Labor Code, apparently fearful of the instability in labor relations that it would introduce. They, together with the trade union opponents of the draft, were able to convince the Junta to postpone promulgation of the code, which the government had originally proposed for the second anniversary of the coup The Ministry of Labor agreed to resubmit the draft code to both workers' and employers' organizations for criticism and amendment, and promised to take such suggestions seriously—although making no specific promises to modify the legislation. Late in July 1975, the minister of labor assured me that the projected Labor Code was still a draft and that no precipitate action would be taken to enact it.[36]

By the end of the fourth year of the Junta, the new Labor Code had still not been enacted.

THE VOCATIONAL TRAINING STATUTE

The other proposed piece of labor legislation upon which the Junta apparently put great store was the so-called Statute of Vocational Training of Workers. This measure established the obligation of employers to provide vocational education for their workers, although not going into detail concerning the nature and duration of such training. It set up a National Council of Vocational Training, with representatives of government, employers, and workers, which would establish the norms for such a program and supervise its fulfillment.[37]

In an interview I had with the minister of labor, General Nicanor Díaz

Estrada in July 1975, he was exceedingly enthusiastic about the long-run implications of this vocational training law. He insisted that it would be the vehicle for the "liberation" of the workers, since it would give every worker the possibility of receiving the training necessary for him to rise to a better job. The minister argued that once the law became a reality, only a worker's individual ambition and personal capacity would limit how far he could rise in the economic and social scale.[38] The trade union leaders tended to be very much less sanguine about the proposal, feeling that it might be of some help to some workers, but that it would not make any fundamental change in their status.

WAGE AND EMPLOYMENT CONSTRAINTS

Whatever the Junta's long-run intentions with regard to the Chilean working class and its trade union movement, the short-run effects of the government's economic policies on labor were catastrophic. There was a violent decline in the level of living of virtually all workers during the first four years of the Junta regime.

The only part of the economy that was not subjected to the free operation of the market was wages. These were strictly controlled by the government, and the tendency consistently was to have the increase in wages lag far behind the increase in the price level.

A government decree providing for general wage increases was being prepared by the Allende regime at the time of its overthrow and was supposed to go into effect in October 1973. The real wage of the workers had fallen massively during the middle months of 1973, a fact of which the Junta was quite aware. In an effort partially to offset this decline, the military government decreed that during the last three months of 1973 all workers were to receive payment for five months instead of three. Then at the beginning of 1974 the regime decreed a 500 percent wage increase. Since inflation had been something in the vicinity of 1,000 percent during 1973, it is doubtful that the government-decreed wage rise anywhere near offset the price increase.

During the first six months of 1974, the inflation was officially estimated at 173.4 percent, while during this same period, wage increases of only 50 percent were permitted. However, the government made some additional adjustments in take-home pay. The family allowance was increased from 200 escudos a head to 5,000 for each dependent member of a worker's family. In addition, "bonuses" of 5,200 escudos a month for transportation and 5,000 a month for lunch taken on the job were also enacted. Nevertheless, these far from prevented the decline in workers' real wages during this period.[39]

Subsequently, a system was adopted whereby wage increases were provided every three months, on the basis of the price increases during the previous quarter. However, wage increases consistently lagged behind the price increases during the period involved. Indeed, in mid-1975, the government decreed that the price increases of 19 and 16 percent which had occurred during May and June would not be included in calculations for wage purposes and that the next wage increase would be in October, covering July, August, and September.

In June 1975, *Latin America Economic Report* calculated that between September 1973 and September 1974 the real income of employed workers had fallen about 42 percent for those in private employment and 50 percent for government workers. Using figures from the May 1975 issue of *Mensaje,* the publication indicated that the cost of a "shopping basket" for a working-class family of five persons, containing only the most essential items, had risen between September 1974 and March 1975 from 1,923.5 escudos to 5,927 escudos, or 302 percent, whereas wages, including family allowances, had gone up 266 percent—this figure representing a further decline in real income of 13 percent for the six-month period.[40]

At the beginning of 1977, it was announced that the system of periodical wage increases would be altered. Instead of being given every three months, they would be enacted only in March, July, and December.[41] This, of course, meant that the workers would have to withstand continuing price increases for longer periods between wage rises, which in any case would only partly make up the loss of real wages in the preceding period.

In August 1975, a group of seventeen leading labor union officials, headed by Eduardo Ríos, sent an open letter to the ministers of economy, finance, and labor stressing the direness of the workers' plight. They argued that according to the official cost of living index, prices had risen 5,000 percent since the Junta had taken over, while wages had gone up only 2,500 percent. They were reported as demanding "wage settlements linked to the cost of living index, with a monthly trigger; subsidies of basic foods, and a price freeze on such items; an immediate bonus to cover the difference between wage settlements of July and the two months' inflation for May and June which these did not take into account; and better conditions for the unemployed."[42] The government paid little or no attention to the union leaders' arguments.

The decline in real wages of those workers still employed was accompanied by a massive increase in unemployment. As mentioned earlier, the government's figures consistently underestimated the real extent of unemployment, and it is not clear whether the official estimates included the several thousand workers who had been dismissed for political reasons, estimated by General Pinochet to number 100,000 by early 1974.[43]

In the early months of the Junta regime, there were provisions for dismissed workers to receive for three months a sum equivalent to three-fourths of the wage which they had been getting, with this subsidy being renewable for three additional periods of three months each.⁴⁴ By mid-1975, many thousands of workers had exhausted these benefits and were totally without money income.

Obviously, under the circumstances of the first four years of the Junta regime, collective bargaining was strictly forbidden. Furthermore, the government made little effort to consult with the leaders of the noncollaborationist trade unions with regard to the labor aspects of its general economic policy. As a result, organized labor had absolutely no input in government decisions vitally affecting the country's workers, since the collaborationist unionists merely parroted the words of the government. Trade union freedom obviously was incompatible with general political tyranny and an economic program that deliberately and drastically reduced the workers' levels of living.

35
The Nature of Chile's Tragedy

Chile's tragedy is the destruction, at least for the time being, of a uniquely open, tolerant, and civilized society. It is the ending of a long process of economic development and institutional transformation that was providing increasing quantities and a more equitable distribution of goods and services, as well as a high degree of freedom for the average citizen. It is the destruction of a stable polity and the opening of a long-run perspective of turbulence and tyranny.

Over a period of many decades, Chile had evolved from an aristocratic republic, in which economic and political power and social prestige were highly concentrated in the hands of a rural and commercial elite, into a democratic republic in which economic power was much more widely diffused among agriculturalists, industrialists, and (through their trade unions), middle-class and working people. At the same time, participation in the political process had been opened to all adult citizens, and the principal actors on the political stage had come to be the parties which drew their support from and represented the middle and working classes.

All of this had been carried out with a minimum of political upheaval and oppression, in conformity with Chile's long history of stable and civilian government. During almost the whole of the first three quarters of the twentieth century, only in the years 1924 to 1932 had there been successful coups and dictatorships. Although Chilean democracy had not worked perfectly—any more than democracy in any other country—and there had been governmental abuses and arbitrariness from time to time, Chile had come to be a nation in which the widest range of political thought and activity had been permitted and even encouraged.

These characteristics had made Chile distinctive in a world in which alternations between chaos and tyranny are all too often the rule. They had made it a country of far greater importance and international prestige than its small population and relatively modest role in world affairs would warrant. They were what made Chile's voice be listened to with respect in hemispheric and world councils.

Of course, this is not to say that Chile was a utopia. By the middle 1960s, it still had much unfinished business: it had to find new ways of continuing the expansion of its economy, of creating a wider distribution of its economic products, and of assuring more effective participation in national decision-making by the less highly placed members of the citizenry.

Major steps were taken in the latter half of the 1960s to complete this unfinished business. Under the aegis of the Christian Democratic government of President Eduardo Frei, rural unionization and land redistribution programs were launched to give the two million people who still worked or lived in agriculture a more effective control over their own destiny. Grass roots organizations of the poorer members of the society—neighborhood clubs, mothers' groups, youth organizations—were established under government patronage and were given legal recognition and encouragement, not only to become effective pressure groups on national and local governments, but also to be able to undertake programs in their localities on their own initiative. The tax system was revised to bear more heavily on the higher income groups. New initiatives and new directions were taken in the effort to give new vitality to economic development. Finally, the country's major source of income from abroad, the mining industry, was brought under national control and majority government ownership.

This apparently hopeful start in solving the major problems facing the country in the late 1960s turned into catastrophe in the first half of the 1970s. Severe economic crisis and almost total polarization of the body politic led to the first successful military coup in more than forty years and to the establishment of a tyranny such as Chile had not known since its early years as an independent nation. As this is being written, the tyranny persists, as does the economic crisis that helped give it birth, and no progress has been made in bridging the gap that has divided the Chilean people into two hostile camps. Indeed, the gap has grown wider.

The tragedy of Chile is that it may never be possible to reestablish the kind of society and polity which it enjoyed for so long. The country may well have been transformed into one more banana republic, where one arbitrary government succeeds another, only occasionally relieved by short periods of relative freedom bordering on chaos. It may not prove possible for Chile to obtain once again the high degree of civilization it once had, in which law and not arbitrary fiat ruled, in which the people were governed by those whom they chose, and in which public decisions were made and governments were changed by public exchange of views and by votes, rather than by organized or disorganized violence.

All elements in Chilean society to some degree share the responsibility for what has occurred to their country. Some bear a much larger burden of this responsibility than others, but there is no one who is completely innocent of blame. The elements of the extreme Right, authoritarian or totalitarian in ideology, contributed their share to the destruction of Chilean democracy. By plotting coups and arming small paramilitary groups, they helped to bring about the polarization of public opinion which destroyed the broad consensus upon which that democracy rested.

The economic and political conservatives—landowners and industrialists and their political expression, the Partido Nacional—also contributed to the process of disintegration. Their resistance to the changes brought about by the Frei regime, and their frequent assertions that the Christian Democratic government was "worse than the Marxists," created difficulties for the process of peaceful transformation of the society and economy. Furthermore, their mounting of the presidential candidacy of Jorge Alessandri, and the clear intention of many of them to use an Alessandri victory as a vehicle for obtaining "revenge" for what had occurred during the Christian Democratic regime, played directly into the hands of the Marxist-Leninists supporting Allende's campaign.

The Christian Democrats also had their share of responsibility. Factional fighting greatly handicapped the execution of the programs of the Frei regime. President Frei himself made major tactical mistakes in not paying sufficient attention to the problems of organized labor, and not supporting measures that would have reduced the ability of the Marxist-Leninist parties to manipulate the labor movement to gain and consolidate their own power. Radomiro Tomic made probably the greatest mistake of all the Christian Democrats in seeking to outflank Allende from the Left in the 1970 election campaign. His action resulted in few gains for his candidacy from that sector and at the same time sacrificed the support of moderate elements who felt that when faced with two nominees who seemed to be talking the same kind of language, they had no alternative but to vote for the third one, Jorge Alessandri.

The parties and leaders of the Unidad Popular had the greatest responsibility for creating the economic, social, and political conditions that led to the coup of September 11, 1973. They pushed ruthlessly ahead to carry forward a program that went considerably beyond their mandate; they deliberately sought "total power," even though theirs was a minority government; they refused any compromises that might have led to the maintenance of an elected civilian regime; and they first sought to manipulate and then to subvert the armed forces while at the same time extensively arming their own supporters. The Unidad Popular leaders thereby created a situation in which force became virtually the only alternative left.

Within the Unidad Popular, the leaders of the Socialist party have the greatest culpability for what happened. It was mainly they who were behind the refusal to compromise, it was they who openly and provocatively conspired in the armed forces, it was they who were more insistent on the right of the regime to do anything it wanted to do in spite of its lack of a popular mandate.

The Communists' responsibility was less and of a different nature. Although they did seek arrangements with the opposition which would have provided a broad basis for carrying out programs mutually agreed to, they were not forthright enough about this effort to pressure Allende into a compromise. They bore the major responsibility for the use of the organized labor movement as a political instrument for organizing demonstrations on behalf of the government, instead of as a tool for cooperation with the government's program in the economic field. Finally, during the last months of the regime, they caved in to pressures from their own Left and joined in the general euphoria and hysteria characterizing the Unidad Popular in that period.

President Salvador Allende had a special responsibility because of the office he held. Although apparently favoring compromises and policies that would have saved his regime from disaster, he hesitated until it was too late to break with those among his followers who not only were provoking a cataclysmic crisis but were welcoming it.

The MIR, too, must take its share of the blame. Continuing to insist on the need for a violent denouement to the situation of the Allende government, it openly called for a coup to liquidate, politically and physically, the elements opposed to the "Chilean Road to Socialism." They got a coup, but not the kind they had advocated.

Of course, the leaders of the armed forces were responsible in several ways for the tragedy of Chile. In the first place, they allowed themselves to be used by the Allende government on several occasions, apparently becoming its partners in pushing to conclusion a program that did not have a popular mandate. Then for their own reasons they overthrew the Allende regime. The military leaders must shoulder the major blame for the kind of regime that was established after this coup, a regime that negates the long tradition of Chilean democracy and tolerance, and that has brought economic misery and degradation to a vast proportion of the Chilean people.

Nor can elements outside of Chile be completely exonerated. The Nixon administration adopted a posture of outright hostility towards the Allende regime which only played into the hands of the more extreme elements within that regime. The CIA conspired ineptly with Right-wing elements in Chilean politics, and although its activities had little or nothing to do with the ultimate overthrow of the Allende regime, they contributed to the intense polarization of public opinion in Chile.

On the other hand, elements of the democratic Left in the United States and Europe—especially the European Socialists—were responsible for spreading the myth that the Allende regime was seeking to use democratic means to establish a democratic Socialist society, when in fact the major parties of that regime were using democratic means to achieve a totalitarian society. In doing so, they undoubtedly contributed to the illusions of many in the Allende regime that it had a degree of foreign support that would allow it to do virtually anything it wanted to do.

For the moment, the future of Chile rests with the top military leaders. They remain confused and uncertain as to their long-range goals and as to how long they intend to retain control. A resolution of these issues will undoubtedly depend upon what happens to the economy, how strong the resistance to the regime becomes and what form it takes, and, in the last instance, on the military leaders' own assessment of their situation and that of Chile as a whole.

Events outside of Chile will also help determine what road the country will take in the near future. Therefore, some foreign governments and public opinion in parts of the world where it can be openly expressed bear their share of the responsibility for what may happen in Chile. Public opinion in the United States is of particular importance. All believers in democracy in this country—whether they are conservative, liberal, or socialist—should exert what pressure they can to convince the military rulers of Chile of the urgent need to return to democracy and to begin to restore the kind of society which made Chile unique among the nations despite its small size. Such urgings cannot be in the name of the regime that has fallen; an apologia for Allende and his government has no place in an appeal for the restoration of democracy in Chile. The real issue is between political and social democracy on the one hand, and authoritarianism and totalitarianism of all kinds on the other—not between existing authoritarianism and a regime that was seeking the establishment of an all-encompassing totalitarianism, "total power."

Appendix 1:
The 91 Firms

Soon after taking office, Allende indicated that his administration wanted to have the following firms transferred from private ownership to either the mixed or social area of the economy.

TO MIXED AREA

Madeco: copper products
Inchalam
Vidrios Planos Lirquen: glass
American Screw
Standard Electric: telephone equipment
Interocean Gas
Aga
Indulsever: soaps and detergents
Hidols Cadena
Philips: electric products
Andona: bottling works
Cia. Chilena Tabacos: tobacco products
Pizarreño
Bata: shoes
Soinco
Catecu
Cia. Chilena Fósforos: matches
Cobre Cerrilos
Fesa
Nieto Hermanos
Burger
Calderón

Oxford
Dos Alamos
Lechera Sur: milk products
Electromat: electrical products
Pollak: food products
Paños Continental: textiles
Comandark
Cotesa
Saavedra Benard
Laja Crown
Sixtex: synthetic textiles
Oxiquim: chemical products
Farmoquímica del Pacifico: pharmaceuticals
Eperva
Macisa
Cholguna

TO SOCIAL AREA

Cia. Chilena de Teléfonos: telephone system
Hirmas: textiles
Yarur: textiles
Progreso: textiles
Oveja Tome: textiles
Rayonhil: textiles
Fanaloza: ceramics
General Electric: electric products
Compañia Industrial
Mademsa: heavy consumer goods
Cristalerias de Chile: glass
Sonap
Carburo y Metalurgia
Sindalen
Conafe
Gildemeister
Dupont: chemicals
Pesquera Industrial: fish products
Aceites y Alcoholes Patria: industrial oils and alcohol
Refractarios Lota Green: ceramics
Cimet
Ferriloza: ceramics
Corese
Mitjans
Coprona
Fanac
Agencias Graham: wholesaling

Tejidos Caupolican: textiles
Lanera Austral: textiles
Banyarte
Volcan
Sudamericana de Vapores: shipping
Copec: oil refining
CRAV
Fensa
Carozzi
Aceros Andes: steel products
Interoceánica: shipping
Cemento Biobio: cement
Sumer: textiles
Cervecerias Unidas: brewing
Rayon Said: textiles
Cia. Manufacturera de Papeles y Cartones: paper and pulp
Gasco: commercial gas
Cic
Indura
Codina
Cia. Teléfonos Valdivia: telephone service
Cia. de Gas de Concepción: commercial gas
Soprola
Chiprodal
Grace
Guanayo

Appendix 2:
The Military's Stated Reasons for Overthrowing Allende

The following is a translation of Edict No. 5 of the Junta Militar, as published in the September 8–15, 1973, issue of the international edition of *El Mercurio*:

Whereas,

1) The Government of Allende had incurred grave illegitimacy through destroying fundamental rights of freedom of expression, freedom of education, right of assembly, right of strike, right of petition, right of property, and right, in general, to a dignified and secure existence;

2) The same Government had broken national unity, fomenting artificially a sterile and in many cases bloody class struggle, losing the valuable contribution which every Chilean might make to seeking the welfare of the Fatherland, and carrying on a fratricidal, blind struggle in favor of ideas foreign to our national character, false and provenly failed;

3) The same Government showed itself incapable of maintaining coexistence among Chileans and by not obeying or enforcing the Law, gravely abused its power on many occasions;

4) Furthermore, the Government had placed itself outside the Constitution on many occasions, using doubtful judgment and tortuous and deliberate interpretations, or in other flagrant cases failing to apply it;

5) Also, using the subterfuge that they themselves have called "legal loopholes" they have failed to apply laws, they have violated others, and they have created illegal de facto situations;

6) Also, on reiterated occasions it destroyed the mutual respect which is due among the branches of the State, failing to carry out decisions of the National Congress, the Courts and the Comptroller General of the Republic, with inadmissable excuses or simply without explanation;

7) The Executive Branch has violated the limits of its authority, in a deliberate and obvious way, succeeding in accumulating in its hands, the greatest political and economic power, to the detriment of vital national activities and putting in grave danger all of the rights and freedoms of the inhabitants of the country;

8) The President of the Republic has demonstrated to the country that his personal power is conditioned upon the decisions of committees and executives of political parties and groups which associate with him, thus losing the image of maximum authority which the Constitution assigns him, and therefore the presidential character of the Government;

9) The agricultural, commercial and industrial economy of the country is paralyzed and in decline and the inflation is at an accelerated rate without there being any indication or preoccupation with this problem on the part of those entrusted with them by the Government, which appears to be a mere spectator;

10) There exists in the country anarchy, asphyxia of freedom, moral and economic deterioration and in the Government an absolute irresponsibility and incapacity which has made the situation of Chile worse, preventing it from taking the position which corresponds to it, as one of the leading nations of the continent;

11) All of the factors noted in the previous numbered paragraphs are sufficient to conclude that the internal and external security of the country were endangered, that the continuance of our existence as an independent State was menaced, and that the continuation of the Government is not in conformity with the high interests of the Republic and its Sovereign People.

12) These same factors are, in terms of classic doctrine which characterizes our historical thinking, sufficient to justify our intervention to depose an illegitimate, immoral Government unrepresentative of the national will, thus avoiding greater evils that the present vacuum of Power might produce, since to obtain this there are no other reasonably successful means of achieving our objective of reestablishing economic and social normality to the country, and the peace, tranquility and security which have been lost.

13) For all the reasons indicated, the Armed Forces have assumed the moral duty which the Fatherland imposes upon them to depose the Government which, although initially legitimate, has fallen into flagrant illegitimacy, assuming power only for so long as circumstances require supported by the evident feeling of the great national majority, which, in the face of God and History, makes just their actions, as well as the resolutions, norms and instructions which they issue to achieve the task for the common good and high patriotic interests which they are fulfilling.

14) Consequently, the legitimacy of these measures bears with it the obligation for the citizenry, and particularly the authorities, to obey and conform to them.

Notes

CHAPTER 5

1. Julio César Jobet, *El Partido Socialista de Chile,* Ediciones Prensa Latinoamericana, Santiago, 1971, Volume 2, page 49.

2. Ibid., page 85.

3. Ibid., page 104.

4. Ibid., page 55.

5. Fernando Monckenberg, *Jaque al Subdesarrollo,* Editora Nacional Gabriela Mistral Ltda., Santiago, 1974, page 61.

6. Ibid., page 62.

7. Ibid., page 67.

CHAPTER 7

1. *Latin American Digest,* March 1968, page 7.

2. *Intercontinental Press*, March 24, 1969, page 303.

CHAPTER 8

1. Lia Cortes and Jordi Fuentes, *Diccionario Político de Chile*, Editorial Orbe, Santiago, 1967, page 346.

2. *El Mercurio*, March 4, 1969, page 1.

3. This information was given to me by a former Socialist party leader who still remains in Chile, and who therefore, for reasons of his own personal safety, must remain anonymous.

4. Ernst Halperin, *Nationalism and Communism in Chile*, MIT Press, Cambridge, Mass., 1965, pages 170-177 has an extensive discussion of the Ampuero-Almeyda struggle.

5. See Julio César Jobet, *El Partido Socialista de Chile*, Ediciones Prensa Latinoamericana, Santiago, 1971, Volume 2, page 123.

6. *El Mercurio*, March 4, 1969, page 1.

7. *El Mercurio*, November 8, 1968.

8. *Intercontinental Press*, March 24, 1969.

9. *El Mercurio*, March 4, 1969.
10. Interview with Oscar Waiss in Santiago, July 3, 1968.
11. *El Mercurio*, September 3, 1969.
12. *El Mercurio*, International Edition, June 2-8, 1969.
13. *El Mercurio*, August 7, 1968.
14. *El Mercurio*, August 9, 1969.
15. *Ercilla*, June 25, 1971, pages 15-16.
16. *El Mercurio*, International Edition, January 6-12, 1969.
17. *El Mercurio*, International Edition, June 23-29, 1969.
18. *El Mercurio*, July 6, 1969.
19. *El Mercurio*, International Edition, January 19-25, 1970.
20. *El Mercurio*, International Edition, May 26-June 1, 1969.
21. *El Mercurio*, International Edition, November 10-18, 1969.
22. *El Mercurio*, March 4, 1969.
23. *Latin American Digest*, May 1968, page 8.
24. *Latin American Digest*, March 1967, page 8.
25. *New York Times*, January 19, 1967.

CHAPTER 9

1. *The Times of the Americas*, November 19, 1969.
2. *El Mercurio*, September 10, 1968.
3. *The Times of the Americas*, November 19, 1969.
4. Editorial in *El Mercurio*, October 13, 1968.
5. *El Mercurio*, International Edition, June 23-29, 1969.
6. *El Mercurio*, International Edition, October 13-19, 1969.
7. *El Mercurio*, International Edition, October 20-26, 1969.
8. All of the foregoing quotations are from *El Mercurio*, International Edition, October 20-26, 1969.
9. *Le Monde*, English language edition, December 3, 1969.
10. *El Mercurio*, International Edition, January 20-28, 1969.
11. *El Mercurio*, International Edition, December 22-28, 1969.

CHAPTER 10

1. Unless otherwise noted, the following observations on rural unionism are drawn from my own study of the problem in July and August 1968. For further discussion, see Robert J. Alexander, "Chilean Agricultural Workers Unionization During the Frei Administration," *Journal of Economic Issues*, September 1972.
2. Julio César Jobet, *El Partido Socialista de Chile*, Ediciones Prensa Latinoamericana, Santiago, 1971, Volume 2, page 78.
3. For the text of Law No. 16,625 and its regulations, see *Sindicación Campesina*, Edición Oficial, Santiago, 1967.
4. *La Verdad Sobre la Reforma Agraria*, Editorial del Pacífico, S.A., Santiago, n.d. (1966?).
5. For a more extensive study of the Frei Agrarian Reform Law, see Joseph R. Thome, "Expropriation in Chile Under the Frei Agrarian Reform," *American Journal of Comparative Law*, Summer 1971.
6. Thome, op. cit., page 496.
7. Ibid., page 513.
8. Ibid., page 513.
9. Ibid., page 513.
10. Interview with Jorge Cerda, president of Confederación de Pequeños Agricultores, in Santiago, July 4, 1968.

11. Eduardo Frei, *Quinto Mensaje del Presidente de la República de Chile, don Eduardo Frei Montalva al inaugurar el periodo de Sesiones Ordinarias del Congreso Nacional, 21 de Mayo de 1969*, Departamento de Publicaciones de la Presidencia de la República, May 1969, page 215.

12. Ibid., page 217.

13. Ibid., page 218.

14. Eduardo Frei, *La Unión Hace la Fuerza: Intervención del Presidente Frei a traves de la Red Nacional de Emisoras y Canales de Televisión los días 27 y 28 de Noviembre de 1967*, Editorial del Pacífico, Santiago, 1967, pages 14-15.

CHAPTER 11

1. For an extensive exposition of the Frei government's Chileanization program, particularly its economic implications, see Raúl Sáez, *Chile y el Cobre, Perspectivas de una Nueva Politica*, Publicidad Condor, Santiago, n.d.

2. Eduardo Frei, *Tercer Mensaje del Presidente de la República de Chile, don Eduardo Frei Montalva al inaugurar el periodo de Sesiones Ordinarias del Congreso Nacional, 21 de Mayo de 1967*, Departamento de Publicaciones de la Presidencia de la República, May 1967, page 411.

3. Ibid., page 412.

4. Ibid., pages 415-416.

5. *Le Monde*, October 25, 1969, page 5.

6. Eric Baklanoff, *Expropriation of U.S. Investments in Cuba, Mexico and Chile*, Praeger Publishers, New York, 1975, page 81.

7. *Chile Economic Notes*, May 8, 1970, page 3.

8. Frei, *Tercer Mensaje*, page 413.

9. *Chile Economic Background Information*, July 31, 1970, page 2.

10. Eduardo Frei, *Tercer Mensaje*, page 414.

11. Ibid., page 418.

12. Eduardo Frei, *Cuarto Mensaje del Presidente de la República de Chile, don Eduardo Frei Montalva al inaugurar el periodo de Sesiones Ordinarias del Congreso Nacional, 21 de Mayo de 1968*, Departamento de Publicaciones de la Presidencia de la República, May 1968, page 480.

13. Gary MacEoin, *No Peaceful Way: The Chilean Struggle for Dignity*, Sheed and Ward, Inc., New York, 1974, pages 51-53.

14. For a description and comment on the Chileanization program, see Baklanoff, op. cit., pages 75-83.

15. Sociedad Minera de Chile, *Informa Sobre la Nacionalización de la Industria Salitrera*, May 1971, pages 13-23.

16. Frei, *Tercer Mensaje*, page 179.

17. Ibid., pages 179-180.

18. Ibid., page 181.

19. *Chile Economic Notes*, June 13, 1970, page 1.

20. Ibid., page 4.

21. Ibid., pages 3-4.

22. Frei, *Tercer Mensaje*, pages 31-32.

23. Frei, *Cuarto Mensaje*, page 7.

24. *Chile Economic Notes*, June 13, 1970, pages 2-3.

25. Frei, *Quinto Mensaje del Presidente de la República de Chile, don Eduardo Frei Montalva al inaugurar el periodo de Sesiones Ordinarias del Congreso Nacional, 21 de Mayo de 1969*, Departamento de Publicaciones de la Presidencia de la República May 1969, page 86.

CHAPTER 12

1. For a more extensive description of Chilean labor relations, see Robert J. Alexander, *Labor Relations in Argentina, Brazil and Chile*, McGraw-Hill, New York, 1962, pages 237-255.

2. See William Thayer, *Trabajo, Empresa y Revolución*, Editorial Zig-Zag, Santiago, 1968.

3. Interview with Hector Alarcón, in Santiago, July 13, 1968.

4. *El Siglo*, July 5, 1968.

5. *El Mercurio*, September 26, 1968.

6. *Intercontinential Press*, December 16, 1968, page 1, 120.

7. *El Mercurio*, International Edition, November 26-December 1, 1968.

8. *El Mercurio*, International Edition, December 2-8, 1968.

9. *El Mercurio*, International Edition, December 1-7, 1969.

10. Eduardo Frei, *Quinto Mensaje del Presidente de la República de Chile, don Eduardo Frei Montalva al inaugurar el periodo de Sesiones Ordinarias del Congreso Nacional, 21 de Mayo de 1969*, Departamento de Publicaciones de la Presidencia de la República, May 1969, page 431.

11. Julio César Jobet, *El Partido Socialista de Chile*, Ediciones Prensa Latinoamericana, Santiago, 1971, Volume 2, page 144.

12. Eduardo Frei, *Cuarto Mensaje del Presidente del la República de Chile, don Eduardo Frei Montalva al inaugurar el periodo de Sesiones Ordinarias del Congreso Nacional, 21 de Mayo de 1968*, Departamento de Publicaciones de la Presidencia de la República, May 1968, page 63.

13. Frei, *Quinto Mensaje*, page 493.

CHAPTER 13

1. *El Siglo*, May 4, 1969.

2. *El Mercurio*, International Edition, April 7-13, 1969; see also *Latin America*, April 18, 1969, page 1.

3. *El Mercurio*, International Edition, August 11-17, 1969.

4. See Julio César Jobet, *El Partido Socialista de Chile*, Ediciones Prensa Latinoamericana, Santiago, 1971, Volume 2, pages 148-157, for further discussion of Socialist thinking about the establishment of Unidad Popular.

5. Ibid., Volume 2, page 157.

6. This information on Allende's nomination was provided by a Socialist friend who is still in Chile and who must therefore remain unidentified.

7. These quotations from the Unidad Popular program are translated from the program as it appeared in *El Mercurio*, December 23, 1969; see also *Programa Básico de Gobierno de la Unidad Popular*, (pamphlet), Santiago, 1970.

8. The full text of the Unidad Popular program can be found in *New Chile*, North American Congress on Latin America, Madison, Wis., 1973, pages 130-142.

9. *El Mercurio*, September 5, 1970, page 1; *El Siglo*, September 5, 1970, page 1; *Chile & Allende*, Facts on File, New York, 1974, page 31.

10. *Últimas Noticias*, September 5, 1970, page 5.

11. Lautaro Silva, *Allende: El Fin de una Aventura*, Ediciones Patria Nueva, Santiago, 1974, page 160.

12. Robert Moss, *El Experimento Marxista Chileno*, Editora Nacional Gabriela Mistral Ltda., Santiago, 1974, pages 41-42.

13. See *Chile & Allende*, pages 34-35.

14. *New York Times*, November 21, 1975, page 54; also see *Covert Action in Chile 1963-1973*, U.S. Government Printing Office, Washington, D.C., 1975, pages 10-11, for a discussion of CIA connection with Schneider murder.

15. *Chile & Allende*, page 35.

16. *El Mercurio*, September 25, 1970.

17. For the text of the Tribunal Constitucional amendment, see *Tribunal Constitucional de la República de Chile, Normas Constitucionales y Autos Acordados*, Editorial Jurídica de Chile, Santiago, 1972; and Silva, op. cit., pages 40-42.

CHAPTER 14

1. Cited in Pablo Baraona Urzua and others, *Fuerzas Armadas y Seguridad Nacional*, Ediciones Portada, Santiago, 1973, page 240.
2. See "La 'Vía Chilena' en Europa," *Plan*, May 31, 1971, page 5.
3. See Oscar Waiss, *Amanecer en Belgrado*, Prensa Latinoamericana, S.A., Santiago, n.d. (1956).
4. Ernst Halperin, *Nationalism and Communism in Chile*, MIT Press, Cambridge, Mass., 1965, page 158.
5. Julio César Jobet, *El Partido Socialista de Chile*, Ediciones Prensa Latinoamericana, Santiago, 1971, Volume 2, page 177.
6. *El Mercurio*, June 27, 1971.
7. *El Mercurio*, International Edition, March 13-19, 1972.
8. Since I do not know the present whereabouts of this individual, and so as not to put him in any more danger than he may now be, I shall leave him unidentified. However, he was one of the more prominent leaders of the Socialist party in the Allende period.
9. Hernan Millas and Emilio Filippi, *Chile 70-73: Crónica de una Experiencia*, Empresa Editora Zig-Zag, Santiago, 1974, pages 15-16.
10. Pedro Ibáñez, *The Chilean Crisis and Its Outcome*, 1974 (mimeographed), pages 11-12.
11. Régis Debray, *Conversations with Allende: Socialism in Chile*, Giangiacome Feltrinelli Editore, London, 1971, page 75.
12. Millas and Filippi, op. cit., page 13.
13. Salvador Allende, "The Chilean Victory Belongs to the People," *Socialist International Information*, December 1970, page 167.
14. Salvador Allende, *La Vía Chilena, del Primer Mensaje del Presidente Allende ante el Congreso Pleno, 21 de Mayo de 1971*, Empresa Editora Nacional Quimantú, Santiago, 1971, page 5.
15. Ibid., page 11.
16. Salvador Allende, *La Lucha por la Democracia Económica y las Libertades Sociales, del Segundo Mensaje del Presidente Allende ante el Congreso Pleno, 21 de Mayo de 1972*, Consejería de Difusión de la Presidencia de la República, Santiago, 1972, page 51.

CHAPTER 15

1. A list of sections of the Chilean economy controlled by the Corporación de Fomento can be found in *Basic Data* 1970, *Corporación de Fomento de la Producción, Chile,* New York and Santiago, 1970; and more extensively in Corporación de Fomento de la Producción, *Monografía de Empresas Filiales*, 1970, Santiago, 1970.
2. Eric Baklanoff, *Expropriation of U.S. Investments in Cuba, Mexico, and Chile,* Praeger Publishers, New York, 1975, page 89.
3. *Chile & Allende*, Facts on File, New York, 1974, page 51.
4. Baklanoff, op. cit., pages 90-91.
5. Ibid., page 90; for a discussion of the validity of Allende's calculations, see Baklanoff, pages 91-194.
6. Régis Debray, *Conversations with Allende: Socialism in Chile,* Giangiacome Feltrinelli

Editore, London, 1971, pages 110-111, quotes Allende as complaining particularly about this situation.

7. Interview with Max Nolf, president, Corporación del Cobre, in Santiago, July 5, 1971.

8. Quoted in Baklanoff, op. cit., page 102.

9. Lautaro Silva, *Allende: El Fin de una Aventura*, Ediciones Patria Nueva, Santiago, 1974, page 51.

10. *Breve Historia de la Unidad Popular: Documento de 'El Mercurio,'* El Mercurio S.A.P., Santiago, 1974, page 35.

11. Ibid., page 37.

12. Ibid., page 52.

13. Ibid., page 158.

14. Ibid., page 88.

15. Ibid., page 40.

16. Interview with a former Citibank Chilean management official, whose present whereabouts are unknown and who thus must remain anonymous.

17. *El Mercurio*, International Edition, January 17-23, 1972, page 7.

18. *El Mercurio*, International Edition, March 17, 1972, page 5.

19. A summary of Sáenz's major speeches during the first thirty months of the Unidad Popular regime can be found in Orlando Sáenz, *Un País en Quiebra: 33 Preguntas a Orlando Sáenz*, Ediciones Portada, Santiago, April 1973.

20. *El Mercurio*, September 26, 1971, page 1, gives the text of this decree.

21. See Carlos Charlin, *Del Avión Rojo a la República Socialista*, Empresa Editora Nacional Quimantú, Santiago, 1972, pages 816-887, for a discussion of the origins of this law and key excerpts from its text.

22. *La Prensa*, July 6, 1971.

23. *El Mercurio*, International Edition, November 20-26, 1972, page 5.

24. *El Mercurio*, February 2, 1973.

25. *El Mercurio*, April 11, 1973.

26. *La Prensa*, June 21, 1972.

27. Jaime Valdes, *La 'Clase' Dorada (o el Gobierno Secreto de la UP)*, privately published, Santiago, n.d. (1972), pages 58-60.

28. Alberto Baltra Cortes, *Gestión Económica del Gobierno de la Unidad Popular*, Editorial Orbe, Santiago, 1973, page 75.

29. *El Mercurio*, January 13, 1973.

CHAPTER 16

1. *Clarín*, January 2, 1972, page 13.

2. *El Mercurio*, International Edition, February 7-13, 1972, page 2.

3. *El Siglo*, June 26, 1972, page 7.

4. *El Siglo*, July 3, 1972.

5. Lautaro Silva, *Allende: El Fin de una Aventura*, Ediciones Patria Nueva, Santiago, 1974, page 48.

6. *Programa Básico de Gobierno de la Unidad Popular*, Santiago, June 1970, page 16.

7. Corporación de la Reforma Agraria, Relaciones Públicas, *ABC de la Reforma Agraria*, Santiago, n.d. (1971).

8. David Baytelman, *Resumen Extractado de la Exposición en Plenaria del Delegado de Chile*, IV Reunión Interamericana de Ejecutivos de Reforma Agraria, Panama, May 1972, page 7.

9. Ibid., page 8.

10. *Clarín*, January 2, 1972, page 13.

11. Interview with Luís Díaz, member of Executive Committee of Confederación Campesina El Triunfo Campesino, in Santiago, July 11, 1973.

12. Baytelman, op. cit., pages 7-8.

13. Corporación de la Reforma Agraria, *Organización Transitoria de la Nueva Area de Reforma Agraria: Los Centros de Reforma Agraria* (mimeographed), n.d., page 9.

14. Alfredo Barahona Zuleta, *Una Verdadera Reforma Agraria Esta en Marcha*, Corporación de la Reforma Agraria, Relaciones Públicas, Santiago (mimeographed), n.d., page 13.

15. Salvador Allende, *La Lucha por la Democracia Ecónomica y las Libertades Sociales, del Segundo Mensaje del Presidente Allende ante el Congreso Pleno, 21 de Mayo de 1972*, Consejería de la Difusión de la Presidencia de la República, Santiago, 1972, page 35.

16. *El Mercurio*, January 27, 1972.

17. *El Mercurio*, June 20, 1972.

18. Robert Moss, *El Experimento Marxista Chileno*, Editora Nacional Gabriela Mistral, Ltda., Santiago, 1974, page 100.

19. Ibid., page 100.

20. *El Mercurio*, April 13, 1973.

21. *El Mercurio*, December 1, 1972.

22. Interview with Eduardo Alessandri, June 21, 1972.

23. *Christian Science Monitor*, March 13, 1971, pages 1-2.

24. *Intercontinental Press* quotes *Le Monde* in issue of October 4, 1971.

25. *El Mercurio*, November 14, 1971.

26. Moss, op. cit., page 101.

27. *El Mercurio*, International Edition, February 21-27, 1972, page 4.

28. Moss, op. cit., page 101.

29. *El Mercurio*, March 29, 1972.

30. Interview with Luís Salamanca, treasurer, Confederación Nacional Campesina el Triunfo Campesino, in Santiago, July 5, 1972.

31. Silva, op. cit., page 65.

32. Ibid., pages 65-66.

33. Moss, op. cit., page 102.

34. *El Mercurio*, January 2, 1972.

35. Moss, op. cit., page 94.

36. Ibid., page 105.

37. Ibid., page 106; "La Agricultura en 1972," an article appearing in the anti-UP periodical *Portada*, last quarter 1972, pages 23-25, describes the growing crisis in agriculture at that time.

38. See Gary MacEoin, *No Peaceful Way: The Chilean Struggle for Dignity*, Sheed and Ward, Inc., New York, 1974, pages 102-103, for instance.

39. Quoted in Moss, page 104.

CHAPTER 17

1. Alberto Baltra Cortes, *Gestión Económica del Gobierno de la Unidad Popular*, Editorial Orbe, Santiago, 1973, page 15.

2. Ibid., page 20.

3. Ibid., page 15.

4. Ibid., page 10.

5. Ibid., page 13.

6. Ibid., page 17.

7. Robert Moss, *El Experimento Marxista Chileno*, Editorial Nacional Gabriela Mistral Ltda., 1974, pages 89-90.

8. Cited by Baltra, op. cit., page 17.

9. Baltra, op. cit., page 12.

10. *Pueblo*, Oficina de Informaciones y Radiodifusión de la Presidencia de la República, Chile, Santiago, n.d. (1971), page 4. The full text of Allende's 1971 May Day speech can be found in Salvador Allende, *El Futuro de la Revolución Chilena Esta en las Manos de los Trabajadores*, Consejería de Difusión de la Presidencia de la República, Santiago, 1971.

11. Baltra, op. cit., page 24.

12. Ibid., page 24-25.

13. Ibid., page 25.

14. Quoted in Baltra, op. cit., page 136.

15. Statement by Professor Paul Rosenstein-Rodan in *Statement Made by Mr. Fernando Leniz and Others*, Editora Nacional Gabriela Mistral, Santiago, 1974, page 27.

16. Baltra, op. cit., page 79.

17. Ibid., page 78.

18. Ibid., page 82.

19. Ibid., pages 82-83.

20. *Pueblo*, op. cit., page 6.

21. Baltra, op. cit., page 82.

22. *Punto Final*, August 15, 1972, page 17.

23. *World Affairs Report*, Volume 2, No. 4, page 269.

24. Baltra, op. cit., page 92.

25. Ibid., page 76.

26. Cited in Baltra, op. cit., page 120.

27. Cited in Baltra, op. cit., page 122.

28. Cited in Baltra, op. cit., page 119.

29. Baltra, op. cit., page 92.

30. Cited in Baltra, op. cit., page 18.

31. Baltra, op. cit., page 98.

32. Ibid., page 99.

33. Ibid., page 99.

34. Ibid., page 101.

35. Ibid., page 102.

36. Ibid., page 103.

37. Moss, op. cit., page 68.

38. Ibid., page 78.

39. Salvador Allende, *La Lucha por la Democracia Económica y las Libertades Sociales, del Segundo Mensaje del Presidente Allende ante el Congreso Pleno, 21 de Mayo de 1972*, Consejería de la Difusión de la Presidencia de la República, Santiago, 1972, page 38.

40. *U.S.: Consejería Nacional de Desarrollo Social*, Departamento Relaciones Públicas, C.N.D.S., Santiago, n.d., page 7.

41. Quoted in *Economía de Chile Durante el Periodo de Gobierno de La Unidad Popular: La Vía Chilena al Marxismo*, Escuela de Negocios de Valparaíso: Fundación Adolfo Ibáñez, March 1974, page 10.

42. Baltra, op. cit., pages 65-67.

43. Ibid., page 67.

44. *Que Pasa?*, November 2, 1973, page 7, reported in Jeffrey B. Gayner and Lawrence D. Pratt, *Allende and the Failure of Chilean Marxism*, Heritage Foundation, Inc., Washington, D.C., 1974, page 1.

45. Baltra, op. cit., page 60.

46. *La Economía de Chile Durante el Periodo*, page 28.

47. Lorenzo Gotuzzo Borlando, *Exposición sobre el Estado de la Hacienda Pública, Presentada por el Ministro de Hacienda Contralmirante don Lorenzo Gotuzzo Borlando, Octubre de 1973*, Dirección de Presupuestos, Santiago, October 1973, Pamphlet No. 124, page 10; also see *Realidad y Destino de Chile*, Editora Nacional Gabriela Mistral, Santiago, 1973, page 42.

48. Boorstein's letter reprinted in Lautaro Silva, *Allende: El Fin de una Aventura*, Ediciones Patria Nueva, Santiago, 1974, pages 120-24.

49. Baltra, op. cit., page 56.

50. Moss, op. cit., page 66.

51. Salvador Allende, *La Vía Chilena, del Primer Mensaje del Preisdente Allende ante el Congreso Pleno, 21 de Mayo de 1971*, Empresa Editora Nacional Quimantú, Santiago, 1971, page 19.

CHAPTER 18

1. *El Mercurio*, International Edition, December 6-12, 1971, page 4.

2. *El Mercurio*, International Edition, December 12-19, 1971.

3. *El Mercurio*, International Edition, December 6-12, 1971, page 4.

4. *El Mercurio*, International Edition, December 13-19, 1971.

5. *El Mercurio*, International Edition, December 13-19, 1971.

6. *El Mercurio*, June 26, 1972.

7. *Puro Chile*, June 20, 1972.

8. *El Popular*, Communist newspaper of Montevideo, Uruguay, June 7, 1972.

9. Article by James and Eva Cockroft, *All You Can Eat*, September 1972, page 11.

10. *New York Times*, July 16, 1972, page 20.

11. Cockroft, op. cit., page 11.

12. *La Prensa*, July 7, 1972.

13. *Que Pasa?*, June 22, 1972, page 43.

14. *La Prensa*, July 2, 1971.

15. *El Mercurio*, December 19, 1971.

16. Salvador Allende, *La Lucha por la Democracia Económica y las Libertades Sociales, del Segundo Mensaje del Presidente Allende ante el Congreso Pleno, 21 de Mayo de 1972*, Consejería de la Presidencia de la República, Santiago, 1972, pages 37-38.

17. *El Mercurio*, February 23, 1972.

18. *El Mercurio*, April 4, 1973.

19. Comité Ejecutivo Nacional CUT-Gobierno de Participación, *Informe, Comité Ejecutivo Nacional CUT-Gobierno para la Participación de los Trabajadores en la Dirección de las Empresas del Area Social y Mixta*, Santiago, n.d. (1971) (mimeographed), page 1.

20. Presidencia de la República, Oficina de Planificación Nacional, *Normas Básicas de Participación de los Trabajadores en la Administración de las Empresas del Area Social y Mixta*, Santiago, n.d. (1971) (mimeographed), page 20.

21. Interview with James Wilson, graduate student of Cornell University, studying the problem of workers' participation in management in Chile, in Santiago, August 21, 1974.

22. Presidencia de la República, Oficina de Planificación Nacional, op. cit., page 6.

23. Ibid., pages 7-11.

24. Cockroft, op. cit., page 11.

25. *El Mercurio*, International Edition, January 12-23, 1972.

26. Article by Andy Zimbalist and Barbara Stallings, "Showdown in Chile," *Monthly Review*, October 1973, page 12.

27. *Puro Chile*, May 23, 1972, page 26.

28. *El Mercurio*, International Edition, August 23-29, 1971.

29. *Puro Chile*, May 23, 1972.

30. *Chile Hoy*, June 16, 1972, page 14.

31. *La Prensa*, June 14, 1972.

32. Central Única de Trabajadores, *Pongale el Hombro a la Patria: Llamamiento de la CUT a los Trabajadores*, Santiago, May 1971, pages 5, 6.

33. *La Segunda*, July 5, 1971; *El Siglo*, July 6, 1971; *La Prensa*, July 6, 1971.

34. *El Mercurio*, October 24, 1971.

35. *El Mercurio,* International Edition, January 17-23, 1972.

36. *La Tribuna*, July 7, 1972.

37. *El Mercurio*, September 29, 1972.

38. *El Mercurio*, September 30, 1972.

39. *El Mercurio*, November 8, 1972.

40. *El Mercurio*, February 22, 1973.

41. *El Mercurio*, December 20, 1972.

42. Editorial in *El Mercurio*, International Edition, August 2-8, 1971.

43. *El Mercurio*, International Edition, May 2-7, 1972.

44. *El Mercurio*, October 16-22, 1972.

45. *El Mercurio*, July 10, 1973.

46. *Wall Street Journal*, June 18, 1973.

47. For a discussion of the El Teniente strike, see *Chile & Allende*, Facts on File, 1974, New York, pages 125-129.

CHAPTER 19

1. *Chile Economic Notes*, May 12, 1972, page 8.

2. *Alliance for Progress Weekly Newsletter*, February 1, 1971, page 1.

3. *El Mercurio*, February 8, 1973.

4. *Chile & Allende*, Facts on File, New York, 1974, page 103.

5. Ibid., page 101.

6. Ibid., pages 65-66.

7. Ibid., page 104.

8. Ibid., page 112.

9. Ibid., page 105.

10. Ibid., page 105.

11. Ibid., page 63.

12. Ibid., page 36.

13. Ibid., page 63.

14. Ibid., page 102.

15. *El Mercurio*, January 3, 1973.

16. The post-Allende government presented the Organization of American States with a list of interventions of the Castro government in Chilean affairs during the Allende period. See Embassy of Chile, Washington, D.C., *Castro's Intervention in Chile*, Washington, D.C., n.d. (1974).

17. *El Mercurio*, November 14, 1971.

18. *El Mercurio*, November 28, 1971.

19. *Intercontinental Press*, December 6, 1971.

21. *New York Times*, December 21, 1971, quoted in Jeffrey B. Gaynor and Lawrence D. Pratt, *Allende and the Failure of Chilean Marxism*, Heritage Foundation, Inc., Washington, D.C., 1974, page 13.

22. Hernan Millas and Emilio Filippi, *Chile 70-73: Crónica de una Experiencia*, Empresa Editorial Zig-Zag, Santiago, 1974, page 96.

23. *Chile & Allende*, page 102.

24. *Socialist International Information*, November 11, 1970, page 164.

25. Speech by Harald Edelstam, former Swedish ambassador to Chile, at Rutgers University, New Brunswick, N.J., March 8, 1974.

26. *Chile Economic Notes*, May 12, 1973.

CHAPTER 20

1. For example, see the books of Lawrence Birns (editor), *The End of Chilean Democracy: An IDOC Dossier on the Coup and Its Aftermath*, Seabury Press, New York, 1974; and Gary MacEoin, *No Peaceful Way: The Chilean Struggle for Dignity*, Sheed and Ward, Inc., New York, 1974.

2. Salvador Allende, *Chile, Speech Delivered by Dr. Salvador Allende, President of the Republic of Chile Before the General Assembly of the United Nations, December 4, 1972*, Embassy of Chile, Washington, D.C., n.d. (1972), page 14.

3. Paul Sigmund, "The 'Invisible Blockade' and the Overthrow of Allende," *Foreign Affairs*, January 1974, page 327.

4. Interview with Edward Korry in New York, September 19, 1973.

5. Sigmund, op. cit., page 327.

6. Ibid., page 328.

7. Ibid., page 329.

8. Ibid., pages 329-330.

9. Allende, op. cit., pages 15-16.

10. Sigmund, op. cit., page 330.

11. Ibid., page 334.

12. Ibid., page 333.

13. Ibid., page 335.

14. *El Mercurio*, February 25, 1972.

15. Sigmund, op. cit., page 335.

16. *El Mercurio*, July 9, 1973.

17. For instance, see the article "El Bloqueo Yanqui Estrángula a Chile," *Punto Final*, June 20, 1972.

18. Ibid.

19. Robert Moss, *El Experimento Marxista Chileno*, Editorial Nacional Gabriela Mistral Ltda., Santiago, 1974, page 83.

20. Sigmund, op. cit., page 333.

21. Ibid., page 332.

22. Ibid., pages 332-333.

23. Ibid., page 333.

24. Ibid., page 336.

25. Speech by Harald Edelstam, former Swedish ambassador to Chile, at Rutgers University, New Brunswick, N.J., March 8, 1974.

26. Alberto Baltra Cortes, *Gestión Económica del Gobierno de la Unidad Popular*, Editorial Orbe, Santiago, 1973, page 110.

27. *Latin America*, July 20, 1973, page 227.

28. Baltra, op. cit., pages 111-112.

29. Ibid., page 113.

30. Sigmund, op. cit., page 333.

31. *Chile Economic Notes*, June 13, 1970, page 2.

32. *Covert Action in Chile 1963-1973*, Staff Report of the Select Committee to Study Governmental Operations with respect to Intelligence Activities, U.S. Senate, U.S. Government Printing Office, Washington, D.C., 1975, page 20.

33. Ibid., page 21.

34. Ibid., pages 21-22.

35. Ibid., page 13; also see *Subversion in Chile: The Complete Set of IT&T Memos*, Non-Intervention in Chile, Madison, Wis., n.d., for documentation on ITT activities during and just after 1970 election in Chile.

36. All foregoing quotations are from *Covert Action in Chile 1963-1973*, page 24.

37. Ibid., page 25.

38. Ibid., page 25.

39. Ibid., page 26.

40. Ibid., page 27.

41. Ibid., pages 28, 29.

42. Ibid., page 31.

43. *Covert Action in Chile*, op. cit., page 31.

44. *El Camionero*, November 1972, page 60.

45. *Covert Action in Chile 1963-1973*, page 28.

46. MacEoin, op. cit., page 100.

47. Sigmund, op. cit., page 334.

48. Birns (editor), op. cit., page 155.

49. *Covert Action in Chile 1963-1973*, page 36.

50. Ibid., page 28.

51. *Chile & Allende*, Facts on File, New York, 1974, page 60.

52. MacEoin, op. cit., page 169.

53. Ibid., page 170.

54. Salvador Allende, *La Vía Chilena, del Primer Mensaje del Presidente Allende ante el Congreso Pleno, 21 de Mayo de 1971*, Empresa Editora Nacional Quimantú, Santiago, 1971, page 31.

55. Summary of Staff Report of Church Committee, *New York Times*, December 5, 1975, page 10.

56. *Chile & Allende*, op. cit., page 60.

57. Sigmund, op. cit., page 325.

CHAPTER 21

1. Transcript of an interview with Fidel Castro by Dan Rather, October 2, 1974, page 6.

2. Tomás MacHale, *El Frente de Libertad de Expresión (1970-1972)*, Ediciones Portada, Santiago, 1972, pages 49-54.

3. A discussion of Allende's relations with *El Mercurio* can be found in MacHale, op. cit., pages 69-95.

4. Ibid., pages 195-198.

5. Ibid., pages 57-58.

6. Ibid., pages 198-202.

7. Ibid., pages 202-205.

8. Ibid., pages 55-56.

9. Ibid., pages 120-122.

10. Ibid., pages 159-160.

11. An extensive discussion of the Allende regime and television can be found in MacHale, op. cit., pages 157-193.

12. An extensive discussion of the Allende regime and radio can be found in MacHale, op. cit., pages 133-155.

13. Ibid., page 18.

14. Ibid., page 19.

15. Ibid., pages 32-33.

16. Ibid., page 32.

17. Ibid., page 34.

18. Ibid., page 37.

19. Ibid., page 36.

20. Robert Moss, *El Experimento Marxista Chileno*, Editora Nacional Gabriela Mistral Ltda., Santiago, 1974, pages 28, 76.

21. See *Programa Básico de Gobierno de la Unidad Popular*, Santiago, June 1970, page 12.

CHAPTER 22

1. *El Mercurio*, April 6, 1971.

2. *Chile & Allende*, Facts on File, New York, 1974, page 43.

3. Ibid., page 69.

4. *Breve Historia de la Unidad Popular: Documento de 'El Mercurio,'* El Mercurio S.A.P., Santiago, 1974, page 145.

5. Ibid., page 146; also see *Chile & Allende*, page 82.

6. *Chile & Allende*, page 82; also *El Mercurio*, International Edition, April 3-9, 1972.

7. *Breve Historia*, page 1974; and interviews with Bernardo Leighton, in Santiago, June 29, 1972, and Renan Fuentealba, in Santiago, August 20, 1974.

8. Salvador Allende, *La Lucha por la Democracia Económica y las Libertades Sociales, del Segundo Mensaje del Presidente Allende ante el Congreso Pleno, 21 de Mayo de 1972*, Consejería de la Difusión de la Presidencia de la República, Santiago, 1972, page 46.

9. Ibid., page 47.

10. Robert Moss, *El Experimento Marxista Chileno*, Editora Nacional Gabriela Mistral Ltda., Santiago, pages 53-54.

11. Quoted in Dale Johnson (editor), *The Chilean Road to Socialism*, Anchor Books, Garden City, N.Y., 1973, page 287.

12. *Breve Historia*, page 305.

13. *Chile & Allende,* page 99.

14. Cited in *Intercontinental Press*, January 25, 1971.

15. Orlando Millas, "La Clase Obrera en las Condiciones del Gobierno Popular," *Punto Final*, June 20, 1972, page 14.

16. *El Siglo*, June 19, 1971.

17. "Declaración del Comité Político, Partido Comunista de Chile, 7 de Junio 1971," *Boletín Informativo del Comité Central del Partido Comunista de Chile*, June 1971, No. 5 (mimeographed).

18. *El Siglo*, June 26, 1971; for the full text of a major polemical article by the Communists against the MIR during the early months of the UP regime, see Johnson (editor), op. cit., pages 371-376.

19. *El Siglo*, June 25, 1971.

20. *El Mercurio*, International Edition, February 1-6, 1972, page 4.

21. Cited in *El Mercurio*, International Edition, February 7-13, 1972, page 4.

22. *El Mercurio*, International Edition, April 20-26, 1972, page 6.

23. *El Siglo*, June 26, 1972.

24. *El Mercurio*, April 4, 1973.

25. *El Siglo*, June 25, 1971, page 4.

26. *El Siglo*, June 23, 1972, page 5.

27. *El Siglo*, June 26, 1972, page 4.

28. Quoted in Johnson (editor), op. cit., page 179.

29. *El Mercurio*, March 16, 1972.

30. *El Mercurio*, September 9, 1973.

31. Quoted in Peter Camejo, *Allende's Chile, Is It Going Socialist?*, Pathfinder Press, New York, 1971, page 12.

32. Quoted in Gerry Foley and Malik Miah, *Tragedy in Chile: Lessons of the Revolutionary Upsurge and Its Defeat*, Pathfinder Press, New York, 1973, page 4.

33. This information was provided me by sources who are still in Chile and must therefore remain anonymous.

34. Julio César Jobet, *El Partido Socialista de Chile*, Ediciones Prensa Latinoamericana, Santiago, 1971, Volume 2, page 169.

35. Ibid., Volume 2, pages 141, 171.

36. Ibid., Volume 2, pages 42, 171.

37. Ibid., Volume 2, page 173.

38. Ibid., Volume 2, page 173.

39. Ibid., Volume 2, page 174.

40. Ibid., Volume 2, page 175.

41. *Latin America*, June 1, 1973, pages 174-175.

42. Jobet, op. cit., Volume 2, pages 180-181.

43. *El Mercurio*, March 8, 1973.

44. *El Mercurio*, June 27, 1971.

45. Moss, op. cit., page 62.

46. Speech of Carlos Altamirano to Socialist Plenum, reported in *El Mercurio*, September 9, 1973.

47. *La Prensa*, June 15, 1972.

48. *El Mercurio*, January 29, 1973.

49. *El Mercurio*, November 13, 1972.

50. *White Book of the Change of Government in Chile 11th September 1973*, Empresa Editora Nacional Gabriela Mistral Ltda., Santiago, n.d., pages 120-121, Document No. 5.

51. *El Mercurio*, March 31, 1973.

52. Régis Debray, *Conversations with Allende: Socialism in Chile*, Giangiacomo Feltrinelli Editore, London, 1971, page 163. A somewhat different translation of this same document is given in *New Chile*, published by the North American Congress on Latin America, Madison, Wis. 1973, pages 143-149.

53. Debray, op. cit., page 188.

54. Ibid., pages 172-173.

55. *Anatomía de un Fracaso (La Experiencia Socialista Chilena)*, Empresa Editora Zig-Zag, S.A., Santiago, 1973, page 47.

56. See ibid., pages 55-63.

57. Allende, *La Lucha por la Democracia*, page 47.

58. Hernan Millas and Emilio Filippi, *Chile 70-73: Crónica de una Experiencia*, Empresa Editora Zig-Zag, Santiago, 1974, page 59.

59. This judgment is based on a conversation with a military leader who was particularly involved in "wiping up" MIR strongholds following the coup of September 11, 1973; see Moss, op. cit., for a description of Comandante Pepe, MIR guerrilla, pages 132-133.

60. Millas and Filippi, op. cit., page 66.

61. *Chile & Allende*, page 123.

62. *Breve Historia de la Unidad Popular*, page 408.

63. *El Mercurio*, International Edition, September 9-15, 1973, page 5.

CHAPTER 23

1. *El Mercurio*, August 4, 1971.

2. *El Mercurio*, August 5, 1971.

3. *El Mercurio*, October 6, 1971.

4. *El Mercurio*, March 29, 1972.

5. *El Mercurio*, International Edition, April 3-9, 1972, editorial; and *Intercontinental Press*, April 24, 1972, page 459.

6. Hernan Millas and Emilio Filippi, *Chile 70-73: Crónica de una Experiencia*, Empresa Editorial Zig-Zag, Santiago, 1974, pages 103-109.

7. *El Mercurio*, International Edition, July 26-August 1, 1971.

8. *El Mercurio*, October 24, 1971.

9. *Times of the Americas*, March 1, 1972.

10. Robert Moss, *El Experimento Marxista Chileno*, Editora Nacional Gabriela Mistral Ltda., Santiago, 1974, page 138.

11. Ibid., page 140.

12. Ibid., page 141.

13. Interview with Bernardo Leighton in Santiago, June 29, 1972.

14. Interview with Renán Fuentealba in Santiago, August 20, 1974.

15. Moss, op. cit., page 141.

16. Interview with Renán Fuentealba in Santiago, August 20, 1974.

17. *El Mercurio*, International Edition, September 9-15, page 5.

CHAPTER 24

1. For more information on the number and equipment of the armed forces, see *The Statesmen's Yearbook 1971/72*, Macmillan, London, 1971, pages 807-808.

2. Robert Moss, *El Experimento Marxista Chileno*, Editora Nacional Gabriela Mistral Ltda., Santiago, 1974, page 169.

3. Quoted in Gary MacEoin, *No Peaceful Way: The Chilean Struggle for Dignity*, Sheed and Ward, Inc., New York, 1974, page 73.

4. Ibid., page 155.

5. Article by Robinson Rojas in *Causa ML*, Santiago, July-August 1971, quoted in Dale Johnson (editor), *The Chilean Road to Socialism*, Anchor Books, Garden City, N.Y., 1973, page 317.

6. *Chile: A Critical Survey*, Institute of General Studies, Santiago, 1972, page 314.

7. *International Socialist Review*, February 1972, page 34.

8. This information was given to me by a source who was close to Allende; as the source is still in Chile, it must stay anonymous.

9. *El Mercurio*, International Edition, September 18-24, 1972, page 3.

10. *Chile: A Critical Survey*, page 315.

11. Moss, op. cit., page 172.

12. Interview with ex-President Gabriel González Videla in Santiago, June 22, 1972.

13. *El Mercurio*, International Edition, October 30-November 5, 1972, page 1.

14. Moss, op. cit., page 167.

15. *Intercontinental Press*, September 10, 1973, page 983.

16. Moss, op. cit., page 204.

17. Ibid., page 205.

18. Ibid., page 207.

19. Ibid., page 206.

20. Ibid., page 160.

21. *Chile & Allende*, Facts on File, New York, 1974, page 99.

22. Ibid., page 96.

23. Moss, op. cit., pages 159-160.

24. *El Mercurio*, October 31, 1971.

25. *El Mercurio*, June 25, 1971.

26. *Breve Historia de la Unidad Popular: Documento de 'El Mercurio,'* El Mercurio, S.A.P., Santiago, 1974, pages 166-167.

27. *El Mercurio*, Extraordinary International Issue, September 1973, page 15; for a more

extensive discussion of this incident, see Hernan Millas and Emilio Filippi, *Chile 70-73: Crónica de una Experiencia*, Empresa Editorial Zig-Zag, Santiago, 1974, page 89-93.

28. *El Mercurio*, April 1, 1972.

29. For a synthesis of Law No. 17,798, see Sergio Miranda C., "Las Fuerzas Armadas en el Ordenamiento Jurídico Chileno," in Pablo Baraona Urzua and others, *Fuerzas Armadas y Seguridad Nacional*, Ediciones Portada, Santiago, 1972, pages 55-60.

30. See *El Mercurio*, International Edition, August 13-19, page 7 (1973).

31. *El Mercurio*, International Edition, September 9-15, 1973, page 5.

CHAPTER 25

1. Salvador Allende, *La Lucha por la Democracia Económica y Libertades Sociales, del Segundo Mensaje del Presidente Allende ante el Congreso Pleno, 21 de Mayo de 1972*, Consejería de la Difusión de la Presidencia de la República, Santiago, 1972, pages 31-32.

2. Interview with Leon Vilarín, in Santiago, August 13, 1974.

3. Ibid.

4. *Breve Historia de la Undiad Popular: Documento de 'El Mercurio,'* El Mercurio, S.A.P., Santiago, 1974, page 230.

5. *El Camionero*, November 1972, page 1.

6. *Breve Historia*, pages 243-244. The October 1972 issue of *El Camionero* gives the statements issued by virtually all of the groups which joined in the strike movement of October 1972. It also contains many of the statements issued by pro-government spokesmen.

7. Robert Moss, *El Experimento Marxista Chileno*, Editora Nacional Gabriela Mistral Ltda., Santiago, 1974, page 159; *Breve Historia*, page 233.

8. *Chile & Allende*, Facts on File, New York, 1974, page 98.

9. Moss, op. cit., page 160.

10. Ibid., pages 160-161; *Chile & Allende,* page 98; *Breve Historia*, page 237.

11. *Chile & Allende*, page 98.

12. *Breve Historia*, page 243.

13. Ibid., page 244.

14. See *Breve Historia*, for a day-by-day account of the October-November 1972 crisis, pages 228-247; also see *Chile & Allende*, pages 98-99. For the text of the government statement resulting in the end of the strike, see *El Camionero*, November 1972, pages 13-14.

15. *Breve Historia*, page 244.

16. *Chile & Allende*, page 113.

17. *Breve Historia*, page 289.

18. Jeffrey B. Gaynor and Lawrence D. Pratt, *Allende and the Failure of Chilean Marxism*, Heritage Foundation, Inc., Washington, D.C., 1974, page 15.

19. *Breve Historia*, page 286.

20. Ibid., page 296.

21. Ibid., page 313.

22. Ibid., page 332.

23. Ibid., page 337.

24. Ibid., page 338.

25. Ibid., page 342.

26. Ibid., page 362.

27. *Latin America*, May 25, 1973, page 165.

28. *Breve Historia*, page 318.

29. Ibid., page 329.

30. Ibid., page 339.

31. Ibid., page 346.
32. Ibid., page 328.
33. Ibid., page 342.
34. Ibid., page 343.
35. Ibid., pages 356-357.
36. Ibid., page 357.
37. Ibid., page 359.
38. Ibid., page 360.
39. Ibid., page 318.
40. Ibid., page 330.
41. Ibid., page 331.
42. Ibid., page 332.
43. Ibid., pages 332-333.
44. Ibid., page 325.
45. Ibid., page 324.
46. Ibid., page 323.
47. Ibid., page 338.
48. Ibid., page 327.
49. Ibid., page 336.
50. Ibid., page 333.
51. Ibid., page 335.
52. Ibid., page 341.
53. Ibid., page 345.
54. Ibid., page 349.
55. Ibid., page 339.
56. Ibid., page 343.
57. Ibid., page 362.
58. Ibid., page 345.
59. Ibid., pages 368-369.
60. A description of and comment on the *tancazo* is to be found in *Latin America*, July 6, 1973, pages 209, 212.
61. *Breve Historia*, pages 369, 371.

CHAPTER 26

1. *Breve Historia de la Unidad Popular: Documento de 'El Mercurio,'* El Mercurio, S.A.P., Santiago, 1974, page 373.
2. Gerry Foley and Malik Miah, *Tragedy in Chile: Lessons of the Revolutionary Upsurge and Its Defeat*, Pathfinder Press, New York, 1973, pages 5-6, gives details on the Sumar incident.
3. *Breve Historia*, page 378. See *Chile: Never Again! How the Revolution Was Betrayed*, Revolutionary Socialist League Publishing Co., 1974, page 11, for a description of the *cordones industriales.*
4. *Breve Historia*, page 396.
5. Ibid., pages 389-390.
6. *Latin America*, August 3, 1973, page 242.
7. All major statements of Congress, the Supreme Court, and the comptroller general questioning the constitutionality of acts of the Allende government can be found in *Algunos Fundamentos de la Intervención Militar en Chile Septiembre 1973*, Editora Nacional Gabriela Mistral Ltda., Santiago, 1974.
8. *Breve Historia*, page 370.

9. Ibid., page 375.

10. Alberto Baltra Cortes, *Gestión Económica del Gobierno de la Unidad Popular*, Editorial Orbe, Santiago, 1973, page 32.

11. Ibid., page 33.

12. Ibid., pages 34-35.

13. Ibid., pages 35-36.

14. Ibid., page 39.

15. *Quiebra del Estado de Derecho Durante el Regimen Marxista de Salvador Allende y Adhesión del Colegio de Abogados al Nuevo Gobierno de Chile: Antecedentes*, Santiago, de Chile, October 1973, page 17.

16. Ibid., page 21.

17. Ibid., page 22.

18. Ibid., page 23.

19. Ibid., pages 24-25.

20. Ibid., page 27.

21. Ibid., page 28.

22. Ibid., page 29.

23. Ibid., pages 29-30.

24. Ibid., page 40.

25. *El Camionero*, March-May, 1973, page 1.

26. *Breve Historia*, page 386.

27. Ibid., page 393.

28. Ibid., page 413.

29. Ibid., page 415.

30. Ibid., page 374.

31. Ibid., page 237.

32. Ibid., page 397.

33. Ibid., page 404.

34. Ibid., page 405.

35. Ibid., page 405.

36. Ibid., page 407.

37. *Latin America*, August 31, 1973, page 273.

38. *Breve Historia*, page 413.

39. Ibid., page 409.

40. Ibid., page 400.

41. Ibid., page 382.

42. Ibid., page 378.

43. Ibid., page 394.

44. Ibid., page 395.

45. Ibid., page 401.

46. Ibid., page 408.

47. Ibid., page 410.

48. *El Mercurio*, International Edition, September 8-15, 1973, page 5.

49. *Breve Historia*, page 384.

50. Ibid., page 403.

CHAPTER 27

1. The foregoing description is based on the Extraordinary International Edition of *El Mercurio*, September 1973, pages 1 and 8; also see Hernan Millas and Emilio Filippi, *Chile 70-73: Crónica de una Experiencia*, Empresa Editora Zig-Zag, Santiago, 1974, pages 7-10. One of the most complete accounts of the coup is to be found in *Ercilla*, September 25-October 2,

1973; see also *Anatomía de un Fracaso (La Experiencia Socialista Chilena)*, Empresa Editora Zig-Zag, Santiago, 1973, pages 7-20.

2. *El Mercurio*, International Edition, September 8-15, 1973, page 6.

3. Hugo Blanco and others, *The Coup in Chile: Firsthand Report and Assessment*, Pathfinder Press, New York, 1973, page 11.

4. *Latin America*, November 9, 1973, page 357.

5. *La Nación*, Buenos Aires, August 9, 1974.

6. This information was supplied to me by someone who was in the presidential palace at the time, but who must remain anonymous.

7. Full details on the alleged Plan Z can be found in *White Book of the Change of Government in Chile 11th September 1973*, Empresa Editora Nacional Gabriela Mistral Ltda., Santiago, n.d. (1973).

8. Laurence Birns (editor), *The End of Chilean Democracy: An IDOC Dossier on the Coup and Its Aftermath*, Seabury Press, New York, 1974, page 40.

9. *El Mercurio*, International Edition, September 8-15, 1973, page 1.

CHAPTER 28

1. *El Mercurio*, Extraordinary International Edition, September 1973, page 2.

2. *El Mercurio*, International Edition, September 8-15, 1973, page 1.

3. *El Mercurio*, International Edition, September 8-15, 1973, page 1.

4. *Latin America*, March 12, 1976, page 81.

5. *Chile & Allende*, Facts on File, New York, 1974, page 169.

6. *Latin America Political Report*, March 18, 1977, page 82.

7. *Latin America Political Report*, February 11, 1977, page 44.

8. Latin America, August 29, 1975, page 266.

9. *Latin America*, January 20, 1976, page 34.

10. This quotation is the author's translation from Augusto Pinochet: *A Seis Mese de la Liberación Nacional, Mensaje al País del Presidente de la Junta de Gobierno, General Augusto Pinochet Ugarte, Pronunciado del Día 11 de Marzo de 1974, al Cumplirse Seis Mese de Gobierno*, Empresa Editora Nacional Gabriela Mistral, Santiago, 1974, page 6. There is also an English version: *Address Delivered by President of Junta, General Augusto Pinochet Ugarte on March 11th 1974, on Occasion of the Sixth Month Anniversary of the New Government*, Junta de Gobierno de Chile, Press Department, Santiago, 1974.

11. Ibid., page 36; see *Chile: Under Military Rule*, IDOC/North America, 1974, for several discussions of the allegedly fascist nature of the Junta regime.

12. "Chile Under the Junta: Eyewitness Report," in *USLA Reporter*, Emergency Issue, November 1973, page 5.

13. *Latin America*, September 20, 1974, page 290.

14. *Latin America*, November 5, 1976, page 336.

15. *El Mercurio*, International Edition, September 24-30, 1973, page 4.

16. *Latin America*, January 17, 1975, page 21.

17. *Latin America*, October 10, 1975, page 314.

18. *Latin America*, November 5, 1976, page 338.

19. *New York Times*, June 19, 1977.

20. Jeffrey B. Gaynor and Lawrence D. Pratt, *Allende and the Failure of Chilean Marxism*, Heritage Foundation, Inc., Washington, D.C., 1974, page 39; also see *Refugees and Humanitarian Problems in Chile*, U.S. Government Printing Office, Washington, D.C., 1973.

21. *Latin America*, December 13, 1974, page 392.

22. Amnesty International, USA, *Desaparecidos: Disappeared in Chile*, n.d. (1977).

23. *Latin America*, May 10, 1974, page 144.

24. *Latin America*, December 6, 1974, page 381.

25. Amnesty International, USA, op. cit., page 3.

26. In my visit to Chile in July 1975, I heard of such cases from people to whom they had happened.

27. Hugo Blanco and others, *The Coup in Chile: Firsthand Report and Assessment*, Pathfinder Press, New York, 1973, page 7.

28. *Chile & Allende*, Facts on File, New York, 1974, pages 168-169.

29. Gaynor and Pratt, op. cit., page 41.

30. *Latin America*, August 15, 1975, pages 254-255.

31. Amnesty International, op. cit.

32. *El Mercurio*, International Edition, September 9-15, 1973, page 1.

33. *El Mercurio*, International Edition, September 24-30, 1973, page 1.

34. *Latin America*, November 5, 1976, page 338.

35. *Latin America Political Report*, April 8, 1977, page 108.

36. *Latin America,* September 19, 1975, page 292.

37. *El Mercurio*, International Edition, September 17-23, 1973, page 1.

38. *Latin America*, May 17, 1974, page 149.

39. *Latin America Political Report*, April 22, 1977, page 130.

40. *Constitutional Acts Proclaimed by the Government of Chile, September 11, 1976*, Impresora Filadelfia, Santiago, n.d. (1976), page 7.

41. Ibid., pages 8-9.

42. *Latin America*, July 16, 1976, page 222.

43. *Latin America Political Report*, March 18, 1977, page 82.

44. *Constitutional Acts*, page 9.

45. Ibid., page 12.

46. Ibid., pages 14-15.

47. *Constitución Política de la República de Chile*, Conforme a la Edición Oficial, incluidas todas las modificaciones hasta el 16 de Julio de 1971, Editorial Nasciemento, Santiago, 1972, page 4.

48. *Constitutional Acts*, page 18.

49. Ibid., page 12.

50. *Constitución Política de la República de Chile*, pages 7-17.

51. *Constitutional Acts*, page 39.

52. *Constitución Política de la República de Chile*, page 36.

53. See Pinochet, *Address Delivered by President of Junta*, page 26.

54. Ibid., page 5.

55. *El Mercurio*, International Edition, May 22-26, 1977, page 1.

56. *El Mercurio*, International Edition, May 15-21, 1977, page 1.

57. *El Mercurio*, International Edition, June 5-11, 1977, page 1.

CHAPTER 29

1. *El Mercurio*, International Edition, September 17-23, 1973, page 1.

2. *El Mercurio*, International Edition, September 24-30, 1973, page 1.

3. *El Mercurio*, International Edition, March 13-19, 1977, page 1.

4. *Latin America Political Report*, March 18, 1977, page 81.

5. *El Socialista*, Paris, December 21, 1976, page 11.

6. *Latin America Political Report*, June 2, 1977, page 161.

7. *Latin America*, October 11, 1974, page 314.

8. *Latin America*, January 2, 1976, page 3.

9. *Intercontinental Press*, December 15, 1975, page 1767.

10. *Latin America*, December 5, 1975, page 384.

11. Cited in Victor Perlo, *End Fascist Terror and U.S. Imperialism in Chile*, New Outlook Publishers, New York, February 1974, page 9.

12. *World Marxist Review*, July 1974, page 89.

13. *World Marxist Review*, July 1974, page 89.

14. *World Marxist Review*, July 1974, page 91.

15. *Latin America*, November 19, 1976, page 360.

16. *Latin America*, December 24, 1976, page 393.

17. *Latin America Political Report*, January 21, 1977, page 20.

18. *El Mercurio*, Extraordinary International Edition, September 1973, page 7.

19. *Latin America*, February 15, 1974, page 54.

20. *Latin America*, December 6, 1974, page 381.

21. *Latin America*, June 6, 1975, page 174.

22. Eduardo Frei, *El Mandato de la Historia y las Exigencias del Porvenir*, 2nd edition, Editorial Democracia y Humanismo, Buenos Aires, March 1976, page 92.

23. Ibid., page 102.

24. *Latin America*, November 22, 1974, page 362.

25. *Latin America*, October 3, 1975, page 306.

26. *Latin America*, July 25, 1975, page 228.

27. Reported in *Latin America*, October 18, 1974, page 326.

28. *Latin America*, August 13, 1976, page 256.

29. *Latin America*, October 10, 1975, page 314.

30. *Latin America Political Report*, March 18, 1977, page 82.

31. *Latin America*, September 24, 1976, page 289.

32. *Latin America Political Report*, June 3, 1977, page 161.

33. *El Mercurio*, International Edition, June 2-8, 1975, page 4; also see *Latin America*, June 20, 1975, page 185.

34. *El Mercurio*, International Edition, December 24-30, 1975, page 5.

35. *El Mercurio*, International Edition, November 17-23, 1975, page 6.

36. *Latin America*, January 23, 1976, page 32.

37. *Latin America*, July 30, 1976, page 239.

38. *Latin America*, April 16, 1976, page 128.

39. *Latin America*, July 30, 1976, page 239.

40. *Latin America*, November 5, 1976, page 338.

41. *Chile & Allende*, Facts on File, New York, 1974, page 171.

42. The events of May Day 1975 are recounted in *Latin Ameria*, May 9, 1975, page 138.

43. *Latin America Political Report*, May 27, 1977, page 159.

44. *Latin America*, September 12, 1975, page 281.

45. *Latin America*, September 17, 1975, page 287.

46. *Latin America Political Report*, April 29, 1977, page 128.

47. *Latin America Political Report*, April 28, 1977, page 108; The bishops' statement was published in full by *El Mercurio*, March 26, 1977, page 27.

48. *Latin America Political Report*, April 29, 1977, page 128.

49. Cited in *Latin American Report*, September 1974, page 2.

50. *Latin America*, October 10, 1975, page 314.

51. *Latin America*, October 31, 1975, page 344.

CHAPTER 30

1. *Latin America Political Report*, February 18, 1977, page 51.

2. *El Mercurio*, International Edition, September 8-15, 1973, page 3.

3. For an early discussion of the sensitiveness of the Junta to foreign criticism, see *Latin America*, December 14, 1973, page 396.

4. *Latin American Report*, November 1974, page 2; see also *World Affairs Report*, March 1975, page 39.

5. *Latin America*, July 18, 1975, page 223.

6. See *The GDR's Fervent Solidarity with the Courageous Chilean People*, Panorama DDR, Berlin, n. d. (1973).

7. *Chile Today*, November 29, 1974, page 1.

8. See *Military Junta Unleashes Terror in Chile; GDR Suspends Relations*, Panorama DDR, Berlin, n.d. (1973); see also *The GDR's Fervent Solidarity with the Courageous Chilean People*.

9. *Latin America*, September 28, 1973, page 312.

10. *World Affairs Report*, June 1975, page 137.

11. *Desafío*, New York, November 11, 1976.

12. *Peking Review*, August 9, 1975, page 39.

13. *Peking Review*, October 15, 1976, page 25.

14. *Peking Review*, October 8, 1976, page 40.

15. *Peking Review*, September 24, 1976, page 30.

16. *Latin America*, August 20, 1976, page 264.

17. *El Mercurio*, March 2, 1976.

18. *Latin America*, June 12, 1976, page 167.

19. *New York Times*, December 18, 1974, page 3.

20. *El Mercurio*, International Edition, March 21-27, 1976, page 3.

21. *El Mercurio*, International Edition, March 7-13, 1976, page 3.

22. *El Mercurio*, International Edition, March 28-April 3, 1976.

23. See *Chile Today*, May 1976, pages 1-2; also *El Mercurio*, International Edition, May 2-8, 1976, page 1.

24. *Intercontinental Press*, June 21, page 962. *El Mercurio* published the text of the Human Rights Commission Report and the Chilean government's reply, International Edition, June 6-12, 1976, page 3.

25. *New York Times*, September 27, 1974, page 18.

26. *El Mercurio*, November 7, 1976, page 3.

27. *Latin America Political Report*, June 3, 1977, page 161.

28. *Latin America*, December 7, 1973, page 392; see also *Latin America*, November 30, 1973, page 384.

29. *Latin America*, December 17, 1976, page 386.

30. *Latin America*, December 24, 1976, page 394.

31. *Latin America*, December 17, 1976, page 386.

32. *Latin America*, December 24, 1976, page 394.

33. *Latin America*, July 18, 1975, page 223.

34. *El Mercurio*, International Edition, November 11-17, 1975, page 3.

35. *Latin America*, January 2, 1976, page 8.

36. *El Mercurio*, January 22, 1975.

37. *El Mercurio*, November 21, 1975.

38. *El Mercurio*, International Edition, November 17-23, 1975, page 3.

39. *El Mercurio*, November 26, 1975, page 1.

40. *El Mercurio*, January 23, 1975.

41. *El Mercurio*, March 13, 1975.

42. *El Mercurio*, March 27, 1976.

43. *Latin America*, October 31, 1975, page 340.

44. *Three Years of Destruction*, Asimpress, Santiago, n.d. (1973), page 34.

45. *World Affairs Report*, March 1975, page 33.

46. *World Affairs Report*, June 1975, page 34.

47. *El Mercurio*, International Edition, December 2-8, 1974.
48. *Latin America*, August 22, 1975, page 264.
49. *FBIS*, November 2, 1976.
50. *Latin America*, May 17, 1974, page 152.
51. *Latin America*, May 24, 1974, page 158.
52. *El Mercurio*, International Edition, April 26-31, 1976, page 1.
53. *El Mercurio*, International Edition, December 2-6, 1974, page 3.
54. *El Mercurio*, International Edition, March 22-28, 1976, page 5.
55. *Latin America*, October 1, 1976, page 304.
56. *Latin America Political Report*, April 8, 1977, page 107.
57. *Latin America*, May 24, 1974, page 158.
58. *El Mercurio*, International Edition, November 7-14, 1976, page 1.
59. *Latin America*, December 19, 1975, page 395.
60. *El Mercurio*, International Edition, May 1-7, 1977, page 1.
61. *Latin America Political Report*, May 6, 1977, page 129.
62. *Latin America*, March 19, 1976, page 93.
63. *Latin America*, November 26, 1976, page 368.
64. *El Mercurio*, November 21-27, 1976, page 1.

CHAPTER 31

1. *Latin America Political Report*, June 17, 1977, page 180.
2. *El Mercurio*, International Edition, March 20-26, 1977, page 6.
3. *El Mercurio*, International Edition, April 10-16, 1977, page 3.
4. *El Mercurio*, October 24, 1976.
5. *Latin America*, November 23, 1973, page 376.
6. This estimate is based on information I received when I was in Chile in July 1974.
7. *Latin America*, December 23, 1973, page 376; see also Patricia Fagen, "Report on the Universities of Chile," in *Newsletter—The International Council on the Future of the University*, July 1974.
8. *El Mercurio*, International Edition, August 11-17, 1975, page 1.
9. *El Mercurio*, International Edition, December 28, 1975-January 4, 1976.
10. *Latin America*, February 6, 1976, page 47.
11. *El Mercurio*, February 15, 1976.
12. *El Mercurio*, December 24, 1975.
13. *El Mercurio*, International Edition, July 11-16, 1976, page 5.
14. *El Mercurio*, International Edition, January 23-28, 1977, page 5.
15. *Latin America Political Report*, June 17, 1977, page 180.
16. *Latin America*, September 12, 1975, page 288.
17. For a discussion of the closing of *La Prensa*, see *Latin America*, March 1, 1976, pages 69-70.
18. *Latin America*, January 25, 1974, page 30.
19. *El Mercurio*, International Edition, September 22-28, 1975, page 5.
20. *El Mercurio*, September 14, 1975.
21. *El Mercurio*, International Edition, September 22-28, 1975.
22. *Latin America Political Report*, February 4, 1977, page 40.
23. *Latin America*, January 23, 1974, page 30.
24. *El Mercurio*, International Edition, January 6-10, 1976, page 7.
25. *El Mercurio*, International Edition, January 25-31, 1976, page 7.
26. *El Mercurio*, International Edition, May 15-21, 1977, page 3.
27. *El Mercurio*, International Edition, September 23-29, 1974.
28. *Presencia*, La Paz, April 3, 1974, page 10.

29. *El Mercurio*, International Edition, March 23-30, 1975, page 5.

30. *El Mercurio*, International Edition, October 26-November 3, 1974, page 5.

CHAPTER 32

1. *Chile Economic News*, February 1977, page 2.

2. *Chile Economic News*, September 1976, page 3.

3. *Latin America*, September 12, 1975, page 281.

4. *Chile Economic News*, February 1977, page 2.

5. *El Mercurio*, International Edition, May 29-June 4, 1977, page 1.

6. *Chile Economic News*, February 1977, page 2.

7. *Realidad y Destino de Chile*, Editora Nacional Gabriela Mistral Ltda., Santiago, 1975, page 39.

8. Interview with Sergio de Castro, subsecretary of economy, in Santiago, August 22, 1974.

9. *Latin America*, October 26, 1973, page 342.

10. Interview with Sergio de Castro, subsecretary of economy, in Santiago, August 22, 1974.

11. *Latin America*, May 2, 1975, page 134.

12. *Latin America Economic Report*, January 14, 1977, page 6.

13. *Latin America*, May 2, 1975, page 134.

14. Interview with Arturo Arrigorriaga Leal, economist of Sociedad de Fomento Fabril, in Santiago, July 25, 1975.

15. This information comes from an opposition economist, who must remain anonymous.

16. *Latin America*, October 24, 1975, page 335; also see *Ercilla*, October 8-14, 1975, pages 35-37.

17. *El Mercurio*, International Edition, April 3-9, 1977, page 2.

18. *Latin America Economic Report*, April 9, 1976, page 58.

19. *Chile Economic News*, June 1975, page 4.

20. *El Mercurio*, International Edition, January 25-31, 1976, page 7.

21. *Ercilla*, October 8-14, 1975, pages 18-19.

22. *Memorandum Económico Latinoamericano*, October 18, 1976, page 4.

23. *Latin America Economic Report*, February 20, 1976, page 32.

24. Interview with Horacio Aranguiz Donoso, secretary general, Confederación de Productores Agrícolas, in Santiago, August 16, 1974.

25. *Latin America*, January 31, 1975, page 39.

26. *El Mercurio*, International Edition, February 27-March 5, 1977, page 6.

27. This information is from an economist who must remain anonymous.

28. *Latin America Economic Report*, January 7, 1977, page 1.

29. *Latin America Economic Report*, January 14, 1977, page 6.

30. *Latin America Economic Report*, January 7, 1977, page 1.

31. *Latin America Economic Report*, January 14, 1977, page 6.

32. *Latin America Economic Report*, June 24, 1977, page 93.

33. *El Mercurio*, International Edition, February 27-March 5, 1977, page 1.

34. *El Mercurio*, International Edition, April 13-19, 1977, page 7.

35. *Latin America Political Report*, February 4, 1977, page 40.

36. *Latin America Political Report*, January 14, 1977, page 15.

37. *Latin America Economic Report*, January 14, 1977, page 6.

38. *El Mercurio*, International Edition, August 11-17, 1975, page 1.

39. *Informe Económico*, October 1975, page 37.

40. *El Mercurio*, International Edition, August 11-17, 1975, page 1.

41. *El Mercurio*, International Edition, May 22-28, 1977, page 2.

42. *Latin America Economic Report*, March 18, 1977, page 43.

43. *Latin America*, February 1, 1974, page 37.

44. *Latin America*, March 28, 1975, page 100.

45. *El Mercurio*, International Edition, February 20-26, 1977, page 3.

46. *El Mercurio*, International Edition, February 27-March 5, 1977, page 1.

47. *Chile Economic News*, June 1976, page 9.

48. *Latin America Commodities Report*, December 10, 1976, page 6.

49. *Latin America Political Report*, May 6, 1977, page 132.

50. *Latin America Economic Report*, June 25, 1976, page 100.

51. *Latin America Commodities Report*, December 10, 1976, page 6.

52. Figures from *El Mercurio*, International Edition, May 8-14, 1977, page 4.

53. *El Mercurio*, International Edition, September 22-28, 1975.

54. *Latin America*, March 12, 1976, page 82, citing the *New York Times*.

55. *El Mercurio*, International Edition, April 17-23, 1977, page 1.

56. *El Mercurio*, International Edition, April 17-23, 1977, page 1.

57. *Chile Economic Notes*, February 1977, page 4.

58. *El Mercurio*, International Edition, April 3-9, 1977, page 2.

59. *Chilegram*, January 1977, page 10.

60. *El Mercurio*, International Edition, February 27-March 5, 1977, page 7.

61. *El Mercurio*, International Edition, April 24-30, 1977, page 8.

CHAPTER 33

1. *El Mercurio*, International Edition, October 20-26, 1975, page 5.

2. *Latin America*, June 6, 1975, page 174.

3. *El Mercurio*, International Edition, October 10-16, 1976, page 1.

4. *Latin America Economic Report*, March 12, 1976, page 43.

5. *El Mercurio*, International Edition, October 10-16, 1976, page 1.

6. *Latin America*, July 18, 1975, page 219.

7. *Latin America Economic Report*, March 4, 1976, page 36.

8. *Latin America Economic Report*, January 14, 1977, page 6.

9. *Bases de la Política Agraria de la Junta de Gobierno*, ICIRA, Santiago, n.d. (1973), page 5.

10. *La Patria*, August 16, 1974, page 3.

11. *El Mercurio*, International Edition, February 20-26, 1977, page 7.

12. *Latin America Economic Report*, March 26, 1976, page 49.

13. *El Mercurio*, International Edition, May 15-21, 1977, page 6.

14. *El Mercurio*, International Edition, May 22-28, 1977, page 4.

15. *El Mercurio*, International Edition, February 20-26, 1977, page 7.

16. *Chile Today*, December 30, 1974, page 1.

17. *Chile Economic News*, April 1977, page 3; for 1974 decree-law, see *Estatuto de la Inversión Extranjera*, Corporación de Fomento de la Producción, Santiago, n. d. (1974).

18. *Latin America Economic Report*, January 16, 1976, page 12.

19. *El Mercurio*, International Edition, October 20-26, 1975, page 2.

20. *Latin America Economic Report*, March 12, 1976, page 43.

21. *Latin America Economic Report*, April 9, 1976, page 58.

22. *El Mercurio*, April 24, 1975.

23. *Latin America Economic Report*, June 17, 1977, page 89.

24. *Chilegram*, October 1976, page 4.

25. *Chile Economic News*, May 1976, page 7.

26. *Chile Economic News*, May 1976, page 8.

27. *Chile Economic News*, October 1976, page 5.

28. *El Mercurio*, International Edition, October 31-November 5, 1976, page 1.

29. *El Mercurio*, International Edition, January 30-February 5, 1977, page 2.

30. See *El Mercurio*, International Edition, January 25-31, 1976, page 5.

31. *El Mercurio*, International Edition, February 13-19, 1977, page 3.

32. *El Mercurio*, International Edition, January 9-15, 1977, page 3.

33. Interview with Sergio de Castro, subsecretary of economy, in Santiago, August 22, 1974.

34. *Latin America*, May 10, 1974, page 139.

35. *El Mercurio*, International Edition, May 1-7, 1977, page 2.

36. Interview with Sergio de Castro, subsecretary of economy, in Santiago, August 22, 1974.

37. *El Mercurio*, International Edition, June 27-July 3, 1976, page 2.

38. *Latin America Economic Report*, October 22, 1976, page 164.

39. *El Mercurio*, International Edition, January 2-8, 1977, page 5.

40. *El Mercurio*, International Edition, October 10-16, 1976, page 2.

41. *El Mercurio*, International Edition, November 21-27, 1976, page 7.

42. *El Mercurio*, International Edition, May 15-21, 1977, page 5.

CHAPTER 34

1. *El Mercurio*, International Edition, September 17-23, 1973, page 7.

2. *El Mercurio*, International Edition, September 24-30, 1973, page 1.

3. *El Mercurio*, Extraordinary International Edition, September 1973, page 2.

4. *El Mercurio*, International Edition, May 1-7, 1977, page 6.

5. *El Mercurio*, International Edition, September 24-30, 1973, page 5.

6. Interview with General Nicanor Díaz Estrada, minister of labor, in Santiago, July 25, 1975.

7. *Latin America*, December 10, 1976, page 384.

8. *El Camionero*, July 1974, pages 57-59, carries the text of Decree-Law No. 198.

9. *Latin America*, June 20, 1975, page 192.

10. *International Trade Union News*, December 15, 1974, page 3.

11. Letter from George Meany to General Pinochet, dated March 20, 1974.

12. *AFL-CIO Free Trade Union News*, September 1974, page 2.

13. *Latin America Political Report*, April 1, 1977, page 99.

14. *International Trade Union News*, October 15, 1974, page 1; see also article by Andrew McLellan in *AFL-CIO Free Trade Union News*, December 1975.

15. *El Mercurio*, International Edition, April 28-May 3, 1974, page 1.

16. This information was supplied during my visit to Chile in July 1975 by members of the 1974 Chilean Workers' Delegation to the International Labor Organization Annual Conference.

17. I was able to observe some of this activity while in Chile in July 1975.

18. *El Mercurio*, International Edition, March 27-April 2, 1977, page 6.

19. *Latin America*, August 29, 1975, page 266.

20. Information concerning leaders of the minority ''collaborationist'' group of trade union leaders was supplied during my visit to Chile in July 1975 by people who were friends of some of them.

21. *Latin America*, October 8, 1976, page 309.

22. *Latin America Political Report*, May 27, 1977, page 159.

23. *Latin America*, October 8, 1976, page 309.

24. *Latin America Policital Report*, May 27, 1977, page 159.

25. See *El Mercurio*, International Edition, April 24-30, 1977, page 5; and *Latin America Political Report*, April 22, 1977, page 120.

26. *Latin America Political Report*, May 27, 1977, page 159.

27. *Chile Economic News*, November 1976, page 5.

28. *Chilegram*, February 1977, page 11.

29. *Boletín Informativo* Confederación de Empleados Particulares de Chile, July 1974.

30. *El Mercurio*, International Edition, May 26-June 1, 1975, pages 1, 7.

31. *Chile Economic News*, November 1976, page 5.
32. *El Mercurio*, International Edition, January 13-19, 1975, page 3.
33. Ministerio del Trabajo y Previsión Social, *Proyectos Decretos Leyes Estatuto Social de la Empresa Y Estatuto de Capacitación Ocupacional de los Trabajadores*, Santiago, January 1975, has the text of the Social Statute of the Enterprises, pages 19-30.
34. *El Mercurio*, International Edition, April 28-May 4, 1975, page 6.
35. The text of the proposed new labor code is given in Ministerio del Trabajo y Previsión Social, *Anteproyecto de Codigo del Trabajo*, Santiago, May 1, 1975.
36. Interview with General Nicanor Díaz Estrada, minister of labor, in Santiago, July 25, 1975.
37. Ministerio del Trabajo y Previsión Social, *Proyectos Decretos Leyes*, pages 17-47.
38. Interview with General Nicanor Díaz Estrada, minister of labor, in Santiago, July 25, 1975.
39. See Robert J. Alexander, "Chile a Year After the Military Coup," *Freedom at Issue*, November-December 1974.
40. *Latin America Economic Report*, June 20, 1975, page 93.
41. *El Mercurio*, International Edition, February 27-March 5, 1977, page 7.
42. *Latin America*, August 29, 1975, page 269.
43. *Chile: State of War, Eyewitness Report*, Women's International League for Peace and Freedom, Philadelphia, 1974, page 4.
44. Interview with Sergio de Castro, subsecretary of economy, in Santiago, August 22, 1974.

Annotated Bibliography

Much of the information and most of the interpretation of events in this book are drawn from my own personal contacts with Chile during fourteen visits there over a period of almost thirty years. I have sought in all possible cases to document statements of fact, as well as statistics, and, of course, to cite sources of any direct quotations. The materials used are of considerable variety, both ideologically and geographically.

Almost all of the sources I have used are listed in the pages that follow. The only exceptions are a handful of cases where information has been gained from interviews with people who remain in Chile, or whose whereabouts I do not know, and for whom an attribution might provoke difficulties with the present authorities in Chile. These cases are few enough, however, that they should not reduce the general reliability of this book.

To facilitate consultation, I have listed the references under a number of separate categories. In most instances, I have annotated the sources.

BOOKS AND PAMPHLETS:

Alexander, Robert J. *Labor Relations in Argentina, Brazil and Chile.* McGraw-Hill, New York, 1962. Extensive study of labor relations under the pre-1973 Labor Code.

Algunos Fundamentes de la Intervención Militar en Chile, Septiembre 1973. Editora Nacional Gabriela Mistral Ltda., Santiago, 1974. Explanations by the Junta regime for the coup and the new government's objectives.

Allende, Salvador. *La Vía Chilena, del Primer Mensaje del Presidente Allende ante el Congreso Pleno, 21 de Mayo de 1971.* Empresa Editora Nacional Quimantú, Santiago, 1971. Excerpts from Salvador Allende's First Annual Message to Congress.

Anatomía de un Fracaso (La Experiencia Socialista Chilena). Empresa Editora Zig-Zag, Santiago, 1973. Unfriendly interpretation of Unidad Popular experience, published after the fall of Allende.

Baklanoff, Eric N. *Expropriation of U.S. Investments in Cuba, Mexico and Chile.* Praeger, New York, 1975. Valuable comparative study of seizures of U.S. property by various Latin American governments; Professor Baklanoff is not favorably disposed towards such seizures.

Baltra Cortes, Alberto. *Gestión Económica del Gobierno de la Unidad Popular.* Editorial Orbe, Santiago, 1973. Study of economic policies of Allende regime by Chilean economist who was one of the principal leaders of the Partido Izquierda Radical, and the Radical party's precandidate for the UP nomination for president in 1970.

Baraona Urzua, Pablo, and others. *Fuerzas Armadas y Seguridad Nacional.* Ediciones Portada, Santiago, 1973 Study of Chilean military from different aspects, by opponents of Allende regime, written and published during that regime.

Birns, Laurence (editor). *The End of Chilean Democracy: An IDOC Dossier on the Coup and Its Aftermath.* Seabury Press, New York, 1974. A collection of documents from diverse sources concerning the UP government and its fall.

Blanco, Hugo, and others. *The Coup in Chile: Firsthand Report and Assessments.* Pathfinder Press, New York, 1973. Report by Peruvian Trotskyite leader and other foreign Leftists on the fall of Allende regime.

Bradfield, Leila A. (editor). *Chile and Peru: Two Paths to Social Justice.* Institute of International and Area Studies, Western Michigan University, 1974. A comparison of the UP government in Chile and the reformist military regime of General Velasco in Peru.

Breve Historia de la Unidad Popular: Documento de 'El Mercurio,' El Mercurio S.A.P., Santiago, 1974. A running account on an almost day-to-day basis of the UP experience, drawn from the pages of *El Mercurio*.

Camejo, Peter. *Allende's Chile. Is It Going Socialist?.* Pathfinder Press, New York, 1971. A Trotskyite pamphlet picturing the Allende regime as "reformist."

Central Única de Trabajadores. *Pongale el Hombro a la Patria: Llamamiento de la CUT a los Trabajadores.* Santiago, May 1971. An exhortation by the CUT to the Chilean workers to support the Allende regime and to intensify production.

Charlin, Carlos. *Del Avión Rojo a la República Socialista.* Empresa Editora Nacional Quimantú, Santiago, 1972. A partial biography of the first leader of the Socialist party of Chile, Marmaduque Grove.

Chile & Allende. Facts on File, New York, 1974. A running account of the Allende regime, its antecedents and its aftermath, drawn from *Facts on File*.

Chile: A Critical Survey. Institute of General Studies, Santiago, 1972. A hostile interpretation of the Allende regime published while it was still in power.

Chile: Never Again. How the Revolution Was Betrayed. Revolutionary Socialist League Publishing Co., 1974. A dissident Trotskyite interpretation of the fall of the UP regime.

Chile: State of War, Eyewitness Report. Women's International League for Peace and Freedom, Philadelphia, 1974. Analysis and criticism of the Junta regime by U.S. pacifist and civil liberties group.

Chile Under Military Rule. IDOC/North America, 1974. Compilation of articles mainly by sympathizers with Allende regime, on causes of the fall of the Unidad Popular, and its aftermath; has some firsthand testimony on mistreatment and torture of political prisoners under the Junta regime.

Cortes, Lia, and Fuentes, Jordi. *Diccionario Político de Chile.* Editorial Orbe, Santiago, 1967. Invaluable source on Chilean politicians and parties.

Debray, Régis. *Conversations with Allende: Socialism in Chile.* Giangiacomo Feltrinelli Editore, London, 1971. A not overly reliable account of interviews by the French pro-Castro Marxist-Leninist with Allende in December 1970.

Foley, Gary, and Miah, Malik. *Tragedy in Chile: Lessons of the Revolutionary Upsurge and Its Defeat.* Pathfinder Press, New York, 1973. A Trotskyite interpretation of the causes of Allende's downfall.

Frei, Eduardo. *El Mandato de la Historia y las Exigencias del Porvenir.* 2nd edition, Editorial Democracia y Humanismo, Buenos Aires, March 1976. The ex-president's book of protest against the Junta regime.

Frei, Eduardo. *La Unión Hace la Fuerza: Intervención del Presidente Frei a Traves de la Red Nacional de Emisores y Canales de Televisión los días 27 y 27 de Noviembre de 1967.* Editorial del Pacífico, Santiago, 1967. A "report to the nation" by President Frei.

Gaynor, Jeffrey, and Pratt, Lawrence D. *Allende and the Failure of Chilean Marxism.* Heritage Foundation, Inc., Washington, D.C., 1974. An unfriendly interpretation of the Allende regime and the causes of its demise.

The GDR's Fervent Solidarity with the Courageous Chilean People. Panorama DDR, Berlin, n.d. (1973). Collection of denunciations of overthrow of Allende regime by governing party and other organizations in East Germany.

Halperin, Ernst. *Nationalism and Communism in Chile.* MIT Press, Cambridge, Mass., 1965. A study of the Socialists, Communists, and Christian Democrats in the 1950s and early 1960s.

Jobet, Julio César. *El Partido Socialista de Chile.* Ediciones Prensa Latinoamericana, Santiago, 1971, 2 volumes. A very valuable history of the Socialist party of Chile, written by one of its early leaders; exceedingly well documented.

Johnson, Dale (editor). *The Chilean Road to Socialism.* Anchor Books, Garden City, N.Y., 1973. A Selection of views on the Allende regime from both friendly and hostile sources.

La Economía de Chile Durante el Periodo de Gobierno de Unidad Popular: La Vía Chilena al Marxismo. Escuela de Negocios de Valparaíso, Fundación Adolfo Ibáñez, March 1974. An analysis of the economic policies of the Allende regime by anti-UP economists, after the fall of the UP.

La Verdad Sobre la Reforma Agraria. Editorial del Pacífico, Santiago, n.d. (1966?). A pro-Christian Democratic analysis of the agrarian reform under Frei.

Leniz, Fernando. *Statements Made by Mr. Fernando Leniz and Others.* Editora Nacional Gabriela Mistral, Santiago, 1974. Statements by the Junta's first civilian minister of finance and other officials on the Chilean economic situation and the policies of the Junta.

Lineas de Acción de la Junta de Gobierno. Empresa Editora Gabriela Mistral, Santiago, n.d. (1973). General statement of policy by the Junta regime.

MacEoin, Gary. *No Peaceful Way: The Chilean Struggle for Dignity.* Sheed and

Ward, New York, 1974. A very pro-Allende study of the UP regime and the causes of its fall.

MacHale, Tomás. *El Frente de Libertad de Expresión (1970-1972)*. Ediciones Portada, Santiago, 1972. A detailed study of the written and oral press during the UP regime, arguing that freedom of the press was in danger.

Millas, Hernán, and Filippi, Emilio. *Chile 70-73: Crónica de una Experiencia*. Empresa Editora Zig-Zag, Santiago, 1974. An unfriendly analysis of the Allende regime and its fall.

Military Junta Unleashes Terror in Chile: GDR Suspends Relations. Panorama DDR, Berlin, n.d. (1973). A strong attack on the Junta regime launched from East Germany.

Monckenberg, Fernando. *Jaque al Subdesarrollo*. Editora Nacional Gabriela Mistral, Santiago, 1974. A study of the continuing unsatisfactory state of economic and social development of Chile, published after Allende's fall.

Moss, Robert. *El Experimento Marxista Chileno*. Editora Nacional Gabriela Mistral Ltda., Santiago, 1974. A study by the Chilean correspondent of *The London Economist*, largely finished while Allende was still in power but published subsequently; unfriendly to the Allende regime. Originally published as *Chile's Marxist Experiment*, David and Charles, Newton, Abbot, London, 1973, but I have used the Chilean edition.

New Chile. North American Congress on Latin America, Madison, Wis., 1973. Pro-MIR interpretation of events in Chile during the Allende regime.

Orrego Vicuña, Francisco (editor). *Chile: The Balanced View*. Institute of International Studies, University of Chile, Santiago, 1975. A collection of articles about the Allende and Junta regimes by Chileans and foreigners; most are friendly to the Junta or hostile to Allende, or both.

Perlo, Victor. *End Fascist Terror and U.S. Imperialism in Chile!*. New Outlook Publishers, New York, 1974. Pamphlet by a leading member of U.S. Communist party, published by Communist publishing firm.

Pinochet Ugarte, Augusto. *A Seis Meses de la Liberación Nacional, Mensaje al País del Presidente de la Junta de Gobierno, General Augusto Pinochet Ugarte, Pronunciado el Día 11 de Marzo de 1974, al Cumplirse Seis Meses de Gobierno*. Empresa Editora Gabriela Mistral, Santiago, 1974. English version: *Address Delivered by President of Junta, General Augusto Pinochet Ugarte on March 11th 1974, on Occasion of the Sixth Month Anniversary of the New Government*. Junta de Gobierno de Chile, Press Department, Santiago, 1974.

Programa Básico de Gobierno de la Unidad Popular. Santiago, June 1970. Program of the Unidad Popular published during the 1970 campaign.

Que es el Comunismo: Preguntas y Respuestas. Editora Austral, Santiago, 1971. Volume originally published in Europe but used as a catechism text in Chilean Communist party training school during the Unidad Popular period.

Quiebra del Estado de Derecho durante el Regimen Marxista de Salvador Allende y Adhesión del Colegio de Abogados al Nuevo Gobierno de Chile: Antecedentes. Santiago de Chile, October 1973. Collection of documents challenging the constitutionality of Allende government policies by Supreme Court, Congress, Bar Association, and other groups.

Sáenz, Orlando. *Un Pais en Quiebra: 33 Preguntas a Orlando Sáenz*. Ediciones Portada, Santiago, April 1973. Attack on Allende regime by the head of Sociedad de Fomento Fabril.

Silva, Lautaro. *Allende: El Fin de una Aventura*. Ediciones Patria Nueva, Santiago, 1974. Hostile discussion of Allende regime and its fall.

Silva, Rene. *Statement on Freedom of the Press in Chile by Mr. Rene Silva, Editor of El Mercurio of Santiago, Chile*. Inter American Press Association, 1973 International Conference, Boston, Mass., October 14-19, 1973. Defense of situation of the press in early months of Junta.

Sociedad de Fomento Fabril. *Analisis Económico de un Año de Gobierno*. Santiago, September 1974. Analysis by economists of the industrialists' Sociedad de Fomento Fabril of Chilean economy during first year of Junta regime.

Statesmen's Yearbook 1971/72. Macmillan, London, 1971.

Thayer, William. *Trabajo, Empresa y Revolución*. Empresa Editora Zig-Zag, Santiago, 1968. Exposition of the ideas of Frei's first minister of labor for revising Chilean labor relations.

Three Years of Destruction. Asimpres (Chilean Printers Association), Santiago, n.d. (1973). Unfriendly description of Allende regime.

Valdés, Jaime. *La 'Clase' Dorada (o el Gobierno Secreto de la UP)*. Privately published, Santiago, 1974. Attack on alleged corruption and self-seeking of Allende regime.

White Book of Change of Government in Chile September 11th 1973. Empresa Editora Nacional Gabriela Mistral Ltda., Santiago, n.d. (1973). Junta's justification for overthrowing Allende government; description of "Plan Z"; contains facsimiles of useful documents.

GOVERNMENT PUBLICATIONS

The sources listed below with one exception, were published by a government printing office, a ministry, autonomous agency, embassy, or government corporation. Other documents that may be equally "official," even if published by a printing concern owned by a government, are listed under the category Books and Pamphlets.

Allende, Salvador. *Chile, Speech Delivered by Dr. Salvador Allende, President of the Republic of Chile, Before the General Assembly of the United Nations, December 4, 1972*. Embassy of Chile, Washington, D.C., n.d. (1972).

Allende, Salvador. *El Futuro de la Revolución Chilena Esta en las Manos de los Trabajadores, Discurso del Presidente de la República, Doctor Salvador Allende, Pronunciado el 1 de Mayo de 1971, Día Internacional del Trabajo*. Consejería de Difusión de la Presidencia de la República, Santiago, 1972. Allende's 1971 May Day speech.

Allende, Salvador. *La Lucha por la Democracia Económica y las Libertades Sociales, del Segundo Mensaje del Presidente Allende ante el Congreso Pleno, 21 de Mayo de 1972*. Consejería de la Difusión de la Presidencia de la República,

Santiago, 1972. Excerpts from Allende's Second Annual Message to Congress.

Barahona Zuleta, Alfredo. *Una Verdadera Reforma Agraria Esta en Marcha*. Relaciones Públicas, Corporación de la Reforma Agraria, 1972 (mimeographed). Explanation and defense of Allende version of agrarian reform program.

Bases de la Pólitica Agraria de la Junta de Gobierno. ICIRA, Santiago, n.d. (1973). Simple exposition of the agrarian policies of the Junta government.

Baytelman, David. *Resumen Extractado de la Exposición en Plenaria del Delegado de Chile*. IV Reunión Interamericana de Ejecutives de Reforma Agraria, Panama, May 1972. Excerpts from speech of head of CORA to meeting of Latin American agrarian reform executives.

Comité Ejecutivo Nacional CUT-Gobierno de Participación. *Informe, Comité Ejecutivo Nacional CUT-Gobierno para la Participación de los Trabajadores en la Dirección de las Empresas del Area Social y Mixta*. n.d. (1971), (mimeographed). Report of joint government-CUT committee on workers' participation in management.

Constitución Política de la República de Chile. Conforme a la Edición Oficial, incluidas todas las modificaciones hasta el 16 de Julio de 1971. Editorial Nascimento, Santiago, 1972.

Constitutional Acts Proclaimed by the Government of Chile, September 11, 1976. Impresora Filadelfia, Santiago, n.d. (1976).

Corporación de Fomento de la Producción. *Basic Data 1970, Corporación de Fomento de la Producción*. New York and Santiago, 1970.

Corporación de Fomento de la Producción. *Monografía de Empresas Filiales 1970*. Santiago, 1970. Study of the firms controlled by CORFO at end of Frei regime.

Corporación de la Reforma Agraria (Relaciones Públicas): *El ABC de la Reforma Agraria*. Santiago, n.d.

Corporación de la Reforma Agraria (Relaciones Públicas): *El ABC de la Reforma Reforma Agraria, Los Centros de Reforma Agraria*. Santiago, n.d. (mimeographed). Official exposition by CORA of *centros de reforma agraria* of the Allende period.

Covert Action in Chile 1963-1973. Staff Report of the Select Committee to Study Government Operations with Respect to Intelligence Activities, U.S. Senate, U.S. Government Printing Office, Washington, D.C., 1975. Staff report of Church Committee on CIA activities in Chile.

Declaración de Principios del Gobierno de Chile. Santiago, March 1974. Junta regime's "declaration of principles."

DS: Consejería Nacional de Desarrollo Social. Departamento Relaciones Públicas, C.N.D.S., Santiago, n.d. (1972). Official explanation of "community development" arm of Chilean government during Allende period.

Embassy of Chile, Washington, D.C. *Castro's Intervention in Chile*. Washington, D.C., n.d. (1974). Junta regime's exposition of influence of Castro regime in Chile under Allende.

Estatuto de la Inversión Extranjera. Corporación de Fomento de la Producción, Santiago, n.d. (1974). Text of Junta regime's law on foreign investment.

Frei, Eduardo. *Cuarto Mensaje del Presidente de la República de Chile, don Eduardo Frei Montalva al inaugurar el periodo de Sesiones Ordinarias del Congreso Nacional, 21 de Mayo de 1968*. Departamento de Publicaciones de la Presidencia de la República, Santiago, May 1968. Complete text of President Frei's Fourth Annual Message to Congress.

Frei, Eduardo. *Quinto Mensaje del Presidente de la República de Chile, don Eduardo Frei Montalva al inaugurar el periodo de Sesiones Ordinarias del Congreso Nacional, 21 de Mayo de 1969.* Departamento de Publicaciones de la Presidencia de la República, Santiago, May 1969. Complete text of President Frei's Fifth Annual Message to Congress.

Frei, Eduardo. *Tercer Mensaje del Presidente de la República de Chile, don Eduardo Frei Montalva al inaugurar el periodo de Sesiones Ordinarias del Congreso Nacional, 21 de Mayo de 1967.* Departamento de Publicaciones de la Presidencia de la República, Santiago, May 1967. Complete text of President Frei's Third Annual Message to Congress.

Gotuzzo Borlando, Lorenzo. *Exposición sobre el Estado de la Hacienda Pública, Presentada por el Ministro de Hacienda Contralmiranto don Lorenzo Gotuzzo Borlando, Octubre de 1973.* Dirección de Presupuestos, Santiago, October 1973. Pamphlet No. 124. Exposition by Junta's first minister of finance of state of Chilean economy and of government finances, on Junta's assumption of power.

The International Telephone and Telegraph Company and Chile, 1970-1971. Report to the Committee on Foreign Relations, U.S. Senate by the Subcommittee on Multinational Corporations, U.S. Government Printing Office, Washington, D.C., 1973. Study of attempts by ITT to prevent election and inauguration of Allende.

Ministerio del Trajabo y Previsión Social. *Anteproyecto de Codigo del Trabajo,* Santiago, May 1, 1975. Text of Junta government's proposed new Labor Code.

Ministerio del Trabajo y Previsión Social. *Proyectos Decretos Leyes Estatuto Social de la Empresa y Estatuto de la Capacitación Ocupacional de los Trabajadores.* Santiago, January 1976. Texts of Junta government's decree-laws on Social Statute of the Enterprise and vocational education.

Presidencia de la República, Oficina de Planificación Nacional. *Normas Básicas de Participación de los Trabajadores en la Administración de las Empresas del Area Social y Mixta.* Santiago, n.d. (1971) (mimeographed). Basic norms for workers' participation in management established by Allende administration.

Pueblo. Oficina de Informaciones y Radiodifusión de la Presidencia de la República, Chile, n.d. (1971). Propaganda leaflet put out by Allende government.

Realidad y Destino de Chile. Editora Nacional Gabriela Mistral Ltda., Santiago, 1975.

Refugee and Humanitarian Problems in Chile. Hearings Before the Subcommittee to Investigate Problems Connected with Refugees and Escapees of the Committee on the Judiciary, U.S. Senate, Ninety-third Congress, First Session, September 28, 1973, U.S. Government Printing Office, Washington, D.C., 1973.

Sáez, Raúl. *Chilean Short- and Medium-Term Development Program.* Dinex, Minirel, Santiago, 1974. Report to Interamerican Economic and Social Conference on Junta regime's economic program.

Sindicación Campesina. Edición Oficial, Santiago, 1967. Text of rural unionization law of Frei regime and its "regulations."

Sociedad Química Minera de Chile. *Informe Sobre la Nacionalización de la Industria Salitrera.* Santiago, May 1971. Report on nationalization of the nitrate industry under Frei and Allende.

NEWSPAPERS AND PERIODICALS

Listed below are all newspapers and other periodicals cited in the text:

AFL-CIO Free Trade Union News. Washington, D.C. Monthly publication of the International Affairs Department of American Federation of Labor-Congress of Industrial Organizations.

Alliance for Progress Weekly Newsletter. Organization of American States, Washington, D.C.

All You Can Eat. New Brunswick, N.J. New Left occasional newspaper, late 1960s and early 1970s.

The American Journal of Comparative Law. Madison, Wis. Scholarly periodical.

Boletín Informativo. Santiago. Occasional mimeographed publication of Confederación de Empleados Particulares de Chile.

Boletín Informativo del Comité Central del Partido Comunista de Chile. Santiago. Occasional mimeographed publication of Central Committee of Communist party of Chile.

Chile Economic Background Information. New York. Occasional publication of Chilean Development Corporation (CORFO) office in New York.

Chile Economic Notes. New York. Monthly publication of Chilean Development Corporation office in New York.

Chilegram. Monthly magazine published and edited by Alvaro Pineda de Castro, Santiago; distributed after the coup by Chilean Embassy in Washington.

Chile Hoy. Santiago. Political weekly, pro-Unidad Popular, founded in June 1972.

Chile: Summary of Recent Events. Washington, D.C. Publication of Chilean Embassy to United States.

Chile Today. Monthly periodical issued by Chilean Embassy in Washington.

Christian Science Monitor. Boston. Daily newspaper.

Clarín. Santiago. Pro-Unidad Popular daily newspaper.

Desafio. Spanish language version of *Challenge,* organ of Progressive Labor party, New York.

El Camionero. Santiago. Official monthly of Confederación Nacional de Dueños de Camiones de Chile.

El Mercurio. Santiago. Conservative daily "newspaper of record."

El Popular. Montevideo. Daily newspaper of Communist party of Uruguay.

El Siglo. Santiago. Official daily newspaper of Communist party of Chile.

El Socialista. Weekly organ of Partido Socialista Obrero Español, published in Paris until 1977, when it was transferred to Madrid.

Ercilla. Santiago. Weekly news magazine, generally pro-Christian Democratic until 1976.

Foreign Affairs. New York. Quarterly publication of Council on Foreign Relations.

Freedom at Issue. New York. Bi-monthly magazine of Freedom House.

Harpers Magazine. New York. Monthly journal of literature and comment.

Informe Económico. Santiago. Monthly publication associated with *Ercilla.*

Intercontinential Press. New York. Weekly news magazine dealing principally with international affairs, sponsored by Trotskyite Socialist Workers party.

International Socialist Review. New York. Quarterly of Socialist Workers party.

International Trade Union News. Brussels. Mimeographed fortnightly newsletter of International Confederation of Free Trade Unions.

Journal of Economic Issues. East Lansing, Mich. Scholarly publication of non-mathematically oriented economists in the United States.

La Nación. Buenos Aires. One of two major dailies in Argentine capital.

La Patria. Santiago. Government daily paper under the Junta regime, formerly *La Nación.*

La Segunda. Santiago. Tabloid daily, part of *El Mercurio* chain.

La Tribuna. Santiago. Tabloid daily, more or less pro-Partido Nacional, Suppressed after September 1973 coup.

Latin America. London. British weekly magazine of news and interpretation of Latin American affairs.

Latin America Commodities Report. London. Sister periodical of *Latin America Political Report* and *Latin America Economic Report.*

Latin America Economic Report. London. Companion periodical of *Latin America,* weekly.

Latin America Political Report. London. Name assumed by *Latin America* in 1977.

Le Monde. Paris. French daily, moderately Left; the English language edition of this periodical is also cited in this book.

Memorandum Económico Latinoamericano. Buenos Aires. Published in association with *Latin America Economic Report* by *Latin American Newsletters Ltd.*

Monthly Review. New York. Independent Marxist-Leninist monthly.

Newsletter. New York. Periodical of International Council on the Future of the University.

New York Times. New York. Daily newspaper "of record."

Peking Review. Weekly publication in various languages published in Peking, China.

Plan. Santiago. Left-wing monthly, pro-Unidad Popular.

Portada. Santiago. Conservative quarterly.

Presencia. La Paz, Bolivia. Pro-Christian Democratic daily paper.

Problems of Communism. Washington, D.C. Scholarly quarterly published by U.S. Information Agency.

Punto Final. Santiago. MIR weekly.

Puro Chile. Santiago. Pro-Communist daily newspaper in early 1970s.

Que Pasa? Santiago. Conservatively oriented weekly magazine of news and comment.

Review of Soviet Press. New York. Publication of Union of Soviet Socialist Republics Mission to the United Nations.

Socialist International Information. London. Monthly periodical of Socialist International.

The Times of the Americas. Miami. Weekly newspaper specializing in Latin American news.

USLA Reporter. New York. Newsletter of U.S. Committee for Justice to Latin American Political Prisoners.

Wall Street Journal. New York. Daily newspaper, more or less conservative.

World Affairs Report. Stanford, Cal. Monthly publication of California Institute of International Studies; treats world news as seen through Soviet press; Ronald Hilton, editor.

World Marxist Review. Toronto. Theoretical and informational journal of Communist and Workers' parties; pro-Moscow.

MISCELLANEOUS PRINTED MATERIAL

The items listed here do not fit into any of the previous categories. All have been cited in the text.

Amnesty International, USA. *Desaparecidos: Disappeared in Chile*, n.d. (1977). Four-page throwaway.
FBIS, Foreign Broadcast Information Service of the U.S. Information Agency. A daily mimeographed report on foreign radio and television broadcasts.
Ibáñez, Pedro. *The Chilean Crisis and Its Outcome.* 1974, mimeographed.
Meany, George. Letter to General Augusto Pinochet, March 20, 1974.
Rather, Dan. Transcript of Interview with Fidel Castro, October 2, 1974.
Subversion in Chile: The Complete Set of IT&T Memos. Non-Intervention in Chile, Madison, Wis., n.d. (mimeographed).

INTERVIEWS

All of the following (each of which is cited in the text) are notes of personal interviews with the people involved, except that of Ambassador Edelstam, which consists of notes on a speech given by him.

Hector Alarcón, leader of Confederación Nacional Campesina, in Santiago, July 13, 1968.
Eduardo Alessandri, former senator, son of ex-President Arturo Alessandri and brother of ex-President Jorge Alessandri, in Santiago, June 21, 1972.
Horacio Aranguez Donoso, secretary general, Confederación de Productores Agrícolas, in Santiago, August 16, 1974.
Arturo Arrigorriaga Leal, economist of Sociedad de Fomento Fabril, in Santiago, July 25, 1975.
Sergio de Castro, subsecretary of economy, in Santiago, August 22, 1974.
Jorge Cerda, president of Confederación de Pequeños Agricultores, in Santiago, July 4, 1968.
Luis Díaz, member of Executive Committee, Confederación Nacional Campesina El Triunfo Campesino, in Santiago, July 11, 1973.
General Nicanor Díaz Estrada, minister of labor, in Santiago, July 25, 1975.
Harald Edelstam, ex-ambassador of Sweden in Chile, speaking to meeting at Rutgers University, New Brunswick, N.J., March 8, 1974.
Renán Fuentealba, former president of Christian Democratic party, in Santiago, August 20, 1974.

Gabriel González Videla, former president of Chile, in Santiago, June 22, 1972.

Edward Korry, ex-U.S. ambassador to Chile, in New York, September 19, 1975.

Bernardo Leighton, Christian Democratic party leader, in Santiago, June 29, 1972.

Max Nol, president, Corporación del Cobre, in Santiago, July 5, 1971.

Luis Salamanca, treasurer, Confederación Nacional Campesina El Triunfo Campesino, in Santiago, July 5, 1972.

Luis Vilarín, president of Confederación Nacional de Dueños de Camiones, in Santiago, August 13, 1974.

James Wilson, Cornell University graduate student, studying workers' participation
in management in Chile, in Santiago, August 21, 1974.

Index

ABC de Reforma Agraria, 162

Acción Democrática of Venezuela, 140, 280

Acción Nacional, 67

Acción Popular Independiente, 75, 76, 122, 133, 168, 256, 261, 306, 358

Acción Revolucionaria Socialista, 20

Acción Sindical Chilena, 87, 91, 111

Acerias del Ecuador, 106

AFL-CIO, 431, 433

Agencias Graham, 156, 308

Agency for International Development, 221, 434

Agrarian Reform Law of 1962, 47, 76, 93

Agrarian Reform Law of 1967, 93, 94, 160, 161, 167, 257, 304, 311, 415, 416

Agrupación Nacional de Empleados Fiscales, 198

Agrupación Nacional de Trabajadores Semifiscales, 198

Aguilar, Mario, 311

Aguirre Cerda, Pedro, 23, 24, 25, 26, 27, 28, 29, 37, 52, 86

Ahora, 238

AID. *See* Agency for International Development

AIFLD. *See* American Institute for Free Labor Development

Alarcón, Hector, 112, 113

Albania, 212

Alberdi, 211

Alemany, Claudio, 259

Alessandri, Eduardo, 48, 167

Alessandri, Fernando, 31, 48

Alessandri, Jorge, 39, 46, 47, 48, 50, 52, 68, 75, 93, 118, 119, 120, 125, 126, 167, 227, 241, 242, 278, 307, 353

Alessandri Palma, Arturo: 5, 10, 11, 12, 13, 14, 15, 16, 17, 18, 19, 20, 21, 22, 23, 24, 25, 29, 30, 32, 35, 37, 48, 52, 118, 167, 289

Alfonso, Pedro Enrique, 37

Aliaga, Serafín, 195

Alianza Liberal, 11, 13

Alianza Popular Libertadora, 24

Alimentos y Fideos Carozzi S.A., 152

Allende, Andrés Pascal, 360

Allende, Laura (president's widow), 380

Allende, Salvador: before presidency, 26, 30, 32, 34, 36, 38, 43, 46, 49, 52, 60, 68, 69, 74, 75, 76, 120, 121, 122, 123, 125, 127, 128, 139, 141, 235, 236, 237, 246, 266, 281, 365; in presidency, xii, 16, 27, 38, 40, 41, 68, 70, 72, 73, 78, 82, 83, 100, 131, 132, 133, 135, 136, 137, 138, 139, 140, 142, 143, 144, 145, 147, 148, 149, 151, 152, 153, 154, 155, 157, 159, 160, 163, 164, 165, 166, 167, 168, 169, 170, 171, 172, 173, 174, 175, 176, 177, 179, 180, 181, 182, 184, 187, 188, 189, 190, 191, 194, 195, 197, 198, 199, 203, 205, 207, 208, 209, 210, 211, 212, 213, 214, 215, 216, 217, 218, 219, 221, 222, 223, 224, 225, 226, 227, 228, 231, 232, 233, 234, 235, 236, 237, 238, 239, 240, 242, 243, 244, 245, 246, 247, 248, 249, 250, 251, 252, 253, 254, 255, 256, 257, 258, 261, 262, 264, 265, 266, 267, 268,

269, 270, 271, 272, 273, 274, 275, 276, 277,
278, 279, 280, 281, 282, 283, 284, 285, 286,
287, 290, 293, 294, 295, 296, 297, 298, 300,
301, 302, 303, 304, 305, 306, 307, 308, 309,
310, 311, 312, 313, 314, 315, 316, 317, 318,
319, 320, 321, 322, 323, 324, 325, 326, 327,
328, 331, 338, 346, 347, 349, 358, 359, 365,
367, 373, 374, 376, 382, 383, 386, 390, 392,
393, 394, 396, 397, 398, 399, 406, 407, 412,
415, 416, 417, 423, 424, 432, 441, 446, 447;
overthrow and death, xii, 177, 211, 232,
233, 234, 236, 331, 332, 333, 334, 335, 336,
337, 338, 339, 341, 347, 361, 374, 391, 426
Alliance for Progress, 47, 48, 50
Alliance for Progress Weekly Newsletter,
210
Almeyda, Clodomiro, 69, 138, 141, 212, 246,
261, 267, 272, 309, 316, 359, 365, 366, 377
Altamirano, Carlos, 138, 141, 241, 242, 260,
266, 267, 269, 270, 271, 272, 273, 276, 277,
287, 288, 300, 315, 316, 325, 326, 327, 328,
335, 359, 365
American Institute for Free Labor Develop-
ment, 433, 434
Amin, General Idi, 343
Amnesty International, 346, 347, 349
Ampuero, Raúl, 34, 36, 44, 69, 70, 72, 137,
138, 141, 266, 307
Amunátegui, Felipe, 286
Anaconda Corporation, 101, 148, 149, 150,
236, 376, 408, 416
Anarchists, 20
Anarchosyndicalists, 22, 32, 41
Andean Bloc. *See* Andean Pact
Andean Group. *See* Andean Pact
Andean Pact, 105, 106, 209, 210, 211, 216,
380, 396, 411, 417, 418, 419
Andean Pact Decisions, 210, 418, 419
ANEF. *See* Agrupación Nacional de Em-
pleados Fiscales
ANOC. *See* Asociación Nacional de Organi-
zaciones Campesinas
API. *See* Acción Popular Independiente
Arab states, 379
Arauco cellulose plant, 417
Arellano, Vladimir, 191
Arellano Stark, General Sergio, 342, 380
Argentina, 6, 40, 47, 51, 183, 211, 225, 226,
232, 235, 341, 382
Arriagada, General Humberto, 18
Arteaga, Domingo, 413
Asamblea popular, 249, 250

Asamblea Radical, 255
ASICH. *See* Acción Sindical Chilena
Asociación Nacional de Organizaciones
Campesinas, 87, 91
Association of Retired Manual Workers, 436
Astilleros Las Mabas, 152
Australia, 225
Aylwin, Patricio, 62, 316, 363, 365

Bachelet Martínez, General Alberto, 308,
309, 348
Bachman, María Elena, 360
Badilla, Luis, 284
Baklanoff, Eric, 147
Balmaceda, José Manuel, 5, 7, 289, 338
Baltra, Mireyra, 349
Baltra Cortes, Alberto, 74, 122, 174, 175,
177, 179, 180, 181, 182, 185, 187, 188, 190,
226, 279, 309
Banco Chileno-Yugoslavo, 403, 404
Banco Continental, 72
Banco de Chile, 151, 333
Banco del Constitución, 151
Banco del Estado, 40, 146, 333, 410
Banco do Brasil, 150
Banco Español, 403
Banco Francés-Italiano de America del Sud,
151
Banco Nacional del Trabajo, 333
Banco Osorno y La Unión, 403
Banco Yugoslavo, 151
Bank of America, 151, 225
Bank of London and South America, 72, 150
Banzer, Colonel Hugo (President of Bolivia),
211, 384
Baraona, Pablo, 396
Barrios, Jaime, 190, 191
Barros Borgoño, Luis, 11
Baytleman, David, 162, 163
Beausire, Mary Ann, 360
Bejares, Hernán, 346
Belaunde, Fernando, 105
Belgium, 44, 378
Beoninger, Rector Eduardo, 244
Berman, Natalio, 29
Bethlehem Steel Corporation, 103, 148
Birns, Laurence, 337
Bitar, Sergio, 365
Blanche, General Bartolomé, 16
Blanco, Hugo, 344
Bogota, 105

Bolivia, 7, 209, 211, 235, 289, 380, 383, 384, 421
Bolivian Pro-Mao Communists, 211
Bolivian Pro-Moscow Communists, 211
Bolivian Trotskyites, 211
Bonilla Bradanovic, Major General Oscar, 340
Boorstein, Edward, 190
Bordaberry, President Juan María, 381
Bossay, Luis, 46, 279
Braden Copper Company, 101
Brady, General Hernán, 342
Bravo, General Hector, 295
Brazil, 79, 183, 189, 211, 212, 226, 381, 382, 409
Brezhnev, Leonid, 212
Briones, Carlos, 316, 317, 324, 332
Brussels, 432
Brzezinski, Zbigniew, 377
Buenos Aires, 211, 363
Bukovsky, Vladimir, 361
Bulgaria, 226, 374
Bulnes, Francisco, 311, 312
Bulnes, General Manuel, 5
Bunster del Solar, Rear Admiral Victor, 294
Bustamante, José, 431
Buzeta, Fernando, 284

Cabieses, Manuel, 260
Cademartori, José, 259, 262
Caldera, Rafael, 210
Calderón, Rolando, 170, 272, 305, 309
Call of the CUT to the Workers, 206
Cambodia, 375
Campos, Roberto, 189
Camus, Bishop Carlos, 370
Canada, 215, 223, 224, 226, 373
Caracas, 359, 365
Carter, Jimmy, 377, 382
Carter administration, 366, 376, 377
Carvajal Prado, Vice-Admiral Patricio, 340, 375
Cassidy, Sheila, 378
Castillo, Bernardino, 428
Castillo, General Sergio, 79
Castillo, Guillermo, 435
Castillo, Jaime, 64, 366
Castillo, René, 360, 361
Castro, Fidel, 41, 61, 71, 140, 143, 191, 192, 193, 212, 213, 214, 215, 234, 237, 275, 283, 294, 298, 336, 361

Catholic University of Santiago, 219, 243, 244, 310, 341, 370, 387
Catholic University of Valparaíso, 219, 243, 244
Cauas, Jorge, 396, 397, 399, 409
CEMADI, 276
CEN. See National Executive Committee of Radical Party
Central Bank, 14, 17, 146, 157, 187, 190, 191, 220, 222, 333, 340, 396, 399, 402, 409, 420
Central Intelligence Agency, 113, 126, 217, 218, 226, 227, 228, 229, 230, 231, 232, 235, 236, 294, 447
Central Nacional Sindical, 428
Central Única de Trabajadores de Chile, 41, 42, 43, 63, 71, 80, 87, 90, 108, 110, 111, 112, 113, 114, 120, 169, 194, 195, 196, 197, 198, 199, 200, 202, 206, 245, 246, 270, 276, 304, 305, 310, 311, 316, 325, 367, 428, 432, 433
CEPCh. See Confederación de Empleados Particulares de Chile
Cerro de Pasco Corporation, 101, 102, 148, 376, 416
Chadwick, Tomás, 70
Chamber Orchestra of Cologne, 394
Chase Manhattan Bank, 225
Chelen Rojas, Alejandro, 239
Chicago Boys, the, 395, 396, 399, 404, 411, 413, 414, 416, 418, 420, 424, 425
Chilean Episcopal Conference, 370
Chilean Institute of the Rational Administration of Firms. See Instituto Chileno de Administración Racional de Empresas
"Chilean Road to Socialism," 121, 124, 129, 131, 177, 206, 231, 248, 249, 257, 447
Chile Economic News, 418, 437
Chile Electric Company, 146
Chilefilms, 393, 417
Chilegram, 410
Chile Hoy, 205, 238, 264
China, People's Republic of, 212, 213, 225, 226, 375, 376, 409
Chinese Communist party. See Communist party, China
Chonchol, Jacques, 63, 122, 161, 166, 170, 191, 284, 305
Christian Democratic parties, 280
Christian Democratic party. See Falange Nacional; Partido Demócrata Cristiano
Christian Science Monitor, 167
Christians for Socialists, 367

Chuqicamata mine, 101, 102, 149, 150, 204, 214, 292
Church Committee of the U.S. Senate, 227, 228, 229, 230, 231
Chu Teh, 375
CIPEC. See Intergovernmental Council of Copper Exporters
CIT. See Compañia Tecno-Industrial
Clarín, 161, 162, 238, 333
Club of Paris-Chile Pact, 223
CNC. See Confederación Nacional Campesina
CNS. See Central Nacional Sindical
Cockcroft, Eva, 203
Cockcroft, James, 203
CODELCO. See Corporación del Cobre
Colegio de Abogados, 166
Coll, Gabriel, 168
Colombia, 105, 106, 209, 210, 212, 217, 380, 419
Comando Nacional de Defensa Gremial, 303, 304, 305, 321
Comintern. See Communist International
Comité de Cooperación para la Paz en Chile, 368, 369, 370
Comité para la Paz. See Comité de Cooperación para la Paz en Chile
Commercial Agricultural Enterprise. See Empresa de Comercio Agricola
Committee for Peace. See Comité de Cooperación para la Paz en Chile
Communist International, 21
Communist movement, pro-Moscow: 360, 373, 374
Communist party. See Partido Comunista de Chile
Communist party, China, 69
Communist party, Cuba, 213
Communist party, France, 133, 136
Communist party, Italy, 135, 136
Communist party, Soviet Union, 71, 135
Communist party, West Germany, 375
Communist party, Yugoslavia, 133
Communists, 20, 372
Compañia de Papeles y Cartones, 104
Compañia de Teléfonos de Chile, 153, 417
Compañia Interoceanica de Navigación, 152
Compañia Manufacturera de Papeles y Cartones. See La Papelera
Compañia Minera Andina S.A., 102
Compañia Minera Exótica, 102
Compañia Salitrera Anglo-Lautaro, 103

Compañia Salitrera de Chile, 14
Compañia Sud Americana de Vapores, 152
Compañia Tecno-Industrial, 421
Concha, Jaime, 284
Confederación de Empleados de Industria y Comercio, 198
Confederación de Empleados Particulares de Chile, 113, 198, 433
Confederación Democrática, 279
Confederación de Sindicatos de Empleadores Agrícolas, 68, 91
Confederación de Trabajadores de Chile, 22, 24, 30, 31, 32, 41
Confederación General de Trabajadores, 22, 41
Confederación Nacional Campesina, 91
Confederación Nacional de Asentiamientos, 169, 170
Confederación Nacional de Dueños de Camiones, 229, 230, 302, 303, 321, 324
Confederación Nacional de Pequeños Agricultores, 91, 169
Confederación Nacional de Sindicatos Legales, 22
Confederación Nacional Sindical Campesina "Libertad," 91, 169, 170
Confederación Unitaria de Campesinos, 169
Confederation of Agricultural Producers, 401
Confederation of Production and Commerce, 303
Confederation of Professionals of Chile, 322
Confederation of Retail Commerce and Small Industry, 303
Confederation of Rural Employers. See Confederación de Sindicatos de Empleadores Agrícolas
Confederation of Truck Owners. See Confederación Nacional de Dueños de Camiones
Confederation of White Collar Workers, 436
Congrevi, 113
Consejería Nacional de Desarrollo Social, 185
Conservative party, 11, 20, 23, 24, 25, 29, 33, 37, 44, 45, 46, 48, 49, 59, 66, 67, 238
Conservative Republic, 5
Conservatives, 4, 8, 9
Constitutional Acts, 352, 353, 354, 355, 370
Constitutional commission, 351, 352
Constitutional tribunal, 83, 128, 285
Constitution of 1925, 13, 17, 18, 29, 31, 33, 76,

81, 82, 83, 84, 155, 246, 248, 249, 252, 253, 285, 293, 311, 312, 317, 318, 319, 320, 326, 336, 339, 351, 352, 353, 354, 355
Construction Workers' Federation, 434, 435
Contreras Labarca, Carlos, 374
Copper Workers' Confederation, 40, 108, 428, 435
CORA: See Corporación de la Reforma Agraria
Cordones industriales, 314, 315, 323
CORFO. See Corporación de Fomento de la Producción
Corporación de Fomento de la Producción, 27, 28, 34, 35, 47, 50, 101, 103, 104, 145, 146, 153, 157, 158, 187, 191, 192, 201, 241, 242, 303, 333, 340, 364, 396, 412, 413, 417, 418, 424
Corporación de la Reforma Agraria, 62, 94, 95, 132, 160, 161, 162, 163, 164, 165, 166, 167, 170, 171, 179, 257, 286, 322, 415, 416
Corporación de la Vivienda, 40
Corporatión del Cobre, 100, 101, 102, 149, 191
Corporación de Reconstrucción y Auxilio, 27
Corps of Retired Generals and Admirals, 313
Correa, Ulises, 75
Corvalán, Luis, 136, 172, 264, 309, 312, 345, 358, 360, 361, 362
COSACh. See Compañía Salitrera de Chile
Council of Copper Exporting Countries, 102
Council of State, 352, 353
Crater, Arthur, 233
Cre, Jaime, 204, 205
Crespo Montero, Colonel Sergio, 340
Creus, Eduardo, 334
Cristalerias de Chile, 152, 333
Cruz, Luciano, 73
Cruz Coke, Eduardo, 31, 45
CTCh. See Confederación de Trabajadores de Chile
Cuba, 50, 51, 61, 71, 180, 192, 195, 213, 214, 215, 227, 298, 361, 374
Cuban Airlines, 298
Cuban extremists, 333
CUTCh. See Central Única de Trabajadores de Chile
Czechoslovakia, 71, 195, 226

Damilano, Renato, 370
Danus Covián, Colonel Luis, 412, 413
Dávila, Carlos, 16, 85, 154
Davis, Captain Ray E., 233

Day of the Jackal, The, 394
Debray, Régis, 141
De Castro, Sergio, 396, 399, 410, 419, 420, 421
Decree-Law No. 1, 339, 340
Decree-Law No. 12, 428
Decree-Law No. 198, 429, 430, 435
Decree-Law No. 520, 285
Decree-Law No. 521, 347
Decree-Law No. 600 (foreign investment statute), 417
Decree-Law No. 1281, 393
Decree-Law No. 1800, 416
Decree-law on labor delegates, 430
DeGaulle, Charles, 119
De la Cruz, Lisandro, 76
De la Ossa, Sergio, 81
Del Canto, Hernán, 195, 197, 272, 298
Del Rio, Arturo, 11
Democratic Front. See Frente Democrático
Democratic Party. See Partido Democrático
Democratic Republic of Germany. See East Germany
Derpsch, Colonel Carlos, 372
Díaz, Victor, 262, 263
Diaz Estrada, General Nicanor, 428, 431, 435, 436, 440, 441
Diez, Sergio, 286, 312
DINA. See Dirección de Investigaciónes Nacionales
DINAC. See Empresa Nacional de Distribución y Comercialización
Dirección de Industria y Comercio, 115, 184, 185, 191, 398
Dirección de Investigaciónes Nacionales, 346, 347, 349, 372
DIRINCO. See Dirección de Industria y Comercio
Duhalde, Alfredo, 26, 30, 44, 75
Durán, Domingo, 401
Durán, Julio, 49, 74, 279

East Berlin, 375
Easter Island, 232
Eastern Europe, 33, 34, 212, 225, 375, 393, 394
East Germany, 195, 226, 308, 346, 373, 374, 375
ECA. See Empresa de Comercio Agrícola
Echeverría, Luis, 210, 211, 309, 380
ECLA. See Economic Commission for Latin America

Economic Commission for Latin America, 189, 385
Ecuador, 105, 106, 209, 210, 380
Edelstam, Harald, 377
Edict No. 5, 336
Edict No. 26, 333
Edict No. 29, 340
Editorial Gabriela Mistral, 390
Editorial National Quimantu. *See* Empresa Nacional Quimantu
Edwards, Agustín, 240
Egypt, 379
Eisenhower, Dwight, 119
El Camionero, 230, 303, 321
El Cronista, 388, 391
El Diario Ilustrado, 113, 238
Elizabeth II, Queen, 382
El Mandato de la Historia y Las Exigencias del Porvenir, 364
El Mercurio, 80, 113, 154, 155, 161, 167, 170, 229, 238, 240, 241, 261, 263, 264, 272, 376, 377, 378, 379, 380, 382, 383, 384, 387, 391, 392, 393, 396, 400, 402, 403, 405, 409, 412, 415, 416, 419, 420, 422
El Salvador mine, 101, 115
El Siglo, 113, 119, 156, 161, 238, 260, 263
El Teniente, 101, 150, 175, 308, 310
Empresa de Comercio Agrícola, 47, 156, 401
Empresa Nacional Avicola, 157, 164, 401
Empresa Nacional de Distribución y Comercialización, 156, 185
Empresa Nacional de Electricidad, S.A., 27, 145
Empresa Nacional de Petroleo, 104
Empresa Nacional Quimantú, 239, 390
ENADI (gas distribution firm), 157
ENAP. *See* Empresa Nacional de Petroleo
ENAVI. *See* Empresa Nacional Avicola
ENDESA. *See* Empresa Nacional de Electricidad
End of Chilean Democracy, The, 337
Engels, 239
Enriquez, Miguel, 275, 276, 300, 326
ENU. *See* Escuela Nacional Unificada
Ercilla, 239, 364, 392
Errázuriz Zañartu, Federico, 6
Escuela Nacional Unificada, 307, 308, 311
Espinoza Carillo, Gerardo, 308
Eyzaguirre, José María, 350

Fabricaciones Militares, 342
Fabrilana textile plant, 203

Facultad Latino Americana de Ciencias Sociales, 385, 388
Faivovich, Angel, 75
Faivovich, Jaime, 322
Falange Nacional, 31, 43, 44, 61, 63
Falange Socialista Boliviana, 211
Fatherland and Liberty. *See Patria y Libertad*
Federación Industrial Ferrovaria de Chile, 109, 110, 429
Federación Obrera de Chile, 21, 22
Federación Social Cristiana, 45
Federation of Metalurgical Unions, 421
Federation of Taxi Chauffeurs' Unions, 303
FENSA (metal company), 155, 421
Fernández, Sergio, 432, 435
Ferriloza (ceramics plant), 155, 421
FIFCh. *See* Federación Industrial Ferroviaria de Chile
Figueroa, Emiliano, 10, 14
Figueroa, Luis, 113, 195, 197, 199, 246, 305, 432
Financieras, 402, 403, 404, 422
Finland, 226
Firestone, 417
First Assembly of Left Journalists, 247
First International Seminar of Social Democratic Youth of Europe and Latin America, 74
First National City Bank, 150, 151
First truckers' strike, 253, 294, 295, 301, 304
FLACSO. *See* Facultad Latino Americana de Ciencias Sociales
Flores, Ermol, 433
Flores, Fernando, 186, 332, 337
Fluxa group, 404, 422
Fontaine, Arturo, 351
France, 8, 195, 226, 378, 393, 419
Franco, Francisco, 226, 378, 379
FRAP. *See* Frente de Acción Popular
Frei, Eduardo: before presidency, 46, 49, 50, 266, 282; in presidency, 55, 56, 58, 59, 60, 61, 62, 63, 64, 65, 66, 67, 68, 69, 70, 71, 72, 73, 75, 76, 77, 78, 79, 80, 81, 82, 83, 84, 86, 87, 88, 89, 90, 93, 94, 95, 96, 97, 98, 99, 100, 101, 102, 103, 104, 105, 106, 107, 110, 111, 112, 114, 115, 116, 119, 120, 121, 146, 161, 166, 171, 181, 222, 226, 243, 266, 274, 281, 286, 293, 298, 365, 388, 415, 417, 424, 425, 445, 446; after presidency, 126, 210, 227, 228, 284, 304, 353, 362, 364, 366, 377
Freistas. *See* Oficialistas
Frente de Acción Popular, 43, 45, 46, 49, 50, 71, 75, 122

Frente del Pueblo, 43
Frente Democrático, 49
Frente de Trabajadores Revolucionarios, 196, 274, 276
Frente Nacional del Pueblo, 43
Frenz, Bishop Helmut, 370
Friedman, Milton, 395
Friedrich Ebert Foundation, 365
Front of the People. *See* Frente del Pueblo
Frota, General Silvio, 381
FTR. *See* Frente de Trabajadores Revolutionarios
Fuentealba, Renán, 62, 64, 205, 284, 285, 286, 304, 347, 364, 365, 366

Gall, Norman, 149, 150
GAP. *See* Grupo de Amigos del Presidente
García Márquez, Gabriel, 217
Garretón, Oscar, 256, 276, 326
Gas Company of Concepción, 155
Gaynor, Jeff, 346
Gazmuri, Jaime, 256
Geisel, president of Brazil, 381
General Tie Corporation, 152
Geneva, 216, 431, 433
Germany, 22, 30, 33, 390
Gibbs wholesale firm, 156
Godoy Urrutia, César, 29
González Acevedo, Major General Rolando, 340
González Alfaro, Raúl, 240
González Córdoba, Luis Renato, 337
González Videla, Gabriel, 26, 31, 32, 33, 34, 35, 36, 38, 44, 51, 86, 88, 90, 136, 137, 141, 143, 353
González von Mareés, Jorge, 22
Goodsell, James, 167
Gotusso Rolando, Rear Admiral Lorenzo, 340, 398
Goulart, Jõao, 350
Government Junta of 1924, 13
Great Britain, 5, 19, 211, 378, 382, 407
Gremios. *See* Comando Nacional de Defensa Gremial
Grove, Marmaduque, 13, 15, 16, 20, 24, 30, 85
Grove-Matte regime, 16, 20
Grupo Andino. *See* Andean Pact
Grupo de Amigos del Presidente, 274, 332
Guatemala, 381
Gugliemetti, Pedro, 200
Guijón, Patricio, 332
Gumucio, Rafael, 63, 365

Gutierrez, Nelson, 258, 259, 360
Gutiérrez Figueroa, Brigadier General Sergio, 340
Guzmán, Jaime, 351, 404

Haiti, 51
Hamburg, 375
Hamilton, Alexander, 4
Hamilton, Juan, 285, 316
Hamilton-Fuentealba amendment, 252
Harbad Valdés, General Diego, 340
Harper's Magazine, 217
Hart, Armando, 213
Havana, 72, 215, 360
Health Workers' Federation, 433, 434
Henriquez, Miguel, 359
Hidalgo, Manuel, 9
History of the Russian Revolution, 239
Holland, 226, 378, 407
Hong Kong, 422
Horman, Charles, 233
Hua Kuo-feng, 375
Huerta Díez, Admiral Ismael, 294, 304, 340, 383
Human Rights Commission of OAS. *See* Organization of American States, Human Rights Commission
Human Rights Commission of UN. *See* United Nations Human Rights Commission
Humeres, Humberto, 155
Hungary, 226

IAMEA (tire company), 417
Ibáñez, Bernardo, 30, 31, 37, 113, 141
Ibáñez, Carlos, 13, 14, 15, 16, 19, 20, 21, 22, 24, 25, 29, 36, 37, 39, 40, 41, 45, 50, 51, 52, 62, 76, 85, 122, 141, 215, 282, 289, 339
Ibáñez, Pedro, 140
Ibáñez Ojeda, Pedro, 353
ICARE. *See* Instituto Chileno de Administración Racional de Empresas
ICFTU. *See* International Confederation of Free Trade Unions
ILO. *See* International Labor Organization
IMF. *See* International Monetary Fund
Impacto, 239
INACAP. *See* Instituto Nacional de Capacitación Profesional
Incami, 386
INDAP. *See* Instituto de Desarrollo Agropecuario
Industrial cordons. *See Cordones industriales*

Instituto Chileno de Administración Racional de Empresas, 51
Instituto de Desarrollo Agropecuario, 62, 90, 94, 95, 256, 402, 415
Instituto de Educación Rural, 87
Instituto Nacional de Capacitación Profesional, 96, 200
Instituto Nacional de Estadísticas, 401, 402
Instituto Pedagógio, 334
Inter American Commission of Human Rights, 346
Inter American Defense Board, 231, 232
Inter American Press Association, 392
Intercontinental Press, 214
Intergovernmental Council of Copper Exporters, 407
International Bank for Reconstruction and Development, 219, 220, 236, 378, 401, 409
International Commission of Jurists, 373, 374
International Confederation of Free Trade Unions, 199, 431, 432
International Court, 212, 382, 431
International Federation of Christian Trade Unions, 42
International Labor Organization, 431, 433, 434
International Monetary Fund, 219, 220, 221, 236
International Telephone and Telegraph Company, 153, 217, 227, 417
International Transport Workers' Federation, 431
International Union of Soviet Youth, 74
Isabel Riquelme Peasant Federation, 167
ITF. *See* International Transport Workers' Federation
ITT. *See* International Telephone and Telegraph Company
IUSY. *See* International Union of Socialist Youth
IVA. *See* Value Added Tax
Izquierda Comunista, 20
Izquierda Cristiana, 63, 132, 133, 166, 169, 196, 250, 252, 362, 365, 366

Jamaica, 25
Janutschek, Hans, 215
Japan, 30, 223
Jaramillo, Alberto, 284
Jarpa, Sergio Onofre, 282, 304
Jerez, Alberto, 63, 284, 316
Jobet, Julio César, 50, 86, 138, 267

Jordan, 378
Journalists Association, 393
Jovín, Colonel Pedro, 340
Juan Carlos I, King of Spain, 378
Juárez, Sergio, 308
Junta de Gobierno of 1924, 13, 16
Junta de Gobierno of 1973. *See* Junta Militar
Junta Militar, 333, 334, 335, 336, 338, 339, 340, 341, 342, 343, 344, 345, 346, 347, 348, 349, 350, 351, 352, 353, 354, 355, 356, 357, 358, 363, 364, 365, 366, 367, 369, 370, 371, 372, 373, 374, 375, 376, 377, 378, 379, 380, 381, 382, 383, 384, 385, 386, 387, 388, 389, 390, 391, 392, 393, 394, 395, 396, 397, 398, 401, 402, 404, 405, 406, 407, 408, 409, 410, 411, 412, 413, 414, 415, 416, 417, 418, 419, 420, 421, 422, 423, 424, 425, 426, 427, 428, 429, 430, 431, 432, 433, 434, 435, 436, 437, 438, 439, 440, 441, 442, 443, 447

Kennecott Corporation, 101, 148, 149, 150, 236, 276, 408, 416
Kennedy, Edward, 376
Kennedy amendment, 376
Kissinger, Henry, 235, 377
Korry, Edward, 219
Kosygin, Prime Minister, 212
Kuwait, 379

Labbe Troncoso, Colonel Alberto, 294
Labor Code, 15, 31, 42, 62, 76, 88, 89, 108, 109, 110, 120, 197, 439; proposed by military regime, 428, 434, 436, 438, 439, 440
Lacrampette Calderón, Brigadier Hector, 324
La Familia *financiera*, 404
Laferte, Elias, 14
LAFTA. *See* Latin American Free Trade Area
La Mañana, 241, 392
La Nación, 113, 138, 238, 332, 391
LAN-Chile airlines, 221, 413
Lanusse, General Alejandro, 211, 212
La Papelera, 241, 242, 253, 286
La Patria, 391, 414
La Paz, 383
La Prensa, 196, 238, 271, 391, 392
La Segunda, 238, 392
Last Tango in Paris, 394
Latin America, 317, 324, 334, 342, 348, 353, 359, 361, 365, 368, 382, 384, 434
Latin America Commodities Report, 408
Latin America Economic Report, 401, 403, 405, 413, 415, 421, 442

Latin American Free Trade Area, 48
Latin America Political Report, 358, 362, 370, 372, 382
La Tribuna, 238, 240, 282, 392
Lavín, Colonel Jaime, 372
Law for the Defense of Democracy, 34, 35, 40, 45
Law no. 16,625. *See* Ley de Sindicación Campesina
Law no. 16,640. *See* Agrarian Reform Law of 1967
Law no. 17,377. *See* Law regulating TV
Law no. 17,798. *See* Law on control of arms
Law of Peasant Unionization. *See* Ley de Sindicación Campesina
Law on control of arms, 299, 323
Law regulating TV, 243
Lazo, Carmen, 365
Lebon, Raúl David, 168
Le Drapeau Rouge, 258, 264
Leigh Guzmán, General Gustavo, 324, 334, 339, 342, 351, 376, 426, 438
Leighton, Bernardo, 62, 286, 347, 365, 366
Le Monde, 81, 101, 167, 348
Lenin, 239, 256, 391
Leniz, Fernando, 396, 397, 398, 436, 437, 438
Leoni, Raúl, 105
Letelier, Orlando, 332
Ley de Reajuste of 1971, 175
Ley de Sindicación Campesina, 68, 88, 89, 90, 91, 110, 127, 169
Liberal party. *See* Partido Liberal
Liberal Republic, 5, 6
Liberals, 4, 5, 6, 8, 11
Liberty Fund, 242
Lima, 418
Lion of Tarapacá, 11
Lleras Restrepo, Carlos, 105
Lopez, Hernán, 392
Luders, Rolf, 421
Lutheran Church of Chile, 370

MacDermot, Neal, 374
MacEoin, Gary, 102, 131, 231, 232, 292
MacHale, Tomás, 245, 246, 247
MacKay Jaraquemada, General Mario, 340
MADEMSA firm, 421
Mahn, General Alfredo, 80
Maira, Luis, 284
Man of La Mancha, 394
Manuel Rodriguez group, 403

Manufacturas de Cobre, 152
Manufacturers Hanover Bank, 225
Mao Tse-tung, 375
MAPU. *See* Movimiento de Acción Popular Unida
Marambio, General Tulio, 80, 81
March of the Pots, 283
Maria Elena nitrate field, 214
Marín, Dr., 284
Marín, Gladys, 258, 259
Maritain, Jacques, 44
Maritime Workers Confederation, 111, 433, 435, 436
Marshall, Major Arturo, 80
Martan, Osvaldo, 433
Martínez, Alberto, 191
Martus, Carlos, 191
Marx, 239, 391
Marxist-Leninists, 21, 34, 44, 69, 74, 77, 165, 209, 239, 256, 266, 368, 381, 391, 446
Marxists, 68, 238, 255, 268, 279, 324, 368, 370, 379, 381, 382, 388, 390, 393, 432
Matos, Hubert, 361
Matte, Eugenio, 15, 20
Matte Larrain, Arturo, 37
Matthei, General Fernando, 386, 387
Matús, Carlos, 305
Mayor, Captain, 337
Mayoría, 239
MCR. *See* Movimiento de Campesinos Revolutionarios
Meany, George, 431, 432
Medina Galvez, Guillermo, 353
Mendoza, General César, 334, 335, 339, 341, 365, 381
Mensaje, 239, 392, 400
Mercau, Andrés, 380
Merino, Vice Admiral José Toribio, 326, 334, 335, 339, 355, 356, 378
Mexico, 210, 211, 212, 225, 380, 386
Milicia Republicano, 18
Military Coup of September 11, 1973, xi, xii, 3, 16, 246, 247, 264, 280, 282, 287, 288, 298, 299, 301, 317, 326, 331, 332, 333, 334, 335, 336, 337, 338, 339, 341, 342, 345, 348, 353, 355, 357, 358, 362, 367, 372, 374, 385, 386, 387, 388, 390, 391, 392, 393, 394, 407, 430, 445, 447
Military Junta of 1924. *See* Junta del Gobierno of 1924
Military Junta of 1973. *See* Junta Militar
Military Justice Code, 240

Millas, Orlando, 224, 225, 226, 258, 261, 263, 271, 272, 308
MIR. *See* Movimiento de Izquierda Revolucionaria
Miranda, Hugo, 365
Miret, Pedro, 213
Molina, Sergio, 400
Monckenberg, Fernando, 51, 52
Mondale, Walter, 377
Montealegre, Hernán, 369
Montero, Juan Esteban, 15
Montero Cornejo, Vice Admiral Raúl, 294, 295, 323, 324, 334, 335
Montes, Jorge, 346
Montt, Admiral Jorge, 339
Montt, Manuel, 5, 6
Montt-Varista party. *See* Partido Nacional
Mora, Marcial, 75
Morales, Carlos, 365
Morales, Hernán, 309
Moreno, Rafael, 263, 286
Moscow, 133, 361, 375
Moss, Robert, 168, 170, 285, 286
Movement of United Popular Action. *See* Movimiento de Acción Popular Unida
Movimiento Campesino Independiente, 87
Movimiento de Acción Popular Unida, 63, 75, 84, 122, 132, 169, 196, 203, 204, 205, 256, 261, 276, 279, 283, 284, 294, 306, 309, 326, 358, 362, 365, 366
Movimiento de Campesinos Revolucionarios, 167, 275
Movimiento de Izquierda Cristiana, 284
Movimiento de Izquierda Revolucionaria, 72, 73, 77, 113, 132, 141, 144, 160, 166, 167, 179, 194, 196, 197, 214, 215, 238, 241, 245, 251, 252, 253, 256, 258, 259, 260, 261, 263, 265, 269, 270, 271, 273, 274, 275, 276, 277, 298, 300, 307, 309, 310, 315, 317, 325, 326, 336, 345, 357, 358, 359, 360, 362, 365, 366, 367, 378, 428, 447
Movimiento de Unidad Nacional, 351
Movimiento Nacional de Liberación Campesina, 87
Movimiento Nacionalista Revolucionario, 211
Movimiento Radical Independiente, 279
Movimiento Revolucionario Manuel Rodríguez, 73
MR-2. *See* Movimiento Revolucionario Manuel Rodríguez
Mujica, Federico, 433

MUN. *See* Movimiento de Unidad Nacional
Musalem, José, 45, 62, 284, 365

National Center for Pedagogic Improvement, Experimentation and Research, 97
National Channel, 243, 244
National Confederation of Small Industry and Artisans, 303
National Council, 243, 244
National Council of Churches, 366
National Council of Distribution and Commercialization, 308
National Executive Committee of the Radical party, 74, 279
National Planning Organization, 292
National Program of Improvement of Teaching, 97
National Revolutionary parties, 280
National Secretariat of Commercialization and Distribution, 308
National Security Council, 352
National Statistical Institute, 178
National Symphony, 394
National Television Enterprise, 243
Navarro Tobar, José, 340
Nazi party. *See* Partido Nacista
Neruda, Pablo, 122, 123
Netherlands. *See* Holland
New China News Agency, 375
New Delhi, 216
New York Times, 221
Nicaragua, 381
Niedergang, Marcel, 101
Nierad, Captain, 80
Nigeria, 382
Nixon, Richard, 228, 234, 235, 236, 447
Normas Básicas de Participación de los Trabajadores en la Administración de las Empresas del Area Social y Mixta, 201
North Korea, 212, 213, 226, 374
North Vietnam, 212
Noticias de la Tarde, 73
Nueva Izquierda Democrática, 49

OAS. *See* Organization of American States
Ochoa, Arnaldo, 213
ODEPLAN. *See* Oficina de Planeamiento
Office of Agricultural Planning, 401, 402
Oficialistas, 61, 62, 63, 64, 65, 111
Oficina de Planeamiento, 175, 181, 191, 192, 200, 202
O'Higgins, Bernardo, 4

OLAS. *See* Organización Latino Americana de Solidaridad

Olguín, Osvaldo, 316, 363

Olivares, Augusto, 332

Olivares, Eduardo, 332

OPEC. *See* Organization of Petroleum Exporting Countries

Operation Unitas, 232, 331

Orden Socialista, 20

Organización Latino Americana de Solidaridad, 72, 141, 213

Organización Regional Inter Americana de Trabajadores, 41, 42

Organization of American States, 213, 230, 346, 376, 377

Organization of American States, Human Rights Commission, 377

Organization of Petroleum Exporting Countries, 102

Organized Vanguard of the People. *See* Vanguardia Organizada del Pueblo

ORIT. *See* Organización Regional Inter Americana de Trabajadores

Osses Santa María, Hernán, 73

Pablo, Tomás, 286, 348

PADENA. *See* Partido Democrático Nacional

Palacios, Brigadier General Pedro, 294

Palacios Ruhmann, General Javier, 342

Palma, Anibal, 346

Palma, Ignacio, 62

Palme, Olav, 215

Panama, 233

Panorama, 370

Paraguay, 381

Paredes, Eduardo, 274, 298

Paris Club, 183, 407

Parodi, Captain Alfonso, 308

Parra, Bosco, 284

Partido Agrario Laborista, 36, 75, 282

Partido Comunista de Chile, 9, 14, 20, 21, 22, 23, 24, 25, 28, 29, 30, 31, 32, 33, 34, 36, 37, 38, 41, 42, 43, 45, 46, 48, 56, 57, 59, 60, 63, 70, 71, 72, 73, 74, 76, 80, 82, 84, 86, 90, 97, 109, 110, 111, 112, 113, 114, 119, 121, 122, 123, 132, 133, 134, 135, 136, 137, 144, 150, 163, 165, 169, 172, 186, 192, 195, 196, 197, 200, 203, 206, 238, 239, 243, 245, 248, 251, 254, 255, 256, 257, 258, 259, 260, 261, 262, 263, 264, 265, 267, 268, 269, 270, 273, 276, 277, 279, 294, 297, 298, 302, 305, 306, 308, 309, 310, 312, 313, 315, 325, 345, 346, 349, 360, 361, 362, 365, 374, 391, 428, 429, 432, 434, 435, 447

Partido Comunista Revolucionario, 195

Partido Conservador Social Cristiano, 44, 45

Partido de la Democracia Radical, 75, 276, 278, 279, 284, 307, 358

Partido Demócrata Cristiano, 44, 45, 46, 48, 49, 50, 52, 55, 56, 57, 58, 59, 60, 61, 62, 63, 64, 65, 66, 67, 68, 69, 71, 73, 74, 75, 76, 77, 78, 79, 81, 82, 83, 84, 85, 86, 87, 88, 90, 91, 93, 94, 95, 97, 98, 99, 100, 104, 107, 108, 110, 111, 112, 113, 114, 115, 116, 117, 118, 119, 120, 121, 125, 126, 127, 128, 133, 139, 140, 144, 146, 147, 165, 166, 169, 194, 195, 196, 197, 199, 200, 204, 205, 206, 210, 227, 238, 239, 242, 243, 245, 251, 252, 253, 256, 257, 259, 262, 263, 264, 267, 268, 269, 270, 271, 274, 276, 277, 278, 279, 280, 281, 282, 283, 284, 285, 286, 287, 291, 297, 304, 307, 310, 312, 316, 317, 336, 340, 342, 347, 348, 358, 359, 360, 362, 363, 364, 365, 366, 374, 391, 392, 393, 396, 408, 428, 429, 433, 435, 445, 446

Partido Democrático, 6, 9, 11, 24, 36, 43, 46, 75, 122, 133, 255

Partido Democrático de Chile, 43

Partido Democrático del Pueblo, 43

Partido Democrático Nacional, 49, 59, 75, 112, 278, 284, 307

Partido Federado Unidad Popular, 306

Partido Feminino, 40, 41

Partido Izquierda Radical, 196, 204, 208, 252, 253, 255, 278, 279, 280, 286, 294, 305, 306, 307, 316, 358

Partido Liberal, 9, 11, 20, 23, 24, 25, 29, 30, 32, 33, 36, 45, 46, 48, 49, 59, 66, 67

Partido Nacional, 67, 70, 74, 76, 84, 97, 101, 113, 140, 196, 197, 204, 238, 240, 243, 262, 267, 278, 279, 280, 281, 282, 284, 286, 304, 307, 311, 312, 358, 446

Partido Nacional Cristiano, 45

Partido Nacional (Montt-Varista), 5, 11

Partido Nacista, 20, 22, 23, 24

Partido Radical, 6, 9, 15, 16, 20, 21, 22, 23, 24, 25, 26, 27, 29, 30, 31, 32, 33, 35, 36, 37, 38, 39, 43, 46, 48, 49, 56, 59, 60, 62, 69, 70, 71, 72, 73, 74, 75, 76, 84, 97, 112, 113, 121, 122, 123, 132, 140, 144, 196, 227, 245, 252, 254, 255, 256, 261, 267, 270, 278, 279, 280, 294, 306, 358, 362, 365, 380

Partido Radical Doctrinario, 36

Partido Social Demócrata, 75, 122, 133, 255, 279
Partido Socialista Auténtico, 30
Partido Socialista de Chile, 16, 20, 21, 22, 23, 24, 25, 28, 29, 30, 31, 32, 33, 34, 38, 40, 42, 43, 44, 46, 48, 49, 56, 59, 63, 69, 70, 71, 72, 73, 74, 76, 80, 82, 84, 86, 90, 97, 110, 111, 113, 114, 121, 122, 123, 132, 133, 137, 139, 140, 141, 143, 163, 166, 169, 179, 192, 195, 196, 197, 200, 208, 213, 215, 238, 239, 241, 245, 248, 251, 252, 254, 255, 256, 257, 258, 260, 261, 265, 266, 267, 268, 269, 270, 271, 272, 273, 274, 276, 277, 279, 286, 287, 294, 298, 299, 302, 305, 306, 307, 309, 312, 315, 316, 317, 322, 324, 325, 326, 327, 335, 336, 359, 361, 362, 365, 380, 391, 428, 435, 446
Partido Socialista Marxista, 20
Partido Socialista Popular, 34, 36, 40, 43, 44, 69
Partido Socialista Unificado, 20
Patria y Libertad, 57, 68, 77, 228, 280, 281, 282, 298, 307, 311, 358, 435
Patria y Libertad, 239, 281
PDC. *See* Partido Demócrata Cristiano
PDR. *See* Partido de la Democracia Radical
Peace Corps, 236
P.E.C., 239, 281, 392
Pedro Aguirre Cerda Peasant Federation, 167
Peking, 375
Peking Review, 375
People's Republic of Korea. *See* North Korea
Pérez Zujovic, Edmundo, 62, 199, 259, 274, 275, 297
Perón, Juan, 40, 41, 215, 241, 382
Peru, 4, 7, 11, 15, 102, 105, 195, 209, 210, 212, 226, 235, 289, 375, 380, 383, 384
"Petition of Chile," 304
Pfizer pharmaceutical company, 156
Philippi Izquierdo, Julio, 353
Philippines, the, 422
Pinochet Ugarte, General Augusto, 292, 293, 295, 324, 334, 339, 341, 342, 343, 344, 345, 346, 347, 350, 351, 355, 356, 357, 361, 363, 368, 373, 377, 378, 379, 380, 381, 382, 383, 384, 390, 409, 410, 426, 427, 430, 431, 432, 433, 434, 438, 442
Pinto Cáceres, Commander Carlos, 375
Pipino, Adelio, 419
PIR. *See* Partido Izquierda Radical
Pizarreño industry, 333
PLAN, 136, 238
Plan Z, 336

Podgorny, President, 212
Poland, 226
Política e Espiritu, 239
Ponce, Aníbal, 305
Popper, David, 377
Popular assembly. *See Asamblea popular*
Popular Front, the, 23, 24, 25, 26, 27, 28, 29, 37, 43, 50, 52, 74, 86, 122, 254
Popular Tribunals. *See* Tribunales Populares
Popular Unity Federated Party. *See* Partido Federado Unidad Popular
Popular Unity regime. *See* Unidad Popular
Portales, Diego, 4, 5
Posición, 238
Prats, General Carlos, 253, 292, 293, 294, 295, 296, 297, 305, 306, 308, 313, 321, 323, 324, 333, 335, 341
Pratt, Lawrence, 346
Precht, Monsignor Christian, 368
Prieto, General Joaquín, 5
Prieto Befalluy, Alfredo, 389
Principios, 238
Production Development Corporation. *See* Corporación de Fomento de la Producción
PSA. *See* Partido Socialista Auténtico
PSCh. *See* Partido Socialista de Chile
PSD. *See* Partido Social Demócrata
PSP. *See* Partido Socialista Popular
Puccio, Osvaldo, 332
Punto Final, 203, 204, 238, 258, 333, 392
Purina firm, 157
Puro Chile, 153, 238

Quadros, Janio, 141
¿Que Es el Comunismo?, 133, 134, 135
¿Que Pasa?, 239
Quintana, Alfonso, 75

Radical Democracy. *See* Partido Radical
Radical Party. *See* Partido Radical
Radicals, 8, 11
Radio Agricultura of Los Andes, 304
Radio Balmaceda, 245, 366
Radio Controllers Union, 245
Radio Corporación, 313
Radio Corporation of America, 152
Radio Luis Emilio Recabarren, 245
Radio Luxemburg of Paris, 426
Railroad Workers Federation. *See* Federación Industrial Ferroviaria de Chile
Ramírez, Pedro Felipe, 208, 346

Ramona Parra Brigades, 264, 313
Ramos, Sergio, 135
Rather, Dan, 237
"Rattling of the Sabres," 12, 85
Ravines, Eudosio, 21
Readjustment Law of 1968, 76
Rebeldes, 61, 62, 63, 64, 65, 71, 110, 111, 113, 256, 283
Recabarren, Luis Emilio, 9
Reconstruction and Relief Corporation. *See* Corporación de Reconstrucción y Auxilio
Refinería de Azúcar de Vina del Mar, 152
Refractarías, 152
Regional Council of Journalists (Santiago), 246, 247
"Revolution in Liberty," 49, 55, 85, 118
Revolution of 1891, 7
Reyes, Tomás, 62, 366
Reyes del Rio, Admiral Olegario, 18
Rio Blanco mine, 102
Rio de Janeiro, 79
Ríos, Eduardo, 433, 436, 442
Ríos, Juan Antonio, 23, 26, 29, 30, 31, 44
Ríos Valdivia, Alejandro, 297
Rocha Aros, Captain Sergio, 313
Rodríguez, Ambrosio, 434
Rodríguez, Aniceto, 70, 126, 266, 267, 270, 354, 365
Rodríguez, General, 388
Rodríguez, Manuel, 197, 433
Rodríguez Elizondo, José, 153
Rojas, Edgardo, 195
Rojas, Patricio, 114
Ross, Gustavo, 19, 23, 24, 25, 44
Ruíz Danyau, General César, 294, 295, 323, 324, 388
Rumania, 195, 226, 375
Russia, 135, 142, 150, 393
Ryan, Lieutenant Colonel Patrick, 233

Saavedra, Patricio, 247
Saenz, Orlando, 153, 397
Sáez, Raúl, 340
Salta, Argentina, 211
Sanhueza, Manuel, 253, 280, 286
Santa María, Domingo, 6
Santos Salas, José, 14
Sarmiento, Domingo, 211
Saudi Arabia, 379
Scandinavian countries, 377, 378
Schindler, Colonel Rubén, 408
Schnake, Oscar, 28, 29, 37

Schneider, General René, 57, 68, 81, 126, 228, 236, 281, 296
School of Fine Arts, 388
Second truckers' strike, 272, 321, 322
Second Vatican Council, 369
Sepa, 239, 240
Sepúlveda, Brigadier General Claudio, 294, 305
Sepúlveda, General José María, 295, 323
Sepúlveda, Lucia, 204
Sepúlveda, Washington, 433
Serani, Edmundo, 73
Servicio Nacional de Salud, 51
Servicio Nacional de Seguro Social, 51, 333, 437, 438, 446
SIAM di Tella, 421
Sigmund, Paul, 219, 220, 221, 222, 225, 231, 235
Silva, René, 392
Silva Henríquez, Cardinal Raúl, 287, 348, 368, 370, 387, 436
Silverman, David, 150
Simon, William, 377
Social Democratic parties of Europe, 21
Social Democratic party of Germany, 365
Social Democratic party of Sweden, 215
Social Democrats of the Socialist party, 266
"Social enterprise" statute. *See* Social Statute of the Enterprise
Socialist International, 6, 74, 132, 138, 215
Socialist parties of Europe, 359
Socialist Party. *See* Partido Socialista de Chile
Socialist party of Spain, 359
Socialist Republic, 15, 16, 20, 21, 85, 154
Socialists of Europe, 447
Social Security Law proposed by military regime, 436, 437
Social Security Service. *See* Servicio Nacional de Seguro Social
Social Security System. *See* Servicio Nacional de Seguro Social
Social Security workers. *See* Health Workers' Federation
Social Statute of the Enterprise, 436, 438
Sociedad Comercializadora de la Reforma Agraria, 156
Sociedad de Fomento Fabril, 153, 178, 397, 400, 409, 413
Sociedad Ganadera de Tierra del Fuego, 162
Sociedad Minera El Teniente, 101
Sociedad Nacional de Agricultura, 68
Sociedad Química Minera de Chile, 103

Soler, Vicente, 284
Somoza, General Anastasio, 381
Souper, Colonel Robert, 313
South Africa, 379
Southern University, 389
Soviet Union, 28, 71, 164, 165, 180, 183, 195, 212, 225, 226, 227, 247, 250, 361, 374, 375, 383
Spain, 226, 289, 378, 393, 407
Special copper tribunal, 147
SQM. *See* Sociedad Química Minera de Chile
Stallings, Barbara, 203
State Bank. *See* Banco del Estado
Statute of Constitutional Guarantees, 246
Statute of Vocational Training of Workers, 440
Stockholm, 431
Stroessner, President, 381, 382
Stuardo, Julio, 308, 310
Suarez, Jaime, 305
Sule, Anselmo, 365
Sumitomo Metal Mining Company, 102
Supreme Court, 144, 248, 249, 253, 299, 318, 319, 320, 321, 348, 349, 350, 351, 352, 353, 369

Tacna, 239, 281, 392
Tacna-Arica question, 15
Taiwan, 422
Tancazo, 301, 308, 311, 314, 315, 319, 325
Tapia, Jorge, 307, 308, 311
Tapia Falk, Colonel Julio, 388
Tarud, Rafael, 74, 75, 76, 122
Teitelboim, Volodia, 260
Terceristas, 61, 62, 63, 64, 65, 111, 283, 284
Thayer, William, 62, 76, 88, 110, 111, 114
Thome, Joseph, 95
"Three Bands," 243
Tito, Josip Broz, 138
Tizona, 239
Toha, Jaime, 332
Toha, José, 235, 267, 332, 348
Tomic, Radomiro, 56, 110, 120, 121, 125, 262, 307, 446
Torres, General Juan José, 211
Torres de la Cruz, General Manuel, 325
Trade Union School of the military regime, 434
Tribunales populares, 248
Troncoso Daroch, Admiral Arturo, 389

Trotsky, Leon, 239, 391
Trotskyites, 20, 21, 29, 72, 302, 334, 344, 391

UCC. *See* Unión de Campesinos Cristianos
Uganda, 353
Ugarte Román, Marta, 349
Última Hora, 238, 260, 316
Ultimas Noticias, 238, 365
Unidad Popular, xii, 26, 31, 38, 56, 60, 71, 74, 75, 118, 121, 122, 123, 124, 127, 131, 132, 133, 135, 136, 137, 138, 139, 143, 144, 145, 146, 147, 150, 152, 155, 158, 159, 160, 161, 163, 164, 166, 168, 169, 170, 171, 174, 176, 184, 185, 186, 190, 192, 193, 194, 195, 199, 200, 203, 204, 205, 206, 209, 210, 211, 212, 213, 217, 224, 227, 232, 234, 235, 236, 237, 238, 239, 240, 241, 242, 243, 244, 245, 246, 247, 248, 249, 250, 251, 252, 253, 254, 255, 256, 257, 258, 259, 260, 261, 262, 263, 264, 265, 266, 267, 268, 269, 270, 271, 272, 273, 274, 275, 276, 277, 278, 279, 280, 281, 283, 284, 285, 288, 291, 292, 294, 295, 296, 297, 299, 302, 304, 305, 307, 308, 309, 310, 312, 315, 316, 322, 323, 327, 334, 345, 347, 349, 357, 358, 359, 360, 361, 362, 365, 366, 367, 383, 386, 387, 392, 393, 394, 395, 403, 412, 423, 425, 428, 446, 447
Unified National School, 308
Unión de Campesinos Cristianos, 87, 90
Unión de Trabajadores de Chile, 112, 113
Unión Nacional, 11
Unión Nacional Laboral, 428
Union of Workers of State Commerce and Consumers Cooperatives of Soviet Union, 198
Unión Socialista Popular, 70, 113, 196, 307
United Nations Conference on Trade and Development, 210, 216
United Nations General Assembly, 218, 297, 373, 378
United Nations High Commission for Refugees, 345, 386
United Nations Human Rights Commission, 369, 373, 379
United Nations Institute of Social Development, 51
United Nations refugee centers, 372
United States (general), 363, 372, 373, 382, 393, 408, 447
United States Export-Import Bank, 101, 102, 219, 221, 222

United States government and military, 13, 28, 30, 32, 47, 50, 51, 76, 91, 183, 209, 217, 218, 219, 221, 223, 225, 228, 230, 231, 232, 233, 234, 235, 293, 331, 347, 359, 369, 373, 376, 377, 378, 407, 409, 434
Universidad del Norte, 389
Universidad Técnica del Estado, 51, 333, 334, 348, 387, 389
University of Chicago, 394
University of Chile, 243, 244, 310, 341, 353, 387, 388, 404, 405
University of Concepción, 72, 73, 214, 276, 387, 388, 389
UP. *See* Unidad Popular
Uraas, Pedro, 284
Urrutia, General Marcial, 18
Urrutia Manzano, Enrique, 349, 350
Uruguay, 195, 211, 381
USSR. *See* Soviet Union
UTRACh. *See* Unión de Trabajadores de Chile

Valente Rossi, Luis, 156
Value Added Tax, 419
Vanguardia Organizada del Pueblo, 73, 274
Varas, José Miguel, 243
Velasco, General Juan, 209
Venezuela, 105, 106, 195, 209, 210, 359, 380
Vergara, Daniel, 332, 337
Viaux, General Roberto, 57, 80, 81, 126, 281
Vicaría de Solidaridad, 349, 350, 368, 369
Vicencio, Hugo, 203, 204
Videl, Colonel Ernesto, 372
Videla, General of Argentina, 382
Videla, Pedro, 284
Vienna Boys Choir, 394
Vietnam, 233
Vilarín, León, 302, 321
Viña Santa Carolina, 333

Vitale, Luis, 72
Vivero Avila, Brigadier General Arturo, 340
Vogel, Ernesto, 196, 199
VOP. *See* Vanguardia Organizada del Pueblo
Vovane Zuñiga, General Arturo, 340
Vuskevic, Pedro, 152, 189, 190, 191

Waiss, Oscar, 72, 138
War of the Pacific, 11, 383
Washington, D.C., 217, 294, 366
Western Europe, 209, 215, 225, 372, 377, 378, 393, 394, 447
West Germany, 50, 226, 378, 407
WFTU. *See* World Federation of Trade Unions
Williams-Balfour wholesale firm, 156
Willoughby, Federico, 357
Workers Assembly, 244
World Affairs Report, 180
World Bank. *See* International Bank for Reconstruction and Development
World Confederation of Labor, 199
World Federation of Trade Unions, 42, 195, 199
World Marxist Review, 360
World Trade Union Assembly, 199

Yarur textile firm, 156, 333

Zaire, 102
Zalaquett, José Fernando, 369
Zaldivar, Andrés, 114, 263, 366
Zambia, 102
Zamorano, Antonio, 46
Zamorano, Mario, 260, 263
Zig-Zag publishing firm, 239
Zimbalist, Andy, 203
Zorilla, Américo, 151
Zuñiga, Colonel Gastón, 375

ABOUT THE AUTHOR

Robert J. Alexander, professor of economics at Rutgers University, New Brunswick, New Jersey, has written twenty books in the fields of economics, political science, history, and Latin American affairs.